LATCHED
VIEWING
PARAMETERS

INTERP
FO
SIMU

POLYGON
TABLE

FRAME
BUFFER

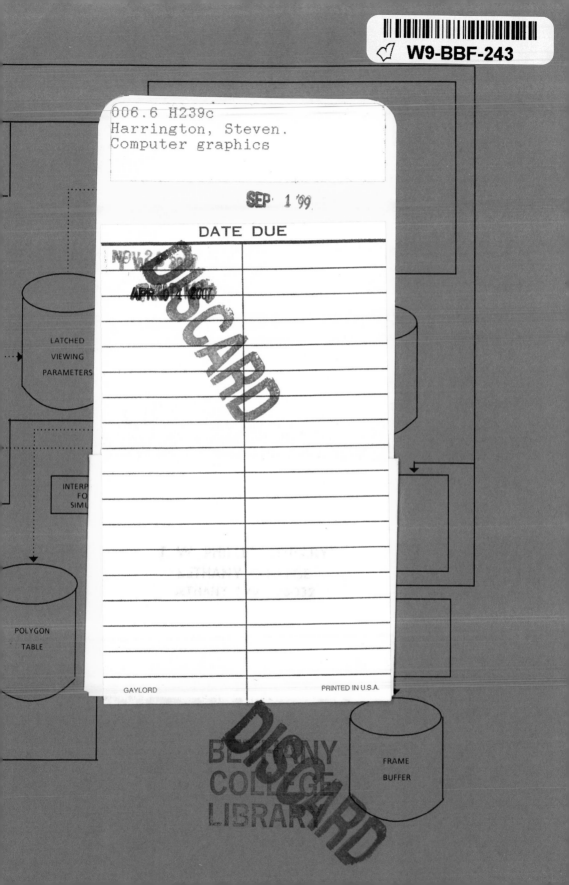

COMPUTER GRAPHICS
A PROGRAMMING APPROACH

COMPUTER
GRAPHICS
A Programming Approach

Second Edition

Steven Harrington

Xerox Corporation

McGraw-Hill Book Company

New York   St. Louis   San Francisco   Auckland   Bogotá   Hamburg   Johannesburg
London   Madrid   Mexico   Milan   Montreal   New Delhi   Panama
Paris   São Paulo   Singapore   Sydney   Tokyo   Toronto

This book was set in Times Roman by Publication Services.
The editors were Kaye Pace and Larry Goldberg;
the cover was designed by Amy Becker;
the production supervisor was Salvador Gonzales;
new drawings were done by Wellington Studios, Ltd.
R. R. Donnelley & Sons Company was printer and binder.

The cover photo was supplied by Abel Image Research, Los Angeles, California. This still image
is from a 30-second commercial entitled *Brilliance*. It was produced by Robert Abel & Associates of
Los Angeles for the canned food information council in collaboration with Ketchum Advertising of
San Francisco.

COMPUTER GRAPHICS

A Programming Approach

1 2 3 4 5 6 7 8 9 0   DOCDOC   8 9 2 1 0 9 8 7

ISBN 0-07-026753-7

Library of Congress Cataloging-in-Publication Data

Harrington, Steven.
    Computer graphics.

    Includes bibliographies and index.
    1. Computer graphics.   2. Programming (Electronic
computers)   I. Title.
T385.H34   1987   006.6   86–21295
ISBN   0–07–026753–7

CONTENTS

PREFACE

HANDS-ON APPROACH

This book, the second edition of an introductory text on interactive computer graphics, presents the basic concepts of that field. The approach is somewhat different from that of previous texts in that it encourages a "hands-on," or "learn-by-doing," attitude. The book provides guidance for developing a graphics system, suggestions for modifications and extensions of the system, and application problems which make use of the system. The advantages of this approach are a high level of student involvement, an understanding of the systems aspects of graphics software, a realistic feeling for graphics system capabilities and ease of use, and a greater feeling of accomplishment.

PREREQUISITES

This book is written at a lower level than previous graphics texts. It is intended for students with a knowledge of high school algebra, analytic geometry, and trigonometry, and with at least one high-level language programming course. Although the necessary information on vectors, matrices, and data structures is presented in the text, students familiar with these topics will find the material easier to follow. The text should be suitable for junior college and undergraduate college levels. Most of computer graphics is based on the mathematics of analytic geometry; a knowledge of this area is appropriate and necessary. This book presents a graphics system as a series of programming problems, so a familiarity with some high-level language is required. The text attempts to present its algorithms in a language-independent fashion and does not require the knowledge of any one particular language. It has been used successfully with Pascal, C, and Fortran.

TIME REQUIREMENTS

The material can be covered at a rate of about one chapter per week. Slightly more time is needed to cover Chapters 8 to 11. Each chapter also provides a programming assignment for a component of the graphics system. The requirement of a weekly program is a heavy but not excessive load for students. If necessary, the less instructive portions of programming projects may be provided by the instructor. At the end of the course, students have not only a working knowledge of computer graphics fundamentals but also a graphics system, or a collection of graphics programs, of which they can rightly be proud. There are several suggested programming problems at the end of each chapter. Some of these problems are much more difficult than others. The difficult problems are marked with an asterisk; very difficult problems have two asterisks.

ORGANIZATION

The text is organized so that each chapter introduces a new topic in computer graphics. The progression is such that new chapters build on previous ones, so the order of presentation is rather fixed. The first chapter begins with a very elementary review of analytic geometry and a discussion of vector generation. The second chapter considers line- and character-drawing commands and provides the interface between the specific display devices being used and the rest of the system. It also presents the basic concept of the display file, or metafile. The third chapter presents polygon surfaces and the rasterization problem. The fourth chapter discusses the basic transformations of translation, scaling, and rotation. The fifth talks about display file segmentation and visibility. These first five chapters, dealing with the management and interpretation of the display file, form a natural group when considering intelligent graphics terminals which maintain their own display files. The sixth chapter completes the discussion of two-dimensional graphics with a discussion of windowing and clipping. The instructor may choose to cover Chapter 6 before Chapter 5. This groups the image construction topics together, followed by the data structuring topic. In the seventh chapter, interactive techniques are discussed. Here again, routines act as an interface between the rest of the system and the particular graphics input hardware available. In Chapter 8 the system is generalized to three-dimensional graphics. The topics of three-dimensional geometry, viewing transformations, parallel projection, perspective projection, and three-dimensional clipping are discussed. Chapter 9 considers hidden surface and line removal. It presents two methods in detail: The first is the simple check for removal of back faces; the second is a priority sort for implementation of the painter's algorithm. The tenth chapter considers shading and color. The eleventh and final chapter considers the drawing of curved lines and surfaces. Arc generations, interpolations, and fractals are covered.

Throughout the text, the generic masculine pronoun "he" has been used solely on account of the ease of expression it affords. Such use of the masculine pronoun should not be interpreted as a wish to exclude women from the use of this text or from the field in general; in fact, all areas of computer science provide excellent career opportunities for women. "The programmer...he" is used only because it is less cumbersome than "the programmer...he or she."

RELATION TO STANDARDS

The original edition of this text was modeled after the GSPC CORE system, with extensions to raster graphics, hidden surfaces, shading, and curves. Although the new edition has modified and extended the system, the basic object-oriented structure and basic input and output primitives have been preserved. Objects are modeled in world-coordinate space, and views of the objects are transformed to normalized device coordinates. Individual graphics primitives can be grouped into segments. This approach is common to many of the current standards, so the student will feel at home with the GKS, PHIGS, CGI, and CGM standards.

SIMPLICITY VS. EFFICIENCY

There are many places in this book where several different algorithms are possible, where the problem may be solved many different ways. As a rule, only one solution is presented in great detail, although others may be described. The particular solution chosen may not be the most clever or the most efficient. The primary objective was not to create the best graphics system but to teach the basic graphics principles. The algorithms selected are, therefore, those which were felt to most readily convey these principles and which were easiest to understand.

APPROACHES TO A GRAPHICS COURSE

There are several ways of using this book. One method is to have students implement the described graphics system. With this approach, the student gets a good understanding of how the components of a graphics system work and interact. Since each extension builds on the previous week's work, the instructor may need to provide solutions to previous assignments. One danger in providing algorithms as complete as those given here is a temptation to copy them without really understanding them. This should be countered with classroom explanation and by assigning some of the exercises which are included.

A second approach is to use the presented graphics system as a base for extensions and modifications. Alternative algorithms and methods may be explored. The book provides a well-documented basic support system, or test bed, on which these methods can be actually programmed. The actual implementation and use of an approach can provide insights into the details of its behavior and its system implications, which may be missed when the algorithm is discussed in isolation. Programming problems suggesting extensions have been included.

A third approach is to emphasize *using* a graphics system rather than building one. With this approach, the algorithms serve as examples of graphics system routines, but not as implementation guides. Students should have this system or some other equivalent system available. Classroom lectures can still explain graphics systems and how they work, but programming projects use these features rather than build them. Applications-oriented programming problems are provided for this purpose.

CHANGES IN THE SECOND EDITION

Computer graphics is a rapidly developing field, and even though this is an introductory text, some revision is needed in order to stay current. In addition, weaknesses in the original text have been addressed. Actual changes include a discussion of the popular Bresenham vector generation algorithm; an introduction to antialiasing techniques and imaging with pixel arrays and patterns; a discussion of the Cohen-Sutherland Outcode clipping algorithm and use of the Blinn shading model; discussions of ray tracing, halftones, and several color topics; and an introduction to Bezier curves, surface patches, and fractals. Three-dimensional clipping was included with the other three-dimensional extensions in Chapter 8, instead of occupying its own chapter. The hidden surface and line chapter was completely redone, providing much more discussion of alternate approaches and less on the algorithm details. It follows Fuch's approach to sorting polygons, simplifying comparison techniques, and does not attempt to discuss polygon decomposition. Other changes include a greatly expanded set of references, an increased selection of exercises and programming problems, and an eight-page insert of full-color photographs (Plates 1 to 16) in Chapter 10.

FURTHER SUPPORT

One thing learned through the first edition of the book is that the text creates the need for information about implementations of the graphics system described. What implementations are available? What languages and computing environments have been tried? What problems or bugs were discovered? What extensions have been carried out? With this edition I shall attempt to act as a clearinghouse for this information. As such, I shall welcome hearing of implementations and requests for implementations. All inquiries can be sent to Steven Harrington, Xerox Corporation, W128-29E, 800 Phillips Rd., Webster, NY 14580.

APPRECIATION

I would like to express my appreciation and thanks to those who reviewed this edition of the text: Steve Cunningham, Rollin Dix, William Grosky, David McAllister, and Spencer Thomas. Their comments and suggestions were very valuable, and I am most grateful for their assistance.

Steven Harrington

CHAPTER
ONE

GEOMETRY
AND LINE
GENERATION

INTRODUCTION

Perhaps our age will be known as the Information Revolution or the Computer Revolution, for we are witnessing a remarkable growth and development of computer technology and applications. The computer is an information processing machine, a tool for storing, manipulating, and correlating data. We are able to generate or collect and process information on a scope never before possible. This information can help us make decisions, understand our world, and control its operation. But as the volume of information increases, a problem arises. How can this information be efficiently and effectively transferred between machine and human? The machine can easily generate tables of numbers hundreds of pages long. But such a printout may be worthless if the human reader does not have the time to understand it. Computer graphics strikes directly at this problem. It is a study of techniques to improve communication between human and machine. A graph may replace that huge table of numbers and allow the reader to note the relevant patterns and characteristics at a glance. Giving the computer the ability to express its data in pictorial form can greatly increase its ability to provide information to the human user. This is a passive form of graphics, but communication can also be a two-way process. It may be convenient and appropriate to input graphical information to the computer. Thus there are both graphical input and graphical output devices. It is often desirable to have the input from the user alter the output presented by the machine. A dialogue can be established through the graphics medium. This is termed *interactive computer graphics* because the user interacts with the machine. Computer graphics allows communication through pictures, charts, and diagrams. It offers

1

a vital alternative to the typewriter's string of symbols. The old adage "A picture is worth a thousand words" is certainly true. Through computer graphics we can pilot spaceships; walk through buildings which have yet to be built; and watch bridges collapse, stars being born, and the rotations of atoms. There are many applications for computer graphics. Management information may be displayed as charts and diagrams. Scientific theories and models may be described in pictorial form. (See Plates 1 through 4.) In computer-aided design we can display an aircraft wing, a highway layout, a printed circuit board, a building "blueprint," or a machine part. (See Plate 15.) Maps can be created for all kinds of geographic information. Diagrams and simulations can enrich classroom instruction. The computer has become a new tool for the artist and animator. (See Plates 5 through 14.) And in video games, computer graphics provides a new form of entertainment.

Over the years many graphics display devices have been developed. There are also many software packages and graphics languages. The problem with such diversity is that it makes it difficult to transfer a graphics program from one installation to another. In the late 1970s, the Graphics Standards Planning Committee of the Association for Computing Machinery developed a proposal for a standard graphics system called the CORE system. This system provided a standardized set of commands to control the construction and display of graphic images. The commands were independent of the device used to create or to display the image and independent of the language in which the graphics program was written. The CORE system defined basic graphics primitives from which more complex or special-purpose graphics routines could be built. The idea was that a program written for the CORE system could be run on any installation using that system. The CORE system contained mechanisms for describing and displaying both two-dimensional and three-dimensional structures. However, it was developed just before the reduction in the cost of computer memory made possible economical raster displays (which allow solid and colored areas to be drawn). It therefore lacked the primitives for describing areas and could only create line drawings. Extensions were soon proposed to provide the CORE system with raster imaging primitives.

A second standard called the graphics kernel system (GKS) was developed in Europe, and it has been steadily gaining in popularity. The GKS system was heavily influenced by CORE, and the minimal GKS implementation is essentially identical to CORE's two-dimensional subset. The GKS standard did contain primitives for imaging areas and colors, but it did not contain the constructs for three-dimensional objects. It introduced the concept of a workstation, which allowed a single graphics program to control several graphics terminals.

Another graphics standard is the programmer's hierarchical interactive graphics standard (PHIGS). It takes input and output functions and viewing model from CORE and GKS, but it is a programmer's toolbox, intended for programming graphics applications. It contains enhanced graphics program structuring features. Two other graphics standards are the computer graphics metafile (CGM) and the computer graphics interface (CGI). The CGM is a file format for picture information that allows device-independent capture, storage, and transfer. The CGI is a companion standard which provides a procedural interface for the CGM primitives.

In this book we are going to present the algorithms for constructing a graphics system which have the flavor of the CORE and GKS standards and, in some areas, go beyond them.

We begin our discussion of computer graphics with the fundamental question of how to locate and display points and line segments. There are several hardware devices (graphics terminals) which may be used to display computer-generated images. Some of these will be discussed in Chapter 2. Before we talk about the devices which display points, we shall review the basic geometry which underlies all of our techniques. We shall consider what points and lines are and how we can specify and manipulate them. We conclude this chapter with a discussion of how the mathematical description of these fundamental geometric building blocks can be implemented on an actual display device. Algorithms are presented for carrying out such an implementation for a line printer or common cathode ray tube (CRT) display. These algorithms will allow us (if needed) to use the line printer or CRT as a somewhat crude, but effective, graphics display device for demonstrating the graphics principles described in the rest of the text.

LINES

We can specify a point (a position in a plane) with an ordered pair of numbers (x, y), where x is the horizontal distance from the origin and y is the vertical distance. Two points will specify a line. Lines are described by equations such that if a point (x, y) satisfies the equations, then the point is on the line. If the two points used to specify a line are (x_1, y_1) and (x_2, y_2), then an equation for the line is given by

$$\frac{y - y_1}{x - x_1} = \frac{y_2 - y_1}{x_2 - x_1} \tag{1.1}$$

This says that the slope between any point on the line and (x_1, y_1) is the same as the slope between (x_2, y_2) and (x_1, y_1).

There are many equivalent forms for this equation. Multiplying by the denominators gives the form

$$(x - x_1)(y_2 - y_1) = (y - y_1)(x_2 - x_1) \tag{1.2}$$

A little more algebra solving for y gives

$$y = \frac{y_2 - y_1}{x_2 - x_1}(x - x_1) + y_1 \tag{1.3}$$

or

$$y = mx + b \tag{1.4}$$

where

$$m = \frac{y_2 - y_1}{x_2 - x_1}$$

and

$$b = y_1 - mx_1$$

This is called the *slope-intercept* form of the line. The *slope* m is the change in height divided by the change in width for two points on the line (the rise over the run). The *intercept* b is the height at which the line crosses the y axis. This can be seen by noting that the point (0, b) satisfies the equation of the line.

A different form of the line equation, called the *general form*, may be found by multiplying out the factors in Equation 1.2 and collecting them on one side of the equal sign.

$$(y_2 - y_1) x - (x_2 - x_1) y + x_2y_1 - x_1y_2 = 0 \tag{1.5}$$

or

$$rx + sy + t = 0 \tag{1.6}$$

where possible values for r, s, and t are

$$r = (y_2 - y_1)$$

$$s = - (x_2 - x_1)$$

$$t = x_2y_1 - x_1y_2$$

We say *possible* values because we see that multiplying r, s, and t by any common factor will produce a new set of r′, s′, and t′ values which will still satisfy Equation 1.6 and, therefore, also describe the same line. The values for r, s, and t are sometimes chosen so that

$$r^2 + s^2 = 1 \tag{1.7}$$

Comparing Equations 1.4 and 1.6 we see that

$$m = - \frac{r}{s}$$

and $\tag{1.8}$

$$b = - \frac{t}{s}$$

Can we determine where two lines will cross? Yes, it is fairly easy to determine where two lines will cross. By the two lines crossing we mean that they share some point in common. That point will satisfy both of the equations for the two lines. The problem is to find this point. Suppose we give the equations for the two lines in their slope-intercept form:

$$\text{line 1:} \quad y = m_1x + b_1 \tag{1.9}$$
$$\text{line 2:} \quad y = m_2x + b_2$$

Now if there is some point (x_i, y_i) shared by both lines, then

$$y_i = m_1x_i + b_1 \quad \text{and} \quad y_i = m_2x_i + b_2 \tag{1.10}$$

will both be true. Equating over y_i gives

$$m_1x_i + b_1 = m_2x_i + b_2 \tag{1.11}$$

Solving for x_i yields

$$x_i = \frac{b_2 - b_1}{m_1 - m_2}$$ (1.12)

Substituting this into the equation for either line 1 or line 2 gives

$$y_i = \frac{b_2 m_1 - b_1 m_2}{m_1 - m_2}$$ (1.13)

Therefore, the point

$$\left(\frac{b_2 - b_1}{m_1 - m_2} , \frac{b_2 m_1 - b_1 m_2}{m_1 - m_2} \right)$$ (1.14)

is the intersection point. Note that two parallel lines will have the same slope. Since such lines will not intersect, it is not at all surprising that the above expression results in a division by zero. When no point exists, we cannot solve for it.

If the Equation 1.6 form is used to describe the lines, then similar algebra yields an intersection point which is given by

$$\left(\frac{s_1 t_2 - s_2 t_1}{s_2 r_1 - s_1 r_2} , \frac{t_1 r_2 - t_2 r_1}{s_2 r_1 - s_1 r_2} \right)$$ (1.15)

LINE SEGMENTS

What are *line segments*? Our equations for lines specify all points in a given direction. The lines extend forever both forward and backward. This is not exactly what we need for graphics. We would like to display only pieces of lines. Let's consider only those points on a line which lie between two endpoints p_1 and p_2. (See Figure 1-1.)

This is called a line segment. A line segment may be specified by its two endpoints. From these endpoints we can determine the equation of the line. From this equation and the endpoints we can decide if any point is or is not on the segment. If the endpoints are $p_1 = (x_1, y_1)$ and $p_2 = (x_2, y_2)$ and these yield equation $y = mx + b$ (or $rx + sy + t = 0$), then another point $p_3 = (x_3, y_3)$ lies on the segment if

1. $y_3 = mx_3 + b$ (or $rx_3 + sy_3 + t = 0$)
2. $\min(x_1, x_2) \le x_3 \le \max(x_1, x_2)$
3. $\min(y_1, y_2) \le y_3 \le \max(y_1, y_2)$

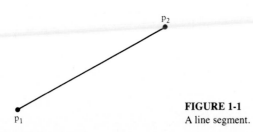

p_2

p_1

FIGURE 1-1
A line segment.

Here the notation $\min(x_1, x_2)$ means the smallest of x_1 and x_2 and $\max(x_1, x_2)$ means the largest of the two numbers.

There is one more useful form of the line equation called the *parametric form* because the x and y values on the line are given in terms of a parameter u. This form is convenient when considering line segments because we can construct it such that line-segment points correspond to values of the parameter between 0 and 1. Suppose we want the line segment between $(x_1, y_1,)$ and (x_2, y_2). We wish the x coordinate to go uniformly from x_1 to x_2. This may be expressed by the equation

$$x = x_1 + (x_2 - x_1)u \tag{1.16}$$

When u is 0, x is x_1. As u increases to 1, x moves uniformly to x_2. But for a line segment, we must have the y coordinate moving from y_1 to y_2 at the same time as x changes.

$$y = y_1 + (y_2 - y_1)u \tag{1.17}$$

The two equations together describe a straight line. This can be shown by equating over u. A little algebra recovers the line equation. Note that with this form, we can generate the point on the line segment by letting u sweep from 0 to 1; also, given the parameter value for a point on the line, we can easily test to see if the point lies within the segment boundaries.

How long is a line segment? If we are given the two endpoints of a line segment p_1 and p_2 we can determine its length L. Construct a right triangle p_1p_2A by attaching a vertical line to p_2 and a horizontal line to p_1. (See Figure 1-2.)

The Pythagorean theorem states that the square of the length of the hypotenuse (p_1p_2) is equal to the sum of the squares of the lengths of the two adjacent sides $(p_1A$ and $p_2A)$. If we call the coordinates of p_1 (x_1, y_1), and the coordinates of p_2 (x_2, y_2), then A will have coordinates (x_2, y_1), and the length of the segment L will be given by

$$L^2 = (x_2 - x_1)^2 + (y_2 - y_1)^2 \tag{1.18}$$

so

$$L = \left[(x_2 - x_1)^2 + (y_2 - y_1)^2\right]^{1/2} \tag{1.19}$$

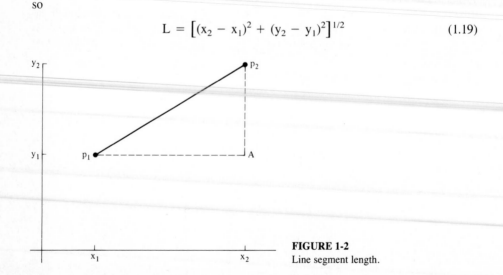

FIGURE 1-2
Line segment length.

What is the *midpoint* of a line segment? The midpoint of a line segment is often useful and easy to calculate. The point halfway between the endpoints of a segment will have an x coordinate halfway between the x coordinates of the endpoints, and a y coordinate halfway between the y coordinates of the endpoints. (See Figure 1-3.) Therefore, the midpoint is

$$(x_m, y_m) = \left[\frac{(x_1 + x_2)}{2}, \frac{(y_1 + y_2)}{2} \right] \qquad (1.20)$$

PERPENDICULAR LINES

Can we tell if two lines are *perpendicular*? We can determine if two lines are perpendicular by examining their slopes. Suppose we have two lines

$$y = m_1 x + b_1$$

and $\qquad (1.21)$

$$y = m_2 x + b_2$$

If the first line is perpendicular to the second, then a line parallel to the first (that is, a line with the same slope) will also be perpendicular to the second. For example, $y = m_1 x$ should be perpendicular to $y = m_2 x + b_2$. The same argument applies to the second line: $y = m_2 x$ will be perpendicular to $y = m_1 x$. Now these are two lines which intersect at the origin. (See Figure 1-4.)

Consider a point (x_1, y_1) on the line $y = m_1 x$ so that $y_1 = m_1 x_1$ and a point (x_2, y_2) on $y = m_2 x$ so that $y_2 = m_2 x_2$. The three points $(x_1 \ y_1)$, (x_2, y_2), and $(0, 0)$ form a triangle. If the two lines are perpendicular, they will form a right triangle and the Pythagorean theorem will apply. The distance between $(0, 0)$ and (x_1, y_1) squared plus the distance between $(0, 0)$ and (x_2, y_2) squared will equal the square of the hypotenuse between (x_1, y_1) and (x_2, y_2). The distance formula gives

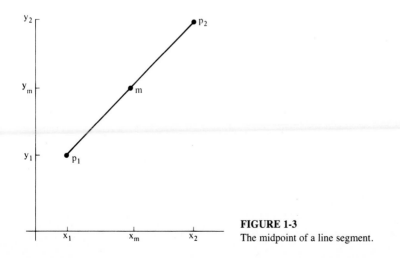

FIGURE 1-3
The midpoint of a line segment.

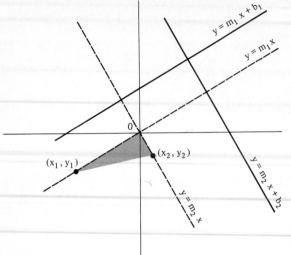

FIGURE 1-4
Construction for test for perpendicular lines.

$$x_1^2 + y_1^2 + x_2^2 + y_2^2 = (x_1 - x_2)^2 + (y_1 - y_2)^2 \tag{1.22}$$

Simplifying gives

$$0 = -2y_1y_2 - 2x_1x_2$$

or $\tag{1.23}$

$$\frac{y_1}{x_1} = -\frac{x_2}{y_2}$$

but since $y_1 = m_1x_1$ and $y_2 = m_2x_2$, we have

$$m_1 = -\frac{1}{m_2} \tag{1.24}$$

Therefore, if two lines are perpendicular, the slope of one will be the negative reciprocal of the slope of the other.

From Equations 1.8 and 1.22 we see that two lines expressed in the general form for a line are perpendicular if

$$r_1r_2 + s_1s_2 = 0 \tag{1.25}$$

It also follows that

$$(x_{b1} - x_{a1})(x_{b2} - x_{a2}) + (y_{b1} - y_{a1})(y_{b2} - y_{a2}) = 0 \tag{1.26}$$

for (x_{a1}, y_{a1}) and (x_{b1}, y_{b1}) on line 1, (x_{a2}, y_{a2}) and (x_{b2}, y_{b2}) on line 2.

DISTANCE BETWEEN A POINT AND A LINE

We shall derive one more formula in our review of geometry. What is the distance between a point and a line in a plane? Suppose we have a point (x_0, y_0) and a line $rx +$

$sy + t = 0$, where r, s, and t were chosen to satisfy Equation 1.7. We can find a line which is perpendicular to the given line and contains the given point. It is

$$-sx + ry + (sx_0 + ry_0) = 0 \qquad (1.27)$$

We can determine the intersection point of the original line and this perpendicular. (See Figure 1-5.) Using Expression 1.15 we find it to be

$$\left(s\,(sx_0 - ry_0) - rt \,,\, -st - r\,(sx_0 - ry_0)\right) \qquad (1.28)$$

Now we can use the distance formula (Equation 1.19) to determine the distance between the point (x_0, y_0) and this intersection point. This is what we mean by the distance between the point and the line.

$$L = (\{x_0 - [s\,(sx_0 - ry_0) - rt]\}^2 + \{y_0 - [-st - r\,(sx_0 - ry_0)]\}^2)^{1/2} \quad (1.29)$$

This will reduce down to

$$L = |\,rx_0 + sy_0 + t\,| \qquad (1.30)$$

Notice that this is just the magnitude of the value obtained by substituting the coordinates of the point into the expression for the line. When the expression is zero, the point is on the line, while other values give the distance of the point from the line. Remember that this only works because we have chosen values for r, s, and t which

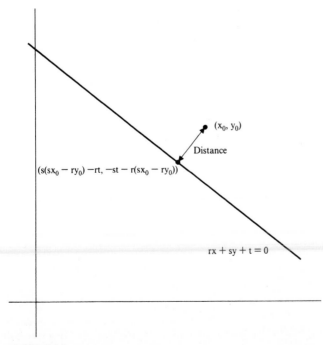

FIGURE 1-5
Distance between a point and a line.

satisfy Equation 1.7, and in fact this simple distance relationship is the motivation for this choice.

VECTORS

What is a *vector*? A vector has a single direction and a length. A vector may be denoted $[D_x, D_y]$, where D_x indicates how far to move along the x-axis direction and D_y indicates how far to move along the y-axis direction. (See Figure 1-6.)

Unlike line segments, vectors have no fixed position in space. They tell us how far and what direction to move, but they do not tell us where to start. The idea of a vector is useful because it closely parallels the manner in which a pen draws lines on paper or an electron beam draws lines on a cathode ray tube. The command to the pen may be to move so far from its current position in a given direction.

Two vectors may be added by adding their respective components.

$$V_1 + V_2 = [D_{x1}, D_{y1}] + [D_{x2}, D_{y2}] = [D_{x1} + D_{x2}, D_{y1} + D_{y2}] \tag{1.31}$$

We can picture this in terms of pen movements. Suppose we start at some point A. The first vector moves the pen from point A to point B; the second, from point B to point C. The right-hand side of the above equation produces a single vector which will move the pen directly from point A to point C.

We can also multiply a vector by a number by multiplying each of its components.

$$nV = n [D_x, D_y] = [nD_x, nD_y] \tag{1.32}$$

This preserves the vector's direction but changes its magnitude. A measure of that magnitude is given by the vector's length.

$$|V| = (D_x^2 + D_y^2)^{1/2} \tag{1.33}$$

If we multiply a vector by the reciprocal of its length, the result is a vector with length equal to 1. Such vectors are called unit vectors. They conveniently capture the direction information.

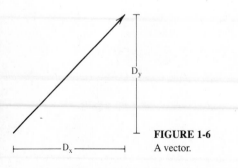

FIGURE 1-6
A vector.

D_y

D_x

We sometimes use vectors as a shorthand way of expressing operations on all coordinates. For example, the parametric equations for a line (Equations 1.16 and 1.17) can be combined into the vector form

$$V = V_1 + u(V_2 - V_1) \qquad (1.34)$$

where $V = [x, y]$, $V_1 = [x_1, y_1]$, and $V_2 = [x_2, y_2]$.

We shall consider additional vector operations in later chapters as the need arises.

PIXELS AND FRAME BUFFERS

How does all this apply to an actual graphics display? To begin with, the mathematical notion of an infinite number of infinitesimal points does not carry over to the actual display. We cannot represent an infinite number of points on a computer, just as we cannot represent an infinite quantity of numbers. The machine is finite, and we are limited to a finite number of points making up each line (usually no more than a few hundred to a few thousand). The maximum number of distinguishable points which a line may have is a measure of the resolution of the display device. The greater the number of points, the higher the resolution. This limitation in the number of points may not bother us too much, because the human eye does not notice much detail finer than 1000 points per line segment. Since we must build our lines from a finite number of points, each point must have some size and so is not really a point at all. It is called a *pixel* (short for picture element). The pixel is the smallest addressable screen element. It is the smallest piece of the display screen which we can control. Each pixel has a name or address. The names which identify pixels correspond to the coordinates which identify points. Computer graphics images are made by setting the intensity and color of the pixels which compose the screen. We draw line segments by setting the intensities, that is, the brightness, of a string of pixels between a starting pixel and an ending pixel. We can think of the display screen as a grid, or array, of pixels. We shall give integer coordinate values to each pixel. Starting at the left with 1, we shall number each column. Starting at the bottom with 1, we shall number each row. The coordinate (i, j) will then give the column and row of a pixel. Each pixel will be centered at its coordinates. (See Figure 1-7.)

We may wish to place the intensity values for all pixels into an array in our computer's memory. Our graphics display device can then access this array to determine the intensity at which each pixel should be displayed. This array, which contains an internal representation of the image, is called the *frame buffer*. It collects and stores pixel values for use by the display device.

VECTOR GENERATION

The process of "turning on" the pixels for a line segment is called *vector generation*. If we know the endpoints which specify the segment, how do we decide which pixels

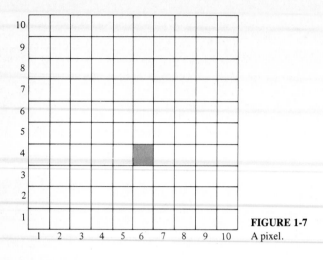

FIGURE 1-7
A pixel.

should have their intensity changed? There are several approaches to this problem. We shall present two examples here. The first is a general algorithm, while the second is a more efficient version for the case where the line segment endpoints are integers.

The problem is to select pixels which lie near to the line segment. We might try to turn on every pixel through which the line segment passes, but there is a problem with this approach. It would not be easy to find all such pixels, and since vector generation may be performed often, especially for animated displays or complex images, we want it to be efficient. Another problem is that the apparent thickness of the line would change with slope and position. An alternative would be to step along the columns of pixels, and for each column ask which row is closest to the line. We could then turn on the pixel in that row and column. We know how to find the row because we can place the x value corresponding to the column into the line equation, solve for y, and note which row it is in. This will work for lines with slopes between −1 and 1 (lines which are closer to being horizontal than vertical). But for the steeply rising or falling lines, the method will leave gaps. This failing can be overcome if we divide the lines into two classes. For the gentle slopes ($-1 < m < 1$) there are more columns than rows. These are the line segments where the length of the x component $D_x = (x_b - x_a)$ is longer than the length of the y component $D_y = (y_b - y_a)$, that is, $|D_x| > |D_y|$. For these cases, we step across the columns and solve for the rows. For the sharp slopes where $|D_x| \leq |D_y|$, we step up the rows and solve for the columns.

It would still be very inefficient if we actually had to solve the line equation to determine every pixel, but fortunately we can avoid this by taking uniform steps and using what we learn about the position of the line at each column (or row) to determine its position at the next column (or row). Consider the gentle slope case where we step across the columns. Each time we move from one column to the next, the value of x changes by 1. But if x always changes by exactly 1, then y will always change by exactly m (the slope). The change in y is

$$y_{i+1} - y_i = (mx_{i+1} + b) - (mx_i + b)$$

$$= m(x_{i+1} - x_i) = m(1) = m \tag{1.35}$$

This means that as we step along the columns, we can find the new value of y for the line by just adding m to the y position at the previous column. So our approach so far is first to find the column at the left end of the line segment and the y value at that column, and then to step through the columns which the line segment crosses, adding m to the y value each time to get a new y value. The y values will be used to select a row at each column, and we turn on a pixel at the selected row and column. (See Figure 1-8.)

The vector generation algorithms (and curve generation algorithms) which step along the line (or curve) to determine the pixels which should be turned on are sometimes called *digital differential analyzers* (DDAs). The name comes from the fact that we use the same technique as a numerical method for solving differential equations. For a line segment, we solve the differential equation for a straight line and plot the result instead of printing it.

We shall make one further refinement in our approach. Instead of determining the full y value of the line segment for each column, we shall only keep track of the current height above the closest row boundary. At each step, the height increases by m along with y. We can check the height at each step to see if we have moved into a new row. If we have entered a new row, then we change the row value used to select pixels and also subtract 1 from our height so that we will now be measuring height from the new row boundary. For lines with negative slopes, we could let the height decrease and check for crossing of a lower row boundary, but instead we use the absolute value of

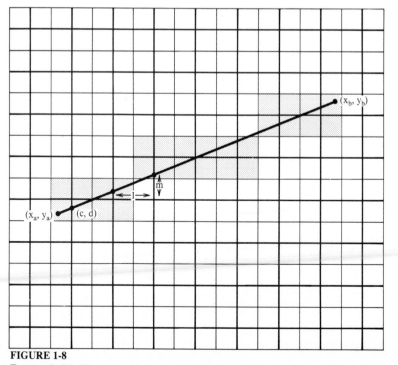

FIGURE 1-8
Turn on pixels with centers closest to the line segment.

height and slope and check as it steps up. This is in order to be consistent with the algorithm presented in the next section.

For lines with sharp slopes, a similar procedure is used, only the roles of x and y are exchanged and a new "height" is found for a new row by adding 1/m to the height value for the old row.

Now a few more words on how our particular vector generator finds the starting point. For the gentle slope cases, we shall turn on pixels in the columns that have a center line which crosses the line segment. We shall center the columns and rows on integer coordinate values, so if x_a is the left end of the line segment and x_b is the right end, then columns between $c = \text{CEILING}(x_a)$ and $f = \text{FLOOR}(x_b)$ inclusive are affected. (The function CEILING returns the smallest integer which is greater than or equal to its argument, and FLOOR returns the largest integer which is less than or equal to its argument.) Our starting y position will correspond to the point at $x = c$, and might not be the endpoint y_a. The starting y value may be determined from the line equation as follows:

$$d = mc + b = mc + (y_a - mx_a) \tag{1.36}$$

$$= y_a + m(c - x_a)$$

To find the index of the closest row, we round the value of y. Rounding may be done by adding 0.5 and then using the FLOOR function.

$$r = \text{FLOOR}(y + 0.5) \tag{1.37}$$

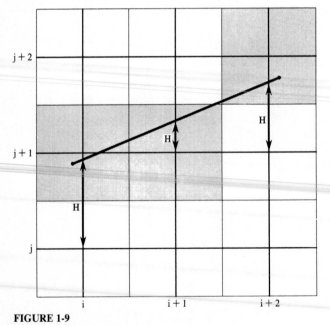

FIGURE 1-9
Height of the line above pixel-row boundaries.

To find the height of y above the row boundary, we take the difference of y (where the line is) and r (the row index). If we then add m to this, we have the height value which should be checked for the next column and so on. (See Figure 1-9.)

We shall now present the full algorithm.

1.1 Algorithm VECGEN(XA, YA, XB, YB, INTENSITY) For changing pixel values of the frame buffer along a line segment

Arguments   XA and YA are the coordinates of one endpoint

                 XB and YB are the coordinates of the other endpoint

                 INTENSITY is the intensity setting to be used for the vector

Global   FRAME the two-dimensional frame buffer array

Local   DX, DY the vector to be drawn

                 R and C the row and column indices for the pixel to be changed

                 F the stopping index

                 D the line segment coordinate at the starting point

                 H the difference between the line segment and the row index

                 M the slope of the line segment

                 M1 the change in H when a boundary is crossed

```
BEGIN
    determine the components of the vector
    DX ← XB – XA;
    DY ← YB – YA;
    decide on whether to step across columns or up rows
    IF |DX| > |DY| THEN
        BEGIN
            the gentle slope case
            M ← DY / DX;
            set up of starting point depends on which point is leftmost
            IF DX > 0 THEN
                BEGIN
                    C ← CEILING(XA);
                    D ← YA + M * (C – XA);
                    F ← FLOOR(XB);
                END
            ELSE
                BEGIN
                    C ← CEILING(XB);
                    D ← YB + M * (C – XB);
                    F ← FLOOR(XA);
                END;
            R ← FLOOR(D + 0.5);
            H ← R – D + M;
            IF M > 0 THEN
                BEGIN
                    the positive slope case
                    M1 ← M – 1;
                    now step through the columns
                    WHILE C ≤ F DO
```

```
                    BEGIN
                        set the nearest pixel in the frame buffer
                        FRAME[C, R] ← INTENSITY;
                        next column
                        C ← C + 1;
                        should row change
                        IF H ≥ 0.5 THEN
                            BEGIN
                                R ← R + 1;
                                H ← H + M1;
                            END
                        ELSE H ← H + M;
                    END;
                END
            ELSE
                BEGIN
                    then negative slope case
                    M ← –M;
                    H ← –H;
                    M1 ← M – 1;
                    WHILE C ≤ F DO
                        BEGIN
                            set the nearest pixel in the frame buffer
                            FRAME[C, R] ← INTENSITY;
                            next column
                            C ← C + 1;
                            should row change
                            IF H > 0.5 THEN
                                BEGIN
                                    R ← R – 1;
                                    H ← H + M1;
                                END
                            ELSE H ← H + M;
                        END;
                END;
            END
        ELSE
            BEGIN
                the sharp slope case
                IF DY = 0.0 THEN RETURN;
                here the above steps are repeated
                with the roles of x and y interchanged
            END;
        RETURN;
    END;
```

The actual algorithm contains a couple of things which were not brought up in the above discussion. The determination of the starting values is complicated by not knowing a priori whether XA is left or right of XB, and YA above or below YB. The algorithm also contains a test on the sign of the slope. It is used to select a loop which moves the line in the proper direction.

BRESENHAM'S ALGORITHM

The above algorithm was chosen because it can be revised into a very efficient and popular form known as *Bresenham's algorithm* for the special case where the coordinates of the line segment endpoints are integers. The attractiveness of Bresenham's algorithm is that it can be implemented entirely with integer arithmetic. Integer arithmetic is usually much faster than floating-point arithmetic. Furthermore, Bresenham's algorithm does not require any multiplication or division. To derive the algorithm, first consider the effect of integer coordinates on determining the starting point. The starting point will just be the endpoint of the line segment. No calculation is needed to move along the line to a pixel center, because it is already there. This eliminates one place where the line slope was needed, but we also used the slope to update H. How can we revise our test for new rows so that it requires only integer arithmetic? To simplify the discussion, consider just the gentle slope case. The test was

$$H > 0.5 \tag{1.38}$$

where

$$H \leftarrow H + M$$

or

$$H \leftarrow H + M - 1$$

at each column. Note first that we can rewrite the test as

$$H - 0.5 > 0$$

Now we can multiply by 2 to get

$$2H - 1 > 0 \tag{1.39}$$

Notice how the 0.5 fraction is removed. But H still has a fractional part, which arises from the denominator in M that is added in at each step. To remove it, we multiply by DX. Assuming we have arranged the endpoints so that DX is positive, the test is then

$$2DX \, H - DX > 0$$

Suppose we define G as

$$G = 2DX \, H - DX \tag{1.40}$$

The test is simply

$$G > 0 \tag{1.41}$$

Then how does G change from one column to the next? Solving for H gives

$$H = \frac{G + DX}{2DX} \tag{1.42}$$

If

$$H_{new} \leftarrow H_{old} + M$$

then

$$\frac{G_{new} + DX}{2DX} \leftarrow \frac{G_{old} + DX}{2DX} + \frac{DY}{DX}$$

or

$$G_{new} \leftarrow G_{old} + 2DY \tag{1.43}$$

For the case

$$H_{new} \leftarrow H_{old} + M - 1$$

we get

$$G_{new} \leftarrow G_{old} + 2DY - 2DX \tag{1.44}$$

Calculating G requires only additions and subtractions and can be done entirely with integers. The trick then is to use the test $G > 0$ to determine when a row boundary is crossed by the line instead of the test $H > 0.5$. For integer endpoints, the initial value of H is M, so the initial value of G is

$$G = 2DX \left(\frac{DY}{DX} \right) - DX = 2DY - DX \tag{1.45}$$

For each column, we check G. If it is positive, we move to the next row and add $2DY - 2DX$ to G. Otherwise, we keep the same row and add $2DY$ to G. The full algorithm follows.

1.2 Algorithm BRESENHAM(XA, YA, XB, YB, INTENSITY) For changing pixel values of the frame buffer along a line segment with integer endpoints

Arguments XA and YA are the coordinates of one endpoint
  XB and YB are the coordinates of the other endpoint
  INTENSITY is the intensity setting to be used for the vector

Global FRAME the two-dimensional frame buffer array

Local DX, DY the vector to be drawn
  R, C the row and column indices for the pixel
  F the final row or column
  G for testing for a new row or column
  INC1 increment for G when row or column is unchanged
  INC2 increment for G when row or column changes
  POS-SLOPE a flag to indicate if the slope is positive

BEGIN
  determine the components of the vector
  DX ← XB – XA;
  DY ← YB – YA;

determine the sign of the slope
POS-SLOPE ← (DX > 0);
IF DY < 0 THEN POS-SLOPE ← NOT POS-SLOPE;
decide on whether to step across columns or up rows
IF |DX| > |DY| THEN
    BEGIN
        this is the gentle slope case
        IF DX > 0 THEN
            BEGIN
                C ← XA;
                R ← YA;
                F ← XB;
            END
        ELSE
            BEGIN
                C ← XB;
                R ← YB;
                F ← XA;
            END;
        INC1 ← 2 * |DY|;
        G ← 2 * |DY| – |DX|;
        INC2 ← 2 * (|DY| – |DX|);
        IF POS-SLOPE THEN
            BEGIN
                now step across line segment
                WHILE C ≤ F DO
                    BEGIN
                        set nearest pixel in the frame buffer
                        FRAME[C, R] ← INTENSITY;
                        next column
                        C ← C + 1;
                        should row change
                        IF G ≥ 0 THEN
                            BEGIN
                                R ← R + 1;
                                G ← G + INC2;
                            END
                        ELSE G ← G + INC1;
                    END;
        END
        ELSE
            BEGIN
                WHILE C ≤ F DO
                BEGIN
                        set nearest pixel in the frame buffer
                        FRAME[C, R] ← INTENSITY;
                        next column
                        C ← C + 1;
                        should row change

```
         IF G > 0 THEN
            BEGIN
               R ← R – 1;
               G ← INC2;
            END
         ELSE G ← G + INC1;
      END;
   END;
END
ELSE
   BEGIN
      this is the sharp slope case
      here the above steps are repeated
      with the roles of x and y interchanged
   END;
RETURN;
END;
```

We have seen how the BRESENHAM algorithm is more efficient than the VEC-GEN algorithm in that it requires only integer addition and subtraction. We might ask, why not always use it? Why not always round line segment endpoints to integers before vector generation? In fact, many systems will do just that, but note that in rounding the line segment endpoint positions, errors are introduced. These errors can be seen in cases where two overlapping line segments are drawn on the display (as when two objects are shown side by side). Another example occurs when a new line segment with a different INTENSITY overlaps an old line segment; we might like to change the old segment's pixels to the appropriate values for the new segment. If we deal with exactly the same line equation for both line segments, then the same pixels should be selected; but if errors in the endpoint positions are introduced, the line equations might not match, and the new line segment can leave pixels from the old line segment peeking out from behind it. Note, however, that even our VECGEN algorithm can have errors introduced in the endpoint position as the result of round-off in the floating point arithmetic of the machine.

Algorithms for vector generation (such as the ones we've seen) may be implemented in hardware where speed is important. This is usually done for displays which avoid the cost of a large frame buffer memory by letting the vector generator directly control the drawing instrument (usually an electron beam in a cathode ray tube). Instead of setting the (x, y) element in a frame buffer, the pen (or electron beam) is moved to position (x, y), where it illuminates the pixel on the screen.

ANTIALIASING OF LINES

Many displays allow only two pixel states, on or off. For these displays, lines may have a jagged or stair-step appearance when they step from one row or column to the next. The lower the resolution, the more apparent the effect. This is one aspect of a phenomenon called *aliasing*. Aliasing produces the defects which occur when the scene being displayed changes faster or more smoothly than every two pixels. Displays which allow setting pixels to gray levels between black and white provide a means to reduce this effect. The technique is called *antialiasing*, and it uses the gray levels to gradually turn off the pixels in one row as it gradually turns on the pixels in the next. (See Figure 1-10.)

The vector generation algorithms can be modified to perform antialiasing. Remember that for gentle sloped lines, we in effect examined the line position for each column index and decided which row was closest. The line segment would lie between two pixels, and we picked one. Suppose that instead of picking the closest, we turned them both on. We should choose the intensity values according to a function of the distance between the pixel index and the line segment so that the pixel closest to the line receives most of its intensity. The sum of the intensity values for the two pixels should match the total intensity value for the line. The function used can be a simple or a complex expression based on intensity patterns, pixel shapes, and how lines cover them. In general, we want the pixel's intensity to match the amount of the line which covers its area. Antialiasing with complicated functions can still be done efficiently by storing the function values in a table. The table is then used to look up the intensity for a distance between the pixel index and the line. (See Figure 1-11.)

THICK LINE SEGMENTS

Raster displays allow the display of lines with thickness greater than one pixel. To produce a thick line segment, we can run two vector generation algorithms in parallel to find the pixels along the line edges. As we step along the line finding successive edge pixels, we must also turn on all pixels which lie between the boundaries. For a gentle sloping line between (x_a, y_a) and (x_b, y_b) with thickness w, we would have a top boundary between the points $(x_a, y_a + w_y)$ and $(x_b, y_b + w_y)$ and a lower boundary between $(x_a, y_a - w_y)$ and $(x_b, y_b - w_y)$ where w_y is given by

$$w_y = \frac{(w-1)}{2} \frac{[(x_b - x_a)^2 + (y_b - y_a)^2]^{1/2}}{|x_b - x_a|} \tag{1.46}$$

This is the amount by which the boundary lines are moved from the line center. The (w − 1) factor is the desired width minus the one-pixel thickness we automatically receive from drawing the boundary. We divide this by 2 because half the thickness will be used to offset the top boundary, and the other half to move the bottom boundary. The factor containing the x and y values is needed to find the amount to shift up and

FIGURE 1-10
Antialiasing of a line.

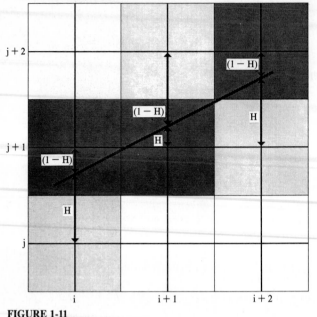

FIGURE 1-11
Using vertical distance from the pixel to determine intensity.

down in order to achieve the proper width w as measured perpendicular to the line direction, not up and down. (See Figure 1-12.) Sharply sloping lines can be handled similarly with the x and y roles reversed.

CHARACTER GENERATION

Along with lines and points, strings of characters are often displayed to label and annotate drawings and to give instructions and information to the user. Characters are almost always built into the graphics display device, usually as hardware but sometimes through software. There are two primary methods for character generation. One is called the *stroke method*. This method creates characters out of a series of line segments, like strokes of a pen. We could build our own stroke-method character generator by calls to the VECGEN algorithm. We would decide what line segments are needed for each character and set up the calls to the VECGEN for each character we wished to draw. In actual graphics displays, the commands for drawing the character line segments may be in either hardware or software. The stroke method lends itself to changes of scale; the characters may be made twice as large by simply doubling the length of each segment.

The second method of character generation is the *dot-matrix* or *bitmap method*. In this scheme, characters are represented by an array of dots. An array of 5 dots wide and 7 dots high is often used, but 7 × 9 and 9 × 13 arrays are also found. High-resolution devices, such as ink-jet or laser printers, may use character arrays that are over 100

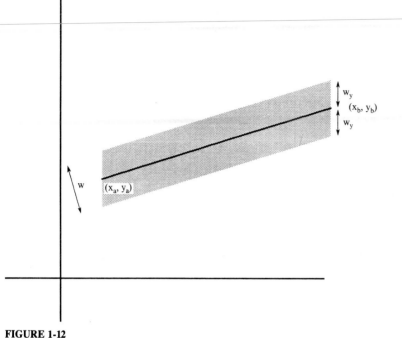

FIGURE 1-12
Thick line construction.

pixels on a side. This array is like a small frame buffer, just big enough to hold a character. The dots are the pixels for this small array. Placing the character on the screen then becomes a matter of copying pixel values from the small character array into some portion of the screen's frame buffer (usually, for common alphanumeric terminals the dot matrix is allowed to directly control the intensity of small parts of the screen, eliminating the need for a large frame buffer). The memory containing the character dot-matrix array is often a hardware device called a *character-generator chip*, but random access memory may also be used when many fonts are desired. The size of a dot is fixed, so the dot-matrix method does not lend itself to variable-sized characters. (See Figure 1-13.)

(a)

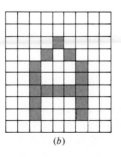

(b)

FIGURE 1-13
Character generation. (a) Stroke method;
(b) dot-matrix method.

Antialiasing techniques can be applied to characters. This can improve the appearance of the character, particularly for very small fonts and characters where the finite resolution of the display interferes with their smooth curved shapes.

DISPLAYING THE FRAME BUFFER

Using algorithms such as VECGEN or BRESENHAM, a frame buffer array may be modified to contain line segments and characters. This array directly corresponds to the screen and holds an intensity-coded form of the image to be displayed. To use this device, some additional operations are required. We must be able to clear the frame buffer. We need to begin with a blank array for the same reason that we start a pen-and-ink drawing with a blank piece of paper. Another operation which is necessary is transfer of the information from the frame buffer to the display medium (the display screen or the paper). For raster graphics displays, this operation is built into the hardware. The frame buffer is continually being scanned by the hardware to form the screen image. Any change in the frame buffer is immediately shown on the screen. For graphics output on a line printer, however, there is no hardware which automatically shows the content of the frame buffer. In this case, the display operation must be done by a software routine. Finally, routines may be necessary for initialization and termination of the graphics system. When starting a graphics program, hardware devices and storage may be allocated and variables may be initialized by an initialization routine. Upon the completion of the job, the deallocation of the storage, the release of hardware devices, and other housekeeping chores may be done by a termination routine.

To complete this chapter, we would like to give the algorithms needed to obtain graphics output from a line printer or common CRT terminal. The first algorithms, the vector generators, have already been presented. We shall need a frame buffer array to hold the image. The size of this array depends upon the resolution of the display device. If a CRT displaying 24 lines of 80 characters each is used, the frame buffer might be dimensioned FRAME[80,24]. This is not the only choice. In many displays we find that setting the lower right-hand pixel will cause automatic scrolling of the image, shifting the top line off the screen. This can be prevented by not using the bottom line, and [80,23] may be more appropriate. Or we may find that the display screen is not square, and for the sake of treating the x and y directions equally, we may select a square subarea like [60,23]. A line printer may use an array FRAME[90,50] or larger, depending on the storage available and the number of characters per line. The frame buffer will be an array of characters. The INTENSITY of algorithm 1.1 will be a character such as the period or asterisk, out of which we will construct the picture. For a clear or empty frame buffer corresponding to a clear display, the array should be filled entirely with blanks. This is done by the following algorithm.

1.3 Algorithm ERASE Clears the frame buffer by assigning every pixel a background value

Global   FRAME the two-dimensional frame buffer array
             WIDTH-START and HEIGHT-START the starting indices of FRAME
             WIDTH-END and HEIGHT-END the ending indices of FRAME
Local   X, Y frame buffer indices

```
BEGIN
    FOR Y = HEIGHT-START TO HEIGHT-END DO
        FOR X = WIDTH-START TO WIDTH-END DO
            FRAME[X, Y] ← ' ';
    RETURN;
END;
```

A call of the ERASE routine clears the display. We can use this whenever we wish to draw a new picture.

The DISPLAY routine is used to show the contents of the frame buffer on a line printer. Note that while our y coordinate begins at the bottom and increases as we move up the display, printers typically begin at the top of the page and work down. This means that the y coordinate must be displayed beginning with its high values and working down.

1.4 Algorithm DISPLAY This displays the contents of the frame buffer

```
Global      FRAME the frame buffer array
            WIDTH-START and HEIGHT-START the starting indices of FRAME
            WIDTH-END and HEIGHT-END the ending indices of FRAME
Local       X,Y the pixel being displayed
BEGIN
    FOR Y = HEIGHT-END TO HEIGHT-START DO
        PRINT FOR X = WIDTH-START TO WIDTH-END, FRAME[X, Y];
    RETURN;
END;
```

To complete this package, we must include a routine to initialize the parameters for the display size and to perform any system-dependent housekeeping. Included in the initialization should be the establishment of frame buffer size parameters and the clearing of the display.

1.5 Algorithm INITIALIZE-1

```
Global      WIDTH-START and HEIGHT-START the starting indices of FRAME
            WIDTH-END and HEIGHT-END the ending indices of FRAME
            WIDTH, HEIGHT the dimensions of FRAME
BEGIN
    perform any needed storage allocation, hardware assignment,
    or other system-dependent housekeeping;
    HEIGHT-START ← starting column index of FRAME;
    WIDTH-START ← starting row index of FRAME;
    HEIGHT-END ← ending column index of FRAME;
    WIDTH-END ← ending row index of FRAME;
    HEIGHT ← HEIGHT-END – HEIGHT-START;
    WIDTH ← WIDTH-END – WIDTH-START;
    ERASE;
    RETURN;
END;
```

1.6 Algorithm TERMINATE
BEGIN
    release any assigned hardware devices;
    perform any necessary final housekeeping;
    STOP;
END;

FURTHER READING

There are a large number of texts on analytic geometry. One book which is oriented toward computer graphics is [ROG76]. Use of a frame buffer was first described in [NOL71]. Bresenham presented his algorithm in [BRE65]. DDAs and Bresenham's algorithm are also discussed in [EAR77], [FIE85], [LOC80], and [SPR82]. An alternative approach to vector generation based on the general form of the line equation rather than on the parametric form is presented in [DAN70]. Another approach based on the structural properties of the line is described in [BRO74] and [CED79]. A symmetric algorithm which allows a sequence of lines to be erased by drawing them in reverse order with "white ink" is given in [TRA82]. An example of a 7 × 9 dot-matrix font may be found in [VAR71]. An example of specialized character-generation hardware may be found in [THO72]. A discussion of antialiasing lines may be found in [CRO78], [GUP81], and [PIT80]. A simple, fast algorithm for antialiased lines is given in [KET85]. Antialiasing of characters is described in [WAR80]. A more general discussion of aliasing and antialiasing is presented in [LEL80]. An early description of CORE was published in [GSPC79]. An overview of the GKS standard is given in [BON82]. The GKS standard is published in [GKS84].

[BON82] Bono, P. R., Encarnacao, J. L., Hopgood, F. R. A., ten Hagen, P. J. W., "GKS—The First Graphics Standard," *IEEE Computer Graphics and Applications*, vol. 2, no. 7, pp. 9–23 (1982).

[BRE65] Bresenham, J. E., "Algorithm for Computer Control of a Digital Plotter," *IBM System Journal*, vol. 4, no.1, pp. 106–111 (1965).

[BRO74] Brons, R., "Linguistic Methods for the Description of a Straight Line on a Grid," *Computer Graphics and Image Processing*, vol. 3, no. 1, pp. 48–62 (1974).

[CED79] Cederberg, R. L. T., "A New Method for Vector Generation," *Computer Graphics and Image Processing*, vol. 9, no. 2, pp. 183–195 (1979).

[CRO78] Crow, F. C., "The Use of Grayscale for Improved Raster Display of Vectors and Characters," *Computer Graphics*, vol. 12, no. 3, pp. 1–5 (1978).

[DAN70] Danielsson, P. E., "Incremental Curve Generation," *IEEE Transactions on Computers*, vol. C-19, no. 9, pp. 783–793 (1970).

[EAR77] Earnshaw, R. A., "Line Generation for Incremental and Raster Devices," *Computer Graphics*, vol. 11, no. 2, pp. 199–205 (1977).

[FIE85] Field, D., "Incremental Linear Interpolation," *ACM Transactions on Graphics*, vol. 4, no. 1, pp. 1–11, (1985).

[GKS84] "Graphics Kernel System, ANSI X3H3/83-25r3," *Computer Graphics*, vol. 18, special issue (Feb. 1984).

[GSPC79] "Status Report of the Graphics Standards Planning Committee of ACM/SIGGRAPH," *Computer Graphics*, vol. 13, no. 3 (1979).

[GUP81] Gupta, S., and Sproull, R. F., "Filtering Edges for Gray-Scale Displays," *Computer Graphics*, vol. 15, no. 3, pp. 1–5 (1981).

[KET85] Ketcham, R. L., "A High-Speed Algorithm for Generating Anti-Aliased Lines," *Society for Information Display 85 Digest*, vol. 16, pp. 308–311 (1985).

[LEL80] Leler, W. J., "Human Vision, Anti-aliasing, and the Cheap 4000 Line Display," *Computer Graphics*, vol. 14, no. 3, pp. 308–313 (1980).

[LOC80] Loceff, M., "A New Approach to High-Speed Computer Graphics: The Line," *Computer*, vol. 13, no. 6, pp. 56–66 (1980).

[NOL71] Noll, A. M., "Scanned-Display Computer Graphics," *Communications of the ACM*, vol. 14, no. 3, pp. 143–150 (1971).

[PIT80] Pitteway, M. L. V., and Watkinson, D. J., "Bresenham's Algorithm with Grey Scale," *Communications of the ACM*, vol. 23, no. 11, pp. 625–626 (1980).

[ROG76] Rogers, D. F., Adams, J. A., *Mathematical Elements for Computer Graphics*, McGraw-Hill, New York (1976).

[SPR82] Sproull, R. F., "Using Program Transformations to Derive Line-Drawing Algorithms," *ACM Transactions on Graphics*, vol. 1, no. 4, pp. 259–273 (1982).

[THO72] Thomas, P. A. V., and Mennie, W. E., "A Logic Character Generator for Use in a CRT Text Display," *Information Display*, vol. 9, no. 2, pp. 9–14 (1972).

[TRA82] Tran-Thong, "A Symmetric Linear Algorithm for Line Segment Generation," *Computers and Graphics*, vol. 6, no. 1, pp. 15–17 (1982).

[VAR71] Vartabedian, A. G., "A Graphic Set for ASCII Using a 7 × 9 Dot Pattern," *Information Display*, vol. 8, no. 6, pp. 11–16 (1971).

[WAR80] Warnock, J. E., "The Display of Characters Using Gray Level Sample Arrays," *Computer Graphics*, vol. 14, no. 3, pp. 302–307 (1980).

EXERCISES

1-1 Give the slope-intercept form of the equation for the line passing through each pair of points.

a) $(0, 0)$ and $(6, 2)$

b) $(1, 0)$ and $(7, 2)$

c) $(2, 3)$ and $(4, 2)$

d) $(1, 1)$ and $(2, 3)$

e) $(0, 2.5)$ and $(-1, 3.5)$

f) $(3, 6)$ and $(-4, 6)$

1-2 Give a general form for the equation of the line passing through each pair of points in Exercise 1-1.

1-3 For the following pairs of lines, state whether or not they intersect. If they do, give the coordinates of the point of intersection.

a) $y = x$ and $y = 2x + 6$

b) $y = x + 4$ and $y = -2x - 1$

c) $y = x + 4$ and $y = 2x + 6$

d) $y = -2x - 1$ and $y = 2x + 6$

e) $y = -x/3 + 6$ and $y = 2x + 6$

f) $y = -x/3 + 6$ and $y = x/3 + 4$

g) $y = -x/3 + 6$ and $y = x + 4$

h) $y = x$ and $y = x + 4$

i) $y = x$ and $y = x/3 + 4$

j) $y = -3$ and $y = x + 4$

1-4 For each line segment specified by the following endpoints, give the midpoint and the middle third line segment.

a) $(0, 0)$ to $(5, 0)$

b) $(1, 3)$ to $(4, 7)$

c) (4, 4) to (1, 7)
d) (1, 1) to (–3, 4)
e) (3, 5) to (–2, –7)
f) (2, 0) to (0, 2)
g) (2, 1) to (2, 4)
h) (2, 1) to (4, 2)

1-5 What is the length of each line segment in Exercise 1-4?

1-6 For each of the segments specified in Exercise 1-4, give parametric equations for x and y with parameter u. The equations should give the first endpoint at u = 0 and the second endpoint at u = 1.

1-7 For the points

$$P_1 = (1, 1)$$

$$P_2 = (4, 5)$$

$$P_3 = (6, 2)$$

find the distance between each point and the line passing through the other two.

1-8 Consider the vectors

$$A = [3, 4]$$

$$B = [-1, 3]$$

$$C = [5, 12]$$

a) Give the length of each vector.
b) Find unit vectors for each of the three vector directions.
c) Show all possible pairwise additions of the vectors.

1-9 Consider the vectors $V_1 = [1, 4]$ and $V_2 = [5, 2]$.
   a) Plot the two vectors and their sum on graph paper such that each vector begins at the origin.
   b) Plot the locus of points (x, y) as u goes from 0 to 1 for

$$[x, y] = V = V_1 + uV_2.$$

c) Plot $V = V_2 + uV_1$
d) Plot $V = uV_1 + (1 - u) V_2$.

1-10 For a 10 × 10 frame buffer, interpret the BRESENHAM algorithm by hand to find which pixels are turned on for the line segments between
   a) (1, 2) and (7, 6)
   b) (3, 2) and (6, 4)
   c) (5, 8) and (9, 5)

1-11 The darkness of a line depends on the density of dark pixels for the line, that is, the number of pixels set divided by the line's true length. Calculate this density as a function of the line's slope for the BRESENHAM algorithm. Suggest ways to reduce this variation.

1-12 Because it only takes one bit to indicate if a pixel is on or off, we often find frame buffers organized such that many pixels are packed into each computer word (one pixel for each bit in the word). Suppose you had an array of 16-bit words for use as a frame buffer; write procedures to set and examine individual pixels.

PROGRAMMING PROBLEMS

1-1 Implement algorithms 1.1 or 1.2, and 1.3 through 1.6 to form a line-drawing system.

1-2 Test the system of Programming Problem 1-1 by writing a program to draw a house. For example:

    a) Call INITIALIZE-1 to set the frame parameters.
    b) Call ERASE to clear the display.
    c) Call the VECGEN or BRESENHAM algorithm to draw a house, such as
        BRESENHAM (10, 5, 10, 10, '*')
        BRESENHAM (10, 10, 25, 15, '*')
        BRESENHAM (25, 15, 40, 10, '*')
        BRESENHAM (40, 10, 40, 5, '*')
        BRESENHAM (40, 5, 10, 5, '*')
    d) Call DISPLAY.
    e) Call TERMINATE to end the program.

1-3 A widget manufacturing firm made the following sales:

Jan.	2000
Feb.	4000
Mar.	7000
Apr.	6000
May	4000
June	8000
July	8000
Aug.	7000
Sept.	5000
Oct.	6000
Nov.	8000
Dec.	9000

Using the line-drawing system of Programming Problem 1-1, write a program to plot a graph of the year's widget sales. (See page 30, top.)

1-4 Using the widget data of Programming Problem 1-3, construct a bar graph of the year's sales. (See page 31, top.)

1-5 Write a routine to draw a square with a side length A centered on the display. The value of A should be given as an argument to the routine. Test this routine by drawing a picture with four squares of different sizes. (See page 32, top.)

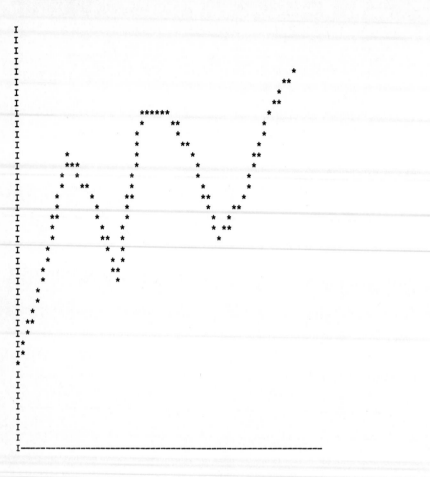

1-6 Write a program to draw an approximation to the curve $x = y^2 / 10$. Do this by dividing the y direction into intervals $y_1, y_2, \ldots, y_n$. Find the point on the curve corresponding to each x value.

$$(x, y) = (y^2 / 10, y)$$

So for y_1 ($y_1^2 / 10, y_1$); for y_2 ($y_2^2 / 10, y_2$); and so on. Connect these points with line segments to get the approximation to the curve. (See page 32, bottom.)

1-7 Modify the BRESENHAM algorithm so that it will produce a dashed-line pattern. The dash length should be independent of slope.

*1-8 Some CRT terminals allow positioning of the cursor by means of control characters or escape sequences. If you have such a terminal, modify the vector generation algorithms so that they alter the characters directly on the screen, instead of changing the value of a frame buffer.

*1-9 a) Modify the VECGEN algorithm to provide antialiasing. To simplify the problem, use the vertical distance to the line (H and H − 1 in the algorithm) to find intensities rather than the

```
I
I
I
I
I
I                                                      *
I                                                      *
I                                                      *
I                                                      *
I                        *       *              *      *
I                        *       *              *      *
I                        *       *              *      *
I                        *       *              *      *
I           *            *       *      *       *      *
I           *            *       *      *       *      *
I           *            *       *      *       *      *
I           *            *       *      *       *      *
I           *    *       *       *      *   *   *      *
I           *    *       *       *      *   *   *      *
I           *    *       *       *      *   *   *      *
I           *    *       *       *      *   *   *      *
I           *    *       *       *      *   *   *      *
I           *    *       *       *   *  *   *   *      *
I           *    *       *       *   *  *   *   *      *
I           *    *       *       *   *  *   *   *      *
I      *    *    *    *   *       *   *  *   *   *      *
I      *    *    *    *   *       *   *  *   *   *      *
I      *    *    *    *   *       *   *  *   *   *      *
I      *    *    *    *   *       *   *  *   *   *      *
I      *    *    *    *   *       *   *  *   *   *      *
I      *    *    *    *   *       *   *  *   *   *      *
I      *    *    *    *   *       *   *  *   *   *      *
I      *    *    *    *   *       *   *  *   *   *      *
I      *    *    *    *   *       *   *  *   *   *      *
I      *    *    *    *   *       *   *  *   *   *      *
I      *    *    *    *   *       *   *  *   *   *      *
I      *    *    *    *   *       *   *  *   *   *      *
I      *    *    *    *   *       *   *  *   *   *      *
I      *    *    *    *   *       *   *  *   *   *      *
I----*----*----*----*----*----*----*----*----*----*----*-----
```

true distance measured perpendicular to the line direction. Also assume that the intensity is prop- ortional to 1 minus the distance. Test your algorithm on a scene containing lines at many differ- ent angles.

b) The true distance between the line and the pixel center can easily be determined from the vertical distance and the line's slope. Note, however, that the sum of the perpendicular dis- tances will not be 1, so they should not be used as a direct measure of pixel intensity. Instead, we can imagine the line overlapping a portion of some extended pixel shape. The actual displayed pixels will be brightest at their centers and then decline with distance, but they may overlap with other pixels to provide uniform intensity areas. The spatial distribution of light from a pixel is called its filter function. We can decide how much of this intensity distribution is claimed by the line for some representative distances between line and pixel center, and store the result in a table. This table provides the intensity for a pixel, given the distance between it and the line. Im- plement this method of antialiasing.

c) We are spreading the line over two pixels instead of just turning on one, so the pixels are gray, each representing part of the line and part of the background. But it can happen that some of the background pixels are not ''off'' (e.g., when one line crosses another). To take this into account, the intensity value determined for the new line should be combined with the exist-

```
****************************************************************
*                                                              *
*                                                              *
*     *********************************************************  *
*     *                                                   *    *
*     *                                                   *    *
*     *                                                   *    *
*     *     ***************************************       *    *
*     *     *                                     *       *    *
*     *     *                                     *       *    *
*     *     *                                     *       *    *
*     *     *                                     *       *    *
*     *     *                                     *       *    *
*     *     *          ***********                *       *    *
*     *     *          *         *                *       *    *
*     *     *          *         *                *       *    *
*     *     *          *         *                *       *    *
*     *     *          *         *                *       *    *
*     *     *          ***********                *       *    *
*     *     *                                     *       *    *
*     *     *                                     *       *    *
*     *     *                                     *       *    *
*     *     *                                     *       *    *
*     *     *                                     *       *    *
*     *     ***************************************       *    *
*     *                                                   *    *
*     *                                                   *    *
*     *                                                   *    *
*     *********************************************************  *
*                                                              *
*                                                              *
****************************************************************
```

ing value, rather than replacing it. Develop a suitable combination scheme and modify your algorithm to use it. Test it on a scene where lines cross.

*1-10 Construct a routine THICK-VECGEN(XA, YA, XB, YB, W, INTENSITY) which takes two endpoints and a line width, and enters into the frame buffer a thick vector with width W centered on the line segment from (XA, YA) to (XB, YB).

```
                              ***
                             *****
                            ****
                           ***
                        ****
                       ***
                      **
                    ***
                  ***
                 **
               ***
              ***
            **
           **
          **
         **
        **
       *
       *
      *
      *
```

CHAPTER
TWO

GRAPHICS
PRIMITIVES

INTRODUCTION

The computer graphics user will not, in general, have to start from scratch in preparing for a project. Instead, he will have a graphics system available. This system will include special hardware for output and input of pictorial information and software routines for performing the basic graphics operations.

The purpose of a graphics system is to make programming easier for the user. Just as high-level computer languages make programming easier by supplying powerful operations and constructs which match the requirements of the problem, a graphics system supplies operations and constructs suited to the creation of graphical images to enhance the development of a graphics program. In fact, some graphics systems are in the form of special high-level graphics languages, languages suitable for solving graphics problems. Other graphics systems are in the form of extensions to general-purpose high-level languages such as FORTRAN, PL/I, or PASCAL. Such extensions may be made through a "package" of subprograms or by the addition of new language constructs.

While the form may vary between different graphics systems, there are certain basic operations which can almost always be found. These are operations such as moving the pen (or electron beam), drawing a line, writing a character or a string of text, and changing the line style. In this chapter we shall begin constructing our own graphics system. We shall start by looking in more detail at some of the types of display devices. We shall present algorithms for some basic graphics operations, and we shall introduce the concepts of device independence and of a display file.

DISPLAY DEVICES

We saw in the last chapter how computer graphics images are composed of a finite number of picture elements, or pixels. A display with good resolution might have 1000 divisions in both the x and y directions. The screen would then have 1000 × 1000 or 1 million, pixels. Each pixel requires at least one bit of intensity information, light or dark, and further bits are needed if shades of gray or different colors are desired. Thus, if we actually store the information for each pixel in the computer's memory, a lot of memory may be required. This is, in fact, what is done in some *raster graphics* displays. As we said in Chapter 1, the portion of the memory used to hold the pixels is called the frame buffer. The memory is usually scanned and displayed by *direct memory access*, that is, special hardware, independent of the central processor (leaving the processor free for generation of the images). (See Figure 2-1.)

In the raster display, the frame buffer may be examined to determine what is currently being displayed. Surfaces, as well as lines, may be displayed on raster display devices. Since images may be displayed on television-style picture tubes, raster display devices can often take advantage of the technological research and mass production of the television industry. The raster terminal can also display color images. One of the problems with the raster display is the time which may be required to alter every pixel whenever the image is changed. Another disadvantage is the cost of the required memory. This has been eased in some displays by using a coarse resolution (fewer pixels). However, technological progress has steadily brought the price of memory down, and at this point in time it appears that raster graphics will play a dominant role in the future.

In the past, the cost of memory made the raster display seem much less promising. Different designs for graphics displays were developed in an effort to reduce expenses. One approach was to let the display medium remember the image, instead of using the computer memory. This is what plotters do. A pen is lowered onto paper and moved under the direction of a vector generation algorithm. (See Figure 2-2.)

Once the line is drawn, the ink on the paper "remembers" it, and the computer need not consider it further. The main disadvantage to this approach is that once drawn, a line cannot be easily removed. If we wish to change the image on the plotter by removing a line, we must get a fresh piece of paper and redraw the picture (without the removed line). This can be time-consuming (and can use a lot of paper). For this reason, plotters are not the best devices for interactive graphics.

The first "low-cost" CRT display (under $5000) was produced by Tektronix. Because of good resolution and low cost, these terminals became widely accepted and may be commonly found today. The terminals use special cathode ray tubes called *direct view storage tubes (DVST)*, which behave much the same way as a plotter. An elec-

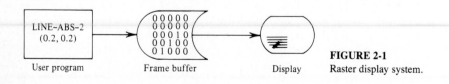

| LINE–ABS–2 | | |
| (0.2, 0.2) | | |

User program   Frame buffer   Display

FIGURE 2-1
Raster display system.

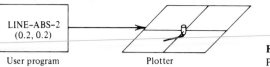

LINE–ABS–2
(0.2, 0.2)

User program   Plotter

FIGURE 2-2
Plotting system.

tron beam is directed at the surface of the screen. The position of the beam is controlled by electric or magnetic fields within the tube. Once the screen phosphors of this special tube have been illuminated by the electron beam, they stay lit. (See Figure 2-3.)

As was the case with the plotter, one cannot alter a DVST image except by erasing the entire screen and drawing it again. This can be done faster than on a plotter, but the process is still time-consuming, making interaction difficult and eliminating these devices from use in real-time animation.

A display device which stores the image (as plotters and storage tubes do) but allows selective erasing is the *plasma panel*. The plasma panel contains a gas at low pressure sandwiched between horizontal and vertical grids of fine wires. A large voltage difference between a horizontal and vertical wire will cause the gas to glow as it does in a neon street sign. A lower voltage will not start a glow but will maintain a glow once started. Normally the wires have this low voltage between them. To set a pixel, the voltage is increased momentarily on the wires that intersect the desired point. To extinguish a pixel, the voltage on the corresponding wires is reduced until the glow cannot be maintained. Plasma panels are very durable and are often used for military applications. They have also been used in the PLATO educational system.

A device which is now becoming economical is the *liquid crystal display*. This is a flat panel display technology, which makes it less bulky than CRTs. Also, because of its low voltage and power requirements, it is lighter in weight, making it the display of choice where portability is required. In a liquid crystal display, light is either transmitted or blocked, depending upon the orientation of molecules in the liquid crystal. An electrical signal can be used to change the molecular orientation, turning a pixel on or off. The material is sandwiched between horizontal and vertical grids of electrodes which are used to select the pixel.

At the present time, liquid crystal televisions are available, but the display is formed on a single semiconductor wafer, which limits its size. Larger but slower displays are also available (640 × 250 pixels). This technology is still young and may compete with CRT displays in the future.

Another approach to the display of graphical information, which has had a profound effect on today's graphics methods, is the *vector refresh display*. The vector re-

LINE–ABS–2
(0.2, 0.2)

User program   DVST Display

FIGURE 2-3
Direct view storage tube system.

fresh display stores the image in the computer's memory, but it tries to be much more efficient about it than a raster display. To specify a line segment, all that is required is the coordinates of its endpoints. The raster frame buffer, however, stores not only the endpoints but also all pixels in between, as well as all pixels not on the line. The vector refresh display stores only the commands necessary for drawing the line segments. The input to the vector generator is saved, instead of the output. These commands are saved in what is called the *display file*. They are examined and the lines are drawn using a vector-generating algorithm. This is done on a normal cathode ray tube, so the image quickly fades. In order to present a steady image, the display must be drawn repeatedly. This means that a vector generator must be applied to all of the lines in an image fast enough to draw the entire image before flicker is noticeable (more than 30 times a second). To do this, the vector generators of refresh displays are usually implemented in hardware. (See Figure 2-4.)

Refresh displays do allow real-time alteration of the image. They also have some disadvantages. The images formed are composed of line segments, not surfaces, and a complex display may flicker because it will take a long time to analyze and draw it.

The concept of a display file has proved to be a useful one. It provides an interface between the image specification process and the image display process. It also defines a compact description of the image, which may be saved for later display. The display-file idea may be applied to devices other than refresh displays. Such files are sometimes called *pseudo display files*, or *metafiles*. Standards are currently under development for metafiles to aid in the transport of images between computers.

Devices such as vector refresh displays, pen plotters, and DVSTs may only directly support *line* drawing. They do not provide support for the solid areas which can be constructed on raster displays. Such line-drawing devices are called *calligraphic* displays.

All the graphics display systems we have described can display the image as it is being constructed. When a command to draw a line segment is issued, the line segment can immediately appear on the screen or paper. The major difference is in whether the display may be altered. To change a vector refresh display, one needs only to change the display file. To change a raster display, one alters the frame buffer. A similar alteration can change a plasma panel. However, to change a plotter or a DVST, one must first call a new-frame routine, which shifts the paper or erases the screen, and then one must redraw the entire image.

We should mention one further class of display device. They are raster printers and plotters that create the image in a single sweep across the page. There are a number of technologies which fall into this category including film printers, laser printers,

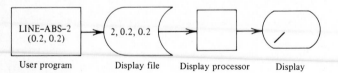

User program Display file Display processor Display

FIGURE 2-4
Vector refresh display system.

electrostatic plotters, thermal and thermal-transfer printers, ink-jet printers, and impact dot-matrix printers. The devices can range in resolution from about 100 pixels per inch for dot-matrix printers to over 1000 pixels per inch for film printers. Dot-matrix printers have an array of wires which can be individually triggered to press an inked ribbon to make a dot on the paper. By sweeping the array across the paper, images can be formed. Ink-jet printers form tiny droplets of ink which can be guided to the paper to form dots. They use nozzles which move across the paper. Laser printers are built on top of copier technology. Instead of copying the light pattern reflected from a piece of paper, a laser is used to supply the light pattern. A rotating mirror sweeps the laser in a raster pattern, and a light valve turns the beam on or off to form the image which is "copied." Film printers use a laser scanning system similar to laser printers, but they focus the laser directly on photographic film to form the picture. Thermal printers have a print head which can burn tiny dots on a heat-sensitive paper. Thermal-transfer printers have a similar print head, but it is used to melt dots of wax-based pigment onto the paper. Electrostatic plotters use an array of wires to which a voltage may be selectively applied. As the paper passes across the wires, it is given a pattern of electrostatic charges. The paper then passes through a liquid toner which is attracted to the pattern on the paper.

As we saw in Chapter 1, one way to produce an image on such raster devices is to first construct it in a frame buffer. The image is constructed by altering the contents of this array, just as may be done for a raster display. The difference from a raster display is that the user will not be able to watch the image being formed. When the user has completed the image, it may output in the order required for printing. These devices require an additional procedure for showing the image.

By creating a frame buffer, alphanumeric terminals and printers may be used for graphics output. They have the same behavior as raster printing devices. The resolution of such devices is usually not very good, but they are readily available and may be sufficient for the user's needs.

PRIMITIVE OPERATIONS

Regardless of the differences in display devices, most graphics systems offer a similar set of graphics primitive commands (although the form of the commands may differ between systems). The first primitive command we shall consider is that for drawing a line segment. While a segment may be specified by its two endpoints, it is often the case that the segments drawn will be connected end to end. (See Figure 2-5.)

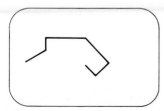

FIGURE 2-5
Connected line segments.

The final point of the last segment becomes the first point of the next segment. To avoid specifying this point twice, the system can keep track of the *current* pen or electron beam position. The command then becomes: draw a line from the current position to the point specified. This is

LINE-ABS-2(X, Y)

and is called an *absolute line command* because the actual coordinates of the final position are passed. (See Figure 2-6.)

There is also a *relative line command*. In this command we only indicate how far to move from the current position (see Figure 2-7):

LINE-REL-2(DX, DY)

The actual endpoint of the segment may be determined from the current position and the relative specification. If we let (XC, YC) denote the current position, then

LINE-REL-2(DX, DY)

is the same as

LINE-ABS-2(XC + DX, YC + DY)

The above procedures are fine for producing a connected string of line segments, but it may happen that we wish to draw two disconnected segments. (See Figure 2-8.)

This can be accomplished by the same mechanism if we picture these two segments as connected by a middle segment which happens to be invisible. We have commands for moving the pen position without leaving a line. Again there can be both absolute and relative moves.

MOVE-ABS-2(X, Y)
MOVE-REL-2(DX, DY)

We can construct a line drawing (say of a house) by a series of line and move commands. If these commands are located in a subprogram, then each time a subprogram is called, an image of the house is produced. If absolute commands are used, then the house will always be located at the same position on the screen. If, however,

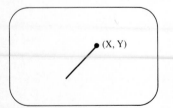

FIGURE 2-6
The absolute line command.

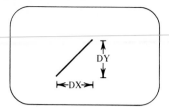

FIGURE 2-7
The relative line command.

only relative commands are used, then the position of the house will depend upon the position of the pen (or beam) at the time when the subprogram was entered. This may be used for the construction of pictures made of repeated instances of basic components. The subprogram for each type of component should be written using only relative commands. Drawing the entire picture is reduced to positioning the beam and calling subprograms. For example, suppose we write the following subprogram for a house.

Subprogram House
```
BEGIN
    LINE-REL-2(0,0.2);
    LINE-REL-2(0.1,0.1);
    LINE-REL-2(0.1–0.1);
    LINE-REL-2(0,–0.2);
    LINE-REL-2(–0.2,0);
END;
```

This will start at the current pen position, which will become the lower-left corner of the drawing. It will draw the left wall, the roof, the right wall, and, finally, the floor. (See Figure 2-9.)

Since only relative commands were used, we can draw three houses by simply calling this subprogram at three different starting positions. (See Figure 2-10.)

```
BEGIN
    MOVE-ABS-2(0.1,0.2);
    HOUSE;
    MOVE-ABS-2(0.4,0.2);
    HOUSE;
    MOVE-ABS-2(0.7,0.2);
    HOUSE;
END;
```

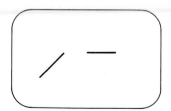

FIGURE 2-8
Disconnected line segments.

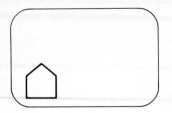

FIGURE 2-9
Subprogram HOUSE.

THE DISPLAY-FILE INTERPRETER

While it might be possible to have the LINE command directly alter the frame buffer, we shall not organize our system in this manner. Instead, we shall insert an intermediate step. We shall have LINE and MOVE commands store their information in what we shall call our display file. We shall then use the information in the display file to create the image. There are several reasons for using this two-step process. First, not every display device has a frame buffer. Different display devices require different programs to drive them. By isolating the driving program in the second of the two steps, we achieve some measure of device independence. Second, it will make it easy for us to change the position, size, and orientation of the image. These image transformations will be carried out during the second step. The techniques involved will be covered in Chapter 4. For now, we shall concentrate on the form of the display file. In Chapter 5 we shall learn how to structure the image and to carry out transformations on portions of it. The display file will support this structuring.

The display file will contain the information necessary to construct the picture. The information will be in the form of instructions such as "draw a line," or "move the pen." Saving instructions such as these usually takes much less storage than saving the picture itself. These instructions can be thought of as a program for creating the image. Each instruction indicates a MOVE, or a LINE, action for the display device. We shall write a *display-file interpreter* to convert these instructions into actual images. (See Figure 2-11.)

Our interpreter may be thought of as a machine which executes these instructions. The result of execution is a visual image. In some graphics systems there is, in fact, a separate computer, called the *display processor*, which is located in the graphics terminal and which is used just for this purpose. In other systems, the behavior of a display processor is simulated. Where there is a separate display processor, some care must be taken when the display file is modified since the display processor may currently be executing the instructions being changed.

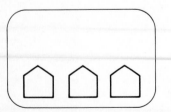

FIGURE 2-10
Three calls of HOUSE, each with a different initial pen position.

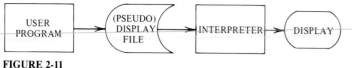

FIGURE 2-11
Display file and interpreter.

Our display-file interpreter serves as an interface between our graphics program and the display device. If we write a graphics program for a particular display device, chances are that it will not run on a different display. The portability of the program is limited. If, on the other hand, we write a program which generates display-file code, all we need is an interpreter for each device which converts our "standard" display instructions to the actions of the particular device. We think of the display device and its interpreter as a machine upon which any standard program may run. The display-file instructions may actually be saved in a file either for display later or for transfer to another machine. Such files of imaging instructions are sometimes called *metafiles*.

NORMALIZED DEVICE COORDINATES

Different display devices may have different screen sizes as measured in pixels. If we wish our programs to be device-independent, we should specify the coordinates in some units other than pixels and then use the interpreter to convert these coordinates to the appropriate pixel values for the particular display we are using. The device-independent units are called the normalized device coordinates. In these units, the screen measures 1 unit wide and 1 unit high. The lower-left corner of the screen is the origin, and the upper-right corner is the point (1, 1). The point (0.5, 0.5) is in the center of the screen no matter what the physical dimensions or resolution of the actual display device may be. (See Figure 2-12.)

The interpreter uses a simple linear formula to convert from the normalized device coordinates to the actual device coordinates. Suppose that for the actual display the index of the leftmost pixel is WIDTH-START and that there are WIDTH pixels in the horizontal direction. Suppose also that the bottommost pixel is HEIGHT-START and the number of pixels in the vertical direction is HEIGHT. In the normalized coordinates the screen is 1 unit wide, but in the actual coordinates it is WIDTH units wide so the normalized x position should be multiplied by WIDTH/1 to convert to actual screen units. At position $x_n = 0$ in normalized coordinates we should get $x_s = $ WIDTH-START in actual screen coordinates, so the conversion formula should be

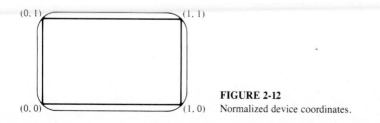

FIGURE 2-12
Normalized device coordinates.

$$x_s = WIDTH * x_n + WIDTH\text{-}START$$

Similarly for the vertical direction

$$y_s = HEIGHT * y_n + HEIGHT\text{-}START$$

One problem in setting up the formula to convert from normalized to device coordinates is that the display surfaces are often not square. The ratio of the height to the width is called the display's aspect ratio. If we have a display which is not square, we can either use the display's full height and width in the conversion formula or use numbers which correspond to a square area. If we use the full dimensions, we take full advantage of the display area, but the image will be stretched or squashed. If we use a square area of the display, the image is correctly proportioned, but some of the display area is wasted. If we use a square area larger than the actual display, we may use all of the screen and have a properly proportioned image, but the image may not entirely fit on the display.

DISPLAY-FILE STRUCTURE

Now let us consider the structure of the display file. Each display-file command contains two parts, an *operation code (opcode)*, which indicates what kind of command it is (e.g., LINE or MOVE), and *operands*, which are the coordinates of a point (x, y). The display file is made up of a series of these instructions. One possible method for storing these instructions is to use three separate arrays: one for the operation code (DF-OP), one for the x coordinate (DF-X), and one for the y coordinate (DF-Y). To piece together the seventh display-file instruction, we would get the seventh element from each of the three arrays DF-OP[7], DF-X[7], and DF-Y[7]. The display file must be large enough to hold all the commands needed to create our image.

We must assign meaning to the possible operation codes before we can proceed to interpret them. At this point there are only two possible instructions to consider, MOVE and LINE. We need to consider only absolute MOVE and LINE commands, since relative commands can be converted to absolute commands before they are entered into the display file. Let us define an opcode of 1 to mean a MOVE command and an opcode of 2 to mean a LINE command. A command to move to position x = 0.3 and y = 0.7 would look like 1, 0.3, 0.7. The statements

DF-OP[3] ← 1;
DF-X[3] ← 0.3;
DF-Y[3] ← 0.7;

would store this instruction in the third display-file position. If DF-OP[4] had the value 2, DF-X[4] had the value 0.5, and DF-Y[4] had the value 0.8, then the display would show a line segment from (0.3, 0.7) to (0.5, 0.8) when display-file instructions 3 and 4 were interpreted. (See Figure 2-13.)

Let us develop the algorithms for inserting display-file instructions. Line segments require two endpoints for their specification, but we shall enter only one endpoint and assume that the other endpoint is the current pen position. We will therefore

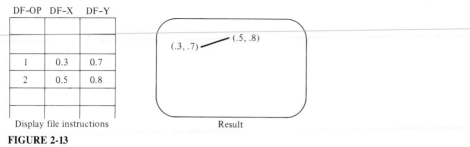

DF-OP DF-X DF-Y

1	0.3	0.7
2	0.5	0.8

Display file instructions   Result

FIGURE 2-13
Display-file instructions.

need variables DF-PEN-X and DF-PEN-Y to keep track of the current pen position. We will need to know this position for the conversion of relative commands to absolute commands. We shall also need a variable FREE to indicate where the next free (unused) cell of the display file is located. These variables, together with the display file itself, are used by several different routines and must be maintained between accesses. They are therefore presented as global variables.

The first algorithm we will consider actually puts an instruction into the display file.

2.1 Algorithm PUT-POINT(OP, X, Y) Place an instruction into the display file
Arguments   OP, X, Y the instruction to be entered
Global   DF-OP, DF-X, DF-Y the three display-file arrays
                  FREE the position of the next free cell
Constant   DFSIZE the length of the display-file arrays
BEGIN
    IF FREE > DFSIZE THEN RETURN ERROR 'DISPLAY FILE FULL';
    DF-OP[FREE] ← OP;
    DF-X[FREE] ← X;
    DF-Y[FREE] ← Y;
    FREE ← FREE + 1;
    RETURN;
END;

This algorithm stores the operation code and the coordinates of the specified position in the display file. The pointer FREE to the next free cell is incremented so that it will be in the correct position for the next entry.

We also wish to access elements in the display file. We isolate the accessing mechanism in a separate routine so that any changes in the data structure used for the display file will not affect the rest of our graphics package.

2.2 Algorithm GET-POINT (NTH, OP, X, Y) Retrieve the NTH instruction from the display file
Arguments   NTH the number of the desired instruction
                  OP, X, Y the instruction to be returned
Global   arrays DF-OP, DF-X, DF-Y the display file

```
BEGIN
    OP ← DF-OP[NTH];
    X ← DF-X[NTH];
    Y ← DF-Y[NTH];
    RETURN;
END;
```

Our MOVE and LINE instructions must update the current pen position and enter a command into the display file. If the update of the pen position is done first, then the new pen position will serve as the operand for the display-file instruction. It will prove convenient in later chapters to have a separate routine which takes the operation code and the pen position and enters them into the display file as an instruction.

2.3 Algorithm DISPLAY-FILE-ENTER(OP) Combine operation and position to form an instruction and save it in the display file

Argument   OP the operation to be entered

Global   DF-PEN-X, DF-PEN-Y the current pen position

```
BEGIN
    PUT-POINT(OP, DF-PEN-X, DF-PEN-Y);
    RETURN;
END;
```

Using DISPLAY-FILE-ENTER to place instructions in the display file, the absolute MOVE routine becomes the following:

2.4 Algorithm MOVE-ABS-2(X, Y) User routine to save an instruction to move the pen

Arguments   X, Y the point to which to move the pen

Global   DF-PEN-X, DF-PEN-Y the current pen position

```
BEGIN
    DF-PEN-X ← X;
    DF-PEN-Y ← Y;
    DISPLAY-FILE-ENTER(1);
    RETURN;
END;
```

The point (DF-PEN-X, DF-PEN-Y) is keeping track of where we wish the pen to go. By setting (DF-PEN-X, DF-PEN-Y) to (X, Y), we are saying the pen is to be at position (X, Y).

The algorithm for entering a LINE command is similar.

2.5 Algorithm LINE-ABS-2(X, Y) User routine to save a command to draw a line

Arguments   X, Y the point to which to draw the line

Global   DF-PEN-X, DF-PEN-Y the current pen position

```
BEGIN
    DF-PEN-X ← X;
    DF-PEN-Y ← Y;
    DISPLAY-FILE-ENTER(2)
    RETURN;
END;
```

Again by changing DF-PEN-X and DF-PEN-Y we indicate that the pen will be placed at (X, Y), but by entering an operation code of 2 instead of 1, we instruct the interpreter to draw a line as the pen is moved.

We can also write algorithms for the relative commands.

2.6 Algorithm MOVE-REL-2(DX, DY) User routine to save a command to move the pen

Arguments   DX, DY the change in the pen position
Global   DF-PEN-X, DF-PEN-Y the current pen position
BEGIN
   DF-PEN-X ← DF-PEN-X + DX;
   DF-PEN-Y ← DF-PEN-Y + DY;
   DISPLAY-FILE-ENTER(1);
   RETURN;
END;

2.7 Algorithm LINE-REL-2(DX, DY) User routine to save a command to draw a line

Arguments   DX, DY the change over which to draw a line
Global   DF-PEN-X, DF-PEN-Y the current pen position
BEGIN
   DF-PEN-X ← DF-PEN-X + DX;
   DF-PEN-Y ← DF-PEN-Y + DY;
   DISPLAY-FILE-ENTER(2);
   RETURN;
END;

The relative LINE and MOVE routines act like the absolute routines in that they tell where the pen is to be placed and how it is to get there. They differ in that the new pen position is calculated as an offset to the old pen position.

DISPLAY-FILE ALGORITHMS

The above algorithms indicate how to enter instructions into the display file. The other half of the problem is to analyze the display file and perform the commands.

Now let us consider algorithms for our display-file interpreter. The interpreter will read instructions from a portion of the display file and carry out the appropriate LINE and MOVE commands by calls on a vector-generating subroutine such as those described in Chapter 1.

The routine which actually causes the LINE or MOVE to be carried out on the display can depend upon the nature of the display device and upon its software. Below are versions of these algorithms which may be used with a vector generator. The DOMOVE routine has only to update the current pen position. The arithmetic involved is the conversion from normalized device coordinates to the actual screen coordinates.

2.8 Algorithm DOMOVE(X, Y) Perform a move of the pen

Arguments   X, Y point to which to move the pen (normalized coordinates)
Global   FRAME-PEN-X, FRAME-PEN-Y the pen position (actual screen coordinates)

WIDTH, HEIGHT the screen dimensions
WIDTH-START, HEIGHT-START coordinates of the lower-left corner
WIDTH-END, HEIGHT-END coordinates of the upper-right corner
BEGIN
    FRAME-PEN-X ← MAX(WIDTH-START, MIN(WIDTH-END, X ∗ WIDTH +
           WIDTH-START));
    FRAME-PEN-Y ← MAX(HEIGHT-START, MIN(HEIGHT-END, Y ∗ HEIGHT +
           HEIGHT-START));
    RETURN;
END;

In this algorithm we see the formula for converting the normalized coordinate
values of the arguments into actual screen coordinates. The MAX and MIN functions
have been added to the formula as a safeguard. They prevent it from ever generating a
value outside the bounds of the actual display. If (X, Y) were to correspond to a point
outside the screen area, the MAX and MIN functions would "clamp" the corresponding screen coordinate position to the display boundary. In algorithm 2.8, it was assumed that WIDTH-START was less than WIDTH-END, and HEIGHT-START less
than HEIGHT-END; however, this is not the case for some devices. In general, we use
the smallest boundary in the MAX test and the largest boundary in the MIN test.

The DOLINE algorithm updates the pen position and calls the Bresenham algorithm (or some other vector generator) to place the line segment in the frame buffer.
It, too, performs a conversion from normalized device coordinates to the actual screen
coordinates. Since the Bresenham algorithm is used in this example, the coordinates
must be rounded to integer pixel positions.

2.9 Algorithm DOLINE(X, Y) This routine draws a line
Arguments   X, Y point to which to draw the line (normalized coordinates)
Global   FRAME-PEN-X, FRAME-PEN-Y the pen position (screen coordinates)
           WIDTH, HEIGHT the screen dimensions
           WIDTH-START, HEIGHT-START coordinates of the lower-left corner
           WIDTH-END, HEIGHT-END coordinates of the upper-right corner
           LINECHR the style of the line
Local   X1, Y1 the old endpoint of the line segment
BEGIN
    X1 ← FRAME-PEN-X;
    Y1 ← FRAME-PEN-Y;
    FRAME-PEN-X ← MAX(WIDTH-START, MIN(WIDTH-END, X ∗ WIDTH +
           WIDTH-START));
    FRAME-PEN-Y ← MAX(HEIGHT-START, MIN(HEIGHT-END, Y ∗ HEIGHT +
           HEIGHT-START));
    BRESENHAM(INT(X1 + 0.5), INT(Y1 + 0.5),
           INT(FRAME-PEN-X + 0.5), INT(FRAME-PEN-Y + 0.5),
           LINECHR);
           RETURN;
END;

Now we can write the interpreter, the routine which examines the display file and
calls DOMOVE and DOLINE according to the instructions that it discovers. It will

prove useful in later chapters to be able to interpret just a portion of the display file. We shall therefore pass as arguments to the interpreter the starting position START and how many instructions to interpret COUNT.

> **2.10 Algorithm INTERPRET(START, COUNT)** Scan the display file performing the instructions
> Arguments   START the starting index of the display-file scan
>   COUNT the number of instructions to be interpreted
> Local   NTH the display-file index
>   OP, X, Y, the display-file instruction
> BEGIN
>   a loop to do all desired instructions
>   FOR NTH = START TO START + COUNT − 1 DO
>   BEGIN
>   GET-POINT(NTH, OP, X, Y);
>   IF OP = 1 THEN DOMOVE(X, Y)
>   ELSE IF OP = 2 THEN DOLINE(X, Y)
>   ELSE RETURN ERROR 'OP-CODE ERROR';
>   END;
>   RETURN;
> END;

A loop steps through all the desired display-file instructions, retrieving them by the GET-POINT routine. The algorithm identifies each instruction as being either a MOVE or a LINE instruction by examining its opcode and calls the routine DOMOVE or DOLINE to actually perform the appropriate action upon the display.

DISPLAY CONTROL

In order to show the picture described in the display file, one might have to do three things. First, the current display may have to be cleared; second, the display file must be interpreted; and third, on some devices (such as line printers and standard CRT terminals) an explicit action is required to show the contents of the frame buffer. For the convenience of the user we shall combine these operations under a single routine. Before presenting the algorithm for this routine, however, we should say a little more about clearing the display (or frame buffer). We may not want to clear the display every time we interpret the display file. If the only changes to the picture have been additions, then there is no need to clear and redraw the rest of the image. In fact, quite complex drawings may be generated a piece at a time. Of course, some changes made to the image do require clearing and redrawing. Deleting a portion of the drawing—or shifting its position, size, or orientation—may require a new image starting with a clear screen. We shall see how to perform these changes in Chapters 4 and 5; the important thing to note here is that the request for a clear screen may be incorporated as part of these changes. In these cases, screen clearing can be done automatically. Still, the user should also be able to explicitly request an erasure of the screen. In Chapter 1 we introduced a display-clearing routine which the user might call; however, sometimes the point at which the user's program discovers that an erasure is needed may occur before the desired time at which the actual clearing should occur. We shall handle clearing of the frame by means of a flag (a variable with the value true or false). We use a true value to indicate that the screen should be cleared before interpreting the display file and a false value to mean that the display-file instructions may be drawn "on top of" the old image. If the machine discovers that an erasure will be needed, it sets the flag to true. If the user decides that there should be a new frame, he sets the flag to true. Nothing happens to the display until the display file is ready to be interpreted. At this point the erase flag is checked, and if true, the frame is cleared and the flag is changed back to false.

2.11 Algorithm NEW-FRAME User routine to indicate that the frame buffer should be cleared before showing the display file

Global   ERASE-FLAG a flag to indicate whether the frame should be cleared
BEGIN
       ERASE-FLAG ← TRUE;
       RETURN;
END;

Now we wish to combine the erasing of the frame buffer, if needed, the interpretation of the display file, and the displaying of the new frame buffer into a single routine called MAKE-PICTURE-CURRENT.

2.12 Algorithm MAKE-PICTURE-CURRENT User routine to show the current display file

Global   FREE the index of the next free display-file cell
               ERASE-FLAG indicates if frames should be cleared
BEGIN
     IF ERASE-FLAG THEN
         BEGIN
             ERASE;
             ERASE-FLAG ← FALSE;
         END;
     IF FREE > 1 THEN INTERPRET(1, FREE – 1);
     DISPLAY;
     FREE ← 1;
     RETURN;
END;

The algorithm first checks for an erasure, as we have discussed. It next checks to be sure the display file is not empty; if it is not, the commands within it are interpreted. Next, any actions necessary to show the results of the interpretation are taken by means of the DISPLAY routine. If a graphics display device which immediately shows the result of each command is used, then the call of DISPLAY is unnecessary or DISPLAY becomes a "dummy" do-nothing routine. Finally, the display-file index is reset to 1, indicating an empty display file ready to accept the next image-drawing commands.

There is one more routine needed to implement this stage of our graphics system. We have some global variables which should be given initial values. This is done by the following algorithm.

2.13 Algorithm INITIALIZE-2A Initialization of variables for line drawings
Global   FREE the index of the next free display-file cell
                DF-PEN-X, DF-PEN-Y the display-file pen position
BEGIN
    INITIALIZE-1;
    FREE ← 1;
    DF-PEN-X ← 0;
    DF-PEN-Y ← 0;
    NEW-FRAME;
    RETURN;
END;

TEXT

Another primitive operation is that of text output. Most graphics displays involve textual, as well as graphical, data. Labels, instructions, commands, values, messages, and so on, may be presented with the image. The primitive command involved here is the output of a character or a string of characters. While one usually has a command available for output of an entire string, there may sometimes be only a command available for output of a single character. A procedure to apply such a primitive to an entire string is not difficult to construct. The characters themselves may be drawn by either the dot-matrix or the stroke method. Their patterns are often copied from memory into the frame buffer or created by special character generation hardware, although software subroutines using line segments are also to be found. The advantage of hardware is speed and a saving of display-file memory. With sophisticated displays there may be options which the user must specify. Among such options are the spacing of the characters, the size of the characters, the ratio of their height to their width, the slope of the character string, the orientation of the characters, and, possibly, which font is to be used.

We will extend our interpreter to include the output of text. We will do this by extending the number of operation codes to include one code for each character. The operand for an instruction will determine where the character will be placed on the screen. We shall use as the opcode for a character the negative of its ASCII character code. (See Figure 2-14.) Our opcodes will range between −32 and −126 inclusive. Using the ASCII character code should facilitate conversion between the instruction and the character value for output in most systems. We shall exclude the ASCII codes for control characters so that a valid code must be less than −31 (the codes 0 through −31 will be used for line and polygon style changes). Character codings other than ASCII can be used, provided that the codes can be mapped to values less than −31.

A character command, then, has an opcode that specifies which character is to be displayed and x, y operands which tell where on the screen that character should be placed. A word or string of text is stored as a sequence of individual character instructions. Since we save the position of each character, we have control over the character spacing within the string. Since we save y position as well as x position, we can cause our strings to be written vertically or diagonally.

We have not introduced any mechanism for specifying the character orientation. Some display devices allow characters to be drawn at any angle. Others allow only 90-

Char	Code	Char	Code	Char	Code	Char	Code
space	32	8	56	P	80	h	104
!	33	9	57	Q	81	i	105
"	34	:	58	R	82	j	106
#	35	;	59	S	83	k	107
$	36	<	60	T	84	l	108
%	37	=	61	U	85	m	109
&	38	>	62	V	86	n	110
'	39	?	63	W	87	o	111
(	40	@	64	X	88	p	112
)	41	A	65	Y	89	q	113
*	42	B	66	Z	90	r	114
+	43	C	67	[	91	s	115
,	44	D	68	\	92	t	116
-	45	E	69	]	93	u	117
.	46	F	70	^	94	v	118
/	47	G	71	—	95	w	119
0	48	H	72	'	96	x	120
1	49	I	73	a	97	y	121
2	50	J	74	b	98	z	122
3	51	K	75	c	99	{	123
4	52	L	76	d	100			124
5	53	M	77	e	101	}	125
6	54	N	78	f	102	~	126
7	55	O	79	g	103		

FIGURE 2-14
ASCII character codes.

degree increments, while many (such as normal output devices) display only upright characters. To maintain device independence and to try to simplify things a little, we shall require all characters within a string to be oriented in the same direction and, in fact, will design our algorithms for a device which allows only upright characters. Writing a string of text can be rather cumbersome if each character requires its own procedure call. We shall therefore write a routine for placing entire strings of text into the display file through a series of character commands. It will be up to this routine to automatically shift the position of each character to achieve the desired spacing. The spacing between characters will be given by global variables XCHRSP and YCHRSP. Of course, we need a routine to set these spacing parameters to whatever values we desire. The CORE and GKS graphics systems have rich selections of text formatting operations; they allow changing the size, orientation, spacing, and font of the character and also the direction of the line of text. We will not be that ambitious here. We shall only control the character spacing and line direction. We shall determine the direction of the line of text from the orientation of the characters. There is a command SET-CHARUP(DX, DY) in which [DX, DY] is a vector specifying the "UP" direction for the characters. The text line then prints to the "right" of this direction. For our system, we will not try to change character orientation with respect to line direction, so a SET-CHARUP command looks a bit awkward. Nevertheless, we shall use it because of its correspondence to graphics standards.

Spacing in the direction of the text line can be changed by the SET-CHARSPACE(CHARSPACE) command. The system will space over one character width automatically. The CHARSPACE parameter indicates any additional spacing. This spacing is specified in units of character size, so a CHARSPACE of 0.5 would mean spacing an additional one-half character (a total of 1.5 character widths between character centers). The CHARSPACE parameter is measured in terms of character width instead of normalized device coordinates, so a widely spaced line on one device will look just as widely spaced on every other device, even though the width of the characters (in normalized device coordinates) may differ. Our problem is to convert the CHARUP and CHARSPACE specifications, and our knowledge about the size of a character, into distances to step in the x and y direction between each character in the string (XCHRSP, YCHRSP). (See Figure 2-15 and Figure 2-16.)

The calculation of step size is complicated by the fact that we are not rotating the character symbols and that the width and height of a character are often unequal. If the text string is to be printed horizontally, then we shall step by the character width. If the string is to be printed vertically, then character height should be the default step size. At other orientations, we wish to use some default step size between the width and height. To use as much of the width as we are stepping horizontally and as much of the height as we are stepping vertically, we calculate a default step size as

$$\text{DEFAULT-STEP} = \frac{|(\text{CHAR-WIDTH})(\text{DY})| + |(\text{CHAR-HEIGHT})(\text{DX})|}{(\text{DX}^2 + \text{DY}^2)^{1/2}} \quad (2.1)$$

Here DX and DY are from the CHARUP vector, and are perpendicular to the line direction; that is why they appear to be reversed.

This default step size can be increased by the user's CHAR-SEPARATION factor.

$$\text{TRUE-STEP} = \text{DEFAULT-STEP}\,(1 + \text{CHAR-SEPARATION}) \quad (2.2)$$

Finally, we decompose the step size into horizontal and vertical components. Once again, since [DX, DY] is a vector perpendicular to the direction of the string, DY will act as the x component and $-$ DX will behave as the y component.

$$\text{XCHRSP} = \text{TRUE-STEP}\,\frac{\text{DY}}{(\text{DX}^2 + \text{DY}^2)^{1/2}}$$

$$\quad (2.3)$$

$$\text{YCHRSP} = \text{TRUE-STEP}\,\frac{-\text{DX}}{(\text{DX}^2 + \text{DY}^2)^{1/2}}$$

This calculation is carried out a bit more efficiently in the following algorithm. (You may notice that upon combining Equations 2.1, 2.2, and 2.3, the square root operation drops out.)

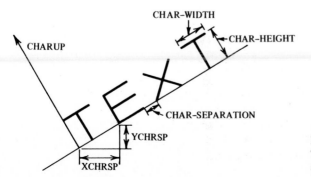

FIGURE 2-15
Text parameters for orientable characters.

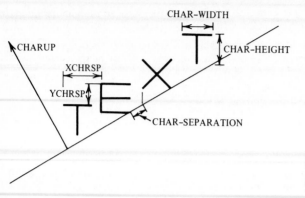

FIGURE 2-16

Text parameters for nonorientable characters.

2.14 Algorithm SET-CHARUP(DX, DY) User routine to indicate in which direction a string should be printed

Arguments DX, DY a vector for the up direction of the string
Global   XCHRSP, YCHRSP spacing between character centers
             CHAR-WIDTH, CHAR-HEIGHT the character size
             CHAR-SEPARATION the proportion of character size separating characters
Local   S, S1, S2 temporary variables used to hold partially completed calculations
Constant   ROUNDOFF some small number greater than any round-off error
BEGIN
    S ← DX ↑ 2 + DY ↑ 2;
    IF S < ROUNDOFF THEN RETURN ERROR 'NO CHARUP DIRECTION';
    S1 ← (|CHAR-WIDTH * DY| + |CHAR-HEIGHT * DX|);
    S2 ← S1 * (1 + CHAR-SEPARATION) / S;
    XCHRSP ← DY * S2;
    YCHRSP ← – DX * S2;
    RETURN;
END;

The SET-CHARSPACE routine should not only change the global CHAR-SEPARATION value but also update the step size currently in use. In the arguments of the call to SET-CHARUP, we again see the switch of x and y which comes from specifying the ''up'' direction in terms of the parameters for the text line direction.

2.15 Algorithm SET-CHARSPACE(SPACE) User routine to set the spacing between characters

Argument   SPACE the fraction of the character size separating characters
Global   CHAR-SEPARATION storage for the character spacing
            XCHRSP, YCHRSP spacing between character centers
BEGIN
    CHAR-SEPARATION ← SPACE;
    SET-CHARUP(– YCHRSP, XCHRSP);
    RETURN;
END;

Now let's write the algorithm to enter a string of text into the display file, beginning at the current pen position.

2.16 Algorithm TEXT(STRING) User routine to place instructions for printing a string into the display file

Argument   STRING the characters to be entered
Global   DF-PEN-X, DF-PEN-Y the pen position
             XCHRSP, YCHRSP the character spacing
Local   LEN the length of the string.
             X, Y the character position
             I an index to count off the characters
             CHR the character being saved
             OP the character's operation-code
BEGIN
    determine the length of the string
    LEN ← LENGTH(STRING)
    save the pen position for restoration after string is entered
    X ← DF-PEN-X;
    Y ← DF-PEN-Y;
    enter the string
    FOR I = 1 TO LEN DO
      BEGIN
          consider the ith character of the string
          CHR ← GETCHR(STRING, I);
          form its character code
          OP ← – DECODE(CHR);
          enter it into the display file
          DISPLAY-FILE-ENTER(OP);
          move the pen to the next character position
          DF-PEN-X ← DF-PEN-X + XCHRSP;
          DF-PEN-Y ← DF-PEN-Y + YCHRSP;
      END;
    restore the pen to its original position
    MOVE-ABS-2(X, Y);
    RETURN;
END;

The routines LENGTH, GETCHR, and DECODE depend upon how strings are represented on the particular system that we are using, and the algorithms for them will not be presented here. The LENGTH routine returns the number of characters in the string. The GETCHR routine returns the ith character in the string. The DECODE routine converts the character to the ASCII code, if necessary.

We must now modify our interpreter to be able to handle these new character commands which we are entering into the display file.

2.17 Algorithm INTERPRET(START, COUNT) (Algorithm 2.10 revisited) Scan the display file performing the instructions

Arguments   START the starting index of the display-file scan
              COUNT the number of instructions to be interpreted

```
Local       NTH the display-file index
            OP, X, Y the display-file instruction
BEGIN
    a loop to do all desired instructions
    FOR NTH = START TO START + COUNT – 1 DO
        BEGIN
            GET-POINT(NTH, OP, X, Y);
            IF OP < –31 THEN DOCHAR(OP, X, Y)
            ELSE IF OP = 1 THEN DOMOVE(X, Y)
            ELSE IF OP = 2 THEN DOLINE(X, Y)
                    ELSE RETURN ERROR 'OP-CODE ERROR';
        END;
    RETURN;
END;
```

The instructions for actually putting the character into the frame buffer have been placed in the DOCHAR routine.

2.18 Algorithm DOCHAR(OP, X, Y) Place a character on the screen

```
Arguments   OP indicates which character should be used
            X, Y indicate the position on the screen
Global      WIDTH, HEIGHT the screen dimensions
            WIDTH-START, HEIGHT-START screen coordinates of lower-left corner
            WIDTH-END, HEIGHT-END screen coordinates of upper-right corner
Local       CHR the character to be displayed
            X1, Y1 screen coordinates of the character
BEGIN
    CHR ← CODE(–OP);
    X1 ← MAX(WIDTH-START, MIN(WIDTH-END, X * WIDTH +
            WIDTH-START));
    Y1 ← MAX(HEIGHT-START, MIN(HEIGHT-END, Y * HEIGHT +
            HEIGHT-START));
    GENERATE-CHAR(X1, Y1, CHR);
    RETURN;
END;
```

Once again we have system-dependent routines, which are named CODE and GENERATE-CHAR. CODE converts from ASCII to whatever form is convenient for GENERATE-CHAR. GENERATE-CHAR generates a character on the screen or in the frame buffer at position (X1, Y1).

Again we have introduced some global variables which should be initialized. The following routine takes care of this.

2.19 Algorithm INITIALIZE-2B Initialization of character parameters

```
Global      CHAR-WIDTH, CHAR-HEIGHT the character size
            CHAR-SEPARATION the proportion of character size to use for additional
            character spacing
```

```
BEGIN
    INITIALIZE-2A;
    CHAR-WIDTH ← the width of a character in normalized coordinates;
    CHAR-HEIGHT ← the height of a character in normalized coordinates;
    CHAR-SEPARATION ← 0;
    SET-CHARUP(0, 1);
    RETURN;
END;
```

THE LINE-STYLE PRIMITIVE

Many display devices offer a selection of line styles. Lines may be continuous, or they may be dashed or dotted. One may be able to select the color of the line or its intensity or thickness. It is desirable to be able to change the line style in the middle of the display process. We therefore need a display-file command for changing line style. When the interpreter encounters such a command, the line style is changed and all subsequent lines are drawn in this new style. Our display-file commands are composed of three parts, the opcode and the two operands for the x and y coordinates. We can use a special opcode to indicate change of line style (or color or intensity), but such a command would not require any operands. Some possible display-file organizations allow different-sized instructions, but we shall take the simpler alternative of providing dummy operands which are ignored. We will use codes between 0 and −15, inclusive, for change of line-style commands. This allows up to 16 possible line styles. The actual identification of opcodes with line styles will depend upon the possible line styles available. We shall, however, assume that a code of 0 corresponds to the normal straight line. This should be the default style when the system is initialized. Other line styles should correspond to the codes −1, −2, and so on. For a line printer display such as discussed in Chapter 1, the line style is the character that is placed in the frame buffer. Changing the line style is a matter of changing this character. (See Figure 2-17.)

We will augment our interpreter to process commands for changing line style. To do this, we will need two new routines, one to place the line-style commands into the display file and another to actually make the change whenever such a command is discovered by the interpreter.

While line-style opcodes in the display file are negative to distinguish them from the MOVE and LINE opcodes, there is no reason to force the user to use negative numbers in his specification. To do so would give the user one more pointless thing to remember. We therefore have the user specify the positive codes 1,2,... for line styles

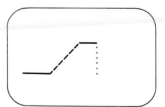

FIGURE 2-17
Changing line style.

and let the SET-LINESTYLE algorithm enter corresponding negatives into the display file. The algorithm for setting the line style would look as follows:

2.20 Algorithm SET-LINESTYLE(LSTYLE) User routine for changing line style
Argument   LSTYLE the user's line-style specification
BEGIN
    DISPLAY-FILE-ENTER(1 − LSTYLE);
    RETURN;
END;

When the interpreter discovers a line-style command, it must perform the change. We isolate this system-dependent process in a separate routine to allow easy interfacing with different display devices.

2.21 Algorithm DOSTYLE(OP) Routine to change the line style
Argument   OP indicates the desired line style
BEGIN
    decode OP;
    set the line style;
    RETURN;
END;

If the vector generation algorithms of Chapter 1 are used for a line printer or CRT with different characters representing different line styles, then algorithm 2.21 would be

2.21A Algorithm DOSTYLE(OP) Routine to change the line style
Global   LINECHR the line character used by the vector generator
BEGIN
    LINECHR ← LINE-CODE(1 − OP);
    RETURN;
END;

where LINE-CODE converts from the integers 1, 2, ... to appropriate character codes, for example '∗', '+', ...

We must once again extend our interpreter so that it will now recognize line-style operation codes.

2.22 Algorithm INTERPRET(START, COUNT) (Algorithm 2.17 revisited) Scan the display file performing the instructions
Arguments   START the starting index of the display-file scan
                    COUNT the number of instructions to be interpreted
Local   NTH the display-file index
                    OP, X, Y the display-file instruction
BEGIN
    a loop to do all desired instructions
    FOR NTH = START TO START + COUNT − 1 DO

```
    BEGIN
        GET-POINT(NTH, OP, X, Y);
        IF OP < –31 THEN DOCHAR(OP, X, Y)
        ELSE IF OP < 1 THEN DOSTYLE(OP)
                ELSE IF OP = 1 THEN DOMOVE(X, Y)
                ELSE IF OP = 2 THEN DOLINE(X, Y)
                        ELSE RETURN ERROR 'OP-CODE ERROR';
    END;
    RETURN;
END;
```

We shall also make a small change in the DISPLAY-FILE-ENTER algorithm so that it will distinguish between instructions which use the coordinate information (LINE and MOVE) and those which do not (STYLE). This distinction will prove useful in later chapters, where we will not enter all of the line-drawing instructions but will still wish to enter all changes of style.

2.23 Algorithm DISPLAY-FILE-ENTER(OP) (Algorithm 2.3 revisited) Combine operation and position to form an instruction and save it in the display file
Argument   OP the operation to be entered
Global   DF-PEN-X, DF-PEN-Y the current pen position
```
BEGIN
    IF OP < 1 AND OP > –32 THEN PUT-POINT(OP, 0, 0)
    ELSE PUT-POINT(OP, DF-PEN-X, DF-PEN-Y);
    RETURN;
END;
```

There is one more routine which is needed to complete this stage of our system. We must supply initial or default values to our global variables. In addition to the previous initializations, we should now also set the initial line style.

2.24 Algorithm INITIALIZE-2 Initialization of variables for lines, characters, and style
```
BEGIN
    INITIALIZE-2B
    DOSTYLE(0)
    RETURN;
END;
```

AN APPLICATION

Let us suppose that we wanted a graphics program to draw a graph of some data. Let us outline how this might be done using some of the algorithms which we have written. To begin, we can plot the horizontal and vertical axes of the graph. These are just two lines, which may be created by a MOVE-ABS-2 to one endpoint and a LINE-ABS-2 to the other endpoint. (See Figure 2-18.)

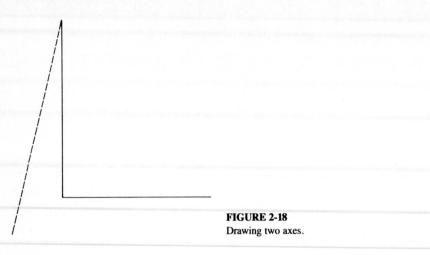

FIGURE 2-18
Drawing two axes.

MOVE-ABS-2(0.2, 0.8);
LINE-ABS-2(0.2, 0.2);
LINE-ABS-2(0.8, 0.2);

The next step might be to label the axes. This can be done by a series of TEXT commands. For example, suppose we wish to label the horizontal axis with the numbers 1 through 5. For each number, we decide where it should be placed on the graph. We issue a MOVE-ABS-2 to place the pen at this position, followed by a TEXT command to write the numeral. (See Figure 2-19.)

MOVE-ABS-2(0.3, 0.15);
TEXT('1');
MOVE-ABS-2(0.4, 0.15);
TEXT('2');

We might also want to label each axis with a string indicating what is being plotted. A MOVE-ABS-2 to the starting position followed by a TEXT command will do this for us. (See Figure 2-20.)

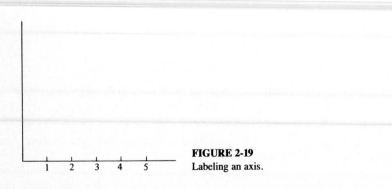

FIGURE 2-19
Labeling an axis.

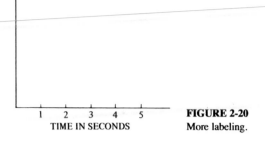

FIGURE 2-20
More labeling.

MOVE-ABS-2(0.35, 0.1);
TEXT('TIME IN SECONDS');

For the vertical axis, it may be useful to change the CHAR-UP direction so that the print line will be vertical. (See Figure 2-21.)

SET-CHARUP(–1, 0);
MOVE-ABS-2(0.1, 0.3);
TEXT('POSITION IN METERS');

Now all that is left for us to do is to plot the data. At this point we might use SET-LINESTYLE to change the style of the line so that our data curve looks different from the axes.

We shall assume that the information to be displayed came into our plotting package as an array of data values or measurements. For each of these measurements we may have to perform some arithmetic to calculate the corresponding position on our display. If we use MOVE-ABS-2 to plot the first data point, and LINE-ABS-2 on the remaining points, we shall get a sequence of line segments connecting the data values. (See Figure 2-22.)

SET-LINE-STYLE(2);
MOVE-ABS-2(0.2, A[1] + 0.2);

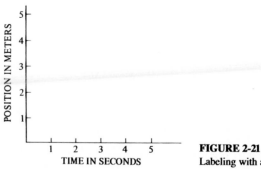

FIGURE 2-21
Labeling with a different CHAR-UP.

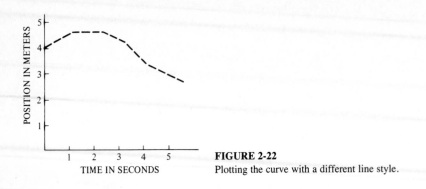

FIGURE 2-22
Plotting the curve with a different line style.

```
FOR I = 2 TO 6 DO
    LINE-ABS-2(0.1 * I + 0.1, A[I] + 0.2);
```

Plotting of all but the first data point can usually be accomplished by a loop which gets the measurement, calculates the corresponding display position, and calls LINE-ABS-2 to display it.

FURTHER READING

Introductory discussions of various imaging technologies may be found in [ALD84], [BAL84], [HOB84], [HUB84], [JER77], [LEE84], [LUC78], [MCC84], [MIL84], [PRE78], [SLO76], [SPR83], [WAT84], [ZAP75], and [ZUC84]. Use of magnetic drum memory as a frame buffer was described in [OPH68], and the first example of the core memory frame buffer is [NOL71]. A frame buffer is also described in [KAJ75]. A display processor and display-file interpreter is described in [DOO84]. Use of a display file for a device-independent system and suggested primitives are presented in [NEW74]. A discussion of graphics primitives is given in [LUC76], and those in the CORE system in [BER78] and [GRA79].

[ALD84] Aldersey-Williams, H., "Liquid Crystals in Flat Panel Displays," *Electronic Imaging*, vol. 3, no. 11, pp. 54–57 (1984).

[BAL84] Baltazzi, E. S., "Reprographic Imaging Techniques," *Electronic Imaging*, vol. 3, no. 12, pp. 53–55 (1984).

[BER78] Bergeron, R. D., Bono, P. R., and Foley, J. D., "Graphics Programming Using the CORE System," *ACM Computing Surveys*, vol. 10, no. 4, pp. 389–394 (1978).

[DOO84] Doornink, D. J., Dalrymple, J. C., "The Architectural Evolution of a High-Performance Graphics Terminal," *IEEE Computer Graphics and Applications*, vol. 4, no. 4, pp. 47–54 (1984).

[GRA79] Graphic Standards Planning Committee, "Status Report Part II: General Methodology and the Proposed Core System," *Computer Graphics*, vol. 13, no. 3, pp. II-1–II-179 (1979).

[HOB84] Hobbs, I. C., "Computer Graphics Display Hardware," *Computer Graphics and Applications*, vol. 1, no. 1, pp. 25–32 (1981).

[HUB84] Hubbold, R. J., "Computer Graphics and Displays," *Computer-Aided Design*, vol. 16, no. 3, pp. 127–133 (1984).

[JER77] Jern, M., "Color Jet Plotter," *Computer Graphics*, vol. 11, no. 1, pp. 18–31 (1977).

[KAJ75] Kajiya, J. T., Sutherland, I. E., Cheadle, E. C., " A Random-Access Video Frame Buffer," *Proceedings of the Conference on Computer Graphics, Pattern Recognition, & Data Structure*, pp. 1–6, IEEE Cat. No. 75CH0981-1c (1975).

[LEE84] Lee, F. C., Mills, R. N., Talke, F. E., "The Application of Drop-on-Demand Ink Jet Technology to Color Printing," *IBM Journal of Research and Development*, vol. 28, no. 3, pp. 307–313 (1984).

[LUC76] Lucido, A. P., "Software Systems for Computer Graphics," *Computer*, vol. 9, no. 8, pp 23–36 (1976).

[LUC78] Lucido, A. P., "An Overview of Directed Beam Graphics Display Hardware," *Computer*, vol. 11, no. 11, pp. 29–37 (1978).

[MCC84] McComrick, J. J., "Present and Future Color Display Technologies for Graphics," *Computers & Graphics*, vol. 8, no. 3, pp. 281–293 (1984).

[MIL84] Miller, R. C., "Introduction to the IBM 3800 Printing Subsystem Models 3 and 8," *IBM Journal of Research and Development*, vol. 28, no. 3, pp. 252–256 (1984).

[NEW74] Newman, W. M., and Sproull, R. F., "An Approach to Graphics System Design," *Proceedings of the IEEE*, vol. 62, no. 4, pp. 471–483 (1974).

[NOL71] Noll, A. M., "Scanned-Display Computer Graphics," *Communications of the ACM*, vol. 14, no. 3, pp. 143–150 (1971).

[OPH68] Ophir, D., Rankowitz, S., Shepherd, B. J., and Spinrad, R. J., "BRAD: the Brookhaven Raster Display," *Communications of the ACM*, vol. 11, no. 6, pp. 415–416 (1968).

[PRE78] Preiss, R. B., "Storage CRT Display Terminals, Evolution and Trends," *Computer*, vol. 11, no. 11, pp. 20–28 (1978).

[SLO76] Slottow, H. G., "Plasma Displays," *IEEE Transactions on Electron Devices*, vol. ED-23, no. 7, pp. 760–772 (1976).

[SPR83] Spruth, W. G., Bahr, G., "Printing Technologies," *Computers and Graphics*, vol. 7, no. 1, pp. 51–57 (1983).

[WAT84] Watkins, H. S., Moore, J. S., "A Survey of Color Graphics Printing," *IEEE Spectrum*, vol. 21, no. 7, pp. 26–37 (1984).

[ZAP75] Zaphiropoulos, R., "Electrostatic Impactless Printing and Plotting," *Information Display*, vol. 12, no. 1, pp. 23–25 (1975).

[ZUC84] Zuckerman, M. M., "Innovative Display Technologies—Why a Flat Panel When You Can Have a CRT?," *Computer Graphics & Applications*, vol. 4, no. 4, pp. 9–15 (1984).

EXERCISES

2-1 Suppose that the display device we are using has resolution 1024×1024. The pixels are numbered from 0 to 1023 for both the x and y directions, so $0 \leq x_s \leq 1023$.

a) Give the conversion function $f(x_n)$ for converting from normalized coordinates x_n to the corresponding screen coordinates x_s, that is

$$x_s = f(x_n)$$

b) If the pixels were numbered from 1 to 1024 ($1 \leq x_s \leq 1024$), what would the conversion function be?

2-2 Write program fragments using LINE-ABS-2 and MOVE-ABS-2 to draw each of the following pictures.

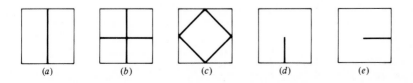

(a)   (b)   (c)   (d)   (e)

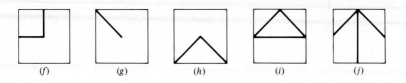

(f)   (g)   (h)   (i)   (j)

2-3 Assuming that the pen is initially positioned at (0, 0) for each case, write program fragments to draw the pictures of Exercise 2-2 using the LINE-REL-2 and MOVE-REL-2 routines.

2-4 Give the call to SET-CHARUP for generating each of the following line orientations.

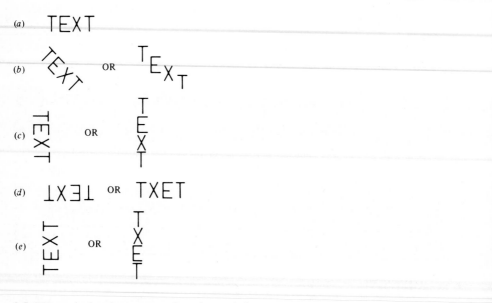

2-5 Write a single subprogram to draw the symbol

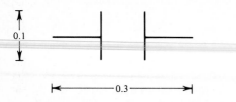

using only relative commands. The entire symbol should be 0.1 unit high and 0.3 unit wide. By calling the subprogram three times, construct the picture:

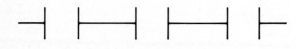

2-6 Using the routines described in this chapter, write program fragments to generate the following displays.

a) +5 VOLTS

b)

c)

d)

e)

2-7 Suppose that MOVE and LINE display-file instructions each take 4 bytes of storage.

a) How much display-file storage is required for 1000 independent line segments?

b) If the line segments are drawn as connected sequences that average four segments in length, how much display-file storage is needed for 250 such sequences?

c) If the image is placed in a 1024 × 1024, 1-bit-per-pixel frame buffer, how much frame buffer memory is required?

2-8 Give the advantages and disadvantages of hard copy displays, DVST displays, vector refresh displays, and raster displays. Suggest an applications area for which each class of device is best suited.

2-9 A high-speed laser printer may print two 8.5 × 11 inch pages each second at a resolution of 600 pixels per inch. How many bits per second does such a device require?

2-10 If a TV screen has 525 scan lines and an aspect ratio of 3:4, and if each pixel contains 8 bits worth of intensity information, how many bits per second are required to show 30 frames each second?

2-11 We have presented a display-file structure in which each entry is the same size. However, a more flexible and space-efficient scheme might allow different instructions to be different sizes (e.g., style instructions smaller than line instructions) or it might even allow an instruction to vary in size (e.g., string instructions instead of character instructions). Design a display-file structure which accommodates dynamic instruction size.

2-12 Discuss the advantages of a display-file structure which contains instructions for entire strings over a structure which contains only individual character instructions, when one wishes to interpret the display file on several different devices.

PROGRAMMING PROBLEMS

2-1 a) Implement algorithms 2.1 through 2.13.

b) Implement algorithms 2.14 through 2.19.

c) Implement algorithms 2.20 through 2.24.

2-2 Test the routines of Programming Problem 2-1 by drawing a house.

a) Use all of LINE-ABS-2, LINE-REL-2, MOVE-ABS-2, and MOVE-REL-2 to construct an image of a house.

b) Test the character routines by labeling the FLOOR with a horizontal string, the WALL with a vertical string, the ROOF with a diagonal string, and the entire HOUSE with a widely spaced string.

c) Draw the roof of the house with a different line style.

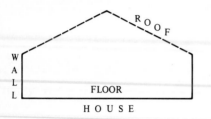

2-3 Write the four routines

INQUIRE-LINESTYLE(L)   INQUIRE-CHARSIZE(W, H)
INQUIRE-CHARSPACE(S)   INQUIRE-CHARUP(DX, DY)

which return to the user the current settings of the line style, character separation, character width and height, and the last specified character up direction.

2-4 Write routines called

POLYLINE-ABS-2 (X-ARRAY, Y-ARRAY, N)
POLYLINE-REL-2 (DX-ARRAY, DY-ARRAY, N)

These routines will enter a connected sequence of lines. The sequence begins at the current pen position, and for POLYLINE-ABS-2 connects the sequence of absolute points stored in X-ARRAY and Y-ARRAY. For POLYLINE-REL-2, the sequence is given by relative changes stored in DX-ARRAY and DY-ARRAY. The number of values in the arrays is given by N.

2-5   a) Using the LINE and MOVE routines of this chapter, or the POLYLINE routines of Programming Problem 2-4, draw a line graph of the following widget sales data.

Jan	Feb	Mar	Apr	May	June	July	Aug	Sept	Oct	Nov	Dec
2000	4000	7000	6000	4000	8000	8000	7000	5000	6000	8000	9000

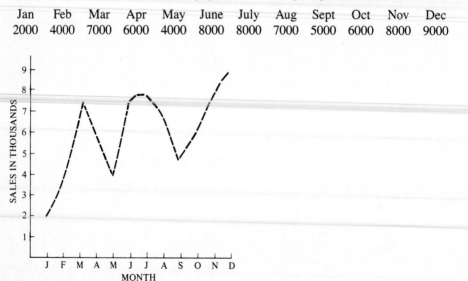

b) Draw and label the axes for the widget graph.

c) Use solid lines for the axes and some other line style for the graph itself.

2-6 Construct a bar graph of the widget data given in Programming Problem 2-5 using LINE and MOVE routines.

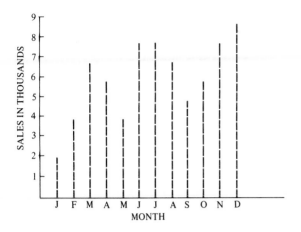

2-7 a) Write three user subprograms called

SET-MARKER-SYMBOL(SYMBOL)

MARKER-ABS-2(X, Y)

MARKER-REL-2(DX, DY)

The SET-MARKER-SYMBOL routine saves a character or symbol to be used by the other two routines. The two MARKER subprograms move the pen without drawing and then place the marker symbol at this position. Thus the commands

SET-MARKER-SYMBOL(2);

MARKER-ABS-2(0.2, 0.3);

MARKER-REL-2(0.2, 0.0);

would result in the picture

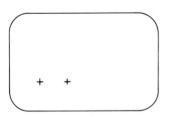

b) Use the marker routines to plot the widget sales information of Programming Problem 2-5. (See page 66, top.)

c) Write routines called

POLYMARKER-ABS-2 (X-ARRAY, Y-ARRAY, N)

POLYMARKER-REL-2 (DX-ARRAY, DY-ARRAY, N)

These routines would draw the current marker symbol at each of the points indicated by the argument arrays. For POLYMARKER-ABS-2, the arrays X-ARRAY and Y-ARRAY contain a

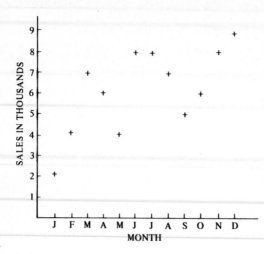

sequence of absolute points. For POLYMARKER-REL-2, the points are described by a sequence of relative position changes in DX-ARRAY and DY-ARRAY. The number of values in the arrays is given by N.

d) Use the POLYMARKER-ABS-2 and the POLYMARKER-REL-2 routines to plot the widget sales information of Programming Problem 2-5.

2-8 Write an automatic graphing procedure which takes an array of values and plots them on a graph

a) Using markers or character symbols to plot points

b) Using connected line segments

2-9 Write routines called

DASHED-ABS-2(X, Y)

DASHED-REL-2(DX, DY)

These procedures enter a sequence of line segments into the display file so that the result is the display of a dashed line.

2-10 a) Write a routine called

ADJUSTED-TEXT(STRING, LENGTH)

which takes a string as an argument and also a length. The routine will find the number of characters in the string, examine the character width (perhaps using INQUIRE-CHARSIZE of Programming Problem 2-3), and call SET-CHARSPACE before calling TEXT, such that the displayed string has the requested length.

b) Using the ADJUSTED-TEXT routine, write a program which reads a stream of text, breaks it up into lines, if necessary, and displays those lines in a column which has both left and right margins justified.

*2-11 The projection of three-dimensional constructions and the display of surfaces will be considered in Chapters 8 and 9; however, in this problem we shall consider an easy way to present three-dimensional information using only the two-dimensional routines which we have studied. Consider a function of two variables $w = f(u,v)$. We can set up three coordinate axes for u, v, w, and plot the (u, v, w) points in space.

The collection of these points forms a surface. We can get some feel for the shape of this surface by plotting sample points and connecting them by line segments.

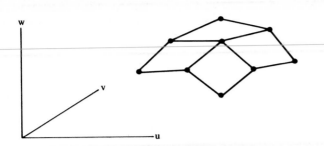

To place the three-dimensional point on our two-dimensional display, note that as w increases the point moves up, as u increases the point moves right, and as v increases the point moves both right and up.

$$x = u + v/2$$

$$y = w + v/2$$

Now as an example of this technique, consider the following array of w values

v/u	0.1	0.2	0.3	0.4	0.5
0.1	0.10	0.10	0.13	0.15	0.20
0.2	0.10	0.12	0.15	0.20	0.25
0.3	0.12	0.15	0.20	0.25	0.30
0.4	0.11	0.15	0.20	0.25	0.30
0.5	0.08	0.11	0.15	0.18	0.20

a) Write a program to plot the table points using the above formula to determine the appropriate (x, y) coordinates.

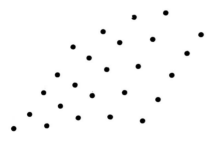

b) Connect the successive elements of each row by line segments.

c) Connect with line segments successive row elements and successive column elements.

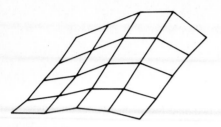

*2-12 To get three-dimensional realism in a display of a function of two variables, we should not draw lines that would be hidden by the surface. The following is a simple but rather crude method to get this effect. We wish to show a function such as $w = f(u, v)$. As in Programming Problem 2-11, we map this into our x and y coordinates by

$$x = u + v/2$$

$$y = w + v/2$$

For given v value, we shall draw curves showing how w varies as u is changed. We do this by stepping through u values; calculating w by the function f; using u, v, and w to get x and y; and connecting successive x and y points by line segments. To get the hidden-line effect, we must draw the curves in front first. That means we start with the smallest v, draw the curve for it, increment v, draw the next curve, and so on. Now suppose we draw a curve which rises to form a peak. This peak might hide the next curve. If this is the case, the y value for the curve in front will be greater than the y value for the curve behind. We can avoid drawing the hidden line if instead of drawing the line segment to the new y value, we draw it to the maximum y value. To do this, we just need an array which holds maximum values. The following is an algorithm which uses this method to draw the function for the range $0 < u < 0.5$, $0 < v < 0.5$; NUM-CURVES is the number of curves drawn, MAX-TABLE is the array of maximum y values and should contain at least three times NUM-CURVES elements.

```
BEGIN
    initialize the array of maximum values
    FOR I = 1 TO 3 * NUM-CURVES DO MAX-TABLE[I] ← 0;
    set the step sizes
    DV ← 0.5 / (NUM-CURVES − 1);
    DU ← DV * 0.5;
    V ← 0;
    loop to draw all curves
    FOR T = 1 TO NUM-CURVES DO
        BEGIN
            U ← 0;
            loop to draw one curve
            FOR K = 1 to 2 * NUM-CURVES − 1 DO
                BEGIN
                    calculate a point on the curve
                    W ← F(U, V);
```

```
      X ← U + V * 0.5;
      Y ← W + V * 0.5;
      plot the point
      MAX-TABLE [T + K – 1] ← MAX(MAX-TABLE[T + K – 1], Y)
      IF K = 1 THEN MOVE-ABS-2(X , MAX-TABLE[T + K – 1])
      ELSE LINE-ABS-2(X, MAXTABLE [T + K –1]);
      step along the curve
          U ← U + DU;
    END;
  step to next curve
      V = V + DV;
  END;
  RETURN;
END;
```

Try it for f(u, v) = (1/2) (sin 8πu) (sin 4πv) for $0 \le u \le 0.5$, $0 \le v \le 0.5$. The illustration was done with NUM-CURVES at a value of 25.

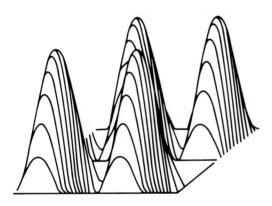

*2-13 Revise the graphics system's display-file structure so that it can handle instructions of varying size. Using this display file, revise the text algorithms so that they use a string instruction instead of individual characters.

*2-14 It is possible to have a single graphics program driving several different display devices or workstations. The program can build a single display file which is examined by different interpreters for the different devices. Extend your graphics system to allow multiple workstations (perhaps some CRTs and some hard-copy devices). Provide the user the ability to select which workstations will be active at any time.

CHAPTER
THREE

POLYGONS

INTRODUCTION

So far our discussion has dealt only with lines and characters. The world might seem
rather dull if it were made out of straight lines. It would be a world of stick figures and
outlines lacking texture, mass, and solidity. How much more interesting is the world of
patterns, colors, and shading. Unfortunately, much of the early graphics dealt only
with line drawings. This was because the available display devices (plotters, DVSTs,
and vector refresh displays) were line-drawing devices. Raster displays, however, can
display solid patterns and objects with no greater effort than that involved in showing
their outlines. Coloring and shading are possible with raster technology. Thus with the
rise in popularity of raster displays has also come an increase in attention to surface
representation. The representation of surface objects is important even for line-drawing
displays. In Chapter 9 we shall look at the problem of not showing lines which would
normally be hidden, such as the edges on the back side of an object. For this problem,
knowledge of the edges is not enough; we must also know what surfaces are present so
that we can decide what can and what cannot be seen.

In this chapter we will extend our system to include a new graphic primitive, the
polygon. We shall discuss what polygons are and how to represent them. We shall learn
how to determine if a point is inside a polygon. Finally, a method for filling in all inside pixels will be developed.

POLYGONS

We wish to be able to represent a surface. Our basic surface primitive is a *polygon* (a
many-sided figure). A polygon may be represented as a number of line segments con-

nected end to end to form a closed figure. Alternatively, it may be represented as the points where the sides of the polygon are connected. The line segments which make up the polygon boundary are called *sides* or *edges*. The endpoints of the sides are called the polygon *vertices*. The simplest polygon is the triangle, having three sides and three vertex points. (See Figure 3-1.)

We can divide polygons into two classes: *convex* and *concave*. A convex polygon is a polygon such that for any two points inside the polygon, all points on the line segment connecting them are also inside the polygon. A concave polygon is one which is not convex. A triangle is always convex. (See Figure 3-2.)

POLYGON REPRESENTATION

If we are to add polygons to our graphics system, we must first decide how to represent them. Some graphics devices supply a polygon drawing primitive to directly image polygon shapes. On such devices it is natural to save the polygon as a unit. Other devices provide a trapezoid primitive. Trapezoids are formed from two scan lines and two line segments. (See Figure 3-3.) The trapezoids are drawn by stepping down the line segments with two vector generators and, for each scan line, filling in all the pixels between them. Every polygon can be broken up into trapezoids by means similar to those described below. In such a system, it would be natural to represent a polygon as a series of trapezoids. Many other graphics devices do not provide any polygon support at all, and it is left up to the software to break up the polygon into the lines or points which can be imaged. In this case, it is again best to represent the polygon as a unit. This is the approach we shall take. We shall store full polygons in our display file and investigate the methods for imaging them using lines and points.

What should a polygon look like in our display file? We might just place line commands for each of the edges into the display file, but there are two deficiencies with this scheme. First, we have no way of knowing which line commands out of all those in the display file should be grouped together to form the polygon graphical unit; and second, we have not correctly positioned the pen for drawing the initial side. We can overcome these problems by prefacing the commands for drawing the polygon sides by a new command. This new command will tell us how many sides are in the polygon, so we will know how many of the following line commands are part of the polygon. Upon interpretation, this new command will act like a move to correctly position the pen for drawing the first side.

We have not yet used the operation codes 3 or greater. We can therefore use these codes to indicate polygons. The value of the code will indicate the number of sides. We

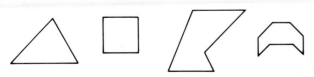

FIGURE 3-1
Polygons.

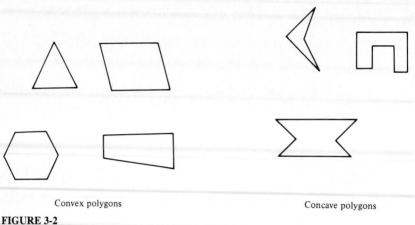

Convex polygons   Concave polygons

FIGURE 3-2
Convex and concave polygons.

will therefore be limited to polygons with no more sides than the maximum possible opcode. The X and Y operands of the polygon command will be the coordinates of the point where the first side to be drawn begins. Since polygons are closed curves, it will also be the final endpoint of the last side to be drawn. Upon execution, the polygon instruction (opcode 3 or greater) will signal that the following instructions belong to a polygon, but will otherwise behave as a move command. (See Figure 3-4.)

ENTERING POLYGONS

We can now consider algorithms for entering polygons into the display file. The information required to specify the polygon is the number of sides and the coordinates of the vertex points. Arrays can be used to pass the coordinates of all vertices to the

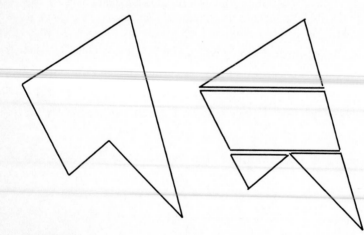

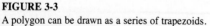

FIGURE 3-3
A polygon can be drawn as a series of trapezoids.

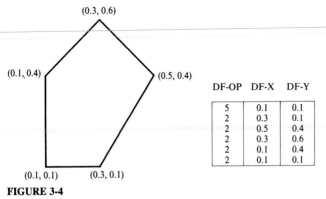

DF-OP	DF-X	DF-Y
5	0.1	0.1
2	0.3	0.1
2	0.5	0.4
2	0.3	0.6
2	0.1	0.4
2	0.1	0.1

FIGURE 3-4
A polygon and its display-file entry.

routine. If we give absolute coordinates, the following algorithm may be employed. (See Figure 3-5.)

3.1 Algorithm POLYGON-ABS-2(AX, AY, N) Entry of an absolute polygon into the display file

Arguments   AX, AY arrays containing the vertices of the polygon
             N the number of polygon sides
Global   DF-PEN-X, DF-PEN-Y the current pen position
Local   I for stepping through the polygon sides
BEGIN
    IF N < 3 THEN RETURN ERROR 'POLYGON SIZE ERROR';
    enter the polygon instruction
    DF-PEN-X ← AX[N];
    DF-PEN-Y ← AY[N];
    DISPLAY-FILE-ENTER(N);
    enter the instructions for the sides
    FOR I = 1 TO N DO LINE-ABS-2(AX[I], AY[I]);
    RETURN;
END;

We might also wish to be able to construct polygons relative to the current pen position. We would then understand the first point specified to be a relative move from

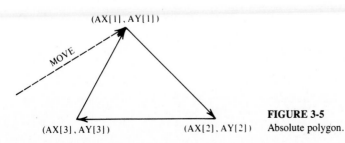

FIGURE 3-5
Absolute polygon.

the current position, and subsequent points to be used in relative line commands for the sides. (See Figure 3-6.)

3.2 Algorithm POLYGON-REL-2(AX, AY, N) Entry of a relative polygon into the display file

Arguments   AX, AY arrays containing the relative offsets of the vertices
                N the number of polygon sides
Global   DF-PEN-X, DF-PEN-Y the current pen position
Local   I for stepping through the polygon sides.
TMPX,TMPY Storage of the point at which the polygon is closed.
BEGIN
   IF N < 3 THEN RETURN ERROR 'POLYGON SIZE ERROR';
   DF-PEN-X ← DF-PEN-X + AX[1];
   DF-PEN-Y ← DF-PEN-Y + AY[1];
   save the starting point for closing the polygon
   TMPX ← DF-PEN-X;
   TMPY ← DF-PEN-Y;
   enter the polygon instruction
   DISPLAY-FILE-ENTER(N);
   enter the instructions for the sides
   FOR I = 2 TO N DO LINE-REL-2(AX[I], AY[I]);
   close the polygon
   LINE-ABS-2(TMPX, TMPY);
   RETURN;
END;

In the above algorithm, the polygon starting position must be calculated from the specified offset and the current pen position. This location must be saved temporarily so that it may be used in the final instruction, which closes the figure.

AN INSIDE TEST

Having entered the commands in the display file, we can show outlined forms for polygons by simply modifying the interpreter so that it treats command codes 3 and greater as move commands. However, we might also wish to be able to show the polygons as solid objects by setting the pixels inside the polygon as well as those on the boundary. Let us consider how we can determine whether or not a point is inside of a polygon. One method of doing this is to construct a line segment between the point in question

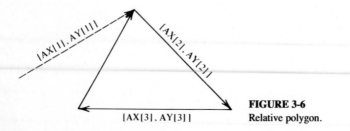

FIGURE 3-6
Relative polygon.

and a point known to be outside the polygon. It is easy to find a point outside the polygon; one could, for example, pick a point with an x coordinate smaller than the smallest x coordinate of the polygon's vertices. One then counts how many intersections of the line segment with the polygon boundary occur. If there are an odd number of intersections, then the point in question is inside; an even number indicates that it is outside. This is called the *even-odd method* of determining polygon interior points. (See Figure 3-7.)

When counting intersection points, one must be cautious when the point of intersection is also the vertex where two sides meet. To handle this case, we must look at the other endpoints of the two segments which meet at this vertex. If these points lie on the same side of the constructed line, then the point in question counts as an even number of intersections. If they lie on opposite sides of the constructed line, then the point is counted as a single intersection. (See Figure 3-8.)

There is an alternative method for defining a polygon's interior points called the *winding-number method*. Conceptually one can stretch a piece of elastic between the point in question and a point on the polygon boundary. The end attached to the polygon is slid along the boundary until it has made one complete circuit. We then examine the point in question to see how many times the elastic has wound around it. If it has wound at least once, then the point is inside. If there is no net winding, then the point is outside. Calculating the winding number for a point is not as difficult as the method just described. We begin, as in the even-odd method, by picturing a line segment running from outside the polygon to the point in question and consider the polygon sides which it crosses. However, in the winding-number method, instead of just counting the intersections, we give each boundary line crossed a *direction number*, and we sum these direction numbers. The direction number indicates the direction the polygon edge was drawn relative to the line segment we constructed for the test. For example, to test a point (x_a, y_a), let us consider a horizontal line segment $y = y_a$ which runs from outside the polygon to (x_a, y_a). We find all of the sides which cross this line segment. Now there are two ways for a side to cross. The side could be drawn starting below the line, cross it, and end above the line (first y value less than the second y value). In this case, we give a direction number of -1 to the side. Or the edge could start above the

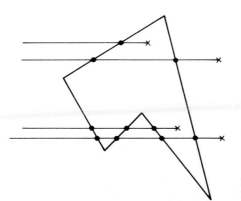

FIGURE 3-7
Even-odd inside test.

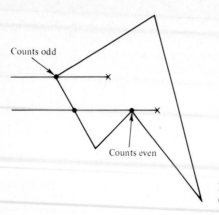

Counts odd

Counts even

FIGURE 3-8
Count of vertex intersections.

line and finish below it (first y value greater than the second y value). This case is given a direction of 1. The sum of the direction numbers for the sides that cross the constructed horizontal line segment yields the winding number for the point in question. (See Figure 3-9.)

Using the winding number to define the interior points can yield different results from the even-odd method when a polygon is allowed to overlap itself. (See Figure 3-10.) The polygon-filling algorithm presented in this book is based on the even-odd method.

POLYGON INTERFACING ALGORITHMS

Before we become too deeply involved in the details of filling a polygon, let us give the algorithm that is needed to interface polygons with the rest of our graphics system.

We shall be able to show polygons either filled or in outline. We shall therefore provide the user with a method of indicating his preference. This is done by setting a global flag which can be checked at the time when the polygon is actually drawn.

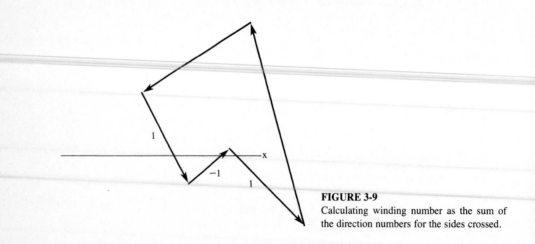

FIGURE 3-9
Calculating winding number as the sum of the direction numbers for the sides crossed.

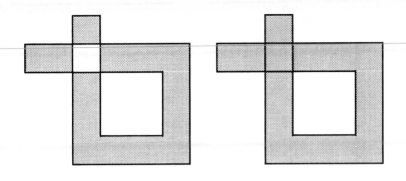

Even-odd method   Winding number method

FIGURE 3-10
Interior points for a polygon that overlaps itself.

3.3 Algorithm SET-FILL(ON-OFF) User routine to set a flag indicating that polygons should be filled
Argument   ON-OFF the user's fill setting
Global   SOLID a flag which indicates filling of polygons
BEGIN
    SOLID ← ON-OFF;
    RETURN;
END;

Just as we have different line styles, we shall provide for different interior styles for polygons. Fill styles may be implemented as different colors, different shades of gray, or different filling patterns. We shall give the user a routine for selecting the desired interior style. Style values between 1 and 16, inclusive, will be acceptable. We map these values to opcodes between −16 and −31.

3.4 Algorithm SET-FILL-STYLE(STYLE) User routine to set the polygon interior style
Argument   STYLE the user's style request
Constant   FIRST-FILL-OP first fill op = −16
BEGIN
    DISPLAY-FILE-ENTER(FIRST-FILL-OP − (STYLE − 1));
    RETURN;
END;

Fill styles are handled in the same manner as line styles. A code indicating the desired style setting is placed in the display file. We can use negative integers as the operation codes for both line and fill styles. In our system, the codes 0 through −15 will be reserved for line styles and codes −16 through −31 will refer to fill styles. The user again specifies a positive integer for the interior style, which is converted to a negative number between −16 and −31 before it is stored in the display file. What the system actually does with a polygon fill style depends upon how fill styles are implemented. The system might select a color or an intensity value (FILLCHR) to be used in filling. Or it might set a SCAN-DECREMENT parameter which indicates the filling of every nth scan line. It might also set an index into a table of patterns (FILL-PATTERN).

The DOSTYLE algorithm of Chapter 2 can be modified to include both line and interior style settings.

3.5 Algorithm DOSTYLE(OP) (Algorithm 2.21 revisited) Routine to interpret change of style commands
Argument   OP indicates the desired style.
Constant   FIRST-FILL-OP first fill op $= -16$
BEGIN
    IF OP $\leq$ FIRST-FILL-OP; THEN decode op and set polygon fill style
    ELSE decode op and set line style;
    RETURN;
END;

The INTERPRET algorithm must also be extended to handle polygon commands. When a polygon command is discovered, control is then transferred to the DOPOLYGON command, which processes the polygon.

3.6 Algorithm INTERPRET(START, COUNT) (Algorithm 2.22 revisited) Scan the display file performing the instructions
Arguments   START the starting index of the display-file scan
                COUNT the number of instructions to be interpreted
Local   NTH the display-file index
         OP, X, Y the display-file instruction
BEGIN
    a loop to do all desired instructions
    FOR NTH = START TO START + COUNT $-$ 1 DO
        BEGIN
            GET-POINT(NTH, OP, X, Y);
            IF OP $<$ -31 THEN DOCHAR(OP, X, Y)
            ELSE IF OP $<$ 1 THEN DOSTYLE(OP)
                  ELSE IF OP $=$ 1 THEN DOMOVE(X, Y)
                      ELSE IF OP $=$ 2 THEN DOLINE(X, Y)
                          ELSE DOPOLYGON(OP, X, Y, NTH);
        END;
        RETURN;
END;

The polygon command indicates that there is a polygon and indicates how many sides it has. If the user has requested filled polygons by setting the SOLID flag, then this information is given to the FILL-POLYGON routine which will do the actual filling in. In all other respects, the polygon command is treated as a move.

3.7 Algorithm DOPOLYGON(OP, X, Y, INDEX) Routine to process a polygon command

Arguments   OP X Y the display-file instruction
                 INDEX the position in the display file of the instruction
Global   SOLID a flag to indicate if the polygon should be filled in
BEGIN
   IF SOLID THEN FILL-POLYGON(INDEX);
   DOMOVE(X, Y);
   RETURN;
END;

FILLING POLYGONS

One way of filling polygons is to first draw the edges of the polygon in a blank frame buffer. Then starting with some "seed" point known to be inside the polygon, we set the intensity to the interior style and examine the neighboring pixels. We continue to set the pixel values in an increasing area until we encounter the boundary pixels. This method is called a *flood fill* because color flows from the seed pixel until reaching the polygon boundary, like water flooding the interior of a container. The flood-fill method can be quite useful in some cases. It will work with any closed shape in the frame buffer, no matter how that shape originated. However, it requires a frame buffer free of pixels with the polygon interior style, in order to avoid confusion. It also requires a seed pixel.

We could draw solid polygons by considering every pixel on the screen, applying our inside test, and setting those pixels which satisfied it. This would avoid the need for a seed pixel, but the method would be rather costly. Many pixels can be immediately eliminated by comparing them with the maximum and minimum boundary points. We really need to consider only those pixels which lie within the smallest rectangle which contains the polygon. If we first find the largest and smallest y values of the polygon, we need to consider only points which lie between them. Let us suppose that we start with the largest y value and work our way down, scanning from left to right as we go, in the manner of a raster display. Our constructed test lines will be the horizontal lines at the current y scanning value. Many problems in computer graphics can be approached a scan line at a time. Algorithms which take this approach are called *scan-line algorithms*. Often we can take advantage of what we learned in processing one scan line to make the calculation easier for the next scan line. (See Figure 3-11.)

We could draw the boundary of the polygon in a blank frame buffer and then examine the pixels in the box around the polygon, scan line by scan line. Moving across the scan line, when we encounter a pixel with the intensity of the boundary, we enter the polygon. Subsequent pixels are given the interior intensity until we encounter a second boundary pixel. The problems with this scheme are that we must start with a frame buffer free of pixels with the polygon boundary intensity and we must be careful about cases where two polygon edges meet at a single pixel. We can avoid these problems by determining the polygon boundary values directly from the polygon instruction, instead of from the frame buffer. Using the display-file instructions, we can deter-

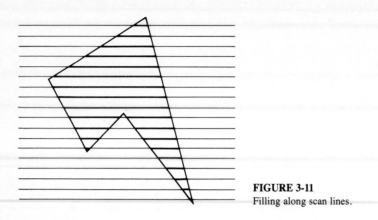

FIGURE 3-11
Filling along scan lines.

mine where the scan line crosses the polygon boundary. To test a point, we do not have to compute the intersection of our scan line with every polygon side. We need to consider only the polygon sides with endpoints straddling the test line. (See Figure 3-12.)

It will be easier to identify which polygon sides should be tested if we first sort the sides in order of their maximum y value. As we scan down the polygon, the order in which the sides must be considered will match the order in which they are stored.

Each time we step down to a lower y value, we can examine the sides being considered, in order to determine whether we have passed their lower endpoints. If we have stepped past the lowest y value of a side, it may be removed from the set of sides being considered. Now for each y value we know exactly which polygon sides can be crossed. (See Figure 3-13.)

We maintain our list of sides so that all the sides which are currently being considered will be grouped together. We shall keep two pointers to mark the boundaries of the group, START-EDGE and END-EDGE. All edges stored with list indices greater or equal to START-EDGE and less than END-EDGE should be considered. An edge in the list before START-EDGE has yet to be encountered. Those which lie behind END-EDGE will have been passed.

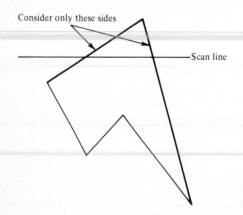

FIGURE 3-12
Consider only the sides which intersect the scan line.

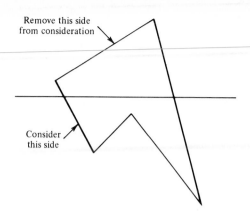

Remove this side
from consideration

Consider
this side

FIGURE 3-13
When the scan line passes the bottom endpoint of
a side, remove it from consideration. When the
scan line passes the top endpoint of a side, consider the side.

Our task becomes setting those pixels on the horizontal scan line which lie inside
the polygon. It is really not necessary to examine every pixel on the horizontal line.
We can think of the polygon as breaking up a horizontal scan into pieces. (See Figure
3-14.) According to the even-odd definition of the polygon interior, the pieces alternate
light and dark. If we know the endpoints of the pieces—that is, the points where the
scan line crosses the polygon's sides—then we can use our vector generator (or equivalent) to fill in the entire piece. We do not have to consider each pixel in the scan-line
segment individually. Suppose we compute the x values for all intersections of polygon sides with a given horizontal line, and then sort these x values. The smallest x
value will be the left polygon boundary. At this point the polygon begins. The next x
value indicates where the polygon ends. Therefore, a line segment drawn between
these values will fill in this portion of the polygon. We can pair up the sorted x values
in this manner for passage to our line-drawing routine. (See Figure 3-15.)

In summary, an algorithm for filling a solid polygon should begin by ordering
the polygon sides on the largest y value. It should begin with the largest y value and
scan down the polygon. For each y, it should determine which sides can be intersected
and find the x values of these intersection points. The x values are sorted, paired, and
passed to a line-drawing routine.

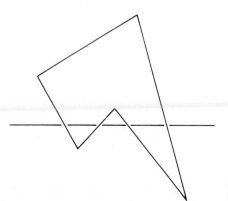

FIGURE 3-14
The polygon breaks the scan line into pieces.

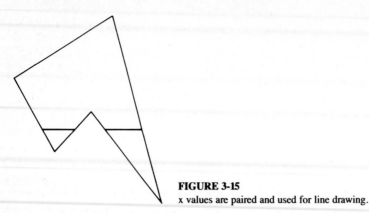

FIGURE 3-15
x values are paired and used for line drawing.

The algorithm which performs the yx scan and fills in the polygon is called FILL-POLYGON. It begins by retrieving the polygon shape information from the display file and sorting it by largest y value. This is accomplished by means of the LOAD-POLYGON algorithm. The filling in of the polygon is done by repeating five steps. The first step is to determine if any additional polygon sides should be considered for this scan line. The INCLUDE routine makes this determination. The second step is to sort the x coordinates of the points where the polygon sides cross the scan line so that they may be easily paired. This is done by the XSORT routine. The third step is to actually turn on the pixels between the polygon edges, which is done by FILL-SCAN. Next, the current scan line is decremented; and finally, the UPDATE-X-VALUES routine determines the points of intersection of the polygon with this new scan line, and removes from consideration any edges which have been passed. These steps are repeated until all polygon edges have been passed by the scanning process.

3.8 Algorithm FILL-POLYGON(INDEX) Fills in a polygon

Arguments   INDEX the display-file index of the instruction

Global   YMAX an array of upper y coordinates for polygon sides

                SCAN-DECREMENT the size of a scan-line decrement

Local   EDGES the number of polygon sides considered

                SCAN the y value of the scan line

                START-EDGE, END-EDGE indicate which polygon sides are crossed by the scan line

BEGIN

    load global arrays with the polygon vertex information

    LOAD-POLYGON(INDEX, EDGES);

    are there enough sides to consider

    IF EDGES < 2 THEN RETURN;

    set scan line

    SCAN ← YMAX[1];

    initialize starting and ending index values for sides considered

    START-EDGE ← 1;

    END-EDGE ← 1;

```
fill in polygon
pick up any new sides to be included in this scan
INCLUDE(END-EDGE, EDGES, SCAN);
repeat the filling until all sides have been passed
WHILE END-EDGE ≠ START-EDGE; DO
    BEGIN
        make sure the x values are in order
        XSORT(START-EDGE, END-EDGE − 1);
        fill in the scan line
        FILL-SCAN(END-EDGE, START-EDGE, SCAN);
        next scan line
        SCAN ← SCAN − SCAN-DECREMENT;
        revise x values
        UPDATE-X-VALUES(END-EDGE − 1, START-EDGE, SCAN);
        and see if any new edges should be considered
        INCLUDE(END-EDGE, EDGES, SCAN);
    END;
    RETURN;
END;
```

Now let's consider in more detail what we would like to know about each polygon edge. We would like to know the largest and smallest y-coordinate values. The largest y value indicates at which point in the scanning process to include this edge. The smallest y value will determine when the line has been passed and need no longer be considered. We shall also need to store x-coordinate information so that we can determine where the edge will intersect the scan line. For this purpose, the x value of the endpoint with largest y value should be saved. Thus we save both x and y coordinates of the endpoint which will first be encountered in the scanning process. Now as we step down through successive scan lines, the point of intersection will shift in x. The amount by which it shifts can be determined if we know the change in x for a change in y along the edge, that is, if we know the reciprocal of the slope of the edge. These four items (X-TOP, Y-TOP, Y-BOTTOM, INVERSE-SLOPE) are all that we need to know about each side. (See Figure 3-16.)

We shall want to store this information for all nonhorizontal lines. Horizontal lines can be ignored because they are parallel to the scan lines and cannot intersect them. We shall want to store this information ordered according to Y-TOP, because this is the order in which it will be accessed. The retrieval and storing of the edge informa-

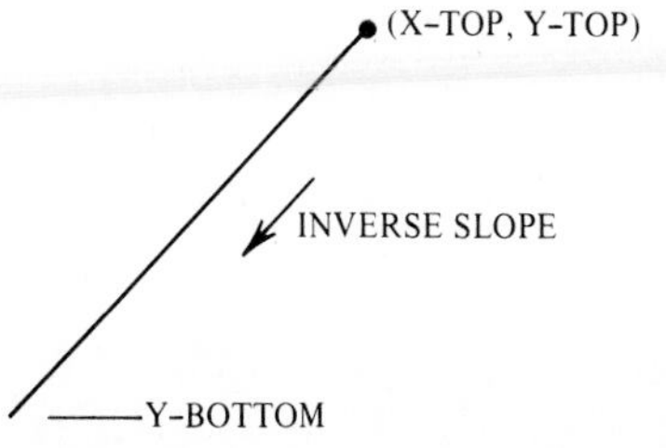

FIGURE 3-16
Parameters stored for each side of the polygon.

tion are performed by a routine which we have called LOAD-POLYGON. The algorithm begins by setting one endpoint of the edge equal to the vertex in the original polygon command. The point is converted from normalized coordinates to actual devices coordinates. We add 0.5 to get the effect of rounding the point to a pixel number. The y value is rounded right away by the INT function, which is the same as FLOOR for positive arguments. The x value will be rounded at every scan line.

The LOAD-POLYGON algorithm next steps through the display file. It retrieves a new vertex by means of the GET-POINT routine. This vertex becomes the second endpoint of a polygon edge (the first endpoint came from the previous step). Horizontal edges are ignored, but information for nonhorizontal lines is saved in order by the POLY-INSERT routine. When all edges have been considered, the algorithm returns the number of edges actually saved.

3.9 Algorithm LOAD-POLYGON(I, EDGES)   A routine to retrieve polygon side information from the display file. Positions are converted to actual screen coordinates

Arguments   I the display-file index of the instruction
            EDGES for return of the number of sides stored

Global   WIDTH-START, HEIGHT-START starting index of the screen
            WIDTH width in pixels of the screen
            HEIGHT height in pixels of the screen

Local   X1, Y1, X2, Y2 edge endpoints in actual device coordinates
            I1 for stepping through the display file
            K for stepping through the polygon sides
            DUMMY for a dummy argument
            SIDES the number of sides on the polygon

BEGIN
    set starting point for a side
    GET-POINT(I, SIDES, X1, Y1);
    X1 ← X1 * WIDTH + WIDTH-START + 0.5;
    adjust y coordinate to nearest scan line
    Y1 ← INT(Y1 * HEIGHT + HEIGHT-START + 0.5);
    get index of first side command
    I1 ← I + 1;
    initialize an index for storing side data
    EDGES ← 1;
    a loop to get information about each side
    FOR K = 1 TO SIDES DO
      BEGIN
        get next vertex
        GET-POINT(I1, DUMMY, X2, Y2);
        X2 ← X2 * WIDTH + WIDTH-START + 0.5;
        Y2 ← INT(Y2 * HEIGHT + HEIGHT-START + 0.5);
        see if horizontal line
        IF Y1 = Y2 THEN X1 ← X2
        ELSE
          BEGIN
            save data about side in order of largest y
            POLY-INSERT(EDGES, X1, Y1, X2, Y2);

```
            increment index for side data storage
            EDGES ← EDGES + 1;
            old point is reset
            Y1 ← Y2;
            X1 ← X2;
         END;
      I1 ← I1 + 1;
   END;
 set EDGES to be a count of the edges stored.
 EDGES ← EDGES − 1;
 RETURN;
END;
```

The POLY-INSERT algorithm is basically an insertion sort. It determines the maximum y value for the two endpoints and compares it with previously entered edges to determine where in the sequence the new edge belongs. It begins with the last element, to see if it belongs at this end. If the new edge's maximum y value is smaller than that of all previous edges, it is entered at this end. If not, the last edge is moved down one position, opening a possible storage location in the next-to-the-last place. This comparison with, and shifting of, the edges is continued until the appropriate position for the new edge is found, at which point information for the new edge is inserted. The data is stored in four separate arrays (one for each type of information). These arrays should be dimensioned to match the maximum number of sides a polygon can have in the system (one entry for each side). We have named the arrays YMAX to save Y-TOP, YMIN to save Y-BOTTOM, XA to save X-TOP, and DX to hold the change in x for each scan decrement. For a constant scan decrement, there will be a fixed change in the x-intersection value for each scan. We can find the amount that the intersection point will shift by multiplying the rate of change in x for a change in y by the scan decrement. The scan decrement is the distance between the scan lines actually being filled. Usually this will be 1, so that every scan line is filled, but by allowing other values, we can achieve different fill styles. For example, a scan decrement of 2 would fill every other scan line. (See Figure 3-17.) We use the INT function to round the x values to integer pixel positions in determining XA and DX. This is so the sides of the polygon will match the boundary drawn with the Bresenham algorithm.

3.10 Algorithm POLY-INSERT (J, X1, Y1, X2, Y2) The ordered insertion of polygon edge information

Arguments   J insertion index
            X1, Y1, X2, Y2 endpoints of the polygon side (y values rounded)
Global   YMAX, YMIN, XA, DX arrays for storage of polygon edge information
            SCAN-DECREMENT step between filled scan lines
Local   J1 for stepping through the stored edges
            YM the maximum y value of the new edge
BEGIN
    insertion sort into global arrays on maximum y
    J1 ← J;
    find the largest y

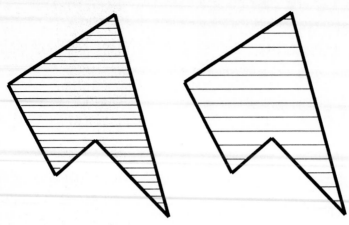

FIGURE 3-17
Using scan decrement for fill styles.

```
YM ← MAX(Y1, Y2);
find correct insertion point, moving items out of the way as we go
WHILE J1 ≠ 1 AND YMAX(J1 − 1) < YM DO
    BEGIN
        move up the insertion slot
        YMAX[J1] ← YMAX[J1 − 1];
        YMIN[J1] ← YMIN[J1 − 1];
        XA[J1] ← XA[J1 − 1];
        DX[J1] ← DX[J1 − 1];
        J1 ← J1 − 1;
    END;
insert information about side
YMAX[J1] ← YM;
DX[J1] ← ((INT(X2) − INT(X1)) / (Y2 − Y1)) * ( − SCAN-DECREMENT);
see which end is on top
IF Y1 > Y2 THEN
    BEGIN
        YMIN[J1] ← Y2;
        XA[J1] ← INT(X1);
    END
ELSE
    BEGIN
        YMIN[J1] ← Y1;
        XA[J1] ← INT(X2);
    END;
    RETURN;
END;
```

The edge information for the polygon has been stored for our use, but we need not consider every edge with every scan line. We need to maintain the START-EDGE and END-EDGE pointers to delimit the edges of interest. (See Figure 3-18.)

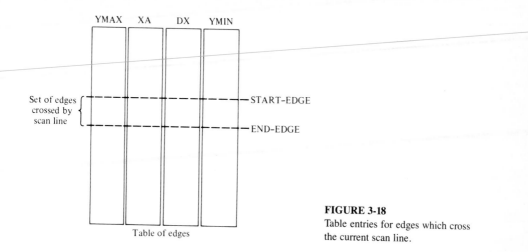

FIGURE 3-18
Table entries for edges which cross the current scan line.

The algorithm we have called INCLUDE adds new edges to the group being considered. Because of the order in which we have stored the edges, the next edge to be included will be the next edge in the array. To include the new edge, we only have to increment the END-EDGE boundary. For each new scan line, the INCLUDE algorithm checks the largest y value for the next edge; if the scan has gone below this value, then END-EDGE is incremented to include the edge.

3.11 Algorithm INCLUDE(END-EDGE, FINAL-EDGE, SCAN) Include any edges newly intersected by the scan line

Arguments   END-EDGE index of the side being considered for inclusion
            FINAL-EDGE index of last side
            SCAN position of current scan line
Global   YMAX, XA, DX arrays of edge information
            SCAN-DECREMENT the size of a scan-line decrement
BEGIN
    WHILE END-EDGE ≤ FINAL-EDGE AND YMAX[END-EDGE] ≥ SCAN DO
        include a new edge
        END-EDGE ← EDGE-END + 1;
    RETURN;
END;

The edge information between START-EDGE and END-EDGE is kept ordered on the x-intersection value. (See Figure 3-19.)

The task of maintaining this ordering belongs to the algorithm called XSORT. The XSORT routine steps through the currently active edges. If the position is correct, then nothing happens. If, however, the element is out of place, it is ''bubbled up'' to its correct position by a series of exchanges with its neighbors. When a new edge is entered, it may have to be shuffled down the array to place it in order. In subsequent checks, however, the edges will almost always be in their correct positions. The exception is when polygon sides are allowed to cross.

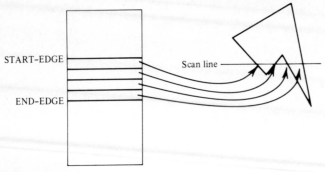

FIGURE 3-19
Table entries sorted on x.

3.12 Algorithm XSORT(START-EDGE, LAST-EDGE) Checking the order of the x intersection

Arguments   START-EDGE index of the first of the edges considered
            LAST-EDGE index of the last edge whose order is to be checked

Global   YMIN, XA, DX arrays of edge information

Local   K, L for stepping through the edges
            T temporary storage for the exchange

BEGIN
    FOR K = START-EDGE TO LAST-EDGE DO
        BEGIN
            L ← K;
            WHILE L > START-EDGE AND XA[L] < XA[L − 1] DO
                BEGIN
                    T ← YMIN[L];
                    YMIN[L] ← YMIN[L − 1];
                    YMIN[L − 1] ← T;
                    T ← XA[L];
                    XA[L] ← XA[L − 1];
                    XA[L − 1] ← T;
                    T ← DX[L];
                    DX[L] ← DX[L − 1];
                    DX[L − 1] ← T;
                    L ← L − 1;
                END;
        END;
    RETURN;
END:

The next algorithm, FILL-SCAN, actually fills in a scan line. It contains a loop which steps through all current intersection points, connecting pairs with line segments. The actual line-segment drawing is done by FILLIN.

3.13 Algorithm FILL-SCAN(END-EDGE, START-EDGE, SCAN) Fill in the scan line

Argument	START-EDGE, END-EDGE indicates which edges are crossed by the scan line
	SCAN the position of the scan line
Global	XA an array of edge intersection positions
Local	NX the number of line segments to be drawn
	J for stepping through the edges
	K for stepping through line segments

```
BEGIN
    NX ← (END-EDGE − START-EDGE) / 2;
    J ← START-EDGE;
    FOR K = 1 TO NX DO
        BEGIN
            FILLIN(XA[J], XA[J + 1], SCAN);
            J ← J + 2;
        END;
    RETURN;
END;
```

The FILLIN routine may depend upon the type of display system being used. If FILLIN uses some vector-generating routine provided by the display, FILLIN may have to store the current line style, set the line style to the polygon interior style, move to one of the endpoints, draw a line to the other endpoint, and reset the line style and pen position to their original values. Alternatively, we can write a simple FILLIN algorithm based on an assumed frame buffer (or some other method of setting individual pixels), as were the vector generation algorithms of Chapter 1.

3.14 Algorithm FILLIN(X1, X2, Y) Fills in scan line Y from X1 to X2

Arguments	X1, X2 end positions of the scan line to be filled
	Y the scan line to be filled
Global	FILLCHR intensity value to be used for the polygon
	FRAME the two-dimensional frame buffer array
Local	X for stepping across the scan line

```
BEGIN
    IF X1 = X2 THEN RETURN;
    FOR X = X1 TO X2 DO FRAME[X, Y] ← FILLCHR;
    RETURN;
END;
```

For each new scan line, we must examine the currently active edges to see if any have been passed. If the edge should still be considered, the intersection value for the new scan line should be calculated; if it has been passed, the edge should be removed from consideration. This is the job of the algorithm called UPDATE-X-VALUES. To determine if an edge still crosses the scan line, the lowest y value is examined. To update the intersection point, the constant step size (determined in INCLUDE) is added. To remove an edge from consideration, the information for previous edges is moved up one position in the arrays. This overwrites the deleted edge and allows incrementing of the START-EDGE boundary. (See Figure 3-20.)

3.15 Algorithm UPDATE-X-VALUES(LAST-EDGE, START-EDGE, SCAN) Update points of intersection between edges and the scan line

Arguments   START-EDGE and LAST-EDGE limits of current edge list

               SCAN the current scan line

Global   XA, DX, YMIN arrays of edge information

Local   K1 index of edge being considered for update

               K2 index of where to store the updated edge

```
BEGIN
    K2 ← LAST-EDGE;
    FOR K1 = LAST-EDGE TO START-EDGE DO
        BEGIN
            check each edge
            IF YMIN[K1] < SCAN THEN
                BEGIN
                    the edge is still active so update its x values
                    XA[K2] ← XA[K1] + DX[K1];
                    IF K1 ≠ K2 THEN
                        BEGIN
                            YMIN[K2] ← YMIN[K1];
                            DX[K2] ← DX[K1];
                        END;
                    decrement K2 so the edge won't get overwritten
                    K2 ← K2 − 1;
                END;
        END;
    START-EDGE ← K2 + 1;
    RETURN;
END;
```

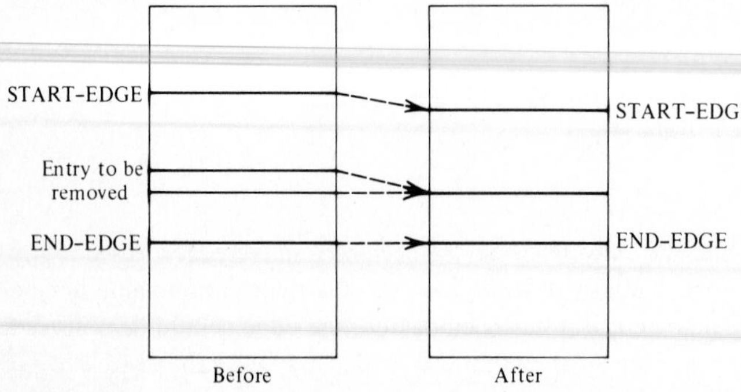

START-EDGE   START-EDGE

Entry to be removed

END-EDGE   END-EDGE

Before   After

FIGURE 3-20
Removal of a table entry.

The above algorithms allow us to fill in the interiors of polygons efficiently. We should note, however, that if we are not careful, the method used for determining the polygon boundary may be different from that used by the line generation algorithm to outline the polygon. The interior may turn out to be a pixel wider than the edge, which can be apparent at low resolution.

FILLING WITH A PATTERN

We mentioned that polygon fill styles might be patterns. Patterns are most easily implemented on raster display devices. A pattern is a grid of pixel values which is replicated like tiles to cover the polygon area. A pattern is often fixed, or *registered,* to the imaging surface so that if two polygons are filled with the pattern and placed side by side, the pattern will match at the boundary. We can imagine taking the pattern and replicating it to cover the entire imaging surface, and then erasing it anywhere outside of the polygons which use it. (See Figure 3-21.)

Assuming a frame buffer (or some other means of setting individual points), we can show how patterns might be added to our graphics system. We can set up a table of patterns and use the fill style to select one. We shall provide a routine for placing patterns into the table. We shall also give a version of FILLIN which uses the table. Some examples of 4 × 4 patterns are shown in Figure 3-22.

The pattern table can be composed of three arrays—PATTERN-X, PATTERN-Y, and PATTERNS—where PATTERN-X and PATTERN-Y are arrays of numbers which

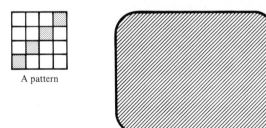

A pattern

Replicated across the display

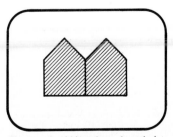

Shown only within polygon boundaries

FIGURE 3-21
Replication of a pattern.

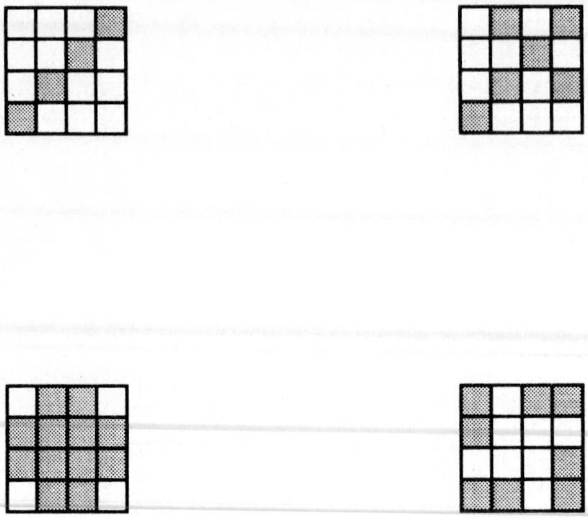

FIGURE 3-22
Some 4 × 4 patterns.

specify the size of each pattern, and PATTERNS is an array of two-dimensional arrays which are the actual patterns. (One way to implement PATTERNS is to make it a three-dimensional array, but this may not be as flexible as alternatives offered by some languages.) We place an individual pattern into the pattern table with the following algorithm.

3.16 Algorithm SET-PATTERN-REPRESENTATION(PATTERN-INDEX, PAT-X, PAT-Y, NEW-PATTERN) Enters a pattern into the pattern table

Arguments   PATTERN-INDEX the place in the pattern table to save the pattern

               PAT-X, PAT-Y the dimensions of the pattern

               NEW-PATTERN the pattern, a two-dimensional array of intensity values

Global   PATTERN-X, PATTERN-Y, PATTERNS the pattern table

BEGIN

     PATTERN-X[PATTERN-INDEX] ← PAT-X;

     PATTERN-Y[PATTERN-INDEX] ← PAT-Y;

     the following statement depends upon the implementation of PATTERNS, and may entail the copying of all the individual intensity values

     PATTERNS[PATTERN-INDEX] ← NEW-PATTERN;

     RETURN;

END;

The FILLIN algorithm is revised as follows:

3.17 Algorithm FILLIN(X1, X2, Y) (Revision of algorithm 3.14) Fills in scan line Y from X1 to X2

Arguments   X1, X2 end positions of the scan line to be filled

               Y the scan line to be filled

Global   FILL-PATTERN pattern table index of the pattern to use

               PATTERN-X, PATTERN-Y, PATTERNS the pattern table

               FRAME the two-dimensional frame buffer array

```
Local       X for stepping across the scan line
            PX, PY for accessing the pattern
            PATTERN-TO-USE the pattern to be used in filling
            PAT-X, PAT-Y the x and y dimensions of the pattern
BEGIN
   IF X1 = X2 THEN RETURN;
   PAT-X ← PATTERN-X[FILL-PATTERN];
   PAT-Y ← PATTERN-Y[FILL-PATTERN];
   if a local array is used as shown in the following statement,
   then the implementation should avoid copying of individual elements
   PATTERN-TO-USE ← PATTERNS[FILL-PATTERN];
   PX ← MOD(X1, PAT-X) + 1;
   PY ← MOD(Y, PAT-Y) + 1;
   FOR X = X1 TO X2 DO
      BEGIN
         FRAME[X, Y] ← PATTERN-TO-USE[PX, PY];
         IF PX = PAT-X THEN PX ← 1
         ELSE PX ← PX + 1;
      END;
   RETURN;
END;
```

The MOD functions give the remainder after division of the first element by the second. This is what causes the replication of the pattern. If we have a value X1 or Y which is larger than the pattern size, the MOD function wraps PX and PY back into values within the pattern, thereby repeating the pattern. The 1s are added into this calculation because we have assumed our arrays are dimensioned with starting index 1. We set the local variables PAT-X, PAT-Y, and PATTERN-TO-USE in order to remove the address computation from the loop. Actually, it would be even better to make these variables global and to set them in DOSTYLE (the only reason we did not do so is that DOSTYLE is too system-dependent for a clean example).

On many devices there are only two pixel states, on or off. For these displays, the frame buffers and pattern tables can be compactly implemented by using individual bits to describe the pixel states. Pattern dimensions can be chosen to lie on word boundaries, and the FILLIN algorithm can be made more efficient by dealing with entire words of pixel values.

INITIALIZATION

To finish this chapter's algorithms, an initialization routine is needed to set default values for filling and fill-style parameters. If filling with patterns is possible, then the pattern table should be initialized to a default set of patterns.

3.18 Algorithm INITIALIZE-3 Routine to initialize the system
Local   P for stepping through the pattern table
Constants   MINIMUM-FILL-OP opcode for first fill style = -16
                NUMBER-OF-PATTERNS the size of the pattern table

```
                    DEFAULT-PAT-X, DEFAULT-PAT-Y size of the default pattern
                    DEFAULT-PATTERN a default pattern array
      BEGIN
         INITIALIZE-2;
         DOSTYLE(MINIMUM-FILL-OP);
         SET-FILL(FALSE);
         the following loop is included only if polygons may be filled with patterns
         FOR P = 1 TO NUMBER-OF-PATTERNS DO
            SET-PATTERN-REPRESENTATION(P, DEFAULT-PAT-X, DEFAULT-PAT-Y,
            DEFAULT-PATTERN);
         RETURN;
      END;
```

ANTIALIASING

In Chapter 1 we mentioned a technique for smoothing the jagged steps in a line which is introduced by the quantization to finite-sized pixels. Aliasing is a problem for the edges of polygons just as it is for lines, and several antialiasing techniques which use the shading of gray-level displays to reduce the effects have been developed. One technique is to calculate what fraction of a pixel is actually covered by the polygon and how much is background. The pixel intensity displayed would then be the average of the background and polygon intensities weighted by their relative areas.

Another approach is to generate the scene at a higher resolution than that which will actually be used, and then to average the intensity values of neighboring pixels to determine the intensity to be displayed. Increasing the resolution between four and eight times gives good results. Note that this need not be as much work as it seems. The antialiasing can be incorporated as part of the polygon-filling algorithm. Antialiasing need only be applied to the points on the edge (interior points will have the full polygon intensity). It can be carried out scan line by scan line, so we don't need excessive amounts of memory.

AN APPLICATION

Before leaving this chapter, let's discuss how we might use some of the routines which we have developed. Let's consider how we might write a package to draw a bar graph of some data. We have already seen in Chapter 2 how the axes might be drawn and labeled, so we shall concentrate on how to generate the bars. We can make a bar out of a four-sided polygon. (See Figure 3-23.)

Suppose that we construct such a polygon with lower-left corner at the current pen position by using the POLYGON-REL-2(AX, AY, 4) command. Then the necessary AX and AY array values would be

$$AX = 0, DX, 0, -DX$$

$$AY = 0, 0, DY, 0$$

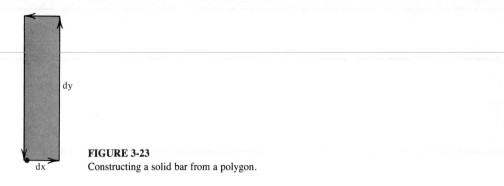

FIGURE 3-23
Constructing a solid bar from a polygon.

Here, DX will give the width of the polygon and DY will give its height. Now we can fix DX at the width which we want our bar graph's bars to have. All bars should have the same width, but the height of each bar depends upon the input data. Each bar might have a different height. We can see, however, that it is easy to change the bar height; we need to change only the value of the DY parameter in the AY array. Thus by poking the appropriate value into the AY array and calling the POLYGON-REL-2 routine, we can generate a bar with any height we choose. Now what we want to do is to draw a series of bars, each at a different horizontal position and each with a height representing the data value for that position. This is easy because we have used a relative polygon command. To position the bar, we need only move the pen to the correct starting position before drawing the polygon. (See Figure 3-24.)

MOVE-ABS-2(X, Y);
POLYGON-REL-2(AX, AY, 4);

Now we can place these instructions within a loop. Each time through the loop, we get one of the data values to be plotted. We increment X in order to position the pen at the starting point for the next bar. We calculate the height of the bar from the data value and put it into the AY array. And we call the MOVE and POLYGON algorithms to actually draw the bar. Each time through the loop, another bar would be drawn until the graph is complete. (See Figure 3-25.)

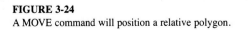

FIGURE 3-24
A MOVE command will position a relative polygon.

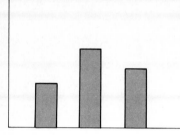

FIGURE 3-25
A bar graph constructed by repeated use of the POLYGON command.

We might note that if the bars are equally spaced and drawn sequentially, the explicit MOVE-ABS-2 command can be replaced by the implicit relative move done by the POLYGON-REL-2 algorithm.

FURTHER READING

A discussion of winding numbers and inside tests may be found in [NEW80]. We represented polygons as a list of vertex coordinates; alternative representations are presented in [BUR77] and [FRA83]. To fill a polygon, we broke it down into individual scan lines. This technique is called scan conversion and is discussed in [BAR73] and [BAR74]. An alternative approach to filling regions such as polygons is to draw their border in the frame buffer and then, starting with a seed pixel within the polygon, progressively examine each pixel, changing its color to the interior style until the boundary is encountered. This technique is called flood fill or seed fill and is discussed in [LIE78]. Instead of filling from a single seed, we can scan the area to be filled, building regions. When two regions merge, we note their equivalence; then on a second pass we shade all regions associated with the interior [DIS82]. The decomposition of polygons into trapezoids or triangles is described in [FOU84], [GAR78], [JAC80], and [LIT79]. Polygons can also be described as the differences of convex polygons [TOR84]. An attempt to save the scan-converted polygons in the display file rather than in a frame buffer is described in [SPR75]. Filling polygons on calligraphic devices with patterns of lines is discussed in [BRA79]. Polygon filling is also discussed in [AGK81], [DUN83], [PAV78], [PAV81], [POL86], and [SHA80]. A discussion of antialiasing of polygons is given in [BAR79] and [CRO81]. Our polygon primitives are based on proposed extensions to the CORE system, which are described in [GSPC79].

[AGK81] Agkland, B. D., "The Edge Flag Algorithm—A Fill Method for Raster Scan Displays," *IEEE Transactions on Computers*, vol. C-30, no. 1, pp. 41–47 (1981).

[BAR73] Barrett, R. C., and Jordan, B. W., Jr., "A Scan Conversion Algorithm with Reduced Storage Requirements," *Communications of the ACM*, vol 16, no. 11, pp. 676–682 (1973).

[BAR74] Barrett, R. C., and Jordan, B. W., Jr., "Scan-Conversion Algorithms for a Cell Organized Raster Display," *Communications of the ACM*, vol. 17, no. 3, pp. 157–163 (1974).

[BAR79] Barros, J., Fuchs, H., "Generating Smooth 2-D Monocolor Line Drawings on Video Displays," *Computer Graphics*, vol. 13, no. 2, pp. 260–269 (1979).

[BRA79] Brassel, K. E., Fegeas, R., "An Algorithm for Shading of Regions on Vector Display Devices," *Computer Graphics*, vol. 13, no. 2, pp. 126–133 (1979).

[BUR77] Burton, W., "Representation of Many-Sided Polygons and Polygonal Lines for Rapid Processing," *Communications of the ACM*, vol. 20, no. 3 , pp. 166–171 (1977).

[CRO81] Crow, F. C., "A Comparison of Antialiasing Techniques," *IEEE Computer Graphics and Applications*, vol. 1, no. 1, pp. 40–48 (1981).

[DIS82] Distante, A., Veneziani, N., "A Two-Pass Filling Algorithm for Raster Graphics," *Computer Graphics and Image Processing*, vol. 20, no. 3, pp. 288–295 (1982).

[DUN83] Dunlavey, M. R., "Efficient Polygon-Filling Algorithms for Raster Displays," *ACM Transactions on Graphics*, vol. 2, no. 4, pp. 264–273 (1983).

[FOU84] Fourner, A., Montuno, D. Y., "Triangulating Simple Polygons and Equivalent Problems," *ACM Transactions on Graphics*, vol. 3, no. 2, pp. 153–174 (1984).

[FRA83] Franklin, W. R., "Rays—New Representation for Polygons and Polyhedra," *Computer Vision, Graphics, and Image Processing*, vol. 22, no. 3, pp. 327–338 (1983).

[GAR78] Garey, M. R., Johnson, D. S., Preparata, F. P., Tarjan, R. E., "Triangulating a Simple Polygon," *Information Processing Letters*, vol. 7, no. 4, pp. 175–179 (1978).

[GSPC79] Graphic Standards Planning Committee, "Status Report Part III: Raster Extensions to the CORE System," *Computer Graphics*, vol. 3, no. 3, pp. III-1–III-39 (1979).

[JAC80] Jackson, J. H., "Dynamic Scan-Converted Images with a Frame Buffer Display Device," *Computer Graphics*, vol. 14, no. 3, pp. 163–169 (1980).

[LIE78] Lieberman, H., "How to Color in a Coloring Book," *Computer Graphics*, vol. 12, no. 3, pp. 111–116 (1978).

[LIT79] Little, W. D., and Heuft, R., "An Area Shading Graphics Display System," *IEEE Transactions on Computers*, vol. c-28, no. 7, pp. 528–531 (1979).

[NEW80] Newell, M. E., and Sequin, C. H., "The Inside Story on Self-Intersecting Polygons," *Lambda*, vol. 1, no. 2, pp. 20–24 (1980).

[PAV78] Pavlidis, T., "Filling Algorithms for Raster Graphics," *Computer Graphics*, vol. 12, no. 3, pp. 161–166 (1978).

[PAV81] Pavlidis, T., "Contour Filling in Raster Graphics," *Computer Graphics*, vol. 15, no. 3, pp. 29–36 (1981).

[POL86] Polik, W. F., "Area Filling Algorithms," *Computer Language*, vol. 3, no. 5, pp. 33–40 (1986).

[SHA80] Shani, U., "Filling Regions in Binary Raster Images: A Graph-Theoretic Approach," *Computer Graphics*, vol. 14, no. 3, pp. 321–327 (1980).

[SPR75] Sproull, R. F., Newman, W. M., "The Design of Gray-Scale Graphics Software," *Proceedings of the Conference on Computer Graphics, Pattern Recognition, & Data Structure*, pp. 18–20, IEEE Cat. No. 75CH0981-1c, (1975).

[TOR84] Tor, S. B., Middleditch, A. E., "Convex Decomposition of Simple Polygons," *ACM Transactions on Graphics*, vol. 3, no. 4, pp. 244–265 (1984).

EXERCISES

3-1 For each of the following polygons, indicate whether it is concave or convex:

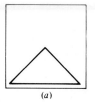

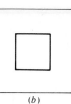

(a)　　　　　　　　　(b)　　　　　　　　　(c)

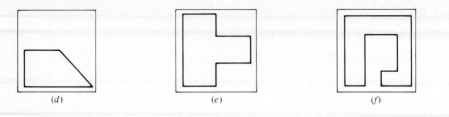

(d)   (e)   (f)

3-2 Sketch what would be drawn by a POLYGON-ABS-2(AX, AY, N) command for each of the following array pairs.

    a) N = 8

        AX = 0.2, 0.2, 0.1, 0.1, 0.4, 0.4, 0.3, 0.3

        AY = 0.1, 0.3, 0.3, 0.4, 0.4, 0.3, 0.3, 0.1

    b) N = 8

        AX = 0.5, 0.5, 0.3, 0.3, 0.5, 0.5, 0.1, 0.1

        AY = 0.1, 0.2, 0.2, 0.3, 0.3, 0.4, 0.4, 0.1

    c) N = 8

        AX = 0.2, 0.3, 0.2, 0.3, 0.2, 0.1, 0.2, 0.1

        AY = 0.1, 0.1, 0.2, 0.3, 0.4, .4, 0.2, 0.2

    d) N = 5

        AX = 0.1, 0.1, 0.5, 0.9, 0.9

        AY = 0.1, 0.6, 0.8, 0.6, 0.1

    e) N = 7

        AX = 0.5, 0.3, 0.4, 0.4, 0.6, 0.6, 0.7

        AY = 0.7, 0.5, 0.5, 0.1, 0.1, 0.5, 0.5

3-3 Sketch what would be drawn by

    MOVE-ABS-2(0, 0)

    POLYGON-REL-2(AX, AY, N)

for each of the following array pairs:

    a) N = 4

        AX = 0.1, 0.1, 0.1, –0.1

        AY = 0.2, –0.1, 0.1, 0.1

    b) N = 10

        AX = 0.4, 0, –0.2, 0.3, 0.1, 0.1, 0.3, –0.2, 0, –0.2

        AY = 0.2, 0.2, 0.2, 0, 0.2, –0.2, 0, –0.2, –0.2, 0.2

    c) N = 5

        AX = 0.1, 0.1, 0.1, 0.1, 0.1

        AY = 0.2, 0.1, –0.1, 0.1, –0.1

    d) N = 10

        AX = 0.5, –0.4, 0, 0.1, 0, 0.1, 0, 0.1, 0, 0.1

        AY = 0.3, 0, –0.1, 0, –0.1, 0, 0.1, 0, –0.1, 0

    e) N = 11

        AX = 0.1, 0.2, –0.1, 0.2, –0.1, 0.2, 0.2, –0.1, 0.2, –0.1, 0.2

        AY = 0.1, 0.2, 0, 0.2, 0, 0.2, –0.2, 0, –0.2, 0, –0.2

3-4 Give suitable values of argument arrays for a POLYGON-ABS-2 command to draw each of the figures in Exercise 3-1.

3-5 Give suitable values of argument arrays for a POLYGON-REL-2 command to draw each of the figures in Exercise 3-1, assuming that the pen begins at the origin for each case.

3-6 For each of the polygons shown, indicate the interior regions
    a) Using the even-odd method
    b) Using the winding-number method

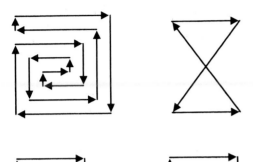

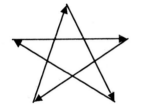

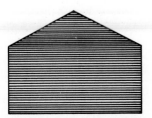

PROGRAMMING PROBLEMS

3-1 Implement algorithms 3.1 through 3.15 and 3.18. Devise DOSTYLE and FILLIN routines appropriate for your system.

3-2 Test the implementation of Programming Problem 3-1 by drawing a house as a five-sided polygon. Show this house in outline and filled with at least two fill styles.

3-3 Write routines named

INQUIRE-FILL-STYLE(I)

and

INQUIRE-FILLED(ON-OFF)

which return the current polygon interior style and the value of the SOLID flag.

3-4 Implement algorithms 3.16 and 3.17 (revised for your system if necessary) to allow filling of polygons with patterns. Show a polygon filled with three different patterns.

3-5 Write a program to construct a picture out of N squares (each square should be a four-sided polygon). The vertices of the squares should be (J/N, 0) (1, J/N), (1 − (J/N), 1), and (0, 1 − (J/N)), where J steps between 1 and N, inclusive.

　a) Show the squares unfilled.

　b) Show each square filled with a different interior style.

3-6　a) Write a program to draw a number of overlapping triangles on the display. The triangles can have random positions, random shapes, and random interior styles.

　　b) Write a program to draw a number of overlapping random polygons. The polygons should vary in the number of sides as well as in the position and interior style.

3-7 Consider the following map showing the four counties in the State of Invention.

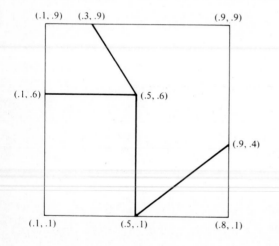

　a) Construct this map out of polygons, using one polygon for each county. (Do *not* label the vertices on your map.)

　b) Show your map with each county filled with a different interior style.

3-8 Consider the following table of widget sales and expenses.

Widget annual report

Month	Jan	Feb	Mar	Apr	May	June	July	Aug	Sept	Oct	Nov	Dec
Sales	2000	4000	7000	6000	4000	8000	8000	7000	5000	6000	8000	9000
Expenses	5000	5000	4000	3000	2000	4000	5000	6000	8000	9000	6000	5000

a) Form a polygon out of the widget sales data and the lower-left and lower-right corners of the graph axis, and display this both unfilled and filled.

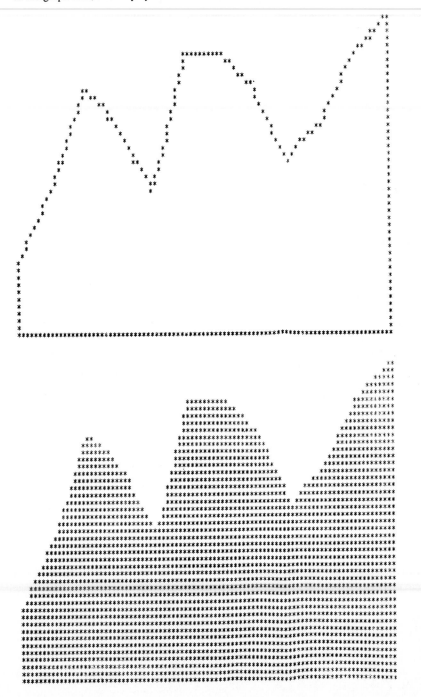

b) Form a similar polygon for widget expense figures and plot both polygons unfilled.

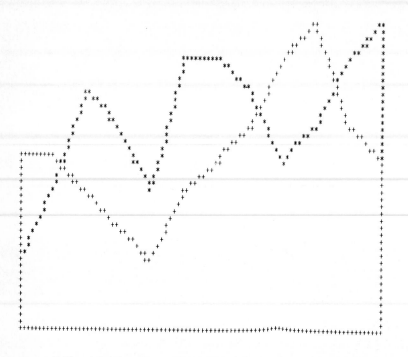

c) First, plot the sales polygon filled, and then superimpose the expense polygon unfilled. Use an expense line style different from the sales interior style.

d) Plot the sales polygon filled, followed by the expense polygon filled, followed in turn by the sales polygon again unfilled.

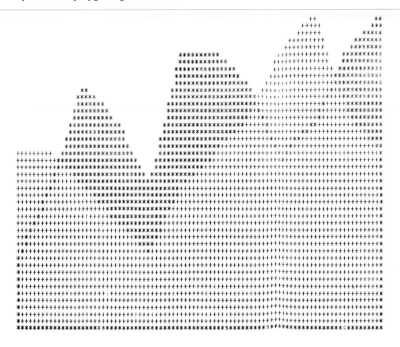

e) Form a single large polygon from an array of sales figures, followed by expense figures entered in reverse chronological order and display filled.

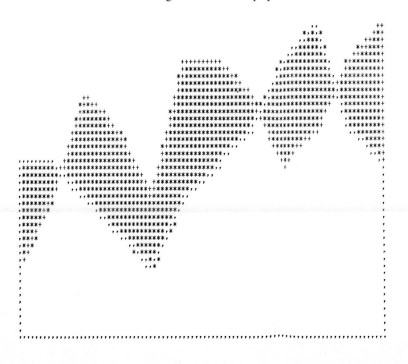

3-9 a) Write a subroutine to draw a filled square with side length 0.1 using only relative commands. Then, by positioning the pen and calling this subroutine, construct a checkerboard.

b) Construct other patterns by repetition of different polygon shapes.

3-10 a) Use rectangular polygons to form a bar graph of data in Programming Problem 3-8.

b) Display both widget sales and expense data on the same bar graph by using bars with different interior and edge styles for the two types of data. Place both bars for each month on top of each other, but enter the larger of the two first.

3-11 Write a graphing procedure which takes an array of values and plots them in a bar graph.

3-12 Write a routine WEDGE(A) which draws a polygon in the shape of a wedge of pie. The wedge should have radius 1 and one edge on the x axis with the point at the origin. The angle of the wedge is A radians. A round border is approximated with line segments connecting points on a circle. The ith border point is given by $Xi = COS(Ai)$, $Yi = SIN(Ai)$, where $Ai = (i * A) / N$ and $N = INT(4 * A)$. The index i will step between O and N, inclusive.

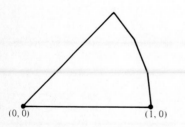

(0, 0)   (1, 0)

3-13 Write a routine called THICK-LINE-ABS-2(X, Y, W) which draws a thick line of width W centered on the line segment between the current position and the point (X, Y). The thick line will actually be a polygon. Design the polygon so that the ends of the thick line are perpendicular to its direction.

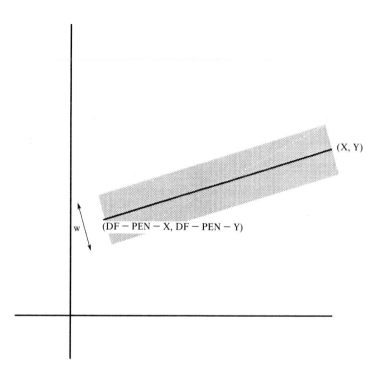

3-14 Extend your graphics system to allow the user to specify whether or not polygon borders should be drawn.

3-15 We allocated opcodes for 16 line styles and 16 fill styles. This may not be enough. A graphics system may have 64 gray levels or 256 colors plus thicknesses and patterns. We can accommodate this variety by assigning generic opcodes (line style, line color, fill style, fill color, etc.) and using the operand field (DF-X or DF-Y) to hold the particular style value. Modify your graphics system to do this.

*3-16 When using a frame buffer to display polygons, the most recently drawn polygon can obscure anything drawn prior to it. We can use this to give a feeling of three-dimensional depth by drawing the background objects prior to the foreground. Develop routines which allow the user to enter each polygon with some depth or priority number. These polygons should then be sorted into priority order so that the most distant (lowest priority) polygons are drawn before the closest (highest priority).

*3-17 Construct a font of large characters and/or digits out of filled polygons. Write a separate procedure for each symbol, and use only relative commands so that the position of the symbol may be changed.

*3-18 Extend the polygon-filling algorithm to provide antialiasing. Do this by in effect doubling the resolution in both x and y directions. Set up a storage buffer for two double-length scan lines. As you step through the polygon-filling algorithm, fill in these buffers with the background values from the display (replicating values to match the higher resolution). Next, fill the pair of scan lines with the polygon. Finally, average the intensities of the four-pixel high-resolution cells to arrive at an intensity value for the corresponding pixels on the actual display.

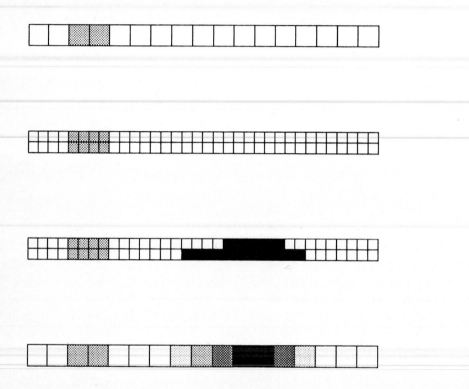

*3-19 Some graphics hardware will directly support the drawing of trapezoids with their parallel sides in the scan-line direction. Write a program which will decompose arbitrary polygons into such trapezoids.

*3-20 We often find convex polygons easier to deal with than concave ones. Triangles are particularly convenient because they are guaranteed to be both convex and planar. Write a program which will decompose arbitrary polygons into triangles.

*3-21 If instead of filling in a polygon, our scan-line program just set the edge pixels, we would have a program which constructs a line drawing from top to bottom. This is just the order that some raster displays (and line printers) need the pixel information in for display. Now imagine that the instructions not only for a single polygon are sorted, but also those for the entire display file. Then pixel settings for the entire picture can be generated in just the order in which the display device needs them. By correctly sorting the display-file instructions, it is possible to avoid the need for the large frame buffer. Assume that the display contains only MOVE and LINE commands. Write DOLINE, DOMOVE, and DISPLAY routines, modeled after FILL-POLYGON and its friends, which eliminate the need for a frame buffer array for line printer output.

FOUR

TRANSFORMATIONS

INTRODUCTION

One of the major assets of computer graphics is the ease with which certain alterations of the picture may be performed. The manager can alter the scale of the graphs in a report. The architect can view a building from a different angle. The cartographer can change the size of a chart. The animator can change the position of a character. These changes are easy to perform because the graphic image has been coded as numbers and stored within the computer. The numbers may be modified by mathematical operations called *transformations*.

Transformations allow us to uniformly alter the entire picture. It is in fact often easier to change the entire computer-drawn image than it is to alter only part of it. This can provide a useful complement to hand drawing techniques, where it is usually easier to change a small portion of a drawing than it is to create an entirely new picture.

In this chapter we shall consider the geometric transformations of scaling, translation, and rotation. We shall see how they can be simply expressed in terms of matrix multiplications. We shall introduce homogeneous coordinates in order to uniformly treat translations and in anticipation of three-dimensional perspective transformations. The algorithms presented in this chapter will describe two-dimensional scale, translation, and rotation routines.

MATRICES

Our computer graphics images are generated from a series of line segments which are represented by the coordinates of their endpoints. Certain changes in an image can be easily made by performing mathematical operations on these coordinates. Before we consider some of the possible transformations, let us review some of the mathematical tools we shall need, namely, matrix multiplication.

For our purposes we will consider a matrix to be a two-dimensional array of numbers. For example,

$$\begin{vmatrix} 1 & 0 \\ 0 & 1 \end{vmatrix} \quad \begin{vmatrix} 1 & 2 & 3 \\ 4 & 5 & 6 \end{vmatrix} \quad \begin{vmatrix} 1 \\ -1 \\ 0 \end{vmatrix} \quad \begin{vmatrix} 1 & 0 & 2 \\ 0 & 1 & 2 \\ 0 & 0 & 1 \end{vmatrix}$$

are four different matrices.

Suppose we define the matrix A to be

$$A = \begin{vmatrix} 1 & 2 & 3 \\ 4 & 5 & 6 \\ 7 & 8 & 9 \end{vmatrix} \tag{4.1}$$

Then the element in the second row and third column would be A(2, 3) and would have the value 6.

The matrix operation which concerns us most is that of multiplication. Matrix multiplication is more complex than the simple product of two numbers; it involves simple products and sums of the matrix elements. Not every pair of matrices can be multiplied. We can multiply two matrices A and B together if the number of columns of the first matrix (A) is the same as the number of rows of the second matrix (B). For example, if we chose the first matrix to be the matrix A defined in Equation 4.1 and matrix B to be

$$B = \begin{vmatrix} 1 & 0 \\ -1 & 2 \\ 0 & 1 \end{vmatrix} \tag{4.2}$$

then we can multiply A times B because A has 3 columns and B has 3 rows. Unlike multiplication of numbers, the multiplication of matrices is not commutative; that is, while we can multiply A times B, we cannot multiply B times A, because B has only 2 columns (which does not match the 3 rows of A). When we multiply two matrices, we get a matrix as a result. This product matrix will have the same number of rows as the first matrix of the two being multiplied and the same number of columns as the second matrix. Multiplying the 3 × 3 matrix A times the 3 × 2 matrix B gives a 3 × 2 matrix result C.

The elements of the product matrix C are given in terms of the elements of matrices A and B by the following formula:

$$C(i, k) = \sum_j A(i, j) \, B(j, k) \tag{4.3}$$

For our particular example of C = AB

$$C = \begin{vmatrix} 1 & 2 & 3 \\ 4 & 5 & 6 \\ 7 & 8 & 9 \end{vmatrix} \begin{vmatrix} 1 & 0 \\ -1 & 2 \\ 0 & 1 \end{vmatrix} \tag{4.4}$$

the element C(1, 1) is found by multiplying each element of the first row of A by the corresponding element of the first column of B and adding these products together.

$$C(1, 1) = A(1, 1)B(1, 1) + A(1, 2)B(2, 1) + A(1, 3)B(3, 1)$$

$$= (1)(1) + (2)(-1) + (3)(0) = -1 \qquad (4.5)$$

The element C(3, 2) would be

$$C(3, 2) = A(3, 1)B(1, 2) + A(3, 2)B(2, 2) + A(3, 3)B(3, 2)$$

$$= (7)(0) + (8)(2) + (9)(1) = 25 \qquad (4.6)$$

Performing this arithmetic for every element of C shows us that

$$C = \begin{vmatrix} -1 & 7 \\ -1 & 16 \\ -1 & 25 \end{vmatrix} \qquad (4.7)$$

Multiplication is associative. This means that if we have several matrices to multiply together, it does not matter which we multiply first. In mathematical notation:

$$A(BC) = (AB)C \qquad (4.8)$$

This is a very useful property; it will allow us to combine several graphics transformations into a single transformation, thereby making our calculations more efficient.

There is a set of matrices with the property that when they multiply another matrix, they reproduce that matrix. For this reason, the matrices in this set are called *identity matrices*. They are square matrices (same number of rows and columns) with all the elements 0 except the elements of the main diagonal, which are all 1. For example,

$$\begin{vmatrix} 1 \end{vmatrix} \qquad \begin{vmatrix} 1 & 0 \\ 0 & 1 \end{vmatrix} \qquad \begin{vmatrix} 1 & 0 & 0 \\ 0 & 1 & 0 \\ 0 & 0 & 1 \end{vmatrix}$$

and so on.

We can see that if

$$I = \begin{vmatrix} 1 & 0 & 0 \\ 0 & 1 & 0 \\ 0 & 0 & 1 \end{vmatrix} \qquad (4.9)$$

then

$$A = AI \qquad (4.10)$$

SCALING TRANSFORMATIONS

Now how does all this apply to graphics? Well, we can consider a point $P_1 = [x_1 \quad y_1]$ as being a 1×2 matrix. If we multiply it by some 2×2 matrix T, we will obtain another 1×2 matrix which we can interpret as another point

$$[x_2 \quad y_2] = P_2 = P_1 T \qquad (4.11)$$

Thus, the matrix T gives a mapping between an original point P_1 and a new point P_2. Remember that our image is stored as a list of endpoints. What will happen if we transform every point by means of multiplication by T and display the result? What will this new image look like? The answer, of course, depends upon what elements are in matrix T. If, for example, matrix T were the identity matrix

$$T = \begin{vmatrix} 1 & 0 \\ 0 & 1 \end{vmatrix} \tag{4.12}$$

then the image would be unchanged.

If, however, we choose T to be T_1

$$T_1 = \begin{vmatrix} 2 & 0 \\ 0 & 1 \end{vmatrix} \tag{4.13}$$

then,

$$[x_2 \quad y_2] = [x_1 \quad y_1] \begin{vmatrix} 2 & 0 \\ 0 & 1 \end{vmatrix} = [2x_1 \quad y_1] \tag{4.14}$$

Every new x coordinate would be twice as large as the old value. Horizontal lines would become twice as long on the new image. The new image would have the same height, but would appear to be stretched to twice the width of the original. (See Figure 4-1.)

The transformation matrix

$$T_2 = \begin{vmatrix} 0.5 & 0 \\ 0 & 1 \end{vmatrix} \tag{4.15}$$

would shrink all x coordinates to one-half their original value. The image would have the original height but would be squeezed to one-half the width.

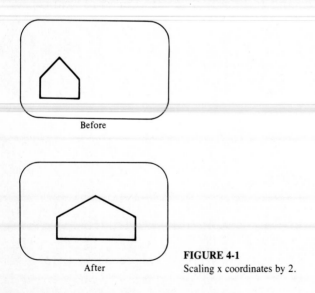

Before

After

FIGURE 4-1
Scaling x coordinates by 2.

Now, if we were to stretch the image to twice the width and then compress it to one-half the new width,

$$P_2 = (P_1 T_1) T_2 \tag{4.16}$$

we would expect to get the original image back again. Let us check that this is so by multiplying the two transformations T_1 and T_2 together first. The associative property for matrix multiplication allows us to write

$$P_2 = P_1 (T_1 T_2) \tag{4.17}$$

Multiplying the two transformations together combines them into a single transformation.

$$T_1 T_2 = \begin{vmatrix} 2 & 0 \\ 0 & 1 \end{vmatrix} \begin{vmatrix} 0.5 & 0 \\ 0 & 1 \end{vmatrix} = \begin{vmatrix} 1 & 0 \\ 0 & 1 \end{vmatrix} \tag{4.18}$$

But this is just the expected identity matrix, which will not change an image.

We can make an image twice as tall with the same width by finding a transformation which just multiplies the y coordinate by 2. Such a transformation is given by

$$T_3 = \begin{vmatrix} 1 & 0 \\ 0 & 2 \end{vmatrix} \tag{4.19}$$

Multiplying an arbitrary point by this matrix shows that this is true. (See Figure 4-2.)

$$[x_2 \quad y_2] = [x_1 \quad y_1] \begin{vmatrix} 1 & 0 \\ 0 & 2 \end{vmatrix} = [x_1 \quad 2y_1] \tag{4.20}$$

By applying both transformations T_1 and T_3, we will make the image both twice as wide and twice as tall. In other words, we would have a similar image, only twice as big.

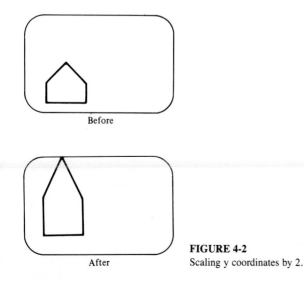

Before

After

FIGURE 4-2
Scaling y coordinates by 2.

$$P_2 = P_1 T_1 T_3 \tag{4.21}$$

Again, by multiplying the two transformation matrices together, we can obtain a single transformation matrix for making the entire image twice as large. (See Figure 4-3.)

$$T_4 = T_1 T_3 = \begin{vmatrix} 2 & 0 \\ 0 & 1 \end{vmatrix} \begin{vmatrix} 1 & 0 \\ 0 & 2 \end{vmatrix} = \begin{vmatrix} 2 & 0 \\ 0 & 2 \end{vmatrix} \tag{4.22}$$

In general, transformations of the form

$$S = \begin{vmatrix} s_x & 0 \\ 0 & s_y \end{vmatrix} \tag{4.23}$$

change the size and the proportion of the image. They are called *scaling transformations*. s_x is the *scale factor* for the x coordinate and s_y for the y coordinate.

Note that when we scale the image, every point except the origin changes. This means that not only the size of an image will change but also its position. A scale in x by a factor greater than 1 will cause the image to shift to the right, along with making it wider. A scale in x by a factor less than 1 will shift the image to the left. A scale in y will shift the image up and down as well as change its height.

SIN AND COS

The next transformation we would like to consider is that for rotation. To prepare for the discussion of rotations we shall review some basic trigonometry. Suppose we have a point $P_1 = (x_1, y_1)$ and we rotate it about the origin by an angle θ to get a new position $P_2 = (x_2, y_2)$. We wish to find a transformation which will change (x_1, y_1) into (x_2, y_2). But, before we can check any transformation to see if it is correct, we must first know what (x_2, y_2) should be in terms of (x_1, y_1) and θ. To determine this we shall need the trigonometric functions *sine* and *cosine* (abbreviated *sin* and *cos*). We can de-

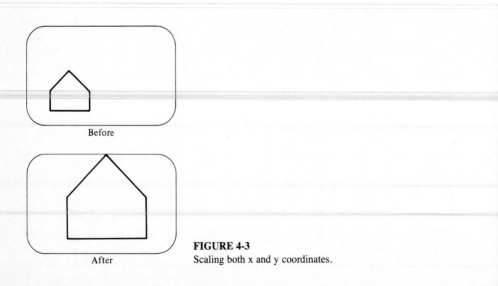

Before

After

FIGURE 4-3
Scaling both x and y coordinates.

fine sin and cos for an angle θ in the following manner. Let us draw a line segment from the origin at the angle θ counterclockwise from the x axis, and suppose that the line segment we have drawn has length L. (See Figure 4-4.)

The line segment will then have endpoints (0, 0) and (x, y) and length

$$L = (x^2 + y^2)^{1/2}$$

Then, the ratio of the height of the (x, y) endpoint above the x axis (the y-coordinate value) and the length of the segment will be the sine of the angle

$$\sin \theta = \frac{y}{(x^2 + y^2)^{1/2}} \qquad (4.24)$$

and the ratio of the distance to the right of the y axis (the x-coordinate value) and the length of the segment will be the cosine of the angle

$$\cos \theta = \frac{x}{(x^2 + y^2)^{1/2}} \qquad (4.25)$$

Note that if we draw a segment with length L = 1, then

$$\sin \theta = y \qquad \text{and} \qquad \cos \theta = x \qquad (4.26)$$

ROTATION

To determine the form for the *rotation transformation matrix*, consider the point (1, 0). If we rotate this point counterclockwise by an angle θ, it becomes $(\cos \theta, \sin \theta)$ (see Figure 4-5), so

$$[\cos \theta \quad \sin \theta] = \begin{vmatrix} 1 & 0 \end{vmatrix} \begin{vmatrix} a & b \\ c & d \end{vmatrix} = \begin{vmatrix} a, & b \end{vmatrix} \qquad (4.27)$$

If we rotate the point (0, 1) counterclockwise by an angle θ, it becomes $(-\sin \theta, \cos \theta)$. (See Figure 4-6.)

$$[-\sin \theta \quad \cos \theta] = \begin{vmatrix} 0 & 1 \end{vmatrix} \begin{vmatrix} a & b \\ c & d \end{vmatrix} = \begin{vmatrix} c, & d \end{vmatrix} \qquad (4.28)$$

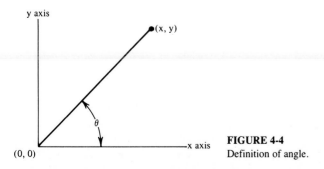

FIGURE 4-4
Definition of angle.

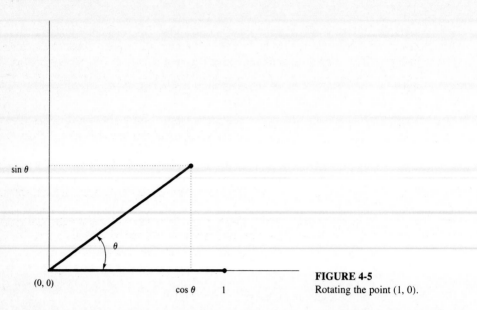

sin θ

θ

(0, 0)

cos θ   1

FIGURE 4-5
Rotating the point (1, 0).

From these equations we can see the values of a, b, c, and d needed to form the rotation matrix. The transformation matrix for a counterclockwise rotation of θ about the origin is

$$R = \begin{vmatrix} \cos\theta & \sin\theta \\ -\sin\theta & \cos\theta \end{vmatrix} \qquad (4.29)$$

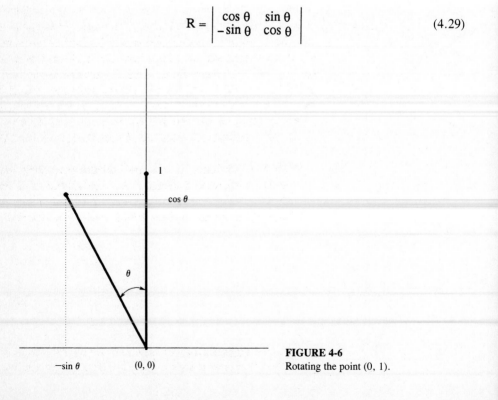

1

cos θ

θ

−sin θ   (0, 0)

FIGURE 4-6
Rotating the point (0, 1).

As an example, suppose we wished to rotate the point (2, 3) counterclockwise by an angle of $\pi/6$ radians. (See Figure 4-7.) Then the rotation matrix would be

$$\begin{vmatrix} \cos\frac{\pi}{6} & \sin\frac{\pi}{6} \\ -\sin\frac{\pi}{6} & \cos\frac{\pi}{6} \end{vmatrix} = \begin{vmatrix} 0.866 & 0.5 \\ -0.5 & 0.866 \end{vmatrix} \tag{4.30}$$

and the rotated point would be

$$\begin{vmatrix} 2 & 3 \end{vmatrix} \begin{vmatrix} 0.866 & 0.5 \\ -0.5 & 0.866 \end{vmatrix} = \begin{vmatrix} 0.232 & 3.598 \end{vmatrix} \tag{4.31}$$

We can rotate an entire line segment by rotating both the endpoints which specify it.

The sign of an angle determines the direction of rotation. We have defined the rotation matrix so that a positive angle will rotate the image in a counterclockwise direction with respect to the axes. In order to rotate in the clockwise direction we use a negative angle, so the rotation matrix for an angle θ clockwise would be

$$R = \begin{vmatrix} \cos(-\theta) & \sin(-\theta) \\ -\sin(-\theta) & \cos(-\theta) \end{vmatrix} \tag{4.32}$$

or since

$$\cos(-\theta) = \cos\theta \tag{4.33}$$

and

$$\sin(-\theta) = -\sin\theta \tag{4.34}$$

this may be rewritten as

$$R = \begin{vmatrix} \cos\theta & -\sin\theta \\ \sin\theta & \cos\theta \end{vmatrix} \tag{4.35}$$

for clockwise rotations about the origin.

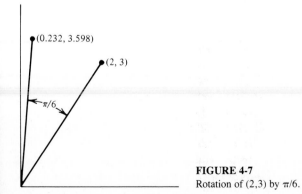

FIGURE 4-7
Rotation of (2,3) by $\pi/6$.

HOMOGENEOUS COORDINATES
AND TRANSLATION

Suppose we wished to rotate about some point other than the origin. If we had some way of moving the entire image around on the screen, we could accomplish such a rotation by first moving the image until the center of rotation was at the origin, then performing the rotation as we just discussed, and finally, moving the image back where it belongs.

Moving the image is called *translation*. It is easily accomplished by adding to each point the amount by which we want the picture shifted. If we wish the image shifted 2 units to the right, we would add 2 to the x coordinate of every point. To move it down 1 unit, add –1 to every y coordinate. (See Figure 4-8.)

In general, in order to translate the image to the right and up by (t_x, t_y), every point (x_1, y_1) is replaced by a new point (x_2, y_2) where

$$x_2 = x_1 + t_x, \qquad y_2 = y_1 + t_y \tag{4.36}$$

Unfortunately, this way of describing translation does not use a matrix, so it cannot be combined with other transformations by simple matrix multiplication. Such a combination would be desirable; for example, we have seen that rotating about a point other than the origin can be done by a translation, a rotation, and another translation. We would like to be able to combine these three transformations into a single transformation for the sake of efficiency and elegance. One way of doing this is to use homogeneous coordinates. In *homogeneous coordinates* we use 3×3 matrices instead of 2×2, introducing an additional dummy coordinate w; points are specified by three numbers instead of two. The first homogeneous coordinate will be the product of x and w, the second will be the product of y and w, and the third will just be w. A coordinate point (x, y) will be represented by the triple (xw, yw, w). The x and y coordinates can easily be recovered by dividing the first and second numbers by the third. We will not really use the extra number w until we consider three-dimensional perspective transforma-

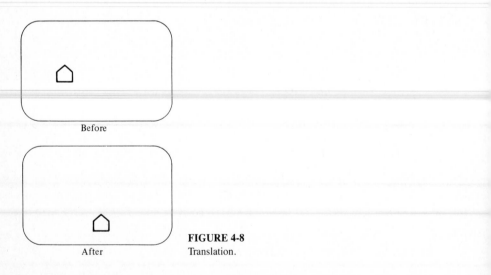

Before

After

FIGURE 4-8
Translation.

tions. In two dimensions its value is usually kept at 1 for simplicity. Still, we will discuss it in its generality in anticipation of the three-dimensional transformations.

In homogeneous coordinates our scaling matrix

$$\begin{vmatrix} s_x & 0 \\ 0 & s_y \end{vmatrix}$$

becomes

$$S = \begin{vmatrix} s_x & 0 & 0 \\ 0 & s_y & 0 \\ 0 & 0 & 1 \end{vmatrix} \qquad (4.37)$$

If we apply this to the point (xw, yw, w), we obtain

$$\begin{vmatrix} xw & yw & w \end{vmatrix} \begin{vmatrix} s_x & 0 & 0 \\ 0 & s_y & 0 \\ 0 & 0 & 1 \end{vmatrix} = \begin{vmatrix} s_x xw & s_y yw & w \end{vmatrix} \qquad (4.38)$$

Dividing by the third number w gives

$$(s_x x, s_y y)$$

which is the correctly scaled point.

The counterclockwise rotation matrix

$$\begin{vmatrix} \cos\theta & \sin\theta \\ -\sin\theta & \cos\theta \end{vmatrix}$$

becomes, using homogeneous coordinates,

$$R = \begin{vmatrix} \cos\theta & \sin\theta & 0 \\ -\sin\theta & \cos\theta & 0 \\ 0 & 0 & 1 \end{vmatrix} \qquad (4.39)$$

Applying it to the point (x, y) with homogeneous coordinate (xw, yw, w) gives

$$[xw \quad yw \quad w] \begin{vmatrix} \cos\theta & \sin\theta & 0 \\ -\sin\theta & \cos\theta & 0 \\ 0 & 0 & 1 \end{vmatrix} =$$

$$[(xw \cos\theta - yw \sin\theta) \quad (xw \sin\theta + yw \cos\theta) \quad w] \qquad (4.40)$$

for the correctly rotated point

$$(x \cos\theta - y \sin\theta, x \sin\theta + y \cos\theta)$$

The homogeneous coordinate transformation matrix for a translation of t_x, t_y is

$$T = \begin{vmatrix} 1 & 0 & 0 \\ 0 & 1 & 0 \\ t_x & t_y & 1 \end{vmatrix} \qquad (4.41)$$

To show that this is so, we apply the matrix

$$[xw \quad yw \quad w] \begin{vmatrix} 1 & 0 & 0 \\ 0 & 1 & 0 \\ t_x & t_y & 1 \end{vmatrix} = [(xw + t_x w) \quad (yw + t_y w) \quad w] \qquad (4.42)$$

for the translated point $(x + t_x, y + t_y)$

COORDINATE TRANSFORMATIONS

We have shown how applying a transformation to a point yields a new point, but transformations may also be used to change coordinate systems. For example, a distance measured in inches can be converted to the same distance measured in centimeters by means of a scale. The actual operation of the transformation is the same as already described; only the interpretation changes. The coordinates of the point, when multiplied by the transformation, represent the same point, only measured in different coordinates.

Translations are useful coordinate transformations when the origins are not aligned. For example, we think of the lower-left corner of the display as being the origin (0, 0), but in some display systems this point may actually correspond to pixel (1, 1). Another example is a display which places the (0, 0) pixel in the upper-left corner and numbers the scan lines from top to bottom. This is sometimes done on alphanumeric printers because it is the order in which the lines are printed, and on raster displays because it is the order that they are actually scanned. To convert between these coordinates and the ones we have been using, we need a scale of 1 in x but –1 in y to reverse the scan-line order, and also a translation in y by the vertical screen dimension to move the origin to the proper corner.

Rotations may also be used in coordinate transformations, but are usually for angles of $\pi/2$ (90 degrees). For example, a printer using 8.5 by 11 inch paper may have the y axis along the long edge and the x axis along the short edge. This is called *portrait mode*. We might prefer to orient the y axis along the short edge and the x axis along the long edge (perhaps so that the orientation of the paper is a better fit to the shape of a television's display). This is termed *landscape mode*. A rotation of $\pi/2$ and a translation to reposition the origin in the lower-left corner will do this.

We have already seen an example of a coordinate transformation, although we did not use transformation-matrix notation. The example is the transformation from normalized device coordinates to actual device coordinates. The arithmetic we used to do the conversion was

X1 ← X * WIDTH + WIDTH-START;
Y1 ← Y * HEIGHT + HEIGHT-START;

We can see now that this is a scale by WIDTH for x and HEIGHT for y, followed by a translation by WIDTH-START and HEIGHT-START. The full transformation matrix for this change in coordinates is

$$D = \begin{vmatrix} \text{WIDTH} & 0 & 0 \\ 0 & \text{HEIGHT} & 0 \\ \text{WIDTH - START} & \text{HEIGHT - START} & 1 \end{vmatrix} \qquad (4.43)$$

ROTATION ABOUT AN ARBITRARY POINT

Now let's determine the transformation matrix for a counterclockwise rotation about point (x_C, y_C). (See Figure 4-9.)

We shall do this by three transformation steps. We shall translate the point (x_C, y_C) to the origin, rotate about the origin, and then translate the center of rotation back where it belongs. (See Figure 4-10.)

Matrix multiplication is not commutative. Multiplying A times B will not always yield the same result as multiplying B times A. We must be careful to order the matrices so that they correspond to the order of the transformations on the image. We shall place the coordinates of the point on the left and the transformation matrix on the right. With this ordering, if an additional matrix product is introduced on the right (*post-multiplication*), then the corresponding transformation will be carried out after the original transformation. If an additional matrix product is introduced on the left of the original transformation matrix (between it and the coordinates of the point), then the new transformation takes place prior to the original transformation. Multiplying on the left is called *pre-multiplication*. We use post-multiplication in the construction of our general rotation.

The translation which moves (x_C, y_C) to the origin is

$$T_1 = \begin{vmatrix} 1 & 0 & 0 \\ 0 & 1 & 0 \\ -x_C & -y_C & 1 \end{vmatrix} \tag{4.44}$$

the rotation is

$$R = \begin{vmatrix} \cos\theta & \sin\theta & 0 \\ -\sin\theta & \cos\theta & 0 \\ 0 & 0 & 1 \end{vmatrix} \tag{4.45}$$

and the translation to move the center point back to its correct position is

$$T_2 = \begin{vmatrix} 1 & 0 & 0 \\ 0 & 1 & 0 \\ x_C & y_C & 1 \end{vmatrix} \tag{4.46}$$

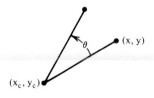

FIGURE 4-9
Rotation about an arbitrary point.

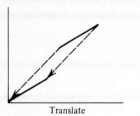 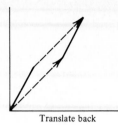

Translate   Rotate   Translate back

FIGURE 4-10
Three steps in the rotation about an arbitrary point.

To transform a point, we would multiply

$$((([xw \quad yw \quad w] T_1)R) T_2)$$

but we reassociate and multiply all the transformation matrices together first to form an overall transformation matrix

$$[xw \quad yw \quad w](T_1(R \, T_2))$$

$$T_1 \, R \, T_2 = \begin{vmatrix} 1 & 0 & 0 \\ 0 & 1 & 0 \\ -x_C & -y_C & 1 \end{vmatrix} \begin{vmatrix} \cos\theta & \sin\theta & 0 \\ -\sin\theta & \cos\theta & 0 \\ 0 & 0 & 1 \end{vmatrix} \begin{vmatrix} 1 & 0 & 0 \\ 0 & 1 & 0 \\ x_C & y_C & 1 \end{vmatrix}$$

$$= \begin{vmatrix} 1 & 0 & 0 \\ 0 & 1 & 0 \\ -x_C & -y_C & 1 \end{vmatrix} \begin{vmatrix} \cos\theta & \sin\theta & 0 \\ -\sin\theta & \cos\theta & 0 \\ x_C & y_C & 1 \end{vmatrix}$$

$$= \begin{vmatrix} \cos\theta & \sin\theta & 0 \\ -\sin\theta & \cos\theta & 0 \\ -x_C\cos\theta + y_C\sin\theta + x_C & -x_C\sin\theta - y_C\cos\theta + y_C & 1 \end{vmatrix} \quad (4.47)$$

This is the overall transformation for a rotation by θ counterclockwise about the point (x_C, y_C). Note that this matrix may also be formed by an initial rotation of θ, followed by a single translation by the values in its third row.

OTHER TRANSFORMATIONS

The three transformations of scaling, rotating, and translating are the most useful and the most common. Other transformations are also possible. Since any 2 × 2 transformation matrix

$$\begin{vmatrix} a & b \\ c & d \end{vmatrix}$$

can be converted to a 3 × 3 homogeneous coordinate matrix as

$$\begin{vmatrix} a & b & 0 \\ c & d & 0 \\ 0 & 0 & 1 \end{vmatrix}$$

we will present only the 2 × 2 form for some of these transformations:

$$\begin{vmatrix} -1 & 0 \\ 0 & 1 \end{vmatrix}$$ reflection in the y axis (see Figure 4-11)

$$\begin{vmatrix} 1 & 0 \\ 0 & -1 \end{vmatrix}$$ reflection in the x axis (see Figure 4-12)

$$\begin{vmatrix} -1 & 0 \\ 0 & -1 \end{vmatrix}$$ reflection in the origin (see Figure 4-13)

$$\begin{vmatrix} 0 & 1 \\ 1 & 0 \end{vmatrix}$$ reflection in the line y = x (see Figure 4-14)

$$\begin{vmatrix} 0 & -1 \\ -1 & 0 \end{vmatrix}$$ reflection in the line y = −x (see Figure 4-15)

$$\begin{vmatrix} 1 & a \\ 0 & 1 \end{vmatrix}$$ y shear (see Figure 4-16)

$$\begin{vmatrix} 1 & 0 \\ b & 1 \end{vmatrix}$$ x shear (see Figure 4-17)

The first three reflections are just scales with negative scale factors. The reflections in the lines y = x and y = –x can be done by a scale followed by a rotation.

The shear transformations cause the image to slant. The y shear preserves all the x-coordinate values but shifts the y value. The amount of change in the y value depends upon the x position. This causes horizontal lines to transform into lines which slope up or down. The x shear maintains the y coordinates, but changes the x values which causes vertical lines to tilt right or left. It is possible to form the shear transformations out of sequences of rotations and scales, although it is much easier to just form the matrix directly. It is also possible to build rotation and some scaling transformations out of shear transformations.

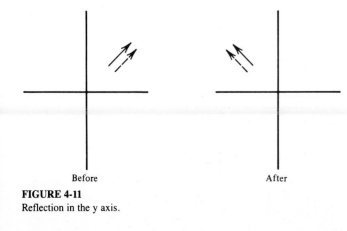

Before   After

FIGURE 4-11
Reflection in the y axis.

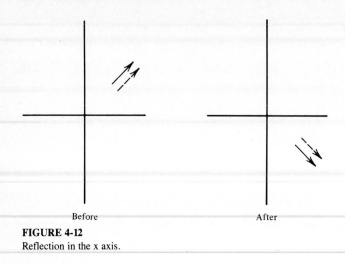

Before   After

FIGURE 4-12
Reflection in the x axis.

INVERSE TRANSFORMATIONS

We have seen how to use transformations to map each point (x, y) into a new point $(x',$ $y')$. Sometimes, however, we are faced with the problem of undoing the effect of a transformation; given the transformed point (x', y'), we must find the original point (x, y). An example occurs when the user indicates a particular position on a displayed image. The display may show an object which has undergone a transformation. If we want to know the corresponding point on the original object, then we must undo the transformation.

Undoing a transformation appears to be a transformation itself. Given any point (x', y'), we need a way of calculating a new point (x, y). Is there perhaps a transformation matrix which will do this? Often there is, and it can be determined by *matrix inver-*

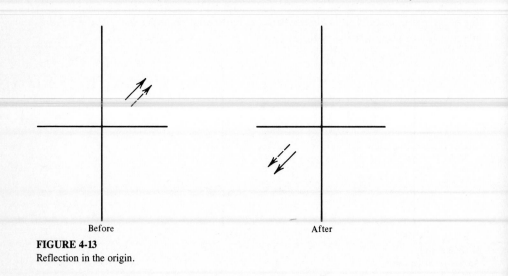

Before   After

FIGURE 4-13
Reflection in the origin.

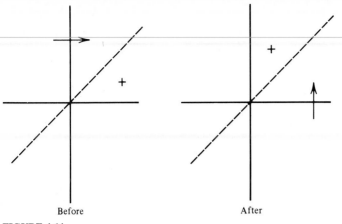

FIGURE 4-14
Reflection in the line y = x.

sion. The inverse of a matrix is another matrix such that when the two are multiplied together, the identity matrix results.

If the inverse of matrix T is T^{-1}, then

$$TT^{-1} = T^{-1}T = I \tag{4.48}$$

To see that this is what we need, consider Equation 4.11 which transforms point P_1 to yield point P_2. If we multiply both sides of this equation by the inverse of transformation matrix T, we get

$$P_2T^{-1} = P_1TT^{-1} = P_1I = P_1 \tag{4.49}$$

This shows that the inverse of T transforms P_2 back into P_1.

This inverse of a matrix can be a handy thing to have, so we shall show how to find it. We shall do so in terms of another matrix calculation called the *determinant*. The

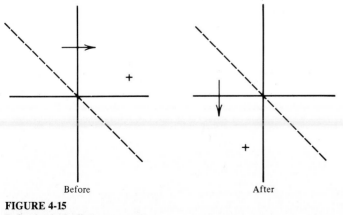

FIGURE 4-15
Reflection in the line y = −x.

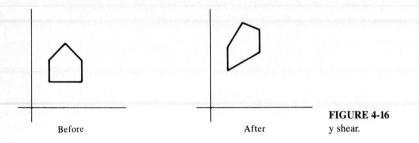

FIGURE 4-16
Before   After   y shear.

determinant of a matrix is a single number calculated from the elements of the matrix. For a single element matrix, the determinant is simply the value of the element.

$$\det|t| = t \tag{4.50}$$

For larger matrices, we express the determinant as a combination of the determinants of smaller matrices. The smaller matrices are called the *minors* and are made by removing a row and column from the larger matrix. Call M_{ij} the matrix formed by removing row i and column j from matrix T. Then the determinant of T is given by

$$\det T_j = \Sigma \, t_{ij}(-1)^{i+j} \det M_{ij} \tag{4.51}$$

This says that we pick some row of the original matrix T and multiply each element in the row by the determinant of the minor for that position, alternating signs. The sum of these numbers is the full determinant.

The determinant of a 2×2 matrix is

$$\det \begin{vmatrix} t_{11} & t_{12} \\ t_{21} & t_{22} \end{vmatrix} = t_{11}t_{22} - t_{12}t_{21} \tag{4.52}$$

The determinant of a 3×3 matrix is

$$\det T = t_{11}(t_{22}t_{33} - t_{23}t_{32}) - t_{12}(t_{21}t_{33} - t_{23}t_{31}) + t_{13}(t_{21}t_{32} - t_{22}t_{31}) \tag{4.53}$$

The determinant of the homogeneous coordinate transformation matrices we usually deal with is

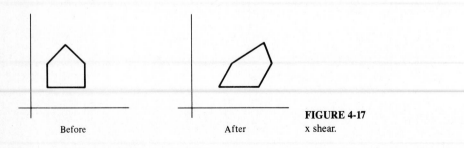

FIGURE 4-17
Before   After   x shear.

$$\det \begin{vmatrix} a & d & 0 \\ b & e & 0 \\ c & f & 1 \end{vmatrix} = ae - bd \tag{4.54}$$

Now we can express the inverse of a matrix in terms of determinants.

$$t'_{ij} = \frac{(-1)^{i+j} \det M_{ji}}{\det T} \tag{4.55}$$

where t'_{ij} is an element of the inverse of matrix T. Note that the order of i and j is reversed on the minor.

The inverse of the homogeneous coordinate transformation matrix is

$$\text{inv} \begin{vmatrix} a & d & 0 \\ b & e & 0 \\ c & f & 1 \end{vmatrix} = \frac{1}{ae - bd} \begin{vmatrix} e & -d & 0 \\ -b & a & 0 \\ bf - ce & cd - af & ae - bd \end{vmatrix} \tag{4.56}$$

TRANSFORMATION ROUTINES

Now that we have seen the mathematics behind transformations, let's look at some algorithms to actually perform them. We shall construct routines for translating, rotating, and scaling. The routines that create the transformations will modify a homogeneous coordinate transformation matrix. This matrix can then be applied to any point to obtain the corresponding transformed point. While we use the notion of homogeneous coordinates, we shall not actually store the third coordinate w; instead, we shall arrange our transformations so that w will always be 1. We can therefore just use 1 whenever we need the coordinate w. For the same reason, we shall not store the last column of the transformation matrix. This column would always contain 0, 0, 1; and since we know this, we can avoid actually storing these numbers. We shall save the 3×3 homogeneous transformation matrix in the 3×2 array named H.

We begin with a routine to set the transformation matrix to the identity matrix. This clears the transformation so that we can start fresh.

4.1 Algorithm IDENTITY-MATRIX (H) Routine to create the identity transformation
Argument   H is a transformation array of 3×2 elements.
Local   I, J variables for stepping through the H array
BEGIN
    FOR I = 1 TO 3 DO
        FOR J = 1 TO 2 DO
            IF I = J THEN H[I, J] $\leftarrow$ 1
            ELSE H[I, J] $\leftarrow$ 0;
        RETURN;
END;

The next algorithm causes a scaling transformation. It has the effect of multiplying the matrix H on the right by a scaling transformation matrix of

$$\begin{vmatrix} SX & 0 & 0 \\ 0 & SY & 0 \\ 0 & 0 & 1 \end{vmatrix}$$

We notice that there are a lot of zeros in this matrix, so if we follow the multiplication steps of Equation 4.3, we will be multiplying and adding many noncontributing terms. The algorithm given here avoids this wasted effort by only dealing with the nonzero terms.

4.2 Algorithm MULTIPLY-IN-SCALE (SX, SY, H) Routine to post-multiply the transformation matrix by a scale transformation

Arguments   SX is the x scale factor

                SY is the y scale factor

                H is a 3 × 2 transformation matrix

Local   I for stepping through the array

BEGIN

    FOR I = 1 TO 3 DO

        BEGIN

            H[I, 1] ← H[I, 1] ∗ SX;

            H[I, 2] ← H[I, 2] ∗ SY;

        END;

    RETURN;

END;

For translation TX, TY, we post-multiply H by the translation matrix

$$\begin{vmatrix} 1 & 0 & 0 \\ 0 & 1 & 0 \\ TX & TY & 1 \end{vmatrix}$$

Again we simplify the multiplication by neglecting zero terms. Since the third column of the transformation matrix is always 0, 0, 1, the algorithm for translation is as follows.

4.3 Algorithm MULTIPLY-IN-TRANSLATION (TX, TY, H) Routine to post-multiply the transformation matrix by a translation

Arguments   TX translation in the x direction

                TY translation in the y direction

                H a 3 × 2 transformation matrix

BEGIN

    H[3, 1] ← H[3, 1] + TX;

    H[3, 2] ← H[3, 2] + TY;

    RETURN;

END;

For a rotation of A radians counterclockwise, we post-multiply by

$$\begin{vmatrix} \cos A & \sin A & 0 \\ -\sin A & \cos A & 0 \\ 0 & 0 & 1 \end{vmatrix}$$

The algorithm takes the angle as an argument, calculates the sine and cosine, and then performs the matrix multiplication for nonzero terms.

> **4.4 Algorithm MULTIPLY-IN-ROTATION(A, H)** Routine to post-multiply the transformation matrix by a rotation
> Arguments   A angle of counterclockwise rotation
> H a 3 × 2 transformation matrix
> Local   S, C the sine and cosine values
> I for stepping through the array
> TEMP temporary storage of the first column
> BEGIN
>   C ← COS(A);
>   S ← SIN(A);
>   FOR I = 1 TO 3 DO
>   BEGIN
>   TEMP ← H[I, 1] * C – H[I, 2] * S;
>   H[I, 2] ← H[I, 1] * S + H[I, 2] * C;
>   H[I, 1] ← TEMP;
>   END;
>   RETURN;
> END;

The above routines serve to create a transformation matrix, but we still need a routine to apply the resulting transformation. The following routine transforms a single point. The point coordinates are passed to the subroutine as arguments, and the transformed point is returned in the same variables.

> **4.5 Algorithm DO-TRANSFORMATION(X, Y, H)** Routine to transform a point
> Arguments   X, Y the coordinates of the point to be transformed
> H a 3 × 2 transformation matrix
> Local   TEMP temporary storage for the new X value.
> BEGIN
>   TEMP ← X * H[1, 1] + Y * H[2, 1] + H[3, 1];
>   Y ← X * H[1, 2] + Y * H[2, 2] + H[3, 2];
>   X ← TEMP;
>   RETURN;
> END;

To perform a transformation, we must form the appropriate transformation matrix and then apply it to the points in our display. There are several ways this might be done. In our approach we shall deny the user access to the MULTIPLY-IN-SCALE, MULTIPLY-IN-TRANSLATION, and MULTIPLY-IN-ROTATION routines. The user will therefore not be able to build up complex transformations by multiplying several scales, translations, or rotations (if he wishes to do this, he will have to write his own routines). Instead, the user will be allowed only one scale, one rotation, and one translation, to be applied in that order. The transformations will be applied as the display file is interpreted. The user can change the values of these transformations at any time, but the image will be formed using the values in effect at the time the display file is in-

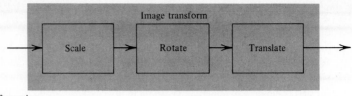

FIGURE 4-18
The image transformation.

terpreted. The following three algorithms describe user routines for saving the transformation parameters until it is time to interpret the display file.

4.6 Algorithm TRANSLATE(TX, TY) User routine to set the translation parameters
Arguments   TX, TY the translation amount
Global   TRNX, TRNY storage for the translation parameters
BEGIN
   TRNX ← TX;
   TRNY ← TY;
   CALL NEWFRAME;
   RETURN;
END;

4.7 Algorithm SCALE(SX, SY) User routine to set the scaling parameters
Arguments   SX, SY the scaling factors
Global   SCLX, SCLY storage for the scale parameters
BEGIN
   SCLX ← SX;
   SCLY ← SY;
   CALL NEWFRAME;
   RETURN;
END;

4.8 Algorithm ROTATE(A) User routine to set the rotation angle
Argument   A the rotation angle
Global   ANGL a place to save the rotation angle
BEGIN
   ANGL ← A;
   CALL NEWFRAME;
   RETURN;
END;

We now need a routine which will take the transformation parameters specified by the user and use them to form a transformation matrix. This is just a matter of passing the values to the transformation matrix multiplication routines which we defined above. (See Figure 4-18.)

4.9 Algorithm BUILD-TRANSFORMATION Routine to build the image transformation matrix
Global   ANGL, SCLX, SCLY, TRNX, TRNY the transformation parameters
          IMAGE-XFORM a 3 × 2 array containing the image transformation

```
BEGIN
    IDENTITY-MATRIX(IMAGE-XFORM);
    MULTIPLY-IN-SCALE(SCLX, SCLY, IMAGE-XFORM);
    MULTIPLY-IN-ROTATION(ANGL, IMAGE-XFORM);
    MULTIPLY-IN-TRANSLATION(TRNX, TRNY, IMAGE-XFORM);
    RETURN;
END;
```

To apply these transformations to a picture, we shall modify three of the algorithms from previous chapters. We shall extend the MAKE-PICTURE-CURRENT algorithm to include a call on BUILD-TRANSFORMATION. Thus the parameter settings at the time the MAKE-PICTURE-CURRENT routine is executed will be the values used for the transformation.

4.10 Algorithm MAKE-PICTURE-CURRENT (Algorithm 2.12 revisited) User routine to show the current display file

Global   FREE the index of the next free display-file cell

               ERASE-FLAG indicates if frames should be cleared

```
BEGIN
    IF ERASE-FLAG THEN
        BEGIN
            ERASE;
            ERASE-FLAG ← FALSE;
        END;
    BUILD-TRANSFORMATION;
    IF FREE > 1 THEN INTERPRET(1, FREE − 1);
    DISPLAY;
    FREE ← 1;
    RETURN;
END;
```

Each point retrieved from the display should be multiplied by the transformation matrix, and the resulting product should be used. This can be accomplished by modifying the INTERPRET and LOAD-POLYGON routines to call GET-TRANSFORMED-POINT instead of GET-POINT. (See Figure 4-19.)

4.11 Algorithm INTERPRET(START, COUNT) (Algorithm 3.6 revisited) Scan the display file performing the instructions

Arguments   START the starting index of the display-file scan

                COUNT the number of instructions to be interpreted

Local   NTH the display-file index

                OP, X, Y the display file instruction

```
BEGIN
    a loop to do all desired instructions
    FOR NTH = START TO START + COUNT − 1 DO
        BEGIN
            GET-TRANSFORMED-POINT(NTH, OP, X, Y);
            IF OP < −31 THEN DOCHAR(OP, X, Y)
```

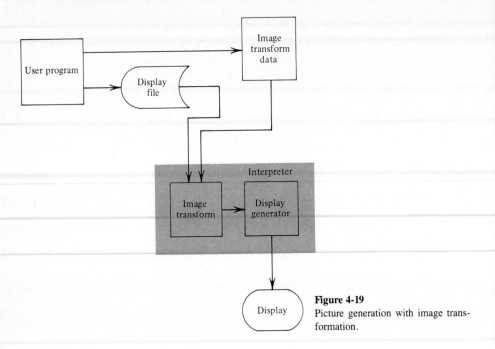

Figure 4-19
Picture generation with image transformation.

```
            ELSE IF OP < 1 THEN DOSTYLE(OP)
                ELSE IF OP = 1 THEN DOMOVE(X, Y)
                    ELSE IF OP = 2 THEN DOLINE(X, Y)
                        ELSE DOPOLYGON(OP, X, Y, NTH);

        END;
      RETURN;
    END;
```

4.12 Algorithm LOAD-POLYGON(I, EDGES) (A modification of algorithm 3.9) A routine to retrieve polygon side information from the display file
Positions are converted to actual screen coordinates

Arguments	I the display-file index of the instruction
	EDGES for return of the number of sides stored
Global	WIDTH-START, HEIGHT-START starting index of the screen
	WIDTH width in pixels of the screen
	HEIGHT height in pixels of the actual screen
Local	X1, Y1, X2, Y2 edge endpoints in device coordinates
	I1 for stepping through the display file
	K for stepping through the polygon sides
	DUMMY for a dummy argument

```
BEGIN
    set starting point for a side
    GET-TRANSFORMED-POINT(I, SIDES, X1, Y1);
    X1 ← X1 * WIDTH + WIDTH-START + 0.5;
    adjust y coordinate to nearest scan line
    Y1 ← INT(Y1 * HEIGHT + HEIGHT-START + 0.5);
```

```
    get index of first side command
    I1 ← I + 1;
    initialize an index for storing side data
    EDGES ← 1;
    a loop to get information about each side
    FOR K = 1 TO SIDES DO
        BEGIN
            get next vertex
            GET-TRANSFORMED-POINT(I1, DUMMY, X2, Y2);
            X2 ← X2 * WIDTH + WIDTH-START + 0.5;
            Y2 ← INT( Y2 * HEIGHT + HEIGHT-START + 0.5);
            see if horizontal line
            IF Y1 = Y2 THEN X1 ← X2
            ELSE
                BEGIN
                    save data about side in order of largest y
                    POLY-INSERT(EDGES, X1, Y1, X2, Y2);
                    increment index for side data storage
                    EDGES ← EDGES + 1;
                    old point is reset
                    Y1 ← Y2:
                    X1 ← X2;
                END;
            I1 ← I1 + 1;
        END;
    set EDGES to be a count of the edges stored.
    EDGES ← EDGES − 1;
    RETURN;
END;
```

The GET-TRANSFORMED-POINT routine retrieves an instruction from the display file and applies the transformation to it.

4.13 Algorithm GET-TRANSFORMED-POINT(NTH, OP, X, Y) Retrieve and transform the Nth instruction from the display file

Argument   NTH the index of the desired instruction
           OP, X, Y the instruction to be returned
Global   IMAGE-XFORM a 3 × 2 array containing the image transformation
BEGIN
    GET-POINT(NTH, OP, X, Y);
    IF OP > 0 OR OP < –31 THEN DO-TRANSFORMATION(X, Y, IMAGE-XFORM);
    RETURN;
END;

TRANSFORMATIONS AND PATTERNS

In Chapter 3 we described how patterns might be used to fill polygons. We showed how to implement patterns which are registered to the imaging surface. This is what is needed for patterns which give gray levels or simple textures such as stripes or weaves.

But there is an alternative use of patterns where it would be better if the pattern could be moved with respect to the imaging surface. This occurs when patterns are used to display pictures. It is sometimes better to represent a picture directly as a pixel pattern, instead of using lines and polygons. This may be because the shapes in the picture are curved (for example, characters). Or it may be that there are no lines at all, as often occurs with pictures extracted from photographs. For this type of pattern we may want to be able to move it around on the display. We might also like to be able to change the scale and orientation. We might like to rotate the picture or make it bigger. In other words, we would like to apply a transformation to the pattern. (See Figure 4-20.)

We shall show one way that this can be done using the image transformation which we have just developed. The resulting program will behave in the following way. Suppose we create a polygon and a pattern for filling it. Now suppose that we apply an image transformation to scale the polygon; we shall also scale the pattern so that the picture looks the same except for size. If we use the image transformation to rotate the polygon, the pattern will rotate with it, and if we use the image transformation to translate the polygon, the pattern it is filled with will be translated, too. The way we shall implement this is by extending the FILLIN algorithm. FILLIN determines the intensity value for each point in the polygon. In Chapter 3 we showed how the intensity for a point [x, y] could be found by looking in a pattern table; but now,

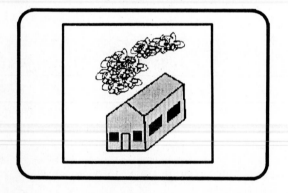

FIGURE 4-20
When the filling pattern is a picture, it should be transformed with the polygon.

FILLIN must find the intensity value for the transformed point $[x', y'] = [x, y]H$, where H is the image transformation and $[x, y]$ is in normalized device coordinates. Given the point $[x', y']$, we need to find the point $[x, y]$ and use it to look up the intensity in the pattern table. In effect, we are asking for the intensity of the original pattern at the point which gets transformed into the point being imaged. To find $[x, y]$ from $[x', y']$, we need the inverse transformation. We can build the inverse transformation from the inverses of the scale, rotation, and translation components.

The inverse of the scaling transformation of Equation 4.37 is

$$S^{-1} = \begin{vmatrix} \frac{1}{s_x} & 0 & 0 \\ 0 & \frac{1}{s_y} & 0 \\ 0 & 0 & 1 \end{vmatrix} \tag{4.57}$$

For example, scaling by one-half undoes the effect of scaling by two.

The inverse of the rotation matrix of Equation 4.39 is

$$R^{-1} = \begin{vmatrix} \cos\theta & -\sin\theta & 0 \\ \sin\theta & \cos\theta & 0 \\ 0 & 0 & 1 \end{vmatrix} = \begin{vmatrix} \cos(-\theta) & \sin(-\theta) & 0 \\ -\sin(-\theta) & \cos(-\theta) & 0 \\ 0 & 0 & 1 \end{vmatrix} \tag{4.58}$$

This says that we can undo the effect of a counterclockwise rotation by a rotation of the same amount in the clockwise direction.

Finally, the inverse of the translation matrix of Equation 4.41 is

$$T^{-1} = \begin{vmatrix} 1 & 0 & 0 \\ 0 & 1 & 0 \\ -t_x & -t_y & 1 \end{vmatrix} \tag{4.59}$$

We undo the effect of a translation by translating the same amount in the opposite direction.

Our image transformation is the product of a scale, a rotation, and a translation. Its inverse can be built from the inverses of its components. However, when we take something apart, we do it in the reverse sequence of when we put it together, and the inverse of the image transformation H is the product of its components in reverse order.

$$H^{-1} = (S\,R\,T)^{-1} = T^{-1}\,R^{-1}\,S^{-1} \tag{4.60}$$

This is almost what we need for transforming the pattern. The image transformation is applied to normalized device coordinates, but the points in FILLIN have been transformed to the actual device coordinates; so in order to apply H^{-1}, we should first convert the point back to the normalized coordinates by applying the inverse of this coordinate transformation. Once we have applied the inverse of the image transformation, we must convert the result back again to the actual device coordinates. This may seem like a lot of work, but actually it is not, because the coordinate transformation matrix (and its inverse) can be multiplied in with the inverse image transformation matrix so that there is only a single net transformation which we must apply to each point.

We saw the transformation from normalized device coordinates to actual device coordinates in Equation 4.43. This is the product of a scale (S_n) by the WIDTH and HEIGHT, followed by a translation (T_n) by WIDTH-START and HEIGHT-START. So the full transformation which should be applied to each point of the polygon being filled is

$$T_n^{-1} \, S_n^{-1} \, H^{-1} \, S_n \, T_n$$

Let's extend the BUILD-TRANSFORMATION algorithm so that it builds both the image transformation and the inverse transformation needed to transform patterns.

4.14 Algorithm BUILD-TRANSFORMATION (Revision of algorithm 4.9) Routine to build the image transformation matrix and its inverse
Global   ANGL, SCLX, SCLY, TRNX, TRNY the transformation parameters
                IMAGE-XFORM a 3 × 2 array containing the image transformation
                INVERSE-IMAGE-XFORM a 3 × 2 array for the inverse of the image
                transformation
BEGIN
    IDENTITY-MATRIX(IMAGE-XFORM);
    MULTIPLY-IN-SCALE(SCLX, SCLY, IMAGE-XFORM);
    MULTIPLY-IN-ROTATION(ANGL, IMAGE-XFORM);
    MULTIPLY-IN-TRANSLATION(TRNX, TRNY, IMAGE-XFORM);
    IDENTITY-MATRIX(INVERSE-IMAGE-XFORM);
    MULTIPLY-IN-TRANSLATION(− WIDTH-START, − HEIGHT-START,
        INVERSE-IMAGE-XFORM);
    MULTIPLY-IN-SCALE(1 / WIDTH, 1 / HEIGHT, INVERSE-IMAGE-XFORM);
    MULTIPLY-IN-TRANSLATION(− TRNX, − TRNY, INVERSE-IMAGE-XFORM);
    MULTIPLY-IN-ROTATION(− ANGL, INVERSE-IMAGE-XFORM);
    MULTIPLY-IN-SCALE(1 / SCLX, 1 / SCLY, INVERSE-IMAGE-XFORM);
    MULTIPLY-IN-SCALE(WIDTH, HEIGHT, INVERSE-IMAGE-XFORM);
    MULTIPLY-IN-TRANSLATION(WIDTH-START, HEIGHT-START,
        INVERSE-IMAGE-XFORM);
    RETURN;
END;

Before presenting the modified FILLIN algorithm, let's define a flag which the user can set to indicate whether or not he wants patterns to be transformed.

4.15 Algorithm SET-TRANSFORM-PATTERN(ON-OFF) User routine to indicate whether polygon fill patterns should undergo the image transformation
Argument   ON-OFF the user's choice
Global   XFORM-PATTERN a flag to indicate transformation of patterns
BEGIN
    XFORM-PATTERN ← ON-OFF;
    RETURN;
END;

Now we shall revise the FILLIN algorithm to allow image transformations on the patterns used to fill polygons.

4.16 Algorithm FILLIN(X1, X2, Y) (Revision of algorithm 3.17) Fills in scan line Y
from X1 to X2

Arguments   X1, X2 end positions of the scan line to be filled

Y the scan line to be filled

Global   FILL-PATTERN pattern table index of the pattern to use

PATTERN-X, PATTERN-Y, PATTERNS the pattern table

FRAME the two-dimensional frame buffer array

XFORM-PATTERN a flag to indicate transformation of patterns

INVERSE-IMAGE-XFORM a 3×2 array for the inverse of the image
transformation

Local   X for stepping across the scan line

PX, PY for accessing the pattern

PATTERN-TO-USE the pattern to be used in filling

PAT-X, PAT-Y the x and y dimensions of the pattern

BEGIN
    IF X1 = X2 THEN RETURN;
    PAT-X ← PATTERN-X[FILL-PATTERN];
    PAT-Y ← PATTERN-Y[FILL-PATTERN];
    if a local array is used as shown in the following statement,
    then the implementation should avoid copying of individual elements
    PATTERN-TO-USE ← PATTERNS[FILL-PATTERN];
    IF XFORM-PATTERN THEN
        BEGIN
            FOR X = X1 TO X2 DO
                BEGIN
                    PX ← X;
                    PY ← Y;
                    DO-TRANSFORMATION(PX, PY, INVERSE-IMAGE-XFORM);
                    PX ← MOD(INT(PX + 0.5), PAT-X) + 1;
                    PY ← MOD(INT(PY + 0.5), PAT-Y) + 1;
                    FRAME[X, Y] ← PATTERN-TO-USE[PX, PY];
                END;
        END
    ELSE
            BEGIN
                PX ← MOD(X1, PAT-X) + 1;
                PY ← MOD(Y, PAT-Y) + 1;
                FOR X = X1 TO X2 DO
                    BEGIN
                        FRAME[X, Y] ← PATTERN-TO-USE[PX, PY];
                        IF PX = PAT-X THEN PX ← 1
                        ELSE PX ← PX + 1;
                    END;
            END;
    RETURN;
END;

Note that for pattern sizes restricted to powers of 2, the MOD operation can be replaced by a logical AND instruction, which is usually much faster.

The algorithm has been extended to include a check for transformation of the pattern. If the transformation should be done, then the inverse image transformation is applied to each point that is to be filled. The result is rounded to the nearest pixel, and MOD operations are used to determine the appropriate pattern element. Although they may look different, this new portion of the algorithm and the portion written in Chapter 3 are really quite similar. In fact, if the transformation is the identity, then the top and bottom halves of the algorithm have exactly the same effect. The difference is that in the untransformed case we can keep track of our position in the pattern, and can thereby avoid doing the MOD operations for every point. In the transformed case we cannot do this, and the MOD operators are needed.

Transformations on patterns should be used for pictures, but should be avoided for simple shading patterns and repetitive designs. There are two reasons for this. One is that the transformation of every pixel in the filled area can be quite time-consuming. The second is that transforming a pattern introduces aliasing effects. When transformed, the pixel positions do not correspond directly to the pattern positions. We must guess the proper pixel intensity from the intensity value of a nearby pattern element. This guess introduces errors. Antialiasing techniques can be used at the expense of more time. For example, we can set the pixel intensity to be a weighted average of the nearby pattern element values.

INITIALIZATION

We need a routine which will initialize the parameters so that the user will not have to set them unless he wishes to. The default parameter values should give the identity transformation.

4.17 Algorithm INITIALIZE-4 Initialization routine
```
BEGIN
    INITIALIZE-3;
    CALL SCALE(1, 1);
    CALL ROTATE(0);
    CALL TRANSLATE(0, 0);
    SET-TRANSFORM-PATTERN(FALSE);
    RETURN;
END;
```

DISPLAY PROCEDURES

There may be times, when the image transformation presented here is inadequate, when the user may wish to perform more than just a single scale, rotation, and translation operation. For example, a rotation about an arbitrary center point is most easily handled by a translation, followed by a rotation, followed by another translation. In these situations, the user should add one or more transformation levels to the system. He should write his own LINE and MOVE routines which multiply their arguments by his own transformation matrix before calling the system LINE-ABS-2 and MOVE-

ABS-2 routines to actually do the drawing. A transformation matrix designed and created by the user may be as complex as necessary, involving many component transformations. Routines written according to this prescription will transform point values before they are entered into the display file. The system extension detailed in the above algorithms, on the other hand, operates on points as they are read from the display file. Transformations may be carried out at both stages of the processing.

One situation in which multiple transformations are useful occurs when a picture is made of a few basic components combined according to some hierarchical structure. For example, we may have a routine which draws a flower petal. By combining petals with different positions and orientations, flowers may be drawn. By combining flowers with different sizes and positions, a flower bush may be created. Transformations of several bushes can form a garden, and so on. (See Figure 4-21.)

Pictures with this structure lend themselves to a subprogram organization. A program to draw a garden could do so by several calls on a subprogram which draws a flower bush. The subprogram which draws the flower bush could do so by several calls on a flower-drawing subprogram. The flower-drawing subprogram could use several calls on the petal subprogram. Notice, however, that these subprogram calls are a little more complicated than those of normal programming languages; they involve the establishment of a transformation matrix. An ordinary subprogram call (CALL PETAL) would always produce the image with the same size and orientation. What is needed is a call which sets up a transformation which is applied to all the points generated in the subprogram before they are entered into the display file, for example,

CALL PETAL WITH SIZE(SX, SY), ANGLE(A), TRANSLATION(TX, TY).

These calls, which involve establishment of a transformation, are named *display procedure calls*, and the subprograms which draw subpictures are known as *display procedures*. Because display procedure calls can be nested, there can be multiple transfor-

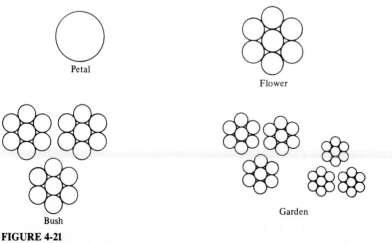

Petal

Flower

Bush

Garden

FIGURE 4-21
Hierarchical picture structure.

mations. Suppose, for example, that the GARDEN program calls the FLOWER-BUSH display procedure with transformation T_1. FLOWER-BUSH calls the FLOWER display procedure with transformation T_2. Finally, FLOWER calls the PETAL display procedure with transformation T_3. Then, the overall transformation applied to points generated in PETAL would be the product $T_3T_2T_1$. We can see that each time a new display procedure call is executed, the overall transformation matrix is multiplied on the left by the transformation for that display procedure. Here is a case where pre-multiplication is appropriate. In the GARDEN procedure, we have the identity matrix I. When FLOWER-BUSH is called, this is multiplied by T_1 to give T_1. When this, in turn, calls FLOWER, the T_2 transformation is multiplied in to give T_2T_1. Finally, when PETAL is called, the third transformation is also present: $T_3T_2T_1$. What happens when PETAL finishes and control is returned to FLOWER? We would expect to have the overall transformation which is appropriate for FLOWER, namely $T_2 T_1$. Likewise, when control is returned to FLOWER-BUSH from FLOWER, the transformation should be T_1, and when control returns to GARDEN, the overall transformation should once again be the identity I. There must therefore be some way of saving the overall transformation before multiplying by the additional transformation for a new display procedure call, so that it may be restored when control returns from that display procedure. When FLOWER calls PETAL, it saves the current overall transformation T_2T_1, multiplies it by T_3 to get the new overall transformation $T_3T_2T_1$, and transfers control to the PETAL. When PETAL is finished and ready to return, it first restores the overall transformation to the value that was saved, T_2T_1, and then returns control to FLOWER. Each display procedure call must save the current overall transformation matrix. Because there can be nested calls, several transformation matrices may have to be stored simultaneously. One possible data structure for storing these matrices is a stack. The last item stored in a stack is the first item to be removed, so it matches the last-entered–first-returned nature of subroutines.

In summary, then, a display procedure call involves the following:

1. Saving the overall transformation matrix
2. Multiplying the overall transformation matrix on the left by the transformation in the call to form a new overall transformation matrix
3. Transferring control to the display procedure

A return from a display procedure involves the following:

1. Restoring the overall transformation matrix from the value saved
2. Returning control to the calling program

The user's LINE and MOVE commands within the body of a display procedure should do the following:

1. Multiply point coordinates by the current overall transformation matrix to get the transformed point.

2. Enter the transformed values into the display file via the system LINE-ABS-2 or MOVE-ABS-2 commands.

AN APPLICATION

Let's consider how our graphics system might be useful in producing animated films. Animation is done by photographing a sequence of drawings, each slightly different from the previous. For example, to show a person moving his arm, a series of drawings is photographed, each drawing showing the arm at a different position. When the images are displayed one after another by a movie projector, we perceive the arm as moving through the sequence. (See Figure 4-22.)

From the artist's point of view, it is desirable to have only a small amount of motion occurring at any one time. The picture can then be constructed of a background which does not change and a foreground which alters from frame to frame. The foreground may be drawn upon a piece of clear plastic and then overlaid upon the background. If the portion of the image which changes is small, then the foreground image which must be redrawn for each frame is small and will require less work. What may be difficult for the human artist is changing the entire scene. For example, if one wished to give the impression of moving into the scene, one might scale the background, making each frame slightly larger. While this sort of change is difficult for the human artist, it is easy for the computer. It may therefore be beneficial to have the computer generate the background scene, while the human artist superimposes the foreground action.

Let's see how our graphics system could be used to generate the background. First, we must construct the full background drawing by using the LINE and POLYGON commands of the previous chapters. Let us assume that this has been done and that we have a routine which will enter appropriate instructions into the display file. By repeatedly executing these commands, the background images for each photograph may be generated. Suppose that the scene is a city street. To show a character moving down the street, we may really want to keep the character centered and move the scenery past him. This can be done by shifting our background image with the TRANSLATE(TX, TY) command. Before each display, we add a little more to TX. Each frame will show the background shifted a little more to the right. This will give the impression that our character has moved to the left. (See Figure 4-23.)

Or suppose that we wish to show our character approaching a building. We could give this effect by having the building grow larger. It could be done by using the SCALE(SX, SY) routine to make the building grow, and the TRANSLATE(TX, TY)

FIGURE 4-22
Animation of arm movement by a series of pictures, each slightly different from the previous.

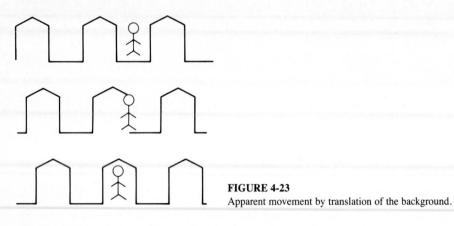

FIGURE 4-23
Apparent movement by translation of the background.

routine to keep it centered. With each frame, SX and SY are increased slightly to make the building appear a little larger. (See Figure 4-24.)

FURTHER READING

Other techniques for transforming patterns are found in [BRA80]. Transforming images is also considered in [CAT80]. Aliasing can be a major problem for transformed patterns. One approach to the problem is to find all pattern elements which transform to part of the displayed pixel and then to average their intensity values. A clever way to find the sum of the pattern element intensities is to store the progressive sums of intensity values in the pattern table so that the total intensity for a rectangular area is given by the difference in the values at the corners [CRO84]. A formal description of trans-

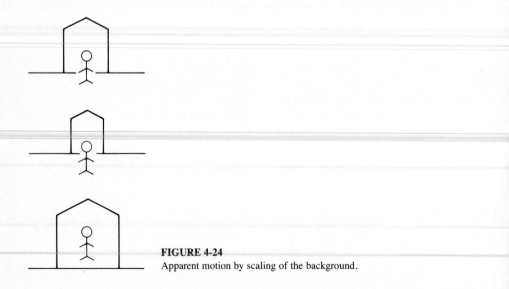

FIGURE 4-24
Apparent motion by scaling of the background.

formations and clipping in a hierarchical picture structure is described in [MAL78]. Display procedures are described in [NEW71].

[AHU68] Ahuja, D. V., and Coons, S. A., "Geometry for Construction and Display," *IBM Systems Journal*, vol. 7, no. 3/4, pp. 188–205 (1968).
[BRA80] Braccini, C., Marino. G., "Fast Geometrical Manipulations of Digital Images," *Computer Graphics and Image Processing*, vol. 13, no. 2, pp. 127–141 (1980).
[CAT80] Catmull, E., Smith, A. R., "3-D Transformations of Images in Scanline Order," *Computer Graphics*, vol. 14, no. 3, pp. 279–285 (1980).
[CRO84] Crow, F. C., "Summed-Area Tables for Texture Mapping," *Computer Graphics*, vol.18, no. 3, pp. 207–212 (1984).
[MAL78] Mallgren, W. R., Shaw, A. C., "Graphical Transformations and Hierarchic Picture Structures," *Computer Graphics and Image Processing*, vol. 8, no. 3, pp. 237–258 (1978).
[NEW71] Newman, W. M., "Display Procedures," *Communications of the ACM*, vol. 14, no. 10, pp. 651–660 (1971).

EXERCISES

4-1 Perform the following indicated matrix multiplications:

a) $\begin{vmatrix} 1 & 0 \\ 2 & 3 \end{vmatrix}$ $\begin{vmatrix} 2 & 1 \\ 1 & 1 \end{vmatrix}$

b) $\begin{vmatrix} 1 & 0 \\ 0 & 1 \end{vmatrix}$ $\begin{vmatrix} 1 & 2 \\ 3 & 4 \end{vmatrix}$

c) $\begin{vmatrix} 0 & 1 \\ 1 & 0 \end{vmatrix}$ $\begin{vmatrix} 1 & 2 \\ 3 & 4 \end{vmatrix}$

d) $\begin{vmatrix} 2 & 4 \end{vmatrix}$ $\begin{vmatrix} 3 & 5 \\ 2 & 0 \end{vmatrix}$

e) $\begin{vmatrix} 3 & 5 \\ 2 & 0 \end{vmatrix}$ $\begin{vmatrix} 2 \\ 4 \end{vmatrix}$

f) $\begin{vmatrix} 3 & 4 & 1 \end{vmatrix}$ $\begin{vmatrix} 1 & 2 & 0 \\ -2 & 3 & 0 \\ 0 & 0 & 1 \end{vmatrix}$

g) $\begin{vmatrix} 0 & 0 & 1 \end{vmatrix}$ $\begin{vmatrix} 0 & 0 & 0 \\ 0 & 0 & 0 \\ 3 & 5 & 1 \end{vmatrix}$

h) $\begin{vmatrix} 1 & 1 & 1 \end{vmatrix}$ $\begin{vmatrix} 3 & 0 & 0 \\ 0 & 4 & 0 \\ 0 & 0 & 1 \end{vmatrix}$

i) $\begin{vmatrix} 1 & 0 & 1 \end{vmatrix}$ $\begin{vmatrix} 0 & 1 & 0 \\ -1 & 0 & 0 \\ 0 & 0 & 1 \end{vmatrix}$

j) $\begin{vmatrix} 2 & 1 & 0 \\ 3 & 1 & 0 \\ 1 & 0 & 1 \end{vmatrix}$ $\begin{vmatrix} 1 & 4 & 0 \\ 1 & 5 & 0 \\ 0 & 2 & 1 \end{vmatrix}$

4-2 Write a 2 × 2 transformation matrix for each of the following scaling transformations:

    a) The entire picture three times as large

    b) The entire picture one-third as large

    c) The x direction four times as large, the y direction unchanged

    d) The y lengths reduced to two-thirds their original value, the x lengths unchanged

    e) The x direction reduced to three-fourths the original, y direction increased by a factor of seven-fifths

4-3 Give 3 × 3 homogeneous-coordinate transformation matrices for each of the scaling transformations given in Exercise 4-2.

4-4 Write a 2 × 2 transformation matrix for each of the following rotations about the origin:

    a) Counterclockwise by π

    b) Counterclockwise by $\pi/2$

    c) Clockwise by $\pi/2$

    d) Counterclockwise by $\pi/4$

    e) Counterclockwise by $5\pi/4$

4-5 Give a 3 × 3 homogeneous-coordinate transformation matrix for each of the rotations of Exercise 4-4.

4-6 Give a 3 × 3 homogeneous-coordinate transformation matrix for each of the following translations:

    a) Shift the image to the right 3 units.

    b) Shift the image up 2 units.

    c) Move the image down $1/2$ unit and right 1 unit.

    d) Move the image down $2/3$ unit and left 4 units.

4-7 Give a single 3 × 3 homogeneous coordinate transformation matrix which will have the same effect as each of the following transformation sequences:

    a) Scale the image to be twice as large and then translate it 1 unit to the left.

    b) Scale the x direction to be one-half as large and then rotate counterclockwise by $\pi/2$ about the origin.

    c) Rotate counterclockwise about the origin by $\pi/2$ and then scale the x direction to be one-half as large.

    d) Translate down $1/2$ unit, right $1/2$ unit, and then rotate counterclockwise by $\pi/4$.

    e) Scale the y coordinate to make the image twice as tall, shift it down 1 unit, and then rotate clockwise by $\pi/6$.

4-8 Show how reflections in the line y = x and in the line y = − x can be performed by a scaling operation followed by a rotation. (Scaling by negative factors is permitted.)

4-9 Suppose that a figure is centered at (0.5, 0.5):

    a) Give the calls to SCALE, ROTATE, and TRANSLATE which will show the figure scaled twice as large and still centered on the screen.

    b) Give the calls to SCALE, ROTATE, and TRANSLATE which scale the figure by a factor S and keep it centered on the screen.

    c) Give the calls to SCALE, ROTATE, and TRANSLATE which will rotate the figure counterclockwise by an angle A and still keep it centered on the screen.

    d) Give the calls to SCALE, ROTATE, and TRANSLATE which will show the figure reflected in the line x = 0.5.

    e) Give the calls to SCALE, ROTATE, and TRANSLATE which will show the figure reflected in the point (0.5, 0.5); that is, $x_1 = 1 - x$ and $y_1 = 1 - y$.

4-10 a) Prove that two scaling transformations commute; that is, $S_1S_2 = S_2S_1$.

b) Prove that two two-dimensional rotations about the origin commute; $R_1R_2 = R_2R_1$.

c) Show that two-dimensional scales and rotations do not commute in general. Under what restriction on scaling transformations is commutation of scales and rotations guaranteed?

4-11 Show how shear transformations may be expressed in terms of rotations and scales. Show how rotations can be expressed in terms of shears and scales. What scaling operations can be expressed as shears?

4-12 a) Show that a rotation about the origin can be done by performing three shearing transformations (with no scaling). This can be a fast way to rotate bitmaps since shears can often be carried out by moving entire blocks of pixels.

b) On each shearing operation, a quantization error in pixel position can be made. What is the maximum cumulative error in pixel position for a rotation conducted as three shears?

4-13 Describe the visual effect on an image of each of the following transformations:

a) $\begin{vmatrix} 0 & 0 \\ 0 & 0 \end{vmatrix}$ b) $\begin{vmatrix} 1 & 0 \\ 0 & 0 \end{vmatrix}$ c) $\begin{vmatrix} 0 & 1 \\ 0 & 0 \end{vmatrix}$

d) $\begin{vmatrix} 1 & 0 \\ 0 & 1 \end{vmatrix}$ e) $\begin{vmatrix} 0 & 1 \\ 1 & 0 \end{vmatrix}$ f) $\begin{vmatrix} 0 & 1 \\ 0 & 1 \end{vmatrix}$

g) $\begin{vmatrix} 1 & 1 \\ 0 & 1 \end{vmatrix}$ h) $\begin{vmatrix} 1 & 1 \\ 1 & 0 \end{vmatrix}$ i) $\begin{vmatrix} 1 & 1 \\ 1 & 1 \end{vmatrix}$

4-14 Find the inverse of each of the matrices in Exercise 4-13, if it exists.

4-15 Express each of the transformations in the OTHER TRANSFORMATIONS section as a product of rotations and scales. Also give the inverse transformation.

PROGRAMMING PROBLEMS

4-1 Implement algorithms 4.1 through 4.13, and 4.17, which extend the graphics system to include image transformations.

4-2 Write a program which draws a house-shaped, five-sided polygon. Show this figure scaled, rotated, translated, and under a combination of all three transformations. Show the figure both filled and unfilled.

4-3 Write the three routines

    INQUIRE-SCALE(SX, SY)
    INQUIRE-ROTATE(A)
    INQUIRE-TRANSLATE(TX, TY)

which will return the current image transformation parameter settings.

4-4 Eye chart program: Using a filled polygon to construct a square letter E, write a program to successively show this letter at different sizes and orientations. The orientation should be one of the four E, Ǝ, ɯ, ɯ and should be picked at random for each image. The size should begin large, but get smaller with each frame. The letter should always be centered on the screen. (See page 144.)

4-5 Write a procedure PIE(A1, A2, R) which draws a pie-shaped segment of a circle by performing an image transformation on the result of the WEDGE procedure of Programming Problem 3-12. The segment of a circle should have its point centered at $(0.5, 0.5)$, should have radius R, and should lie between angles A_1 and A_2.

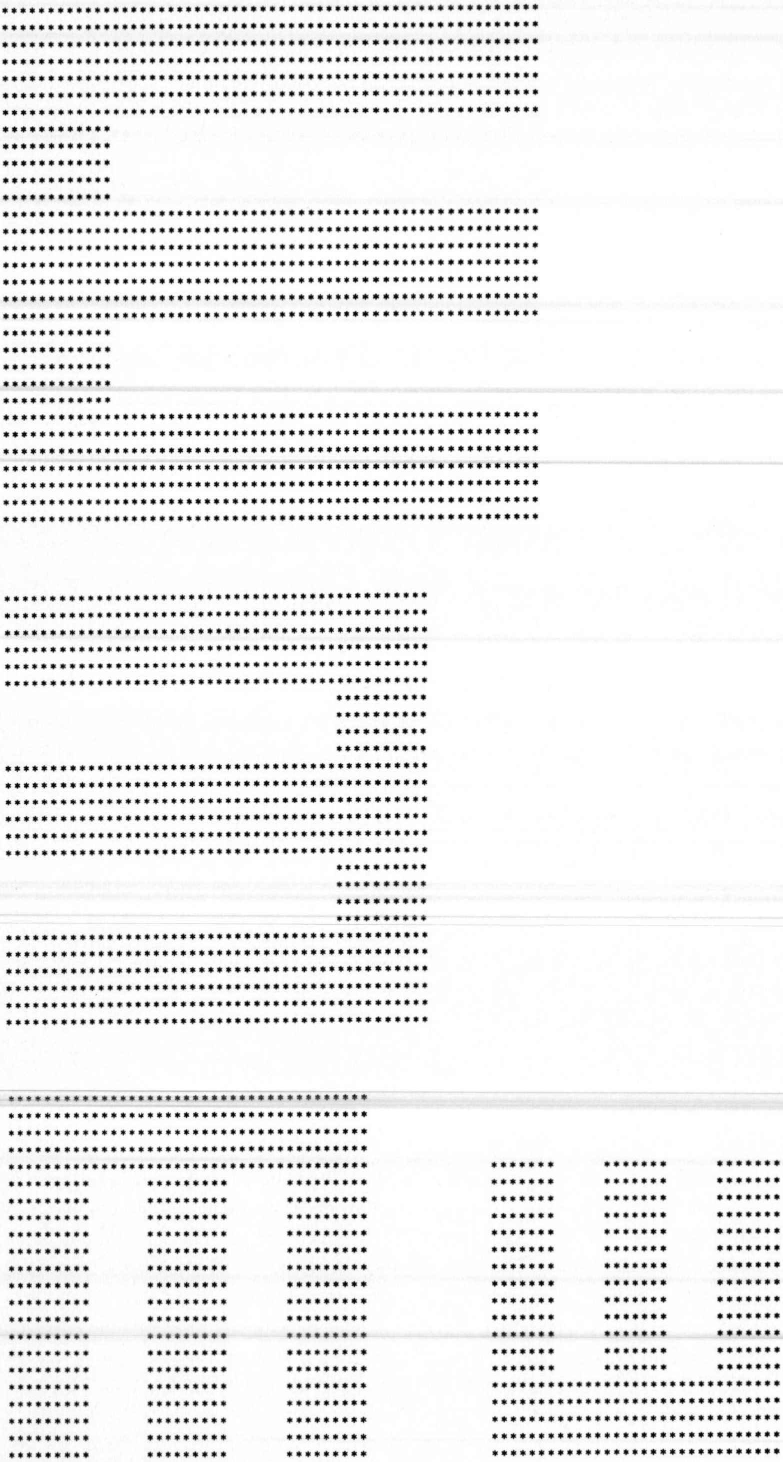

4-6 Suppose that procedure FOO has LINE, MOVE, and POLYGON drawing commands for some image. Write a program to repeat the following steps.

    a) Call FOO to create the image.

    b) Form a new image transformation which will show the image rotated $\pi/5$ counterclockwise and scaled by 0.8 from the last image displayed. The image should remain centered on the screen.

    c) Display the resulting image.

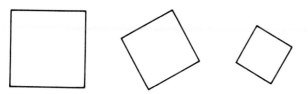

Test this program for five iterations, where FOO draws the square (0, 0), (0, 1), (1, 1), (1, 0).

4-7 Implement algorithms 4.14 through 4.17 for transformation of a polygon-filling pattern. Test your implementation by showing a polygon filled with a pattern when untransformed, translated, scaled, rotated, and under a combination of all three transformations. Show it under both settings of the XFORM-PATTERN flag.

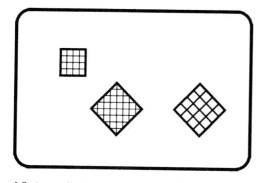

4-8 An application program can make greater use of transformation than we have provided. One might wish more general transformations such as the reflections and shears, or one might want to apply long sequences of transformations. Write user procedures T-MOVE-ABS-2(X, Y), T-MOVE-REL-2(DX, DY), T-LINE-ABS-2(X, Y), T-LINE-REL-2(DX, DY), T-POLYGON-ABS-2(AX, AY, N), and T-POLYGON-REL-2(AX, AY, N), which apply a general transformation to the coordinates before passing them on the MOVE-ABS-2, MOVE-REL-2, etc. Also write procedures T-CLEAR, which sets this application transformation to the identity transformation, and T-MULT-XFORM(A, B, C, D, E, F), which multiplies the application transformation by

$$\begin{vmatrix} A & D & 0 \\ B & E & 0 \\ C & F & 1 \end{vmatrix}$$

Optionally, you might write individual translation, scale, rotation, and shear routines which are special cases of the T-MULT-XFORM. Note that the "absolute" operations have full coordinates for arguments and are multiplied by the full transformation, but the "relative" operations have vectors as arguments. Vectors undergo the 2 × 2 scale and rotation transformations because they have length and direction, but they do not undergo translation because they do not have position.

***4-9** Implement a display procedure mechanism.

CHAPTER
FIVE

SEGMENTS

INTRODUCTION

In the preceding chapters we have organized our display as a single picture. In reality, however, the image on the display screen is often composed of several pictures or items of information. A single image may contain several views of an object. It may have a picture of the overall object and a close-up of a particular component. It may also contain information about the object, instructions for the user, and, possibly, error information. As an example, we may wish to display the design plans for a building. The plans may contain structural diagrams, electrical diagrams, plumbing diagrams, and heating diagrams. We might wish to show all this information simultaneously or, at other times, look at the individual elements. As another example, consider an animated display of a spaceship in motion. We might want to show the spaceship at different positions while the background remains fixed, or we might choose to keep the ship centered on the screen and move the background. The transformations of the last chapter tell us how to shift the position of the image, but now we wish to apply them to only a portion of the scene (either the ship or the background, but not both).

We would like to organize our display file to reflect this subpicture structure. We would like to divide our display file into *segments,* each segment corresponding to a component of the overall display. We shall associate a set of *attributes* with each segment. One such attribute is *visibility.* A visible segment will be displayed, but an invisible segment will not be shown. By varying the settings of the visibility attribute, we can build a picture out of the selected subpictures. Consider the building plan applica-

146

tion. We might, for example, in one display select structural and electrical information for a building by making the first and second segments visible and the third and fourth segments invisible. In another display we could select structural and plumbing information by making only the first and third segments visible. While all display information may be present in the machine, we can selectively show portions of it by designating which segments of the display file are to be interpreted.

Another attribute which can be associated with each segment is an image transformation. This will allow the independent scaling, rotating, and translating of each segment. For the spaceship, we could put the ship in one segment and the background in a different segment. We could then shift either of them by means of an image transformation, while leaving the other unchanged. (See Figure 5-1.)

In this chapter we shall consider segmentation of the display file. We shall learn how to create, close, rename, and delete segments. We shall also consider such display-file attributes as visibility and image transformation.

THE SEGMENT TABLE

We shall begin our discussion by considering some of the information that must be associated with each segment and how this information might be organized. We must give each segment its own unique name so that we can specify it. If we are to change the visibility of a segment, we must have some way to distinguish that segment from all the others. When we refer to a display-file segment, we must know which display-file instructions belong to it. This may be determined by knowing where the display-file instructions for the segment begin and how many of them there are. For each segment, we shall need some way of associating its display-file position information and its attribute information with its name. We need to organize this information so that given the segment name, we can look up or alter its attributes, or given its name, we can interpret the corresponding display-file instructions. In our system we shall do this

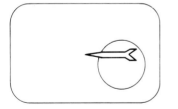

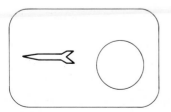

FIGURE 5-1
Transformation of a portion of the display.

by forming a segment table. We shall use a number for the name of the segment. Simple arrays will serve to hold segment properties, and the segment name will be used as the index into these arrays. We shall have one array containing display-file starting locations. A second array will hold segment size information, while a third will indicate visibility, and so on. To find out the size of, say, the third segment, we would look for the third element in the size array. (See Figure 5-2.)

The number 1 will refer to the first named segment of the table, 2, to the second named table entry, and so on. We shall have table entries (arrays) for holding the display-file starting position, for the segment size, and for attributes such as visibility and the image transformation parameters. If we wish not to show segment number 3, we will set the corresponding entry in the visibility array to off. When we show our picture, we shall consult the segment table to determine which segments are visible. For each visible segment, we shall look up its starting point and size and pass this information along to our display-file interpreter. The interpreter will therefore only interpret those segments which are visible.

There are other possible schemes for implementing the segment table, many with substantial advantages over the one which we have chosen here. We have selected this design because it allows simple accessing. It does not require any new data-structuring concepts, and its updating is straightforward.

We would like this extension to our graphics system to be compatible with our previous programs, which did not specify any segments. Perhaps the easiest way to do this is to say that when no segment name is specified, the instructions will be placed in a special "unnamed" segment. Information, such as display-file starting position and segment size, must be stored for the unnamed segment just as it is for named segments. We shall do this by placing a special entry in the segment table for the unnamed

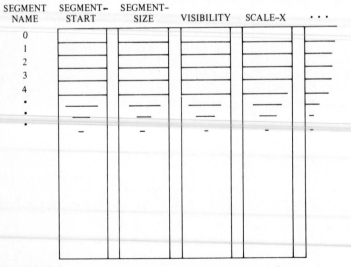

FIGURE 5-2
The segment table.

segment. In this implementation, we have chosen to associate the unnamed segment with table index 0. That is, the segment table arrays will be dimensioned with lower bound 0 instead of 1. Thus SEGMENT-SIZE[1] will still be the number of instructions of the segment with name 1, but SEGMENT-SIZE[0] will be the number of instructions in the unnamed segment.

SEGMENT CREATION

Let us consider the process of creating or opening a segment. When we create a segment, we are saying that all subsequent LINE, MOVE, TEXT, or POLYGON commands will be members of this segment. We must give the segment a name so that we can identify it. We might, for example, say that this is segment number 3. Then all following MOVE and LINE commands would belong to segment 3. We could then close segment 3 and open another segment, say segment 5. The next MOVE and LINE commands would belong to segment 5.

The first thing we do when we create a segment is check to see whether some other segment is still open. We cannot have two segments open at the same time because we would not know to which segment we should assign the drawing instructions. If there is a segment still open, we have an error. If no segment is currently open, we should check to make sure that we have a valid segment name. If the segment name is correct, check to see whether there already exists a segment under this name. If so, we again have an error. We initialize the items in the segment table under our segment name to indicate that this is a fresh new segment. The first instruction belonging to this segment will be located at the next free storage area in the display file. The current size of the segment is zero since we have not actually entered any instructions into it yet. The attributes are initialized to those of the unnamed segment, which provides the default attribute values. Finally we indicate that there is now a segment open (the one which we just created).

5.1 Algorithm CREATE-SEGMENT(SEGMENT-NAME) User routine to create a named segment

Argument   SEGMENT-NAME the segment name
Global   NOW-OPEN the segment currently open
              FREE the index of the next free display-file cell
              SEGMENT-START, SEGMENT-SIZE, VISIBILITY
              ANGLE, SCALE-X, SCALE-Y, TRANSLATE-X, TRANSLATE-Y
              arrays that make up the segment table
Constant   NUMBER-OF-SEGMENTS size of the segment table
BEGIN
     IF NOW-OPEN > 0 THEN RETURN ERROR 'SEGMENT STILL OPEN';
     IF SEGMENT-NAME < 1 OR SEGMENT-NAME > NUMBER-OF-SEGMENTS
     THEN
         RETURN ERROR 'INVALID SEGMENT NAME';
     IF SEGMENT-SIZE[SEGMENT-NAME] > 0 THEN
         RETURN ERROR 'SEGMENT ALREADY EXISTS';
     SEGMENT-START[SEGMENT-NAME] ← FREE;

```
        SEGMENT-SIZE[SEGMENT-NAME] ← 0;
        VISIBILITY[SEGMENT-NAME] ← VISIBILITY[0];
        ANGLE[SEGMENT-NAME] ← ANGLE[0];
        SCALE-X[SEGMENT-NAME] ← SCALE-X[0];
        SCALE-Y[SEGMENT-NAME] ← SCALE-Y[0];
        TRANSLATE-X[SEGMENT-NAME] ← TRANSLATE-X[0];
        TRANSLATE-Y[SEGMENT-NAME] ← TRANSLATE-Y[0];
        NOW-OPEN ← SEGMENT-NAME;
        RETURN;
    END;
```

CLOSING A SEGMENT

With the segment open we can proceed with the entry of display-file instructions, as we did in previous chapters. Now, however, all commands which are entered are associated with the open segment. Once we have completed the drawing instructions for the segment, we should close it. At this point, all that is necessary in closing the segment is to change the value of the NOW-OPEN variable, which indicates the name of the currently open segment. We must change it to something, so we shall set it to 0 and make the unnamed segment the one which is open. In our algorithm below we do this by placing a 0 in the NOW-OPEN variable. We don't want to have two unnamed segments around because we shall only show one of them and the other would just waste storage. So we delete any unnamed segment instructions which may have been saved. We initialize the unnamed segment to have no instructions, but to be ready to receive them in the next free display-file location.

5.2 Algorithm CLOSE-SEGMENT User routine to close the currently open segment

```
    Global      NOW-OPEN the name of the currently open segment
                FREE the index of the next free display-file cell
                SEGMENT-START, SEGMENT-SIZE start and size of the segments
    BEGIN
        IF NOW-OPEN = 0 THEN RETURN ERROR 'NO SEGMENT OPEN';
        DELETE-SEGMENT(0);
        SEGMENT-START[0] ← FREE;
        SEGMENT-SIZE[0] ← 0;
        NOW-OPEN ← 0;
        RETURN;
    END;
```

DELETING A SEGMENT

The most complex algorithm for this chapter is that for deleting a segment. If a segment is no longer needed, we would like to recover the display-file storage occupied by its instructions. Since these instructions will never again be executed, we would prefer to use this storage for some other segment. At the same time, we would rather not have to destroy and re-form the entire display file. We may be altering some small portion of an image which is very costly to generate. We would like to be able to delete (and perhaps re-create with modifications) just one segment, while preserving the rest of the display file. The method of doing this depends upon the data structure used for the display file. We have used arrays. Recovery of a block of storage in an array is both simple and straightforward, but it is not as efficient as some other storage techniques. What we shall do is take all display-file instructions entered after the segment which we are deleting was closed, and move them up in the display file so that they lie on top of the deleted segment. Thus we fill in the gap left by the deleted block and recover an equivalent amount of storage at the end of the display file. (See Figure 5-3.)

We begin our segment deletion algorithm by checking to make sure that we have a valid segment name. If the name is correct, we next check that it is not open. Open segments are still in use; if an attempt is made to delete an open segment, we shall treat it as an error. We next check to see whether the size of the segment is 0. A segment with no instructions has nothing to remove from the display file, so no further processing is necessary. We can now shift the instructions in the display file. We wish to place instructions on top of the deleted segment. So our first relocated instruction will be put on top of the first instruction of our deleted segment. We will get the instruction to be moved from the first location beyond the deleted segment. We shall move through the display file, getting instructions and shifting them down until we come to an unused display-file location. When we have completed moving the display-file instructions, we can reset the index of the next free instruction to reflect the recovered storage. Finally, we must adjust not only the display file but also the segment table, since the starting positions of segments created after the segment which was deleted will now have changed. We can do this by scanning the segment table and noting any segments whose starting position lies beyond the starting position of the segment which we deleted. We change the starting positions by subtracting the size of the deleted segment. We can set the size of the segment which we deleted to be 0 to indicate that this segment no longer exists. If we delete a visible segment, a NEW-FRAME action is required. These steps are detailed in the following algorithm:

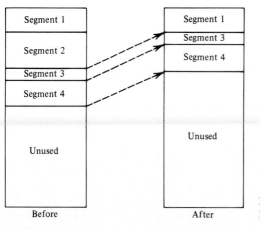

FIGURE 5-3
Deleting segment 2 from the display file.

5.3 Algorithm DELETE-SEGMENT(SEGMENT-NAME) User routine to delete a segment

Argument	SEGMENT-NAME the segment name
Global	NOW-OPEN the currently open segment
	FREE the index of the next free display-file cell
	DF-OP, DF-X, DF-Y the display-file arrays
	SEGMENT-START, SEGMENT-SIZE, VISIBILITY part of the segment table arrays
Constant	NUMBER-OF-SEGMENTS the size of the segment table
Local	GET the location of an instruction to be moved
	PUT the location to which an instruction should be moved
	SIZE the size of the deleted segment
	I a variable for stepping through the segment table

BEGIN
   IF SEGMENT-NAME < 0 OR SEGMENT-NAME > NUMBER-OF-SEGMENTS THEN
      RETURN ERROR 'INVALID SEGMENT NAME';
   IF SEGMENT-NAME = NOW-OPEN AND SEGMENT-NAME ≠ 0 THEN
      RETURN ERROR 'SEGMENT STILL OPEN';
   IF SEGMENT-SIZE[SEGMENT-NAME] = 0 THEN RETURN;
   PUT ← SEGMENT-START[SEGMENT-NAME];
   SIZE ← SEGMENT-SIZE[SEGMENT-NAME];
   GET ← PUT + SIZE;
   shift the display-file elements
   WHILE GET < FREE DO
     BEGIN
       DF-OP[PUT] ← DF-OP[GET];
       DF-X[PUT] ← DF-X[GET];
       DF-Y[PUT] ← DF-Y[GET];
       PUT ← PUT + 1;
       GET ← GET + 1;
     END;
   recover the deleted storage
   FREE ← PUT;
   update the segment table
   FOR I = 0 TO NUMBER-OF-SEGMENTS DO
     IF SEGMENT-START[I] > SEGMENT-START[SEGMENT-NAME] THEN
       SEGMENT-START[I] ← SEGMENT-START[I] − SIZE;
   SEGMENT-SIZE[SEGMENT-NAME] ← 0;
   IF VISIBILITY[SEGMENT-NAME] THEN NEW-FRAME;
   RETURN;
END;

We also shall have a routine to delete all of the segments. This will be useful to the user should he wish to start a completely new picture and will also be useful for initialization. One way of doing this is to delete all segments individually. This approach is independent of the data structure used for the display file. A somewhat more efficient approach for our particular array structure is to simply set the size value of all segments to 0 and initialize the free cell index FREE to be the first cell in the display file. We also set all starting positions to 1 so that after initialization there will not be any garbage in these locations which might upset the DELETE-SEGMENT routine.

5.4 Algorithm DELETE-ALL-SEGMENTS User routine to delete all segments

Global   NOW-OPEN the segment currently open
              FREE the index of the next available display-file cell
              SEGMENT-SIZE the segment size array
              SEGMENT-START the segment starting index array
Constant   NUMBER-OF-SEGMENTS the size of the segment table
Local   I a variable for stepping through the segment table
BEGIN
    FOR I = 0 TO NUMBER-OF-SEGMENTS DO
        BEGIN
            SEGMENT-START[I] ← 1;
            SEGMENT-SIZE[I] ← 0;
        END;
    NOW-OPEN ← 0;
    FREE ← 1;
    NEW-FRAME;
    RETURN;
END;

RENAMING A SEGMENT

Another routine which is easy to implement and often useful is renaming a segment. As an example of how it might be used, consider a display device with an independent display processor. The display processor is continuously reading the display file and showing its current contents. (We would not need a MAKE-PICTURE-CURRENT routine for such a device because the picture is always current.) Now suppose we wish to use this device to show an animated character moving on the display. This would be done by presenting a sequence of images, each with a slightly different drawing of the character. Assume we have a segment for the character. Then, for each new image, we could delete the segment, re-create it with the altered character, and show the result. The problem with this is that during the time after the first image is deleted but before the second image is completed, only a partially completed character can be seen. Since we may begin working on the next image as soon as the last one is completed, we may in fact be continually looking at only partially completed characters. To avoid this problem we should not delete a segment until a replacement for it is completed. This means that both segments must exist in the display file at the same time. We do this by building the new invisible image under some temporary segment name. When it is completed, we can delete the original image, make the replacement image visible, and rename the new segment to become the old segment. These steps can be repeated to achieve apparent motion. The idea of maintaining two images, one to show and one to build or alter, is called *double buffering*. The renaming is carried out by our RENAME-SEGMENT algorithm. The algorithm checks that the segment names are valid and that they are not still open. It also checks against using the name of an already existing segment. If these conditions are met, the segment table entries for the old name are copied into the new name position and the size of the old segment is set back to 0.

5.5 Algorithm RENAME-SEGMENT(SEGMENT-NAME-OLD, SEGMENT-NAME-NEW) User routine to rename SEGMENT-NAME-OLD to be SEGMENT-NAME-NEW

Arguments   SEGMENT-NAME-OLD old name of segment
             SEGMENT-NAME-NEW new name of segment
Global   SEGMENT-START, SEGMENT-SIZE, VISIBILITY, ANGLE, SCALE-X, SCALE-Y, TRANSLATE-X, TRANSLATE-Y the segment table arrays
Constant   NUMBER-OF-SEGMENTS the size of the segment table
BEGIN
   IF SEGMENT-NAME-OLD < 1 OR SEGMENT-NAME-NEW < 1 OR
       SEGMENT-NAME-OLD > NUMBER-OF-SEGMENTS OR
       SEGMENT-NAME-NEW > NUMBER-OF-SEGMENTS THEN
          RETURN ERROR 'INVALID SEGMENT NAME';
   IF SEGMENT-NAME-OLD = NOW-OPEN OR
       SEGMENT-NAME-NEW = NOW-OPEN THEN
       RETURN ERROR 'SEGMENT STILL OPEN';
   IF SEGMENT-SIZE[SEGMENT-NAME-NEW] ≠ 0 THEN
       RETURN ERROR 'SEGMENT ALREADY EXISTS';
  copy the old segment table entry into the new position
  SEGMENT-START[SEGMENT-NAME-NEW]
      ← SEGMENT-START[SEGMENT-NAME-OLD];
  SEGMENT-SIZE[SEGMENT-NAME-NEW]
      ← SEGMENT-SIZE[SEGMENT-NAME-OLD];
  VISIBILITY[SEGMENT-NAME-NEW] ← VISIBILITY[SEGMENT-NAME-OLD];
  ANGLE[SEGMENT-NAME-NEW] ← ANGLE[SEGMENT-NAME-OLD];
  SCALE-X[SEGMENT-NAME-NEW] ← SCALE-X[SEGMENT-NAME-OLD];
  SCALE-Y[SEGMENT-NAME-NEW] ← SCALE-Y[SEGMENT-NAME-OLD];
  TRANSLATE-X[SEGMENT-NAME-NEW]
      ← TRANSLATE-X[SEGMENT-NAME-OLD];
  TRANSLATE-Y[SEGMENT-NAME-NEW]
      ← TRANSLATE-Y[SEGMENT-NAME-OLD];
  delete the old segment
  SEGMENT-SIZE[SEGMENT-NAME-OLD] ← 0;
  RETURN;
END;

VISIBILITY

We have talked about the property of visibility. Each segment is given a visibility attribute. The segment's visibility is stored in an array as part of the segment table. We are therefore able to look up the value of each segment's visibility. By checking this array we can determine whether or not the segment should be displayed. We should give the user some method of changing the value of a segment's visibility, so that he can choose to show or not to show the segment. The following algorithm does this, while freeing the user from any concern about global variables and segment table representation. If the visibility is being turned off, then a new-frame action is needed. (See Figure 5-4.)

5.6 Algorithm SET-VISIBILITY(SEGMENT-NAME, ON-OFF) User routine to set the visibility attribute

Arguments SEGMENT-NAME the name of the segment
                         ON-OFF the new visibility setting
Global   VISIBILITY the array of visibility flags
Constant   NUMBER-OF-SEGMENTS the size of the segment table
BEGIN
     IF SEGMENT-NAME < 1 OR SEGMENT-NAME > NUMBER-OF-SEGMENTS
     THEN
          RETURN ERROR 'INVALID SEGMENT NAME';
     VISIBILITY[SEGMENT-NAME] ← ON-OFF;
     IF NOT ON-OFF THEN NEW-FRAME;
     RETURN;
END;

IMAGE TRANSFORMATION

An image transformation is carried out on the contents of the display file. If we think of the display file as containing the picture which we have constructed, then the image

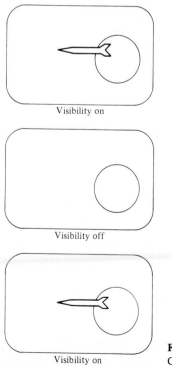

Visibility on

Visibility off

Visibility on

FIGURE 5-4
Changing the visibility attribute.

transformation provides some variety as to how that picture is displayed. This transformation may be supported by the hardware which reads the display file and generates the image. In the following chapters we shall see how other transformations may be used in the picture-creation process.

We would like to give each segment its own image transformation attributes. Let us now consider how this might be done. As we saw in the last chapter, our image transformation can be specified by five numbers: x and y scale factors, a rotation angle, and x and y translation amounts. These are, then, five more attributes to be saved for each segment. In Chapter 4 we used global variables to hold the image transformation parameters. Now, however, we shall use arrays so that individual parameters may be stored for each of the display-file segments. We shall have an array for each type of parameter as part of the segment table. Of course, the user must be able to set the image transformation parameters. Translation may be set by the following algorithm:

5.7 Algorithm SET-IMAGE-TRANSLATION(SEGMENT-NAME, TX, TY) User routine to set the image translation for a segment

Arguments   SEGMENT-NAME the segment being transformed
               TX, TY the translation parameters
Global   TRANSLATE-X, TRANSLATE-Y segment translation parameter table
Constant   NUMBER-OF-SEGMENTS the size of the segment table
BEGIN
  IF SEGMENT-NAME < 1 OR SEGMENT-NAME > NUMBER-OF-SEGMENTS
  THEN
      RETURN ERROR 'INVALID SEGMENT NAME';
  TRANSLATE-X[SEGMENT-NAME] ← TX;
  TRANSLATE-Y[SEGMENT-NAME] ← TY;
  IF VISIBILITY[SEGMENT-NAME] THEN NEW-FRAME;
  RETURN;
END;

The above algorithm saves translation amounts for the SEGMENT-NAME segment. Notice that a new-frame action is called only if the segment which is being modified happens to be visible.

A graphics system may not have individual routines for setting image scale and rotation. This is because almost every time a scale or rotation is performed, a translation adjustment is also needed. Our system will provide a single routine which sets all of the image's transformation parameters. (See Figure 5-5.)

5.8 Algorithm SET-IMAGE-TRANSFORMATION(SEGMENT-NAME, SX, SY, A, TX, TY) User routine to set the image transformation parameters of a segment

Arguments   SEGMENT-NAME the segment being transformed
               SX, SY, A, TX, TY the new image transformation parameters
Global   VISIBILITY, SCALE-X, SCALE-Y, ANGLE, TRANSLATE-X,
               TRANSLATE-Y arrays for attribute part of the segment table
Constant   NUMBER-OF-SEGMENTS the size of the segment table

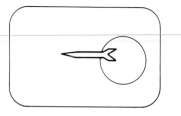

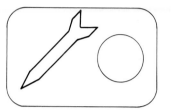

FIGURE 5-5
Changing the image transformation.

```
BEGIN
    IF SEGMENT-NAME < 1 OR SEGMENT-NAME > NUMBER-OF-SEGMENTS
    THEN
        RETURN ERROR 'INVALID SEGMENT NAME';
    SCALE-X[SEGMENT-NAME] ← SX;
    SCALE-Y[SEGMENT-NAME] ← SY;
    ANGLE[SEGMENT-NAME] ← A;
    TRANSLATE-X[SEGMENT-NAME] ← TX;
    TRANSLATE-Y[SEGMENT-NAME] ← TY;
    IF VISIBILITY[SEGMENT-NAME] THEN NEW-FRAME;
    RETURN;
END;
```

REVISING PREVIOUS TRANSFORMATION ROUTINES

We can modify the algorithms of Chapter 4 that set the image parameters to be compatible with the segmented display file by making them correspond to the unnamed segment.

5.9 Algorithm TRANSLATE(TX, TY) (Upgrade of algorithm 4.6) Setting the translation parameters for the unnamed segment

Argument TX, TY the user translation specification
Global   TRANSLATE-X, TRANSLATE-Y arrays for translation part
          of the segment table

```
BEGIN
    TRANSLATE-X[0] ← TX;
    TRANSLATE-Y[0] ← TY;
    NEW-FRAME;
    RETURN;
END;
```

5.10 Algorithm SCALE(SX, SY) (Upgrade of algorithm 4.7) Image scaling transformation
Arguments   SX, SY the scaling parameters
Global   SCALE-X, SCALE-Y the segment scaling parameter tables
BEGIN
   SCALE-X[0]← SX;
   SCALE-Y[0] ← SY;
   NEW-FRAME;
   RETURN;
END;

5.11 Algorithm ROTATE(A) (Upgrade of algorithm 4.8) Image rotation
Argument   A the angle of rotation
Global   ANGLE the segment-angle parameter table
BEGIN
   ANGLE[0]← A;
   NEW-FRAME;
   RETURN;
END;

The algorithm for building the complete transformation matrix should now specify which segment's image transformation parameters should be used.

5.12 Algorithm BUILD-TRANSFORMATION (SEGMENT-NAME) (Upgrade of algorithm 4.14) Build the image transformation matrix
Argument   SEGMENT-NAME the segment which we are transforming
Global   SCALE-X, SCALE-Y, ANGLE, TRANSLATE-X, TRANSLATE-Y
         arrays for attribute part of the segment table
         IMAGE-XFORM a 3 × 2 array containing the image transformation
         INVERSE-IMAGE-XFORM a 3 × 2 array for the inverse of the image
         transformation
BEGIN
   IF SEGMENT-NAME < 0 OR SEGMENT-NAME > NUMBER-OF-SEGMENTS
   THEN
      RETURN ERROR 'INVALID SEGMENT NAME';
   IDENTITY-MATRIX(IMAGE-XFORM);
   MULTIPLY-IN-SCALE(SCALE-X[SEGMENT-NAME],SCALE-Y[SEGMENT-
      NAME],IMAGE-XFORM);
   MULTIPLY-IN-ROTATION(ANGLE[SEGMENT-NAME], IMAGE-XFORM);
   MULTIPLY-IN-TRANSLATION(TRANSLATE-X[SEGMENT-NAME],
      TRANSLATE-Y[SEGMENT-NAME], IMAGE-XFORM);
   IDENTITY-MATRIX(INVERSE-IMAGE-XFORM);
   MULTIPLY-IN-TRANSLATION(− WIDTH-START, − HEIGHT-START,
      INVERSE-IMAGE-XFORM);
   MULTIPLY-IN-SCALE(1 / WIDTH, 1 / HEIGHT, INVERSE-IMAGE-XFORM);
   MULTIPLY-IN-TRANSLATION(− TRANSLATE-X[SEGMENT-NAME],
       − TRANSLATE-Y[SEGMENT-NAME],INVERSE-IMAGE-XFORM);
   MULTIPLY-IN-ROTATION(− ANGLE[SEGMENT-NAME],INVERSE-IMAGE-
      XFORM);

MULTIPLY-IN-SCALE(1/SCALE-X[SEGMENT-NAME],1/SCALE-Y[SEGMENT-
    NAME],INVERSE-IMAGE-XFORM);
MULTIPLY-IN-SCALE(WIDTH, HEIGHT, INVERSE-IMAGE-XFORM);
MULTIPLY-IN-TRANSLATION(WIDTH-START,HEIGHT-START,
    INVERSE-IMAGE-XFORM);
    RETURN;
END;

We shall also need an initialization routine for this chapter. At the start of processing, all segments should be empty. A call on DELETE-ALL-SEGMENTS ac-
complishes this. The unnamed segment should always be visible, and this attribute can
be initialized here. At the start of the program, no named segments should be open, so
the NOW-OPEN variable is initialized to 0.

5.13 Algorithm INITIALIZE-5
Global   VISIBILITY the segment visibility table
               NOW-OPEN the currently open segment
BEGIN
    INITIALIZE-4;
    DELETE-ALL-SEGMENTS;
    VISIBILITY[0] ← TRUE;
    NOW-OPEN ← 0;
    RETURN;
END;

SAVING AND SHOWING SEGMENTS

So far we have given a lot of algorithms for creating and storing information about segments in a segment table. We still have to attach this segment structure to the routines
for saving and for showing display-file instructions. (See Figure 5-6.)

The first routine we must alter is PUT-POINT. We must add to this routine a
statement which increments the size of the segment currently open every time a new
instruction is added to a display file.

5.14 Algorithm PUT-POINT(OP, X, Y) Extension of algorithm 2.1 to include updating
the segment table
Arguments   OP, X, Y a display-file instruction
Global   NOW-OPEN the segment currently open
            SEGMENT-SIZE the segment size array
            DF-OP, DF-X, DF-Y the three display-file arrays
            FREE the position of the next free display-file cell
BEGIN
    SEGMENT-SIZE[NOW-OPEN] ← SEGMENT-SIZE[NOW-OPEN] + 1;
    IF FREE > DFSIZE THEN RETURN ERROR 'DISPLAY FILE FULL';
    DF-OP[FREE] ← OP;
    DF-X[FREE] ← X;
    DF-Y[FREE] ← Y;

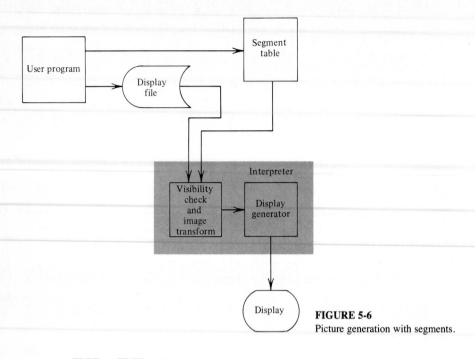

FIGURE 5-6
Picture generation with segments.

```
        FREE ← FREE + 1;
        RETURN;
END;
```

The second routine we must change is MAKE-PICTURE-CURRENT. This routine contained an instruction to display the entire display file, beginning with instruction 1 and ending with index FREE − 1. We replace this statement by a loop which steps through the segment table, examining each segment to see if its size is greater than 0 and if it is also visible. If both of these conditions are met, then its image transformation matrix is formed and the segment is interpreted. The segment table tells us where to begin and how many instructions to interpret. We pass this information to our INTERPRET routine as its arguments.(See Figure 5-7.)

5.15 Algorithm MAKE-PICTURE-CURRENT (Revision of algorithm 4.10)

Global   SEGMENT-START, SEGMENT-SIZE, VISIBILITY the segment table
            ERASE-FLAG a flag indicating that the display should be erased
Local   I a variable for stepping through the segment table
Constant   NUMBER-OF-SEGMENTS the size of the segment table
BEGIN
    IF ERASE-FLAG THEN
        BEGIN
            ERASE;
            ERASE-FLAG ← FALSE;
        END;

```
FOR I = 0 TO NUMBER-OF-SEGMENTS DO
    IF SEGMENT-SIZE[I] ≠ 0 AND VISIBILITY[I] THEN
        BEGIN
            BUILD-TRANSFORMATION(I);
            INTERPRET(SEGMENT-START[I], SEGMENT-SIZE[I]);
        END;
    DISPLAY;
    DELETE-SEGMENT(0);
    RETURN;
END;
```

OTHER DISPLAY-FILE STRUCTURES

The necessary operations on the display file are insertion, when we construct a drawing; selection, when we interpret and display; and deletion, when we are finished with a segment. There are many possible data structures which might be used. We have chosen a simple one, the array. While insertion, selection, and deletion are easy for an array, deletion may not be very efficient. If we wish to remove an instruction at the beginning of the display file, we must move all succeeding instructions. If the display file is large, this could mean a lot of processing to recover only a small amount of storage. One alternative data structure which might be used is the *linked list*. (See Figure 5-8.)

In a linked list the instructions are not stored in order; rather a new field is added to the instruction. This field, called the link or pointer, gives the location of the next instruction. We step through the instructions by following the chain of links. The instruction cells which have not yet been used are also linked to form a *list of available space*.

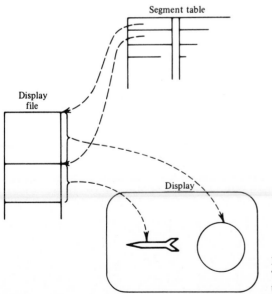

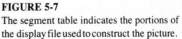

FIGURE 5-7
The segment table indicates the portions of the display file used to construct the picture.

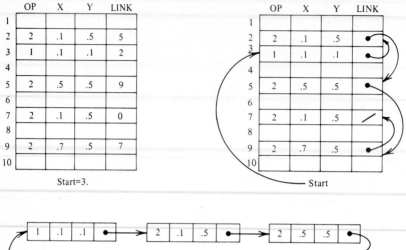

Start=3.

Start

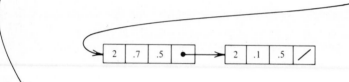

Start

FIGURE 5-8
The display file as a linked list (drawn three different ways).

When a new instruction is added to a display file, a cell is obtained from the list of available space, the correct instruction operation code and operands are stored, and the cell is linked to the display-file list. Deletion of cells from a linked list is very easy. To remove a cell, we need only change the pointer which points to that cell so that it points to the succeeding cell. (See Figure 5-9.)

We could also link the cell which we have removed to the list of available space. In the linked list scheme, deleting the cell means changing two links. This can be much more efficient than moving a number of instructions, as we did for the array. The disadvantages of the linked list scheme are that it requires more storage to hold the links and that it is costly to locate arbitrary cells.

A third scheme, which is between the array and linked list methods, is a *paging scheme*. In this method the display file is organized into a number of small arrays called pages. The pages are linked to form a linked list of pages. Each segment begins at the beginning of a page. If a segment ends at some point other than a page boundary,

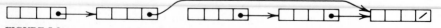

FIGURE 5-9
Deleting display-file instructions from a linked list.

then the remainder of that page is not used. In this scheme, display-file instructions can be accessed within a page just as they were accessed in an array. When the end of a page is reached, a link is followed to find the next page. (See Figure 5-10.)

By grouping the instructions into pages, we have reduced the number of links involved, yet we are still able to delete a segment by simply altering links. A list of unused or available pages provides a source of new pages when the display file is extended, and deleted pages may be returned to this list for reuse. Some disadvantages of this scheme are that storage is lost at the end of the page if a segment does not completely fill it and that accessing is a bit more complex.

In the above discussion, once a display-file segment has been closed, it can no longer be altered. There is no way to replace display-file instructions, and once closed, the segment cannot even be extended. While we have built this restriction into our system, other systems might allow such operations (although some questions may arise, for instance, whether modification commands should follow the current attributes, such as line style and character spacing, or those that were in effect in the original segment at the point of modification). When editing of the display file is allowed, a linked structure may be much more natural than our array scheme. The extension of our array scheme is considered in Programming Problem 5-12.

There are many other possible storage schemes besides the three we have mentioned. We have tried to isolate access to the display file in the routines GET-POINT and PUT-POINT, although the segment deletion routine also depends on the display-file structure. We have organized our program in this way so that different display-file data structures might be employed with a minimum of alteration to the algorithms.

SOME RASTER TECHNIQUES

In the graphics package we are developing, the only method available for altering an image is to change the display file or image transformation and reinterpret the entire picture. This method works well for storage tube and vector refresh displays, but may prove inefficient for raster displays, where clearing and recomputing the pixel values for the entire frame buffer can be costly. The principle behind fast modification of a raster display is to change as little as possible. Special techniques have been developed for raster displays which allow altering a portion of the display while leaving the re-

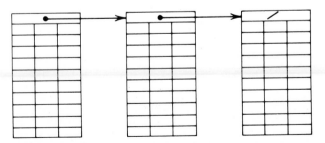

FIGURE 5-10
Linked pages of display-file instructions.

mainder of the frame buffer intact. For example, suppose we wished to make one segment invisible while maintaining the current status on all remaining segments. Instead of clearing the frame buffer and redrawing the entire picture, we might just redraw the segment which we wish to make invisible, only in this drawing use a background value for the setting of each pixel. This in effect erases all lines which were previously drawn by the segment. The segment would be removed without clearing the entire display. This technique could leave gaps in lines belonging to other segments if the segments shared pixels with the invisible segment (for example, points where a line from the invisible segment crosses a line from the visible segment). This damage could be repaired by reinterpreting the segments which are still visible. Again this can be done without first clearing the frame buffer. (See Figure 5-11.)

Another frame buffer technique can sometimes be used for efficient translation of an image. The image may be moved from one portion of the screen to a different portion of the screen by simply copying those pixels involved in the image from one position in the frame buffer to their new position. If the image is confined to a box, then only those pixels within that box need be copied. Pixels outside can be left unchanged. This could be much more efficient than setting all pixels in the frame buffer to their background value and recomputing the pixel settings for the translated image. (See Figure 5-12.)

There is an operation called a *RasterOp* or *bit block-transfer (BITBLT)* which can be quite useful in working with raster displays. The idea is to perform logic operations on bit-addressed blocks of memory. The BITBLT works on subarrays of the frame buffer. It performs simple operations on subarrays (such as turning all pixels on or off, shifting all values by a row or a column, and copying values from another subarray); and for one-bit-per-pixel frame buffers, it forms the logical AND, OR, or EXCLUSIVE-OR of pixel values in two subarrays. For example, we might use a BITBLT to copy a rectangular area of the display to some other area on the screen. Or we might use the BITBLT to clear a portion of the display. We have already introduced

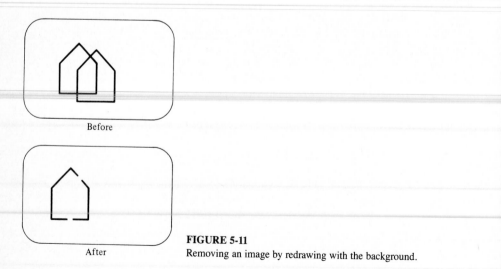

Before

After

FIGURE 5-11
Removing an image by redrawing with the background.

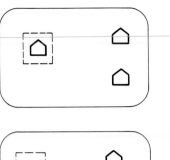

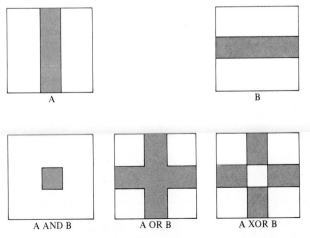

FIGURE 5-12
Alter only the pixels contained by the box.

this idea in connection with character generation. Pixel values for a character may be copied into a subarray of the frame buffer from some fixed template. BITBLT operations may be implemented in hardware so that they are very fast. (See Figure 5-13.)

AN APPLICATION

Let us suppose that a computer graphics display system is to be used to aid in the docking of a large ship. The relative position of the ship and the dock (measured by the ship's sensors) is to be presented graphically by showing an image of the ship and dock as they might be seen from above. How might such a program be written in our system? We can use our LINE and POLYGON commands to generate images for the dock and for the ship. If the instructions for these images are placed in different display-file

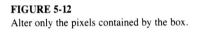

FIGURE 5-13
Logical operations on scenes.

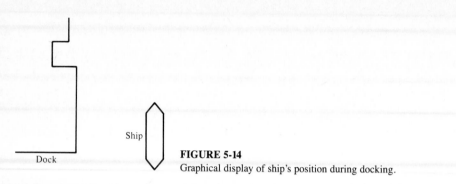

FIGURE 5-14
Graphical display of ship's position during docking.

segments, then we can use the image transformation to position each independently. (See Figure 5-14.)

```
CREATE-SEGMENT(1);
draw the ship
CLOSE-SEGMENT;
CREATE-SEGMENT(2);
draw the dock
CLOSE-SEGMENT;
```

Now we need a loop to repeatedly update the ship's position on the display. This loop will obtain the position from the ship's sensors and determine the rotation and translation parameters required. These parameters are used in the image transformation to place the ship and dock in their correct positions on the display. Of course, if the ship's position has not altered since the last check, then no updating is necessary. We can extend this program to handle docking at several ports-of-call by entering, in separate segments, the shape of the dock at each port. We then make the dock at the current port-of-call visible, while all the others are made invisible.

FURTHER READING

A segmented display file and the operations on it are described in [NEW74]. A system which builds pictures from subpictures composed of instances of segments is described in [JOS84]. An overview of several segmentation schemes is given in [FOL76]. Special hardware which supports BITBLT or RasterOp functions on 8 × 8 pixel squares is described in [SPR83]. Techniques for producing animation on different hardware architectures are described in [BAE79]. A bibliography on computer animation is given in [THA85].

[BAE79] Baecker, "Digital Video Display Systems and Dynamic Graphics," *Computer Graphics*, vol. 13, no. 2, pp. 48–56 (1979).

[FOL76] Foley, J. D., "Picture Naming and Modification: An Overview," *Computer Graphics*, vol. 10, no. 1, pp. 49–53 (1976).

[JOS84] Joshi, R. R., Arunachalam, H., "Multilevel Picture Segmentations in the Graphics System—GRASP," *Computers & Graphics*, vol. 8, no. 2, pp. 167–176 (1984).

[NEW74] Newman, W. M., and Sproull, R. F., "An Approach to Graphics System Design," *Proceedings of the IEEE*, vol. 62, no. 4, pp. 471–483 (1974).

[SPR83] Sproull, R. F., Sutherland, I. E., Thompson, A., Gupta, S., Minter, C., "The 8 by 8 Display," *ACM Transactions on Graphics*, vol. 2, no. 1, pp. 32–56 (1983).

[THA85] Thalmann, N., Thalmann, D., "An Indexed Bibliography on Computer Animation," *IEEE Computer Graphics and Applications*, vol. 5, no. 7, pp. 76–86 (1985).

EXERCISES

5-1 Suppose that the segment table contains room for only five named segments and the unnamed segment. Describe the segment table built by each of the following program fragments.

   a) INITIALIZE-5
      MOVE-ABS-2(0.5, 0.5)
      LINE-ABS-2(0.5, 1.0)
      LINE-ABS-2(0.0, 1.0)
      LINE-ABS-2(0.5, 0.5)

   b) INITIALIZE-5
      CREATE-SEGMENT(1)
      MOVE-ABS-2(0.5, 0.5)
      LINE-ABS-2(0.5, 1.0)
      LINE-ABS-2(0.0, 1.0)
      LINE-ABS-2(0.5, 0.5)
      CLOSE-SEGMENT

   c) INITIALIZE-5
      CREATE-SEGMENT(4)
      MOVE-ABS-2(0.5, 0.5)
      LINE-ABS-2(0.5, 1.0)
      LINE-ABS-2(0.0, 1.0)
      LINE-ABS-2(0.5, 0.5)
      CLOSE-SEGMENT

   d) INITIALIZE-5
      CREATE-SEGMENT(3)
      MOVE-ABS-2(0.5, 0.5)
      LINE-ABS-2(0.5, 1.0)
      CLOSE-SEGMENT
      LINE-ABS-2(0.0, 1.0)
      LINE-ABS-2(0.5, 0.5)

   e) INITIALIZE-5
      MOVE-ABS-2(0.5, 0.5)
      CREATE-SEGMENT(2)
      LINE-ABS-2(0.5, 1.0)
      LINE-ABS-2(0.0, 1.0)
      CLOSE-SEGMENT
      LINE-ABS-2(0.5, 0.5)

   f) INITIALIZE-5
      CREATE-SEGMENT(2)

        MOVE-ABS-2(0.5, 0.5)
        LINE-ABS-2(0.5, 1.0)
        CLOSE-SEGMENT
        CREATE-SEGMENT(4)
        LINE-ABS-2(0.0, 1.0)
        LINE-ABS-2(0.5, 0.5)
        CLOSE-SEGMENT
    g) INITIALIZE-5
        CREATE-SEGMENT(2)
        MOVE-ABS-2(0.5, 0.5)
        LINE-ABS-2(0.5, 1.0)
        CLOSE-SEGMENT
        CREATE-SEGMENT(4)
        LINE-ABS-2(0.0, 1.0)
        LINE-ABS-2(0.5, 0.5)
        CLOSE-SEGMENT
        DELETE-SEGMENT(4)
    h) INITIALIZE-5
        CREATE-SEGMENT(2)
        MOVE-ABS-2(0.5, 0.5)
        LINE-ABS-2(0.5, 1.0)
        CLOSE-SEGMENT
        CREATE-SEGMENT(4)
        LINE-ABS-2(0.0, 1.0)
        LINE-ABS-2(0.5, 0.5)
        CLOSE-SEGMENT
        DELETE-SEGMENT(2)
    i) INITIALIZE-5
        CREATE-SEGMENT(2)
        MOVE-ABS-2(0.5, 0.5)
        LINE-ABS-2(0.5, 1.0)
        CLOSE-SEGMENT
        RENAME-SEGMENT(2, 4)

5-2 Suggest other attributes besides visibility and the image transformation which might be associated with a display-file segment.

5-3 In our implementation, we have used one segment-table entry for each possible name, so that if we want 1000 possible names, arrays of size 1000 would be needed. Suppose, however, that we wish to allow the user to use any name between 1 and 10,000, but restrict him to using no more than 100 segments at any one time. Suggest a segment-table organization which will allow him to do this using arrays of only 100 elements.

5-4 Suggest other possible data structures which could be used for holding display-file segments. Discuss their advantages and disadvantages.

5-5 Outline PUT-POINT, GET-POINT, and DELETE-SEGMENT algorithms for a linked list display-file data structure.

5-6 Consider a graphics system which allows the user to have more than one segment open at a time. Suggest how we might implement such a system. What would be the advantages and disadvantages?

5-7 We have mentioned the binary operations of AND, OR, and EXCLUSIVE-OR as being useful in combining raster images. Generalize these operations to gray-level displays, where each pixel has a multibit intensity value.

5-8 List all of the possible logical operations which can be used to combine two binary raster images and describe their effects. (The full list contains 16 operations.)

PROGRAMMING PROBLEMS

5-1 Implement algorithms 5.1 through 5.15 to extend the system to allow segmentation of the display file.

5-2 Write the routines

INQUIRE-SEGMENT-OPEN(SEGMENT-NAME)
INQUIRE-VISIBILITY(SEGMENT-NAME, ON-OFF)
INQUIRE-IMAGE-TRANSFORMATION(SEGMENT-NAME, SX, SY, A, TX, TY)

which return to the user the name of the currently open segment, the visibility status of a segment, and the image transformation parameters for a segment.

5-3 Write a subroutine DIE(N) which displays the image of a die showing N dots (N ranges between 1 and 6). Use one segment to draw the cube

and four other segments with the dot patterns

Display N dots by setting the visibility attributes of the four dot-pattern segments. For example, if N were 5, the first three patterns should be visible and the fourth invisible, giving

which when drawn on the cube background gives

5-4 Consider the map of Programming Problem 3-7. We wish to draw this map again (unfilled this time) but with other information superimposed. We would like to show the map as follows:

    a) With the location of widget distributors

    b) With the locations of the competitive doohickey distributors

    c) With the locations of both

To do this, put the map in one display-file segment, markers for widget locations in a second segment, and different markers for doohickey locations in a third segment. Produce the appropriate maps by setting the segment's visibility attribute. The distributors should be shown at the following locations.

    Widget (0.2, 0.7), (0.3, 0.5), (0.8, 0.8), (0.6, 0.5)

    Doohickey (0.8, 0.2), (0.2, 0.3), (0.3, 0.7), (0.7, 0.7)

5-5 Write a subprogram which will draw four images to give a kaleidoscope effect. Each image will be formed by redrawing the picture with a new display image transformation. The first image will have the identity transformation, the second will be reflected in the line x = 0.5, the third will be reflected in the line y = 0.5, and the fourth will be reflected in the point (0.5, 0.5).

5-6 Consider the polygon command for drawing a square with vertices (0.0), (0.1), (1.1), (1.0), and an image transformation which will shrink the square by 0.8, rotate it by $\pi/5$, and center it at (0.5, 0.5). For each segment you have available, construct a square which is smaller and further rotated than that in the previous segment. Show all segments.

5-7 Write a subroutine PIE-CHART(FA, N, R) which takes as arguments an array FA of fractions, a number N which tells how many fractions are in this array, and a radius R. The program should draw separate pie-shaped wedges for each fraction which fit together in a circle. Construct each wedge by a call to the PIE routine of Programming Problem 4-5. Each wedge should be in its own display-file segment so that it can have its own image transformation. As an example, suppose that FA contained 0.3, 0.5, and 0.2, then PIE-CHART(FA, 3, 0.4) should look like this:

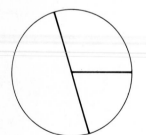

5-8 Construct a graphing program that allows the user to view several graphs either independently or overlaid.

5-9 a) Construct a face using separate segments for the head, eyes, nose, and mouth.

    b) Change the face by applying image transformations to the features.

5-10 Construct a cartoon character which can be shown in different positions on different backgrounds (using the visibility and image transformation attributes of segments). Allow the character to change by placing parts of the character in different segments.

5-11 Show an "exploded" view of the components which make up some object. Place each component in a separate segment and allow the user to enlarge it.

*5-12 There are two routines which are very useful for some applications. The first routine COPY-SEGMENT(SEGMENT-1, SEGMENT-2) makes SEGMENT-2 draw the same picture (possibly with a different image transformation) as SEGMENT-1. One way to do this is to actually copy all the instructions in SEGMENT-1 to the end of the display file and associate these duplicate instructions with SEGMENT-2. Another method requiring less storage is to give SEGMENT-2 the same display-file starting index as SEGMENT-1. In this case, the instructions are entered only once, but both segments use them. The problem with this approach is that the DELETE-SEGMENT routine becomes a little more complex. A second useful routine is EXTEND-SEGMENT(SEGMENT). This routine reopens a segment which has been closed. It does not delete any of the existing instructions in that segment, but allows new instructions to be added.

    a) Design and implement a COPY-SEGMENT routine.

    b) Design and implement an EXTEND-SEGMENT routine.

*5-13 Consider the simple animation problem of a square wheel rolling across the screen, obscuring a row of houses in the background as it rolls.

    a) Determine the timings of the basic operations on your system (arithmetic operations, procedure calls, frame buffer rendering, etc.). Using these timings, analyze the algorithms involved and estimate how many frames per second your system can produce (30 frames per second are required for smooth animation).

    b) Implement the animation problem and compare its speed with the result of your calculation.

*5-14 It is often useful to be able to save an image. A drawing could be saved and later examined. If the image is saved in the form of a display file, then when redisplayed, the visibility and image transformation attributes can be used to provide desired versions. Retrieved images can also be modified by adding or deleting segments. Extend your system to allow the saving of a display-file image. The system should be capable of reloading and displaying the stored image. The user should be able to load from a library of saved images.

CHAPTER
SIX

WINDOWING
AND
CLIPPING

INTRODUCTION

An architect may have a graphics program to draw an entire building but be interested in only the ground floor. A businessman may have a map of sales for the entire nation but be interested in only the northeast and southwest. An integrated circuit designer may have a program for displaying an entire chip but be interested in only a few registers. Often, the computer is used in design applications because it can easily and accurately create, store, and modify very complex drawings. When drawings are too complex, however, they become difficult to read. In such situations it is useful to display only those portions of the drawing that are of immediate interest. This gives the effect of looking at the image through a window. Furthermore, it is desirable to enlarge these portions to take full advantage of the available display surface. The method for selecting and enlarging portions of a drawing is called *windowing*. The technique for not showing that part of the drawing which one is not interested in is called *clipping*. (The term windowing has been used to mean several different things, all related to partitioning of the display. A single consistent definition is used within this text, but other definitions are found in the literature and may be a source of confusion.)

In this chapter we shall consider the ideas of windowing, clipping, and viewing transformation. We will add to our graphics package the routines for setting windows and viewports and for removing lines which lie outside the region we wish to display. The transformation routines of Chapter 4 will guide us in setting up a viewing transformation which will be applied to each display-file instruction as the instruction is created.

THE VIEWING TRANSFORMATION

It is often useful to think of two models of the item we are displaying. There is the object model and there is the image of the object which appears on the display. When we speak of the object, we are actually referring to a model of the object stored in the computer. The object model is said to reside in *object space*. This model represents the object using the physical units of length. In the object space, lengths of the object may be measured in any units from light-years to angstroms. The lengths of the image on the screen, however, must be measured in screen coordinates (we have normalized the screen coordinates so that they range between 0 and 1). (See Figure 6-1.)

   We must have some way of converting from the object space units of measure to those of the *image space* (screen space). This can be done by the scaling transformation of Chapter 4. By scaling, we can uniformly reduce the size of the object until its dimensions lie between 0 and 1. Very small objects can be enlarged until their overall dimension is almost 1 unit. The physical dimensions of the object are scaled until they are suitable for display. (See Figure 6-2.)

   It may be, however, that the object is too complex to show in its entirety or that we are particularly interested in just a portion of it. We would like to imagine a box about a portion of the object. We would only display what is enclosed in the box. Such a box is called a *window*. (See Figure 6-3.)

   It might also happen that we do not wish to use the entire screen for display. We would like to imagine a box on the screen and have the image confined to that box. Such a box in the screen space is called a *viewport*. (See Figure 6-4.)

   When the window is changed, we see a different part of the object shown at the same position on the display. (See Figure 6-5.) If we change the viewport, we see the same part of the object drawn at a different place on the display. (See Figure 6-6.)

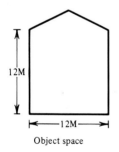

Object space

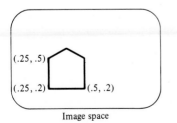

Image space

FIGURE 6-1

In the object space, position is measured in physical units, such as meters. In the image space, position is given in normalized screen coordinates.

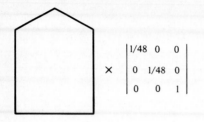

$$\times \begin{vmatrix} 1/48 & 0 & 0 \\ 0 & 1/48 & 0 \\ 0 & 0 & 1 \end{vmatrix}$$

=

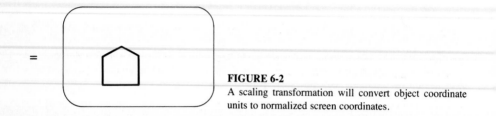

FIGURE 6-2
A scaling transformation will convert object coordinate units to normalized screen coordinates.

In specifying both window and viewport, we have enough information to determine the translation and scaling transformations necessary to map from the object space to the image space. This can be done with the following three steps. First, the object together with its window is translated until the lower-left corner of the window is at the origin. Second, the object and window are scaled until the window has the dimensions of the viewport. In effect, this converts object and window into image and

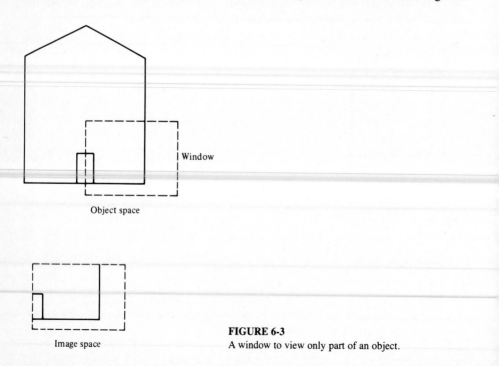

Window

Object space

Image space

FIGURE 6-3
A window to view only part of an object.

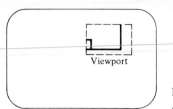

FIGURE 6-4
A viewport to define the part of the screen to be used.

viewport. The final transformation step is another translation to move the viewport to its correct position on the screen. (See Figure 6-7.)

We are really trying to do two things. We are changing the window size to become the size of the viewport (scaling) and we are positioning it at the desired location on the screen (translating). The positioning is just moving the lower-left corner of the window to the viewport's lower-left corner location, but we do this in two steps. We first move the corner to the origin and second move it to the viewport corner location. We take two steps because while it is at the origin, we can perform the necessary scaling without disturbing the corner's position.

The overall transformation which performs these three steps we shall call the *viewing transformation*. It creates a particular view of the object. (See Figure 6-8.)

Let us consider an example of a viewing transformation. If our window has left and right boundaries of 3 and 5 and lower and upper boundaries of 0 and 4, then the first translation matrix would be

$$\begin{vmatrix} 1 & 0 & 0 \\ 0 & 1 & 0 \\ -3 & 0 & 1 \end{vmatrix}$$

Suppose the viewport is the upper-right quadrant of the screen with boundaries at 0.5 and 1.0 for both x and y directions. The length of the window is $5 - 3 = 2$ in the

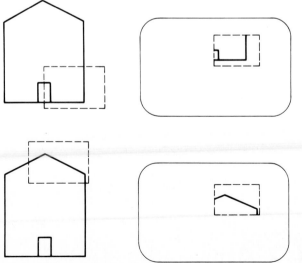

FIGURE 6-5
Different windows, same viewports.

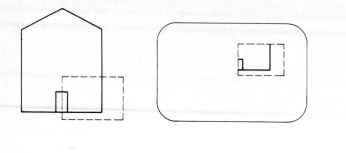

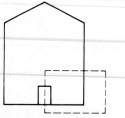

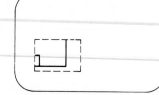

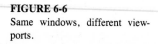

FIGURE 6-6
Same windows, different viewports.

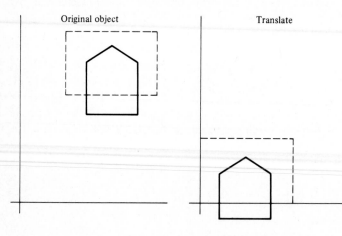

Original object

Translate

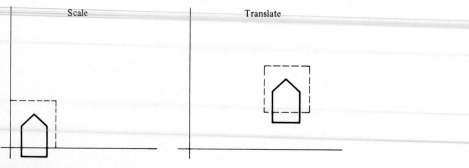

Scale

Translate

FIGURE 6-7
Steps in the viewing transformation.

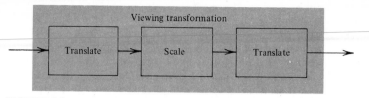

FIGURE 6-8
The viewing transformation.

x direction. The length of the viewport is $1.0 - 0.5 = 0.5$, so the x scale factor is $0.5/2 = 0.25$. In the y direction, we have the factor $0.5/4 = 0.125$, so the scaling transformation matrix will be

$$\begin{vmatrix} 0.25 & 0 & 0 \\ 0 & 0.125 & 0 \\ 0 & 0 & 1 \end{vmatrix}$$

Finally, to position the viewport requires a translation of

$$\begin{vmatrix} 1 & 0 & 0 \\ 0 & 1 & 0 \\ 0.5 & 0.5 & 1 \end{vmatrix}$$

The viewing transformation is then

$$\begin{vmatrix} 1 & 0 & 0 \\ 0 & 1 & 0 \\ -3 & 0 & 1 \end{vmatrix} \begin{vmatrix} 0.25 & 0 & 0 \\ 0 & 0.125 & 0 \\ 0 & 0 & 1 \end{vmatrix} \begin{vmatrix} 1 & 0 & 0 \\ 0 & 1 & 0 \\ 0.5 & 0.5 & 1 \end{vmatrix} = \begin{vmatrix} 0.25 & 0 & 0 \\ 0 & 0.125 & 0 \\ -0.25 & 0.5 & 1 \end{vmatrix} \quad (6.1)$$

In general, the viewing transformation is

$$\begin{vmatrix} 1 & 0 & 0 \\ 0 & 1 & 0 \\ -WXL & -WYL & 1 \end{vmatrix} \begin{vmatrix} \dfrac{(VXH-VXL)}{(WXH-WXL)} & 0 & 0 \\ 0 & \dfrac{(VYH-VYL)}{(WYH-WYL)} & 0 \\ 0 & 0 & 1 \end{vmatrix} \begin{vmatrix} 1 & 0 & 0 \\ 0 & 1 & 0 \\ VXL & VYL & 1 \end{vmatrix}$$

$$= \begin{vmatrix} \dfrac{(VXH-VXL)}{(WXH-WXL)} & 0 & 0 \\ 0 & \dfrac{(VYH-VYL)}{(WYH-WYL)} & 0 \\ VXL-WXL\dfrac{(VXH-VXL)}{(WXH-WXL)} & VYL-WYL\dfrac{(VYH-VYL)}{(WYH-WYL)} & 1 \end{vmatrix} \quad (6.2)$$

The variables have been named according to the rule that V stands for viewport and W for window, X for the position of a vertical boundary and Y for a horizontal boundary, H for the high boundary and L for the low boundary.

Note that if the height and width of the window do not have the same proportions as the height and width of the viewport, then the viewing transformation will cause some distortion of the image in order to squeeze the shape selected by the window into the shape presented by the viewport.

VIEWING TRANSFORMATION
IMPLEMENTATION

The first step of our viewing transformation is specifying the size of the window. We will confine our window to a rectangular shape parallel with the x and y axes. By doing this, we need only specify the smallest and largest possible x values and the smallest and largest possible y values. Our routine for specifying the size of the window will store these boundary values in global variables so that they will be available when it comes time to perform the transformation. Likewise, we must specify the boundaries of the viewport. The length of the viewport or window in either the x or the y dimension is determined by subtracting the lower boundary from the upper boundary. Note that we cannot have the lower boundary equal to the upper boundary for a window because this would cause us to divide by zero when we try to determine the scaling transformation. Algorithms for setting the viewport and window dimensions are given below.

> **6.1 Algorithm SET-VIEWPORT(XL, XH, YL, YH)** User routine for specifying the viewport
>
> Arguments   XL, XH the left and right viewport boundaries
> YL, YH the bottom and top viewport boundaries
> Global   VXL-HOLD, VXH-HOLD, VYL-HOLD, VYH-HOLD
> storage for the viewport boundaries
> BEGIN
>   IF XL ≥ XH OR YL ≥ YH THEN RETURN ERROR 'BAD VIEWPORT';
>   VXL-HOLD ← XL;
>   VXH-HOLD ← XH;
>   VYL-HOLD ← YL;
>   VYH-HOLD ← YH;
>   RETURN;
> END;

> **6.2 Algorithm SET-WINDOW(XL, XH, YL, YH)** User routine for specifying the window
>
> Arguments   XL, XH the left and right window boundaries
> YL, YH the bottom and top window boundaries
> Global   WXL-HOLD, WXH-HOLD, WYL-HOLD, WYH-HOLD
> storage for the window boundaries
> BEGIN
>   IF XL ≥ XH OR YL ≥ YH THEN RETURN ERROR 'BAD WINDOW';
>   WXL-HOLD ← XL;

```
        WXH-HOLD ← XH;
        WYL-HOLD ← YL;
        WYH-HOLD ← YH;
        RETURN;
END;
```

In our system we shall not change viewing parameters in the middle of a segment. Each segment is treated as a snapshot of the object. The viewing transformation describes how the camera is positioned. In this model it is reasonable to prohibit movement of the camera while taking the picture. We shall follow this rule by keeping two sets of viewing parameters, one set for the user to change and a second set to actually be used in the windowing and clipping routines. Changing the window in our system becomes a two-step process. First, the user changes his set of window and viewport boundaries. Second, the user's values are copied into the variables actually used by the windowing and clipping routines. By performing this copying as part of the segment-creation process, we ensure that changes in the viewing parameters being used cannot occur in the middle of a segment. (See Figure 6-9.)

We should note that this restriction on changing viewing parameters is just a rule for the particular viewing model we have chosen. There is no fundamental reason why a system could not be written which would allow changing the view at any point; in fact, while the CORE graphic system matches our approach, the GKS system does allow change of the viewing transformation within segments.

We shall write an algorithm for copying the user's specifications into the system's viewing parameters. This routine also calculates the window-to-viewport scale factors.

6.3 Algorithm NEW-VIEW-2 Set the clipping and viewing parameters from the current window and viewport specifications

Global   WXL-HOLD, WYL-HOLD, WXH-HOLD, WYH-HOLD
            the user's window parameters
            VXL-HOLD, VYL-HOLD, VXH-HOLD, VYH-HOLD
            the user's viewport parameters
            WXL, WYL, WXH, WYH, VXL, VYL, VXH, VYH
            the current clipping parameters
            WSX, WSY the window-to-viewport scale factors

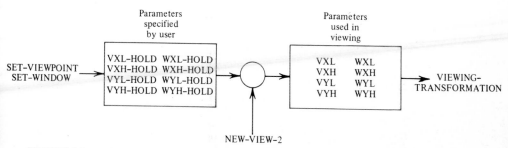

FIGURE 6-9

A NEW-VIEW action is required to make the user's specification that which is used in viewing.

```
BEGIN
    WXL ← WXL-HOLD;
    WYL ← WYL-HOLD;
    WXH ← WXH-HOLD;
    WYH ← WYH-HOLD;
    VXL ← VXL-HOLD;
    VYL ← VYL-HOLD;
    VXH ← VXH-HOLD;
    VYH ← VYH-HOLD;
    WSX ← (VXH − VXL) / (WXH − WXL);
    WSY ← (VYH − VYL) / (WYH − WYL);
    RETURN;
END;
```

We wish any given window setting to apply to an entire display-file segment. We can enforce this restriction by only allowing the above copying of parameters to occur when a segment is created. We shall therefore modify our segment-creation routine to reset the viewing transformation to match the latest user request.

6.4 Algorithm CREATE-SEGMENT(SEGMENT-NAME) (Modification of Algorithm 5.1) User routine to create a named segment

Argument   SEGMENT-NAME the segment name

Global   NOW-OPEN the segment currently open
             FREE the index of the next free display-file cell
             SEGMENT-START, SEGMENT-SIZE, VISIBILITY ANGLE, SCALE-X, SCALE-Y, TRANSLATE-X, TRANSLATE-Y the segment-table arrays

Constant   NUMBER-OF-SEGMENTS size of the segment table

```
BEGIN
    IF NOW-OPEN > 0 THEN RETURN ERROR 'SEGMENT STILL OPEN';
    IF SEGMENT-NAME < 1 OR SEGMENT-NAME > NUMBER-OF-SEGMENTS
    THEN
        RETURN ERROR 'INVALID SEGMENT NAME';
    IF SEGMENT-SIZE[SEGMENT-NAME] > 0 THEN
        RETURN ERROR 'SEGMENT ALREADY EXISTS';
    NEW-VIEW-2;
    SEGMENT-START[SEGMENT-NAME] ← FREE;
    SEGMENT-SIZE[SEGMENT-NAME] ← 0;
    VISIBILITY[SEGMENT-NAME] ← VISIBILITY[0];
    ANGLE[SEGMENT-NAME] ← ANGLE[0];
    SCALE-X[SEGMENT-NAME] ← SCALE-X[0];
    SCALE-Y[SEGMENT-NAME] ← SCALE-Y[0];
    TRANSLATE-X[SEGMENT-NAME] ← TRANSLATE-X[0];
    TRANSLATE-Y[SEGMENT-NAME] ← TRANSLATE-Y[0];
    NOW-OPEN ← SEGMENT-NAME;
    RETURN;
END;
```

We wish to perform the following transformations. First, we wish to translate by the lower x and y boundaries of the window. This moves the lower-left corner of the window to the origin. Second, we wish to scale by the size of the viewport divided by the size of the window. This changes the dimensions of the window to those of the viewport. Finally, we wish to translate by the lower x and y boundary values of the viewport. This moves the lower-left corner from the origin to the correct viewport position. We can form each of these transformation matrices as we did in Chapter 4. We can multiply the matrices together to form a single transformation (Equation 6.2) and then apply it to a general point. This yields the following viewing transformation algorithm:

6.5 Algorithm VIEWING-TRANSFORM(OP, X, Y) Viewing transformation of a point
Arguments   OP, X, Y the instruction to be transformed
Global   WXL, WYL, WSX, WSY, VXL, VYL window and viewport parameters
Local   X1, Y1 the transformed point
BEGIN
    X1 ← (X − WXL) * WSX + VXL;
    Y1 ← (Y − WYL) * WSY + VYL;
    PUT-POINT(OP, X1, Y1);
    RETURN;
END;

Note that the above algorithm not only performs the viewing transformation but also enters the resulting instruction into the display file. The display file will hold the image space model.

CLIPPING

Now that we have seen how our picture may be correctly scaled and positioned, we shall consider how to cut off the lines which are outside the window so that only the lines within the window are displayed. This process is called *clipping*. In clipping we examine each line of the display to determine whether or not it is completely inside the window, lies completely outside the window, or crosses a window boundary. If it is inside, the line is displayed; if it is outside, nothing is drawn. If it crosses the boundary, we must determine the point of intersection and draw only the portion which lies inside. (See Figure 6-10.)

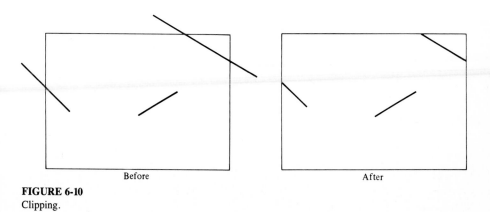

Before   After

FIGURE 6-10
Clipping.

Different graphic elements may require different clipping techniques. A character, for example, may be either entirely included or omitted depending on whether or not its center lies within the window. This technique will not work for lines, and some methods used for lines will not work for polygons.

THE COHEN-SUTHERLAND OUTCODE ALGORITHM

A popular method for clipping lines is the *Cohen-Sutherland Outcode algorithm*. The algorithm quickly removes lines which lie entirely to one side of the clipping region (both endpoints above, or below, or right, or left). The algorithm makes clever use of bit operations (outcodes) to perform this test efficiently. Segment endpoints are each given 4-bit binary codes. The high-order bit is set to 1 if the point is above the window; the next bit is set to 1 if the point is below the window; the third and fourth bits indicate right and left of the window, respectively. The lines which form the window boundary divide the plane into nine regions with the outcodes shown in Figure 6-11.

If the line is entirely within the window, then both endpoints will have outcode 0000. Segments with this property are accepted (segment ST in Figure 6-12). If the line segment lies entirely on one side of the window (say entirely above it), then both endpoints will have a 1 in the outcode bit position for that side (the first bit will be 1 for both endpoints). We can check to see if the line is entirely on one side of the window by taking the logical AND of the outcodes for the two endpoints. If the result of the AND operation is nonzero, then the line segment may be rejected. Thus one test decides if the line segment is entirely above, or entirely below, or entirely to the right, or entirely to the left of the window. For example, segments AB and CD in Figure 6-12 would be quickly removed.

The difficult cases occur when a line crosses one or more of the lines which contain the clipping boundary (such as segments EF and IJ). For these cases, the point of

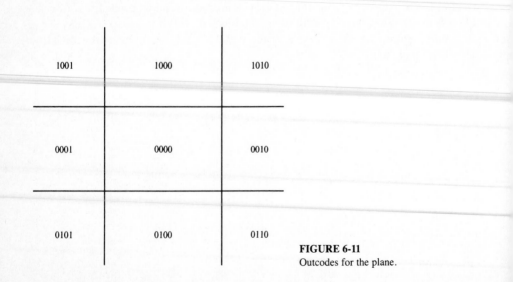

FIGURE 6-11
Outcodes for the plane.

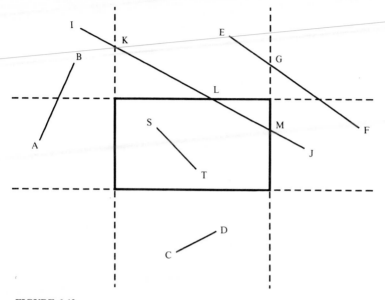

FIGURE 6-12
Testing and dividing line segments.

intersection between the line segment and clipping boundary lines may be used to break up the line segment. The resulting pieces may be tested for acceptance or rejection. Segment EF may be broken into EG and GF, where EG lies above and GF lies to the right, so both would be rejected. Segment IJ might be divided into IK and KJ. IK can be rejected because it lies to the left, but KJ must be further divided. Forming KL and LJ, we see that KL may be rejected as lying above but LJ must still be divided into LM and MJ. LM is contained and accepted, while MJ is to the right and rejected. At worst, the intersections with all four boundary lines will be calculated in order to clip the line.

The following is a brief outline of the algorithm (the details are left as an exercise): First, we compute the outcodes for the two endpoints (p_1 and p_2) of the segment. Next, we enter a loop. Within the loop we check to see if both outcodes are zero; if so, we enter the segment into the display file, exit the loop, and return. If the outcodes are not both zero, then we perform the logical AND function and check for a nonzero result. If this test is nonzero, then we reject the line, exit the loop, and return. If neither of these tests is satisfied, we must subdivide the line segment and repeat the loop. If the outcode for p_1 is zero, exchange the points p_1 and p_2 and also their outcodes. Find a nonzero bit in the outcode of p_1. If it is the high-order bit, then find the intersection of the line with the top boundary of the window. If it is the next bit position, then subdivide along the bottom boundary. The other two bits indicate that the right and left boundaries should be used. Replace the point p_1 with the intersection point and calculate its outcode. Repeat the loop.

THE SUTHERLAND-HODGMAN ALGORITHM

The Cohen-Sutherland algorithm works well for lines, but we would like a method which may be used with polygons as well. Our clipping routines will be based on a method discovered by Sutherland and Hodgman. The method unbundles the clipping test to clip against each of the four boundaries individually. The idea behind the algorithm is that we can easily clip a line segment against any one of the window boundaries. We can then perform the complete clipping by clipping against each of the four boundaries in turn.

To clip at a boundary, we step through the drawing instructions. As we consider each new endpoint, we decide whether it belongs to a line which crosses the boundary. If it does, the point of intersection is determined and is passed on to the next routine. Then each point is examined to see whether it lies within the boundary. If so, it is also passed to the next routine. In this procedure, all line-segment endpoints lying within the boundary and all points where lines intersect the boundary are passed on, while points lying outside the boundary are filtered out. (See Figure 6-13.)

We can think of the process as clipping the entire figure against each window boundary before moving on to the next boundary. (See Figure 6-14.) However, since our clipping process steps sequentially through the figure-drawing instructions, it is possible to begin clipping on a second boundary before the clipping of the entire figure against the first boundary is completed. In fact, each point may be run through all four clipping routines and entered into the display file before the next point is considered.

Algorithms for clipping a figure against each of the four window boundaries are given below. They all follow the same outline. They first check to see if the new point is the first point of a polygon, and if so, they save it. This is used in closing polygons and is discussed below. They examine the new point and last point to see whether the line segment with these endpoints crosses the boundary. The algorithms are called for each new point. We can picture this as pen movements. We start with the pen at some location (the last point, which is stored for each clipping boundary in the arrays XS and YS) and ask to move it to some new position (the new point, X and Y). The clipping routine examines this path to see if it encounters the clipping boundary. If it does,

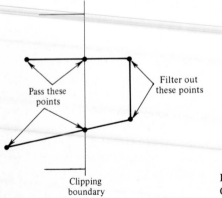

Pass these points

Filter out these points

Clipping boundary

FIGURE 6-13
Clipping against an edge.

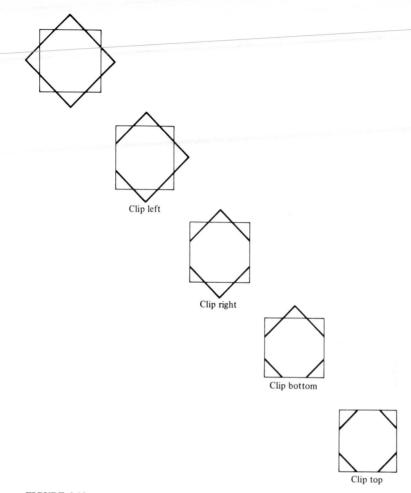

Clip left

Clip right

Clip bottom

Clip top

FIGURE 6-14
Clipping against all four window boundaries.

the pen is moved only to the boundary; a new command, corresponding to the clipped point, is entered. If the side is drawn from outside the window to inside the window or the command is for character drawing, then we introduce a MOVE command; otherwise, the command is the same as the original. This means that if our figure passes outside of the window boundary, the pen will move along the boundary to the point where the figure reenters the window region. The algorithms update the last point to be the current point and check the current point to see whether it is inside the window. If so, this instruction is also entered. When we say a command is "entered," we mean that it is passed on to the next routine. For the first three clipping algorithms, the next routine is the algorithm for clipping along the next boundary. The last clipping algorithm actually enters commands into the display file. (See Figure 6-15.)

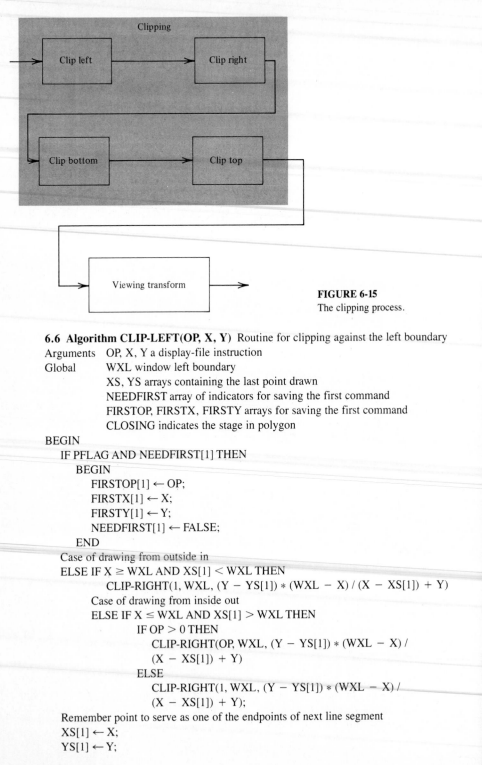

FIGURE 6-15
The clipping process.

6.6 Algorithm CLIP-LEFT(OP, X, Y) Routine for clipping against the left boundary

Arguments   OP, X, Y a display-file instruction

Global   WXL window left boundary

XS, YS arrays containing the last point drawn

NEEDFIRST array of indicators for saving the first command

FIRSTOP, FIRSTX, FIRSTY arrays for saving the first command

CLOSING indicates the stage in polygon

BEGIN

IF PFLAG AND NEEDFIRST[1] THEN

BEGIN

FIRSTOP[1] ← OP;

FIRSTX[1] ← X;

FIRSTY[1] ← Y;

NEEDFIRST[1] ← FALSE;

END

Case of drawing from outside in

ELSE IF X ≥ WXL AND XS[1] < WXL THEN

CLIP-RIGHT(1, WXL, (Y − YS[1]) ∗ (WXL − X) / (X − XS[1]) + Y)

Case of drawing from inside out

ELSE IF X ≤ WXL AND XS[1] > WXL THEN

IF OP > 0 THEN

CLIP-RIGHT(OP, WXL, (Y − YS[1]) ∗ (WXL − X) /

(X − XS[1]) + Y)

ELSE

CLIP-RIGHT(1, WXL, (Y − YS[1]) ∗ (WXL − X) /

(X − XS[1]) + Y);

Remember point to serve as one of the endpoints of next line segment

XS[1] ← X;

YS[1] ← Y;

Case of point inside
IF X ≥ WXL AND CLOSING ≠ 1 THEN CLIP-RIGHT(OP, X, Y);
RETURN;
END;

The calculation which occurs inside the calls to CLIP-RIGHT in the above routine is the determination of the y coordinate of the point where the line intersects the window boundary. The x coordinate of this point is the window boundary position.

6.7 Algorithm CLIP-RIGHT(OP, X, Y) Routine for clipping against the right boundary

Arguments OP, X, Y a display-file instruction
Global   WXH window right boundary
           XS, YS arrays containing the last point drawn
           NEEDFIRST array of indicators for saving the first command
           FIRSTOP, FIRSTX, FIRSTY arrays for saving the first command
           CLOSING indicates the stage in polygon
BEGIN
  IF PFLAG AND NEEDFIRST[2] THEN
    BEGIN
      FIRSTOP[2] ← OP;
      FIRSTX[2] ← X;
      FIRSTY[2] ← Y;
      NEEDFIRST[2] ← FALSE;
    END
  ELSE IF X ≤ WXH AND XS[2] > WXH THEN
      CLIP-BOTTOM(1, WXH, (Y − YS[2]) ∗ (WXH − X) / (X − XS[2]) + Y)
      ELSE IF X ≥ WXH AND XS[2] < WXH THEN
        IF OP > 0 THEN
          CLIP-BOTTOM(OP, WXH, (Y − YS[2]) ∗ (WXH − X) / (X − XS[2]) + Y)
        ELSE
          CLIP-BOTTOM(1, WXH, (Y − YS[2]) ∗ (WXH − X) / (X − XS[2]) + Y);
  XS[2] ← X;
  YS[2] ← Y;
  IF X ≤ WXH AND CLOSING ≠ 2 THEN CLIP-BOTTOM(OP, X, Y);
  RETURN;
END;

6.8 Algorithm CLIP-BOTTOM(OP, X, Y) Routine for clipping against the lower boundary

Arguments OP, X, Y a display-file instruction
Global   WYL window lower boundary
           XS, YS arrays containing the last point drawn
           NEEDFIRST array of indicators for saving the first command
           FIRSTOP, FIRSTX, FIRSTY arrays for saving the first command
           CLOSING indicates the stage in polygon
BEGIN
  IF PFLAG AND NEEDFIRST[3] THEN

```
BEGIN
    FIRSTOP[3] ← OP;
    FIRSTX[3] ← X;
    FIRSTY[3] ← Y;
    NEEDFIRST[3] ← FALSE;
END
ELSE IF Y ≥ WYL AND YS[3] < WYL THEN
        CLIP-TOP(1, (X − XS[3]) * (WYL − Y) / (Y − YS[3]) + X, WYL)
    ELSE IF Y ≤ WYL AND YS[3] > WYL THEN
        IF OP > 0 THEN
            CLIP-TOP(OP, (X − XS[3]) * (WYL − Y) /
            (Y − YS[3]) + X, WYL)
        ELSE
            CLIP-TOP(1, (X − XS[3]) * (WYL − Y) /
            (Y − YS[3]) + X, WYL);
    XS[3] ← X;
    YS[3] ← Y;
    IF Y ≥ WYL AND CLOSING ≠ 3 THEN CLIP-TOP(OP, X, Y);
    RETURN;
END;
```

6.9 Algorithm CLIP-TOP(OP, X, Y) Routine for clipping against the upper boundary

Arguments   OP, X, Y a display-file instruction
Global   WYH window upper boundary
             XS, YS arrays containing the last point drawn
             NEEDFIRST array of indicators for saving the first command
             FIRSTOP, FIRSTX, FIRSTY arrays for saving the first command
             CLOSING indicates the stage in polygon

```
BEGIN
    IF PFLAG AND NEEDFIRST[4] THEN
        BEGIN
            FIRSTOP[4] ← OP;
            FIRSTX[4] ← X;
            FIRSTY[4] ← Y;
            NEEDFIRST[4] ← FALSE;
        END
    ELSE IF Y ≤ WYH AND YS[4] > WYH THEN
            SAVE-CLIPPED-POINT(1, (X − XS[4]) * (WYH − Y) / (Y − YS[4]) +
            X, WYH)
        ELSE IF Y ≥ WYH AND YS[4] < WYH THEN
            IF OP > 0 THEN
                SAVE-CLIPPED-POINT(OP, (X − XS[4]) * (WYH − Y) /
                (Y − YS[4]) + X, WYH)
            ELSE
                SAVE-CLIPPED-POINT(1, (X − XS[4]) * (WYH − Y) /
                (Y − YS[4]) + X, WYH);
    XS[4] ← X;
    YS[4] ← Y;
    IF Y ≤ WYH AND CLOSING ≠ 4 THEN SAVE-CLIPPED-POINT(OP, X, Y);
    RETURN;
END;
```

The SAVE-CLIPPED-POINT routine is used to enter the commands into the display file. It will be described below.

Let's walk through an example to see how these routines operate. Consider the window and sequence of line segments shown in Figure 6-16. Suppose we start with the pen at (2, 2) and attempt to draw the lines to (4,2), (4, 4), (2, 4), and back to (2, 2). The XS and YS array values will be initialized to the current position XS[i] = 2 and YS[i] = 2. The CLIP-LEFT routine is entered with the point X = 4, Y = 2, and the work begins. The CLIP-LEFT routine will compare the segment from (2, 2) to (4, 2) against the window boundary WXL = 1. The segment will not require clipping at this boundary. XS[1] is set to 4 and YS[1] is set again at 2. This point is then passed to the CLIP-RIGHT routine. It compares the segment against the window boundary WXH = 3. The third IF statement in this algorithm discovers that clipping is required and passes the point X = 3, Y = 2 to the CLIP-BOTTOM routine. The XS[2] and YS[2] values are set to 4 and 2, respectively. The CLIP-BOTTOM and CLIP-TOP routines do not have to clip but just pass along the point and remember the (3, 2) position in their XS, YS array elements. The command to draw the line from (2, 2) to (3, 2) is entered into the display file by SAVE-CLIPPED-POINT. The next line segment is seen by CLIP-LEFT as going from (4, 2) to (4, 4). Since this does not cross the left boundary, the point (4, 4) is passed along and remembered. The CLIP-RIGHT routine will also consider the line from (4, 2) to (4, 4). Since both points are outside the right window boundary, this routine will not pass along the point to CLIP-BOTTOM. It will only remember the point (4, 4) as its current pen position. The next point is (2, 4). Again the CLIP-LEFT routine will remember the (2, 4) position in the XS[1], YS[1] array elements and pass the point to clip right. In CLIP-RIGHT the second IF statement will realize that this line crosses from outside the right boundary to inside. It will send a command to MOVE to the point (3, 4) to the CLIP-BOTTOM routine. It remembers the point (2, 4) and finally passes a LINE command to this point. The first of these two calls to CLIP-BOTTOM is for the move from (3, 2) to (3, 4). This does not cross the bottom boundary, so the routine remembers the current position (3, 4) and passes the move command to CLIP-TOP. The CLIP-TOP routine will clip this command at (3, 3) and enter this move into the display file. It will set its current position to (3, 4). Now back to the second call to CLIP-BOTTOM by CLIP-RIGHT. This is a line

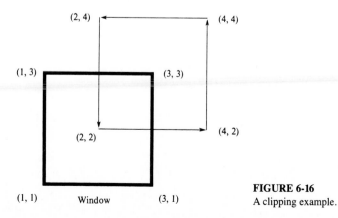

FIGURE 6-16
A clipping example.

command to the point (2, 4). CLIP-BOTTOM will remember this point and pass the command to CLIP-TOP. CLIP-TOP will also remember the point, but will not pass the command any further because the line from (3, 4) to (2, 4) is above the window. Finally, we give the point (2, 2) to the CLIP-LEFT routine. It passes the command to CLIP-RIGHT, which passes it to CLIP-BOTTOM, which passes it in turn to CLIP-TOP. The CLIP-TOP routine sees the segment from (2, 4) to (2, 2). The second IF statement in the routine forwards a command to MOVE to the point (2, 3) to the display file. The final IF statement sends the command to draw a line to the point (2, 2). The net result has been a line from (2, 2) to (3, 2), a move to (3, 3), a move to (2, 3), and a line back to (2, 2).

THE CLIPPING OF POLYGONS

We would like our clipping routine to handle polygons as well as line segments. What will happen if a polygon crosses our window boundary? Our clipping routine will remove some of the polygon's sides, and it will insert a move command instead of a line command along the window boundary. This change in the number of sides in the polygon must be reflected in our initial polygon-drawing operation code. We will consider the move command to be an invisible side since it occupies one instruction and moves the pen just as a line-drawing command. Because of the change in the number of sides, we cannot know what polygon command to enter (if any at all) until the entire polygon has been clipped. We will therefore not enter polygon instructions into the display file immediately. Instead, we shall store them in a temporary area. When all sides have been clipped, we can count how many sides remain, form an appropriate polygon command, and then enter this new command (along with the instructions that were saved for the sides) into the display file. The instructions which survive the clipping routines are therefore treated in two different ways. Instructions which do not belong to a polygon are given a viewing transformation and placed in the display file, while instructions which are part of a polygon are placed in a temporary storage buffer. This decision is made in the algorithm SAVE-CLIPPED-POINT based on a flag PFLAG which indicates polygon processing. The algorithm also keeps track of how many polygon sides have been saved. (See Figure 6-17.)

> **6.10 Algorithm SAVE-CLIPPED-POINT(OP, X, Y)** Saves clipped polygons in the T buffer and sends lines and characters to the display file
> Arguments   OP, X, Y a display-file instruction
> Global   COUNT-OUT a counter of number of sides on clipped polygon
>   PFLAG indicates if a polygon is being clipped
> BEGIN
>   IF PFLAG THEN
>   BEGIN
>   COUNT-OUT ← COUNT-OUT + 1;
>   PUT-IN-T(OP, X, Y, COUNT-OUT);
>   END
>   ELSE VIEWING-TRANSFORM(OP, X, Y);
>   RETURN;
> END;

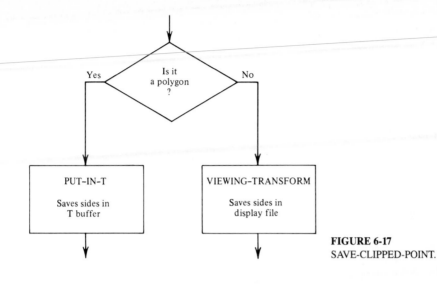

FIGURE 6-17
SAVE-CLIPPED-POINT.

We have called the arrays providing temporary storage for polygons IT, XT, and YT. They must be large enough to hold the maximum number of polygon sides. The above algorithm uses the routine PUT-IN-T to save instructions in these arrays. The algorithm for PUT-IN-T is as follows:

6.11 Algorithm PUT-IN-T(OP, X, Y, INDEX) Save an instruction in the T buffer
Arguments   OP, X, Y the instruction to be stored
             INDEX the position at which to store it
Global   IT, XT, YT arrays for temporary storage of polygon sides
BEGIN
    IT[INDEX] ← OP;
    XT[INDEX] ← X;
    YT[INDEX] ← Y;
    RETURN;
END;

For polygons, we have an overall clipping routine which counts how many sides of the original polygon have been considered. When all sides are considered, we need to make sure that the polygon is closed. The closing problem is illustrated in Figure 6-18. Clipping against the left boundary results in a starting point above the bottom boundary and an ending point which is below this boundary. Now clipping this sequence of points against the bottom boundary results in a polygon which is not closed because there is no command to move across the boundary, and intersection points are only calculated when the boundary is crossed.

To fix this problem we require each clipping stage to close its version of the polygon. (See Figure 6-19.) To do this each clipping stage stores the first instruction it receives from the polygon. This is done by the first IF statement in each of algorithms 6.6 through 6.9. The NEEDFIRST flag is used to tell if the instruction is the first.

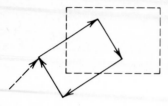

Clipping all sides . . .

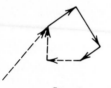

. . . gives unclosed polygon

Correct

FIGURE 6-18
Closing the polygon.

After all commands have been sent we set the CLOSING variable and output the saved instruction to each clipping stage. This causes each stage to check the edge between the last point of the polygon and the first point for intersection with the clipping boundary. If it does intersect, the intersection point is entered which completes the polygon. For this final check we want to enter the intersection point, but we do not want to enter the first point of the polygon a second time. This is what the CLOSING variable is for. It prevents the reentry of the first point when closing the polygon. After closing the polygon, the final number of sides of the clipped polygon is checked to see whether it is greater than 3. If it is less than 3, then the polygon has collapsed or has been clipped away and no entry at all should be made. If the new polygon has an acceptable number of sides, then we must update the polygon command to reflect this. We must also enter the x and y coordinates of this command so that we begin drawing the polygon at the point where drawing of the sides will terminate. All of this is done by the algorithm CLIP-POLYGON-EDGE.

6.12 Algorithm CLIP-POLYGON-EDGE(OP, X, Y) Close and enter a clipped polygon into the display file
Arguments   OP, X, Y a display-file instruction

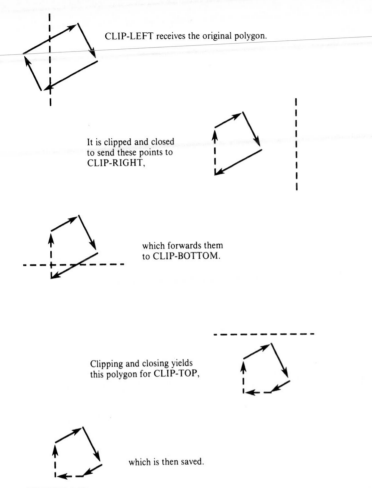

CLIP-LEFT receives the original polygon.

It is clipped and closed
to send these points to
CLIP-RIGHT,

which forwards them
to CLIP-BOTTOM.

Clipping and closing yields
this polygon for CLIP-TOP,

which is then saved.

FIGURE 6-19
Each clipping stage closes its polygon.

Global	PFLAG indicates that a polygon is being drawn
	COUNT-IN the number of sides remaining to be processed
	COUNT-OUT the number of sides to be entered in the display file
	IT, XT, YT temporary storage arrays for a polygon
	NEEDFIRST array of indicators for saving the first command
	FIRSTOP, FIRSTX, FIRSTY arrays for saving the first command
	CLOSING indicates the stage in polygon
Local	I for stepping through the polygon sides

BEGIN
    COUNT-IN ← COUNT-IN − 1;
    CLIP-LEFT(OP, X, Y);

```
    IF COUNT-IN ≠ 0 THEN RETURN;
    close the clipped polygon
    CLOSING ← 1;
    IF NOT NEEDFIRST[1] THEN CLIP-LEFT(FIRSTOP[1], FIRSTX[1], FIRSTY[1]);
    CLOSING ← 2;
    IF NOT NEEDFIRST[2] THEN CLIP-RIGHT(FIRSTOP[2], FIRSTX[2],
    FIRSTY[2]);
    CLOSING ← 3;
    IF NOT NEEDFIRST[3] THEN CLIP-BOTTOM(FIRSTOP[3], FIRSTX[3],
    FIRSTY[3]);
    CLOSING ← 4;
    IF NOT NEEDFIRST[4] THEN CLIP-TOP(FIRSTOP[4], FIRSTX[4], FIRSTY[4]);
    CLOSING ← 0;

    PFLAG ← FALSE;

    IF COUNT-OUT < 3 THEN RETURN;
    enter the polygon into the display file
    VIEWING-TRANSFORM(COUNT-OUT, XT[COUNT-OUT], YT[COUNT-OUT]);
    FOR I = 1 TO COUNT-OUT DO VIEWING-TRANSFORM(IT[I], XT[I], YT[I]);
    RETURN;
END;
```

We must catch and handle polygon commands so that when a polygon is discovered, it is entered into the temporary file. Counters are set for the number of sides to be expected and the number of sides of the result. Last-point variables for each of the clipping routines are initialized, and a flag is set so that future calls to the clipping routine will be recognized as polygon sides. This is done by the algorithm CLIP. This is the top-level clipping routine. Basically, it decides between handling polygons and handling other graphics primitives.

6.13 Algorithm CLIP(OP, X, Y) Top-level clipping routine
Arguments   OP, X, Y the instruction being clipped
Global   PFLAG indicates that a polygon is being processed
            COUNT-IN number of polygon sides still to be input
            COUNT-OUT number of clipped polygon sides stored
            XS, YS arrays for saving the last point drawn
Local   I for initializing the four clipping routines
BEGIN
    IF PFLAG THEN CLIP-POLYGON-EDGE(OP, X, Y)
    ELSE IF OP > 2 THEN
            BEGIN
                PFLAG ← TRUE;
                COUNT-IN ← OP;
                COUNT-OUT ← 0;
                FOR I = 1 TO 4 DO
                    BEGIN
                        XS[I] ← X;
```
```

```
                YS[I] ← Y;
            END;
        END
    ELSE CLIP-LEFT(OP, X, Y);
  RETURN;
END;
```

ADDING CLIPPING TO THE SYSTEM

The CLIP algorithm will clip, transform, and save drawing instructions in the display file. We have only to include it as part of the display-file instruction storage process. To do this, we modify our DISPLAY-FILE-ENTER routine. This routine will now get the current object-space pen position and place it on the display file through the clipping routine, transforming it to image space dimensions in the process. (See Figure 6-20.)

> **6.14 Algorithm DISPLAY-FILE-ENTER(OP)** (Modification of algorithm 2.23) Combine operation and position to form an instruction and save it in the display file
> Argument   OP the operation to be entered
> Global   DF-PEN-X, DF-PEN-Y the current pen position
> BEGIN
>   IF OP < 1 AND OP > − 32 THEN PUT-POINT(OP, 0, 0)
>   ELSE CLIP(OP, DF-PEN-X, DF-PEN-Y);
>   RETURN;
> END;

We would also like to have an initialization routine which sets the boundaries of the viewport and window to be the same as our normalized screen coordinates, that is, from 0 to 1 in both the x and y directions. This makes the window and viewport transformation transparent for the user who does not wish to use it.

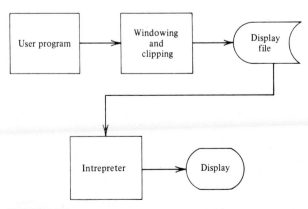

FIGURE 6-20
Adding windowing to the system.

6.15 Algorithm INITIALIZE-6

Global   PFLAG polygon processing flag
               XS, YS position of the pens confined by clipping boundaries
               NEEDFIRST array of indicators for saving the first command
               CLOSING indicates the stage in polygon
Local   I for initialization of the four clipping routines
BEGIN
  INITIALIZE-5
  SET-VIEWPORT(0.0, 1.0, 0.0, 1.0);
  SET-WINDOW(0.0, 1.0, 0.0, 1.0);
  NEW-VIEW-2;
  FOR I = 1 to 4 DO
    BEGIN
      NEEDFIRST[I] ← FALSE;
      XS[I] ← 0;
      YS[I] ← 0;
    END;
  CLOSING ← 0;
  PFLAG ← FALSE;
  RETURN;
END;

GENERALIZED CLIPPING

We have used four separate clipping routines, one for each boundary. But these routines are almost identical. They differ only in their test for determining whether a point is inside or outside the boundary. It is possible to write these routines in a more general form, so that they will be exactly identical and information about the boundary is passed to the routines through their parameters. In a recursive language this would mean that instead of having four separate routines, only one routine would be needed. This routine would be entered four times (recursively), each time with a different boundary specified by its parameters. Furthermore, the routine can be generalized to clip along any line (not just horizontal and vertical boundaries). This form of the algorithm is not limited to clipping along rectangular windows parallel to the axis. Clipping along arbitrary lines means that the window sides may be at any angle, and by recursively calling the clipping algorithm as many times as needed (not just four), the window can have more than four sides. The generalized algorithm in a recursive language can be used to clip along an arbitrary convex polygon. (See Figure 6-21.)

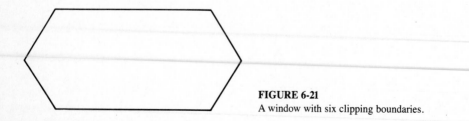

FIGURE 6-21
A window with six clipping boundaries.

POSITION RELATIVE TO
AN ARBITRARY LINE

A line divides a plane into two half planes. Let us consider briefly a half-plane test to determine on which side of a line a point lies. Suppose we have a line specified by the points (x_1, y_1) and (x_2, y_2). Recall from Chapter 1 that if a third point (x, y) is on the line, then

$$(x - x_2)(y_1 - y_2) = (y - y_2)(x_1 - x_2) \qquad (6.3)$$

If the left-hand side does not equal the right-hand side, then the point is not on the line. If the left expression is greater than the right

$$(x - x_2)(y_1 - y_2) > (y - y_2)(x_1 - x_2) \qquad (6.4)$$

then the point lies on one side; if it is less

$$(x - x_2)(y_1 - y_2) < (y - y_2)(x_1 - x_2) \qquad (6.5)$$

then the point lies on the other side. (See Figure 6-22.) The choice of which of the two sides corresponds to the "greater than" case depends upon which of the two line points is named (x_1, y_1).

As an example, consider the line containing points $(x_1, y_1) = (1, 2)$ and $(x_2, y_2) = (4, 5)$. The point $(x, y) = (3, 4)$ is on the line because

$$(3 - 4)(2 - 5) = (4 - 5)(1 - 4) \qquad (6.6)$$

The point $(2, 5)$ is in the half plane above and to the left of the line

$$(2 - 4)(2 - 5) > (5 - 5)(1 - 4) \qquad (6.7)$$

For this identification of the points (x_1, y_1) and (x_2, y_2), all points (x, y) which result in the left-hand side greater than the right-hand side are above and left of the line.

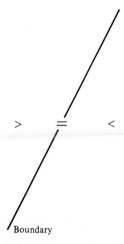

> = <

Boundary

FIGURE 6-22
Deciding on which side of a line a point lies.

The point (4, 3) is below and right. As we can easily verify, it results in the "less than" relation

$$(4 - 4)(2 - 5) < (3 - 5)(1 - 4) \tag{6.8}$$

This test may be used in a clipping algorithm to determine if a point lies inside or outside an arbitrary boundary line.

Other forms of the test are possible. We saw that another form of the line equation is $rx + sy + t = 0$ (Equation 1.6). Substituting the (x, y) coordinates of a point not on the line into the left-hand side of this expression will also give a positive number for one side of the line and a negative number for the other side. Furthermore, we found in Equation 1.30 that for proper normalization of r, s, and t, the magnitude of this expression is the distance of the point from the line.

MULTIPLE WINDOWING

Some systems allow the use of *multiple windowing*; that is, a first image is created by one or more window transformations on the object. Then, windows are applied to this first image to create a second image. Further windowing transformations may be done until the desired picture is created. Every application of a window transformation allows the user to slice up a portion of the picture and reposition it on the screen. Thus multiple windowing gives the user freedom to rearrange components of the picture. The same effect may be achieved, however, by applying a number of single-window transformations to the object. (See Figure 6-23.)

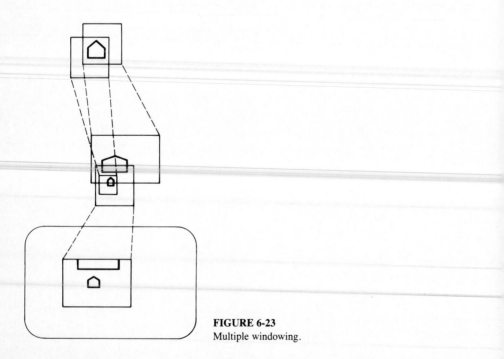

FIGURE 6-23
Multiple windowing.

AN APPLICATION

One important application of computer graphics is the design of integrated circuits. These miniature components may be produced by photographic techniques from large drawings of their circuitry. The drawings describe the areas of the conducting, semiconducting, and insulating materials. Certain patterns or geometries of these materials produce the individual diodes and transistors. A single integrated circuit may have tens of thousands of transistors. Producing a correct drawing for such a complex structure can be quite a task, and computer graphics is an invaluable aid. There is usually a great deal of regularity and repetition within the circuit structure. Our ability to reproduce a pattern by repeated calls upon a single image-generating subroutine is helpful here. Furthermore, the graphics program which draws the circuit may be part of a larger program which provides some checks of the circuit's correctness.

The full drawing of the circuit may be 1 to 2 meters square. If this is reduced to the size of the designer's terminal, the detail will be too fine and too complex to be useful (if it can be displayed at all). What is needed is a clipping window which displays only the portion of the circuit which the designer is currently working on. A call on our SET-WINDOW routine will provide this. If the designer should need to look at two separate portions of the circuit at the same time, the display surface may be separated into two viewports and the portions of the circuit selected by two windows. The designer could specify one window-viewport pair, open a display-file segment, draw the circuit (clipping away all but the portion of interest), close the segment, and then repeat the process for the second portion of the circuit to be displayed. (See Figure 6-24.)

```
SET-WINDOW(20.0, 30.0, 40.0, 50.0);
SET-VIEWPORT(0.2, 0.8, 0.6, 1.0);
CREATE-SEGMENT(1);
DRAW-CIRCUIT;
CLOSE-SEGMENT;
SET-WINDOW(20.0, 30.0, 10.0, 20.0);
SET-VIEWPORT(0.2, 0.8, 0.0, 0.4);
```

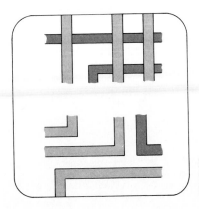

FIGURE 6-24
Use of windows and viewports to examine two portions of an integrated circuit.

CREATE-SEGMENT(2);
DRAW-CIRCUIT;
CLOSE-SEGMENT;

FURTHER READING

Some other clipping methods for lines may be found in [CYR78], [LIA83], [LIA84], and [ROG85]. The Cohen-Sutherland algorithm is also presented in [FOL82]. An implementation of the Cohen-Sutherland algorithm is given in [WHI86]. The Sutherland-Hodgman algorithm is presented in [SUT74]. The Sutherland-Hodgman algorithm requires a convex clipping region; it also results in a single polygon, even when a division into several independent polygons might seem more natural. An alternative clipping method which overcomes these problems is given by [WEI77]. It is possible to find the intersection between a line segment and a clipping boundary by repeatedly dividing the segment into halves. This is particularly useful on systems which do not support fast division. A clipping method based on this technique is given in [SPR68]. A theoretical discussion and algorithms for the general problem of deciding if a point is inside, outside, or on the boundary of a shape are presented in [LEE77] and [TIL80]. The problem of finding the intersection of two polygons is also considered in [ORO82], [YAM72], and [WEI80]. A formal description of transformations and clipping in a hierarchical picture structure is given in [MAL78].

[CYR78] Cyrus, M., Beck, J., "Generalized Two and Three-Dimensional Clipping," *Computers and Graphics*, vol. 3, no. 1, pp. 23–28 (1978).

[FOL82] Foley, J. D., Van Dam, A., *Fundamentals of Interactive Computer Graphics*, Addison-Wesley, Reading, Mass., pp. 146–149 (1982).

[LEE77] Lee, D. T., Preparata, F. P., "Location of a Point in a Planar Subdivision and Its Applications," *SIAM Journal on Computing*, vol. 6, no. 3, pp. 594–606 (1977).

[LIA83] Liang, Y., Barsky, B. A., "An Analysis and Algorithm for Polygon Clipping," *Communications of the ACM*, vol. 26, no. 11, pp. 868–877 (1983).

[LIA84] Liang, Y., Barsky, B. A., "A New Concept and Method for Line Clipping," *ACM Transactions on Graphics*, vol. 3, no. 1, pp. 1–22 (1984).

[MAL78] Mallgren, W. R., Shaw, A. C., "Graphical Transformations and Hierarchic Picture Structures," *Computer Graphics and Image Processing*, vol. 8, no. 2, pp. 237–258 (1978).

[NEW75] Newman, W. M., "Instance Rectangles and Picture Structure," *Proceedings of the Conference on Computer Graphics, Pattern Recognition, & Data Structures*, pp. 297–301, IEEE Cat. No. 75CH0981-1c (1975).

[ORO82] O'Rourke, J., Chen, C., Olson, T., Naddor, D., "A New Linear Algorithm for Intersecting Convex Polygons," *Computer Graphics and Image Processing*, vol. 19, no. 4, pp. 384–391 (1982).

[ROG85] Rogers, D. F., Rybak, L. M., "A Note on an Efficient General Line-Clipping Algorithm," *IEEE Computer Graphics and Applications*, vol. 5, no. 1, pp. 82–86 (1985).

[SPR68] Sproull, R. F., Sutherland, I. E., "A Clipping Divider," *AFIPS FJCC*, vol. 33, pp. 765–776 (1968).

[SUT74] Sutherland, I. E., Hodgman, G. W., "Reentrant Polygon Clipping," *Communications of the ACM*, vol. 17, no. 1, pp. 32–42 (1974).

[TIL80] Tilove, R. B., "Set Membership Classifications: A Unified Approach to Geometric Intersection Problems," *IEEE Transactions on Computers*, vol. C-29, no. 10, pp. 874–883 (1980).

[WEI77] Weiler, K., Atherton, P., "Hidden Surface Removal Using Polygon Area Sorting," *Computer Graphics*, vol. 11, no. 2, pp. 214–222 (1977).

[WEI80] Weiler, K., "Polygon Comparison Using a Graph Representation," *Computer Graphics*, vol. 14, no. 3, pp. 10–18 (1980).

[WHI86] White, M. A., Reppert, R. J., "Clipping and Filling Polygons," *Computer Language*, vol. 3, no. 5, pp. 45–58 (1986).

[YAM72] Yamin, M., "Derivation of All Figures Formed by the Intersection of Generalized Polygons," *Bell System Technical Journal*, vol. 51, no. 7, pp. 1595–1610 (1972).

EXERCISES

6-1 If the viewport is the entire view screen [SET-VIEWPORT (0, 1, 0, 1)], what will be the homogeneous-coordinate viewing transformation matrix for each of the following window settings?

    a) SET-WINDOW (0, 1, 0, 1)

    b) SET-WINDOW (0, 1, 0, 2)

    c) SET-WINDOW (0, 3, 0, 1)

    d) SET-WINDOW (2, 3, 0, 1)

    e) SET-WINDOW ($-$10, 10, $-$2, 2)

6-2 If the window is left at the default setting [SET-WINDOW (0, 1, 0, 1)], what will be the homogeneous transformation matrix for each of the following viewports?

    a) SET-VIEWPORT (0, 0.5, 0, 1)

    b) SET-VIEWPORT (0, 1, 0, 0.3)

    c) SET-VIEWPORT (0.5, 1, 0, 1)

    d) SET-VIEWPORT (0, 1, 0.25, 0.75)

    e) SET-VIEWPORT (0.25, 0.75, 0.5, 1.0)

6-3 For each window-viewport pair specified below, give the viewing transformation matrix as homogeneous coordinates.

    a) SET-VIEWPORT (0, 1, 0.25, 0.75)
       SET-WINDOW (0, 1, 0, 0.5)

    b) SET-VIEWPORT (0, 0.5, 0, 0.5)
       SET-WINDOW (0, 2, 0, 4)

    c) SET-VIEWPORT (0.5, 1, 0.5, 1)
       SET-WINDOW (10, 20, 0, 10)

6-4 Consider the following figure.

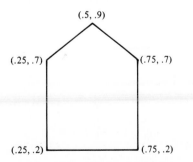

Sketch what will appear on the screen for each of the following window and viewport settings.

    a) SET-VIEWPORT (0, 1, 0, 1)
       SET-WINDOW (0, 2, 0, 2)

b) SET-VIEWPORT (0, 0.5, 0, 0.5)
    SET-WINDOW (0, 1, 0, 1)
c) SET-VIEWPORT (0, 1, 0, 1)
    SET-WINDOW (0, 0.5, 0, 0.7)
d) SET-VIEWPORT (0.5, 1, 0.5, 1)
    SET-WINDOW (0, 1, 0, 1)
e) SET-VIEWPORT (0, 1, 0, 0.5)
    SET-WINDOW (0, 1, 0.5, 1)

6-5 Think of a set of coordinate units which are convenient for some application area. Give a window and viewport specification which allows the use of these coordinates in creating an image.

6-6 Suppose that a window has its lower-left corner at $(-2, -1)$ and its upper-right corner at $(3, 2)$. For each of the following line segments, state whether it will be totally visible, totally hidden, or partially visible; and for the partially visible segments, give the coordinates at which it is clipped.

a) $(-1, 0)$ to $(1, 1)$
b) $(1, 3)$ to $(1.6, 1)$
c) $(-1.5, 0)$ to $(-5, -2)$
d) $(-3, 1)$ to $(4, 1)$
e) $(-2, 3)$ to $(1, 4)$
f) $(-1, 3)$ to $(4, 0.5)$
g) $(2, 3)$ to $(4, 1.5)$
h) $(0, 1.5)$ to $(2.5, 0)$

6-7 Show that clipping may be done in any coordinate units (e.g., the world coordinates in which the image is created, the normalized device coordinates, or the actual device coordinates). Show that clipping can also be easily done in coordinates where the clipping boundaries are rotated multiples of 90 degrees. Discuss clipping when the clipping boundaries are rotated by arbitrary angles.

6-8 What is the maximum number of additional vertices which can be created when
a) An n-sided convex polygon is clipped by a line.
b) An n-sided concave polygon is clipped by a line.
c) An n-sided convex polygon is clipped by a rectangle.
d) An n-sided concave (possibly self-overlapping) polygon is clipped by a rectangle.

6-9 Show why the Sutherland-Hodgman clipping algorithm will only work for convex clipping regions.

6-10 Devise a clipping algorithm for clipping against a line so that it returns two polygons, one for each side of the line.

PROGRAMMING PROBLEMS

6-1 Implement algorithms 6.1 through 6.15 to extend your graphics system to include windowing and clipping.

6-2   a) Construct a circle of radius 1 centered at the origin by connecting, with line segments, points on the circle (cos A , sin A) which are separated by an angle of $\pi/15$ or less.
    b) By using a window on the circle and a line segment, construct the symbol for an AND gate.

c) By using three windows on the circle construct the symbol for an OR gate.

6-3 Use windows on the map of Programming Problem 3-7 to draw maps of each of the four counties.

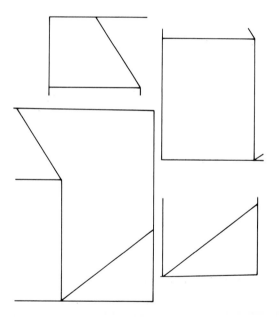

6-4 Consider the following (long) shaft.

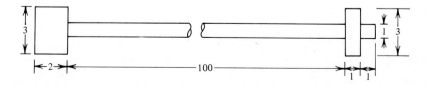

a) Try drawing the entire shaft on the full screen using a square window (bigger than 104) and a viewport.

b) Use a rectangular window which is much longer than it is high (like a box that "fits" the shaft) so that the length is compressed.

c) Use two windows and two viewports to display only the ends of the shaft.

6-5 Extend a graphing routine (such as suggested in Programming Problems 2-8 and 3-11) so that the graph is automatically scaled to be as large as possible and still fit on the display. Do this by creating the appropriate window on the graph.

6-6 Our viewing transformation includes only scales and translations, but in general any transformation could be used. In particular, a rotation can give us a viewport which can be rotated on the display. Modify the graphics system to allow the user to specify a rotated rectangular viewport.

*6-7 Implement the Cohen-Sutherland clipping algorithm and integrate it into the system for use when polygons are not filled.

*6-8 Generalize the Sutherland-Hodgman algorithm for clipping against a boundary so that it will clip against any arbitrary line. Assume that the boundary is specified by four parameters x_1, y_1, x_2, y_2 which are passed to the algorithm and that a point (x, y) is visible when

$$(x - x_2) (y_1 - y_2) > (y - y_2) (x_1 - x_2)$$

**6-9 If your programming language allows recursion, formulate the generalized clipping algorithm of Programming Problem 6-8 in such a way that clipping against all boundaries of the window may be carried out as a series of recursive calls of a single clipping routine. Such a routine would permit clipping against windows which are arbitrary convex polygons.

**6-10 Devise and implement a method for clipping against an arbitrary polygon. Include user routines for setting the clipping region as well as system routines for doing the clipping. (One way to approach this problem is to decompose the clipping polygon into convex regions and then apply the Sutherland-Hodgman method for each region.)

CHAPTER
SEVEN

INTERACTION

INTRODUCTION

Computer graphics gives us added dimensions for communication between the user and the machine. Data about size, shape, position, and orientation can be presented to the user in a natural manner. Complex organizations and relationships can be conveyed clearly to the user. But communication should be a two-way process. It is desirable to allow the user to respond to this information. The most common form of computer output is a string of characters printed on the page or on the surface of a CRT terminal. The corresponding form of input is also a stream of characters coming from a keyboard. Computer graphics extends the form of output to include two-dimensional images, lines, polygons, arcs, colors, and intensities. The graphic display can show the positions of objects and the relationships between objects. We might ask what is the appropriate form of input for a user's response to these images. First consider what sorts of responses a user might wish to make to such a display. The user may wish to select a particular object on the display. He may wish to specify a position on the display. He may wish to alter an object's orientation, size, or location. He may wish to enter a new object onto the display. We find the usual keyboard character input to be quite unnatural for these functions. The user does not wish to determine the coordinates of some point relative to some reference system and then enter them into the machine as decimal digits; he would much rather just point to the position he is interested in. It is awkward to create a drawing by typing coordinates of the endpoints of line segments or by typing instructions for moving the imaginary pen. Most users would prefer to be able to take a real pen and move it across the screen. Some effective methods have been developed for the input of graphic information. A user might move a penlike stylus and see lines appear on the display as if real pen and ink were being used. He may ''attach'' a portion of an image to the stylus and reposition it by moving the stylus. Scale and orientation might be altered by pushing levers or twisting dials. A portion of the display may be selected by just pointing at it. In this chapter we shall consider the devices which allow the user to respond to graphical information in a natural manner. We shall also consider some of the techniques which may be employed to take advantage of this interaction between man and machine.

HARDWARE

Various hardware devices have been developed to enable the user to interact in this more natural manner. These devices can be separated into two classes, *locators* and *selectors*. Locators are devices which give position information. The computer typically receives from a locator the coordinates for a point. Using a locator we can indicate a position on the screen. Selector devices are used to select a particular graphical object. A selector may pick a particular item but provide no information about where that item is located on the screen.

Let us first consider some locator devices. One example of a locator is a pair of *thumbwheels* such as are found on the Tektronix 4010 graphics terminal. These are two potentiometers mounted on the keyboard, which the user can adjust. One potentiometer is used for the x direction, the other for the y direction. Analog-to-digital converters change the potentiometer setting into a digital value which the computer can read. The potentiometer settings may be read whenever desired. The two potentiometer readings together form the coordinates of a point. To be useful, this scheme must also present the user with information as to which point the thumbwheels are specifying. Some *feedback* mechanism is needed. This may be in the form of a special *screen cursor*, that is, a special marker placed on the screen at the point which is being indicated. It might also be done by a pair of *cross hairs* which cross at the indicated point. As a thumbwheel is turned, the marker or cross hair moves across the screen to show the user which position is being read. (See Figure 7-1.)

Another locator device is a *joystick*. A joystick has two potentiometers, just as a pair of thumbwheels. However, they have been attached to a single lever. Moving the

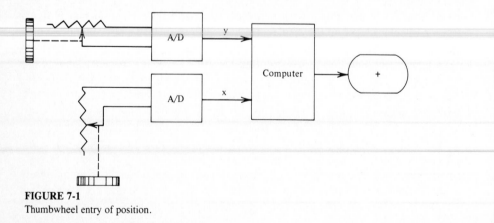

FIGURE 7-1
Thumbwheel entry of position.

lever forward or back changes the setting on one potentiometer. Moving it left or right changes the setting on the other potentiometer. Thus with a joystick both x- and y-coordinate positions can be simultaneously altered by the motion of a single lever. The potentiometer settings are processed in the same manner as they are for thumbwheels. Some joysticks may return to their zero position when released, whereas thumbwheels remain at their last position until changed. Joysticks are inexpensive and are quite common on displays where only rough positioning is needed. (See Figure 7-2.)

Some locator devices use switches attached to wheels instead of potentiometers. As the wheels are turned, the switches produce pulses which may be counted. The count indicates how much a wheel has rotated. This mechanism is often found in *mice* and *track balls*. A mouse is a palm-sized box with a ball on the bottom connected to such wheels for the x and y directions. As the mouse is pushed across a surface, the wheels are turned, providing distance and direction information. This can then be used to alter the position of a cursor on the screen. A mouse may also come with one or more buttons which may be sensed. A track ball is essentially a mouse turned upside down. The ball which turns the wheels is large and is moved directly by the operator. (See Figure 7-3.) There are also mice which use photocells rather than wheels and switches to sense position. An optical mouse is moved across a surface which contains a special grid pattern. Photocells in the bottom of the mouse sense the movement across the grid and produce pulses to report the motion.

If we had a paper drawing or a blueprint which we wished to enter into the machine, we would find that the joystick was not very useful. Although the joystick could indicate a position on the screen, it could not match the screen position to the corresponding blueprint position. For applications such as tracing we need a device called a *digitizer*, or a *tablet*. A tablet is composed of a flat surface and a penlike stylus or windowlike tablet cursor. (See Figure 7-4.) The tablet is able to sense the position of the *stylus* or *tablet cursor* on the surface. A number of different physical principles have been employed for the sensing of the stylus. Most do not require actual contact between the stylus and the tablet surface, so that a drawing or blueprint might be placed upon the surface and the stylus used to trace it. A feedback mechanism on the screen is

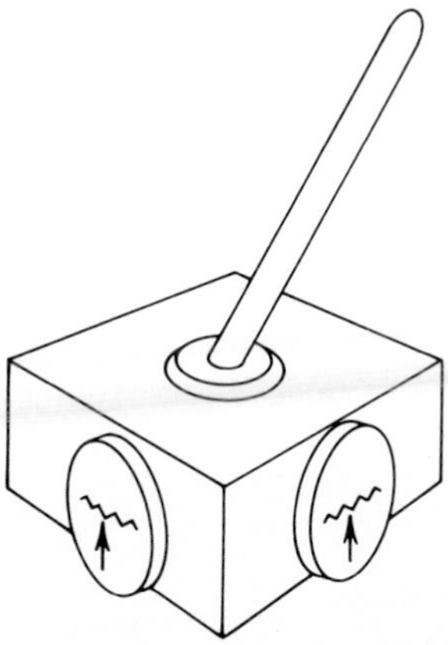

FIGURE 7-2
Joystick.

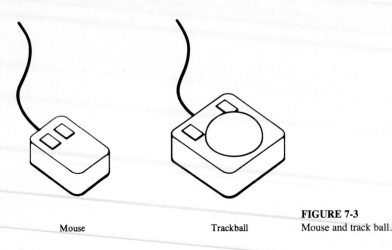

FIGURE 7-3

Mouse   Trackball   Mouse and track ball.

not as necessary for a graphics tablet as it is for a joystick because the user can look at the tablet to see what position he is indicating. Nevertheless, if tablet entries are to be coordinated with items already on the screen, then some form of feedback, such as a screen cursor, is useful.

The user may not wish to have every stylus position entered into the machine. Some of the time he may be moving the stylus about in order to position it for the next entry. It is therefore desirable to have some means of turning the tablet off and on, so that the computer can only read coordinate values when the user is ready. A convenient way of doing this is to build a switch into the tip of the stylus which turns on only when the stylus is pressed down. The user can then lift the stylus, position it, and press down to enter a point.

An example of a selector device is a *light pen*. A light pen is composed of a photocell mounted in a penlike case. (See Figure 7-5.) This pen may be pointed at the screen on a refresh display. The pen will send a pulse whenever the phosphor below it is illuminated. While the image on a refresh display may appear to be stable, it is in fact blinking on and off faster than the eye can detect. This blinking is not too fast, however, for the light pen. The light pen can easily determine the time at which the

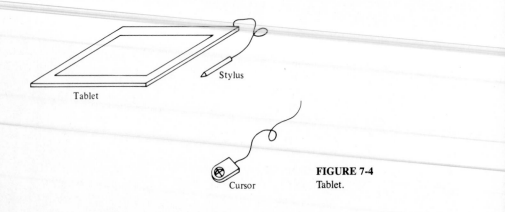

Tablet   Stylus

Cursor

FIGURE 7-4

Tablet.

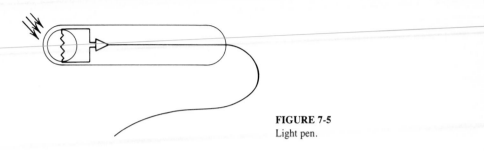

FIGURE 7-5
Light pen.

phosphor is illuminated. Since there is only one electron beam on the refresh display, only one line segment can be drawn at a time and no two segments are drawn simultaneously. When the light pen senses the phosphor beneath it being illuminated, it can interrupt the display processor's interpreting of the display file. The processor's instruction register tells which display-file instruction is currently being drawn. Once this information is extracted, the processor is allowed to continue its display. Thus the light pen tells us which display-file instruction was being executed in order to illuminate the phosphor at which it was pointing. By determining which part of the picture contained the instruction that triggered the light pen, the machine can discover which object the user is indicating. It is often possible to turn the interrupt mechanism on or off during the display process and thereby select or deselect objects on the display for sensing by the light pen.

A light pen is an example of an *event-driven* device. Unlike a locator, which can be sampled at any time, the processor must wait on the light pen until it encounters an illuminated phosphor on the screen. The computer must wait for this to happen before it can obtain the desired information. A keyboard is a more familiar example of an event-driven device. The machine must wait for a key to be pressed before it can determine what character the user wishes to send. Buttons and switches may also be available as input devices. Again, these are event-driven devices. Handling of event-driven devices can be conducted in two different ways. The first is to enter a *polling loop*, that is, a loop which checks the status of the device until an event is indicated. When an event occurs, the loop is exited with the results of the event. (See Figure 7-6.) Reading of terminal input is often handled this way in high-level languages. A disadvantage of this scheme is that the processor is essentially idle while it is waiting for an event. This would be disastrous on a device where the processor is also needed to maintain the display.

An alternative approach is to enable an *interrupt* which is sent by the device when an event occurs. An interrupt is an electrical signal which causes the processor to break the normal execution sequence and transfer control to a special interrupt-handling routine. By using the interrupt mechanism, the processor is free to carry out some other operation while it is waiting for an event to take place. When the event occurs, processing is interrupted and the device which caused it is serviced. After servicing the device, processing can continue. (See Figure 7 -7.)

The interrupt approach to event handling allows handling of events which may occur at times other than when the processor is expecting them. Suppose that one is

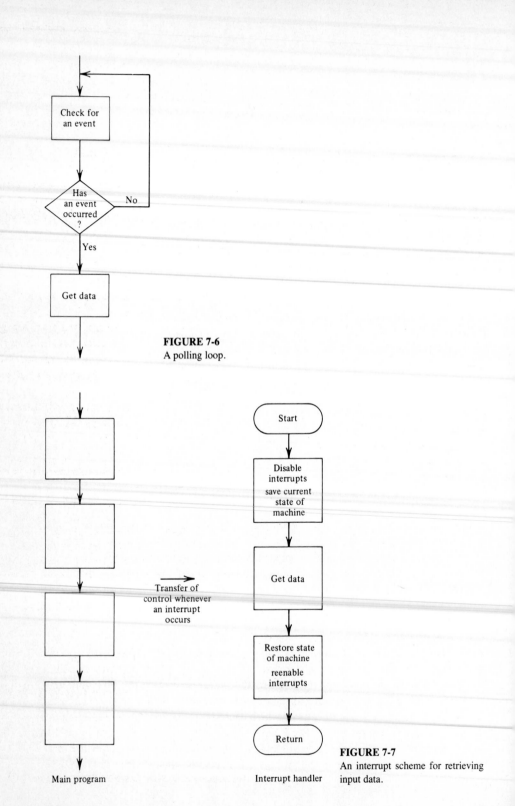

FIGURE 7-6
A polling loop.

Transfer of
control whenever
an interrupt
occurs

Start

Disable
interrupts
save current
state of
machine

Get data

Restore state
of machine
reenable
interrupts

Return

Main program

Interrupt handler

FIGURE 7-7
An interrupt scheme for retrieving
input data.

using a program which presents a display and then requests a keyboard input from the user. The familiar user might anticipate the correct keyboard input and enter it before the system has finished processing and presenting the display. If polling techniques are used, this input could be lost because the computer is not ready for it. An interrupt scheme, on the other hand, would temporarily stop processing and store the input so that it can be reexamined at the appropriate time. The processing of events is broken into two parts. When events occur, the associated information is entered onto an *event queue*. Several events could occur before the program is ready for them, but they would all be stored and would therefore be accessible. When information from an event-driven device is finally needed, the event queue is searched to see what events have transpired. If an appropriate event has occurred, the information is removed from the queue. If no event has occurred and the queue is empty, a polling loop can still be employed to repeatedly check the status of the event queue, instead of checking the status of individual devices.

We may have more than one event-driven device causing interrupts. Input data from different devices may have different sizes or forms. We may wish, therefore, not to save this information directly in a queue, but in some other location. We can use the queue entry to save a ''pointer'' which tells us where to find the information for the event. Another alternative is to have a separate specialized queue for each class of device.

Seeking the information about an event is a two-step operation. The first step is to examine the queue to determine whether the event occurred. The second step is to recover any information which may have been stored when the event transpired. Thus the first step is to await the event, whereas the second is to get the results.

INPUT DEVICE–HANDLING ALGORITHMS

Once again we are dealing with an area which depends heavily on the particular hardware devices available. The graphics standards achieve device independence by specifying what routines should be available and what they should do (but not how they do it); a user can then depend on these features being available. The system acts as an interface between a device-independent user program and the particular devices available. The ''insides'' of the interface routines will depend on the devices, but the ''outsides'' which the user sees will always look the same. This is great for the user but difficult for us, because we cannot just give an algorithm. Each particular input device will have its own version of the algorithm. This will make the routines of this chapter a bit more nebulous than previous routines. Nevertheless, we can state in general terms what we want our algorithms to do. All graphic input may be simulated using only a keyboard device if necessary.

For the keyboard simulation, the internal form of the routines is substantially altered from that of the general case. This is because of two factors. First, input from a keyboard via a high-level language appears to be a sampled, rather than event-driven, mechanism. A READ may be done at any time and will always return some value. In effect, processing is suspended until the input is obtained. So, like a sampled device, whenever a READ occurs, a value is returned. To act as an event-driven device, the READ statement would have to return whether or not some new information has been placed in an input buffer. But this is just not the case for most high-level languages. The second area of difference is the fact that we can assume that there is only one actual device and, therefore, need not worry about problems such as what to do when two events occur at the same time.

Let us consider the general forms of routines to handle input devices. We shall consider five classes of devices. The first is the *button*. The button is an event-driven device that sends an interrupt when it is pressed. It sends no information other than the fact that it has been pressed. The second class of device is the *pick*. The pick is typified by a light pen. It is an event-driven device which selects some portion of the display. The third class is the *keyboard*, and the fourth is the *locator*. A locator is a sampled device that returns the coordinates of some position. Finally, we shall include a *valuator*, which, like a locator, is a sampled device, but which returns only one value. A valuator might be a dial or knob which can be set by the user. There is nothing to prevent a system from having several buttons, light pens, keyboards, locators, or valuators. Therefore, to specify a particular piece of hardware we have to indicate not only its class but also which member of that class the device happens to be.

We assume that some mechanism is available for turning these devices logically on or off, so that routines should be provided which allow the user to *enable* or *disable* each device. When a device is disabled, its inputs, if any, are ignored. The user must, therefore, enable the device before it may be used.

Let us begin our discussion of the interactive graphics routines with the enabling and disabling of devices. Instead of enabling and disabling individual devices, we shall simplify this process to the enabling and disabling of device classes. We shall create a flag for each class. The setting of the flags will determine whether or not a particular class is enabled. We can give numerical names to the various classes to aid in their specification. (See Table 7-1.) The disable routine, then, takes as its argument a class number, performs whatever actions are needed to turn this class of device logically off, and sets the corresponding device flag to false. The enable routine similarly takes a class number, performs any necessary actions to turn the devices logically on, and sets the corresponding device flag to true.

7.1 Algorithm ENABLE-GROUP(CLASS) Routine to enable an input device class
Argument   CLASS the code for the class to be enabled
Global   BUTTON, PICK, KEYBOARD, LOCATOR, VALUATOR device flags
BEGIN
    IF CLASS = 1 THEN

TABLE 7-1
Input class numbering

Input device type	Class number
Button	1
Pick	2
Keyboard	3
Locator	4
Valuator	5

```
      BEGIN
         PERFORM ALL OPERATIONS NEEDED TO PERMIT INPUT FROM THE
            BUTTON DEVICES;
         BUTTON ← TRUE;
      END;
   IF CLASS = 2 THEN
      BEGIN
         PERFORM ALL OPERATIONS NEEDED TO PERMIT INPUT FROM THE
            PICK DEVICES;
         PICK ← TRUE;
      END;
   IF CLASS = 3 THEN
      BEGIN
         PERFORM ALL OPERATIONS NEEDED TO PERMIT INPUT FROM THE
            KEYBOARDS;
         KEYBOARD ← TRUE;
      END;
   IF CLASS = 4 THEN
      BEGIN
         PERFORM ALL OPERATIONS NEEDED TO PERMIT INPUT FROM THE
            LOCATOR DEVICES;
         LOCATOR ← TRUE;
      END;
   IF CLASS = 5 THEN
      BEGIN
         PERFORM ALL OPERATIONS NEEDED TO PERMIT INPUT FROM THE
            VALUATOR DEVICES;
         VALUATOR ← TRUE;
      END;
   RETURN;
END;
```

7.2 Algorithm DISABLE-GROUP(CLASS) Routine to disable an input device class
Argument   CLASS the code for the class to be disabled
Global   BUTTON. PICK. KEYBOARD. LOCATOR. VALUATOR device flags

```
BEGIN
   IF CLASS = 1 THEN
      BEGIN
         PERFORM ALL OPERATIONS NEEDED TO PROHIBIT INPUT FROM THE
            BUTTON DEVICES;
         BUTTON ← FALSE;
      END;
   IF CLASS = 2 THEN
      BEGIN
         PERFORM ALL OPERATIONS NEEDED TO PROHIBIT INPUT FROM THE
            PICK DEVICES;
         PICK ← FALSE;
      END;
   IF CLASS = 3 THEN
```

```
      BEGIN
          PERFORM ALL OPERATIONS NEEDED TO PROHIBIT INPUT FROM THE
              KEYBOARDS;
          KEYBOARD ← FALSE;
      END;
   IF CLASS = 4 THEN
      BEGIN
          PERFORM ALL OPERATIONS NEEDED TO PROHIBIT INPUT FROM THE
              LOCATOR DEVICES;
          LOCATOR ← FALSE;
      END;
   IF CLASS = 5 THEN
      BEGIN
          PERFORM ALL OPERATIONS NEEDED TO PROHIBIT INPUT FROM THE
              VALUATOR DEVICES;
          VALUATOR ← FALSE;
      END;
   RETURN;
END;
```

We can also provide the user with a single routine for disabling all input devices.

7.3 Algorithm DISABLE-ALL Routine to disable all input devices
Local   CLASS for stepping through the possible classes of devices
```
BEGIN
   FOR CLASS = 1 TO 5 DO DISABLE-GROUP(CLASS);
   RETURN;
END;
```

EVENT HANDLING

In theory we picture an event-driven device as one which generates an interrupt. When the processor detects the interrupt, it stops its current activity and services the device. When the device has been serviced, normal processing resumes. What is involved in servicing an interrupt? What will an algorithm to do this servicing look like? An outline for such an algorithm is given below. It assumes that there is a single event queue. In general, however, there could be many queues instead of only one. Servicing the interrupt means identifying which device caused the interrupt and obtaining the input data from that device. This information is then stored on the event queue. Strings are handled a little differently because they may require more storage. The string may be stored in a special string storage area. On the event queue, instead of trying to store the entire string in a data field, we store a pointer which tells us where the string may be found.

7.4 Algorithm EVENT This algorithm is a model for the processing of an input-device interrupt
```
BEGIN
   DISABLE THE PHYSICAL INTERRUPT;
   to prevent interruption of the interrupt processing
```

```
    SAVE PROCESSOR STATUS;
    DETERMINE WHICH DEVICE (CLASS AND NUMBER) CAUSED THE
        INTERRUPT;
    IF DEVICE IS LOGICALLY ENABLED THEN
        BEGIN
            IF EVENT FROM A STRING INPUT DEVICE THEN
                BEGIN
                    GET THE INPUT STRING;
                    ADD-STRING-Q(STRING, DATA);
                END
            ELSE GET THE DATA FROM THE DEVICE;
            ADD-EVENT-Q(CLASS, NUMBER, DATA);
        END;
    RESTORE PROCESSOR STATUS;
    REENABLE PHYSICAL INTERRUPT;
    RETURN;
END;
```

A *queue* is a first-in–first-out data structure like a ticket line. The first one in line is the first to get a ticket. As new patrons arrive, they take their place at the rear of the line. We want our algorithm to add new events to the rear of the queue. We set up arrays to hold the queue data and a pointer QREAR which tells us at which point the last entry was made. We increment this position to store the next event (if we step past the end of the array, we wrap around to the first array position). We also have a pointer to the next element to be removed from the queue, QFRONT. A special value of QFRONT = 0 means that the queue is empty, so this should be checked and set to 1 when we enter the first queue element. (See Figure 7-8.)

7.5 Algorithm ADD-EVENT-Q(CLASS, NUMBER, DATA) Adds an event to the event queue

Arguments   CLASS class of the input device
            NUMBER number of the input device
            DATA data from the input device
Global   EVENTQC, EVENTQN, EVENTQD
            arrays of size QSIZE which form the event queue
            QFRONT, QREAR pointers to front and rear of event queue
Constant   QSIZE the maximum size of the event queue
BEGIN
```
    IF QREAR = QSIZE THEN QREAR ← 1 ELSE QREAR ← QREAR + 1;
    IF QFRONT = QREAR THEN RETURN ERROR 'EVENT Q OVERFLOW';
```

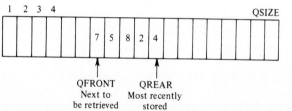

QFRONT   QREAR
Next to   Most recently
be retrieved   stored

FIGURE 7-8
An array used as a queue containing
7, 5, 8, 2, and 4.

EVENTQC[QREAR] ← CLASS;
EVENTQN[QREAR] ← NUMBER;
EVENTQD[QREAR] ← DATA;
IF QFRONT = 0 THEN QFRONT ← 1;
RETURN;
END;

The string queue is handled in a simpler fashion. Each new string is added to an array of strings. When the end of the array is reached, we wrap around to the beginning.

7.6 Algorithm ADD-STRING-Q(STRING, DATA) Saves STRING and returns a pointer to it in DATA
Arguments   STRING a string to be saved in the string array
            DATA for return of the index of the stored string
Global   STRINGQ an array of strings
            SQREAR next free string storage area
Constant   SQSIZE the size of the string queue array
BEGIN
    IF SQREAR = SQSIZE THEN SQREAR ← 1 ELSE SQREAR ← SQREAR + 1;
    STRINGQ[SQREAR] ← STRING;
    DATA ← SQREAR;
    RETURN;
END;

The user must be able to determine if an event has taken place. We must therefore have an "await-event" routine. This routine checks the event queue and returns information about which device has caused an event. If no event has taken place and the queue is empty, the routine may poll the queue for a specified period of time. If at the end of this time the queue is still empty, a failure indicator may be returned.

Now let us consider the routine for checking the event queue. In the interrupt case, this routine polls the queue until the event has occurred or time runs out. It then obtains from the queue the class and number of the device which caused the event. However, if the input device does not generate interrupts, then the event process should be simulated through polling the device directly. There are two ways that the polling may be done. It may be built into the programming language and/or operating system we are using. Input will then act as if from a sampled device; an example is a high-level language READ statement. Polling may also be done in a loop which we have written ourselves. We call this a polled device. In general, our AWAIT-EVENT routine may involve a combination of these techniques. For example, picks may be done through true interrupts, but buttons might be detected with a "homemade" polling loop, and keyboard input might be obtained by a simple READ statement. In the upcoming algorithm we give examples of all three methods. The actual implementation should include only those portions appropriate to the available hardware.

7.7 Algorithm AWAIT-EVENT(WAIT, CLASS, DEVICE) Routine to check the event queue
Arguments   WAIT the time to wait for an event to occur

CLASS, DEVICE to return the type of event which occurred
Global   BUTTON, PICK, KEYBOARD device enabled flags
INPUT-STRING, PICKED-SEGMENT storage for keyboard and pick input
DETECTABLE segment detectability attribute array
BUTTON-POLL, PICK-POLL, KEYBOARD-POLL flag indicating
the status of polled devices
Local   TIME-LIMIT the time at which to stop waiting
DATA for receiving data from the event queue

```
BEGIN
    if buttons are simulated by a sampled device, then include the following conditional
    statement
    IF BUTTON THEN
        BEGIN
            READ DEVICE;
            CLASS ← 1;
            RETURN;
        END;
    if picks are simulated by a sampled device, then include the following conditional
    statement
    IF PICK THEN
        BEGIN
            PICKED-SEGMENT ← 0;
            WHILE PICKED-SEGMENT < 1 OR PICKED-SEGMENT > NUMBER-OF-
                SEGMENTS OR NOT DETECTABLE(PICKED-SEGMENT) DO
                READ PICKED-SEGMENT;
            CLASS ← 2;
            DEVICE ← 1;
            RETURN;
        END;
    if the keyboard is simulated by a sampled device, then include the following condi-
    tional statement
    IF KEYBOARD THEN
        BEGIN
            READ INPUT-STRING;
            CLASS ← 3;
            DEVICE ← 1;
            RETURN;
        END;
    if interrupt-generating or polled devices are available, then include the following loop
    TIME-LIMIT ← TIME( ) + WAIT;
    WHILE TIME( ) ≤ TIME-LIMIT DO
        BEGIN
            if interrupt-generating devices are adding to the event queue, then check the
            queue with the following statements
            BEGIN
                GETQ(CLASS, DEVICE, DATA);
                IF CLASS ≠ 0 THEN
                    IF CLASS = 2 THEN PICKED-SEGMENT←DATA
                    ELSE IF CLASS = 3 THEN INPUT-STRING ← STRINGQ[DATA];
                RETURN;
```

```
        END;
if buttons are simulated on a polled device, then include the following condi-
tional statement
IF BUTTON AND BUTTON-POLL THEN
    BEGIN
        CLASS ← 1;
        READ-BUTTON(DEVICE);
        RETURN;
    END;
if a pick is simulated on a polled device, then include the following conditional
statement
IF PICK AND PICK-POLL THEN
    BEGIN
        READ-PICK(DEVICE,PICKED-SEGMENT);
        IF DETECTABLE[PICKED-SEGMENT] THEN
            BEGIN
                CLASS ← 2;
                RETURN;
            END;
    END;
if the keyboard is treated as a polled device, then include the following condi-
tional statement
IF KEYBOARD AND KEYBOARD-POLL THEN
    BEGIN
        CLASS ← 3;
        READ-KEYBOARD(DEVICE, INPUT-STRING);
        RETURN;
    END;
    END;
  CLASS ← 0;
  DEVICE ← 0;
  RETURN;
END;
```

If interrupts and a true event queue are used, then we must have a routine to get
the foremost item in queue. The algorithm uses the pointer QFRONT to indicate the
position of the leading element. If QFRONT is zero, the queue is empty; if not, the
value of the leading item is returned and the QFRONT pointer is advanced to the next
entry.

7.8 Algorithm GETQ(CLASS, DEVICE, DATA) Returns the event at the front of the
event queue
If the queue is empty, zero is returned
Arguments   CLASS class of the event
            DEVICE device of the event
            DATA input data from the event
Global   EVENTQC, EVENTQN, EVENTQD the event queue arrays
            QFRONT, QREAR pointers to front and rear of event queue

Constant   QSIZE the size of the event queue
BEGIN
   CLASS ← 0;
  IF QFRONT = 0 THEN RETURN;
  CLASS ← EVENTQC[QFRONT];
  DEVICE ← EVENTQN[QFRONT];
  DATA ← EVENTQD[QFRONT];
  IF QFRONT = QREAR THEN
    BEGIN
      QFRONT ← 0;
      QREAR ← 0;
    END
  ELSE IF QFRONT = QSIZE THEN QFRONT ← 1
    ELSE QFRONT ← QFRONT + 1;
  RETURN;
END;

The event queue allows several events to occur before the information is used. The queue provides storage for the event information until it is needed. But we may sometimes want to start fresh, ignoring old events which have not been processed. We can design a routine which will clear the event queue, discarding the unwanted events.

7.9 Algorithm FLUSH-ALL-EVENTS Removes all events from event queue
Global   QFRONT, QREAR event queue front and rear pointers
            SQREAR string file pointer
BEGIN
  QFRONT ← 0;
  QREAR ← 0;
  SQREAR ← 1;
  RETURN;
END;

The AWAIT-EVENT routine simulates the occurrence of some event. For keyboard or pick events, we still must retrieve the information saved when the event occurred. We must therefore provide the user with a GET-KEYBOARD-DATA routine. This routine returns the string which was input, along with its length. A GET-PICK-DATA routine returns the name of the segment which the user selected.

7.10 Algorithm GET-KEYBOARD-DATA(STRING, LEN) Routine to return the stored keyboard input
Arguments   STRING for the return of the string
            LEN the string's length
Global   INPUT-STRING keyboard input storage
BEGIN
  LEN ← LENGTH(INPUT-STRING);
  STRING ← INPUT-STRING;
  RETURN;
END;

7.11 Algorithm GET-PICK-DATA(SEGMENT-NAME) Routine to return the selected pick value

Argument   SEGMENT-NAME the name of the selected segment
Global   PICKED-SEGMENT pick input storage
BEGIN
     SEGMENT-NAME ← PICKED-SEGMENT;
     RETURN;
END;

The AWAIT-EVENT routine allows several input devices to be in use at the same time. Many applications, however, require input from only one device at a time, and furthermore, some time-sharing systems prohibit the simultaneous use of several devices. For these situations, the generality of the event queue becomes a needless overhead. To avoid this, we can provide routines which await input from only a single class of device, either button, pick, or keyboard. Once again, the routines will be device- and system-dependent, but outlines for possible implementations for button and pick routines are given below.

7.12 Algorithm AWAIT-BUTTON(WAIT, BUTTON-NUM) User routine to await the pressing of a button

Arguments   WAIT the time to wait for a button event
               BUTTON-NUM for return of the number of the button device
Global   BUTTON device enabled flag
               BUTTON-POLL status flag if button is a polled device
Local   TIME-LIMIT the time at which to stop waiting
               DUMMY a dummy argument
BEGIN
     IF NOT BUTTON THEN RETURN ERROR 'BUTTON NOT ENABLED';
     if buttons are simulated by a sampled device, then include the following statement
     READ BUTTON-NUM;
     if interrupt-generating or polled devices are used, then include the following loop
     TIME-LIMIT ← TIME( ) + WAIT;
     WHILE TIME( ) ≤ TIME-LIMIT DO
        BEGIN
            if interrupt-generating buttons are used, they may be found by
               BEGIN
                   GETQ(CLASS, BUTTON-NUM, DUMMY);
                   IF CLASS = 1 THEN RETURN;
               END;
            if buttons are simulated on a polled device, then include the following conditional statement
            IF BUTTON-POLL THEN
               BEGIN
                   READ-BUTTON(BUTTON-NUM);
                   RETURN;
               END;
        END;
     BUTTON-NUM ← 0;

RETURN;
END;

7.13 Algorithm AWAIT-PICK(WAIT, PICK-NUM) User routine to await a pick
Arguments   WAIT the time to wait for a pick event
                     PICK-NUM for return of the number of the picked segment
Global   PICK device enabled flag
                     PICK-POLL status flag if pick is a polled device
Local   TIME-LIMIT the time at which to stop waiting
BEGIN
    IF NOT PICK THEN RETURN ERROR 'PICK NOT ENABLED';
    if picks are simulated by a sampled device, then include the following statement
    READ PICK-NUM;
    if interrupt-generating or polled devices are used, then include the following loop
    TIME-LIMIT ← TIME( ) + WAIT;
    WHILE TIME( ) ≤ TIME-LIMIT DO
        BEGIN
            if interrupt-generating picks are used, they may be found by
                BEGIN
                    GETQ(CLASS, DUMMY, PICK-NUM);
                    IF CLASS = 2 THEN RETURN;
                END;
            if picks are simulated on a polled device, then include the following conditional
            statement
            IF PICK-POLL THEN
                BEGIN
                    READ-PICK(PICK-NUM);
                    RETURN;
                END;
        END;
    PICK-NUM ← 0;
    RETURN;
END;

SAMPLED DEVICES

The locator is a sampled device and, therefore, may be read at any time; there is no
need to wait for an event to be placed on the event queue. We need only a routine
which reads the locator and returns its x, y values.

Since locators are sampled devices, our simulation of a locator need not involve
the AWAIT-EVENT routine. For an actual locator device, the current coordinate values
are read from the device and returned. In a keyboard simulation, coordinate values will
be read from the keyboard and returned.

7.14 Algorithm READ-LOCATOR(X, Y)
Global   LOCATOR the locator enabled flag
BEGIN
    IF NOT LOCATOR THEN RETURN ERROR 'LOCATOR NOT ENABLED';

OBTAIN (X, Y) FROM LOCATOR DEVICE OR ITS SIMULATION;
CONVERT TO NORMALIZED DEVICE COORDINATES IF NECESSARY;
RETURN;
END;

Valuators are treated in essentially the same way as locators—one variable is returned instead of a coordinate pair.

7.15 Algorithm READ-VALUATOR(V)
Global   VALUATOR the valuator enabled flag
BEGIN
    IF NOT VALUATOR THEN RETURN ERROR 'VALUATOR NOT ENABLED';
    OBTAIN V FROM VALUATOR DEVICE OR ITS SIMULATION;
    RETURN;
END;

THE DETECTABILITY ATTRIBUTE

A useful feature for pick devices is the ability to set the *detectability* of portions of the display. We may wish to be able to pick an item from a subset of the items actually appearing on display. We want all other items of the display to be ignored by the pick device. This can be done by disabling the interrupt mechanism when portions of the display which we wish to ignore are being drawn. The interrupt mechanism is reenabled when detectable items are being drawn. We would therefore like to present the user with some routine for setting the detectability of portions of his display. We can give segments a detectability attribute so that a segment may or may not be detectable by a pick device. We do this by giving each segment a detectability flag. We provide the user with a routine to set this flag to on or off (the default value would be off). The detectability flag may be checked by the display-generating routines in a vector refresh device to disable or enable light-pen interrupts. For other simulations the flag can still be used to determine whether a segment is a candidate for a pick. An example is the above AWAIT-EVENT routine for sampled pick simulations. In the case where a pick for a particular segment is simulated by a keyboard, the detectability flag for that segment is checked by the AWAIT-EVENT routine. If the segment turns out not to be detectable, then another input is requested. If the segment is detectable, then its name is saved and AWAIT-EVENT returns, indicating that a valid pick has occurred.

If actual interrupts are used for picks, then the MAKE-PICTURE-CURRENT or INTERPRET routine should be extended to include enabling and disabling of interrupts according to the detectability flag for the segment being interpreted.

The following algorithm allows the user to set the detectability attribute.

7.16 Algorithm SET-DETECTABILITY(SEGMENT-NAME, ON-OFF) User routine to set the detectability attribute
Arguments   SEGMENT-NAME the display-file segment being set
                    ON-OFF the detectability setting
Global   DETECTABLE the detectability attribute array
Constant   NUMBER-OF-SEGMENTS the size of the DETECTABLE array

```
BEGIN
    IF SEGMENT-NAME < 1 OR SEGMENT-NAME > NUMBER-OF-SEGMENTS
    THEN
        RETURN ERROR 'INVALID SEGMENT';
    DETECTABLE[SEGMENT-NAME] ← ON-OFF;
    RETURN;
END;
```

We have added a new segment attribute. This means that our routines which manage the segment table must be extended to include this new property. There are two routines which must be changed: the CREATE-SEGMENT routine, which initializes all attributes, and the RENAME-SEGMENT routine, which copies all attributes to a new position in the table. The modified versions of these routines are given below.

7.17 Algorithm CREATE-SEGMENT(SEGMENT-NAME) (Modification of algorithm 6.4) User routine to create a named segment

Argument   SEGMENT-NAME the segment name
Global   NOW-OPEN the segment currently open
            FREE the index of the next free display-file cell
            SEGMENT-START, SEGMENT-SIZE, VISIBILITY
            ANGLE, SCALE-X, SCALE-Y, TRANSLATE-X, TRANSLATE-Y
            DETECTABLE the segment-table arrays
Constant   NUMBER-OF-SEGMENTS size of the segment table

```
BEGIN
    IF NOW-OPEN > 0 THEN RETURN ERROR 'SEGMENT STILL OPEN';
    IF SEGMENT-NAME < 1 OR SEGMENT-NAME > NUMBER-OF-SEGMENTS
    THEN
        RETURN ERROR 'INVALID SEGMENT NAME';
    IF SEGMENT-SIZE[SEGMENT-NAME] > 0 THEN
        RETURN ERROR 'SEGMENT ALREADY EXISTS';
    NEW-VIEW-2
    SEGMENT-START[SEGMENT-NAME] ← FREE;
    SEGMENT-SIZE[SEGMENT-NAME] ← 0;
    VISIBILITY[SEGMENT-NAME] ← VISIBILITY[0];
    ANGLE[SEGMENT-NAME] ← ANGLE[0];
    SCALE-X[SEGMENT-NAME] ← SCALE-X[0];
    SCALE-Y[SEGMENT-NAME] ← SCALE-Y[0];
    TRANSLATE-X[SEGMENT-NAME] ← TRANSLATE-X[0];
    TRANSLATE-Y[SEGMENT-NAME] ← TRANSLATE-Y[0];
    DETECTABLE[SEGMENT-NAME] ← DETECTABLE[0];
    NOW-OPEN ← SEGMENT-NAME;
    RETURN;
END;
```

7.18 Algorithm RENAME-SEGMENT(SEGMENT-NAME-OLD, SEGMENT-NAME-NEW) (Modification of algorithm 5.5) User routine to rename SEGMENT-NAME-OLD to be SEGMENT-NAME-NEW

Arguments   SEGMENT-NAME-OLD old name of segment
            SEGMENT-NAME-NEW new name of segment

Global SEGMENT-START, SEGMENT-SIZE, VISIBILITY
     ANGLE, SCALE-X, SCALE-Y, TRANSLATE-X, TRANSLATE-Y
     <u>DETECTABLE</u> the segment-table arrays
     NOW-OPEN the segment currently open
Constant NUMBER-OF-SEGMENTS the size of the segment table
BEGIN
 IF SEGMENT-NAME-OLD < 1 OR SEGMENT-NAME-NEW < 1
  OR SEGMENT-NAME-OLD > NUMBER-OF-SEGMENTS
  OR SEGMENT-NAME-NEW > NUMBER-OF-SEGMENTS THEN
  RETURN ERROR 'INVALID SEGMENT NAME';
 IF SEGMENT-NAME-OLD = NOW-OPEN OR
  SEGMENT-NAME-NEW = NOW-OPEN THEN
  RETURN ERROR 'SEGMENT STILL OPEN';
 IF SEGMENT-SIZE[SEGMENT-NAME-NEW] $\neq$ 0 THEN
  RETURN ERROR 'SEGMENT ALREADY EXISTS';
copy the old segment-table entry into the new position
SEGMENT-START[SEGMENT-NAME-NEW]
 ← SEGMENT-START[SEGMENT-NAME-OLD];
SEGMENT-SIZE[SEGMENT-NAME-NEW]
 ← SEGMENT-SIZE[SEGMENT-NAME-OLD];
VISIBILITY[SEGMENT-NAME-NEW] ← VISIBILITY[SEGMENT-NAME-OLD];
ANGLE[SEGMENT-NAME-NEW] ← ANGLE[SEGMENT-NAME-OLD];
SCALE-X[SEGMENT-NAME-NEW] ← SCALE-X[SEGMENT-NAME-OLD];
SCALE-Y[SEGMENT-NAME-NEW] ← SCALE-Y[SEGMENT-NAME-OLD];
TRANSLATE-X[SEGMENT-NAME-NEW]
 ← TRANSLATE-X[SEGMENT-NAME-OLD];
TRANSLATE-Y[SEGMENT-NAME-NEW]
 ← TRANSLATE-Y[SEGMENT-NAME-OLD];
DETECTABLE[SEGMENT-NAME-NEW]
 ← DETECTABLE[SEGMENT-NAME-OLD];
delete the old segment
SEGMENT-SIZE[SEGMENT-NAME-OLD] ← 0;
 RETURN;
END;

As in previous chapters, we shall provide the user with an initialization routine. This routine sets the default values so that no device is enabled, no events are in the event queue, and no segments are detectable.

7.19 Algorithm INITIALIZE-7 Initialization
Global DETECTABLE the detectability attribute array
BEGIN
 INITIALIZE-6;
 DISABLE-ALL;
 FLUSH-EVENT-Q;
 DETECTABLE[0] ← FALSE;
 RETURN;
END;

SIMULATING A LOCATOR WITH A PICK

While the light pen can be used to select an object on the screen, it does not give that object's position. Nor can it be used to indicate a position where there is no object, as can be done with a joystick or tablet. In order to use a light pen for position information, a *tracking cross* is employed. A tracking cross is a small cross made of four or more separate line segments. This is placed at some known position on the screen and selected so that it is detectable by the light pen. (See Figure 7-9.)

The pen is positioned at the center of the cross. Then as the pen is moved, it will encounter one of the cross arms. If the pen is moved slightly to the right, it will encounter the right arm of the cross. This information is used to move the cross slightly to the right. After each refresh the cross will be moved until the light pen is once again centered. (See Figure 7-10.)

A similar action is taken for all of the other arms of the cross so that the tracking cross will follow the movements of the light pen. Since the position of the center of the tracking cross is known, positional information can be entered by "grabbing" the cross with the light pen and moving it to the desired location.

SIMULATING A PICK WITH A LOCATOR

Suppose we have a locator, but no pick device. How can we use the locator to get the effect of a pick? We know that the user is interested in the part of the picture located at position (x, y), but do not know which segment is being drawn there. To find out, we shall step through the display-file instructions segment by segment as if we were drawing the image. But instead of generating line and character images, we will ask how close the lines and characters are to the locator position. If a line or a character is sufficiently close, we will assume that it is the item at which the user is pointing. We will note what segment we are considering and return it as the value of the pick selection.

How can we determine the distance between a point (x, y) and a character? We simplify the problem by treating the character as if it were a point (x_c, y_c). Then we can use the distance formula to give

$$D = [(x - xc)^2 + (y - yc)^2]^{1/2} \tag{7.1}$$

If this distance is close enough

$$D < APERTURE \tag{7.2}$$

then we have found the segment. (See Figure 7-11.)

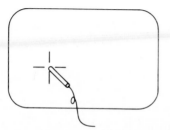

FIGURE 7-9
Light pen and tracking cross.

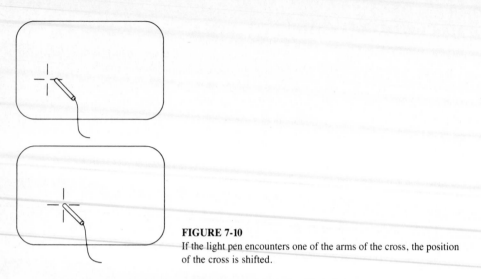

FIGURE 7-10
If the light pen encounters one of the arms of the cross, the position
of the cross is shifted.

This formula will select a character if its point lies within a circle of radius APERTURE centered on the locator point. But this formula involves multiplications which are computationally costly. A more efficient test is to select a point lying within a square with side 2 * APERTURE centered on the locator point. In this case, the test condition becomes

$$|(x - x_c)| + |(y - y_c)| < \text{APERTURE} \tag{7.3}$$

Absolute values are much easier to calculate than squares. (See Figure 7-12.)

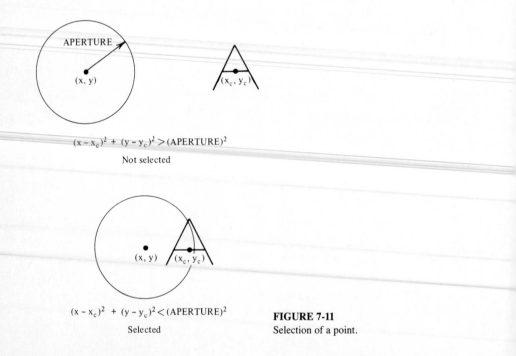

FIGURE 7-11
Selection of a point.

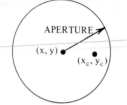

$(x - x_c)^2 + (y - y_c)^2 < (APERTURE)^2$

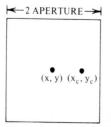

$|x - x_c| + |y - y_c| < APERTURE$

FIGURE 7-12

A square test area results in a more efficient test.

We can also find the distance between a point and a line segment. We already found an expression for this in Equation 1.30 which is

$$D = |rx + sy + t| \qquad (7.4)$$

where (x, y) is the locator point, and r, s, and t are parameters which describe the line (see Equation 1.6) and also satisfy the normalization condition (Equation 1.7). The values for r, s, and t satisfying these constraints for a line with endpoints (x_1, y_1), (x_2, y_2) are

$$r = (y_2 - y_1)/d$$
$$s = -(x_2 - x_1)/d \qquad (7.5)$$
$$t = (x_2 y_1 - x_1 y_2/d$$

where

$$d = [(x_2 - x_1)^2 + (y_2 - y_1)^2]^{1/2}$$

With a little algebra, Equations 7.4 and 7.5 can be distilled into the formula

$$D = \frac{|(x - x_1)(y_2 - y_1) - (y - y_1)(x_2 - x_1)|}{[(x_2 - x_1)^2 + (y_2 - y_1)^2]^{1/2}} \qquad (7.6)$$

This measure applies to the entire line containing the line segment. A preliminary test should be made to determine if the point lies too far beyond the segment endpoints. That is, we can reject the segment if

$$x < \min(x_1, x_2) - \text{APERTURE}$$

$$\text{or } x > \max(x_1, x_2) + \text{APERTURE} \qquad (7.7)$$

$$\text{or } y < \min(y_1, y_2) - \text{APERTURE}$$

$$\text{or } y > \max(y_1, y_2) + \text{APERTURE}$$

Here again we have a number of costly multiplications because we are accepting lines which fall within a circle about the locator point. By considering a square about the locator point we can use the following more efficient formula. (See Figure 7-13.)

$$\min\left(\left|\frac{(y_2-y_1)(x-x_1)}{x_2-x_1} + y_1 - y\right|, \left|\frac{(x_2-x_1)(y-y_1)}{y_2-y_1} + x_1 - x\right|\right)$$

$$<\text{APERTURE} \quad (7.8)$$

Vertical and horizontal line segments must be treated as special cases. An algorithm for simulating a pick with a light pen is given below. It steps through the seg-

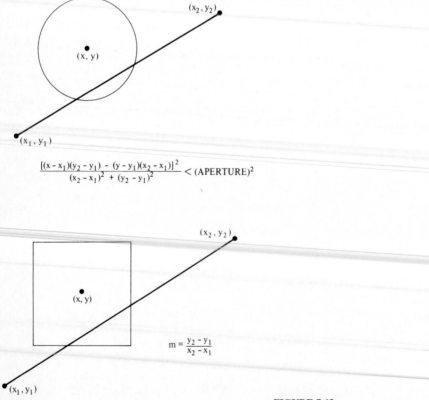

$$\frac{[(x-x_1)(y_2-y_1) - (y-y_1)(x_2-x_1)]^2}{(x_2-x_1)^2 + (y_2-y_1)^2} < (\text{APERTURE})^2$$

$$m = \frac{y_2 - y_1}{x_2 - x_1}$$

$$\min\left(|m(x-x_1) + y_1 - y|, \left|\frac{(y-y_1)}{m} + x_1 - x\right|\right) < \text{APERTURE}$$

FIGURE 7-13
Tests for selecting a line segment.

ment table as does our MAKE-PICTURE-CURRENT routine, but considers only visible, detectable, named segments. For each segment, it steps through the display file as does our INTERPRET routine, but instead of performing the instruction, it applies the above tests. The first segment which satisfies a test is returned as the result. If no such segment is found, then zero is returned.

7.20 Algorithm PICK-SEARCH (PICK, X, Y) Routine used to simulate a pick with a locator

It indicates which segment image is at location X, Y

Arguments   PICK used to return the discovered segment

              X, Y position of the simulated pick

Global   APERTURE sensitivity of the pick

              SEGMENT-START, SEGMENT-SIZE the segment-table arrays

              DETECTABLE the segment detectability attribute array

              VISIBILITY the segment visibility attribute array

              IMAGE-XFORM a 3×2 array containing the image transformation

Local   SEGMENT for stepping through the possible segments

              INSTRUCTIONS for stepping through the display-file segments

Constant   ROUNDOFF some small number greater than any round-off error

              NUMBER-OF-SEGMENTS size of the segment table

```
BEGIN
    X1 ← 0;
    Y1 ← 0;
    FOR SEGMENT = 1 TO NUMBER-OF-SEGMENTS DO
        IF SEGMENT-SIZE[SEGMENT] ≠ 0
            AND VISIBILITY[SEGMENT] AND DETECTABLE[SEGMENT] THEN
            BEGIN
                BUILD-TRANSFORMATION(SEGMENT);
                DO-TRANSFORMATION(X1, Y1, IMAGE-XFORM);
                PICK ← SEGMENT;
                FOR INSTRUCTION = SEGMENT-START[SEGMENT] TO
                    SEGMENT-START[SEGMENT] + SEGMENT-SIZE[SEGMENT] −
                    1 DO
                BEGIN
                    GET-POINT(INSTRUCTION, OP, X2, Y2);
                    IF OP > 0 OR OP < − 31 THEN
                        BEGIN
                            DO-TRANSFORMATION(X2, Y2, IMAGE-XFORM);
                            IF OP < − 31
                                AND |X − X2| + |Y − Y2| < APERTURE THEN
                                RETURN;
                        IF OP = 2 THEN
                            IF X > MIN(X1, X2) − APERTURE AND
                                X < MAX(X1, X2) + APERTURE AND
                                Y > MIN(Y1, Y2) − APERTURE AND
                                Y < MAX(Y1, Y2) + APERTURE THEN
                                    IF |Y2 − Y1| < ROUNDOFF OR
                                        |X2 − X1| < ROUNDOFF THEN RETURN
                                    ELSE IF MIN(|(Y2 − Y1) ∗ (X − X1) / (X2 − X1)
```

$$+ Y1 - Y|, |(X2 - X1) * (Y - Y1) / (Y2 - Y1)$$
$$+ X1 - X|)$$
$$< \text{APERTURE THEN RETURN};$$

```
                        X1 ← X2;
                        Y1 ← Y2;
                    END;
                END;
            END;
        PICK ← 0;
        RETURN;
    END;
```

ECHOING

An important part of an interactive system is *echoing*. Echoing provides the user with information about his actions. This allows the user to compare what he has done against what he wanted to do. For keyboard input, echoing usually takes the form of displaying the typed characters. Locators may be echoed by a screen cursor displayed at the current locator position. This allows the user to see the current locator setting and to relate its position to the objects on the display. (See Figure 7-14.)

A pick may be echoed by identifying the selected objects on the display. The selected objects may be flashed or made brighter or, perhaps, altered in color. This will allow the user to determine whether or not he has selected the intended objects. (See Figure 7-15.)

Buttons, when used to select menu items, can be echoed by flashing or highlighting the selected items. (See Figure 7-16.)

For a valuator, display of the current setting in numerical form or as a position on a scale is possible. (See Figure 7-17.)

It is important that some form of echoing be present, no matter what form it takes. Without it, the user feels that he is working in the dark and may never feel comfortable with the program.

INTERACTIVE TECHNIQUES

We should include in our discussion of graphics input some of the techniques for interactively creating and modifying pictures. Let us first consider how to add new pic-

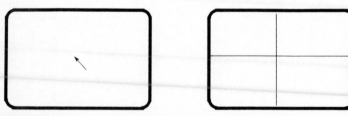

FIGURE 7-14
Echoing a location.

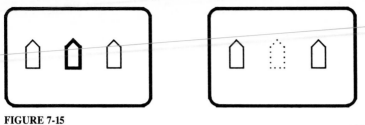

FIGURE 7-15
Echoing a pick.

ture elements to the image. *Point plotting* gives the user the capability of selecting a particular point on the screen. This is usually done by a combination of a locator and a button. The locator is used to tell which point the user selects. The button indicates when the locator is correctly positioned. The algorithm to perform point plotting must await the button event; as soon as it occurs, the locator may be read. The selection of points can be used in many different ways. For example, it can give endpoints of line segments, positions for text, or translations of picture segments. It occurs so often that a system routine for it is worthwhile.

7.21 Algorithm AWAIT-BUTTON-GET-LOCATOR(WAIT, BUTTON-NUM, X, Y)
User routine to interactively select a point
Arguments   WAIT the time to wait for a button event
                 BUTTON-NUM for return of the user's button selection
                 X, Y the point the user selects
BEGIN
    AWAIT-BUTTON(WAIT, BUTTON-NUM);
    READ-LOCATOR(X, Y);
    RETURN;
END;

One use for the point-plotting routine is to enter line segments. The idea here is to connect the successive points selected by the user with line segments, like a child's "connect-the-dots" drawing. The user can indicate whether to continue or terminate the process by which button is pushed. (See Figure 7-18.)

A program fragment for point plotting is as follows:

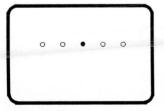

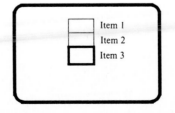

FIGURE 7-16
Echoing buttons and menu selection.

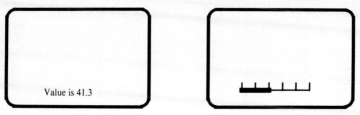

FIGURE 7-17
Echoing a value.

```
BEGIN
    BUTTON-NUM ← CONTINUE;
    WHILE BUTTON-NUM = CONTINUE DO
      BEGIN
          AWAIT-BUTTON-GET-LOCATOR(WAIT, BUTTON-NUM, X, Y);
          LINE-ABS-2(X, Y);
          MAKE-PICTURE-CURRENT;
      END;
END;
```

A variation of this technique is called *inking*. Inking makes the locator automatically leave a trail of line segments the way a pen leaves a trail of ink. It does not re-

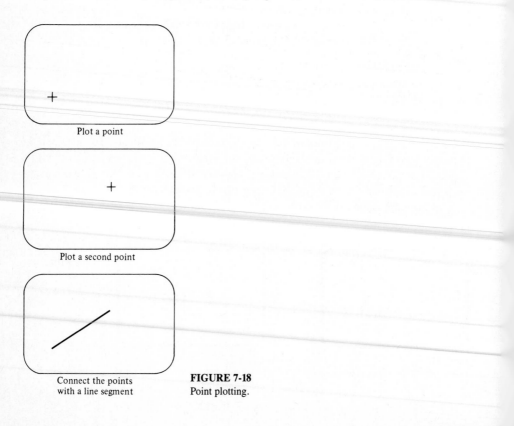

Plot a point

Plot a second point

Connect the points
with a line segment

FIGURE 7-18
Point plotting.

quire the user to push a button for every line segment; instead, a new segment is drawn whenever the locator moves a sufficient distance. (See Figure 7-19.)

The following program fragment outlines the inking techniques.

```
BEGIN
    PEN-ON ← TRUE;
    READ-LOCATOR(XOLD, YOLD);
    WHILE PEN-ON DO
        BEGIN
            READ-LOCATOR(X, Y);
            IF |(X − XOLD)| + |Y − YOLD| > NO-MOVEMENT THEN
            BEGIN
                LINE-ABS-2(X, Y);
                XOLD ← X;
                YOLD ← Y;
                MAKE-PICTURE-CURRENT;
            END;
            UPDATE(PEN-ON);
        END;
END;
```

The UPDATE(PEN-ON) determines whether inking should cease. This may be governed by an event, such as lifting the stylus, or by the passing of a time limit or a limit on the allowed number of line segments. Note that we could collect the sequence of locator positions without connecting them with line segments. Such a sequence of points is called a *stroke*. Inking displays strokes.

Raster displays can extend inking to *painting* with a *brush*. A brush is a pattern of pixel values. When painting, we repeatedly sample the locator position. Each time the position changes we copy the brush pattern into the frame buffer. The pattern is centered on the current locator position. The effect is to draw this pattern repeatedly on the display along the path of the locator. The instances of the pattern usually overlap, resulting in a shape that looks as though the brush has moved across the display leaving a trail of paint. The shape of the trail depends on both the path of the locator and the shape of the brush. (See Figure 7-20.)

It is often the case that the user wants to connect endpoints of several lines, and frequently horizontal and vertical lines predominate. But it can be difficult to position to a single point, and it may be hard to get a line perfectly horizontal or vertical. A technique to aid in such constructions is a *grid*. A grid is a pattern of special points. (See Figure 7-21.) Often the user can make these points either visible or invisible.

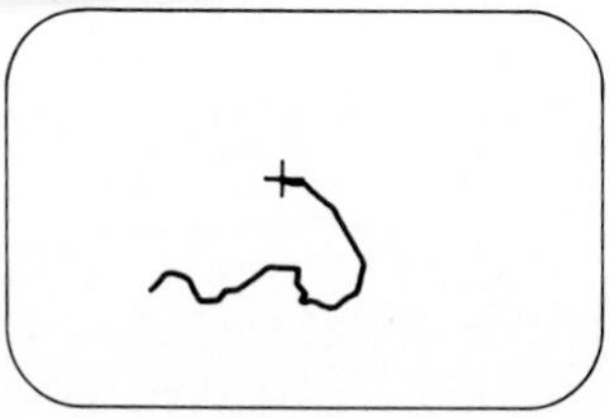

FIGURE 7-19
Inking.

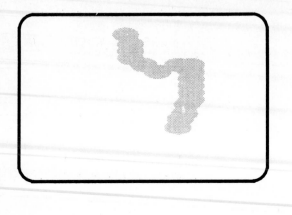

Brush

FIGURE 7-20
Painting.

What is special is that values obtained from the locator are rounded to the nearest grid point. All lines begin and end exactly on a grid point. This makes it easy to ensure that endpoints meet and that lines are vertical or horizontal. The following program fragment draws a grid; it should be placed in its own display-file segment so that it can be made visible or invisible.

```
BEGIN
    FOR X = 0 TO NUMBER-OF-GRIDPOINTS DO
        BEGIN
            FOR Y = 0 TO NUMBER-OF-GRIDPOINTS DO
                BEGIN
                    MOVE-ABS-2(X/NUMBER-OF-GRIDPOINTS - DX/2,
                        Y/NUMBER-OF-GRIDPOINTS);
                    LINE-REL-2(DX, 0);
                    MOVE-REL-2( - DX / 2,  - DX / 2);
```

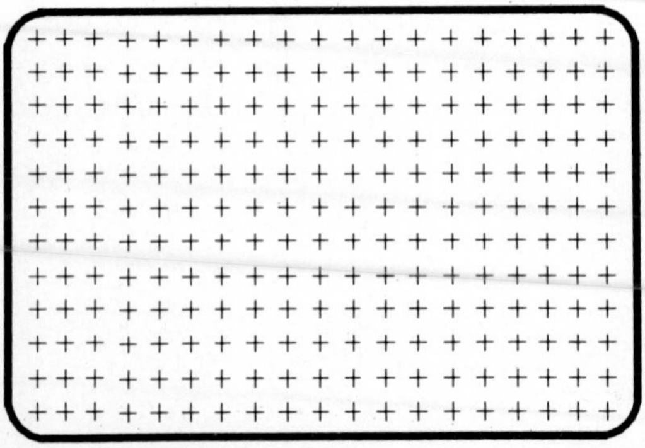

FIGURE 7-21
A grid.

```
                    LINE-REL-2(0, DX);
            END;
        END;
    END;
```

In the above fragment, NUMBER-OF-GRIDPOINTS is a count of how many grid points to display across the screen and DX is the width of a small cross which will be imaged at each grid point.

The rounding to the nearest grid point would look like the following:

```
READ-LOCATOR(X, Y);
X ← INT(X * NUMBER-OF-GRIDPOINTS + 0.5) / NUMBER-OF-GRIDPOINTS;
Y ← INT(Y * NUMBER-OF-GRIDPOINTS + 0.5) / NUMBER-OF-GRIDPOINTS;
```

Vector refresh and some raster displays allow a technique called *rubber band lines*. This technique allows the user to see what a line will look like before fixing it in place. The basic process is the same as line plotting; the user adjusts the locator to place the endpoint of the next line segment. The user presses a button when the locator is correctly positioned. The difference is that a line is constantly drawn between the last endpoint and the locator. As the locator moves, the line is redrawn in a new position, giving the appearance of a rubber band stretched between the fixed endpoint and the locator point. (See Figure 7-22.)

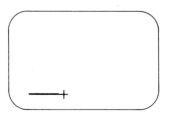

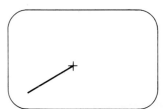

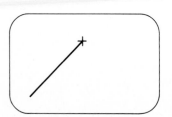

FIGURE 7-22
Rubber band lines.

This technique is difficult to implement in a straightforward manner in our system without adding either the ability to alter portions of the display file without opening and closing segments, or the ability to append new instructions onto a previously closed segment. It can, however, be done by using the image transformation on a single fixed line in a closed segment to create the rubber band line, and another open segment to hold the user's final drawing. The details of this are left as an exercise.

The user might wish not only to create new images but to alter and adjust existing images as well. The first thing necessary is often identifying which part of the image is to be changed. This is naturally a pick operation. Suppose the user wants to remove portions of the image. An AWAIT-PICK operation will determine which segment should be removed and the SET-VISIBILITY routine can make it invisible. Notice that this technique cannot be used to bring the item back, since one cannot pick what one cannot see. (See Figure 7-23.)

Another desirable modification might be a change in the image transformation. For example, the user may wish to change the position of a segment's image. It is usually most convenient for the user to indicate the new position by pointing at it with a locator. The user can use a pick to select the segment to be moved and then select some point on the image with the locator. Finally, the locator is moved to the place to where the point on the image should be moved. (See Figure 7-24.)

A program fragment to do this is given below. INQUIRE-IMAGE-TRANSLATION(TX, TY) is a routine which returns the current image translation parameters.

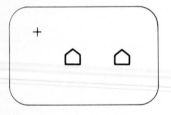

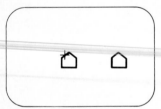

Select a segment

Make it invisible

FIGURE 7-23
Selecting a segment with a pick.

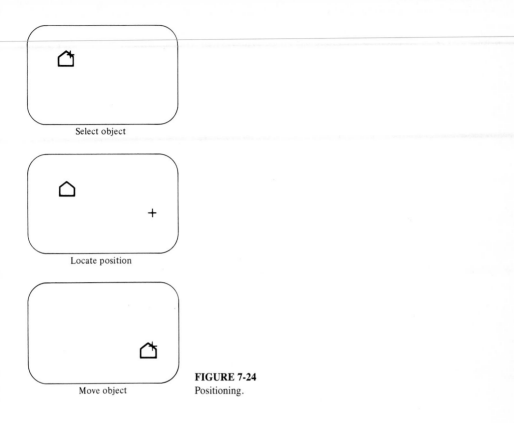

Select object

Locate position

Move object

FIGURE 7-24
Positioning.

```
BEGIN
    AWAIT-PICK(WAIT, SEGMENT);
    AWAIT-BUTTON-GET-LOCATOR(WAIT, BUTTON-NUM, XOLD, YOLD);
    AWAIT-BUTTON-GET-LOCATOR(WAIT, BUTTON-NUM, XNEW, YNEW);
    INQUIRE-IMAGE-TRANSLATION(SEGMENT, TX, TY);
    SET-IMAGE-TRANSLATION(SEGMENT, TX + XNEW − XOLD,
        TY + YNEW − YOLD);
    MAKE-PICTURE-CURRENT;
END;
```

On a vector refresh and some raster displays, the image can be continuously shifted and redrawn to follow the locator movements. The image appears to be attached to the locator. The user can see how the picture will look before fixing the new image translation values. This technique is called *dragging*. (See Figure 7-25.)

An outline for a possible dragging procedure is given below.

```
BEGIN
    AWAIT-PICK(WAIT, SEGMENT);
    AWAIT-BUTTON-GET-LOCATOR(WAIT, BUTTON-NUM, XOLD, YOLD);
    DRAGGING ← TRUE;
    WHILE DRAGGING DO
```

```
        BEGIN
            INQUIRE-IMAGE-TRANSLATION(SEGMENT, TX, TY);
            READ-LOCATOR(XNEW, YNEW);
            IF XNEW ≠ XOLD OR YNEW ≠ YOLD THEN
                BEGIN
                    SET-IMAGE-TRANSLATION(SEGMENT, TX + XNEW − XOLD,
                        TY + YNEW − YOLD);
                    XOLD ← XNEW;
                    YOLD ← YNEW;
                    MAKE-PICTURE-CURRENT;
                END;
            UPDATE(DRAGGING);
        END;
    END;
```

The UPDATE(DRAGGING) routine is used to stop the dragging process. This is usually done by detecting the occurrence of some event, but might also be triggered by the passing of a time limit.

Changes in orientation and scale may also be done interactively. The techniques are basically the same as for changes of the translation parameters, except that the natural input device might be a valuator instead of a locator. A valuator may be simulated using a locator and a scale drawn on the screen (usually parallel to the x or y axis). The

FIGURE 7-25
Dragging.

locator cursor can be positioned on the scale by the user and this position can then be converted into a valuator value. (See Figure 7-26 and Plate 3.)

An interactive program may provide the user with several options. For example, the user might be able to enter a single new line, ink, make a segment visible, move a segment, or quit. The user must select which option to follow. Such a selection can be made with the buttons by assigning a button for each option. The user makes a selection by pressing the appropriate button. We may wish to inform the user just what his options and what the corresponding buttons are. Such a list of options is called a menu. (See Figure 5-7 and Plate 1.) When there are a large number of options, a menu can become excessively long and hard to read. To avoid this the menu can be broken up into several smaller submenus. A top-level menu can be used to select the submenu containing the desired item. Thus menus can be structured into a hierarchy. In a complex selection process one might have to step through several levels of menus to reach the final selection, but at each level the menu is small and the selection easy.

Menus should be placed in a segment or segments different from the main picture so that they can be made invisible when no longer needed. A user may find it inconvenient to transfer his attention back and forth between buttons (or keyboard) and locator (or pick). It's for this reason that a light pen or tablet stylus will often have a switch built into its tip or handle. To avoid switching back and forth between different devices, we may wish to use the light pen or stylus to indicate the desired menu item. Menu selections can be made by a pick instead of a button if we place each selection in a separate segment so that it can be identified. When a light pen is the pick device, such selection items are called *light-buttons*. They behave as buttons, but do not require the user to shift his attention from the screen.

FURTHER READING

Description and classification of graphics input devices are found in [OHL78]. Early descriptions of tablets are given in [DAV64] and [TEI68]. One input device we did not

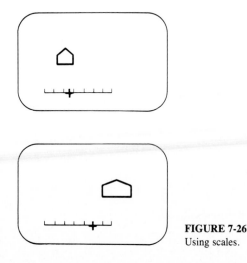

FIGURE 7-26
Using scales.

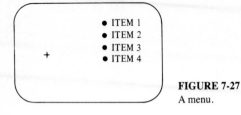

FIGURE 7-27
A menu.

mention is a touch panel, which acts as a locator attached to the display so that positions can be indicated by touching the screen with a finger or with a special pen. An example of this class of device is described in [NAG85]. A version of a mouse which detects changes in position optically is described in [LYO82]. An event queue for graphical input is suggested in [SPR75]. Graphic interaction techniques are described in [BER78], [FOL74], and [NEW68]. A detailed model of device-independent virtual input devices is given in [ROS82]. A description of virtual input is given in [WAL76]. In some cases, the virtual devices we have described may not be a good match to the actual devices; an alternative approach is to describe devices by the state they manage, the events they notice, and the actions they cause [ANS79]. A discussion of some interactive techniques for raster displays and encodings of raster data to support them may be found in [BAU80]. The distinction between the handling of an interaction and the applications program which uses the information is made clear in [KAM83]. The use of picks in interactive graphics is described in [WEL80]. An algorithm for simulating a pick with a locator is given in [GAR80]. Simulating valuators with a locator is described in [EVA81] and [THO79]. In [TUR84] a distinction is made between program variables (set by assignment statements) and graphics variables (set by hardware). An extension of graphics systems to allow attributes and coordinates to be graphics variables allows the display to be dynamically altered for interaction. Issues in interactive graphics and a bibliography are given in [THO83].

[ANS79] Anson, E., "The Semantics of Graphical Input," *Computer Graphics*, vol. 13, no. 2, pp. 113–120 (1979).

[BAU80] Baudelaire, P., Stone, M., "Techniques for Interactive Raster Graphics," *Computer Graphics*, vol. 14, no. 3, pp. 314–320 (1980).

[BER78] Bergeron, R. D., Bono, P. R., Foley, J. D., "Graphics Programming Using the CORE System," *ACM Computing Surveys*, vol. 10, no. 4, pp. 389–394 (1978).

[DAV64] Davis, M. R., Ellis, T. O., "The Rand Tablet: A Man-Machine Graphical Communication Device," *AFIPS FJCC*, vol. 26, pp. 325–331 (1964).

[EVA81] Evans, K. B., Tanner, P. P., Wein, M., "Tablet-Based Valuators That Provide One, Two, or Three Degrees of Freedom," *Computer Graphics*, vol. 15, no. 3, pp. 91–97 (1981).

[FOL74] Foley, J. D., Wallace, V. L., "The Art of Natural Graphic Man-Machine Conversation," *Proceedings of the IEEE*, vol. 62, no. 4, pp. 462–470 (1974).

[FOL84] Foley, J. D., Wallace, V. L., Chan, P., "The Human Factors of Computer Graphics Interaction Techniques," *IEEE Computer Graphics and Applications*, vol. 4, no. 11, pp. 13–48 (1984).

[GAR80] Garret, M. T., "Logical Pick Device Simulation Algorithms for the CORE System," *Computer Graphics*, vol. 13, no. 4, pp. 301–313 (1980).

[KAM83] Kamran, A., Feldman, M. B., "Graphics Programming Independent of Interaction Techniques and Styles," *Computer Graphics*, vol. 17, no. 1, pp. 58–66 (1983).

[LYO82] Lyon, R. F., Haeberli, M. P., "Designing and Testing the Optical Mouse," *VLSI Design*, vol. 3, no. 1, pp. 20–30 (1982).

[NAG85] Nagayama, T., Shibuya, J., Kawakita, T., "Pen-Touch-Type Electro-Magnetic Transparent Touch Panel," *SID Digest*, vol. 16, pp. 32–35 (1985).

[NEW68] Newman, W. M., "A Graphical Technique for Computer Input," *Computer Journal*, vol. 11, no. 1, pp. 63–64 (1968).

[OHL78] Ohlson, M., "System Design Considerations for Graphics Input Devices," *Computer*, vol. 11, no. 11, pp. 9–19 (1978).

[ROS82] Rosenthal, D. S. H., Michener, J. C., Pfaff, G., Kessener, R., Sabin, M., "The Detailed Semantics of Graphics Input Devices," *Computer Graphics*, vol. 16, no. 3, pp. 33–38 (1982).

[SPR75] Sproull, R. F., Newman, W. M., "The Design of Gray-Scale Graphics Software," *Proceedings of the Conference on Computer Graphics, Pattern Recognition, & Data Structure*, pp. 18–20, IEEE Cat. No. 75CH0981-1c (1975).

[TEI68] Teixeira, J. F., Sallen, R. P., "The Sylvania Data Tablet: A New Approach to Graphic Data Input," *AFIPS SJCC*, vol. 32, pp. 315–321 (1968).

[THO79] Thornton, R. W., "The Number Wheel: A Tablet Based Valuator for Interactive Three-Dimensional Positioning," *Computer Graphics*, vol. 13, no. 2, pp. 102–107 (1979).

[THO83] Thomas, J. J., Hamlin, G., "Graphical Input Interaction Technique (GIIT) Workshop Summary," *Computer Graphics*, vol. 17, no. 1, pp. 5–30 (1983).

[TUR84] Turner, J. U., "A Programmer's Interface to Graphics Dynamics," *Computer Graphics*, vol. 18, no. 3, pp. 263–270 (1984).

[WAL76] Wallace, V. L., "The Semantics of Graphic Input Devices," *Computer Graphics*, vol. 10, no. 1, pp. 61–65 (1976).

[WEL80] Weller, D. L., Carlson, E. D., Giddings, G. M., Palermo, F. P., Williams, R., Zilles, S. N., "Software Architecture for Graphical Interaction," *IBM System Journal*, vol. 19, no. 3, pp. 314–330 (1980).

EXERCISES

7-1 Design a routine RUBBERBAND which repeatedly shows a line connecting the point where the locator was positioned when the routine was entered and the current locator position. When an event occurs, the segment which was open when the routine was entered will receive a command to draw a line to the current locator position and the routine will be exited. Write algorithms for RUBBERBAND under each of the following conditions.

a) Our system is extended by a routine REPLACE-INSTRUCTION(OP, X, Y) which replaces the last entered display-file instruction by its arguments.

b) Our system is extended by a routine EXTEND-SEGMENT(SEGMENT-NAME) which reopens a segment so that additional instructions may be added.

c) Our system is not extended at all, so that the image transformation routines must be used.

7-2 Outline an algorithm for a light-pen tracking cross.

7-3 a) Compare the time required on your machine to calculate the nearness of two points using the measure in Equation 7.1 and that of Equation 7.3.

b) Compare the time required on your machine to calculate the nearness of a point to a line using the measure in Equation 7.6 and that in Equation 7.8. Also compare the time required if lines were stored in the general form and Equation 7.4 could be used.

c) Describe under what conditions the two measures used for determining nearness will yield different decisions.

7-4 It can be very frustrating to make mistakes in an interactive graphics session, particularly if one accidentally deletes a complex object. List a set of graphics editing commands you would like to provide a user. For each command, discuss how easy it would be for the user to undo the command. For those commands which would be difficult to undo (e.g., delete), discuss how a special "undo" operation might be included in the system.

PROGRAMMING PROBLEMS

7-1 Using algorithms 7.1 through 7.19 as a guide, extend your graphics system to include interactive capabilities.

7-2 Write a program which will allow a user to interactively create a picture by using the locator and buttons. Use a button value of 1 to move the pen to the locator position without drawing a line (MOVE-ABS-2). Use a button value of 2 to mean draw a line to the locator position (LINE-ABS-2). Use a button value of 3 to stop the program (TERMINATE).

7-3   a) Revise the line-drawing program of Programming Problem 7-2 so that locator points are rounded to grid points for some reasonably spaced grid. Allow the user to either display or not display the grid.

b) Allow the user to interactively change the grid spacing.

7-4 Write a program for inking. Use the pressing of buttons to start and stop the inking process. Your program should repeatedly sample the locator position. If the locator has moved sufficiently from the end of the inked line, extend the line to the current locator position by the addition of an instruction to the display file.

7-5   Revise Programming Problem 7-4 so that the angle between any two line segments is always less than a maximum angle which may be set as a parameter.

7-6 Write a program for moving an image. Select an image to be moved by a pick. When the pick occurs, read the locator position. Then wait for a button to be pressed. When this second event occurs, read the new locator position. Determine the change in locator position and add this change to the current image translation for the selected segment.

7-7   a) Write a program which creates three shapes (a triangle, a square, and a cross) in three different display-file segments. Set the visibility for these shapes to be false. Display a menu which allows the user to make the shapes visible by the pressing of buttons.

b) Place each menu selection in a different display-file segment, so that it may be selected by a pick instead of a button.

c) Let a pick of one of the three images itself cause that image to become invisible again.

7-8 Write a simple "pong" game where a "ball" bounces off four enclosing walls and a paddle, which is controlled by a valuator. (There are several ways to make an object appear to move. One is to use the image transformation, erasing and redrawing the entire object. Another is to add pixels to the forward side of the object and to remove them from the back side. Use the method which is best for your hardware.)

7-9 One of the problems with using a tracking cross and light pen to act as a locator is that a quick motion of the pen can lose the tracking cross. Write a procedure which will search for the lost light pen whenever it is lost. Your procedure should take a starting position as an argument (this might be the last known position of the pen). It should draw a search pattern of line segments. It stops when a line segment encounters the light pen and returns that location.

***7-10** Using image transformations on a closed segment containing a single horizontal line of length 1, implement rubber band lines.

*7-11 Implement rubber band rectangles where one corner is anchored and the opposite corner is attached to the locator. As the locator is moved, the sides of the rectangle stretch or shrink.

*7-12 Systems with frame buffers usually allow the programmer to inquire as to the value of a pixel as well as to set it. We can use this to extract patterns from images on the display. Write a program which allows the user to specify a rectangular boundary on the display. When the user signals that the rectangle is correctly sized and positioned, your program should extract the pattern of pixel values which the rectangle surrounds. The user should then be allowed to use this pattern to fill polygons (possibly with transformations applied as described in Chapter 4).

*7-13 We have described the locator as returning the coordinates of a point in the normalized device coordinates. However, the user would often prefer to receive the point in the same coordinates as he specified the drawing (before the image transformation). We can apply the inverse of the image transformation to the locator position to obtain this value, but if there are several display-file segments on the screen, there can be several image transformations to choose from. One approach to resolving this question is to first try to identify which segments have been drawn in the area near the locator position. An algorithm such as 7.20 for identifying a segment from a position may be used. But it is still possible to have more than one segment drawn in the region. To further resolve the choice, the system can require the user to assign priorities to the segments. When we must choose between segments, we select the one with the highest priority. Design and implement such a mechanism.

*7-14 A computer graphics layout program can find uses in many applications (for example, positioning stories and advertisements in a newspaper, or walls in a building, or equipment in a room). Write an interactive layout program. Allow the user to draw the boundary area (e.g., the walls of a room or the boundaries of a page). Provide grids and rubber band lines to make this easy. Allow the user to select standard items for positioning from a menu (e.g., the pieces of equipment). Selecting an item from the menu should cause an instance of it to be drawn on the display. The user should then be able to drag this item around the display for positioning. The user should also be able to drag any item. You may also wish to allow the user to scale or rotate any item.

*7-15 Extend the multiple workstation idea of Programming Problem 2-14 to include multiple input sources. Devise a means of receiving input from whichever workstations are currently active. You should also be able to identify which workstation provided events or to select which workstation will be sampled.

**7-16 Often when constructing pictures, the user will want to connect a line segment's endpoint to another endpoint. The careful positioning of the locator needed to connect the new segment exactly on the old segment may be difficult and tedious. We can make life easier for the user by writing a routine which returns a point right on a line segment when the locator is near to that line segment, and right on an endpoint when the locator is near that endpoint. Using algorithm 7.16 as a guide, write such a routine.

CHAPTER
EIGHT

THREE
DIMENSIONS

INTRODUCTION

Some graphics applications are two-dimensional; charts and graphs, certain maps, and some artist's creations may be strictly two-dimensional entities. But we live in a three-dimensional world, and in many design applications we must deal with describing three-dimensional objects. If the architect would like to see how the structure will actually look, then a three-dimensional model can allow him to view the structure from different viewpoints. The aircraft designer may wish to model the behavior of the craft under the three-dimensional forces and stresses. Here again, a three-dimensional description is required. Some simulation applications, such as docking a spaceship or landing an airplane, also require a three-dimensional view of the world.

In this chapter we shall generalize our system to handle models of three-dimensional objects. We shall extend our transformations to allow translation and rotation in three-dimensional space. Since the viewing surface is only two-dimensional, we must consider ways of projecting our object onto this flat surface to form the image. Both parallel and perspective projections will be discussed.

3D GEOMETRY

Let us begin our discussion of three dimensions by reviewing the methods of analytic geometry for specifying objects. The simplest object is, of course, the point. As in the case of two dimensions, we can specify a point by establishing a coordinate system and listing the coordinates of the point. We will need an additional coordinate axis for the third dimension (three axes in all, one for height, one for width, and a third for depth). We can arrange the three axes to be at right angles to each other and label the

244

width and height axes x and y, respectively, to correspond to the two-dimensional case. The third axis, for depth, is named the z axis. We have a choice as to which end of the z axis will be given positive values. (See Figure 8-1.)

The orientation of the coordinate system is determined as follows. If the thumb of the right hand points in the positive z direction as one curls the fingers of the right hand from x into y, then the coordinates are called a *right-handed* system. If, however, the thumb points in the negative z direction then it is *left-handed*. Whereas most of geometry uses a right-handed system, computer graphics often prefers the left-handed coordinates. We shall adopt the right-handed system for our use. (The right-handed system is normally used in mathematics, although in computer graphics we also find the left-handed system in use so that objects behind the display screen will have positive z values.) Any point in space may now be specified by telling how far over, up, and out it is from the origin, where the three axes intersect. These distances are written as the ordered triple (x, y, z). (See Figure 8-2.)

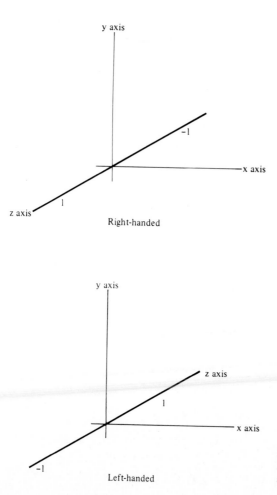

Right-handed

Left-handed

FIGURE 8-1
Right-handed and left-handed coordinate systems.

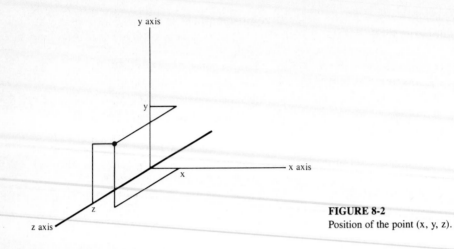

FIGURE 8-2
Position of the point (x, y, z).

We can use the coordinates to specify a line. In two dimensions a line was given by an equation involving x and y.

$$\frac{y - y_1}{x - x_1} = \frac{y_2 - y_1}{x_2 - x_1} \tag{8.1}$$

This equation states that as x changes, the y coordinate changes proportionately. The ratio of the change in y to the change in x is always the same. In three dimensions, as we move along the line, both y and z coordinates will change proportionately to x. A line in three dimensions is given by a pair of equations

$$\frac{y - y_1}{x - x_1} = \frac{y_2 - y_1}{x_2 - x_1}$$

$$\frac{z - z_1}{x - x_1} = \frac{z_2 - z_1}{x_2 - x_1} \tag{8.2}$$

It requires the coordinates of two points to form these equations: (x_1, y_1, z_1) and (x_2, y_2, z_2). Thus it still takes two points to specify a line, as we might expect. A more symmetrical expression for a line is the parametric form, where each of the coordinates is expressed in terms of a parameter u.

$$x = (x_2 - x_1)u + x_1$$

$$y = (y_2 - y_1)u + y_1 \tag{8.3}$$

$$z = (z_2 - z_1)u + z_1$$

We shall also want to work with planes. A plane is specified by a single equation of the form.

$$Ax + By + Cz + D = 0 \tag{8.4}$$

Notice that one of the constants (for example A, if it is not zero) may be divided out of the equation so that

$$x + B_1y + C_1z + D_1 = 0 \qquad (8.5)$$

is an equation for the same plane when

$$B_1 = B/A, \qquad C_1 = C/A, \qquad \text{and} \qquad D_1 = D/A \qquad (8.6)$$

It therefore requires only three constants B_1, C_1, and D_1 to specify the plane. The equation for a particular plane may be determined if we know the coordinates of three points (not all in a line) which lie within it: (x_1, y_1, z_1), (x_2, y_2, z_2), and (x_3, y_3, z_3). We can determine the equation in the following manner. Since each point is in the plane, it must satisfy the plane's equation

$$x_1 + B_1y_1 + C_1z_1 + D_1 = 0$$
$$x_2 + B_1y_2 + C_1z_2 + D_1 = 0 \qquad (8.7)$$
$$x_3 + B_1y_3 + C_1z_3 + D_1 = 0$$

We have three equations to solve for the three unknowns B_1, C_1, and D_1, and standard algebra techniques for solving simultaneous equations will yield their values.

Another normalization is

$$A_2 = A/d, \qquad B_2 = B/d, \qquad C_2 = C/d, \qquad \text{and} \qquad D_2 = D/d \quad (8.8)$$

where

$$d = (A^2 + B^2 + C^2)^{1/2} \qquad (8.9)$$

The value of this selection is that the distance between a point (x, y, z) and the plane is given by

$$L = |A_2x + B_2y + C_2z + D_2| \qquad (8.10)$$

The sign of the quantity in the absolute value bars indicates on which side of the plane the point lies. This is an extension of Equation 1.30 for lines.

Another way of specifying a plane is by a single point in the plane and the direction perpendicular to the plane. A vector perpendicular to a plane is called a normal vector. We can call $[N_x \quad N_y \quad N_z]$ the displacements for the normal vector, and (x_p, y_p, z_p) are the coordinates of a point in the plane. (See Figures 8-3 and 8-4.)

If (x, y, z) is to be an arbitrary point in the plane, then $[(x - x_p) \quad (y - y_p) \quad (z - z_p)]$ is a vector parallel to the plane. We can derive an equation for the plane by using the *vector dot product*. The dot product of two vectors is the sum of the products of their corresponding components. For example, if $A = [A_x \quad A_y \quad A_z]$ and $B = [B_x \quad B_y \quad B_z]$, then their dot product is

$$A \cdot B = A_xB_x + A_yB_y + A_zB_z \qquad (8.11)$$

The result of the dot product is equal to the product of the lengths of the two vectors times the cosine of the angle between them. (See Figure 8-5.)

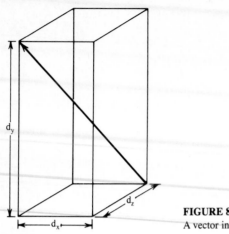

FIGURE 8-3
A vector in three dimensions.

$$A \cdot B = |A||B|\cos\theta \qquad (8.12)$$

Now the angle between any vector parallel to a plane and the normal vector to the plane is $\pi/2$ radians (because that is what we mean by a normal vector). Since the cosine of $\pi/2$ is 0, we know that the dot product of the normal vector with a vector parallel to the plane is 0. We can find a vector parallel to the plane by taking the difference of two points within the plane. Therefore, if

$$N_x (x - x_p) + N_y (y - y_p) + N_z (z - z_p) = 0 \qquad (8.13)$$

is a true equation then the vector formed by the difference between (x, y, z) and (x_p, y_p, z_p) must be parallel to the plane. And since (x_p, y_p, z_p) is in the plane and we can get to (x, y, z) by moving along a vector parallel to the plane, we know that (x, y, z) is also a point in the plane. (See Figure 8-6.) So Equation 8.13 is then an equation for the plane.

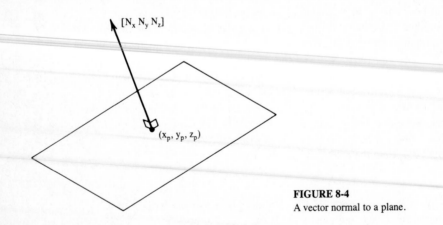

FIGURE 8-4
A vector normal to a plane.

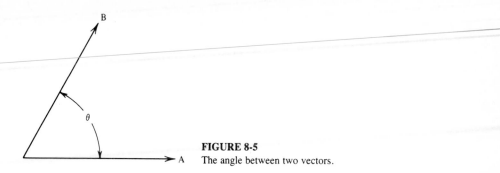

FIGURE 8-5
The angle between two vectors.

3D PRIMITIVES

Now that we know how to express points, lines, and planes in three dimensions, let us consider algorithms which allow the user to model three-dimensional objects. We have provided the user with commands for moving the "pen" and drawing lines and polygons in two dimensions. Extending these operations to three dimensions will mean requesting the user to provide three coordinate specifications instead of two. At some time in the display process we must project these three coordinates onto the two screen coordinates, but we shall place this burden on the DISPLAY-FILE-ENTER routine and postpone its discussion for the moment. As in the case of two dimensions, we picture an imaginary pen or pointer which the user commands to move from point to point. We save this pen's current position in some global variables, only now three variables are required: DF-PEN-X, DF-PEN-Y, and DF-PEN-Z, one for each of the three coordinates. The three-dimensional LINE and MOVE algorithms are as follows:

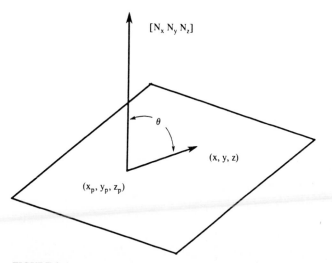

FIGURE 8-6
The angle between a vector normal to a plane and a vector parallel to the plane is 90 degrees.

8.1 Algorithm MOVE-ABS-3(X, Y, Z) The 3D absolute move

Arguments   X, Y, Z world coordinates of the point to move the pen to

Global   DF-PEN-X, DF-PEN-Y, DF-PEN-Z current pen position

BEGIN
   DF-PEN-X ← X;
   DF-PEN-Y ← Y;
   DF-PEN-Z ← Z;
   DISPLAY-FILE-ENTER(1);
   RETURN;
END;

8.2 Algorithm MOVE-REL-3(DX, DY, DZ) The 3D relative move

Arguments   DX, DY, DZ changes to be made to the pen position

Global   DF-PEN-X, DF-PEN-Y, DF-PEN-Z the current pen position

BEGIN
   DF-PEN-X ← DF-PEN-X + DX;
   DF-PEN-Y ← DF-PEN-Y + DX;
   DF-PEN-Z ← DF-PEN-Z + DZ;
   DISPLAY-FILE-ENTER(1);
   RETURN;
END;

8.3 Algorithm LINE-ABS-3(X, Y, Z) The 3D absolute line-drawing routine

Arguments   X, Y, Z coordinates of the point to draw the line to

Global   DF-PEN-X, DF-PEN-Y, DF-PEN-Z the current pen position

BEGIN
   DF-PEN-X ← X;
   DF-PEN-Y ← Y;
   DF-PEN-Z ← Z;
   DISPLAY-FILE-ENTER(2);
   RETURN;
END;

8.4 Algorithm LINE-REL-3(DX, DY, DZ) The 3D relative line-drawing routine

Arguments   DX, DY, DZ displacements over which a line is to be drawn

Global   DF-PEN-X, DF-PEN-Y, DF-PEN-Z the current pen position

BEGIN
   DF-PEN-X ← DF-PEN-X + DX;
   DF-PEN-Y ← DF-PEN-Y + DY;
   DF-PEN-Z ← DF-PEN-Z + DZ;
   DISPLAY-FILE-ENTER(2);
   RETURN;
END;

Polygon commands can also be extended by simply processing an additional array of coordinates. We assume that the user will provide coordinates which all lie in a plane, but a check could be placed in the algorithms to guarantee it. The following are the three-dimensional versions of our routines for entering polygons.

8.5 Algorithm POLYGON-ABS-3(AX, AY, AZ, N) The 3D absolute polygon-drawing routine

Arguments   N the number of polygon sides

AX, AY, AZ arrays of the coordinates of the vertices

Global   DF-PEN-X, DF-PEN-Y, DF-PEN-Z the current pen position

Local   I for stepping through the polygon sides

BEGIN

   IF N < 3 THEN RETURN ERROR 'SIZE ERROR';

   DF-PEN-X ← AX[N];

   DF-PEN-Y ← AY[N];

   DF-PEN-Z ← AZ[N];

   DISPLAY-FILE-ENTER(N);

   FOR I = 1 TO N DO LINE-ABS-3(AX[I], AY[I], AZ[I]);

   RETURN;

END;

8.6 Algorithm POLYGON-REL-3(AX, AY, AZ, N) The 3D relative polygon-drawing routine

Arguments   N the number of polygon sides

AX, AY, AZ arrays of displacements for the polygon sides

Global   DF-PEN-X, DF-PEN-Y, DF-PEN-Z the current pen position

Local   I for stepping through the polygon sides

TMPX, TMPY, TMPZ storage of point at which the polygon is closed

BEGIN

   IF N < 3 THEN RETURN ERROR 'SIZE ERROR';

   move to starting vertex

   DF-PEN-X ← DF-PEN-X + AX[1];

   DF-PEN-Y ← DF-PEN-Y + AY[1];

   DF-PEN-Z ← DF-PEN-Z + AZ[1];

   save vertex for closing the polygon

   TMPX ← DF-PEN-X;

   TMPY ← DF-PEN-Y;

   TMPZ ← DF-PEN-Z;

   DISPLAY-FILE-ENTER(N);

   enter the polygon sides

   FOR I = 2 TO N DO LINE-REL-3(AX[I], AY[I], AZ[I]);

   close the polygon

   LINE-ABS-3(TMPX, TMPY, TMPZ);

   RETURN;

END;

3D TRANSFORMATIONS

Using the above routines the user can construct a three-dimensional "drawing" of his object. But the actual display surface is two-dimensional. The two-dimensional image corresponds to a particular view of the three-dimensional object. The process of find-ing which points on the flat screen correspond to the lines and surfaces of the object involves a viewing transformation. We have seen how it is useful to translate, scale, and rotate images. We shall begin by considering the generalization of these transformations to three dimensions. We shall then extend our transformations to include parallel and perspective projections.

We saw that a two-dimensional scaling transformation matrix was of the form

$$\begin{vmatrix} s_x & 0 \\ 0 & s_y \end{vmatrix}$$

or in homogeneous coordinates,

$$\begin{vmatrix} s_x & 0 & 0 \\ 0 & s_y & 0 \\ 0 & 0 & 1 \end{vmatrix}$$

Three dimensions gives us a third coordinate which can have its own scaling factor, so we shall require a 3×3 matrix rather than a 2×2.

$$\begin{vmatrix} s_x & 0 & 0 \\ 0 & s_y & 0 \\ 0 & 0 & s_z \end{vmatrix}$$

If using homogeneous coordinates, a 4×4 matrix is required.

$$\begin{vmatrix} s_x & 0 & 0 & 0 \\ 0 & s_y & 0 & 0 \\ 0 & 0 & s_z & 0 \\ 0 & 0 & 0 & 1 \end{vmatrix} \tag{8.14}$$

Transformation of a point is done by multiplication by the matrix, just as in Chapter 4.

$$\begin{vmatrix} x_1 & y_1 & z_1 & w_1 \end{vmatrix} = \begin{vmatrix} x & y & z & w \end{vmatrix} \begin{vmatrix} s_x & 0 & 0 & 0 \\ 0 & s_y & 0 & 0 \\ 0 & 0 & s_z & 0 \\ 0 & 0 & 0 & 1 \end{vmatrix} = \begin{vmatrix} s_x x & s_y y & s_z z & w \end{vmatrix} \tag{8.15}$$

We used the bottom row of the homogeneous coordinate matrix for translation values. This will still be the case for three dimensions, only the matrix is now 4×4 instead of 3×3. To translate by t_x in the x direction, t_y in the y direction, and t_z in the z direction, we multiply by the matrix

$$T = \begin{vmatrix} 1 & 0 & 0 & 0 \\ 0 & 1 & 0 & 0 \\ 0 & 0 & 1 & 0 \\ t_x & t_y & t_z & 1 \end{vmatrix} \tag{8.16}$$

When we considered rotation of an object in two dimensions, we developed a matrix for rotation about the origin.

$$\begin{vmatrix} \cos\theta & \sin\theta \\ -\sin\theta & \cos\theta \end{vmatrix}$$

We can generalize this to a three-dimensional rotation about the z axis. If we rotate about the z axis, all z coordinates remain unchanged, while the x and y coordinates behave the same as in the two-dimensional case. (See Figure 8-7.)

A matrix which does this in homogeneous coordinates is

$$R_z = \begin{vmatrix} \cos\theta & \sin\theta & 0 & 0 \\ -\sin\theta & \cos\theta & 0 & 0 \\ 0 & 0 & 1 & 0 \\ 0 & 0 & 0 & 1 \end{vmatrix} \qquad (8.17)$$

In the above rotation, we are thinking of the axes as fixed while some object in the space is moved. We could also think in terms of the object being fixed while the axes are moved. The difference between these two interpretations is the direction of rotation. Fixing the axes and rotating the object counterclockwise is the same as fixing the object and moving the axes clockwise.

Rotation about the x or y axis is done by a matrix of the same general form as in Equation 8.17, as we might expect from the symmetry of the axes. To rotate about the x axis so that y is turned into z, we use the homogeneous coordinate matrix

$$R_x = \begin{vmatrix} 1 & 0 & 0 & 0 \\ 0 & \cos\theta & \sin\theta & 0 \\ 0 & -\sin\theta & \cos\theta & 0 \\ 0 & 0 & 0 & 1 \end{vmatrix} \qquad (8.18)$$

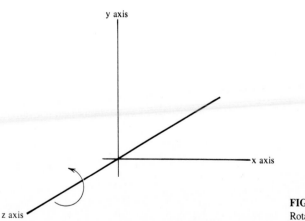

FIGURE 8-7
Rotation about the z axis.

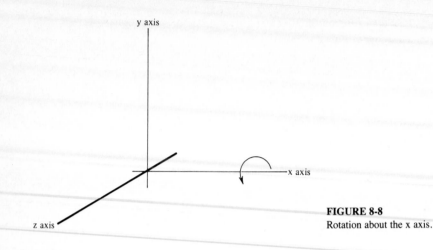

y axis

x axis

z axis

FIGURE 8-8
Rotation about the x axis.

(See Figure 8-8.) To rotate about the y axis so that z is turned into x, we use the homogeneous coordinate matrix

$$Ry = \begin{vmatrix} \cos\theta & 0 & -\sin\theta & 0 \\ 0 & 1 & 0 & 0 \\ \sin\theta & 0 & \cos\theta & 0 \\ 0 & 0 & 0 & 1 \end{vmatrix} \qquad (8.19)$$

(See Figure 8-9.)

Three-dimensional transformations are useful in presenting different views of an object. An example of a program which lets the user interactively specify the transformation parameters for viewing a molecule is shown in Plate 3. Since we will find translation and rotation about an axis useful in creating a viewing transformation, we will develop algorithms for creating transformation matrices involving these operations. We shall do this by means of a routine which creates an identity transformation matrix (NEW-TRANSFORMATION-3) and routines which have the effect of multiplying the current transformation matrix by a matrix for translation or rotation about one of the principal axes. We will use the homogeneous coordinate techniques. For the viewing transformation, we can arrange matters so that the fourth column is always three 0s and a 1. Knowing this, we do not actually need to store these numbers, so a 4 × 3 array of storage is all that is needed. We will call this transformation matrix TMATRIX. The following algorithm sets it to the identity transformation.

8.7 Algorithm NEW-TRANSFORM-3 Initializes the viewing transformation matrix to the identity
Global   TMATRIX a 4 × 3 transformation matrix array
Local   I, J for stepping through the array elements
BEGIN
    FOR I = 1 TO 4 DO
        BEGIN
            FOR J = 1 TO 3 DO TMATRIX[I, J] ← 0;

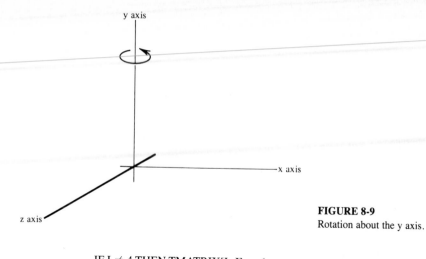

FIGURE 8-9
Rotation about the y axis.

```
                IF I ≠ 4 THEN TMATRIX[I, I] ← 1;
            END;
        RETURN;
    END;
```

The next algorithm has the effect of multiplying the TMATRIX array by a translation matrix.

8.8 Algorithm TRANSLATE-3(TX, TY, TZ) Post-multiplies the viewing transformation matrix by a translation
Arguments   TX, TY, TZ the amount of the translation
Global   TMATRIX a 4 × 3 transformation matrix array
```
BEGIN
    TMATRIX[4, 1] ← TMATRIX[4, 1] + TX;
    TMATRIX[4, 2] ← TMATRIX[4, 2] + TY;
    TMATRIX[4, 3] ← TMATRIX[4, 3] + TZ;
    RETURN;
END;
```

Algorithms for rotating about each of the major axes are given below. The arguments are the sine and cosine of the rotation angle rather than the angle itself.

8.9 Algorithm ROTATE-X-3(S, C) Post-multiplication for a rotation about the x axis
(y into z)
Arguments   S, C the sine and cosine of the rotation angle
Global   TMATRIX a 4 × 3 transformation matrix array
Local   I for stepping through the matrix elements
              TMP temporary storage
```
BEGIN
    FOR I = 1 TO 4 DO
        BEGIN
            TMP ← TMATRIX[I, 2] * C − TMATRIX[I, 3] * S;
            TMATRIX[I, 3] ← TMATRIX[I, 2] * S + TMATRIX[I, 3] * C;
```

```
            TMATRIX[I, 2] ← TMP;
        END;
    RETURN;
END;
```

8.10 Algorithm ROTATE-Y-3(S, C) Post-multiplication for a rotation about the y axis (z into x)

Arguments	S, C the sine and cosine of the angle of rotation
Global	TMATRIX a 4 × 3 transformation matrix array
Local	I for stepping through the matrix elements
	TMP temporary storage

```
BEGIN
    FOR I = 1 TO 4 DO
        BEGIN
            TMP ← TMATRIX[I, 1] * C + TMATRIX[I, 3] * S;
            TMATRIX[I, 3] ← −TMATRIX[I, 1] * S + TMATRIX[I, 3] * C;
            TMATRIX[I, 1] ← TMP;
        END;
    RETURN;
END;
```

8.11 Algorithm ROTATE-Z-3(S, C) Post-multiplication for a rotation about the z axis (x into y)

Arguments	S, C the sine and cosine of the angle of rotation
Global	TMATRIX a 4×3 transformation matrix array
Local	I for stepping through the matrix elements
	TMP temporary storage

```
BEGIN
    FOR I = 1 TO 4 DO
        BEGIN
            TMP ← TMATRIX[I, 1] * C − TMATRIX[I, 2] * S;
            TMATRIX[I, 2] ← TMATRIX[I, 1] * S + TMATRIX[I, 2] * C;
            TMATRIX[I, 1] ← TMP;
        END;
    RETURN;
END;
```

ROTATION ABOUT AN ARBITRARY AXIS

Let us take a moment to become more familiar with three-dimensional transformations by solving a problem. While we have developed transformations for rotation about a coordinate axis, in general any line in space can serve as an axis for rotation. The problem is to derive a transformation matrix for a rotation of angle θ about an arbitrary line. We will build this transformation out of those which we have already encountered. We shall perform a translation to move the origin onto the line. We shall then make rotations about the x and y axes to align the z axis with the line. The rotation about the line then becomes a rotation about the z axis. Finally, we apply inverse transformations for the rotations about the y and x axes and for the translation to restore the line and coordinates to their original orientation. (See Figure 8-10.)

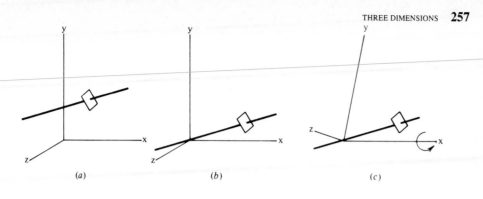

(a)   (b)   (c)

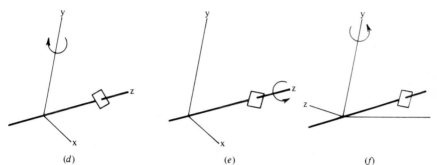

(d)   (e)   (f)

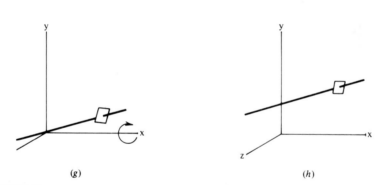

(g)   (h)

FIGURE 8-10

(a) To rotate about an arbitrary axis, (b) first translate the axis to the origin, (c) rotate about x until the axis of rotation is in the xz plane, (d) rotate about y until the z axis corresponds to the axis of rotation, (e) rotate about z (the axis of rotation) instead of fixing the object and rotating the axes (we have in this figure fixed the axes and rotated the object), (f) reverse the rotation about y, (g) reverse the rotation about x, and (h) reverse the translation.

We should decide upon a convenient representation for the line which is to be the axis of rotation. A point on the line, together with the line's direction, is sufficient to specify the line. This will prove to be a good form for our purposes. The point provides information for the translation, and the direction will tell us the correct angles of rotation for aligning the z axis. We can find this form from the parametric equations for the line in the following manner. Given the line

$$x = Au + x_1$$

$$y = Bu + y_1 \qquad (8.20)$$

$$z = Cu + z_1$$

a point on the line is (x_1, y_1, z_1) and the direction is specified by the vector of [A B C].

We can now determine the transformation matrix needed for our general rotation. The initial translation to move the origin to the rotation axis should be

$$T = \begin{vmatrix} 1 & 0 & 0 & 0 \\ 0 & 1 & 0 & 0 \\ 0 & 0 & 1 & 0 \\ -x_1 & -y_1 & -z_1 & 1 \end{vmatrix} \qquad (8.21)$$

After this translation, the point on the line (x_1, y_1, z_1) will be moved to the origin. We will also require the inverse of this translation to place the origin back at its original position once our rotations are completed. This is just a translation by the same amount in the opposite direction

$$T^{-1} = \begin{vmatrix} 1 & 0 & 0 & 0 \\ 0 & 1 & 0 & 0 \\ 0 & 0 & 1 & 0 \\ x_1 & y_1 & z_1 & 1 \end{vmatrix} \qquad (8.22)$$

The next step in the process is a rotation about the x axis. We wish to rotate until our general rotation axis lies in the xz plane. To determine the necessary angle of rotation, let us place our direction vector at the new origin and consider its projection in the yz plane. We can picture this in the following way: The line segment between (0, 0, 0) and (A, B, C) will be in the direction of the arbitrary rotation axis, and since we have translated so that the point (0, 0, 0) is on this axis, the entire segment must lie along the axis. Now imagine shining a beam of light parallel with the x axis and looking at the shadow of the line segment formed on the yz plane. The shadow will extend from (0, 0, 0) to (0, B, C). (See Figure 8-11.)

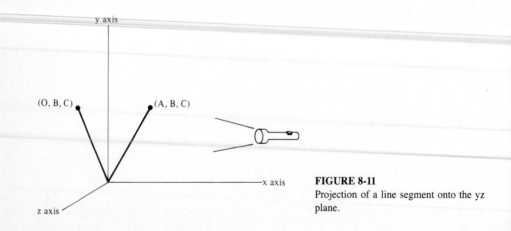

FIGURE 8-11
Projection of a line segment onto the yz plane.

If we now rotate about the x axis until the arbitrary axis is in the xz plane, the line segment's shadow will lie along the z axis. How large an angle I is needed to place this shadow on the z axis? (See Figure 8-12.)

We know that the length of the shadow V will be

$$V = (B^2 + C^2)^{1/2} \tag{8.23}$$

and from the definition of the sine and cosine, we see that

$$\sin I = B/V \tag{8.24}$$
$$\cos I = C/V$$

The rotation about the x axis should be

$$R_X = \begin{vmatrix} 1 & 0 & 0 & 0 \\ 0 & \cos I & \sin I & 0 \\ 0 & -\sin I & \cos I & 0 \\ 0 & 0 & 0 & 1 \end{vmatrix} \tag{8.25}$$

So we have

$$R_X = \begin{vmatrix} 1 & 0 & 0 & 0 \\ 0 & C/V & B/V & 0 \\ 0 & -B/V & C/V & 0 \\ 0 & 0 & 0 & 1 \end{vmatrix} \tag{8.26}$$

The inverse transformation is a rotation of equal magnitude in the opposite direction. Reversing the direction of the angle changes the sign of the sine elements, but leaves the cosine elements unchanged.

$$R_X^{-1} = \begin{vmatrix} 1 & 0 & 0 & 0 \\ 0 & C/V & -B/V & 0 \\ 0 & B/V & C/V & 0 \\ 0 & 0 & 0 & 1 \end{vmatrix} \tag{8.27}$$

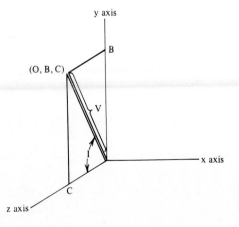

FIGURE 8-12
Parameters of the line segment projection.

Now we can picture our rotation axis as lying in the xz plane. (See Figure 8-13.)

The rotation about the x axis has left the x coordinate unchanged. We also know that the overall length of the segment

$$L = (A^2 + B^2 + C^2)^{1/2} \tag{8.28}$$

is unchanged. The z coordinate will be

$$(L^2 - A^2)^{1/2} = (B^2 + C^2)^{1/2} = V \tag{8.29}$$

We wish to rotate by an angle J about the y axis so that the line segment aligns with the z axis.

$$\sin J = A/L$$
$$\cos J = V/L \tag{8.30}$$

The rotation matrix will be

$$R_y = \begin{vmatrix} \cos J & 0 & \sin J & 0 \\ 0 & 1 & 0 & 0 \\ -\sin J & 0 & \cos J & 0 \\ 0 & 0 & 0 & 1 \end{vmatrix}$$

$$= \begin{vmatrix} V/L & 0 & A/L & 0 \\ 0 & 1 & 0 & 0 \\ -A/L & 0 & V/L & 0 \\ 0 & 0 & 0 & 1 \end{vmatrix} \tag{8.31}$$

The signs are different in Equation 8.31 from those in Equation 8.19 because we are rotating from x into z instead of from z into x. The inverse for this transformation is

$$R_y^{-1} = \begin{vmatrix} V/L & 0 & -A/L & 0 \\ 0 & 1 & 0 & 0 \\ A/L & 0 & V/L & 0 \\ 0 & 0 & 0 & 1 \end{vmatrix} \tag{8.32}$$

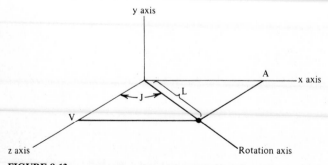

FIGURE 8-13
The rotation axis lying within the xz plane.

Finally we are in a position to rotate by an angle θ about the arbitrary axis. Since we have aligned the arbitrary axis with the z axis, a rotation by θ about the z axis is needed.

$$R_z = \begin{vmatrix} \cos\theta & \sin\theta & 0 & 0 \\ -\sin\theta & \cos\theta & 0 & 0 \\ 0 & 0 & 1 & 0 \\ 0 & 0 & 0 & 1 \end{vmatrix}$$ (8.33)

The actual transformation for a rotation θ about an arbitrary axis is given by the product of the above transformations.

$$R_\theta = TR_xR_yR_zR_y^{-1}R_x^{-1}T^{-1}$$ (8.34)

PARALLEL PROJECTION

We have talked about creating and transforming three-dimensional objects, but since our viewing surface is only two-dimensional, we must have some way of *projecting* our three-dimensional object onto the two-dimensional screen. (See Figure 8-14.)

Perhaps the simplest way of doing this is just to discard the z coordinate. This is a special case of a method known as *parallel projection*. A parallel projection is formed by extending parallel lines from each vertex on the object until they intersect the plane

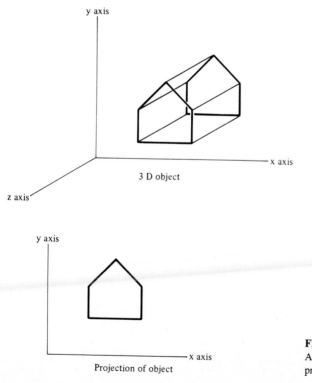

y axis

x axis

3 D object

z axis

y axis

x axis

Projection of object

FIGURE 8-14
A three-dimensional object and its projection.

of the screen. The point of intersection is the projection of the vertex. We connect the projected vertices by line segments which correspond to connections on the original object. (See Figure 8-15.)

Our special case of discarding the z coordinate is the case where the screen, or viewing surface, is parallel to the xy plane, and the lines of projection are parallel to the z axis. As we move along these lines of projection, only the z coordinate changes; x and y values remain constant. So the point of intersection with the viewing surface has the same x and y coordinates as does the vertex on the object. The projected image is formed from the x and y coordinates, and the z value is discarded.

In a general parallel projection, we may select any direction for the lines of projection (so long as they do not run parallel to the plane of the viewing surface). Suppose that the direction of projection is given by the vector $[x_p \quad y_p \quad z_p]$ and that the image is to be projected onto the xy plane. If we have a point on the object at (x_1, y_1, z_1), we wish to determine where the projected point (x_2, y_2) will lie. Let us begin by writing the equations for a line passing through the point (x, y, z) and in the direction of projection. This is easy to do using the parametric form

$$x = x_1 + x_p u$$

$$y = y_1 + y_p u \tag{8.35}$$

$$z = z_1 + z_p u$$

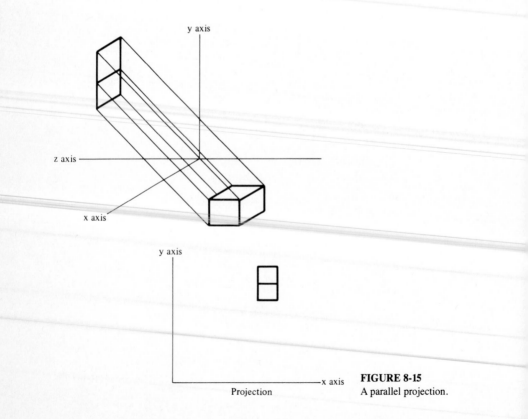

FIGURE 8-15
A parallel projection.

Now we ask, where does this line intersect the xy plane? That is, what are the x and y values when z is 0? If z is 0, the third equation tells us that the parameter u is

$$u = -\frac{z_1}{z_p} \tag{8.36}$$

Substituting this into the first two equations gives

$$x_2 = x_1 - z_1 (x_p / z_p)$$
$$y_2 = y_1 - z_1 (y_p / z_p) \tag{8.37}$$

This projection formula is in fact a transformation which may be written in matrix form

$$[\, x_2 \; y_2 \,] = [\, x_1 \; y_1 \; z_1 \,] \begin{vmatrix} 1 & 0 \\ 0 & 1 \\ -x_p/z_p & -y_p/z_p \end{vmatrix} \tag{8.38}$$

or in full homogeneous coordinates

$$[\, x_2 \; y_2 \; z_2 \; 1 \,] = [\, x_1 \; y_1 \; z_1 \; 1 \,] \begin{vmatrix} 1 & 0 & 0 & 0 \\ 0 & 1 & 0 & 0 \\ -x_p/z_p & -y_p/z_p & 0 & 0 \\ 0 & 0 & 0 & 1 \end{vmatrix} \tag{8.39}$$

This transformation always gives 0 for z_2, the z position of the view plane, but it is often useful to maintain the z information. We will find it useful in Chapter 9 when we order projected objects according to their z position as part of the hidden-surface removal process. A transformation that includes determining a z-coordinate value z_2 (which turns out to be the same as z_1) is as follows:

$$[\, x_2 \; y_2 \; z_2 \; 1 \,] = [\, x_1 \; y_1 \; z_1 \; 1 \,] \begin{vmatrix} 1 & 0 & 0 & 0 \\ 0 & 1 & 0 & 0 \\ -x_p/z_p & -y_p/z_p & 1 & 0 \\ 0 & 0 & 0 & 1 \end{vmatrix} \tag{8.40}$$

We will just ignore the z value when drawing the projected image.

Let us write an algorithm for performing parallel projections. We shall assume that the ratios

$$SXP = x_p / z_p$$
$$SYP = y_p / z_p \tag{8.41}$$

have been calculated and stored, so as to avoid recomputing them for every point projected.

8.12 Algorithm PARALLEL-TRANSFORM(X, Y, Z) Parallel projection of a point
Arguments   X, Y, Z the point to be projected, also for return of result
Global   SXP, SYP the parallel projection vector ratios
BEGIN
    $X \leftarrow X - Z * SXP$;
    $Y \leftarrow Y - Z * SYP$;
    RETURN;
END;

PERSPECTIVE PROJECTION

An alternative projection procedure is a *perspective projection*. In a perspective projection, the further away an object is from the viewer, the smaller it appears. This provides the viewer with a depth cue, an indication of which portions of the image correspond to parts of the object which are close or far away. In a perspective projection, the lines of projection are not parallel. Instead, they all converge at a single point called the *center of projection*. It is the intersections of these converging lines with the plane of the screen that determine the projected image. The projection gives the image which would be seen if the viewer's eye were located at the center of projection. The lines of projection would correspond to the paths of the light rays coming from the object to the eye. (See Figure 8-16.)

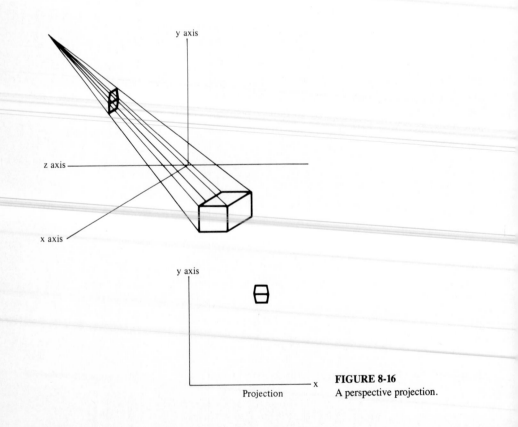

FIGURE 8-16
A perspective projection.

If the center of projection is at (x_c, y_c, z_c) and the point on the object is (x_1, y_1, z_1), then the projection ray will be the line containing these points and will be given by

$$x = x_c + (x_1 - x_c)u$$

$$y = y_c + (y_1 - y_c)u \qquad (8.42)$$

$$z = z_c + (z_1 - z_c)u$$

The projected point (x_2, y_2) will be the point where this line intersects the xy plane. The third equation tells us that u, for this intersection point $(z = 0)$, is

$$u = -\frac{z_c}{z_1 - z_c} \qquad (8.43)$$

Substituting into the first two equations gives

$$x_2 = x_c - z_c \frac{x_1 - x_c}{z_1 - z_c}$$

$$\qquad (8.44)$$

$$y_2 = y_c - z_c \frac{y_1 - y_c}{z_1 - z_c}$$

With a little algebra, we can rewrite this as

$$x_2 = \frac{x_c z_1 - x_1 z_c}{z_1 - z_c}$$

$$\qquad (8.45)$$

$$y_2 = \frac{y_c z_1 - y_1 z_c}{z_1 - z_c}$$

This projection can be put into the form of a transformation matrix if we take full advantage of the properties of homogeneous coordinates. The form of the matrix is

$$P = \begin{vmatrix} -z_c & 0 & 0 & 0 \\ 0 & -z_c & 0 & 0 \\ x_c & y_c & 0 & 1 \\ 0 & 0 & 0 & -z_c \end{vmatrix} \qquad (8.46)$$

To show that this transformation works, consider the point (x_1, y_1, z_1). In homogeneous coordinates we would have

$$[x_1 w_1 \quad y_1 w_1 \quad z_1 w_1 \quad w_1]$$

Multiplying by the transformation matrix gives

$$[x_2 w_2 \ y_2 w_2 \ z_2 w_2 \ w_2] = [x_1 w_1 \ y_1 w_1 \ z_1 w_1 \ w_1] \begin{vmatrix} -z_c & 0 & 0 & 0 \\ 0 & -z_c & 0 & 0 \\ x_c & y_c & 0 & 1 \\ 0 & 0 & 0 & -z_c \end{vmatrix}$$

$$= [-x_1 w_1 z_c + z_1 w_1 x_c \quad -y_1 w_1 z_c + z_1 w_1 y_c \quad 0 \quad z_1 w_1 - z_c w_1] \qquad (8.47)$$

so

$$w_2 = z_1 w_1 - z_c w_1 \tag{8.48}$$

and

$$z_2 w_2 = 0 \tag{8.49}$$

which gives

$$z_2 = 0 \tag{8.50}$$

and

$$x_2 w_2 = -x_1 w_1 z_c + z_1 w_1 x_c \tag{8.51}$$

which gives

$$x_2 = \frac{x_c z_1 - x_1 z_c}{z_1 - z_c} \tag{8.52}$$

and

$$y_2 w_2 = -y_1 w_1 z_c + z_1 w_1 y_c \tag{8.53}$$

which gives

$$y_2 = \frac{y_c z_1 - y_1 z_c}{z_1 - z_c} \tag{8.54}$$

The resulting point (x_2, y_2) is then indeed the correctly projected point.

An equivalent form of the projection transformation is

$$P_1 = \begin{vmatrix} 1 & 0 & 0 & 0 \\ 0 & 1 & 0 & 0 \\ -x_c/z_c & -y_c/z_c & 0 & -1/z_c \\ 0 & 0 & 0 & 1 \end{vmatrix} \tag{8.55}$$

The change is the factor of $-1/z_c$. Because we divide the first three coordinates (x_w, y_w, z_w) by w to obtain the actual position, changing all four coordinates by some common factor has no net effect. In the literature, the perspective transformation is often defined such that the center of projection is located at the origin and the view plane is positioned at $z = d$. For this situation, the transformation is given by

$$P_2 = \begin{vmatrix} 1 & 0 & 0 & 0 \\ 0 & 1 & 0 & 0 \\ 0 & 0 & 0 & 1/d \\ 0 & 0 & 0 & 1 \end{vmatrix} \tag{8.56}$$

We can show that the descriptions are equivalent as follows. To get the perspective transformation with the center of projection at (x_c, y_c, z_c), we can first translate this point to the origin, and then use the perspective transformation matrix P_2 given in Equation 8.55, where d is $-z_c$. We finally translate back to the original coordinates. The details of the proof are left as an exercise.

The above transformation maps points on an object to points on the view plane. We shall, however, find it useful to use a modified version of this transformation. We want a form which yields the same x and y values so that we can still display the image, but we would like to compute a z value different from zero. We would like to find z values such that we can preserve the depth relationship between objects, even after they are transformed. If object A lies in front of object B, we want the perspective transformation of object A to lie in front of the perspective transformation of object B. Furthermore, we want to compute z values such that after transforming the points on a straight line, we still have a straight line. We want the transformation to preserve planarity so that polygons are not warped into nonpolygons. The reason we want to do this is to allow us to establish depth order for hidden-surface removal (in Chapter 9) after having performed the perspective transformation. A form of the perspective transformation which meets these requirements is as follows:

$$P = \begin{vmatrix} -z_c & 0 & 0 & 0 \\ 0 & -z_c & 0 & 0 \\ x_c & y_c & -1 & 1 \\ 0 & 0 & 0 & -z_c \end{vmatrix} \qquad (8.57)$$

This yields a transformed z value given by

$$z_2 = \frac{z_1}{z_1 - z_c} \qquad (8.58)$$

We shall now present an algorithm for performing a perspective transformation of a point.

8.13 Algorithm PERSPECTIVE-TRANSFORM(X, Y, Z) For perspective projection of a point
Arguments X, Y, Z the view plane coordinates of the point
Global XC, YC, ZC the center of projection
Local D the denominator in the calculations
Constant ROUNDOFF some small number greater than any round-off error
VERY-LARGE a very large number approximating infinity
BEGIN
    D ← ZC − Z
    IF |D| < ROUNDOFF THEN
        BEGIN
            X ← (X − XC) * VERY-LARGE
            Y ← (Y − YC) * VERY-LARGE
            Z ← VERY-LARGE
        END

```
        ELSE
          BEGIN
            X ← (X * ZC − XC * Z) / D;
            Y ← (Y * ZC − YC * Z) / D;
            Z ← Z / D;
          END;
        RETURN;
      END;
```

VIEWING PARAMETERS

We have seen how parallel and perspective projections can be used to form a two-dimensional image from a three-dimensional object as seen from the front. But suppose we wish to view the object from the side, or the top, or even from behind. How can this be done? All that we need to do is to apply some rotation transformations before projecting. There are two equivalent ways of thinking about this. We can think of the *view plane* (that is, the plane of our display surface) as fixed and the object as rotated, or we can picture the object as fixed and the view plane as repositioned. (See Figure 8-17.)

In our system we shall use this second description. It is as if the view plane were the film in a camera. Every display-file segment represents a photograph taken by this camera. (See Figure 8-18.)

We can move the camera anywhere, so we can view the object from any angle. The picture taken by this synthetic camera is what is shown on the display surface, as if the film is developed and stuck upon the screen. The user is given routines by which he may change a number of viewing parameters. By setting the parameters, he can position the synthetic camera.(See Figure 8-19.)

The first parameters we shall consider are the coordinates of the *view reference point* (XR, YR, ZR). The view reference point is the center of attention. All other viewing parameters are expressed relative to this point. If we rotate the view, it will be a rotation about the view reference point (not about the origin). We can think of the view reference point as an anchor to which we have tied a string. The synthetic camera is attached to the other end of the string. By changing other viewing parameters, we can swing the camera through an arc or change the length of the string. One end of the string is always attached to the view reference point.

The direction of this imaginary string is given by the *view plane normal* vector [DXN DYN DZN]. This normal vector is the direction perpendicular to the view plane (the view plane is the film in the camera). This means that the camera always looks along the string toward the view reference point. The camera is pointed in the direction of the view plane normal.

The length of the string is given by the VIEW-DISTANCE parameter. This tells how far the camera is positioned from the view reference point. The view plane is positioned VIEW-DISTANCE away from the view reference point in the direction of the view plane normal.

We now have two coordinate systems. We have the object coordinates which we used to model our object, and we have *view plane coordinates*, which are attached to the

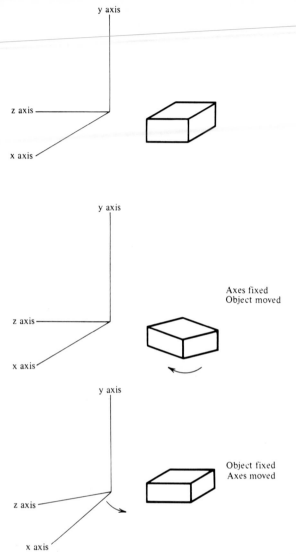

Axes fixed
Object moved

Object fixed
Axes moved

FIGURE 8-17
Rotating an object is equivalent to rotating the axes in the opposite direction.

view plane. Think of the *object coordinates* as being painted on the "floor" which supports the object, while the view plane coordinates have been printed on the film in the synthetic camera. We can place the origin of the view plane coordinates at the point where the string attaches to the film, that is, where a line parallel to the view plane normal, passing through the view reference point, intersects the view plane.

There is one more viewing parameter we need to discuss. Imagine holding the string fixed and spinning the camera on it so that the string serves as the axis of rotation. At each angle, the photograph will show the same scene, but rotated so that a different part of the object is up. (See Figure 8-20.)

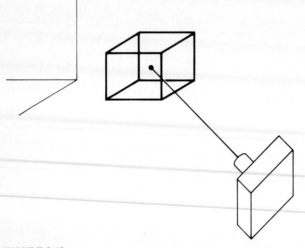

FIGURE 8-18
The synthetic camera analogy.

The *view-up* direction [XUP   YUP   ZUP] fixes the camera angle. Imagine an arrow extending from the view reference point in the view-up direction. We look through the camera's viewfinder and spin the camera until the arrow appears to be in the camera's ''up'' direction.

Changing the view reference point will change the part of the object that is shown at the origin. (See Figure 8-21.)

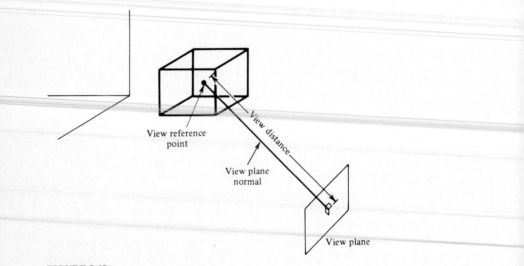

FIGURE 8-19
Three-dimensional viewing parameters.

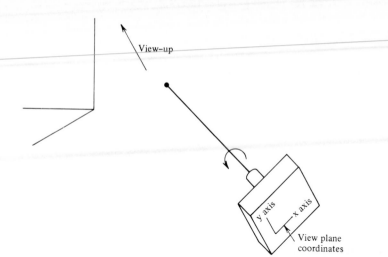

FIGURE 8-20
View-up and the view plane coordinates.

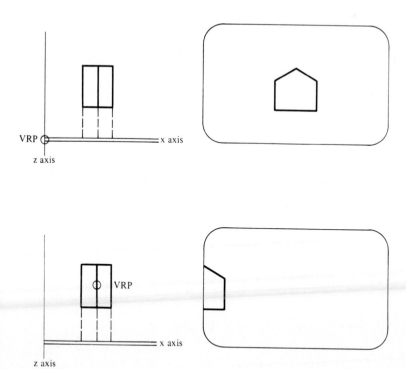

FIGURE 8-21
Changing the view reference point.

Changing the view plane normal will move the camera so as to photograph the object from a different orientation, but the same part of the object is always shown at the origin. (See Figure 8-22.)

Changing the view distance determines how far away from the object the camera is when it takes the picture. (See Figure 8-23.)

When changing view-up, we can imagine always pointing the camera at the same object from the same direction, but twisting the camera in our hands so that the picture, when developed, will turn out sideways or upside-down. (See Figure 8-24.)

These parameters allow the user to select how to view the object. Our system must provide the user with a means of setting the parameters to the values which he desires. The values are saved as global variables. The following algorithms provide an interface between the user and the three-dimensional viewing transformation system.

8.14 Algorithm SET-VIEW-REFERENCE-POINT(X, Y, Z) For changing the view reference point

Arguments   X, Y, Z the new view reference point
Global   XR, YR, ZR permanent storage for the reference point
BEGIN
    XR ← X;
    YR ← Y;
    ZR ← Z;
    RETURN;
END;

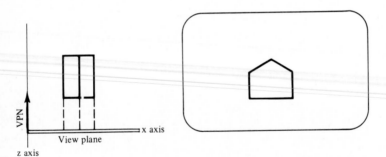

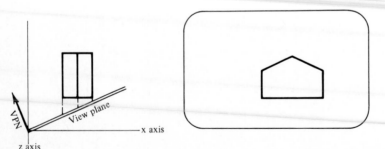

FIGURE 8-22
Changing the view plane normal.

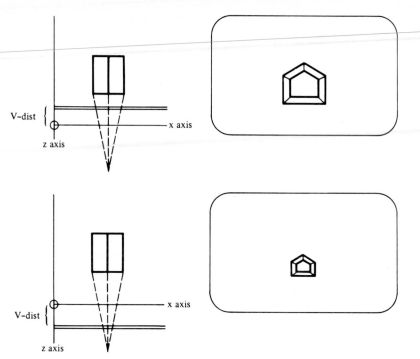

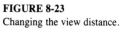

FIGURE 8-23
Changing the view distance.

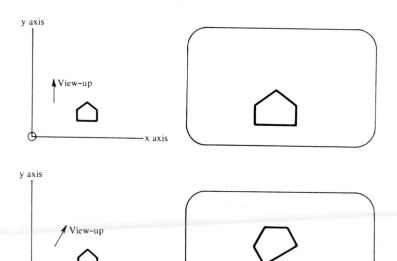

FIGURE 8-24
Changing the view-up direction.

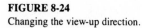

8.15 Algorithm SET-VIEW-PLANE-NORMAL(DX, DY, DZ) For changing the view plane normal

Arguments   DX, DY, DZ the new view plane normal vector

Global   DXN, DYN, DZN permanent storage for the view plane normal

Local   D the length of the user's specification vector

Constant   ROUNDOFF some small number greater than any round-off error

BEGIN
    D ← SQRT(DX ↑ 2 + DY ↑ 2 + DZ ↑ 2);
    IF D < ROUNDOFF THEN
        RETURN ERROR 'INVALID VIEW PLANE NORMAL';
    DXN ← DX / D;
    DYN ← DY / D;
    DZN ← DZ / D;
    RETURN;
END;

8.16 Algorithm SET-VIEW-DISTANCE(D) For changing distance between view reference point and view plane

Argument   D the new distance

Global   VIEW-DISTANCE the permanent storage for the view distance

BEGIN
    VIEW-DISTANCE ← D;
    RETURN;
END;

8.17 Algorithm SET-VIEW-UP(DX, DY, DZ) For changing the direction which will be vertical on the image

Global   DXUP, DYUP, DZUP permanent storage for the view-up direction

Constant   ROUNDOFF some small number greater than any round-off error

BEGIN
    IF |DX| + |DY| + |DZ| < ROUNDOFF THEN
        RETURN ERROR 'NO SET-VIEW-UP DIRECTION';
    DXUP ← DX;
    DYUP ← DY;
    DZUP ← DZ;
    RETURN;
END;

In the above algorithm we use an approximation to the length in order to avoid a zero-length vector. It is easier and faster to sum absolute values than to calculate the square root required for the true length (as we did in algorithm 8.15). The approximation will be no smaller than the true length and will be larger by no more than a factor of $\sqrt{3}$. It therefore provides a good indication of the vector's length and will catch the zero cases.

We must also provide the user with a means for setting the projection. (See Figures 8-25 and 8-26.)

For a parallel projection, the user must specify the direction of the projection lines. A perspective projection requires the location of the center of a projection point. The values are saved in global variables. A flag is used to indicate whether a perspec-

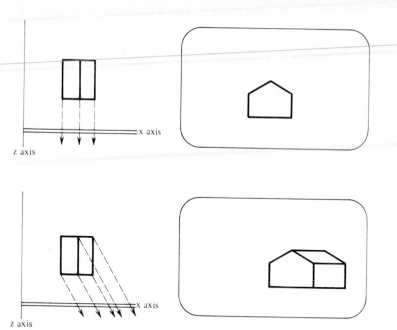

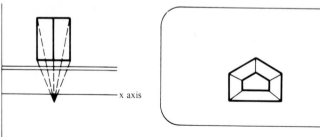

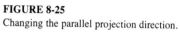

FIGURE 8-25
Changing the parallel projection direction.

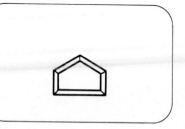

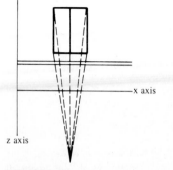

FIGURE 8-26
Changing the center of perspective projection.

tive or a parallel projection is desired. The flag is set to correspond to whichever type of projection was last specified.

8.18 Algorithm SET-PARALLEL(DX, DY, DZ) For user input of the direction of parallel projection

Arguments   DX, DY, DZ the new parallel projection vector

Global   PERSPECTIVE-FLAG the perspective vs. parallel projection flag
              DXP, DYP, DZP permanent storage for the direction of projection

Constant   ROUNDOFF some small number greater than any round-off error

BEGIN
      IF |DX| + |DY| + |DZ| < ROUNDOFF THEN
            RETURN ERROR 'NO DIRECTION OF PROJECTION';
      PERSPECTIVE-FLAG ← FALSE;
      DXP ← DX;
      DYP ← DY;
      DZP ← DZ;
      RETURN;
END;

8.19 Algorithm SET-PERSPECTIVE(X, Y, Z) Indicate a perspective projection and save the center of projection

Arguments   X, Y, Z the new center of projection

Global   XPCNTR, YPCNTR, ZPCNTR the permanent storage for the center
              of projection
              PERSPECTIVE-FLAG perspective vs. parallel projection flag

BEGIN
      PERSPECTIVE-FLAG ← TRUE;
      XPCNTR ← X;
      YPCNTR ← Y;
      ZPCNTR ← Z;
      RETURN;
END;

SPECIAL PROJECTIONS

The problem of rendering a two-dimensional view of a three-dimensional object existed long before the computer was used. One class of projection often used in drafting is called an *axonometric* projection. This is a parallel projection for which the direction of projection is perpendicular to the view plane. We can alter the direction of an axonometric projection to get a different view of an object, provided we also change the view plane normal to match the projection direction. Suppose that we are looking at a cube that has edges parallel to the object coordinate axes. We might start with a view looking straight at one of the faces so that the cube would appear to be a square. (See Figure 8-27.)

If we change our direction of projection slightly to the side, then one of the side faces will become visible, while the edges of the front face will shorten. If we raise our angle of view, the top edges lengthen to make the top face visible, while the edges on the side faces appear to shrink. (See Figure 8-28.)

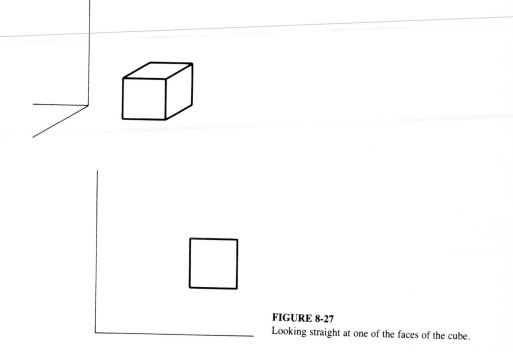

FIGURE 8-27
Looking straight at one of the faces of the cube.

There is a particular direction of projection for which all edges will appear short-ened from their three-dimensional length by the same factor. This special direction is called an *isometric* projection. (See Figure 8-29.)

An isometric projection of a cube will show a corner of the cube in the middle of the image surrounded by three identical faces. From the symmetry of the situation, we can see that the commands needed for an isometric projection of an object with sides parallel to the axes are:

SET-PARALLEL(1, 1, 1);
SET-VIEW-PLANE-NORMAL(−1, −1, −1);

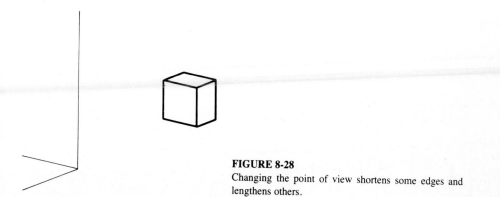

FIGURE 8-28
Changing the point of view shortens some edges and lengthens others.

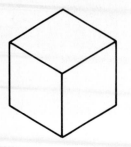

FIGURE 8-29
Isometric projection shortens all axes equally.

This projection will focus on the upper right-front corner of the object. The appropriate commands for projections of the other seven corners are left to the reader as an exercise.

If a viewing transformation is chosen such that edges parallel to only two of the axes are equally shortened, then the projection is called *dimetric*. (See Figure 8-30.)

A *trimetric* projection is one in which none of the three edge directions is equally shortened. There are no symmetries in the angles between the direction of projection and the directions of the object edges. (See Figure 8-31.)

If the direction of parallel projection is not parallel to the view plane normal, then we have what is called an *oblique* projection. We shall describe two special types of oblique projections, called *cavalier* projections and *cabinet* projections.

Let us first discuss the cavalier projection. Let us assume that we are viewing an object with edges parallel to the coordinate axes. The view plane will be parallel to the front face (parallel to the xy plane). For a cavalier projection, the direction of projection is slanted so that points with positive z coordinates will be projected down and to the left on the view plane. Points with negative z coordinates will be projected up and to the right. The angle of the projected z axis (the ratio of up to right) can be whatever we desire, but the distance the point shifts in the projected z direction must equal the actual three-dimensional z distance from the view plane. The projection command which will create a cavalier projection at angle A is

SET-PARALLEL(COS(A), SIN(A), 1).

Actually, any SET-PARALLEL command with arguments in the same ratio as those above will work as well. (See Figure 8-32.)

We stated that for a cavalier projection, the distance shifted along the projected z axis was equal to the actual z-axis distance. This restriction makes it easy to construct

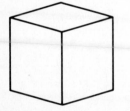

FIGURE 8-30
Dimetric projection shortens two axes equally.

FIGURE 8-31
Trimetric projection shortens all axes differently.

these drawings. However, the result is an object which appears elongated along the z direction. An alternative which is still easy to construct with a scale and triangle is to shift only half the actual z distance along the projected z axis. This is called a cabinet projection. (See Figure 8-33.) It can be created by a SET-PARALLEL call with arguments in the ratio of

SET-PARALLEL(COS(A), SIN(A), 2).

Perspective projections can be classified as one-point, two-point, or three-point. These names refer to the number of vanishing points required for a construction of the drawing. Our routines are sufficiently general to generate all three types of perspective projection. A *one-point perspective* projection occurs when one of the faces of a rectangular object is parallel to the view plane. (See Figure 8-34.)

A *two-point perspective* projection refers to the situation where one set of edges runs parallel to the view plane, but none of the faces is parallel to it. (See Figure 8-35.)

A *three-point perspective* projection is the case where none of the edges is parallel to the view plane. (See Figure 8-36.)

CONVERSION TO VIEW PLANE COORDINATES

The user enters the description of the object in terms of the object coordinates. But our particular point of view corresponds to expressing the object in the view plane coordinates. The process of generating a particular view of the object is one of transforming from one coordinate system to another. While this problem may appear complex, it is actually one which we have already solved. The steps to be taken are the same as those

y axis

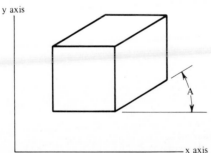

x axis

FIGURE 8-32
A cavalier projection.

y axis

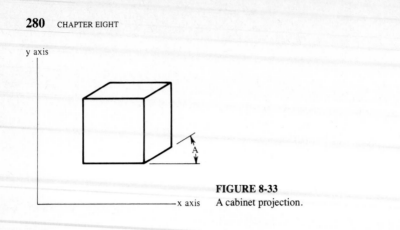

FIGURE 8-33   A cabinet projection.

x axis

which were used for a rotation about an arbitrary axis. We wish to perform a series of transformations which will change the object coordinates into the view plane coordinates. The first step is a translation to move the origin to the correct position for the view plane coordinate system. This is a shift first to the view reference point, and then along the view plane normal by the VIEW-DISTANCE. After the origin is in place, we align the z axis. In the rotation problem, we saw how to rotate a line onto the z axis.

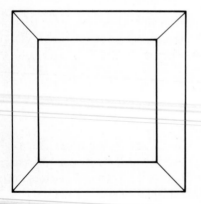

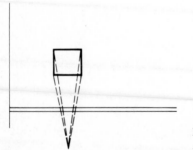

FIGURE 8-34
A one-point perspective.

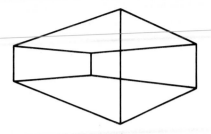

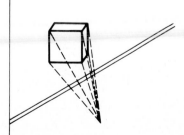

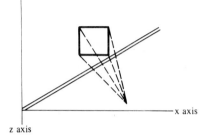

FIGURE 8-35
A two-point perspective.

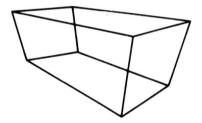

x axis

z axis

FIGURE 8-36
A three-point perspective.

281

Here, we wish that line to be the object coordinate's z axis, and we shall rotate it into the view plane coordinate's z axis (the view plane normal). This is done in two steps. First, a rotation about the x axis places the line in the view plane coordinate's xz plane. Then a rotation about the y axis moves the z axis to its proper position. Now all that is needed is to rotate about the z axis until the x and y axes are in their place in the view plane coordinates. The entire transformation sequence is given by

$$\text{TMATRIX} = \text{TR}_x\text{R}_y\text{R}_z \tag{8.59}$$

where

$$T = \begin{vmatrix} 1 & 0 & 0 & 0 \\ 0 & 1 & 0 & 0 \\ 0 & 0 & 1 & 0 \\ -(XR + DXN * VIEW\text{-}DISTANCE) & -(ZR + DZN * VIEW\text{-}DISTANCE) \\ & -(YR + DYN * VIEW\text{-}DISTANCE) & & 1 \end{vmatrix} \tag{8.60}$$

$$R_X = \begin{vmatrix} 1 & 0 & 0 & 0 \\ 0 & -DZN/V & -DYN/V & 0 \\ 0 & DYN/V & -DZN/V & 0 \\ 0 & 0 & 0 & 1 \end{vmatrix} \tag{8.61}$$

and

$$V = (DYN^2 + DZN^2)^{1/2} \tag{8.62}$$

also

$$R_y = \begin{vmatrix} V & 0 & -DXN & 0 \\ 0 & 1 & 0 & 0 \\ DXN & 0 & V & 0 \\ 0 & 0 & 0 & 1 \end{vmatrix} \tag{8.63}$$

and

$$R_z = \begin{vmatrix} YUP\text{-}VP/RUP & XUP\text{-}VP/RUP & 0 & 0 \\ -XUP\text{-}VP/RUP & YUP\text{-}VP/RUP & 0 & 0 \\ 0 & 0 & 1 & 0 \\ 0 & 0 & 0 & 1 \end{vmatrix} \tag{8.64}$$

where

$$[XUP\text{-}VP \quad YUP\text{-}VP \quad Z \quad 1] = [DXUP \quad DYUP \quad DZUP \quad 1] R_xR_y \tag{8.65}$$

and

$$RUP = (XUP\text{-}VP^2 + YUP\text{-}VP^2)^{1/2} \tag{8.66}$$

What are these XUP-VP and YUP-VP variables? We are trying to finish up the transformation process by rotating the x and y axes into position. The correct position is obtained when the y axis is aligned with the projection on the view plane of the view-up vector. But the view-up vector was specified in the object coordinates. It is much easier to work in the (as yet incomplete) view plane coordinate system. In the view plane system, we can project the view-up vector onto the view plane by just ignoring the z coordinate. The x and y values will be in the ratio of the sine and cosine of the angle needed to correctly align the up direction. So what we are doing is performing our partial transformation $(R_x R_y)$ on the view-up direction. The translation part is not needed because we are working on a vector (which has no position, only magnitude and direction). The z coordinate is ignored to project onto the view plane, and the distance from the origin to the projected point is calculated. Dividing the x and y values by this distance yields the sine and cosine of the needed rotation angle. The following algorithm will create the view plane coordinate transformation.

8.20 Algorithm MAKE-VIEW-PLANE-TRANSFORMATION For making the viewing transformation

Global   XR, YR, ZR the view reference point
DXN, DYN, DZN the view plane normal
DXUP, DYUP, DZUP the view-up direction
TMATRIX a 4 × 3 transformation matrix array
PERSPECTIVE-FLAG the perspective projection flag
VIEW-DISTANCE distance between view reference point and view plane
Local   V, XUP-VP, YUP-VP, RUP for storage of partial results
Constant   ROUNDOFF some small number greater than any round-off error
BEGIN
    start with the identity matrix
    NEW-TRANSFORM-3;
    translate so that view plane center is new origin
    TRANSLATE-3(−(XR + DXN * VIEW-DISTANCE),
        −(YR + DYN * VIEW-DISTANCE), −(ZR + DZN * VIEW-DISTANCE));
    rotate so that view plane normal is z axis
    V ← SQRT(DYN ↑ 2 + DZN ↑ 2);
    IF V > ROUNDOFF THEN ROTATE-X-3(− DYN / V, − DZN / V);
    ROTATE-Y-3(DXN, V);
    determine the view-up direction in these new coordinates
    XUP-VP ← DXUP * TMATRIX[1, 1] + DYUP * TMATRIX[2, 1] +
        DZUP * TMATRIX[3, 1];
    YUP-VP ← DXUP * TMATRIX[1, 2] + DYUP * TMATRIX[2, 2] +
        DZUP * TMATRIX[3, 2];
    determine rotation needed to make view-up vertical
    RUP ← SQRT(XUP-VP ↑ 2 + YUP-VP ↑ 2);
    IF RUP < ROUNDOFF THEN
        RETURN ERROR 'SET-VIEW-UP ALONG VIEW PLANE NORMAL';
    ROTATE-Z-3(XUP-VP / RUP, YUP-VP / RUP);
    IF PERSPECTIVE-FLAG THEN MAKE-PERSPECTIVE-TRANSFORMATION
    ELSE MAKE-PARALLEL-TRANSFORMATION;
    RETURN;
END;

The above algorithm also converts the parallel or perspective projection parameters from object coordinates to view plane coordinates. This is done by calling either the MAKE-PARALLEL-TRANSFORMATION or the MAKE-PERSPECTIVE-TRANSFORMATION routine. The MAKE-PERSPECTIVE-TRANSFORMATION routine just applies the transformation matrix to the center of the projection point. An error occurs if the center of projection is on the wrong side of the view plane, that is, if the observer is on the same side of the screen as the object. The MAKE-PARALLEL-TRANSFORMATION routine converts the direction of parallel projection to the view plane coordinates. Since the direction is specified by a vector (no position), the translation portion of the transformation is omitted. An error occurs if the direction of projection turns out to be parallel to the view plane.

8.21 Algorithm MAKE-PERSPECTIVE-TRANSFORMATION Convert center of projection to view plane coordinates

Global   XPCNTR, YPCNTR, ZPCNTR the center of projection

               XC, YC, ZC the center of projection in view plane coordinates

BEGIN

    XC ← XPCNTR;

    YC ← YPCNTR;

    ZC ← ZPCNTR;

    VIEW-PLANE-TRANSFORM(XC, YC, ZC);

    IF ZC < 0 THEN

        RETURN ERROR 'CENTER OF PROJECTION BEHIND VIEW PLANE';

    RETURN;

END;

8.22 Algorithm MAKE-PARALLEL-TRANSFORMATION Calculation of direction of projection in view plane coordinates

Global   TMATRIX a 4×3 coordinate transformation matrix array

               DXP, DYP, DZP the parallel projection vector

               VXP, VYP, VZP direction of projection in view plane coordinates

               SXP, SYP the slopes of the projection relative to z direction

Constant   ROUNDOFF some small number greater than any round-off error

BEGIN

    VXP ← DXP * TMATRIX[1, 1] + DYP * TMATRIX[2, 1] +

      DZP * TMATRIX[3, 1];

    VYP ← DXP * TMATRIX[1, 2] + DYP * TMATRIX[2, 2] +

      DZP * TMATRIX[3, 2];

    VZP ← DXP * TMATRIX[1, 3] + DYP * TMATRIX[2, 3] +

      DZP * TMATRIX[3, 3];

    IF |VZP| < ROUNDOFF THEN

        RETURN ERROR 'PROJECTION PARALLEL VIEW PLANE';

    SXP ← VXP / VZP;

    SYP ← VYP / VZP;

    RETURN;

END;

CLIPPING IN THREE DIMENSIONS

In Chapter 6 we introduced the idea of a window, which served as a clipping boundary in two-dimensional space. In three-dimensional space the concept can be extended to a clipping volume or view volume. This is a three-dimensional region or box. Objects within the view volume may be seen, while those outside are not displayed. Objects crossing the boundary are cut, and only the portion within the view volume is shown. A view volume may clip the front or back of an object as well as its sides. For example, imagine the image of a building. The picture centers on the door of the building. The size of the entrance increases as you seem to approach it. Passing through the doorway, the outside walls disappear. The display now shows the entry hall. Clipping may be used to remove the front wall of the building, which was hiding its interior. (See Figure 8-37.)

The extension from two-dimensional to three-dimensional clipping is not a difficult one. The methods remain basically the same. The difference lies in the test to see whether or not a point is inside the visible region. Instead of comparing the point against a line, we now must compare the point against a plane. In general, any plane

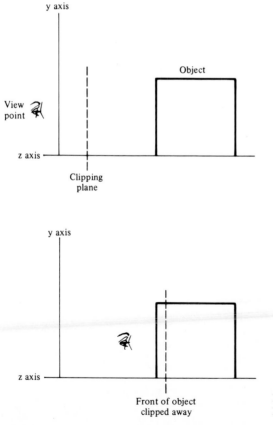

FIGURE 8-37
Moving a clipping plane through an object.

may be used as a boundary, and clipping regions can be arbitrary polyhedra; but there are two *view volume* shapes which are usually used because they are easy to work with. The type of view volume used depends on whether a parallel or a perspective projection is to be employed. For a parallel projection, imagine planes that are in the direction of projection extending from the edges of the window. These planes form a rectangular tube in space. Front and back clipping planes can be added to section this tube into a box. Objects within the box are visible, whereas those outside are clipped away. (See Figure 8-38.) An application of front and back clipping is shown in Plate 2, where the clipping planes are used to show a slice of a molecule. For a perspective projection, we picture rays from the center of projection passing through the window to form a viewing pyramid. This pyramid can be truncated by the front and back clipping planes to form the volume in which objects may be seen. (See Figure 8-39.)

The reason for choosing these regions becomes apparent when we consider what happens when the objects are projected. After projection, objects within the view volume will lie within the window on the view plane. After projection, the clipping planes run parallel to the z axis through the window boundaries, and their equations look the same as the window boundary line equations. This means that if we project the objects before clipping, then the left, right, top, and bottom clipping cases are essentially the same as the window clipping we have already seen in Chapter 6.

We must provide a means to specify where the front and back clipping planes are located. We shall provide algorithms to set these parameters in the same way that the window boundary was specified. The planes will be positioned relative to the view reference point in the direction of the view plane normal. (See Figure 8-40.)

For both the parallel and perspective cases, we have a view volume bounded by six clipping planes. The top, bottom, and side planes can be determined from the window and projection information, but additional routines are needed to allow the user to specify the front and back clipping planes. This is just a matter of saving the position specified by the user in some global variables. The following algorithm will save the positions given in terms of the distance from the view reference point in the direction of the view plane normal.

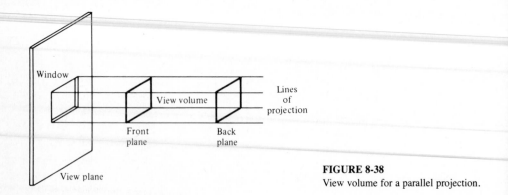

FIGURE 8-38
View volume for a parallel projection.

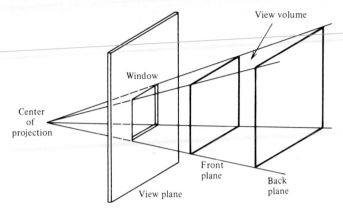

FIGURE 8-39
View volume for a perspective projection.

8.23 Algorithm SET-VIEW-DEPTH(FRONT-DISTANCE, BACK-DISTANCE) User
routine to specify the position of front and back clipping planes

Arguments   FRONT-DISTANCE, BACK-DISTANCE plane distance from the view
              reference point along the view plane normal

Global   FRONT-HOLD, BACK-HOLD storage for plane positions

BEGIN
   IF FRONT-DISTANCE > BACK-DISTANCE THEN
      RETURN ERROR 'FRONT PLANE BEHIND BACK PLANE';
   FRONT-HOLD ← FRONT-DISTANCE;
   BACK-HOLD ← BACK-DISTANCE;
   RETURN;
END;

We could, if we wished, omit the front and/or back clipping tests. All that is
needed is a flag which indicates whether to compare a point against the clipping plane

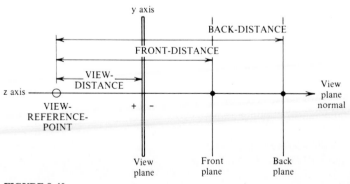

FIGURE 8-40
Front and back clipping plane specification.

or to pass it to the next routine without checking. With very little effort, we can give the user the ability to turn the front and back clipping on or off. Routines which will set clipping flags for this purpose are given below.

8.24 Algorithm SET-FRONT-PLANE-CLIPPING(ON-OFF) User routine to set the front clipping flag
Argument   ON-OFF the user's clipping flag setting
Global   FRONT-FLAG-HOLD the front clipping flag set by the user
BEGIN
    FRONT-FLAG-HOLD ← ON-OFF;
    RETURN;
END;

8.25 Algorithm SET-BACK-PLANE-CLIPPING(ON-OFF) User routine to set the back clipping flag
Argument   ON-OFF the user's clipping flag setting
Global   BACK-FLAG-HOLD the back clipping flag set by the user
BEGIN
    BACK-FLAG-HOLD ← ON-OFF;
    RETURN;
END;

We need to decide whether to perform the z-plane clipping before or after projection. Clipping can be done at either point, provided that the $Z/(Z_C - Z)$ transformation is used on the clipping plane position if we are clipping after a perspective projection. The argument for clipping in z after the projection is that CLIP-FRONT and CLIP-BACK algorithms can simply be incorporated into the clipping sequence. The reason why clipping before projection is desirable is that perspective projection requires that objects lie behind the center of projection. Now if we wish to construct programs where the center of projection (the eye of the viewer) moves among objects and perhaps even through them, then we would like to remove from consideration all objects which lie in front of the center of projection before that projection is carried out. That is, we want to employ front clipping to remove the objects that the viewer has passed and then to project the remaining objects which might be seen. (See Figure 8-41.) We shall present algorithms for the simpler case of clipping after projection and leave clipping before projection as a programming problem.

We shall use the MAKE-Z-CLIP-PLANES algorithm to capture and save the user's front and back clipping specification (which can be changed at any time). This will give fixed clipping characteristics for the life of a display-file segment, as is done in NEW-VIEW-2 for the window clipping planes.

8.26 Algorithm MAKE-Z-CLIP-PLANES Establish the front and back clipping planes
Global   FRONT-HOLD, BACK-HOLD storage for plane positions
              FRONT-Z position of the front clipping plane
              BACK-Z position of the back clipping plane
              FRONT-FLAG-HOLD the front clipping flag set by the user
              BACK-FLAG-HOLD the back clipping flag set by the user

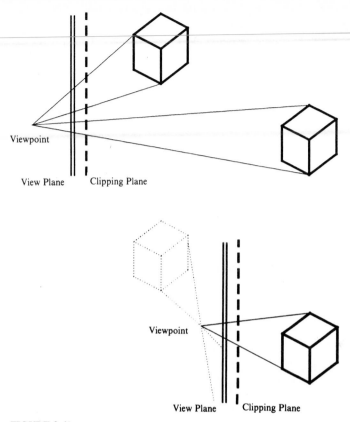

FIGURE 8-41
Front clipping before projection can remove objects that should not be projected.

> FRONT-FLAG the front clipping flag
> BACK-FLAG the back clipping flag
> VIEW-DISTANCE the permanent storage for the view distance
> PERSPECTIVE-FLAG the perspective projection flag
> XC, YC, ZC the center of projection in view plane coordinates

```
BEGIN
   FRONT-FLAG ← FRONT-FLAG-HOLD;
   BACK-FLAG ← BACK-FLAG-HOLD;
   FRONT-Z ← VIEW-DISTANCE − FRONT-HOLD;
   BACK-Z ← VIEW-DISTANCE − BACK-HOLD;
   IF PERSPECTIVE-FLAG THEN
      BEGIN
         FRONT-Z ← FRONT-Z / (ZC − FRONT-Z);
         BACK-Z ← BACK-Z / (ZC − BACK-Z);
      END;
   RETURN;
END;
```

CLIPPING PLANES

The clipping problem becomes one of deciding on which side of a plane a point lies. This is similar to the problem of deciding on which side of a line a point lies in a plane. Remember that the equation of a plane has the form

$$Ax + By + Cz + D = 0 \tag{8.67}$$

Suppose we plug the coordinate values of a point (x_1, y_1, z_1) into this equation. Then if the point is on the plane, the equation will be satisfied.

$$Ax_1 + By_1 + Cz_1 + D = 0 \tag{8.68}$$

But if the point is not on the plane, the result will not be zero. It will be positive if the point is on one side of the plane

$$Ax_1 + By_1 + Cz_1 + D > 0 \tag{8.69}$$

and negative if the point is on the other side.

$$Ax_1 + By_1 + Cz_1 + D < 0 \tag{8.70}$$

We can therefore tell if a point is within the clipping boundary by checking the sign of the expression obtained from the equation of the plane.

Let's consider what the equations describing our actual clipping planes will be. The front and back clipping planes are particularly simple. We shall take them to be parallel to the view plane, so in the view plane coordinate system they are given by

$$z = \text{FRONT-Z} \quad \text{and} \quad z = \text{BACK-Z} \tag{8.71}$$

where FRONT-Z and BACK-Z are constants giving the positions of these planes on the z axis. (See Figure 8-42.)

For the point (x_1, y_1, z_1) to be visible, it must be behind or on the front plane and in front of or on the back plane. The tests should then be

$$z_1 \leq \text{FRONT-Z} \quad \text{and} \quad z_1 \geq \text{BACK-Z} \tag{8.72}$$

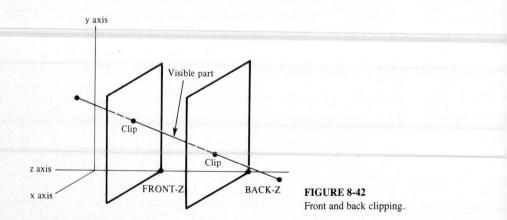

FIGURE 8-42
Front and back clipping.

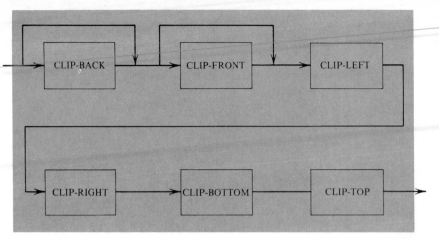

FIGURE 8-43
The clipping process.

Using these tests, we may write algorithms similar to those of Chapter 6 for clipping against back and front planes. These algorithms may be included with upgraded versions of the two-dimensional algorithms to give us three-dimensional clipping. Each visible point passes from one algorithm to the next until it has been checked against all clipping planes. (See Figure 8-43.)

8.27 Algorithm CLIP-BACK(OP, X, Y, Z) Routine for clipping against the back boundary
Arguments   OP, X, Y, Z a display-file instruction
Global   BACK-Z position of the back clipping plane
             BACK-FLAG the back clipping flag
             XS, YS, ZS arrays containing the last point drawn
             NEEDFIRST array of indicators for saving the first command
             FIRSTOP, FIRSTX, FIRSTY, FIRSTZ arrays for saving the first command
             CLOSING indicates the stage in polygon
BEGIN
    IF BACK-FLAG THEN
        BEGIN
            IF PFLAG AND NEEDFIRST[5] THEN
                BEGIN
                    FIRSTOP[5] ← OP;
                    FIRSTX[5] ← X;
                    FIRSTY[5] ← Y;
                    FIRSTZ[5] ← Z
                    NEEDFIRST[5] ← FALSE;
                END
            ELSE
                IF Z ≤ BACK-Z AND ZS[5] < BACK-Z THEN

CLIP-FRONT(1, $(X - XS[5]) * (BACK-Z - Z) / (Z - ZS[5]) + X,$
$(Y - YS[5]) * (BACK-Z - Z) / (Z - ZS[5]) + Y,$
BACK-Z)

ELSE
IF $Z \leq$ BACK-Z AND ZS[5] > BACK-Z THEN
IF OP > 0 THEN
CLIP-FRONT(OP, $(X - XS[5]) * (BACK-Z - Z) / (Z - ZS[5])$
$+ X,$
$(Y - YS[5]) * (BACK-Z - Z) / (Z - ZS[5])$
$+ Y,$ BACK-Z)

ELSE
CLIP-FRONT(1, $(X - XS[5]) * (BACK-Z - Z) / (Z - ZS[5])$
$+ X,$
$(Y - YS[5]) * (BACK-Z - Z) / (Z - ZS[5])$
$+ Y,$ BACK-Z);

XS[5] ← X;
YS[5] ← Y;
ZS[5] ← Z;
IF $Z \geq$ BACK-Z AND CLOSING $\neq$ 5 THEN CLIP-FRONT(OP, X, Y, Z);
END
ELSE CLIP-FRONT(OP, X, Y, Z);
RETURN;
END;

8.28 Algorithm CLIP-FRONT(OP, X, Y, Z) Routine for clipping against the front
boundary
Arguments   OP, X, Y, Z a display-file instruction
Global   FRONT-Z position of the front clipping plane
            FRONT-FLAG the front clipping flag
            XS, YS, ZS arrays containing the last point drawn
            NEEDFIRST array of indicators for saving the first command
            FIRSTOP, FIRSTX, FIRSTY, FIRSTZ arrays for saving the first command
            CLOSING indicates the stage in polygon
BEGIN
    IF FRONT-FLAG THEN
        BEGIN
            IF PFLAG AND NEEDFIRST[6] THEN
                BEGIN
                    FIRSTOP[6] ← OP;
                    FIRSTX[6] ← X;
                    FIRSTY[6] ← Y;
                    FIRSTZ[6] ← Z;
                    NEEDFIRST[6] ← FALSE;
                END
            ELSE
                IF $Z \leq$ FRONT-Z AND ZS[6] > FRONT-Z THEN
                    CLIP-LEFT(1, $(X - XS[6]) * (FRONT-Z - Z) / (Z - ZS[6]) + X,$
                    $(Y - YS[6]) * (FRONT-Z - Z) / (Z - ZS[6]) + Y,$
                    FRONT-Z)

```
    ELSE
        IF Z ≥ FRONT-Z and ZS[6] < FRONT-Z THEN
            IF OP > 0 THEN
                CLIP-LEFT(OP, (X − XS[6]) * (FRONT-Z − Z) / (Z − ZS[6])
                    + X
                    (Y − YS[6]) * (FRONT-Z − Z) / (Z − ZS[6])
                    + Y, FRONT-Z)
            ELSE
                CLIP-LEFT(1, WXH, (X − XS[6]) * (FRONT-Z − Z) /
                    (Z − ZS[6]) + X,
                    (Y − YS[6]) * (FRONT-Z − Z) /
                    (Z − ZS[6]) + Y, FRONT-Z);
        XS[6] ← X;
        YS[6] ← Y;
        ZS[6] ← Z;
        IF Z ≤ FRONT-Z AND CLOSING ≠ 6 THEN CLIP-LEFT(OP, X, Y, Z);
    END;
    ELSE CLIP-LEFT(OP, X, Y, Z);
    RETURN;
END;
```

The following routines are extensions of those presented in Chapter 6. In many cases all that is needed is to include a z coordinate along with x and y. In the four routines which actually do the clipping, the z coordinate of any intersection with the clipping plane must be calculated, as well as the x or the y coordinate. We are maintaining the z-coordinate information in anticipation of its use in the hidden-surface routines of the next chapter.

8.29 Algorithm CLIP-LEFT(OP, X, Y, $\underline{Z}$). (An extension of algorithm 6.6 to three dimensions) Routine for clipping against the left boundary

Arguments OP, X, Y, $\underline{Z}$ a display-file instruction
Global WXL window left boundary
XS, YS, $\underline{ZS}$ arrays containing the last point drawn
NEEDFIRST array of indicators for saving the first command
FIRSTOP, FIRSTX, FIRSTY, $\underline{FIRSTZ}$ arrays for saving the first command
CLOSING indicates the stage in polygon

```
BEGIN
    IF PFLAG AND NEEDFIRST[1] THEN
        BEGIN
            FIRSTOP[1] ← OP;
            FIRSTX[1] ← X;
            FIRSTY[1] ← Y;
            FIRSTZ[1] ← Z;
            NEEDFIRST[1] ← FALSE;
        END
    Case of drawing from outside in
    ELSE
        IF X ≥ WXL AND XS[1] < WXL THEN
```

CLIP-RIGHT(1, WXL, (Y − YS[1]) ∗ (WXL − X) / (X − XS[1]) + Y,

(Z − ZS[1]) ∗ (WXL − X) / (X − XS[1]) + Z)

Case of drawing from inside out

ELSE

IF X ≤ WXL AND XS[1] > WXL THEN

IF OP > 0 THEN

CLIP-RIGHT(OP, WXL, (Y − YS[1]) ∗ (WXL − X) / (X − XS[1])

+ Y,

(Z − ZS[1]) ∗ (WXL − X) / (X − XS[1])

+ Z)

ELSE

CLIP-RIGHT(1, WXL, (Y − YS[1]) ∗ (WXL − X) / (X − XS[1])

+ Y,

(Z − ZS[1]) ∗ (WXL − X) / (X − XS[1])

+ Z);

Remember point to serve as one of the endpoints of next line segment

XS[1] ← X;

YS[1] ← Y;

ZS[1] ← Z;

Case of point inside

IF X ≥ WXL AND CLOSING ≠ 1 THEN CLIP-RIGHT(OP, X, Y, Z);

RETURN;

END;

8.30 Algorithm CLIP-RIGHT(OP, X, Y, Z) (An extension of algorithm 6.7 to three dimensions) Routine for clipping against the right boundary

Arguments   OP, X, Y, Z a display-file instruction

Global   WXH window right boundary

XS, YS, ZS arrays containing the last point drawn

NEEDFIRST array of indicators for saving the first command

FIRSTOP, FIRSTX, FIRSTY, FIRSTZ arrays for saving the first command

CLOSING indicates the stage in polygon

BEGIN

IF PFLAG AND NEEDFIRST[2] THEN

BEGIN

FIRSTOP[2] ← OP;

FIRSTX[2] ← X;

FIRSTY[2] ← Y;

FIRSTZ[2] ← Z;

NEEDFIRST[2] ← FALSE;

END

ELSE

IF X ≤ WXH AND XS[2] > WXH THEN

CLIP-BOTTOM(1, WXH, (Y − YS[2]) ∗ (WXH − X) / (X − XS[2]) + Y,

(Z − ZS[2]) ∗ (WXH − X) / (X − XS[2]) + Z)

ELSE

IF X ≥ WXH and XS[2] < WXH THEN

IF OP > 0 THEN

CLIP-BOTTOM(OP, WXH, (Y − YS[2]) ∗ (WXH − X) / (X − XS[2])

+ Y,

$$\frac{(Z - ZS[2]) * (WXH - X) / (X - XS[2])}{+ Z)}$$

ELSE
      CLIP-BOTTOM(1, WXH, $\underline{(Y - YS[2]) * (WXH - X) / (X - XS[2])}$
            + Y,
            $\underline{(Z - ZS[2]) * (WXH - X) / (X - XS[2])}$
            + Z);

XS[2] ← X;
YS[2] ← Y;
ZS[2] ← Z;
IF X ≤ WXH AND CLOSING ≠ 2 THEN CLIP-BOTTOM(OP, X, Y, Z);
RETURN;
END;

8.31 Algorithm CLIP-BOTTOM(OP, X, Y, Z) (An extension of algorithm 6.8 to three dimensions) Routine for clipping against the lower boundary

Arguments   OP, X, Y, Z a display-file instruction
Global   WYL window lower boundary
              XS, YS, ZS arrays containing the last point drawn
              NEEDFIRST array of indicators for saving the first command
              FIRSTOP, FIRSTX, FIRSTY, FIRSTZ arrays for saving the first command
              CLOSING indicates the stage in polygon
BEGIN
  IF PFLAG AND NEEDFIRST[3] THEN
    BEGIN
      FIRSTOP[3] ← OP;
      FIRSTX[3] ← X;
      FIRSTY[3] ← Y;
      FIRSTZ[3] ← Z;
      NEEDFIRST[3] ← FALSE;
    END
  ELSE
    IF Y ≥ WYL AND YS[3] < WYL THEN
      CLIP-TOP(1, (X − XS[3]) * (WYL − Y) / (Y − YS[3]) + X, WYL,
          (Z − ZS[3]) * (WYL − Y) / (Y − YS[3]) + Z)
    ELSE
      IF Y ≤ WYL AND YS[3] > WYL THEN
        IF OP > 0 THEN
          CLIP-TOP(OP, (X − XS[3]) * (WYL − Y) / (Y − YS[3]) + X, WYL,
             (Z − ZS[3]) * (WYL − Y) / (Y − YS[3]) + Z)
        ELSE
          CLIP-TOP(1, (X − XS[3]) * (WYL − Y) / (Y − YS[3]) + X, WYL,
             (Z − ZS[3]) * (WYL − Y) / (Y − YS[3]) + Z);
XS[3] ← X;
YS[3] ← Y;
ZS[3] ← Z;
IF Y ≥ WYL AND CLOSING ≠ 3 THEN CLIP-TOP(OP, X, Y, Z);
RETURN;
END;

8.32 Algorithm CLIP-TOP(OP, X, Y, Z) (An extension of algorithm 6.9 to three dimensions) Routine for clipping against the upper boundary

Arguments   OP, X, Y, Z a display-file instruction

Global   WYH window upper boundary

XS, YS, ZS arrays containing the last point drawn

NEEDFIRST array of indicators for saving the first command

FIRSTOP, FIRSTX, FIRSTY, FIRSTZ arrays for saving the first command

CLOSING indicates the stage in polygon

BEGIN
  IF PFLAG AND NEEDFIRST[4] THEN
    BEGIN
      FIRSTOP[4] ← OP;
      FIRSTX[4] ← X;
      FIRSTY[4] ← Y;
      FIRSTZ[4] ← Z;
      NEEDFIRST[4] ← FALSE;
    END
  ELSE
    IF Y ≤ WYH AND YS[4] > WYH THEN
      SAVE-CLIPPED-POINT(1, (X − XS[4]) ∗ (WYH − Y) /
                  (Y − YS[4]) + X, WYH,
                  (Z − ZS[4]) ∗ (WYH − Y) / (Y − YS[4]) + Z);
    ELSE
      IF Y ≥ WYH AND YS[4] < WYH THEN
        IF OP > 0 THEN
          SAVE-CLIPPED-POINT(OP, (X − XS[4]) ∗ (WYH − Y) /
                     (Y − YS[4]) + X, WYH,
                    (Z − ZS[4]) ∗ (WYH − Y) /
                    (Y − YS[4]) + Z)
        ELSE
          SAVE-CLIPPED-POINT(1, (X − XS[4]) ∗ (WYH − Y) /
                     (Y − YS[4]) + X, WYH,
                    (Z − ZS[4]) ∗ (WYH − Y) /
                    (Y − YS[4]) + Z);
  XS[4] ← X;
  YS[4] ← Y;
  ZS[4] ← Z;
  IF Y ≤ WYH AND CLOSING ≠ 4 THEN SAVE-CLIPPED-POINT(OP, X, Y, Z);
  RETURN;
END;

8.33 Algorithm SAVE-CLIPPED-POINT(OP, X, Y, Z) (An extension of algorithm 6.10 to three dimensions) Saves clipped polygons in T-buffer and sends lines and characters to the display file

Arguments   OP, X, Y, Z a display-file instruction

Global   COUNT-OUT a counter of number of sides on clipped polygon

PFLAG indicates if a polygon is being clipped

BEGIN
  IF PFLAG THEN
    BEGIN

```
            COUNT-OUT ← COUNT-OUT + 1;
            PUT-IN-T(OP, X, Y, Z, COUNT-OUT);
        END
    ELSE VIEWING-TRANSFORM(OP, X, Y);
    RETURN;
END;
```

8.34 Algorithm PUT-IN-T(OP, X, Y, Z, INDEX) (An extension of algorithm 6.11 to three dimensions)

Arguments   OP, X, Y, Z the instruction to be stored
            INDEX the position at which to store it
Global   IT, XT, YT, ZT arrays for temporary storage of polygon sides

```
BEGIN
    IT[INDEX] ← OP;
    XT[INDEX] ← X;
    YT[INDEX] ← Y;
    ZT[INDEX] ← Z;
    RETURN;
END;
```

8.35 Algorithm CLIP-POLYGON-EDGE(OP, X, Y, Z) (An extension of algorithm 6.12 to three dimensions) Close and enter a clipped polygon into the display file

Arguments   OP, X, Y, Z a display-file instruction
Global   PFLAG indicates that a polygon is being drawn
            COUNT-IN the number of sides remaining to be processed
            COUNT-OUT the number of sides to be entered in the display file
            IT, XT, YT, temporary storage arrays for a polygon
            NEEDFIRST array of indicators for saving the first command
            FIRSTOP, FIRSTX, FIRSTY, FIRSTZ arrays for saving the first command
            CLOSING indicates the stage in polygon
            FRONT-FLAG, BACK-FLAG indicate whether front and back clipping is done
Local   I for stepping through the polygon sides

```
BEGIN
    COUNT-IN ← COUNT-IN − 1;
    CLIP-BACK(OP, X, Y, Z);
    IF COUNT-IN ≠ 0 THEN RETURN;
    close the clipped polygon
    CLOSING ← 5;
    IF BACK-FLAG AND NOT NEEDFIRST[5] THEN
    CLIP-BACK(FIRSTOP[5], FIRSTX[5], FIRSTY[5], FIRSTZ[5]);
    CLOSING ← 6;
    IF FRONT-FLAG AND NOT NEEDFIRST[6] THEN
    CLIP-FRONT(FIRSTOP[6], FIRSTX[6], FIRSTY[6], FIRSTZ[6]);
    CLOSING ← 1;
    IF NOT NEEDFIRST[1] THEN
    CLIP-LEFT(FIRSTOP[1], FIRSTX[1], FIRSTY[1], FIRSTZ[1]);
    CLOSING ← 2;
    IF NOT NEEDFIRST[2] THEN
    CLIP-RIGHT(FIRSTOP[2], FIRSTX[2], FIRSTY[2], FIRSTZ[2]);
```

```
    CLOSING ← 3;
    IF NOT NEEDFIRST[3] THEN
    CLIP-BOTTOM(FIRSTOP[3], FIRSTX[3], FIRSTY[3], FIRSTZ[3]);
    CLOSING ← 4;
    IF NOT NEEDFIRST[4] THEN
    CLIP-TOP(FIRSTOP[4], FIRSTX[4], FIRSTY[4], FIRSTZ[4]);
    CLOSING ← 0;

    PFLAG ← FALSE;
    IF COUNT-OUT < 3 THEN RETURN;
    enter the polygon into the display file
    VIEWING-TRANSFORM(COUNT-OUT, XT[COUNT-OUT], YT[COUNT-OUT]);
    FOR I = 1 TO COUNT-OUT DO VIEWING-TRANSFORM(IT[I], XT[I], YT[I]);
    RETURN:
END;
```

8.36 Algorithm CLIP(OP, X, Y, Z) (An extension of algorithm 6.13 to three dimensions) Top-level clipping routine

```
Arguments   OP, X, Y, Z the instruction being clipped
Global      PFLAG indicates that a polygon is being processed
            COUNT-IN number of polygon sides still to be input
            COUNT-OUT number of clipped polygon sides stored
            XS, YS, ZS arrays for saving the last point drawn
Local       I for initializing the four clipping routines
BEGIN
    IF PFLAG THEN CLIP-POLYGON-EDGE(OP, X, Y, Z)
    ELSE IF OP > 2 THEN
            BEGIN
                PFLAG ← TRUE;
                COUNT-IN ← OP;
                COUNT-OUT ← 0;
                FOR I = 1 TO 6 DO
                    BEGIN
                        XS[I] ← X;
                        YS[I] ← Y;
                        ZS[I] ← Z;
                    END;
            END
            ELSE CLIP-BACK(OP, X, Y, Z);
    RETURN;
END;
```

THE 3D VIEWING TRANSFORMATION

We finally have all of the tools which are needed to process the user's three-dimensional drawing. We assume that the user has specified the desired viewing parameters, and that the MAKE-VIEW-PLANE-TRANSFORMATION routine has been used to create a view plane coordinate transformation. The user now calls a three-dimensional drawing command such as LINE-ABS-3(X, Y, Z). This command updates the pen position and calls the DISPLAY-FILE-ENTER routine which transforms and projects the position onto the view plane before entering it into the display file. The steps are to first multiply by the view plane transformation matrix to convert the point to view plane coordinates. This in effect changes the viewpoint to that of our synthetic camera. Second, we perform a projection to place the two-dimensional image on the "film." Finally, we save the image in the display file by means of our clipping routine. Doing the clipping after the view plane transformation makes it seem as if our clipping window is attached to the view plane. It governs the size of the "film" in the synthetic camera. (See Figure 8-44.)

An algorithm to multiply a point by the view plane transformation matrix and thereby convert it from object to view plane coordinates is given next.

8.37 Algorithm VIEW-PLANE-TRANSFORM(X, Y, Z) Transforms a point into the view plane coordinate system
Arguments   X, Y, Z point to be transformed, also for return of result
Global   TMATRIX a 4 × 3 transformation matrix array
Local   T three-element array to hold results until calculation finished
              I index for stepping through the TMATRIX columns
BEGIN
    FOR I = 1 TO 3 DO
        T[I] ← X * TMATRIX[1, I] + Y * TMATRIX[2, I] +
        Z * TMATRIX[3, I] + TMATRIX[4, I];
    X ← T[1];
    Y ← T[2];
    Z ← T[3];
    RETURN;
END;

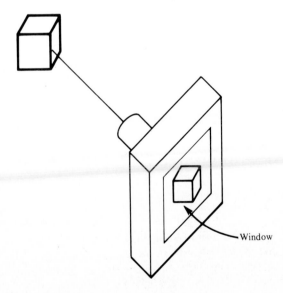

Window

FIGURE 8-44
The window is attached to the view plane.

The modified DISPLAY-FILE-ENTER routine is as follows:

8.38 Algorithm DISPLAY-FILE-ENTER(OP) (Revision of algorithm 6.14) Routine to enter an instruction into the display file

Argument   OP opcode of instruction to be entered
Global   DF-PEN-X, DF-PEN-Y, DF-PEN-Z the current pen position
            PERSPECTIVE-FLAG perspective vs. parallel projection flag
Local   X, Y, Z hold the point that is transformed
BEGIN
   IF OP < 1 AND OP > −32 THEN PUT-POINT(OP, 0, 0)
   ELSE
     BEGIN
        X ← DF-PEN-X;
        Y ← DF-PEN-Y;
        Z ← DF-PEN-Z;
        VIEW-PLANE-TRANSFORM(X, Y, Z);
        IF PERSPECTIVE-FLAG THEN PERSPECTIVE-TRANSFORM(X, Y, Z)
        ELSE PARALLEL-TRANSFORM(X, Y, Z);
        CLIP(OP, X, Y, Z);
     END;
   RETURN;
END;

To finish up, we will extend the CREATE-SEGMENT routine to call an algorithm named NEW-VIEW-3 that forms a new viewing transformation and establishes clipping parameters. This means that a new viewing transformation can be established for each display-file segment. The three-dimensional viewing parameters are therefore established in the same manner as the window specification. The user may set new values at any time, but the new values will not go into effect until a display-file segment is created. Furthermore, a particular viewing specification will remain in effect throughout the segment.

8.39 Algorithm NEW-VIEW-3 Create a new overall viewing transformation
BEGIN
   MAKE-VIEW-PLANE-TRANSFORMATION;
   NEW-VIEW-2;
   MAKE-Z-CLIP-PLANES;
   RETURN;
END;

8.40 Algorithm CREATE-SEGMENT(SEGMENT-NAME) (Modification of algorithm 7.17) User routine to create a named segment

Argument   SEGMENT-NAME the segment name
Global   NOW-OPEN the segment currently open
            FREE the index of the next free display-file cell
            SEGMENT-START, SEGMENT-SIZE, VISIBILITY, ANGLE, SCALE-X,
            SCALE-Y, TRANSLATE-X, TRANSLATE-Y,
            DETECTABLE the segment-table arrays
Constant   NUMBER-OF-SEGMENTS size of the segment table

```
BEGIN
    IF NOW-OPEN > 0 THEN RETURN ERROR 'SEGMENT STILL OPEN';
    IF SEGMENT-NAME < 1 OR SEGMENT-NAME > NUMBER-OF-SEGMENTS
    THEN
        RETURN ERROR 'INVALID SEGMENT NAME';
    IF SEGMENT-SIZE[SEGMENT-NAME] > 0 THEN
        RETURN ERROR 'SEGMENT ALREADY EXISTS';
    NEW-VIEW-3
    SEGMENT-START[SEGMENT-NAME] ← FREE;
    SEGMENT-SIZE[SEGMENT-NAME] ← 0;
    VISIBILITY[SEGMENT-NAME] ← VISIBILITY[0];
    ANGLE[SEGMENT-NAME] ← ANGLE[0];
    SCALE-X[SEGMENT-NAME] ← SCALE-X[0];
    SCALE-Y[SEGMENT-NAME] ← SCALE-Y[0];
    TRANSLATE-X[SEGMENT-NAME] ← TRANSLATE-X[0];
    TRANSLATE-Y[SEGMENT-NAME] ← TRANSLATE-Y[0];
    DETECTABLE[SEGMENT-NAME] ← DETECTABLE[0];
    NOW-OPEN ← SEGMENT-NAME;
    RETURN;
END;
```

We also need an initialization routine to establish default viewing parameters. The default parameters we shall choose are a view reference point at the origin, the view plane in the object coordinate xy plane, the view-up along the object coordinate's y direction, and a parallel projection in the z direction. Front and back clipping will initially be off.

8.41 Algorithm INITIALIZE-8 Initialization of global data

```
Local       I for initialization of the clipping routines
BEGIN
    initialize
    INITIALIZE-7;
    SET-VIEW-REFERENCE-POINT(0, 0, 0);
    SET-VIEW-PLANE-NORMAL(0, 0, −1);
    SET-VIEW-DISTANCE(0);
    SET-VIEW-UP(0, 1, 0);
    SET-PARALLEL(0, 0, 1);
    SET-FRONT-PLANE-CLIPPING(FALSE);
    SET-BACK-PLANE-CLIPPING(FALSE);
    SET-VIEW-DEPTH(0, 0);
    NEW-VIEW-3;
    FOR I = 1 to 6 DO
        BEGIN
            NEEDFIRST[I] ← FALSE;
            XS[I] ← 0;
            YS[I] ← 0;
            ZS[I] ← 0;
        END;
    RETURN;
END;
```

AN APPLICATION

One application relying heavily upon three-dimensional graphics is an airplane flight simulator. A flight simulator can be used as part of a pilot's training. The simulator may look like the real cockpit, only the windshield is replaced by a computer-generated image of the world. This image alters under the pilot's actions in the same manner as his view of the world would change if he were actually flying. In the simulator, the pilot may practice, and even err, without endangering anything but his pride. (See Figure 8-45.)

Let us consider how our three-dimensional graphics system might be used in a flight simulator program. The first thing to be done is to construct a model of the world over which the pilot is to fly. Buildings, runways, fields, lakes, and other landscape features may be constructed using our three-dimensional LINE and POLYGON primitives. Windowing allows us to use real-world dimensions, such as meters. The construction may be somewhat tedious, but it is straightforward. Let us assume that it has been done, that we have a procedure named BUILD-WORLD which contains the commands for drawing the model landscape. We must still project this landscape onto the display screen. We wish to do it in such a manner as to produce the view which the pilot should see from his airplane. We shall consider the view plane to be the cockpit windshield. The view reference point will be attached to the airplane, so as it moves, the windshield (view plane) moves with it. A VIEW-DISTANCE value of zero will do nicely.

It may be convenient to think of the view reference point as centered on the windshield. We can accomplish this with our SET-WINDOW command.

SET-WINDOW(− 0.5, 0.5, − 0.5, 0.5);

The orientation of the plane corresponds to the orientation of its windshield, which is set by the SET-VIEW-PLANE-NORMAL command. The pilot may bank or roll the plane. This would change its view-up direction. And finally, we must indicate the projection, which should be a perspective view centered on the pilot's eye. This is behind the windshield, say about 0.5 meters away. (See Figure 8-46.)

Let us outline two routines, one which is called whenever the plane changes its position, and another to be called when the pilot alters the orientation of the plane. To update the plane's position, we change the view reference point and the center of projection.

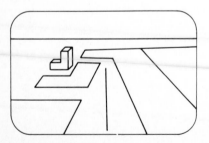

FIGURE 8-45
Airplane flight simulation.

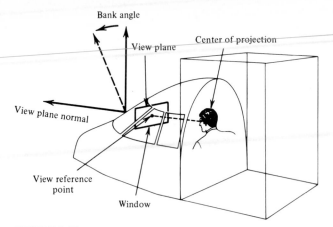

FIGURE 8-46
Parameters for flight simulation.

```
BEGIN
    SET-VIEW-REFERENCE-POINT(EAST-WEST, ALTITUDE, NORTH-SOUTH);
    SET-PERSPECTIVE(EAST-WEST − 0.5 * EW-DIRECTION,
        ALTITUDE − 0.5 * AL-DIRECTION, NORTH-SOUTH
        − 0.5 * NS-DIRECTION);
    CREATE-SEGMENT(2);
    SET-VISIBILITY(2, FALSE);
    BUILD-WORLD;
    CLOSE-SEGMENT;
    SET-VISIBILITY(1, FALSE);
    SET-VISIBILITY(2,TRUE);
    DELETE-SEGMENT(1);
    RENAME-SEGMENT(2, 1);
    RETURN;
END;
```

Here we have used (EAST-WEST, ALTITUDE, NORTH-SOUTH) as the coordinates of the plane's position. The vector [EW-DIRECTION AL-DIRECTION NS-DIRECTION] gives the plane's orientation and is assumed to be normalized. In the SET-PERSPECTIVE command, 0.5 is used as the distance of the pilot from the windshield. It is multiplied by the plane's direction and subtracted from the plane's position to give the pilot's position. The visibility property and segment renaming are used to ensure that the old image of the world is maintained until the new one is ready for display.

A routine to update the plane's orientation might look something like the following:

```
BEGIN
    SET-VIEW-PLANE-NORMAL(EW-DIRECTION, AL-DIRECTION, NS-DIREC-
    TION);
    SET-VIEW-UP(SIN(BANK-ANGLE) * NS-DIRECTION,
```

```
        COS(BANK-ANGLE) * (EW-DIRECTION ↑ 2 + NS-DIRECTION ↑ 2) ↑ 0.5,
        − SIN(BANK-ANGLE) * EW-DIRECTION);
    RETURN;
END;
```

In the above, BANK-ANGLE is how much the plane is banked to the left. A value of zero means level flight, and a negative value means banking to the right. The arithmetic which occurs within the call to SET-VIEW-UP finds a vector in the world coordinates which, if attached to the plane, would correspond to the vertical direction in level flight.

A program for flight simulation might also take advantage of three-dimensional clipping. Such a program should not display what is behind the airplane. We should extend the program so that it clips any object which lies behind the windshield (the view plane). We can do this with our front clipping plane. If the pilot has unlimited visibility, then the back clipping plane should not be used. If, on the other hand, we wish to simulate the limiting effects of bad weather on visibility, an approach might be to simply clip away all objects that exceed the range of vision.

Instructions to set up the front and back clipping might look as follows:

```
SET-VIEW-DEPTH(0, VISIBILITY-DISTANCE);
SET-FRONT-PLANE-CLIPPING(TRUE);
SET-BACK-PLANE-CLIPPING(BAD-WEATHER);
```

In the above, VISIBILITY-DISTANCE is the distance which the pilot is able to see. BAD-WEATHER is TRUE if the pilot's visibility is limited, and FALSE otherwise.

FURTHER READING

The mathematics of transformations and projections is further discussed in [ROG76]. An excellent discussion of homogeneous coordinates and transformations is available in [AHU68]. A mathematical discussion of rotations and reflection matrix properties is given in [FIL84]. There is a fine discussion of the homogeneous form of points, lines, and planes in [BLI77]. Homogeneous coordinates and the relationship between projected and Euclidean space are considered in [RIE81]. Homogeneous coordinates and clipping are considered in [BLI78]. A formal description of transformations and clipping in a hierarchical picture structure is described in [MAL78]. A discussion of projections and how they are specified is given in [CAR78]. A discussion of how to use our viewing system is presented in [BER78]. The viewing process is described in [ROG83]. In [MIC80] there is a critical evaluation of the CORE viewing parameters which we have used, and an alternative scheme for describing the view is presented. Perspective projections help to give some realism to three-dimensional objects but still only give a two-dimensional image. Work has been done on devising display hardware that will create three-dimensional images by presenting a different view to each eye. A survey of these techniques is found in [LAN82]. We have shown how to describe three-dimensional objects by their two-dimensional polygon surfaces, but they may also be described by three-dimensional structures. This is called solid modeling and is often used for computer-aided design. Three-dimensional image representation is also useful for medical applications such as computerized tomography. Some of these techniques are described in [AGG81], [BAD78], [HER82], [JAC80], [MEA82], [REQ80], [SRI81], and [WOO77]. A discussion of flight simulation may be found in [SCH81].

[AGG81] Aggarwal, J. K., Davis, L. S., Martin, W. N., Roach, J. W., "Survey: Representation Methods for Three-Dimensional Objects," *Progress in Pattern Recognition*, vol. 1, pp. 377–391 (1981).

[AHU68] Ahuja, D. V., Coons, S. A., "Geometry for Construction and Display," *IBM Systems Journal*, vol. 7, nos. 3 & 4, pp. 188–205 (1968).

[BAD78] Badler, N., Bajcsy, R., "Three-Dimensional Representations for Computer Graphics and Computer Vision," *Computer Graphics*, vol. 12, no. 3, pp. 153–160 (1978).

[BER78] Bergeron, R. D., Bono, P. R., Foley, J. D., "Graphics Programming Using the CORE System," *ACM Computing Surveys*, vol. 10, no. 4, pp. 389–394 (1978).

[BLI77] Blinn, J. F., "A Homogeneous Formulation for Lines in 3-Space," *Computer Graphics*, vol. 11, no. 2, pp. 237–241 (1977).

[BLI78] Blinn, J. F., Newell, M. E., "Clipping Using Homogeneous Coordinates," *Computer Graphics*, vol. 12, no. 3, pp. 245–251 (1978).

[CAR78] Carlbom, I., Paciorek, J., "Planar Geometric Projections and Viewing Transformations," *ACM Computing Surveys*, vol. 10, no. 4, pp. 465–502 (1978).

[FIL84] Fillmore, J. P., "A Note on Rotation Matrices," *IEEE Computer Graphics and Applications*, vol. 4, no. 2, pp. 30–33 (1984).

[HER82] Herman, G. T., Reynolds, R. A., Udupa, J. K., "Computer Techniques for the Representation of Three-Dimensional Data on a Two-Dimensional Display," *Proceedings of the SPIE*, vol. 367, pp. 3–14 (1982).

[JAC80] Jackins, C. L., Tanimoto, S. L., "Oct-Trees and Their Use in Representing Three-Dimensional Objects," *Computer Graphics and Image Processing*, vol. 14, no. 3, pp. 249–270 (1980).

[LAN82] Land, B., "Stereoscopic Displays," *Proceedings of SPIE*, vol. 367, pp. 20–32 (1982).

[MAL78] Mallgren, W. R., Shaw, A. C., "Graphical Transformations and Hierarchic Picture Structures," *Computer Graphics and Image Processing*, vol. 8, no. 3, pp. 237–258 (1978).

[MEA82] Meagher, D., "Geometric Modeling Using Octree Encoding," *Computer Graphics and Image Processing*, vol. 19, no. 2, pp. 129–147 (1982).

[MIC80] Michener, J. C., Carlbom, I. B., "Natural and Efficient Viewing Parameters," *Computer Graphics*, vol. 14, no. 3, pp. 238–245 (1980).

[REQ80] Requicha, A. A. G., "Representations for Rigid Solids: Theory, Methods, and Systems," *Computing Surveys*, vol. 12, no. 4, pp. 437–464 (1980).

[RIE81] Riesenfeld, R. F., "Homogeneous Coordinates and Projective Planes in Computer Graphics," *IEEE Computer Graphics and Applications*, vol. 1, no. 1, pp. 50–55 (1981).

[ROG76] Rogers, D. F., Adams, J., A., *Mathematical Elements for Computer Graphics*, McGraw-Hill, New York (1976).

[ROG83] Rogers, G., "Viewing," *Computers & Graphics*, vol. 7, no. 1, pp. 83–85 (1985).

[SCH81] Schachter, B. J., "Computer Image Generation for Flight Simulation," *IEEE Computer Graphics and Applications*, vol. 1, no. 10, pp. 29–68 (1981).

[SRI81] Srihari, S. N., "Representation of Three-Dimensional Digital Images," *Computing Surveys*, vol. 13, no. 4, pp. 399–424 (1981).

[WOO77] Woo, T. C., "Progress in Shape Modeling," *Computer*, vol. 10, no. 12, pp. 40–46 (1977).

EXERCISES

8-1 Write the parametric form for the line passing through the following points:
    a) $(0, 0, 0)$ and $(1, 2, 3)$
    b) $(1, 5, 4)$ and $(2, 2, 3)$
    c) $(8, 4, 1)$ and $(5, 2, -1)$

8-2 Give an equation for the following planes:

 a) Containing the point (0, 0, 0) and normal to vector [0, 0, 1]
 b) Containing the point (0, 0, 0) and normal to vector [0, 0, −1]
 c) Containing the point (0, 0, 0) and normal to vector [1, 1, 0]
 d) Containing the point (1, 1, 2) and normal to vector [4, 2, 3]
 e) Containing the points (1, 0, 0), (0, 1, 0), and (0, 0, 1)
 f) Containing the points (0, 0, 0), (1, 0, 0), and (0, 1, 1)
 g) Containing the points (0, 0, 0), (1, 2, 3), and (2, 3, 1)
 h) Containing the points (−1, 0, 1), (0, 1, 0), and (−1, 1, −2)

8-3 Write the three-dimensional homogeneous transformation matrix for each of the following transformations:

 a) Shift 0.5 in x, 0 in y, and −0.2 in z.
 b) Scale z to be half as large.
 c) Scale x and y to be three times as large.
 d) Rotate by $\pi/4$ about the x axis (y into z).
 e) Rotate by $\pi/3$ about the y axis (x into z).
 f) Rotate by π about the line passing through the points (0, 0, 0) and (1, 0, 1).

8-4 Suppose we wish to rotate about the origin so that a point (x, y, z) is moved to the positive z axis. Prove that the following four methods all result in the same transformation matrix.

 a) Rotate about the x axis to place the point in the xz plane. Then rotate about the y axis to place the point on the z axis.

 b) Rotate about the y axis to place the point in the yz plane. Then rotate about the x axis to place the point on the z axis.

 c) Rotate about the z axis to place the point in the xz plane. Then rotate about the y axis to place the point on the z axis.

 d) Rotate about the z axis to place the point in the yz plane. Then rotate about the x axis to place the point on the z axis.

8-5 Given the object

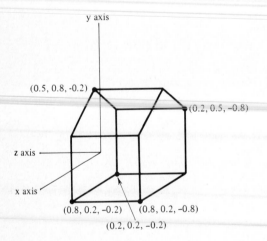

show how it would appear on the screen for each of the following viewing parameter specifications.

a) Default settings except SET-VIEW-REFERENCE-POINT(0.2, 0.2, −0.2)
b) Default settings except SET-PARALLEL(0.2, 0, 1)
c) Default settings except SET-PARALLEL(−0.2, 0, 1)
d) Default settings except SET-PARALLEL(0, −0.2, 1)
e) Default settings except SET-PARALLEL(0, 0.2, 1)
f) Default settings except SET-VIEW-PLANE-NORMAL(−0.5, 0, −1)
g) Default settings except SET-VIEW-PLANE-NORMAL(0, 0.5, −1)
h) Default settings except SET-PARALLEL(0.5, 0, 1)
   SET-VIEW-PLANE-NORMAL(−0.5, 0, −1)
i) Default settings except SET-PARALLEL(0, 0.5, 1)
   SET-VIEW-PLANE-NORMAL(0, −0.5, −1)
j) Default settings except SET-PARALLEL(0.5, 0.5, 1)
   SET-VIEW-PLANE-NORMAL(−0.5, −0.5, −1)
k) Default settings except SET-PARALLEL(0.5, 0, 1)
   SET-VIEW-PLANE-NORMAL(−0.5, 0, −1)
   SET-VIEW-REFERENCE-POINT(0.2, 0.2, −0.2)
l) Default settings except SET-PARALLEL(1, 0, 0)
   SET-VIEW-PLANE-NORMAL(−1, 0, 0)
   SET-VIEW-REFERENCE-POINT(0.2, 0.2, −0.2)
m) Default settings except SET-PARALLEL(0.2, 0, 1)
   SET-VIEW-DISTANCE(0.2)
n) Default settings except SET-PARALLEL(0.2, 0, 1)
   SET-VIEW-DISTANCE(−0.2)
o) Default settings except SET-VIEW-PLANE-NORMAL(−1, 0, 0)
   SET-PARALLEL(1, 0, 0)
   SET-VIEW-REFERENCE-POINT(0.8, 0.2, −0.2)
p) Default settings except SET-VIEW-UP(1, 1, 0)
q) Default settings except SET-PARALLEL(0, 1, 0)
   SET-VIEW-PLANE-NORMAL(0, −1, 0)
   SET-VIEW-REFERENCE-POINT(0.2, 0.2, −0.2)
   SET-VIEW-UP(0, 0, −1)
r) Default settings except SET-VIEW-UP(−1, 0, 0)
   SET-VIEW-REFERENCE-POINT(0.8, 0.2, −0.2)
   SET-VIEW-PLANE-NORMAL(0, −1, 0)
   SET-PARALLEL(0, 1, 0)

8-6 Consider the figure in Exercise 8-5. With the default viewing parameter except for
   SET-PERSPECTIVE(0.5, 0.5, 1)
   SET-DEPTH-CLIPPING-PLANES(0.3, 0.7)
sketch what would be shown for
   a) SET-FRONT-CLIPPING(TRUE)
      SET-BACK-CLIPPING(FALSE)
   b) SET-FRONT-CLIPPING(FALSE)
      SET-BACK-CLIPPING(TRUE)
   c) SET-FRONT-CLIPPING(TRUE)
      SET-BACK-CLIPPING(TRUE)
   d) SET-VIEW-REFERENCE-POINT(0, 0, −0.2)
      SET-FRONT-CLIPPING(TRUE)
      SET-BACK-CLIPPING(TRUE)

8-7 a) Prove that the perspective projection description expressed in Equation 8.46 is equivalent to that for Equation 8.55.

b) Prove that the perspective projection description expressed in Equation 8.55 is equivalent to that for Equation 8.56.

8-8 Prove that the perspective projection of a line segment is equal to the line segment between the perspective projection of the endpoints.

8-9 Develop three-dimensional clipping algorithms which may be applied before projection.

8-10 Develop a general three-dimensional clipping algorithm for clipping against an arbitrary plane. The clipping plane should be specified by the arguments to your algorithm as well as by the line to be clipped. Recursive or repeated calls to your algorithm should allow clipping to view volumes that are arbitrary convex polyhedra.

PROGRAMMING PROBLEMS

8-1 Implement algorithms 8.1 through 8.41 and extend your graphics system to three dimensions.

8-2 Test your graphics system by entering and viewing a three-dimensional house. Show the house in both parallel and perspective projection. Test the action of each of the viewing parameters by making small changes and observing the result.

8-3 Test the three-dimensional clipping algorithms by constructing a three-dimensional object model, such as a house, and in separate views for each, clip using the front, back, top, bottom, and side clipping planes. Try for both parallel and perspective projections.

8-4 Write the routines

    INQUIRE-VIEW-REFERENCE-POINT(X, Y, Z)
    INQUIRE-VIEW-PLANE-NORMAL(DX, DY, DZ)
    INQUIRE-VIEW-DISTANCE(D)
    INQUIRE-VIEW-UP(DX, DY, DZ)
    INQUIRE-PARALLEL(ON-OFF, DX, DY, DZ)
    INQUIRE-PERSPECTIVE(ON-OFF, X, Y, Z)
    INQUIRE-DEPTH-CLIPPING-PLANES(FRONT, BACK)
    INQUIRE-FRONT-CLIPPING(ON-OFF)
    INQUIRE-BACK-CLIPPING(ON-OFF)

which return to the user the last settings for the viewing parameters.

8-5 a) Show a cube in isometric, dimetric, and trimetric projection.

b) Show a cube in cavalier and in cabinet projection.

c) Show a cube in one-point, two-point, and three-point perspective projection.

8-6 Construct a program which gives successive views of a three-dimensional object generated by procedure FOO. The views should give the effect of walking around the object. Assume that the object is contained within the cube with corners $(0, 0, 0)$ and $(1, 1, -1)$.

8-7 Write a program which given the function

$$Y = FUN(X, Z)$$

will show the indicated surface by constructing lines of constant z for $z = 0.2, 0.4, 0.6, 0.8$ by connecting the values at $x = 0.2, 0.4, 0.6, 0.8$. Select a viewing transformation which best displays the surface. Try this for $FUN(X, Z) = SIN(X) * SIN(Z)$, or $FUN(X, Z) = X * Z$, or $FUN(X, Z) = 1 + X \uparrow 2 - Z \uparrow 2$.

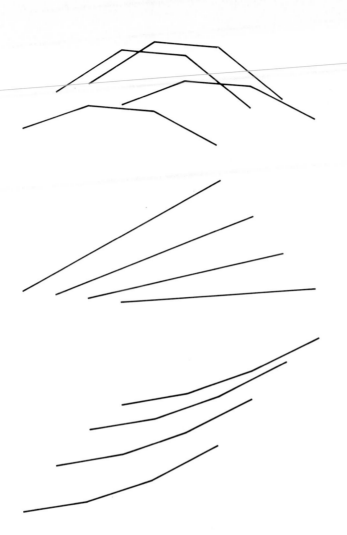

8-8 Display some solid object in perspective projection. Turn on the front clipping and, in successive views, move the clipping plane through the object by changing the view reference point and the center of projection. (Caution: If your routines clip after projection, be careful that the center of projection stays in front of the object.)

8-9 Write a program to move the viewer through a world of objects by setting the view reference point to successive positions along a path. Set the view plane normal to the vector between successive view reference point positions.

8-10 For a truly three-dimensional image of a scene we must present separate stereo views of the scene to each eye (corresponding to the two separate viewpoints). A number of methods have been tried in order to present each eye with its own picture, including systems of mirrors and lenses, shutters, polarized filters, and color filters. Write a graphics program which will produce the two stereo views required for three-dimensional display. (Hint: Consider the viewing parameter settings which will generate the scene as seen by each eye.)

8-11 Write a procedure which takes a polygon as an argument and enters into the graphics system a number of instances of the polygon rotated about the z axis. Using the procedure create a cylinder from a rectangle, a sphere from a circle.

8-12 Write a three-dimensional interactive point plotting program. Use three valuators to set the x, y, and z positions. Echo the position by displaying three intersecting cross hairs with tic marks.

*8-13 Construct a font of characters which can be positioned in three-dimensional space. Generalize the TEXT procedure to allow placement of a string of characters in any orientation on any three-dimensional plane. Show some text written on the top, sides, and bottom of a box. Display it using both parallel and perspective projections.

*8-14 Write an interactive program which repeatedly draws some three-dimensional object, allowing the user to select from a menu and alter the three-dimensional viewing and clipping parameters.

*8-15 Revise your graphics system so that the front and back clipping is carried out prior to projection.

*8-16 Write procedures for clipping against a view volume bounded by six arbitrary planes.

NINE

HIDDEN SURFACES AND LINES

INTRODUCTION

In the last chapter we described how to obtain different views of a scene. We developed perspective projections which made constructed objects look more realistic. But for a realistic scene, we should only draw those lines and polygons which could actually be seen, not those which would be hidden by other objects. What is hidden and what is visible depend upon the point of view. As seen from the front, the front of a building is visible, while the back of the structure is hidden; but as seen from the rear, this situation is reversed. We cannot see the contents of the building from outside because they are hidden by the building's walls, but from a point of view inside the building, some of the contents should be displayed. So far, we have learned how to model and project three-dimensional objects, but all parts of the objects are always displayed. This gives our drawings a transparent quality. Such figures are called *wire-frame drawings* because they look as if they are wire outlines of the supposedly solid objects. Complex objects can easily turn into a confusing clutter of line segments. It may be difficult to judge which lines belong to the front of the object and which to the back. The removal of hidden portions of objects is essential to producing realistic-looking images. (See for example Plates 4 through 15.) In this chapter we consider the problem of removing those lines which would normally be hidden by part of the object. If we can assign this task to the machine, then the user will be free to construct the entire model (front, back, inside, and outside) and still be able to see it as it will actually appear. This problem is not nearly as easy as it might seem at first. What nature does with ease (and a lot of parallel processing) we must do through extensive computation. There exist many solutions to the hidden surface and line problem. Many approaches have been tried; perhaps the best solution has yet to be found. We shall discuss several approaches, but only one solution will be implemented. The first section considers *back-face detection* and removal. This is sufficient for single convex objects. The second section considers the removal of hidden surfaces by means of the *painter's algorithm*.

BACK-FACE REMOVAL

Hidden-line removal can be a costly process, and so it behooves us to apply easy tests to simplify the problem as much as possible before undertaking a thorough analysis. There is a simple test which we can perform which will eliminate most of the faces which cannot be seen. This test identifies surfaces which face away from the viewer. They are the surfaces which make up the back of the object. They cannot be visible because the bulk of the object is in the way. This does not completely solve the hidden-surface problem because we can still have the front face of an object obscured by a second object or by another part of itself. But the test can remove roughly half of the surfaces from consideration and thus simplify the problem.

We begin our discussion by noting that we shall only consider polygons. Lines cannot obscure anything, and although they might be obscured, they are usually found only as edges of surfaces on an object. Because of this, polygons suffice for most drawings. Now a polygon has two surfaces, a front and a back, just as a piece of paper does. We might picture our polygons with one side painted light and the other painted dark. But given the arrays of vertex coordinates which represent polygons, how can we tell which face is which? Easy! We shall say that when we are looking at the light surface, the polygon will appear to be drawn with counterclockwise pen motions. If we move our point of view to the other side, so that the dark surface may be seen, the pen drawing the polygon will appear to move clockwise. (See Figure 9-1.)

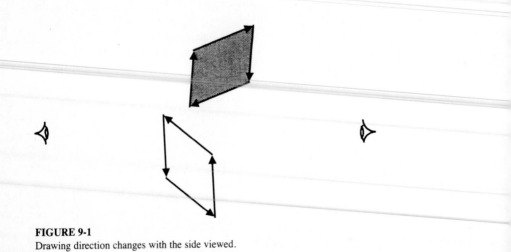

FIGURE 9-1
Drawing direction changes with the side viewed.

Now a little mathematics will give us the direction that the polygon surface is facing (the normal to the plane of the polygon). We shall describe two methods of finding the vector normal to the plane of the polygon. The first method uses an operation that is called the *vector cross product*. The cross product of two vectors is a third vector with the length equal to the product of the lengths of the two vectors times the sine of the angle between them and, most important to us, a direction perpendicular to the plane containing the two vectors. (See Figure 9-2.)

The formulas for a three-dimensional cross product in a right-handed coordinate system are as follows. For

$$[R_x \quad R_y \quad R_z] = [P_x \quad P_y \quad P_z] \times [Q_x \quad Q_y \quad Q_z] \tag{9.1}$$

we have

$$R_x = P_y Q_z - P_z Q_y$$
$$R_y = P_z Q_x - P_x Q_z \tag{9.2}$$
$$R_z = P_x Q_y - P_y Q_x$$

Now two sides of a polygon describe two vectors in the plane of the polygon, so the cross product of two polygon sides forms a vector pointing out from the polygon face. Will this vector point out from the dark face or the light face? That depends on whether the two sides form a convex or concave angle.

Let's assume that we are dealing with two adjacent sides which do not lie in the same line and which meet in a convex vertex, that is, a vertex where two sides meet to form a convex angle. The vector cross product will yield a vector which points out of the light face. (See Figure 9-3.)

The problem with this first approach to finding the vector normal to the polygon is that some searching and checking are required to find a vertex at a convex corner of noncollinear sides. The second method (which we shall use) is suggested by Newell and described in [SUT74]. The calculation is as follows: If the n vertices of the polygon are (x_i, y_i, z_i), then form the sums over all vertices

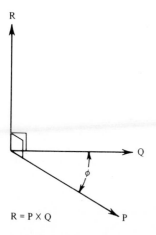

R = P × Q

FIGURE 9-2
The vector cross product.

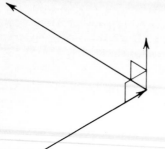

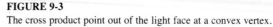

FIGURE 9-3
The cross product point out of the light face at a convex vertex.

$$a = \sum_{i=1}^{n} (y_i - y_j)(z_i + z_j)$$

$$b = \sum_{i=1}^{n} (z_i - z_j)(x_i + x_j) \qquad (9.3)$$

$$c = \sum_{i=1}^{n} (x_i - x_j)(y_i + y_j)$$

where if $i = n$, then $j = 1$; otherwise, $j = i + 1$.

The result [a b c] is a vector normal to the polygon. Each of these sums gives twice the area of the projections of the polygon on a plane. That is, if we project the polygon along the x direction to the yz plane, then the area of that projected polygon is $a/2$. The values $b/2$ and $c/2$ are the areas of the projections on the xz and xy planes, respectively. (The proof of this is left as an exercise.) So a, b, and c describe the projection of the polygon in the x, y, and z directions. But this is directly related to the direction of the plane. The amount of area projected along the z direction, for example, is proportional to the z component of the polygon's normal vector. So [a b c] is a normal vector to the plane of the polygon. The virtue of this method is that there are no special cases to check; we simply compute the sums.

Now, suppose that we make the rule that all solid objects are to be constructed out of polygons in such a way that only the light surfaces are open to the air; the dark faces meet the material inside the object. This means that when we look at an object face from the outside, it will appear to be drawn counterclockwise. (See Figure 9-4.)

If a polygon is visible, the light surface should face toward us and the dark surface should face away from us. Since a cross product or sum can be formed which gives the direction of the light face, this vector should point toward us. So if the normal vector points toward the viewer, the face is visible (a front face), otherwise, the face is hidden (a back face) and should be removed.

How can we tell whether or not a vector points toward the viewer? To do this, we examine the z component of the normal vector. If the z component is positive, then the polygon faces toward the viewer; if negative, it faces away.

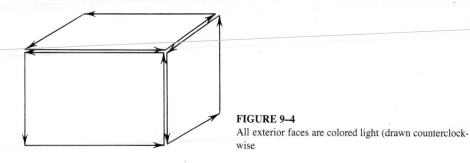

FIGURE 9-4
All exterior faces are colored light (drawn counterclock-wise

This is a special case of the general problem of comparing two vectors. If we have two vectors (say R and S) and wish to compare their directions, we use the vector dot product.

$$a = R \cdot S = |R||S| \cos \theta \qquad (9.4)$$

As we saw in Chapter 8, the dot product gives the product of the lengths of the two vectors times the cosine of the angle between them. This cosine factor is important to us because if the vectors are in the same direction ($0 \le \theta < \pi/2$), then the cosine is positive and the overall dot product is positive; but if the directions are opposing ($\pi/2 < \theta \le \pi$), then the cosine and the overall dot product are negative. (See Figure 9-5.)

The formula for computing a dot product is as follows:

$$a = R \cdot S$$
$$= [R_x \quad R_y \quad R_z] \cdot [S_x \quad S_y \quad S_z] \qquad (9.5)$$
$$= R_x S_x + R_y S_y + R_z S_z$$

For the back-face check, one vector is the normal to the polygon and the other is the depth direction $[0 \quad 0 \quad 1]$. So the test for a back face is then a check on the sign of the z component of the normal vector. (See Figure 9-6.)

Where should all of this checking be done? Certainly it should be done after the transformation to view plane coordinates. It should follow projection (the projection can affect whether the polygon image is drawn clockwise or counterclockwise). We should also wait until after clipping has been performed so that we won't bother with polygons outside of the window. There is a point in the CLIP-POLYGON-EDGE

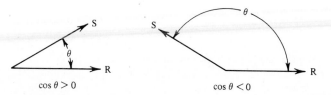

$$\cos \theta > 0 \qquad\qquad \cos \theta < 0$$

FIGURE 9-5
Cosine of the angle is positive if the vectors are pointing somewhat in the same direction and negative if they point away from each other.

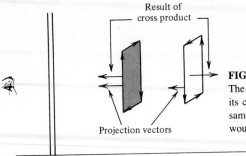

Result of cross product

Projection vectors

FIGURE 9-6
The left plane would be visible from the left because its cross product and projection vectors point in the same direction (positive dot product). The right plane would be a back face.

routine where the clipped polygon is sitting in a temporary storage buffer waiting to be placed into the display file. We test to be sure that the number of sides is at least 3 before the polygon is saved. At this point we can also perform our back-face check, requiring the polygon to also be a front face before it is saved.

BACK-FACE ALGORITHMS

Now let us detail the algorithms which will remove back faces. To begin with, we may not always want hidden lines removed, so we should provide the user with the means of turning the process on or off.

9.1 Algorithm SET-HIDDEN-LINE-REMOVAL(ON-OFF) User routine to set the hidden-line removal indicator
Argument   ON-OFF user specification for removing hidden lines
Global   HIDDEN hidden-line removal flag.
BEGIN
    HIDDEN ← ON-OFF;
    RETURN;
END;

The following is the modified CLIP-POLYGON-EDGE routine, which now includes a check for back faces when the HIDDEN flag is true.

9.2 Algorithm CLIP-POLYGON-EDGE(OP, X, Y, Z) (Revision of algorithm 8.35)
Close and enter a clipped polygon into the display file
Arguments   OP, X, Y, Z a display-file instruction
Global   PFLAG indicates that a polygon is being drawn
           COUNT-IN the number of sides remaining to be processed
           COUNT-OUT the number of sides to be entered in the display file
           IT, XT, YT temporary storage arrays for a polygon
           NEEDFIRST array of indicators for saving the first command
           FIRSTOP, FIRSTX, FIRSTY, FIRSTZ arrays for saving the first command
           CLOSING indicates the stage in polygon

FRONT-FLAG, BACK-FLAG indicate whether front and back clipping is
done
HIDDEN flag for hidden-line removal
Local   I for stepping through the polygon sides
BEGIN
    COUNT-IN ← COUNT-IN − 1;
    CLIP-BACK(OP, X, Y, Z);
    IF COUNT-IN ≠ 0 THEN RETURN;
    close the clipped polygon
    CLOSING ← 5;
    IF BACK-FLAG AND NOT NEEDFIRST[5] THEN
    CLIP-BACK(FIRSTOP[5], FIRSTX[5], FIRSTY[5], FIRSTZ[5]);
    CLOSING ← 6;
    IF FRONT-FLAG AND NOT NEEDFIRST[6] THEN
    CLIP-FRONT(FIRSTOP[6], FIRSTX[6], FIRSTY[6], FIRSTZ[6];
    CLOSING ← 1;
    IF NOT NEEEDFIRST[1] THEN
    CLIP-LEFT(FIRSTOP[1], FIRSTX[1], FIRSTY[1], FIRSTZ[1]);
    CLOSING ← 2;
    IF NOT NEEDFIRST[2] THEN
    CLIP-RIGHT(FIRSTOP[2], FIRSTX[2], FIRSTY[2], FIRSTZ[2]);
    CLOSING ← 3;
    IF NOT NEEDFIRST[3] THEN
    CLIP-BOTTOM(FIRSTOP[3], FIRSTX[3], FIRSTY[3], FIRSTZ[3]);
    CLOSING ← 4;
    IF NOT NEEDFIRST[4] THEN
    CLIP-TOP(FIRSTOP[4], FIRSTX[4], FIRSTY[4], FIRSTZ[4]);
    CLOSING ← 0;
    PFLAG ← FALSE;
    IF COUNT-OUT < 3 THEN RETURN;
    enter the polygon into the display file
    IF HIDDEN THEN CALL BACK-FACE-CHECK(COUNT-OUT);
    ELSE
        BEGIN
            VIEWING-TRANSFORM(COUNT-OUT, XT[COUNT-OUT],
                YT[COUNT-OUT]);
            FOR I = 1 TO COUNT-OUT DO
                VIEWING-TRANSFORM(IT[I], XT[I], YT[I]);
        END;
    RETURN;
END;

The algorithm above uses the BACK-FACE-CHECK function to actually decide
whether the polygon is a back face and enters it into the display file. It computes the z
component of the vector normal to the polygon according to Equation 9.3. It then
checks the sign and enters the polygon only if the z component is positive. Thus, only
front faces are entered.

9.3 Algorithm BACK-FACE-CHECK(POLYSIZE) Filters out polygon drawn clockwise

Argument   POLYSIZE the number of sides on the polygon

Global   XT, YT, ZT T-buffer array storage of the vertex points

Local   C z component of a vector for the normal to the plane of the polygon

             I, J for stepping through the vertices

```
BEGIN
    C ← 0;
    FOR I = 1 TO POLYSIZE DO
        BEGIN
            IF I = POLYSIZE THEN J ← 1
            ELSE J ← I + 1;
            C ← C + ( (XT[I] − XT[J]) * (YT[I] + YT[J]));
        END;
    IF C ≤ 0 THEN RETURN;
    VIEWING-TRANSFORM(POLYSIZE, XT[POLYSIZE], YT[POLYSIZE]);
    FOR I = 1 TO POLYSIZE DO VIEWING-TRANSFORM(IT[I], XT[I], YT[I]);
    RETURN;
END;
```

We have added a new global flag, so we should include it in the initializations. We shall make the default hidden-line removal setting FALSE, so that hidden lines will not be removed unless such action is explicitly requested by the user.

9.4 Algorithm INITIALIZE-9A Initialization routine

```
BEGIN
    INITIALIZE-8;
    SET-HIDDEN-LINE-REMOVAL(FALSE);
    RETURN;
END;
```

We have just seen how to remove many of the lines which would be hidden by an object's bulk. The method will suffice for single convex objects, but may be inadequate when several objects or concave surfaces are involved. (See Figure 9-7.) We now survey some of the techniques used to solve the full hidden-surface and hidden-line problems.

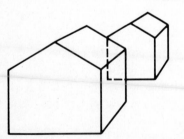

FIGURE 9-7
Hidden lines among front faces.

Z BUFFERS

Consider raster displays backed by a frame buffer. These displays can show surfaces (filled polygons) as well as lines. If we are using such a display, another way to state the hidden-surface problem is that we want to arrange the frame buffer so that the color displayed at any pixel is that of the surface closest to the viewer for that point. To do this, we must somehow compare all of the surfaces which are projected onto the pixel and decide which one can be seen. We must sort the polygons according to their position in space. This notion of *geometrically sorting* the surfaces is central to hidden surface and line removal.

One simple approach to this problem relies on a device called a *Z buffer*. The Z buffer was described by Catmull [CAT74]. It is a large array with an entry for each pixel on the display (like a frame buffer). The Z buffer is used to save the z coordinate values. It helps us to sort out the polygons by keeping track of the z position of the surfaces being displayed. When the frame buffer is cleared, the Z-buffer elements are all set to a very large negative value (a value which is beyond anything which will be imaged). The initial value may be thought of as the z position of the background. Polygons will be entered one by one into the frame buffer by the display-file interpreter, using scan conversion algorithms such as those discussed in Chapter 3. Suppose that the algorithm which turns on each pixel of the polygon knows the projected z position of the point being displayed. It could then compare the z position of the polygon point with the Z-buffer value and decide if the new surface is in front of or behind the current contents of the frame buffer. If the new surface has a z value greater than the Z-buffer value, then it lies in front; its intensity value is entered into the frame buffer, and its z value is entered into the Z buffer. If the z value of the new surface is less than the value in the Z buffer, then it lies behind some polygon which was previously entered. The new surface will be hidden and should not be imaged. No frame buffer or Z-buffer entries will be made. The comparison is carried out on a pixel-by-pixel basis, and we must be able to find the z position of the projected point for every pixel of the polygon.

If we were to modify our system to use a Z buffer for hidden-surface removal, we might extend our display file to keep the z coordinates of the polygon vertices. From the z coordinates of the vertices, we can find the z coordinate of any interior point. We have seen in Chapter 3 (Algorithm 3.15 UPDATE-X-VALUES) how to incrementally find the x values for the polygon edges as we step through the scan lines. The same technique can be used to find the z values along the edges at each step. All we need is the starting z value and the change in z for each step in y for the polygon edges. So for each scan line, then, we still generate pairs of x coordinates which indicate where to fill; but in addition, we know a z value for each of the fill-span endpoints. By reapplying this linear interpolation technique, this time using the span's change in z for each step in the x direction, the z values at each pixel can be calculated. THE FILLIN algorithm would have to obtain the endpoint z coordinates as arguments, perform the interpolation in x, and compare the resulting z values to the Z-buffer values to decide whether to change the frame buffer intensity.

A Z buffer can be expensive. It requires a lot of memory (one entry for each pixel), and each entry must have a sufficient number of bits to distinguish the possible z values. It can also be time-consuming in that a decision must be made for every pixel instead of for the entire polygon. However, it is a very simple method, simple enough to implement in hardware to overcome the speed problems. And the time required to process a scene is proportional to the number of objects in the scene. (Some other techniques which compare every polygon against every other polygon require time proportional to the square of the number of polygons.) This, together with the continuing drop in the cost of memory, makes this method (or its extensions) an increasingly popular approach to the hidden-surface problem.

SCAN-LINE ALGORITHMS

Actually, if we are willing to collect the polygons and process them together, then a full-screen Z buffer is not needed; a scan-line Z buffer will suffice and requires much less memory. The idea was suggested by Carpenter [CAR76]. The reason a large amount of memory is needed for a Z buffer is that we process each polygon independently. As each polygon is rasterized, we must in effect be able to remember the depth of each of its pixels so that they may be compared against later polygons. A polygon may be as large as the screen, so we need a full-screen Z buffer. But we can reduce the memory requirements by processing all of the polygons together on a scan-line by scan-line basis. This in effect is repeatedly doing a Z-buffer hidden-surface removal for a screen that is only one pixel high (a single scan line). The Z buffer only needs to hold one scan line's worth of depth information. When the scan line is done, we save the result, reinitialize the Z buffer, move to the next scan line, and do the next scan-line Z-buffer sort. The key here is that all polygons are processed together. Instead of considering all scan lines for a polygon before moving on to the next polygon, we consider all polygons for a scan line before moving on to the next scan line. This can be done using algorithms much like those of Chapter 3, only instead of entering the edges of a single polygon into the edge list, we enter the sides of all the polygons. We must also be careful when pairing edges for filling that we pair edges belonging to the same polygon.

A variation of the scan-line approach does not require a Z buffer at all. Where a scan line cuts a polygon, a line segment or span is described. It is these spans which are being sorted for the scan line's hidden-surface removal. To order them, we need only determine the depth of the spans at a few points. The interesting points are the span endpoints (and intersection points if polygon faces can penetrate one another). At the x position where a span begins, we could compare its depth with that of the other spans active at that point to decide which is closest to the viewer. Likewise, when a span ends, we could determine which of the remaining spans active at that point should be shown. But often we can get by with even less work. Usually each scan line looks much like its neighbors and we can use this to simplify the calculation. If faces do not interpenetrate, and the order in x of the span ends does not change from one scan line to the next, then the depth ordering is the same for the two scan lines and no new sorting in z is needed. Depth reordering is needed only when the sweep through the scan lines encounters a new polygon, passes a polygon, or finds a change in the order of span endpoints.

THE PAINTER'S ALGORITHM

There is a property of frame buffers used by Newell [NEW72], which has become known as the *painter's algorithm*. The algorithm gets its name from the manner in which an oil painting is created. The artist begins with the background. He can, if he wishes, fill the entire canvas with the background scene. The artist then paints the foreground objects. There is no need to erase portions of the background; the artist simply paints on top of them. The new paint covers the old so that only the newest layer of paint is visible. A frame buffer has this same property. We enter a filled polygon into the frame buffer by changing the proper pixels to values corresponding to the polygon's interior style. If we then enter a second polygon "on top of" the first, some of those same pixels will be changed to correspond to the second polygon's interior style. Wherever the second polygon lies, the first polygon's pixel settings have been forgotten. The second polygon has "covered up" the first. The painter's algorithm tells us to enter first those polygons which are farthest from the viewer (the background) and enter last the objects closest to the viewer (the foreground). Hidden surfaces can be covered up by choosing the correct order to draw them and taking advantage of the properties of frame buffers. (See Figure 9-8.)

The painter's algorithm is a simple idea, but let's look at what is involved in its implementation. First of all, we cannot process each polygon independently, as we did

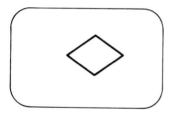

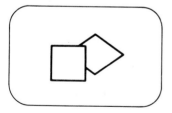

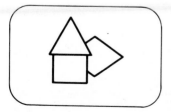

FIGURE 9-8
The most recent filled polygon overwrites previous pixel values.

in the back-face check or the full-screen Z buffer. We must compare each polygon with all of the rest to see which is in front of which. We must, in effect, sort the polygons to determine a priority for their display. The sorting will determine the order in which they will be entered into the display file (the order in which they will be drawn). For efficiency, we try to limit the number of comparisons and we try to make the comparison process fast.

COMPARISON TECHNIQUES

There are several techniques for determining the relevancy and relative position of two polygons. Not all tests may be used with all hidden-surface algorithms, and some of the tests are not always conclusive. Sometimes we can use simple tests for many of the cases and resort to more costly tests only when all else fails.

One technique that is often useful is called the *minimax test* or *boxing test*. We may not need to know the order of every polygon relative to every other polygon; it may suffice to know just the relative orderings of those polygons that overlap. So a test that can quickly tell us if two polygons do not overlap is useful. The minimax test will do just that. This test says that if we place boxes around two polygons and if the two boxes don't overlap, then the polygons within them cannot overlap. (See Figure 9-9.)

We want the boxes to be as small as possible and still contain the polygons. That means we want the top of the box to be as low as possible. The lowest we can make the top of the box is where it just touches the highest point on the polygon, that is, the

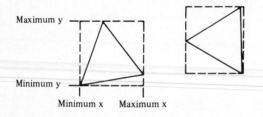

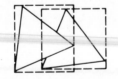

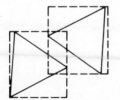

FIGURE 9-9
The minimax test. If the boxes do not overlap, then the polygons cannot overlap.

maximum of the y coordinates of the polygon's vertices. Similarly, the highest position of the bottom of the box is the minimum of the y coordinates of the vertices. Two boxes will not overlap if one is above the other, that is, if the bottom of one box is higher than the top of the other box. This means that the minimum of the y coordinates of one polygon is greater than the maximum of the y coordinates of the other polygon. We can, of course, switch the roles of the two polygons. We can also compare left and right sides by a similar test using the x coordinates.

If the minimax test is true, then the polygons do not overlap; but if the boxes do overlap, we still are not certain whether the polygons within them overlap. We will have to perform further tests.

A minimax test applied to the z coordinates can often tell the relative ordering of two polygons which do overlap in x and y. If the smallest z value for one polygon is larger than the largest z value for the other polygon, then the first polygon lies in front.

Another test which is useful is to see if all the vertices of one polygon lie on the same side of the plane containing the other polygon. If polygon P has all its vertices on the same side of the plane of polygon Q as the viewer, then P is in front of Q. If all the vertices lie in the other half-space, then P is behind Q. (See Figure 9-10.)

This test may also be inconclusive because the plane of polygon Q may intersect polygon P. If this should happen, we can try comparing the vertices of Q against the plane of P. Again, this may or may not yield results. (See Figure 9-11.)

If the above tests fail, we might break up the polygons into pieces such that the tests succeed, or we might try to find an xy point common to both polygons and compare the corresponding z-coordinate values.

WARNOCK'S ALGORITHM

An interesting approach to the hidden-surface problem was presented by Warnock [WAR69]. His method does not try to decide exactly what is happening in the scene but rather just tries to get the display right. As the resolution of the display increases, the amount of work which the algorithm must do to get the scene right also increases.

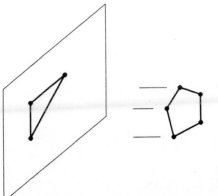

FIGURE 9-10
Vertices of one polygon on one side of the plane of another polygon.

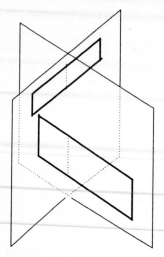

FIGURE 9-11
Vertices of each polygon straddle the plane of the other.

(This is also true for scan-line algorithms.) The algorithm divides the screen up into sample areas. In some sample areas it will be easy to decide what to do. If there are no faces within the area, then it is left blank. If the nearest polygon completely covers it, then it can be filled in with the color of that polygon. If neither of these conditions holds, then the algorithm subdivides the sample area into smaller sample areas and considers each of them in turn. This process is repeated as needed. (See Figure 9-12.) It stops when the sample area satisfies one of the two simple cases or when the sample area is only a single pixel (which can be given the color of the foremost polygon). The process can also be allowed to continue to half or quarter pixel-sized sample areas, whose color may be averaged over a pixel to provide antialiasing.

The test for whether a polygon surrounds or is disjoint from the sample area is much like a clipping test to see if the polygon sides cross the sample-area boundaries.

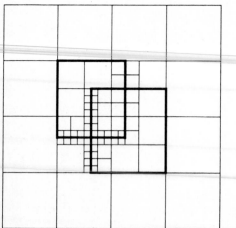

FIGURE 9-12
Subdivision of a scene.

Actually, the minimax test can be employed to identify many of the disjoint polygons. A simple test for whether a polygon is in front of another is a comparison of the z coordinates of the polygon planes at the corners of the sample area.

At each subdivision, information learned in the previous test can be used to simplify the problem. Polygons which are disjoint from the tested sample area will also be disjoint from all of the subareas and do not need further testing. Likewise, a polygon which surrounds the sample area will also surround the subareas.

FRANKLIN ALGORITHM

We mentioned how the number of possible comparisons of polygons grows as the square of the number of polygons in the scene. Many of the hidden-surface algorithms exhibit this behavior and have serious performance problems on complex scenes. Franklin [FRA80] developed an approach which gives linear time behavior for most scenes. This is done by overlaying a grid of cells on the scene (similar to Warnocks approach, only these cells are not subdivided). The size of the cells is on the order of the size of an edge in the scene. At each cell the algorithm looks for a covering face and determines which edges are in front of this face. It then computes the intersections of these edges and determines their visibility. (See Figure 9-13.) The idea is that as objects are added to the scene and the number of polygons increases, the new objects will either be hidden by objects already in the scene or will hide other objects in the scene. While the number of objects increases, the complexity of the final scene (after hidden portions are removed) does not increase. By considering only the edges in front of the covering face for a cell, the algorithm considers only the edges likely to be in the final image. Although the total number of edges may increase, this increase occurs, for the most part, behind the covering faces, and the number of edges in front will remain small.

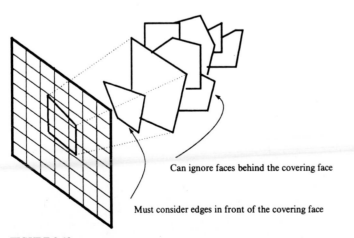

Can ignore faces behind the covering face

Must consider edges in front of the covering face

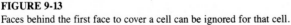

FIGURE 9-13
Faces behind the first face to cover a cell can be ignored for that cell.

HIDDEN-LINE METHODS

The hidden-surface techniques such as the painter's algorithm, which rely on the properties of the frame buffer, are not sufficient for calligraphic displays. On such displays we must not draw the hidden portions of lines. This means that for each line, we must decide not only what objects lie in front of it but also just how those objects hide it. Calligraphic displays were available long before raster displays became economical, and the hidden-line problem was attacked before the hidden-surface problem.

The first solution [ROB63] compared lines to objects. For each object, it considered relevant edges to see if the object hid them. The object might not hide an edge at all or might hide it entirely. It might hide an end, making the visible portion of the edge smaller, or hide the middle, making two smaller visible line segments. After comparison of the line and object, the resulting visible line segments were compared in turn to the remaining objects. A segment which survives comparison to all objects is drawn.

We do not have to compare the line against all of the polygon edges in an object in order to tell if the object hides the line. The only edges which can change whether the line is visible or not are those on the boundary where a front face meets a back face. These are called *contour edges*. We can find the contour edges by examining the object. For a solid object, each edge has two polygons adjacent to it. If the polygons which meet at the edge are both front faces or both back faces, then we have an *interior edge*; but if one is a front face and the other a back face, then it is a contour edge. (See Figure 9-14.)

Instead of comparing all lines to each object, we can compare the contour edges of all objects to each line. For each intersection of a line with a contour edge, the line either passes behind an object or emerges from it. So with each such intersection, the number of faces hiding the line either increases or decreases by 1. Appel [APP67] has termed the number of faces hiding a line its *quantitative invisibility*. His method for hidden-line removal is to find the quantitative invisibility for an initial point on a line, and then to follow along the connected lines, finding intersections with the contour edges

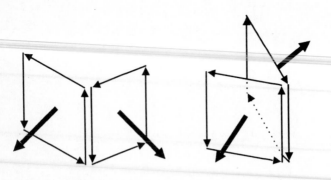

Interior edge   Contour edge

FIGURE 9-14
Interior and contour edges.

and maintaining the quantitative invisibility. The portions of the lines with quantitative invisibility 0 are drawn.

BINARY SPACE PARTITION

Now let's implement a hidden-surface algorithm. The method we shall use is based on the painter's algorithm and is credited to Fuchs [FUC80]. It is called binary space partition (BSP). The idea is to sort the polygons for display in back-to-front order. To order the polygons we use the test which compares all the vertices of one polygon against the plane of another polygon. We extend this test so that if the plane intersects the polygon, we divide the polygon along the plane. Using this test we can pick one polygon and compare all the other polygons to it, splitting them into two groups, those in front and those behind. For each of these two subgroups we can again select a polygon and use it to separate the subgroup. This process is repeated until all polygons have been sorted. The sort works in the same fashion as Hoare's Quicksort algorithm, repeatedly separating the polygons into smaller and smaller groups. The result may be pictured as a binary tree. At each node of the tree is a polygon. In one subtree, or branch, are all the polygons in front of the plane of this polygon, and in the other branch are those polygons which lie behind it. (See Figure 9-15.) Once we have created this tree, we can perform an in-order traversal to obtain the polygons in back-to-front order.

Before discussing the details of the algorithm, we note that it requires the collection and sorting of all the polygons before any of them are drawn. We shall need some storage area to collect the polygon instructions until we are ready to sort them. We shall need to know when to start collecting polygons and also when all polygons have been collected so that sorting can proceed. We shall also need to save more information about a polygon than just its vertices. We shall need to save the edge and fill styles for

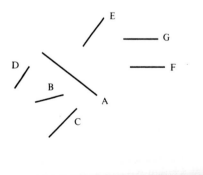

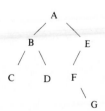

FIGURE 9-15
An ordered tree of polygons.

CHAPTER NINE

the polygon. The change-of-style commands will have to be inserted to match the order in which the polygons are actually drawn (not the order that they are entered by the user). It will also be useful to save the equation for the plane of the polygon. This can be used in the polygon comparison.

Let's first consider when to save and when to sort the polygons. In our system we shall limit hidden-line processing to single display-file segments. We shall sort out all the objects within a segment, but we will not check to see if an object in one segment hides an object in a different segment. With this organization, a reasonable point at which to sort and save the polygons is just before the display-file segment is closed. When the segment is closed, we know that all relevant polygons have been entered and no other display-file segment's polygons will be around to confuse us. We shall therefore modify the CLOSE-SEGMENT algorithm to include a call to our hidden-surface removal routine. We shall use the HIDDEN flag to tell us to save polygons, so polygons will be saved any time this flag is TRUE; but with each CLOSE-SEGMENT, the collected polygons will be sorted and moved to the display file. This groups them according to segment.

The modified CLOSE-SEGMENT routine calls the HIDDEN-SURFACE-CHECK routine to actually do the sorting and saving. It looks as follows:

9.5 Algorithm CLOSE-SEGMENT (Modification of algorithm 5.2)
Global   NOW-OPEN the name of the currently open segment
           FREE the index of the next free display-file cell
           HIDDEN the hidden-surface removal flag
           SEGMENT-START, SEGMENT-SIZE arrays for start and size of the segments
BEGIN
    IF NOW-OPEN = 0 THEN RETURN ERROR 'NO SEGMENT OPEN';
    DELETE-SEGMENT(0);
    IF HIDDEN THEN HIDDEN-SURFACE-CHECK;
    SEGMENT-START[0] ← FREE;
    SEGMENT-SIZE[0] ← 0;
    NOW-OPEN ← 0;
    RETURN;
END;

To save the polygons we shall use some new arrays. We shall use arrays ID, XD, YD, and ZD to hold the polygon edge instructions (the polygon vertices). We shall call this the D buffer. The arrays must be large enough to hold all of the vertices of all of the polygons being sorted. We shall also use arrays POLY-START, POLY-SIDES, POLY-FILL-STYLE, POLY-EDGE-STYLE, POLY-A, POLY-B, POLY-C, POLY-D, POLY-FRONT, and POLY-BACK to form a table of information about each polygon. There is one entry for each polygon drawn. POLY-START will indicate where in the D buffer the vertices for the polygon may be found. POLY-SIDES is the number of edges on the polygon. POLY-FILL-STYLE and POLY-EDGE-STYLE remember the style of the polygon. The arrays POLY-A, POLY-B, POLY-C, and POLY-D contain the coefficients for the equation of the plane of the polygon. POLY-FRONT and POLY-BACK will hold the indices of other polygon entries. They are the branches that will form our sorted tree of polygons.

We shall modify our BACK-FACE-CHECK algorithm to save the polygons. The modifications will be to calculate the entire normal vector to the polygon plane (not just its z component) and to check the solid flag, calling the SAVE-POLY-FOR-HSC routine if the polygon is filled.

9.6 Algorithm BACK-FACE-CHECK(POLYSIZE) (Revision of algorithm 9.3) Filters out polygon drawn clockwise

Argument   POLYSIZE the number of sides on the polygon
Global   XT, YT, ZT T-buffer array storage of the vertex points
              SOLID a flag which indicates polygon filling
Local   A, B, C a vector for the normal to the plane of the polygon
              I, J for stepping through the vertices

```
BEGIN
    A ← 0;
    B ← 0;
    C ← 0;
    FOR I = 1 TO POLYSIZE DO
        BEGIN
            IF I = POLYSIZE THEN J ← 1
            ELSE J ← I + 1;
            A ← A + ( (YT[I] − YT[J]) * (ZT[I] + ZT[J]));
            B ← B + ( (ZT[I] − ZT[J]) * (XT[I] + XT[J]));
            C ← C + ( (XT[I] − XT[J]) * (YT[I] + YT[J]));
        END;
    IF C ≤ 0 THEN RETURN;
    IF SOLID THEN SAVE-POLY-FOR-HSC(POLYSIZE, A, B, C)
    ELSE
        BEGIN
            VIEWING-TRANSFORM(POLYSIZE, XT[POLYSIZE], YT[POLYSIZE]);
            FOR I = 1 TO POLYSIZE DO VIEWING-TRANSFORM(IT[I], XT[I],
                YT[I]);
        END;
    RETURN;
END;
```

The SAVE-POLY-FOR-HSC algorithm enters the polygon information into the polygon table at POLY and into the D buffer starting at DFREE. Most of the entries are straightforward. As we saw in Chapter 8, the A, B, and C coefficients in the equation of the plane (Equation 8.4) can be the elements of the normal vector which is determined in BACK-FACE-CHECK. The fourth coefficient D may be found by substituting for x, y, and z in the equation the coordinates of a point known to be on the plane. This is what is done for the POLY-D array.

By setting POLY-FRONT to POLY − 1, we form a linked list of all the polygons (each linked to its predecessor). We shall use the linked list to access the polygons when sorting.

9.7 Algorithm SAVE-POLY-FOR-HSC(POLYSIZE, A, B, C) Save a polygon in the polygon table for the hidden-surface check

Arguments   POLYSIZE the number of sides on the polygon

                A, B, C a vector normal to the plane of the polygon

Global   POLY index of the next free polygon-table cell

                CURRENT-FILL-STYLE the interior style of the polygon

                CURRENT-LINE-STYLE the edge style of the polygon

                IT, XT, YT, ZT arrays containing the vertices of one polygon

                ID, XD, YD, ZD D-buffer arrays containing the vertices of all polygons involved in the hidden-surface check

                DFREE the next free D-buffer cell

                POLY-START, POLY-SIDES, POLY-FILL-STYLE, POLY-EDGE-STYLE, POLY-A, POLY-B, POLY-C, POLY-D, POLY-FRONT, POLY-BACK the polygon table

Local   I for stepping through the polygon vertices

Constant   POLYGON-TABLE-SIZE the size of the polygon-table arrays

                D-BUFFER-SIZE the size of the D buffer

```
BEGIN
    IF POLY = POLYGON-TABLE-SIZE THEN
        RETURN ERROR 'POLYGON TABLE OVERFLOW';
    POLY-START[POLY] ← DFREE;
    POLY-SIDES[POLY] ← POLYSIZE;
    POLY-FILL-STYLE[POLY] ← CURRENT-FILL-STYLE;
    POLY-EDGE-STYLE[POLY] ← CURRENT-LINE-STYLE;
    POLY-A[POLY] ← A;
    POLY-B[POLY] ← B;
    POLY-C[POLY] ← C;
    POLY-D[POLY] ← − (A * XT[1] + B * YT[1] + C * ZT[1]);
    POLY-FRONT ← POLY − 1;
    POLY-BACK ← 0;
    POLY ← POLY + 1;
    FOR I = 1 TO POLYSIZE DO
        BEGIN
            IF DFREE > D-BUFFER-SIZE THEN
                RETURN ERROR 'D BUFFER OVERFLOW';
            ID[DFREE] := IT[I];
            XD[DFREE] := XT[I];
            YD[DFREE] := YT[I];
            ZD[DFREE] := ZT[I];
            DFREE := DFREE + 1;
        END;
    RETURN;
END;
```

Now let's consider what happens when a display-file segment is closed and the HIDDEN-SURFACE-CHECK algorithm is called. This procedure first determines if there is anything to sort and save. If so, it picks one of the polygons to start the sorting process. This polygon will be the root of the sorted tree of polygons. The algorithm sorts the polygons, saves them in the display file in back-to-front order, and then resets the polygon table and D buffer so that future polygons will be sorted as a new set.

9.8 Algorithm HIDDEN-SURFACE-CHECK   A routine to remove hidden surfaces

Global	POLY index of next free cell in the polygon table
	SOLID the polygon-filling flag
	DFREE the next free D-buffer cell
Local	ROOTPOLY the root of the space partition tree

BEGIN
   IF POLY = 1 THEN RETURN;
   ROOTPOLY ← POLY − 1;
   SORT-POLYGONS(ROOTPOLY);
   SAVE-POLYGONS-IN-ORDER(ROOTPOLY);
   POLY ← 1;
   DFREE ← 1;
   RETURN;
END;

The sorting routine is given in recursive form (it calls itself). Nonrecursive versions are possible, but they are more complex. The algorithm checks to see if there is something to sort; if not, it returns. It uses a loop to step through the polygons in a linked list. The index of the next polygon in the list is found in the POLY-FRONT array for the current polygon. It compares the first polygon in the list (ROOT-NODE) against all of the other polygons in the list (TEST-POLY). The COMPARE-POLYS procedure not only decides on which side of ROOT-NODE each TEST-POLY lies but also links the TEST-POLY onto a sublist accordingly. When the loop has finished, the list will have been divided into two sublists. There will be a list of the polygons in front of the ROOT-NODE, which will be attached to the ROOT-NODE's POLY-FRONT entry, and there will be a list of those behind, attached to POLY-BACK for the ROOT-NODE. The algorithm, then, recursively sorts each of these two sublists.

9.9 Algorithm SORT-POLYGONS(ROOT-NODE)   A routine to build a sorted binary tree of polygons

Argument	ROOT-NODE the polygon at the root of the tree
Global	POLY-FRONT, POLY-BACK links for the tree branches
Local	TEST-POLY, NEXT-POLY polygons to be compared to the root

BEGIN
   IF ROOT-NODE = 0 THEN RETURN;
   TEST-POLY ← POLY-FRONT[ROOT-NODE];
   POLY-FRONT[ROOT-NODE] ← 0;
   WHILE TEST-POLY ≠ 0 DO
     BEGIN
       NEXT-POLY ← POLY-FRONT[TEST-POLY];
       COMPARE-POLYS(ROOT-NODE, TEST-POLY);
       TEST-POLY ← NEXT-POLY;
     END;

```
      SORT-POLYGONS(POLY-FRONT[ROOT-NODE]);
      SORT-POLYGONS(POLY-BACK[ROOT-NODE]);
      RETURN;
   END;
```

There is actually a lot of work that goes on in the COMPARE-POLYS algorithm. It compares each vertex of the TEST polygon against the plane of the ROOT polygon and decides which side it is on. But it will also split the TEST polygon into two separate polygons if it is intersected by the plane. The technique is very similar to what we used for clipping. When clipping, we compare points against a clipping plane and only keep those points which lie on one side. In COMPARE-POLYS we keep the points on both sides but in two separate groups, so we end up with two polygons. As with clipping, when an edge crosses the plane, we calculate the intersection point, using it to build an ''invisible'' edge along the plane boundary. (See Figure 9-16.)

The algorithm determines on which side of the plane a point lies by checking the sign of the result of substituting the coordinates of the point into the expression for the plane (see Equations 8.69 and 8.70). It finds the first vertex point which is not on the plane and then compares following vertices, checking for a change in sign which indicates a crossing of the plane. If a side ever crosses the plane, then we will have to split the polygon. To do this, we form a new polygon starting at DFREE (the next free cell in the D buffer). The new polygon begins with the first intersection point. We must also save the points for the other side of the split. This side will also include the intersection point. Since the split polygon can have more vertices that the original, we cannot store them in place, so we use arrays IE, XE, YE, and ZE (the E buffer) to save the other half of the split polygon. The E buffer must be large enough to hold one polygon. After the first intersection is discovered, vertices are copied to either the D-buffer piece or the E-buffer piece. Intersection points go to both.

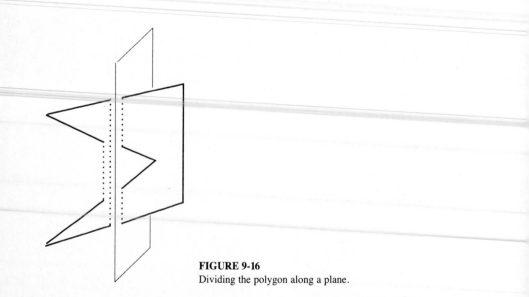

FIGURE 9-16
Dividing the polygon along a plane.

Although we are finding the sign of each vertex, we are actually looking for changes in sign between two vertices; that is, we are considering the edge between the vertex pair. After stepping through all vertices, we must consider the first once again in order to characterize the final edge, that is, to close the polygon.

9.10 Algorithm COMPARE-POLYS(ROOT, TEST) Finds on which side of ROOT the TEST polygon lies and links it to that branch. If the plane of ROOT intersects the TEST polygon, then it is split

Arguments	ROOT the polygon providing the plane used in the comparison
	TEST the polygon being compared and linked (and possibly split)
Global	POLY-START, POLY-SIDES, POLY-A, POLY-B, POLY-C, POLY-D,
	POLY-FRONT the polygon table
	ID, XD, YD, ZD the D-buffer arrays containing polygon vertices
	DFREE the next free D-buffer cell
	IE, XE, YE, ZE the E-buffer arrays for vertices of split-off polygon
	EFREE the next free E-buffer cell
Local	FIRST-V index of the first vertex of the polygon
	LAST-V index of the last vertex of the polygon
	CROSS-V index of the vertex just before the polygon crosses the test plane
	SPLIT-V index of the first vertex of the split polygon
	J for stepping through the polygon vertices
	STEST the first nonzero sign parameter
	SLAST the sign parameter of the previous vertex
	SNEW the sign parameter for the current vertex
	U0, U, V test point parameters
	W parameter for the intersection point
	XP, YP, ZP the intersection point
	CHANGED-BEFORE a flag to indicate the first time the polygon crosses the plane
	CROSSED a flag to indicate if the polygon edge crossed the plane

```
BEGIN
    FIRST-V ← POLY-START[TEST];
    LAST-V ← FIRST-V + POLY-SIDES[TEST] − 1;
    CROSS-V ← FIRST-V;
    U0 ← POLY-A[ROOT] * XD[FIRST-V] + POLY-B[ROOT] * YD[FIRST-V]
        + POLY-C[ROOT] * ZD[FIRST-V] + POLY-D[ROOT];
    STEST ← SIGNOF[U0];
    find the first vertex not on the plane
    U ← U0;
    WHILE STEST = 0 AND CROSS-V < LAST-V DO
        BEGIN
            CROSS-V ← CROSS-V + 1;
            U ← POLY-A[ROOT] * XD[CROSS-V] + POLY-B[ROOT] * YD[CROSS-V]
                + POLY-C[ROOT] * ZD[CROSS-V] + POLY-D[ROOT];
            STEST ← SIGNOF(U);
        END;
    IF STEST = 0 THEN
        BEGIN
            test polygon was contained in the plane so treat as in front
```

```
                    POLY-FRONT[TEST] ← POLY-FRONT[ROOT];
                    POLY-FRONT[ROOT] ← TEST;
                    RETURN;
                END;
            SLAST ← STEST;
            EFREE ← 1;
            SPLIT-V ← DFREE;
            CHANGED-BEFORE ← FALSE;
            FOR J = CROSS-V + 1 TO LAST-V DO
                BEGIN
                    step through all vertices
                    V ← POLY-A[ROOT] * XD[J] + POLY-B[ROOT] * YD[J]
                        + POLY-C[ROOT] * ZD[J] + POLY-D[ROOT];
                    SNEW ← SIGNOF(V);
                    IF SNEW = − SLAST THEN
                        BEGIN
                            point has crossed the plane, find intersection
                            CROSSED ← TRUE;
                            W ← U / (U − V);
                            XP ← (XD[J] − XD[J − 1]) * W + XD[J − 1];
                            YP ← (YD[J] − YD[J − 1]) * W + YD[J − 1];
                            ZP ← (ZD[J] − ZD[J − 1]) * W + ZD[J − 1];
                            CALL PUT-IN-D(ID[J], XP, YP, ZP);
                            CALL PUT-IN-E(ID[J], XP, YP, ZP);
                            SLAST ← SNEW;
                        END
                    ELSE CROSSED ← FALSE;
                    IF SNEW = STEST OR (SNEW = 0 AND SLAST = STEST) THEN
                        BEGIN
                            point belongs on the first side of the plane
                            IF CROSSED THEN IE[EFREE − 1] ← 1;
                            IF CHANGED-BEFORE THEN PUT-IN-E(ID[J], XD[J], YD[J], ZD[J])
                            ELSE CROSS-V ← CROSS-V + 1;
                        END;
                    ELSE
                        BEGIN
                            point belongs on the second side of the plane
                            CHANGED-BEFORE ← TRUE;
                            IF CROSSED THEN ID[DFREE − 1] ← 1;
                            CALL PUT-IN-D(ID[J], XD[J], YD[J], ZD[J]);
                        END;
                    U ← V;
                END;
            now we must close the polygon
            IF SLAST ≠ STEST THEN
                BEGIN
                    W ← V / (V − U0);
                    XP ← (XD[FIRST-V] − XD[J]) * W + XD[J];
                    YP ← (YD[FIRST-V] − YD[J]) * W + YD[J];
                    ZP ← (ZD[FIRST-V] − ZD[J]) * W + ZD[J];
```

CALL PUT-IN-D(ID[FIRST-V], XP, YP, ZP);
CALL PUT-IN-E(1, XP, YP, ZP);
END;
finally, hang the polygon(s) on the ROOT node
IF SPLIT-V ≠ DFREE THEN SET-UP-SPLIT-POLY(ROOT, TEST, SPLIT-V, STEST);
ADJUST-ORIGINAL-POLY(ROOT, TEST, FIRST-V, CROSS-V, STEST);
RETURN;
END;

Once the polygon has been tested (and split if necessary), two routines are used to clean things up. If the polygon is split, then the vertices for one half are copied in the D buffer. But we do not have a corresponding polygon-table entry. The routine SET-UP-SPLIT-POLY forms this table entry. It also links the polygon onto either the POLY-FRONT or POLY-BACK branch of the ROOT polygon, depending on whether it lies in front or in back of the ROOT polygon plane.

9.11 Algorithm SET-UP-SPLIT-POLY(ROOT, TEST, SPLIT-V, STEST) Completes a polygon-table entry for the split-off polygon and attaches it to the root polygon

Arguments   ROOT the root polygon
                TEST the original test polygon
                SPLIT-V index of the first vertex of the split-off polygon
                STEST indicates on which side of the root the split polygon lies

Global   POLY-START, POLY-SIDES, POLY-FILL-STYLE, POLY-EDGE-STYLE,
                POLY-A, POLY-B, POLY-C, POLY-D, POLY-FRONT, POLY-BACK the
                polygon table
                POLY index of the next free polygon-table cell

BEGIN
  POLY-START[POLY] ← SPLIT-V;
  POLY-SIDES[POLY] ← DFREE − SPLIT-V;
  POLY-FILL-STYLE[POLY] ← POLY-FILL-STYLE[TEST];
  POLY-EDGE-STYLE[POLY] ← POLY-EDGE-STYLE[TEST];
  POLY-A[POLY] ← POLY-A[TEST];
  POLY-B[POLY] ← POLY-B[TEST];
  POLY-C[POLY] ← POLY-C[TEST];
  POLY-D[POLY] ← POLY-D[TEST];
  POLY-BACK[POLY] ← 0;
  IF STEST < 0 THEN
    BEGIN
      POLY-FRONT[POLY] ← POLY-FRONT[ROOT];
      POLY-FRONT[ROOT] ← POLY;
    END
  ELSE
    BEGIN
      POLY-FRONT[POLY] ← POLY-BACK[ROOT];
      POLY-BACK[ROOT] ← POLY;
    END;
  POLY ← POLY + 1;
  RETURN;
END;

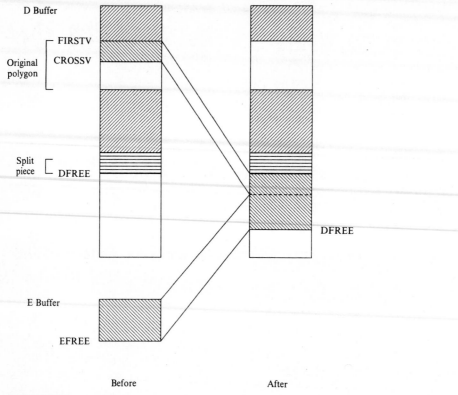

FIGURE 9-17
Case where the number of sides increases with the split.

The second cleanup routine is called ADJUST-ORIGINAL-POLY. If the polygon was split, then the points for one of the subpolygons may be found partly in the D buffer and partly in the E buffer. The D buffer holds the vertices up to the first intersection with the ROOT polygon plane. The remainder is in the E buffer. These two parts must be recombined. If this subpolygon now has fewer vertices than the original, then the vertices in the E buffer can be copied back into the original D-buffer locations. If, however, the size of the polygon has grown, then both the D-buffer piece and the E-buffer piece are copied to a new D-buffer location. The result is linked onto the appropriate branch of the ROOT polygon. (See Figures 9-17 and 9-18.)

9.12 Algorithm ADJUST-ORIGINAL-POLY(ROOT, TEST, FIRST-V, CROSS-V, STEST) Combines all vertices of the polygon in the D buffer and attaches it to the root polygon

Arguments   ROOT the root polygon
               TEST the original test polygon
               FIRST-V index of the first vertex of the polygon
               CROSS-V the vertex just before the polygon crosses the test plane
               STEST indicates on which side of the root the split polygon lies

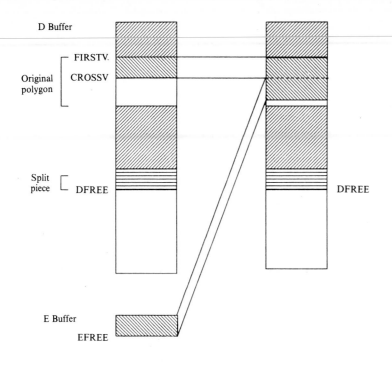

Before   After

FIGURE 9-18
Case where the number of sides does not increase with the split.

Global   POLY-START, POLY-SIDES, POLY-FRONT, POLY-BACK from the polygon
             table
             ID, XD, YD, ZD the D-buffer arrays
             DFREE the next free D-buffer cell
             IE, XE, YE, ZE the E-buffer arrays
             EFREE the next free E-buffer cell
Local   J an index for stepping through the vertices
             SIDES the number of sides on the polygon
BEGIN
    SIDES ← EFREE + CROSS-V − FIRST-V;
    IF SIDES ≤ POLY-SIDES[TEST] THEN
        BEGIN
            the adjusted polygon will fit in the original D-buffer space
            FOR J = 1 TO EFREE − 1 DO
                BEGIN
                    ID[CROSS-V + J] ← IE[J];
                    XD[CROSS-V + J] ← XE[J];
                    YD[CROSS-V + J] ← YE[J];

```
                    ZD[CROSS-V + J] ← ZE[J];
                END;
            END
        ELSE
            BEGIN
                POLY-START[TEST] ← DFREE;
                FOR J = FIRST-V TO CROSS-V DO PUT-IN-D(ID[J], XD[J], YD[J], ZD[J]);
                FOR J = 1 TO EFREE DO PUT-IN-D(IE[J], XE[J], YE[J], ZE[J]);
            END;
        POLY-SIDES[TEST] ← SIDES;
        IF STEST < 0 THEN
            BEGIN
                POLY-FRONT[TEST] ← POLY-BACK[ROOT];
                POLY-BACK[ROOT] ← TEST;
            END
        ELSE
            BEGIN
                POLY-FRONT[TEST] ← POLY-FRONT[ROOT];
                POLY-FRONT[ROOT] ← TEST;
            END;
        RETURN;
    END;
```

The comparison algorithms use the following utility routines to characterize the sign of a number and to save a vertex in the D buffer or E buffer.

9.13 Algorithm SIGNOF(X) Returns -1, 0, or 1 to indicate the sign of X

Argument   X a value from which the sign is to be extracted
Constant   ROUNDOFF some small number greater than any round-off error

```
BEGIN
    SIGNOF ← 0;
    IF X < −ROUNDOFF THEN SIGNOF ← −1;
    IF X > ROUNDOFF THEN SIGNOF ← 1;
    RETURN;
END;
```

9.14 Algorithm PUT-IN-D(OP, X, Y, Z) Saves an instruction in the D buffer

Arguments   OP, X, Y, Z a display-file instruction
Global   ID, XD, YD, ZD the D-buffer arrays
            DFREE the next free D-buffer cell

```
BEGIN
    ID[DFREE] ← OP;
    XD[DFREE] ← X;
    YD[DFREE] ← Y;
    ZD[DFREE] ← Z;
    DFREE ← DFREE + 1;
    RETURN;
END;
```

9.15 Algorithm PUT-IN-E(OP, X, Y, Z) Saves an instruction in the E buffer
Arguments   OP, X, Y, Z a display-file instruction
Global   IE, XE, YE, ZE the E-buffer arrays
                 EFREE the next free E-buffer cell
BEGIN
    IE[EFREE] ← OP;
    XE[EFREE] ← X;
    YE[EFREE] ← Y;
    ZE[EFREE] ← Z;
    EFREE ← EFREE + 1;
    RETURN;
END;

Once we have the sorted tree of polygons, we can traverse it to enumerate them in back-to-front order. This is an in-order traversal of the tree which is most simply expressed as the following recursive algorithm.

9.16 Algorithm SAVE-POLYGONS-IN-ORDER(ROOT) Enter polygons into the display file in back-to-front order
Argument   ROOT the root polygon of the spatially sorted tree
Global   POLY-FRONT, POLY-BACK arrays of the polygon table for the branch links
BEGIN
    IF ROOT = 0 THEN RETURN;
    SAVE-POLYGONS-IN-ORDER(POLY-BACK[ROOT]);
    SEND-TO-DF(ROOT);
    SAVE-POLYGONS-IN-ORDER(POLY-FRONT[ROOT]);
    RETURN;
END;

The algorithm first checks that there is something in the tree. If so, it recursively enters into the display file (in back-to-front order) all of the polygons behind the ROOT polygon. It next enters the ROOT polygon into the display file. Finally, it enters all of the polygons in front of the ROOT polygon by means of another recursive call.

In SEND-TO-DF we first make sure that the proper edge and fill styles are in effect. Then we enter the polygon-drawing command. Finally, we enter the polygon sides.

9.17 Algorithm SEND-TO-DF(POLYGON) Enters a polygon into the display file
Argument   POLYGON the polygon to be entered
Global   POLY-START, POLY-SIDES arrays that are part of the polygon table
                 ID, XD, YD arrays that make up the D buffer
Local   I for stepping through the polygon vertices
                 F the final vertex of the polygon
BEGIN
    CHECK-STYLE(POLYGON);
    F ← POLY-START[POLYGON] + POLY-SIDES[POLYGON] − 1;
    enter the polygon instruction
    VIEWING-TRANSFORM(POLY-SIDES[POLYGON], XD[F], YD[F]);

enter the polygon sides
FOR I = POLY-START[POLYGON] TO F DO
    VIEWING-TRANSFORM(ID[I], XD[I], YD[I]);
RETURN;
END;

Checking for the proper edge and fill style is done through the CHECK-STYLE utility.

9.18 Algorithm CHECK-STYLE(POLYGON) Makes sure that the polygon is drawn in the correct style
Argument · POLYGON the polygon to be drawn
Global   CURRENT-FILL-STYLE the interior style of the polygon
            CURRENT-LINE-STYLE the edge style of the polygon
            POLY-FILL-STYLE, POLY-EDGE-STYLE the style entries in the polygon
            table
BEGIN
    IF CURRENT-LINE-STYLE ≠ POLY-EDGE-STYLE[POLYGON] THEN
        BEGIN
            DISPLAY-FILE-ENTER(POLY-EDGE-STYLE[POLYGON]);
            CURRENT-LINE-STYLE ← POLY-EDGE-STYLE[POLYGON];
        END;
    IF CURRENT-FILL-STYLE ≠ POLY-FILL-STYLE[POLYGON] THEN
        BEGIN
            DISPLAY-FILE-ENTER(POLY-FILL-STYLE[POLYGON]);
            CURRENT-FILL-STYLE ← POLY-FILL-STYLE[POLYGON];
        END;
    RETURN;
END;

All that remains for our hidden-surface check is an initialization procedure. We use it to set the default edge and fill styles, and we empty the D buffer and polygon table.

9.19 Algorithm INITIALIZE-9 Initialization for hidden-surface routines
Global   CURRENT-FILL-STYLE the interior style of the polygon
            CURRENT-LINE-STYLE the edge style of the polygon
            DFREE the next free D-buffer cell
            POLY index of the next free polygon-table cell
BEGIN
    INITIALIZE-9A;
    CURRENT-LINE-STYLE ← 0;
    CURRENT-FILL-STYLE ← − 16;
    POLY ← 1;
    DFREE ← 1;
    RETURN;
END;

This completes the algorithms needed for hidden-surface removal. Our graphics system does not take full advantage of the power of the binary space partition. With each change of viewing parameters we require the applications program to redraw the scene, constructing fresh display-file segments and causing us to resort the polygons. But note that if only the view changes, and not the objects in the scene, then the sort is essentially the same each time. Different views may change whether a sublist of polygons is in front or in back of the root polygon, but it will not change the way that the polygons were divided into sublists. For some applications which show different views of a fixed world, we can take advantage of this, doing the sort only once, building a single tree. This tree is then traversed in the appropriate order for each scene. To do this, the sorted tree and hidden-surface removal must be incorporated into the applications program.

AN APPLICATION

A major application of computer graphics is in computer-aided design (CAD). The computer can aid in the design process in many areas from architecture to machine parts to electronic circuits. The machine can maintain a data base describing the object being designed. Design components and properties of mating parts may also be available. A model for the part can be constructed and its behavior studied via computer simulation. Of course, it is often quite helpful to be able to draw and to view the part, and this is where computer graphics comes in.

Consider a computer-aided design system for designing machine parts. Such a system might provide a set of primitive shapes and operations for combining them to produce the desired object. But a complex object, if shown in wire frame, may be too confusing. To make a realistic-looking object we should remove hidden lines and surfaces. We should also be able to view the object from different directions so as to inspect all sides of it. We might even employ clipping planes to inspect the interior. To do this on our system we would first set the viewing and clipping parameter for the desired view. We would next turn on the HIDDEN flag and open a display-file segment. We would then draw the part using POLYGON-ABS-3 and POLYGON-REL-3 calls. Finally, we would close and display the segment. The hidden-surface software will produce a realistic image.

FURTHER READING

The first solution to the hidden-line problem was described in [ROB63]. Other hidden-line solutions are described in [APP67], [GAL69], and [LOU70]. Back-face removal is discussed in [LOU70]. The Z buffer is described in [CAT74]. A scan-line Z buffer is suggested in [CAR76]. Other scan-line algorithms are described in [BOU70], [GEA77], and [WYL67]. Some of the hidden-surface algorithms first decompose the polygons into triangles or trapezoids. This ensures that the objects are convex and provides a uniformity which makes them easier to manipulate. Methods for this decomposition are described in [JAC80] and [LIT79]. Sorting into priority order and the painter's algorithm are described in [NEW72]. Warnock's algorithm may be found in [WAR69]. Binary space partition is presented in [FUC80]. Its use for fast generation of different views of a scene is described in [FUC83]. An excellent description and comparison of hidden-surface techniques are found in [SUT74], with a shorter version in [SUT73]. A review of some hidden-surface methods and a discussion of how hierarchical structuring of objects can improve quality and performance are given in [CLA76]. A bibliography of hidden-line and hidden-surface papers of the 1960s and 1970s appears in [GRI78].

[APP67] Appel, A. "The Notion of Quantitative Invisibility and the Machine Rendering of Solids," *Proceedings of the ACM National Conference*, pp. 387–393 (1967).

[BOU70] Bouknight, W. J., "A Procedure for Generation of Three Dimensional Half-Tone Computer Graphics Representations," *Communications of the ACM*, vol. 13, no. 9, pp. 527–536 (1970).

[CAR76] Carpenter, L., "A New Hidden Surface Algorithm," *Proceedings of NW76*, ACM, Seattle, WA, (1976).

[CAT74] Catmull, E., "A Subdivision Algorithm for Computer Display of Curved Surfaces," University of Utah, Salt Lake City (Dec. 1974).

[CLA76] Clark, J. H., "Hierarchical Geometric Models for Visible Surface Algorithms," *Communications of the ACM*, vol. 19, no. 10, pp. 547–554 (1976).

[FUC80] Fuchs, H., Kadem, Z., "On Visible Surface Generation by a Priori Tree Structures," *Computer Graphics*, vol. 14, no. 3, pp. 124–133 (1980).

[FUC83] Fuchs, H., "Near Real-Time Shaded Display of Rigid Objects," *Computer Graphics*, vol. 17, no. 3, pp. 65–72 (1983).

[GAL69] Galimberti, R., Montanari, U., "An Algorithm for Hidden-Line Elimination ," *Communications of the ACM*, vol. 12, no. 4, pp. 206–211 (1969).

[GRI78] Griffiths, J. G., "Bibliography of Hidden-Line and Hidden-Surface Algorithms," *Computer Aided Design*, vol. 10, no. 3, pp. 203–206 (1978).

[HAM77] Hamlin, G., Gear, C. W., "Raster-Scan Hidden Surface Algorithm Techniques," *Computer Graphics*, vol. 11, no. 2, pp. 206–213 (1977).

[JAC80] Jackson, J. H., "Dynamic Scan-Converted Images with a Frame Buffer Display Device," *Computer Graphics*, vol. 14, no. 3, pp. 163–169 (1980).

[LIT79] Little, W. D., and Heuft, R., "An Area Shading Graphics Display System," *IEEE Transactions on Computers*, vol. C-28, no. 7, pp. 528–531 (1979).

[LOU70] Loutrel, P. P., "A Solution to the Hidden-Line Problem for Computer-Drawn Polyhedra," *IEEE Transactions on Computers*, vol. C-19, no. 3, pp. 205–213 (1970)

[NEW72] Newell, M. E., Newell, R. G., Sancha, T. L., "A New Approach to the Shaded Picture Problem," *Proceedings of the ACM National Conference* (1972).

[ROB63] Roberts, L. G., "Machine Perception for Three-Dimensional Solids," MIT Lincoln Laboratory, TR 315 (May 1963).

[SUT73] Sutherland, I. E., Sproull, R. F., Schumacker, R. A., "Sorting and the Hidden-Surface Problem," *Proceedings of the National Computer Conference*, vol. 42, pp. 685–693, AFIPS Press (1973).

[SUT74] Sutherland, I. E., Sproull, R. F., Schumacker, R. A., "A Characterization of Ten Hidden-Surface Algorithms," *Computing Surveys*, vol. 6, no. 1, pp. 1–55 (1974).

[WAR69] Warnock, J. E., "A Hidden-Surface Algorithm for Computer-Generated Halftone Pictures," Computer Science Department, University of Utah, TR 4-15 (1969).

[WYL67] Wylie, C., Romney, G., Evans, D., Erdahl, A., "Half-Tone Perspective Drawings by Computer," *AFIPS FJCC*, vol. 31, pp. 49–58 (1967).

EXERCISES

9-1 For each of the following triangles give a vector normal to the plane which contains it.

a) $(0, 1, 2)$, $(2, 1, 2)$, $(3, 5, 2)$

b) $(4, 3, 1)$, $(2, 3, 1)$, $(3, 3, 2)$

c) $(0, 1, 1)$, $(1, 0, 1)$, $(0, 0, 0)$

d) $(3, 2, 1)$, $(1, 3, 2)$, $(2, 1, 3)$

e) $(-5, 3, 7)$, $(4, -2, 1)$, $(0, 6, -2)$

9-2 Consider the vectors

$$A = [1 \quad 0 \quad 0]$$

$$B = [0 \quad 1 \quad 0]$$

$$C = [1 \quad 1 \quad 1]$$

$$D = [2 \quad 3 \quad 4]$$

$$E = [-4 \quad 2 \quad -3]$$

Calculate the following dot and cross products:

$A \cdot B, A \cdot D, B \cdot D, C \cdot D, D \cdot E$

$A \times B, A \times C, A \times D, B \times C, B \times D, C \times D, D \times C, D \times E, E \times D$

9-3 Suppose that POLYGON-ABS-3 commands are issued for the triangles in Exercises 9-1, with the argument arrays containing the points in the same order as listed above. Under the default viewing parameters, state for each triangle whether it is a front or a back face.

9-4 Show that the sums in Equation 9.3 do compute twice the area of the projections of the polygon in the x, y, and z directions. Hint: Consider the area of the triangle between vertex i, vertex j, and the origin.

9-5 Some special cases which cause problems for some hidden-surface algorithms are penetrating faces and cyclic overlap. A penetrating face occurs when polygon A passes through polygon B. Cyclic overlap occurs when polygon A is in front of polygon B, which is in front of polygon C, which is in front of Polygon A. Actually, we need only two polygons for cyclic overlap; imagine a rectangle threaded through a polygon shaped like the letter C so that it is behind the top of the C but in front of the bottom part. For the various hidden-surface methods we have presented, discuss whether or not they can handle penetrating faces and cyclic overlap.

9-6 a) Show that no polygon subdivision takes place in applying the binary space partition method to a convex object.

b) For the case of a convex object compare the cost of the back-face removal method with that of the binary space partition method for a single view.

c) Suppose we wish to display a sequence of views of a convex object. How would the cost of using back-face removal compare to the binary space partition scheme?

PROGRAMMING PROBLEMS

9-1 Implement algorithms 9.1 through 9.4 to extend the graphics system for back-face removal.

9-2 Test the back-face removal algorithm by drawing a house built from unfilled polygons. Select a single view which shows front, side, and roof.

9-3 Test the back-face removal algorithm by drawing a die. Provide different views of the die so that each face is displayed at least once.

9-4 Modify the back-face algorithm for unfilled polygons so that instead of removing back faces it draws them in a less pronounced line style (e.g., as dashed lines).

9-5 Implement algorithms 9.5 through 9.19 to provide the painter's algorithm for hidden-surface removal.

9-6 Test the painter's algorithm by showing several filled polygons with different interior styles, and different states of overlap, entered in mixed order.

9-7 Test the painter's algorithm by showing two houses composed of filled polygons with different interior styles. Select a view such that one house partially obscures the other house.

9-8 Write a program which gives successive views of an object drawn by procedure FOO within the cube $0 < x < 1, 0 < y < 1, 0 < z < 1$. The images should be those seen by the viewer as he walks around the object.

*9-9 Functions of the form $y = F(x, z)$ may be shown by a number of polygons composed of the curve at fixed z for sample x and the boundaries. For example, a polygon might connect points for $z = 0.5$ and $x = 0.0, 0.2, 0.4, 0.6, 0.8, 1.0$, and the boundaries at $x = 1, y = 0$, and $x = 0$. In this manner, each polygon shows a slice of the function. Several slices may be shown by displaying polygons for several z values.

    a) Write a program which does this for a curve such as

$$y = \sin(\pi * x) + \cos(\pi * z)$$

    b) Use the hidden-surface removal algorithm to remove portions hidden by nearer slices. (You can get the effect of hidden-line removal by using polygons filled with white having black edges.)

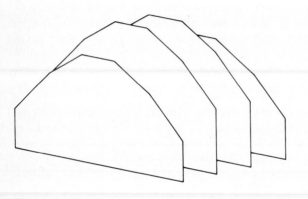

    c) Select viewing parameters which best display the surface.

**9-10 Modify your graphics system to use a Z buffer to remove hidden surfaces.

TEN

LIGHT,
COLOR,
AND
SHADING

INTRODUCTION

In previous chapters, we have seen how to construct three-dimensional objects out of polygons. We can now project and display perspective images of objects to get a feeling of depth. We have also learned how to remove hidden lines and surfaces to give the images a greater degree of realism. The polygons from which the objects are created can be filled in. Often, we will be able to draw polygons with different interior styles, and different styles may give the effect of different intensities or shades for the polygon surfaces. In this chapter we shall consider the shading of three-dimensional objects. We shall learn how to automatically set the polygon interior styles to give further realism to the image. We shall develop a model for the manner in which light sources illuminate objects, and use this model to determine how bright each polygon face should be. We shall also discuss how colors are described and how the model may be extended to colored objects.

DIFFUSE ILLUMINATION

Let us begin our discussion of illumination by considering an indirect lighting source. We will assume that our object is illuminated by light which does not come from any particular source but which comes from all directions. This is background light, light which is reflected from walls, floor, and ceiling. We assume that this light is uniform, that there is the same amount everywhere. There will be no bright spots, and no particular direction will be favored. We will assume that there is as much light going up as there is going down and that there is the same amount going right as there is going left. A surface will therefore receive the same amount of *diffuse* light energy no matter what its orientation may be.

Now, some of this energy will be absorbed by the surface, while the rest will be reflected or reemitted. The ratio of the light reflected from the surface to the total incoming light is called the *coefficient of reflection* or the *reflectivity*. A white surface reflects or reemits nearly all of the incoming radiation; hence its coefficient of reflection is close to 1. A black surface, on the other hand, absorbs most of the incoming light; hence its reflectivity is near zero. A gray surface would have a reflection coefficient somewhere in between. Most objects will reflect some colors of light better than other colors. Suppose that we have an object which has a high coefficient of reflection for red light and a low value for the other colors. If we illuminate the object with white light (which has equal amounts of all colors), then the red portion of the light will be reflected from the object while the other colors will be absorbed. The object will look red. In fact, this is the mechanism which gives objects their colors. If we are using a color graphics display which gives each pixel a red, green, and blue intensity value, we would have to specify three reflectivity values (one for each of the three colors) in order to know the color and shading properties of the object. But to keep things simple, we will begin by considering gray-level displays, and a single reflection coefficient number (R) will tell us what shade of gray our object is painted.

We said that the amount of light striking the object will not change with the object's position because the light is coming uniformly from all directions, but will the intensity of the light reflected to our eye change with different orientations? The answer is that the object will look equally bright no matter how it is positioned. This result arises from the cancellation of two effects. The first effect is that more light is emitted perpendicular to the surface than parallel to it. The precise relation is called *Lambert's law*, and it states that the reflection of light from a perfectly diffusing surface varies as the cosine of the angle between the normal to the surface and the direction of the reflected ray. (See Figure 10-1.)

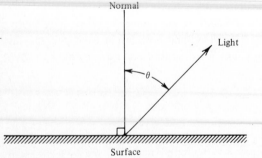

FIGURE 10-1
The direction of light is measured from the surface normal.

Thus the amount of light coming from a point on the surface would decrease as the cosine of the angle as that surface is rotated away from our viewpoint. The compensating effect arises from the fact that we don't see points but areas.

As the surface is turned away from our eyes, the number of light-emitting points within an area of view increases, and this increase happens to be by the reciprocal of the cosine. Therefore, as the surface is turned away from our eyes, we get less light from each point; but the points appear to be squeezed closer together, and the net effect is that the brightness of the surface is unchanged. (See Figure 10-2.)

A similar cancellation of effects occurs as the surface is moved farther from the viewpoint. Light coming from the surface is then spread out over a larger area. The area increases by the square of the distance, so the amount of the light reaching the eye is decreased by this same factor. By the same arguments, however, the objects being viewed will appear to be smaller, again by the same factor. So, while we have less light, it is applied to a smaller area on the retina and the brightness of the surface remains unchanged. (See Figure 10-3.)

We can now give an expression for the brightness of an object illuminated by diffuse background light. If B is the intensity of the background light and R is the object's reflectivity, then the intensity of light coming from any visible surface will be

$$v = BR \tag{10.1}$$

If we allow the user to set the values of B and R, he can create light or dark scenes and "paint" his objects different shades of gray. But in this simple model, every plane on a particular object will be shaded equally. This is not, however, the way real objects

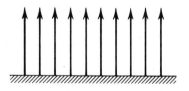

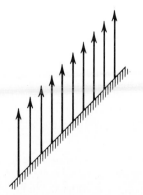

FIGURE 10-2
Viewing the surface at an angle increases the light-producing area in view.

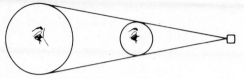

The amount of light decreases with distance

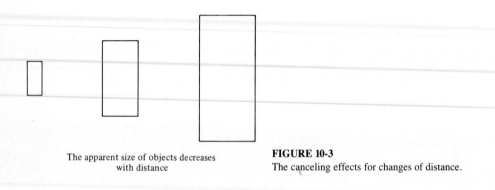

The apparent size of objects decreases
with distance

FIGURE 10-3
The canceling effects for changes of distance.

look; and for a more realistic shading model, we must also include point sources of illumination.

POINT-SOURCE ILLUMINATION

Point sources are abstractions of real-world sources of light such as light bulbs, candles, or the sun. The light originates at a particular place, it comes from a particular direction over a particular distance. For point sources, the position and orientation of the object's surface relative to the light source will determine how much light the surface will receive and, in turn, how bright it will appear. Surfaces facing toward and positioned near the light source will receive more light than those facing away from or far removed from the illumination. Let's begin by considering the effects of orientation. By arguments similar to those we made earlier, we can see that as a face is turned away from the light source, the surface area on which a fixed-sized beam of light falls increases. This means that there is less light for each surface point. The surface is less brightly illuminated. (See Figure 10-4.)

The illumination is decreased by a factor of cos I, where I is the angle between the direction of the light and the direction normal to the plane. The angle I is called the *angle of incidence*. (See Figure 10-5.)

If we have a vector of length 1 called L pointing toward the light source and a vector of length 1 called N in the direction normal to the surface, then the vector dot product gives

$$\cos I = L \cdot N \qquad (10.2)$$

Suppose that P amount of light comes from the point source. Then the shade of a surface of an object will be given by

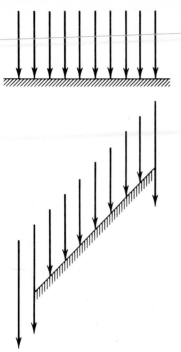

FIGURE 10-4
A surface facing the light source will receive more light than one at an angle.

$$v = BR + PR(L \cdot N) \tag{10.3}$$

The point-source term has the light from the point source, times the cosine of the angle of incidence (giving us how much light illuminates each point on the surface), multiplied by the coefficient of reflection (giving us how much of this light is reemitted to reach the viewer).

SPECULAR REFLECTION

Our model can be improved even more. Light can be reflected from an object in two ways: there is a diffuse reflection, which we have included above, and there is *specular* reflection. The diffuse reflection depends only upon the angle of incidence, and the re-

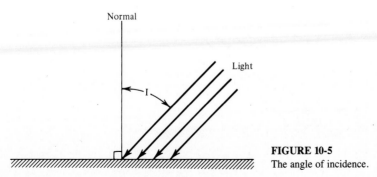

FIGURE 10-5
The angle of incidence.

flected light can be colored, since the coefficient of reflection is involved. Specular reflection acts quite differently. It is the type of reflection which occurs at the surface of a mirror. (Note the reflected light in Plates 5 and 6.) Light is reflected in nearly a single direction (not spread out over all directions in accordance with Lambert's law). Plastics and many metals have a specular reflection which is independent of color; all colors are equally reflected. We shall assume this is the case for our model.

For specular reflection, light comes in, strikes the surface, and bounces right back off. The angle that the reflected beam makes with the surface normal is called the *angle of reflection* O, and is equal in magnitude to the angle of incidence. (See Figure 10-6.)

The model for specular reflection which we shall present was proposed by Blinn [BLI77]. According to this model, there are four factors which contribute to specular reflection. They are the distribution of the surface facets, the direction of the surface, the absorption of the surface, and the blockage of light due to the surface roughness.

The model assumes that the surface is not perfectly smooth, but rather is made of tiny mirrorlike *facets*. Most of the facets will face about the same direction as the overall surface, but some will be a little different and will reflect some of the light in different directions. How glossy an object is depends on how much variation there is in the surface facets. A very glossy object has almost all facets aligned, and light is reflected in a sharp ray. An object with a broader distribution of facet directions will spread out the light; reflections will blur and merge; the object's surface will appear flat. A function which describes the distribution of facets is given by

$$D = \left[\frac{k}{k + 1 - (N \cdot H)} \right]^2 \tag{10.4}$$

The vector H is a unit vector in the direction halfway between the light and the eye. The light from the specular reflection can be seen when the direction from the object to the eye is the same direction as that of the reflected light. Another way to state this is to form a vector halfway between the direction of the incident light and the direction to the eye. (See Figure 10-7.)

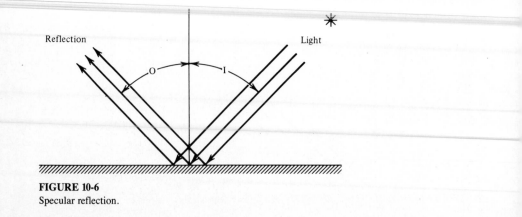

FIGURE 10-6
Specular reflection.

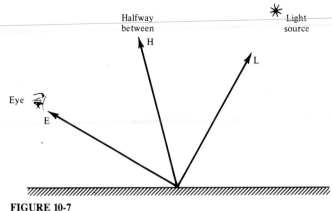

FIGURE 10-7
Defining the vector halfway between the light source and the viewer's eye.

Compare this vector to the surface normal, which is halfway between the incident and reflected rays. (See Figure 10-8.) If the directions match, then the eye can see
the reflected rays. Let's first see how to compute the vector H. If L is a vector of length
1 in the direction out of the surface along the incident light ray, and E is a vector of
length 1 in the direction of the eye, then

$$H = \frac{L + E}{|L + E|} \tag{10.5}$$

will be a vector of length 1 pointing halfway between them. Now we want to show that
Equation 10.4 gives the desired behavior for light reflected from a surface of facets,
most of which are aligned with the surface normal. If N is a vector of length 1 in the
direction of the surface normal, then the dot product $N \cdot H$ will give the cosine of the
angle between the halfway vector and the surface normal. When the angle between

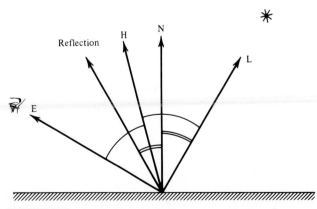

FIGURE 10-8
Vectors used to determine when the eye can see the reflection.

these two vectors is zero, the eye will see reflections from the facets which are aligned with the overall surface direction. Since this is the majority of the facets, we expect D to be largest for this case. At angles near 0, the cosine will be near 1. In Equation 10.4 the term $1 - (N \cdot H)$ will be close to 0, which causes the denominator to be small, and D is its strongest for this direction. But the denominator can never be smaller than k, and D cannot become larger than 1. Here k is a positive parameter which describes the glossiness of the material. For k close to 0, the material is glossy; as the eye moves away from the angle of reflection, the $1 - (N \cdot H)$ term moves away from 0 and quickly overwhelms k. So for small k, we see that D will be small unless N is close to H, at which point the expression approaches 1. We will only be able to see light if we are looking along the angle of reflection. But for large k, the surface is uniform or flat. D will always be close to 1, so we will see some of the light no matter which direction we look. (See Figure 10-9.)

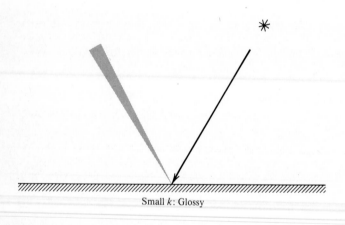

Small k: Glossy

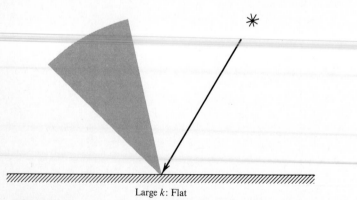

Large k: Flat

FIGURE 10-9
The effect of k.

A second factor is how much of the lighted surface is turned away from our eyes. As we have seen, when a surface is turned away from our eyes, the number of light-emitting points increases by a factor of the reciprocal of the cosine of the angle [i.e., $1 / (N \cdot E)$]. For the diffuse case, this effect was canceled by Lambert's law, but for specular reflection we should retain it.

The third factor is that not all of the light is reflected; some of it is absorbed (or transmitted if the object is transparent). This depends upon the angle of view. The theoretical expression for the amount of light reflection for nonabsorbing materials is given by the *Fresnel equation*

$$F = \frac{(g - c)^2}{2(g + c)^2} \left\{ 1 + \frac{[c(g + c) - 1]^2}{[c(g - c) + 1]^2} \right\} \tag{10.6}$$

where

$$c = E \cdot H \tag{10.7}$$

is the cosine of half the angle between the eye and the light, and g is given by

$$g = (n^2 + c^2 - 1)^{1/2} \tag{10.8}$$

Here n is the effective index of refraction for the material. Transparent objects have an index of refraction near 1, giving small F values; whereas metals have a high value of n which results in F near 1, meaning that most of the light is reflected.

Finally, the roughness of the surface may block some of the light. (See Figure 10-10.) An expression for the amount of reflected light blocked by the surface roughness is

$$G_r = 2 (N \cdot H)(N \cdot E) / (E \cdot H) \tag{10.9}$$

The incident light can also be blocked by the surface roughness

$$G_i = 2 (N \cdot H)(N \cdot L) / (E \cdot H) \tag{10.10}$$

The light blockage factor G which should be used is

$$G = \min[1, \min(G_r, G_i)] \tag{10.11}$$

Putting these factors together gives the net proportion of the light available for specular reflection.

$$\frac{DGF}{E \cdot N} \tag{10.12}$$

We can now extend our shading function to include specular reflection.

$$v = BR + PR(L \cdot N) + PDGF / (E \cdot N) \tag{10.13}$$

Finally, let's include the effects of distance. In theory, the illumination from a point source should decrease as the square of the distance between it and the object being illuminated. Using this relation, however, seems to give too much change with

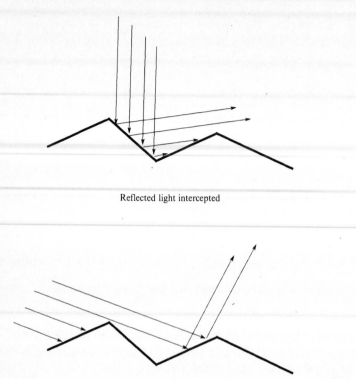

Reflected light intercepted

Incident light blocked

FIGURE 10-10
The effects of surface roughness.

distance. Perhaps this is partly due to the fact that most light sources are much larger than points. An object illuminated by a very large nearby light source would hardly show any change in illumination with small changes in distance. In any case, we want some function which decreases with distance less rapidly than the square. And we may also wish it to approach some finite limit for very small distances, so that we need not worry about division by zero for a badly positioned light source. We suggest the following function

$$W = \frac{1}{C + U} \tag{10.14}$$

where C is a positive constant and U is the distance from the light source to the object. Our shading expression then becomes

$$v = BR + \frac{P[R(L \cdot N) + DGF/(E \cdot N)]}{C + U} \tag{10.15}$$

We could generalize this to several point light sources if we wished.

$$v = BR + \sum_j \frac{P_j[R(L \cdot N) + D_jG_jF/(E \cdot N)]}{C + U_j} \tag{10.16}$$

SHADING ALGORITHMS

Now let's consider how to introduce automatic shading into our graphics system. We begin by creating a means to turn the automatic shading on or off. The flag SHADE-FLAG can be set by the user to indicate whether or not automatic shading should occur.

> **10.1 Algorithm SET-SHADING(ON-OFF)** User routine to indicate automatic shading
> Argument   ON-OFF the user's shading setting
> Global   SHADE-FLAG a flag to indicate automatic shading
> BEGIN
>   SHADE-FLAG ← ON-OFF;
>   RETURN;
> END;

The shading formulas which we presented make use of the dot product of vectors of length 1 for the determination of cosines. We shall therefore often be normalizing vectors (scaling to length 1). It will be convenient to have a utility procedure to do this. The following routine normalizes a vector by dividing by its length. The vector's original length is also returned.

> **10.2 Algorithm UNITY(DX, DY, DZ, LENGTH)** Utility routine to normalize a vector and compute its length
> Arguments   DX, DY, DZ the vector to be normalized
>   LENGTH for return of the vector's original length
> BEGIN
>   LENGTH ← SQRT(DX ↑ 2 + DY ↑ 2 + DZ ↑ 2);
>   DX ← DX / LENGTH;
>   DY ← DY / LENGTH;
>   DZ ← DZ / LENGTH;
>   RETURN;
> END;

We must determine the shade of each polygon, using vectors and angles between it and the light sources and viewpoint. These vectors and angles must be determined before projection (which alters them). We shall alter the DISPLAY-FILE-ENTER routine to include setting of the CURRENT-FILL-STYLE to the proper shade.

> **10.3 Algorithm DISPLAY-FILE-ENTER(OP)** (Revision of algorithm 8.38) Routine to enter an instruction into the display file
> Argument   OP opcode of instruction to be entered
> Global   DF-PEN-X, DF-PEN-Y, DF-PEN-Z the current pen position
>   PERSPECTIVE-FLAG perspective vs. parallel projection flag
> Local   X, Y, Z hold the point that is transformed
> BEGIN
>   IF OP < 1 AND OP > − 32 THEN PUT-POINT(OP, 0, 0)
>   ELSE
>   BEGIN
>   X ← DF-PEN-X;

```
                    Y ← DF-PEN-Y;
                    Z ← DF-PEN-Z;
                    VIEW-PLANE-TRANSFORM(X, Y, Z);
                    IF SHADE-FLAG THEN SHADE-CHECK(OP, X, Y, Z);
                    IF PERSPECTIVE-FLAG THEN PERSPECTIVE-TRANSFORM(X, Y, Z)
                    ELSE PARALLEL-TRANSFORM(X, Y, Z);
                    CLIP(OP, X, Y, Z);
                END;
            RETURN;
        END;
```

We have called SHADE-CHECK in order to calculate the appropriate shade for polygons. The statements in SHADE-CHECK determine the polygon's normal vector and its center. The routine then calls MAKE-SHADE to actually find the shading factor. The SHADE-CHECK procedure is called for every vertex of the polygon, but will calculate the shade only on the last vertex call. The first call will be for the polygon instruction. This causes initializations of the variables and sets a counter for the number of vertices. For each of the following vertices, we accumulate the average position and calculate the normal vector as we did for back-face removal. On the last vertex of the polygon, we complete the center position calculation by averaging the accumulated vertex coordinates. We then use MAKE-SHADE to determine the appropriate interior style. Note that the method we use to find the normal vector for the polygon will give reasonable results when the vertex coordinates are close to but not exactly planar. This can be useful in finding the shade of small curved surface patches as are discussed in Chapter 11.

10.4 Algorithm SHADE-CHECK(OP, X, Y, Z) Calculates the shade of polygons
Determines the normal and center; then calls MAKE-SHADE
Arguments   OP, X, Y, Z a display-file instruction
Global   A-SHADE, B-SHADE, C-SHADE for accumulating the polygon normal
            X-SHADE, Y-SHADE, Z-SHADE for accumulating the polygon center
            X-PREV, Y-PREV, Z-PREV the previous vertex
            SIZE-SHADE the polygon size
            SIDE-COUNT a counter of polygon sides seen

```
BEGIN
    IF OP > 2 THEN
        BEGIN
            new polygon instruction
            SIZE-SHADE ← OP;
            A-SHADE ← 0;
            B-SHADE ← 0;
            C-SHADE ← 0;
            X-SHADE ← 0;
            Y-SHADE ← 0;
            Z-SHADE ← 0;
            X-PREV ← X;
            Y-PREV ← Y;
            Z-PREV ← Z;
```

```
            SIDE-COUNT ← 0;
            RETURN;
        END;
    IF SIZE-SHADE > 0 THEN
        BEGIN
            enter another side
            A-SHADE ← A-SHADE + (Y-PREV − Y) * (Z-PREV + Z);
            B-SHADE ← B-SHADE + (Z-PREV − Z) * (X-PREV + X);
            C-SHADE ← C-SHADE + (X-PREV − X) * (Y-PREV + Y);
            X-SHADE ← X-SHADE + X;
            Y-SHADE ← Y-SHADE + Y;
            Z-SHADE ← Z-SHADE + Z;
            X-PREV ← X;
            Y-PREV ← Y;
            Z-PREV ← Z;
            SIDE-COUNT ← SIDE-COUNT + 1;
            IF SIDE-COUNT = SIZE-SHADE THEN
                BEGIN
                    all vertices seen, so average center position
                    X-SHADE ← X-SHADE / SIZE-SHADE;
                    Y-SHADE ← Y-SHADE / SIZE-SHADE;
                    Z-SHADE ← Z-SHADE / SIZE-SHADE;
                    now determine the shade
                    MAKE-SHADE;
                    SIZE-SHADE ← 0;
                END;
        END;
    RETURN;
END;
```

Now let's discuss the MAKE-SHADE shading routine. This routine obtains as global variables the polygon's normal vector and a center point. It also obtains the position of the light source and the surface properties of the object. The normal vector should be scaled to length 1 by the UNITY routine. The difference between the position of the light source and the position of the polygon gives a vector for the direction to the light. The calculation for the direction to the eye depends upon whether a parallel or perspective projection is used. For a parallel projection, we take the parallel projection vector. For a perspective projection, the direction to the eye is the difference between the center of projection and the average polygon position.

After normalizing the light- and eye-direction vectors, they can be added to calculate the vector midway between them. Now the cosines can be determined. The cosine of the angle of incidence is the dot product of the normal vector and the light vector. A negative result means that the light is behind the surface and the shade will result only from the background illumination. We can plug all the parameters into our shading formula to get a number characterizing the object's brightness. Here the background illumination B (named BKGRND in the algorithm) is assumed to have values between zero and 1, and the point source is given by

$$P = 1 - B \tag{10.17}$$

The result is then scaled by an overall brightness factor BRIGHT. After determining the brightness of a polygon, the result is passed to the routine INTENSITY, which sets the appropriate polygon interior style.

10.5 Algorithm MAKE-SHADE Routine to calculate and set the shading style for a polygon

Global	XL, YL, ZL the location of the light point source
	PERSPECTIVE-FLAG the perspective vs. parallel projection flag
	XC, YC, ZC the center of perspective projection
	VXP, VYP, VZP the direction of parallel projection
	BKGRND the proportion of the light in background illumination
	REFL the reflectivity of the polygon
	K-GLOSS the polygon shininess
	BRIGHT the overall illumination scale vector
	X-SHADE, Y-SHADE, Z-SHADE the position of the polygon
	A-SHADE, B-SHADE, C-SHADE the normal vector to the polygon
	NRF the index of refraction of the surface
Local	DXL, DYL, DZL the direction of the light source
	U the distance to the light source
	DXE, DYE, DZE the direction of the eye
	DXH, DYH, DZH vector halfway between eye and light
	COSNL the cosine of the angle of incidence
	COSNH the cosine of angle between normal and halfway vectors
	COSNE the cosine of the angle between normal and eye vectors
	COSEH the cosine of the angle between eye and halfway vectors
	G factor for self-shading due to surface roughness
	GF, T intermediate values
	F reflection factor from Fresnel's equation
	D facet distribution of the surface
	SHADE-SETTING resulting shading value
	DUMMY a dummy variable

```
BEGIN
    normalize the surface normal vector
    UNITY(A-SHADE, B-SHADE, C-SHADE, DUMMY);
    calculate other vectors
    DXL ← XL − X-SHADE;
    DYL ← YL − Y-SHADE;
    DZL ← ZL − Z-SHADE;
    UNITY( DXL, DYL, DZL, U)
    IF PERSPECTIVE-FLAG THEN
        BEGIN
            DXE ← XC − X-SHADE;
            DYE ← YC· − Y-SHADE;
            DZE ← ZC − Z-SHADE;
        END
    ELSE
        BEGIN
            DXE ← VXP;
            DYE ← VYP;
```

```
            DZE ← VZP;
        END;
    UNITY(DXE, DYE, DZE, DUMMY);
    DXH ← DXE + DXL;
    DYH ← DYE + DYL;
    DZH ← DZE + DZL;
    UNITY(DXH, DYH, DZH, DUMMY);
    calculate the cosines
    COSNE ← A-SHADE * DXE + B-SHADE * DYE + C-SHADE * DZE;
    IF COSNE ≤ 0 THEN RETURN;
    it's a back face
    COSNL ← A-SHADE * DXL + B-SHADE * DYL + C-SHADE * DZL;
    IF COSNL ≤ 0 THEN
        BEGIN
            does not face the light source
            SHADE-SETTING ← MIN(1, BRIGHT * BKGRND * REFL);
            SET-FILL-STYLE(INTENSITY(SHADE-SETTING));
            RETURN;
        END;
    COSNH ← A-SHADE * DXH + B-SHADE * DYH + C-SHADE * DZH;
    COSEH ← DXH * DXE + DYH * DYE + DZH * DZE;
    surface roughness
    IF COSNE < COSNL THEN G ← 2 * COSNE * COSNH / COSEH
    ELSE G ← 2 * COSNL * COSNH / COSEH;
    IF G > 1 THEN G ← 1;
    reflection factor
    GF ← SQRT(NRF * NRF + COSEH * COSEH − 1);
    T ← ((GF + COSEH) * COSEH − 1) / ((GF − COSEH) * COSEH + 1);
    F ← T * T + 1;
    T ← (GF − COSEH) / (GF + COSEH);
    F ← F * T * T / 2;
    facet distribution
    D ← K-GLOSS / (K-GLOSS + 1 − COSNH);
    D ← D * D;
    calculate the shading value
    SHADE-SETTING ← MIN(1, (BKGRND * REFL + (1 − BKGRND) * (REFL *
        COSNL + G * F * D / COSNE) / (1 + U) ) * BRIGHT);
    SET-FILL-STYLE( INTENSITY(SHADE-SETTING));
    RETURN;
END;
```

The INTENSITY routine converts shading values into settings for the polygon interior style. The actual implementation of this routine can depend upon the display device being used. In particular, the number of intensity values actually available and their corresponding fill-style parameters can differ for different implementations. The range of SHADE-SETTING values passed to the INTENSITY routine is 0 to 1. If the display device has possible intensity settings of 1 through N, these values may be generated by

$$\text{INT(SHADE-SETTING} * (N - 1) + 1)$$

This is a linear transformation which assumes that the intensity varies linearly between settings. This is not true for some display devices, and in such cases, different formulas which compensate for the nonlinear hardware may have to be used. This is discussed further in the section on gamma correction. If the system has been written such that fill style 1 is the darkest, style 2 is lighter, and so on up through style N, then the above formula will give the correct style settings. An example of a case where the intensities may not correspond simply to the interior style numbers is the case where output is done on a line printer and different characters are used to get the different intensities. When the relation of style number to intensity is complex, an array can be used for the conversion. We store the fill-style codes in the array. The code for the darkest style is saved in the first array cell, the next darkest in the second cell, and so on, so that the code for the lightest style is in the Nth cell. Then we use the above formula to determine which cell to examine, and we retrieve from that cell the correct style setting. To actually make the change of style, we put the new style instruction into the display file. An example of an INTENSITY routine which could be used with a line printer is given below.

10.6 Algorithm INTENSITY(SHADE-SETTING) Example of routine to enter correct interior style for shading
Argument   SHADE-SETTING the polygon's shading value
Global   SHADE-STYLES an array of 16 interior styles for shading
Local   SHADE-INDEX index of the style setting for the shade
BEGIN
    SHADE-INDEX ← INT(15 * SHADE-SETTING + 1);
    INTENSITY ← SHADE-STYLE[SHADE-INDEX];
    RETURN;
END;

We have used a number of parameters to characterize the light source and the object being illuminated. Of course, we must provide the means for the user to set the values for these parameters. We shall therefore write routines for placing the user's specifications into global variables. Objects will be characterized by their reflectivity (REFL), their index of refraction (NFR), and their glossiness (K-GLOSS). The following routine sets the object parameters.

10.7 Algorithm SET-OBJECT-SHADE(REFLECTIVITY, REFRACTION, GLOSS) User routine to set an object's shading parameters
Arguments   REFLECTIVITY object's coefficient of reflection
            REFRACTION the index of refraction
            GLOSS the narrowness of the reflected rays
Global   REFL, NRF, K-GLOSS global storage for the object's parameters
BEGIN
    REFL ← REFLECTIVITY;
    NRF ← REFRACTION;

```
    K-GLOSS ← GLOSS;
    RETURN;
END;
```

We have allowed the object parameters to be changed at any time, so that as the scene is constructed, different objects may be given different appearances. We wish, however, to treat the lighting parameters somewhat differently. The lighting arrangement will be considered part of the viewing specification, and like the other viewing parameters discussed in Chapter 8, the lighting parameters should be fixed throughout the display-file segment. To do this, we shall have two sets of parameters: one set which the user can alter at any time, and a second set which is given the current user's specification whenever a display-file segment is created. It is the second set which is actually used in the shading calculation. The following routine gets the user's specification.

10.8 Algorithm SET-LIGHT(X, Y, Z, BRIGHTNESS, BACKGROUND) User routine for saving the lighting parameters

```
Arguments   X, Y, Z the location of the light source
            BRIGHTNESS an overall-intensity scaling factor
            BACKGROUND the portion of the light which is indirect
Global      XL1, YL1, ZL1, BRT, BKG storage for the user's specification
BEGIN
    XL1 ← X;
    YL1 ← Y;
    ZL1 ← Z;
    BRT ← BRIGHTNESS;
    BKG ← MAX(0, MIN(1, BACKGROUND));
    RETURN;
END;
```

When a display-file segment is created, we shall copy the current lighting parameters into the global variables which will be used in the shading calculation. We shall also convert the light-source position to the view plane coordinate system. The COPY-LIGHT routine carries out these operations.

10.9 Algorithm COPY-LIGHT Routine to update the current lighting parameters

```
Global      XL1, YL1, ZL1 the current light-source position
            BRT the current brightness
            BKG the current background illumination
            XL, YL ZL lighting position for the display-file segment
            BRIGHT the brightness for the display-file segment
            BKGRND the background illumination for the display-file segment
BEGIN
    BRIGHT ← BRT;
    BKGRND ← BKG;
    XL ← XL1;
    YL ← YL1;
```

```
        ZL ← ZL1;
        VIEW-PLANE-TRANSFORM(XL, YL, ZL);
        RETURN;
    END;
```

The COPY-LIGHT routine should be called as part of the establishment of the viewing parameters. We therefore modify the NEW-VIEW-3 routine as follows:

10.10 Algorithm NEW-VIEW-3 (Revision of algorithm 8.39) Create a new overall viewing transformation
```
BEGIN
    MAKE-VIEW-PLANE-TRANSFORMATION;
    MAKE-Z-CLIP-PLANES;
    NEW-VIEW-2;
    COPY-LIGHT;
    RETURN;
END;
```

To complete our shading algorithm, we must include initializations for the parameters which we have created.

10.11 Algorithm INITIALIZE-10 Initialization of the shading parameters
```
BEGIN
    SIZE-SHADE ← 0;
    SET-LIGHT(0, 0, 1, 1, 0);
    INITIALIZE-9;
    SET-OBJECT-SHADE(1, 10, 10)
    SET-SHADING(FALSE);
    RETURN;
END;
```

The light source is initialized to location $(0, 0, 1)$ with brightness 1. Brightness values will normally be about 1 to 2, but may be larger to compensate for a distant light source or low reflectivity of an object. The background illumination is initialized to 0. This parameter should range between 0 (no indirect lighting) and 1 (totally indirect illumination). Objects are initialized as totally reflective but not very glossy.

SMOOTH SHADING OF SURFACE APPROXIMATIONS

So far we have dealt only with flat polygons. If we wanted to draw a curved shape (a doughnut, ball, can, cup, or airplane), we could approximate it with many small polygons. (See Figure 10-11.)

If we shade the approximate surface, we can often see the individual polygon edges. The edges are enhanced by the properties of our eyes to produce an effect called *Mach banding*. When a uniform dark surface meets a uniform light surface, the dark surface appears even darker along the edge, and the light surface even lighter. This makes the edge stand out. (See Figure 10-12.)

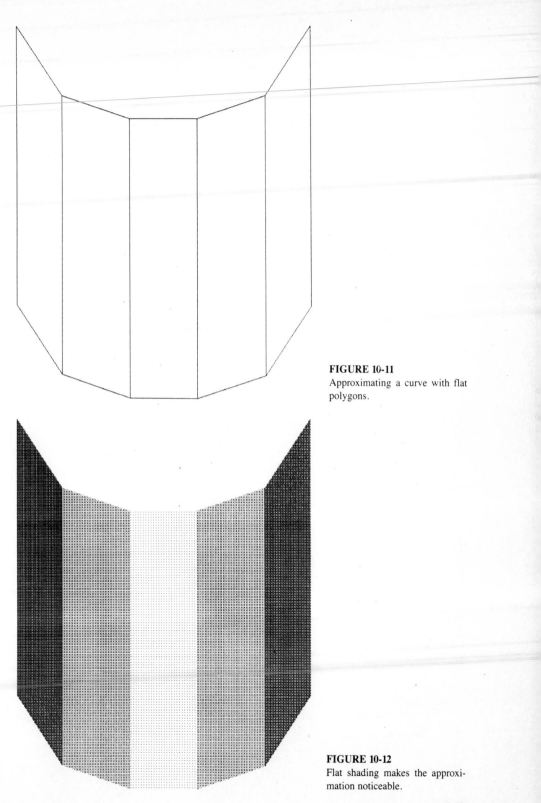

FIGURE 10-11
Approximating a curve with flat polygons.

FIGURE 10-12
Flat shading makes the approximation noticeable.

A method was suggested by Henri Gouraud for varying the shade across polygon surfaces so that the shade at a polygon's edge matches that of its neighbor. (See Figure 10-13.) To do this, we need more information than just a single shade value per polygon. Instead, we need a shade value at each vertex.

We could, for example, extend our polygon routines to enter an intensity value at each vertex, along with the position. This information would have to be included in the display file. The rest of the work would be done by the polygon-filling routines. We use the same method that is used to determine depth values for every polygon point for use in a Z buffer. Recall that our polygon-filling method moves down the polygon a scan line at a time, calculating the x edge values and setting the pixels between them. The new x values could be found by subtracting the inverse slope from the current values. In a similar way we can arrive at a shade value for the edge at each scan line. We start with s_1 at y_1, and for each step down in y, we change the shade by $(s_2 - s_1) / (y_2 - y_1)$. Now for each scan line we have bounding x values (x_a to x_b) and bounding shade values (s_a to s_b). We modify our FILLIN algorithm to change pixel intensities smoothly between these limits. At x_a, shade s_a is used. At $x_a + 1$, the shade $s_a + [(s_b - s_a) / (x_b - x_a)]$ is used. At $x_a + n$, the shade is $s_a + n [(s_b - s_a) /(x_b - x_a)]$. So shading changes linearly along edges and between edges, yielding a smoother, more natural appearance.

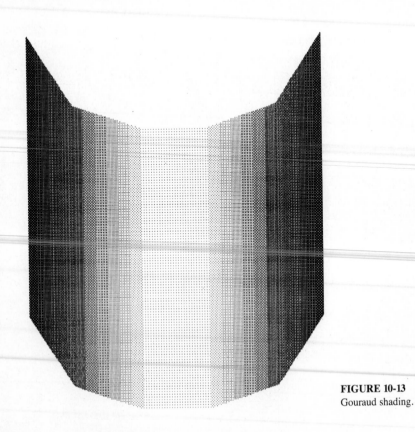

FIGURE 10-13
Gouraud shading.

Specifying the shade of each vertex in the polygon routine leaves it up to the user to determine the appropriate shading. It is also possible to perform automatic shading of curved surfaces using Gouraud's interpolation scheme. The problem is to automatically determine the shade of the surface at each vertex. The formulas that we have presented may be used, only the shade value at a vertex should be based on the direction of the true surface at that point and not the direction of the polygon approximation. (See Figure 10-14.)

TRANSPARENCY

Our shading model has not considered transparent objects. The surface of a transparent object may receive light from behind as well as from in front. Such objects have a *transparency coefficient* T as well as values for reflectivity and specular reflection. The transparency coefficient may depend upon the thickness of the object. If one layer of tinted glass lets through only half of the light, then two layers will let through only one quarter. The transmission of light depends exponentially on the distance which the light ray must travel within the object.

$$T = te^{-ad} \tag{10.18}$$

In this expression, (d) is the distance the light must travel in the object. The coefficients (t) and (a) are properties of the material. The (t) determines how much of the light is transmitted at the surface (instead of reflected), and (a) tells how quickly the material absorbs or attenuates the light. (See Figure 10-15.)

If we view a light source through a transparent object, the properties of the surface (t) may be modeled in much the same way as for a reflecting surface. We are mainly interested in how much light passes through the surface. This is the light which is not reflected and is given by the Fresnel factor $(1 - F)$. For most objects, the light both enters and exits, and a factor is needed for both surfaces.

The transparency and absorption coefficients can depend on color. Some objects let only red light through, while others attenuate the red and blue, letting only green pass. If we are dealing with colored objects, we need three pairs of transparency and absorption coefficients. For very clear objects, we can neglect the attenuation with distance or include it as an average value as part of (t).

A proper treatment of transparent objects should also consider the fact that light changes direction when it crosses the boundary between two media. (See Figure 10-16.) This effect is called *refraction*. The change in direction is related to a property of materials called the index of refraction (n). The exact relation is called *Snell's law*.

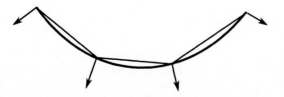

FIGURE 10-14
Use the direction of the true curve at each vertex of the approximation.

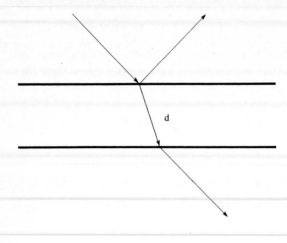

FIGURE 10-15
The absorption of light by an object depends on the length of the optical path within the object.

$$\frac{\sin \theta_1}{\sin \theta_2} = \frac{n_2}{n_1} \tag{10.19}$$

The light ray is bent both when it enters a transparent object and when it leaves. To correctly show transparent objects, then, we have to retain back faces so that we can calculate the light path in and out of objects and also determine the length of the path within the object. This would be difficult to add to our system; however, there is a simple extension which can yield transparency effects.

If we assume that (1) for a given surface, the transparency coefficient for the object is a constant, (2) refraction effects can be ignored, and (3) no light source can be seen directly through the object, then the light coming through the object is just the transparency coefficient times the light coming from objects behind it. Our painter's algorithm overwrites objects in the back of the scene with the objects in the front. In effect, the light from the back object is replaced by that from the front object. But we can make the front object appear transparent if instead of blindly replacing old shading values, we multiply them by the transparency coefficient and add them to the values for the new surface. The shade actually displayed will correspond to light from the new object's surface plus the light behind, which is transmitted through the object.

$$v = v_r + tv_t \tag{10.20}$$

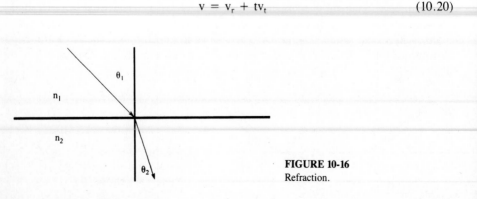

FIGURE 10-16
Refraction.

Here (v) is the total amount of light, (v_r) is the amount reflected from the surface as is given in Equation 10.16, (t) is the transparency coefficient, and (v_t) is the light coming from behind the object, which may be determined from the frame buffer value. We will require an inverse function for INTENSITY so that given the value in the frame buffer, we can determine the original SHADE-SETTING of the background object for use in the transparency calculation. Transparent objects often have a low reflectivity, and the reflected light (v_r) comes from specular reflection.

This simple approximation does not always yield realistic images, particularly where curved surfaces are being constructed. To improve it, we would like to include the angular behavior of the Fresnel reflection vs. transmission at the surface and also the attenuation due to thickness. Imagine light coming from some background object, passing through a transparent object, and reaching the eye. (See Figure 10-17.) If the transparent object has parallel sides (as do glasses, bottles, and windows), then the distance the light must travel through the object depends on the angle at which we view it. When viewed straight on, the distance the light travels within the object is less than when viewed at a glancing angle. Also, when the object's surface is perpendicular to the path of the light, the maximum amount is transmitted (instead of reflected). A simple approximation for this behavior is

$$t = (t_{max} - t_{min}) (N \cdot E)^{\alpha} + t_{min} \qquad (10.21)$$

This is the cosine of the angle between the eye and the surface normal raised to a power. The cosine is strongest when we view the surface straight on and drops off for glancing views. The power just enhances the effect. Values of α of 2 or 3 give reasonable effects.

REFLECTIONS

We have seen how to determine the effects of light coming directly from illumination sources, but in a realistic scene, every object can act as a light source. We should be able to see the specular reflections of objects, not just of lights. We look at a point p_1 on an object and ask what light is coming from that point and from where does it originate. We have seen how to find the light coming from diffuse illumination and directly from point sources. We can also follow a reflected ray back from our eye to the point and determine the incident ray. If we move back along the incident ray and reach a point p_2 on some other surface, then we know that the light (I) from this second point will be reflected at p_1. (See Figure 10-18.)

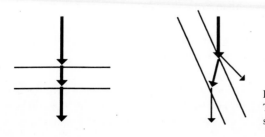

FIGURE 10-17
The reduction in light from reflection and absorption depends on the orientation.

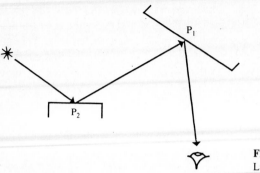

FIGURE 10-18
Light reflected from another object.

This will add a term to Equation 10.16 for the contribution of p_2 of the form

$$\frac{IF'/(E \cdot N)}{C + U} \tag{10.22}$$

where F' is calculated according to Equation 10.6 just as F, only c used in this calculation is given by

$$c = E \cdot N \tag{10.23}$$

The light (I) for the point p_2 should be calculated as if the eye is located at p_1. For such calculations, all surfaces must be considered, even back faces (because a back face may be visible in a reflection). The method is discussed further in the section on ray tracing.

SHADOWS

The problem of shadows is very similar to the hidden-surface problem. A shadowed object is one which is hidden from the light source. Shadow and hidden-surface calculations are often performed together for efficient computation.

One approach to the shadow problem is to repeat the hidden-surface calculation using the light source as the viewpoint. This second hidden-surface calculation divides the polygons into shadowed and unshadowed groups. Surfaces which are visible and which are also visible from the light source are shown with both the background illumination and the light-source illumination. Surfaces which are visible but which are hidden from the light source are displayed with only the background illumination.

Another approach to the shadow problem is the use of *shadow volumes*. Consider a polygon and a light source. There is a volume of space hidden from the light by the polygon. This is the polygon's shadow volume. We can construct this volume from the polygon itself and from the rays from the light which touch the polygon edges. (See Figure 10-19.)

We can compare all other visible polygons to this volume. Portions which lie inside of the volume are shadowed. Their intensity calculation should not include a term from this light source. Polygons which lie outside the shadow volume are not shaded

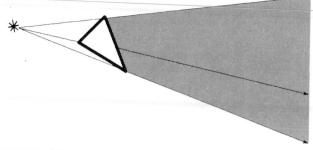

FIGURE 10-19
Shadow volume.

by this polygon, but might be shaded by some other polygon so they must still be checked against the other shadow volumes.

For simplicity, assume that all polygons are convex. (There are techniques for breaking up any polygon into convex components. In particular, polygons can be decomposed into triangles or trapezoids, which are always convex.) The shadow volume for a convex polygon is a convex object, which means that we can use the generalized clipping techniques to find shadowed areas. Points within the shadow volume are shadowed, and a point lies within the volume if it lies on the interior side of the polygon plane and all the shadow planes. So shadowing can be done by "clipping" all visible polygons to all possible shadow volumes.

The shadow volumes may be included as part of the hidden-surface processing. We include the surfaces of the shadow volumes along with the object surfaces. We include both front and back faces for shadow volumes, but tag them as such. We sort all polygons to determine their visibility. Shadow surfaces are invisible, and are not drawn but are counted. Where the number of front shadow faces in front of the visible polygon exceeds the number of back shadow faces, the polygon is in shadow.

We can use Z-buffer techniques to simplify the sorting. Suppose we have two Z buffers, one for determining the foremost visible surface and one for finding shadows. We begin with the Z-buffer hidden-surface removal algorithm described in Chapter 9. After this step, the visible surface Z buffer will contain the z coordinates of all visible points. The next step is to determine the shadow volumes for the scene. We can examine the surfaces in these shadow volumes to find which are the front and back faces. For each shadow volume, we can enter the z coordinate of the back-face pixels in the shadow Z buffer. We can also determine the z values for the pixels of the front faces on the shadow volume. Now if the z value of the front face of the shadow (which we just calculated) is in front of the visible surface (the z value in the visible surface Z buffer) and this in turn is in front of the back of the shadow volume (the z value in the shadow Z buffer), then the visible surface lies within the shadow volume. (See Figure 10-20.)

Shadows from point sources of light are sharp and harsh. In the real world we seldom find light coming from points. The sun and moon are disks; artificial light comes in a variety of shapes. Shadows from these finite shapes have softer edges.

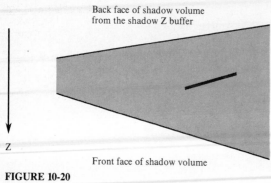

Back face of shadow volume
from the shadow Z buffer

Object's front face
from the visible
surface Z buffer

Z

Front face of shadow volume

FIGURE 10-20
Using a shadow Z buffer to find shaded objects.

Much of the current work on shadows is in modeling these finite light sources to give more realistic results.

RAY TRACING

There is a simple brute-force technique which can yield startlingly realistic computer-generated images. (See Plate 15.) Its basic form is easy to implement and requires little of the machinery of the graphics system we have been constructing. It can handle curved surfaces as well as flat polygons. It includes perspective projection, hidden-surface removal, reflections, shadows, and transparency. The technique is called *ray tracing*, and the problem with it is that it is notoriously slow. The idea is to determine the intensity for each pixel one at a time by following a ray back from the viewpoint through the pixel and into the object space. We can compute the intersection of that ray with all the surfaces. If none is encountered, then the pixel has the background shade. If one or more surfaces are impacted by the ray, we find the one closest to the viewpoint. It is the one which will be seen (the rest are hidden by it). This, in effect, solves the hidden-surface problem for every pixel. (See Figure 10-21.)

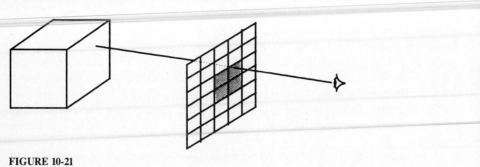

FIGURE 10-21
Ray tracing.

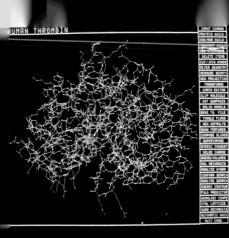

Plate 1

Use of a menu for interaction with the program. (Courtesy D.N.J. White, Chemistry Department, Glasgow University, Scotland. Dr. White's figures were also published in *IEEE Computer Graphics and Applications*, vol. 5, no. 10, pp. 8–14, 1985. © 1985 IEEE, reprinted by permission.)

ate 2

is figure uses front and back clipping display a slice of a molecule. (Courtesy N.J. White, Chemistry Department, asgow University, Scotland. © 1985 IEEE, rinted by permission.)

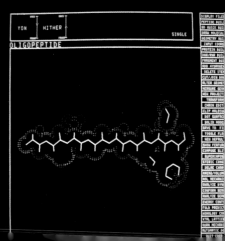

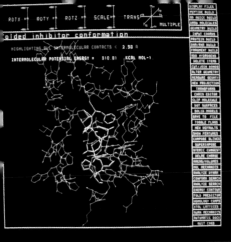

Plate 3

The viewing transformation for this molecule can be interactively set by a series of valuators which are simulated by a locator and scales on the display. (Courtesy D.N.J. White, Chemistry Department, Glasgow University, Scotland. © 1985 IEEE, reprinted by permission.)

Plate 4

A molecule composed of atoms displayed as spheres with hidden-surface removal. (Courtesy D.N.J. White, Chemistry

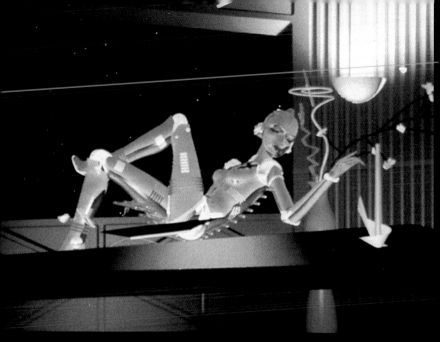

Plate 5

The "Sexy Robot" from the commercial "BRILLIANCE" for the Canned Food Information Council. Randy Roberts Director/Designer. (Courtesy of Abel Image Research, Los Angeles, California. 1985 Abel Image Research.)

Plate 6

night from the opening sequence of *Amazing Stories.* Animation of the complex motion is accomplished by analyzing the actions of a live model. Randy Roberts Director/Designer. (Courtesy of Abel Image Research, Los Angeles, California. 1985 Abel Image Research.)

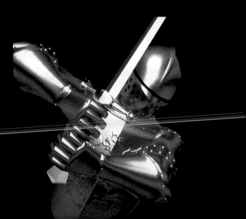

Plate 7

An image from "High Fidelity" of Ava dancing with her umbrellas. Ava's texture was digitized as a flat 2D image and then wrapped around her 3D geometric shapes. Randy Roberts Director/Designer. (Courtesy of Abel Image Research, Los Angeles, California. © 1985 Abel Image Research.)

Plate 8

Andre's Forest. The trees, grass, and flowers in this scene were stochastically generated using particle systems. A specialized shading function was used to cast sunlight on the trees and to simulate self-shadowing. The shadows on the grass were generated using a shadow mask derived from the trees. Created by William Reeves, John Lasseter, and Eben Ostby. (Courtesy Lucasfilm, Ltd., San Rafael, California. The techniques used to create Andre's forest are discussed in *Computer Graphics*, vol. 19, no. 3, pp. 313–322, 1985 © 1985 Lucasfilm. Ltd.)

Plate 9

A scene from "The Adventures of Andre & Wally B." This film demonstrates full classic character animation, motion blur of the characters, and very complex 3D background sets. (Courtesy Alvy Ray Smith, Lucasfilm Ltd., San Rafael, California. © 1985 Lucasfilm, Ltd.)

Plate 10

"Happy Drinking Birds" by Richard Cohen (Courtesy Pacific Data Images, Sunnyvale, California. © 1985 Pacific Data Images.)

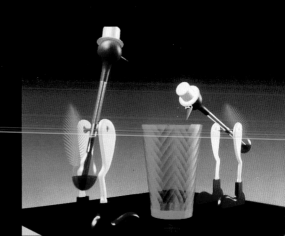

_te 11

_romosaurus" by Don Venhaus. (Courtesy Pacific Data Images, Sunnyvale, California.
_85 Pacific Data Images.)

_te 12

_shwasher" from a Kitchen Aide
_mmercial by S. Cohen and S. Legensky.
_ourtesy Intelligent Light, Fair Lawn,
_w Jersey. © 1984 Intelligent Light.)

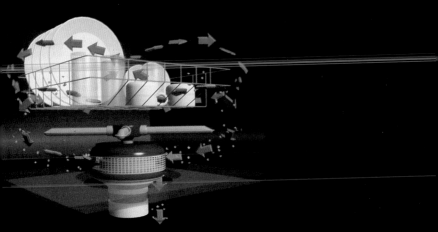

Plate 13

"Backhoe," a frame from a Tenneco commercial by J. Butler, D. Stipe, S. Legensky. (Courtesy Intelligent Light, Fair Lawn, New Jersey. © 1984 Intelligent Light.)

Plate 14

(Courtesy Intelligent Light, Fair Lawn, New Jersey. © 1986 Intelligent Light.)

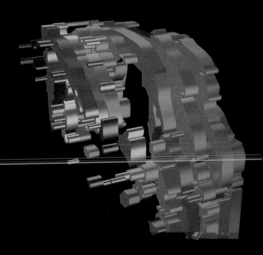

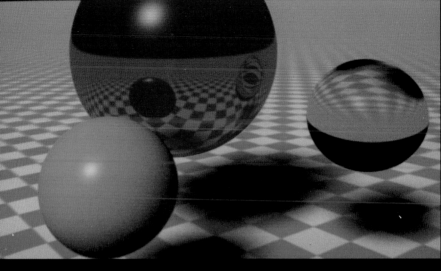

Plate 15

The scene was produced by a ray tracing with cones. This gives more fidelity, better antialiasing, fuzzy shadows, and dull reflections. (Courtesy John Amanatides, University of Toronto, Canada. The creation of this image is discussed in *Computer Graphics,* vol. 18, no. 3, pp. 129-135, 1984. © 1984, Association for Computing Machinery, Inc., reprinted by permission.)

Plate 16

The 1931 CIE chromaticity diagram.
(Courtesy Photo Research, Burbank,
California.)

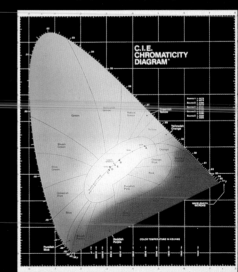

Next we can find the illumination of the surface point by calculations such as Equation 10.16. We may, however, as part of this calculation, look for the intersection of the rays between the surface point and the light sources with other objects in the scene. If a ray is cut by another surface, then the corresponding light source is shadowed for the pixel. This solves the shadow problem for every pixel. The same ray-following routines that were used to find the surface being drawn can be used to find shadows, only the starting point and direction of the ray are different. (See Figure 10-22.)

We must add to the intensity value for the surface point the amount of light reflected from other objects and, if the point belongs to a transparent object, the light transmitted through it. The reflected light is equal to the coefficient of specular reflection times the amount of light coming in along an incident ray. We find the light along this incident ray by recursively applying the method which we are describing. We imagine the surface point as the viewpoint and ask how much light comes to it along a given direction. We examine this new ray for intersections with objects and find the light from the closest. This may entail further recursive calls, until either the ray makes no intersections or the accumulated spectral reflection coefficients have reduced the light to where it is no longer significant. (See Figure 10-23.)

If objects are transparent, then we must also calculate and add in the transmitted light. As with the reflection case, we calculate the refracted ray which would give rise to the light along the ray we followed. We recursively apply our method to this ray to determine the light coming along it. We multiply the amount of light by the transparency and attenuation factors and add it to the total. (See Figure 10-24.)

Most of the time spent in ray tracing is in finding the intersection of a ray with the nearest surface. As the complexity of the image goes up, the number of surfaces which must be checked against the ray also increases. There is much interest and research into ray-tracing techniques, both in modeling the properties of objects and light

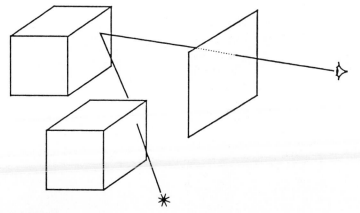

FIGURE 10-22
Ray tracing to find shadows.

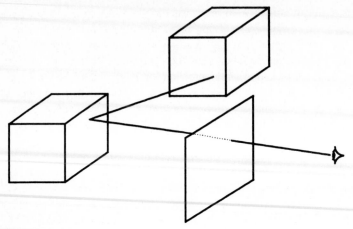

FIGURE 10-23
Ray tracing to find reflections.

sources to make them more realistic and in finding data structures and algorithms which make it more efficient.

HALFTONES

Many display devices allow only two imaging states per pixel (on or off, black or white). This is fine for line drawings, but when displaying surfaces, we would often like more variety than just black or white. There would be little point to the shading calculations we have discussed if there were no way to produce gray images. We discussed in Chapter 3 how our polygon-filling algorithm could be extended to display patterns. Using such patterns allows us to give different polygons different appear-

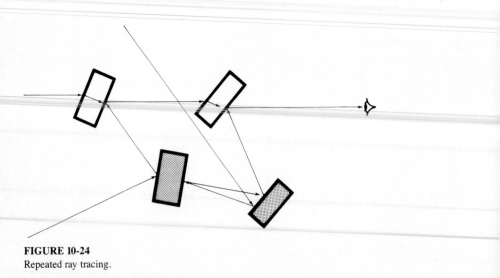

FIGURE 10-24
Repeated ray tracing.

ances, and with a judicious choice of patterns, this mechanism can also provide gray levels for use in shading. But for realistic images, as might be generated by ray tracing or might be input from a television camera or scanner, we must make further extensions so as to be able to control the apparent intensity in finer detail than we did for entire polygons. We have as a guide the work done by the printing industry. Photographs are routinely reproduced in books and newspapers using only two states (ink or no ink). The technique is called *halftoning*. A continuous tone image is shown through a *screen*. This produces a regularly spaced pattern of small dots. The dots vary in size according to the original image intensity; so where the image is light, the dots are small and the background color of the paper predominates. Where the image is dark, the dots are large and merge together to cover the paper with ink. (See Figure 10-25.)

How can we produce halftones? Our first try might be to divide our binary pixels into groups corresponding to the halftone cells, and call each group a single gray-level pixel. We could develop a set of dot patterns for the groups, making dot patterns for the group correspond to intensity values for the gray-level pixel. Every time we set a gray-level pixel to an intensity value, we would really be copying a binary dot pattern into the group of binary pixels which form it. For example, we could make each 2×2 pixel square our gray-level pixel. This would give us five possible intensity settings. We could design a pattern for each setting. (See Figure 10-26.)

Our effective resolution would be half of the binary resolution of the device, but we would have five intensity values instead of just two. (See Figure 10-27.)

The scheme we have outlined will work, but we can do better. We can produce images with a better effective resolution and still have as many gray levels. The reason this can be done is that there exists more than a single possible pattern for many of the intensity levels. Consider the intensity level of two active pixels for the 2×2 halftone cell. There are six possible patterns. (See Figure 10-28.)

The idea is to select patterns which closely match the structure of the image. For example, if we are looking at a polygon edge which crosses the halftone cell, as in Fig-

FIGURE 10-25
Enlarged halftone image of a bird in flight.

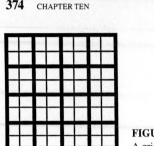

FIGURE 10-26
A grid of halftone cells.

ure 10-29, then for a dark polygon on a light background the pattern with the right two pixels shaded would be most appropriate. For a lighter polygon, perhaps only one of the two right pixels would be colored, but the left pixels should remain light. A simple method which comes close to implementing this kind of halftoning is an *ordered dither*. It is done by constructing a pattern of threshold values, called a *dither matrix*, which correspond to the individual pixels in the halftone cell. The pattern can be replicated to cover the screen so that every binary pixel has an associated threshold value. We then determine the intensity value for every pixel (full resolution, not just gray-level pixels). We compare the intensity of each pixel against its threshold value to determine whether the pixel is turned on or off.

This method also has the advantage of allowing intensity values to range over any scale of values desired. An image could be constructed in which each pixel has one of 256 possible intensity values. The image could be shown on a display using a halftone screen with 5 gray levels, or one with 50 gray levels, or one with 256 gray levels by just designing the corresponding cell of threshold values. For example, suppose we display such pixels using the five-level 2×2 cell. A possible dither matrix is shown in Figure 10-30. With this pattern, the lower right pixel would be turned on if it were set to an intensity greater than 50. The upper left pixel would be turned on only if it were set to an intensity greater than 200.

Notice that we can alter the appearance of the image by changing the threshold values. The intensity at the display need not correspond linearly to that of the source image. This is useful when the source image originates from real life, such as a scanned photograph. Altering the thresholds can adjust for under or over exposure and can be used to enhance the image. The thresholds also can be used to compensate for nonlinearities in either the scanning, the display hardware, or our eyes. Our eyes are in fact sensitive to intensity ratios rather than absolute intensities, so to achieve a set of gray levels which look equally spaced, we might select threshold values which change exponentially (1, 2, 4, 8, 16) or cubically (1, 9, 27, 64).

Implementation of this halftoning scheme is very similar to the method described in Chapter 3 for filling a polygon with a pattern. In that scheme we used the polygon

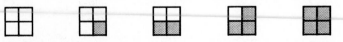

FIGURE 10-27
Intensity settings for the halftone cell.

FIGURE 10-28
Possible patterns for two active pixels.

style to select a pattern and set the frame buffer pixel to the corresponding pixel element. For halftoning, when filling a polygon, we look up the threshold value for each pixel and compare it with the intensity value for the polygon. The results of the comparison are used to decide where to set the pixel. A replacement algorithm for FILLIN which does this halftoning is as follows:

10.12 Algorithm HALFTONE-FILLIN(X1, X2, Y) Fills in scan line Y from X1 to X2 using halftoning

Arguments   X1, X2 end positions of the scan line to be filled
             Y the scan line to be filled
Global   HALFTONE-CELL array of intensity thresholds
             FRAME the two-dimensional (binary) frame buffer array
             FILLCHR the intensity of the polygon
Local   X for stepping across the scan line
             HX, HY for accessing the halftone cell
Constants   HALF-X, HALF-Y the x and y dimensions of the halftone cell
             ON, OFF the possible pixel values
BEGIN
    IF X1 = X2 THEN RETURN;
    HX ← MOD(X1, HALF-X) + 1;
    HY ← MOD(Y, HALF-Y) + 1;
    FOR X = X1 TO X2 DO
        BEGIN
            IF FILLCHR > HALFTONE-CELL[HX, HY] THEN FRAME[X, Y] ← ON
            ELSE FRAME[X, Y] ← OFF;
            IF HX = HALF-X THEN HX ← 1
            ELSE HX ← HX + 1;
        END;
    RETURN;
END;

Note that the above halftoning scheme and the pattern filling of Chapter 3 can be combined to allow filling polygons with gray level and photographic style patterns (or

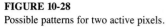

FIGURE 10-29
Select patterns to match the image shape.

200	150
100	50

FIGURE 10-30
A dither pattern for the 2×2 cell.

Gouraud shading) on a bilevel display. In the combined scheme we would look up both the threshold value from the halftone description and the intensity value from the pattern or polygon for the given pixel. These would then be compared to determine if the pixel should be set.

COLOR

Light is an electromagnetic wave and has wave properties. One of these properties is *frequency* (v). The frequency describes how many cycles of the wave occur every second. A related property is the *wavelength* (λ), the distance in space between crests of the wave. They are related properties because light moves at a constant speed ($c = 3 \times 10^8$ meters/second in a vacuum). The speed must be the length of a cycle times how many cycles pass per second, so

$$c = v\lambda \tag{10.24}$$

Our eyes are able to detect differences in frequency (or wavelength) for a small range of the possible values. We can see light with wavelength between about 4×10^{-7} meters and 7×10^{-7} meters. Each wavelength appears to us as a color from violet at 400 nanometers(nm) through the rainbow to red at 700 nm. The reason we can see these colors is that our eyes have three different color sensors which are sensitive to different parts of the visible spectrum. They are called the blue, green, and red *photopigments*, and they give respective peak responses at blue, green, and yellow light, but also give lesser responses at other values so as to cover the entire visible range. (See Figure 10-31.)

We are not equally sensitive to all colors. Our eyes give the greatest response to green. We are less sensitive to red and blue light, and cannot see infrared or ultraviolet light at all. Because of this, the *luminosity* or perceived brightness of the light does not correspond directly to the energy of the light. It takes less energy to increase the brightness of green 1 *lumen* (a unit of brightness) than it takes to increase red 1 lumen, which is in turn less than the energy needed to increase the perceived intensity of blue light the same amount. (See Figure 10-32.)

Light with a single wavelength produces the sensation of a "pure" color. But note that there may be other ways to achieve the same response from the eye. For example, light at 490 nm excites all three photopigments, but the same effect could be achieved with two less intense lights, one at 450 nm to excite the blue and one at about 540 nm to excite the green and red photopigments. Thus blue-green can be seen either from a blue-green light or from a mixture of blue light and green light.

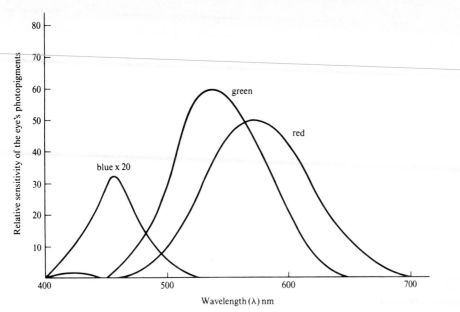

FIGURE 10-31
Relative response of the eye's photopigments.

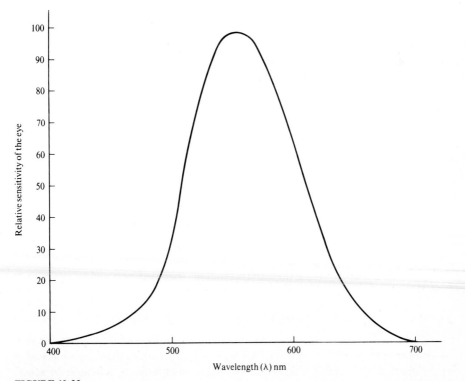

FIGURE 10-32
Total luminosity response of the eye.

We can easily mix colors to achieve relative responses from the photopigments which will not correspond to any of the response patterns for single wavelength (monochromatic) light. But such patterns can be separated into a piece which looks like the response from light with equal amounts of all wavelengths and a remainder which appears like a pure color or its complement. Light with equal amounts of all wavelengths present looks white to us. Thus mixtures of lights will often appear the same as some pure color mixed with white. The pure color determines the hue (e.g., red), while the amount of white light determines the tint (pink). The more white light the less *saturated* is the color. The total amount of light determines its shade or intensity. A diagram was developed by the Commission Internationale L'Eclairage (CIE) which graphically portrays the eye's response to colors. (See Plate 16.) On the diagram, every point represents some color. The diagram is designed such that all colors on a line between two color points may be produced by mixing the light of the end-point colors. Three points will form a triangle of colors, and all colors within the triangle may be produced from mixtures of the vertex colors. The colors within the triangles are called the gamut of colors producible from the colors at the triangle vertices. (See Figure 10-33.) In the center of the diagram is a region corresponding to white. Along the tongue-shaped boundary are the pure colors of monochromatic light. Across the base are the purples, which have no monochromatic representative.

The color of light is determined by the relative responses of the three photopigments in the eye. There is also the absolute response which tells us how much total light there is (how bright it is). In the CIE diagram, just the intensity ratios of the light are used, so the color is described but not the intensity. This is done as follows: Imagine we have sensors for measuring light. Imagine further that the sensors have response curves with peaks at three specially chosen primary colors. Let X, Y, and Z measure the absolute response of these sensors. Then we can compute the ratios

$$x = \frac{X}{X + Y + Z} \qquad y = \frac{Y}{X + Y + Z} \qquad z = \frac{Z}{X + Y + Z} \qquad (10.25)$$

It is the x, y values that are shown in the CIE diagram. Note that

$$z = 1 - x - y \qquad (10.26)$$

so we have only two independent color choices, and they may be shown in a two-dimensional diagram. The CIE definition is arranged so that Y is the eye's total photopic luminosity-function curve, the eye's total sensitivity to light, which is greatest for green. The Y value gives the luminance (brightness of the color). The hue which gives the maximum luminance is green.

Given a *chromaticity* value (hue and saturation) specified by x and y and an overall luminosity Y, we can easily solve for the CIE XYZ coordinates.

$$X = x \,(Y/y) \qquad \text{and} \qquad Z = z \,(Y/y) \qquad (10.27)$$

The response of the eye to light and color is not as straightforward as the response of a physicist's instruments. The perceived intensity of light coming from an object may vary greatly with the amount of light from the surrounding area, even though the actual radiation is the same. The perceived dominant frequency or hue may appear to shift

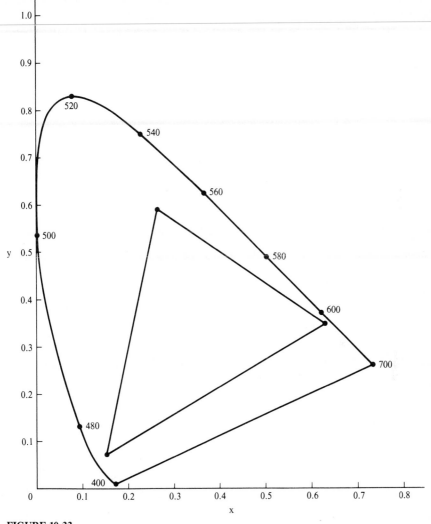

FIGURE 10-33
The color gamut for a color monitor.

slightly as white light is added. The perceived hue and saturation may also change with intensity, dropping out altogether for low radiation levels. In the remainder of the discussion we shall largely ignore these differences, giving rules for specifying the physical light and color rather than the psychophysical perception.

COLOR MODELS

There are several other ways to parameterize colored light. These are called color models. The *red-green-blue* (RGB) model is often encountered in computer graphics. It corresponds to the red, green, and blue intensity settings of a color monitor or television display. Color television has red, blue, and green phosphors forming a triangle on the CIE diagram which includes most, but not all, of the possible colors. The RGB color space may be pictured as rectangular coordinates with black at the origin. Red is measured on the x axis (R axis), green on the y axis (G axis), and blue on the z axis (B axis). The grays are on the diagonal line G = R, B = R. The farther from the origin, the brighter the light. (See Figure 10-34.)

A color display cannot increase its intensity indefinitely; it has some maximum value. Furthermore, how bright that value appears to the eye depends upon the ambient room light. It will appear much brighter in a darkened room than it will in bright sunlight. Because of this absolute intensity, values are not very useful. Instead, we often normalize the intensity scale so that full intensity corresponds to a value of 1. Then the set of realizable colors for the device is described by a unit cube.

The XYZ primary colors defined by the CIE are theoretical extensions and not really the visible red, green, and blue, but we can convert from one coordinate system to the other with a linear transformation. The transformation depends upon just what is meant by red, green, and blue. The CIE standard defines

Standard CIE spectral red	(700 nm)	x = 0.73467, y = 0.26533
Standard CIE spectral green	(546.1 nm)	x = 0.27367, y = 0.71741
Standard CIE spectral blue	(435.8 nm)	x = 0.16658, y = 0.00886

But for the standard television red, green, and blue we have

NTSC red	x = 0.670, y = 0.330
NTSC green	x = 0.210, y = 0.710
NTSC blue	x = 0.140, y = 0.080

And for modern graphics monitors we have

Monitor red	x = 0.628, y = 0.346, z = 0.026
Monitor green	x = 0.268, y = 0.588, z = 0.144
Monitor blue	x = 0.150, y = 0.070, z = 0.780

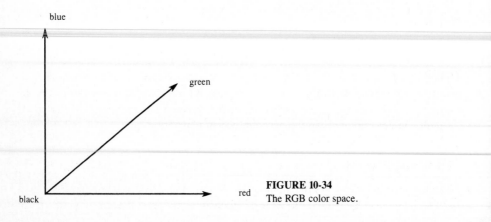

FIGURE 10-34
The RGB color space.

Usually only x and y values are listed because we can find the z values using Equation 10.26. These values are not enough to tell us how to convert between RGB and XYZ. We know the colors but not their relative strengths. If we just pick three colors and add them together, we are unlikely to get white; but we want to weight or scale the primaries we have chosen so that if we do select equal amounts of the red, green, and blue, we do come out with white. The amount to scale depends on just what we mean by white, and there are several choices (the color of an electric light, the color of sunlight at noon, the color of the overcast sky, and others). Monitors are often factory realigned to the color of a black body heated to 6500 degrees Kelvin (K). This has CIE values

$$x = 0.313, \qquad y = 0.329 \qquad\qquad (10.28)$$

which for luminancy of 1 give

$$X_w = 0.950, \qquad Y_w = 1.000, \qquad Z_w = 1.086 \qquad (10.29)$$

So if we were considering the monitor primaries, we would have to supply the scaling factors r, b, g such that

$$x_r r + x_g g + x_b b = X_w$$
$$y_r r + y_g g + y_b b = Y_w \qquad\qquad (10.30)$$
$$z_r r + z_g g + z_b b = Z_w$$

Substituting the actual values gives

$$0.628r + 0.268g + 0.150b = 0.950$$
$$0.346r + 0.588g + 0.070b = 1.000 \qquad\qquad (10.31)$$
$$0.026r + 0.144g + 0.780b = 1.089$$

We can solve this set of linear equations for r, g, and b. Doing so gives

$$r = 0.758, \qquad g = 1.116, \qquad b = 1.165 \qquad (10.32)$$

Multiplying the chromaticities of the primary colors by these weighting factors tells us how much of the X, Y, Z primaries is contributed by each of the R, G, B primary colors. For example, for the red primary, the amount of X contributed is

$$X_r = (0.628)(0.758)R \qquad\qquad (10.33)$$

The total X amount is the sum of the contributions from the R, G, and B components of a color.

$$X = x_r r R + x_g g G + x_b b B \qquad\qquad (10.34)$$
$$= (0.628)(0.758)R + (0.268)(1.116)G + (0.150)(1.165)B$$
$$= 0.476R + 0.299G + 0.175B$$

Similar statements may be made about Y and Z. We can perform the multiplications and combine the three equations into a matrix expression. The result is a transformation for converting from the RGB coordinates of the monitor to XYZ coordinates.

$$[X \ Y \ Z] = [R \ G \ B] \begin{vmatrix} 0.476 & 0.262 & 0.020 \\ 0.299 & 0.656 & 0.161 \\ 0.175 & 0.082 & 0.909 \end{vmatrix} \qquad (10.35)$$

Finding the inverse matrix, we can write

$$[R \ G \ B] = [X \ Y \ Z] \begin{vmatrix} 2.750 & -1.118 & 0.138 \\ -1.149 & 2.026 & -0.333 \\ -0.426 & 0.033 & 1.104 \end{vmatrix} \qquad (10.36)$$

Hard-copy devices may use cyan, magenta, and yellow as the primary colors rather than red, green, and blue. These are the colors of the inks which are placed on the white paper. They begin with white and use the inks to absorb and remove some colors. Cyan removes red, magenta absorbs green, and yellow removes the blue. This complementary relationship between red, green, blue, and cyan, magenta, yellow makes it easy to convert from one color model to the other. Assuming units where 1 means full color and 0 means no color, and assuming that the cyan, magenta, and yellow colors are exact complements of red, green, and blue, then

$$C = 1 - R, \qquad M = 1 - G, \qquad \text{and} \qquad Y = 1 - B \qquad (10.37)$$

or

$$[C \quad M \quad Y] = [1 \quad 1 \quad 1] - [R \quad G \quad B]$$

We can also picture this relation. Start with the unit cube of all colors, with black at a corner which serves as the origin of the RGB coordinate system. The R, G, and B axes along the edges of the cube meet at the black corner. The opposite corner on the cube will correspond to white, and will serve as the origin for the CMY coordinates. The C, M, and Y axes on the edges of the cube meet at the white corner. Each of the other corners of the cube can be labeled with one of the primary colors. (See Figure 10-35.)

Printers often use the four colors cyan, magenta, yellow, and black. In theory, only the three inks cyan, magenta, and yellow (CMY) should be needed. Mixing the three should produce an ink which absorbs all the light, yielding black; but in practice, the inks may not absorb completely or mix well, so a fourth black ink is used to set the shade.

Color television specifies colors by the YIQ color model. The Y is the same as the Y in the CIE primaries and corresponds to the luminosity or brightness. It is the Y component which is displayed on a black-and-white television. The I and Q coordinates determine the hue and saturation. The transformation from RGB coordinates is as follows:

$$[I \ Q \ Y] = [R \ G \ B] \begin{vmatrix} 0.60 & 0.21 & 0.30 \\ -0.28 & -0.52 & 0.59 \\ -0.30 & 0.32 & 0.11 \end{vmatrix} \qquad (10.38)$$

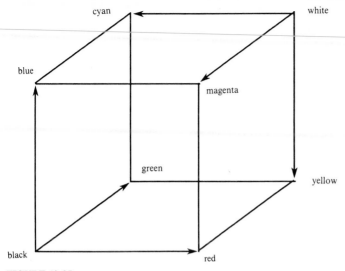

FIGURE 10-35
The RGB-CMY color cube.

Human vision is much more sensitive to intensity than it is to color. For this reason, we do not need to provide as much color information as intensity information. We can quantize the I and Q coordinates in bigger steps (fewer bits) and give fine detail (more bits) to the Y coordinate. This allows an overall reduction in the amount of information which must be sent to achieve a high-quality image. The YIQ model allows a more efficient representation of a color image intended for a human observer.

Another color model is the hue, saturation (or chroma), and intensity(brightness) model (*HSI*). The *hue* or *tone* is the pure color of the light. It is the dominant color we see. *Saturation* indicates how much white light is mixed with the color (the tint). Saturation of 0 means no color; we see white or gray. The intensity tells how much total light there is (the shade). Hue, saturation, and intensity are often plotted in cylindrical coordinates with hue the angle, saturation the radius, and intensity the axis. (See Figure 10-36.)

The conversion between HSI and RGB models can be done in two steps. To convert from RGB to HSI we first rotate the coordinates so that the third axis is along $G = R$, $B = R$ line. This gives a rectangular coordinate version of the HSI space. The second step is a change to cylindrical coordinates and proper scaling of the intensity. The coordinates of the rectangular HSI space will be labeled M_1, M_2, I_1 where I_1 is the intensity and M_1, M_2 describe the hue-saturation plane. (See Figure 10-37.)

The transformation is

$$[M_1 \ M_2 \ I_1] = [R \ G \ B] \begin{vmatrix} 2/\sqrt{6} & 0 & 1/\sqrt{3} \\ -1/\sqrt{6} & 1/\sqrt{2} & 1/\sqrt{3} \\ -1/\sqrt{6} & -1/\sqrt{2} & 1/\sqrt{3} \end{vmatrix} \qquad (10.39)$$

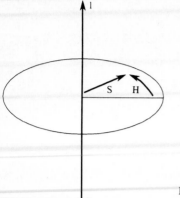

FIGURE 10-36
HSI coordinates.

The conversion to cylindrical coordinates in HSI is

$$H = \arctan(M_1 / M_2)$$
$$S = (M_1^2 + M_2^2)^{1/2} \qquad (10.40)$$
$$I = I_1 \sqrt{3}$$

Conversion from HSI to RGB takes the inverse steps

$$M_1 = S \sin H$$
$$M_2 = S \cos H \qquad (10.41)$$
$$I_1 = I / \sqrt{3}$$

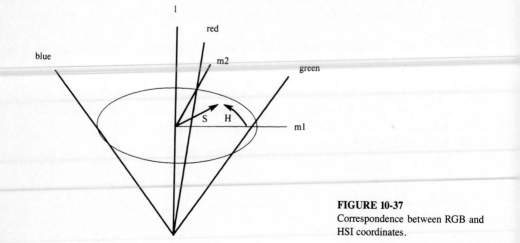

FIGURE 10-37
Correspondence between RGB and
HSI coordinates.

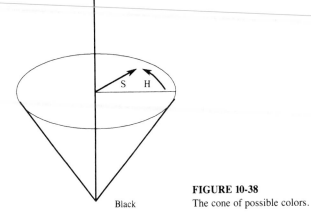

FIGURE 10-38
The cone of possible colors.

Black

$$[R \ G \ B] = [M_1 \ M_2 \ I_1] \begin{vmatrix} 2/\sqrt{6} & -1/\sqrt{6} & -1/\sqrt{6} \\ 0 & 1/\sqrt{2} & -1/\sqrt{2} \\ 1/\sqrt{3} & 1/\sqrt{3} & 1/\sqrt{3} \end{vmatrix} \qquad (10.42)$$

When dealing with inks on paper, we sometimes use a color space with cylindrical coordinates where the angle is hue, brightness is along the axis, and the radius is how much of the colored ink is on the paper. This gives a cone of colors. At the point is black, along the axis is saturation 0 (grays), and along the surface of the cone is the most saturated color. As you move up or down, the amount of black ink changes. Moving out or in adds or removes color from the portion of the paper not covered by black. The radial saturation measure is usually normalized so that it is 1 on the cone's surface. A value of 1 then specifies the maximum saturation achievable by the inks for the given brightness. (See Figure 10-38.)

Sometimes hue, saturation, and value (HSV) are used to specify colors. Value is the intensity of the maximum of the red, blue, and green components of the color. Value has the same "feel" as brightness (as value decreases, the shade looks darker) but is easier to calculate. Also to make the calculation easier, the hue can be approximated by the distance along the edge of a hexagon. The relation between HSV and RGB is given by the next two algorithms:

10.13 Algorithm RGB-TO-HSV(R, G, B. H, S, V) Converts from red, green, blue values in the range 0 to 1 to hue, saturation, and value
Hue is expressed in degrees
Arguments   R, G, B the red, green, blue coordinates
            H, S, V for return of the hue, saturation, and value
Local   R1, G1, B1, how relatively close the color is to red, green, and blue
            X intensity of the minimum primary color
BEGIN
   H ← 0;

```
        find dominant primary color
        V ← MAX(R, MAX(G, B));
        find the amount of white
        X ← MIN(R, MIN(G, B));
        determine the normalized saturation
        S ← (V − X) / V;
        IF S = 0 THEN RETURN;
        R1 := (V − R) / (V − X);
        G1 := (V − G) / (V − X);
        B1 := (V − B) / (V − X);
        in which section of the hexagon does the color lie?
        IF R = V THEN
            IF G = X THEN H ← 5 + B1
            ELSE H ← 1 − G1
        ELSE IF G = V THEN
            IF B = X THEN H ← R1 + 1
            ELSE H ← 3 − B1
        ELSE
            IF R = X THEN H ← 3 + G1
            ELSE H ← 5 − R1;
        convert to degrees
        H ← H * 60
        RETURN;
    END;
```

The algorithm first finds the value parameter, which is simply the intensity of the dominant primary color. Next, it finds the minimum primary color. This can be mixed with equal amounts of the other two colors to form white and is therefore a measure of how much white is in the color. The expression $V − X$ is the amount of the dominant color left after part is used to make the white component of the color. The relative strength of this net color becomes our normalized saturation measure. If the saturation is 0 then there is no hue (we have a gray), so the algorithm returns with a default hue of 0. The R1, G1, and B1 variables are used to tell how much of the second most important color there is relative to the dominant color. The IF statements then find the dominant color and move the hue away from it by this amount.

10.14 Algorithm HSV-TO-RGB(H, S, V, R, G, B) Converts hue, saturation, value coordinates to red, green, blue

Arguments   H, S, V the hue, saturation, and value

             R, G, B for return of the red, green, blue coordinates

Local   H1 the hue in units of 1 to 6

             I integer part of the H1 hue, indicates the dominant color

             F fractional part of the H1 hue, used to determine second color

             A an array that holds the three color values while deciding which is which

BEGIN

    convert from degrees to hexagon section

    H1 ← H / 60;

    find the dominant color

```
    I ← INT[H1];
    F ← H1 − I;
    A[1] ← V;
    A[2] ← V;
    A[3] ← V * (1 − (S * F));
    A[4] ← V * (1 − S);
    A[5] ← A[4];
    A[6] ← V * (1 − (S * (1 − F)));
    map strengths to rgb
    IF I > 4 THEN I ← I − 4 ELSE I ← I + 2;
    R ← A[I];
    IF I > 4 THEN I ← I − 4 ELSE I ← I + 2;
    B ← A[I];
    IF I > 4 THEN I ← I − 4 ELSE I ← I + 2;
    G ← A[I];
    RETURN;
END;
```

In this algorithm the integer part of the hue determines the dominant color. Its intensity V is saved in the first and second array cells. The fractional part describes the second most important color. Its value is in either the third or sixth array cell, depending on which side of the dominant color it lies. The weakest color intensity is saved in the fourth and fifth cells. Then the values are copied from the array to the R, G, B parameters according to which color was dominant (the original I).

Because of the simple way that HSV calculates hue, the colors are mapped onto a hexagonal pyramid or hexcone instead of a circular cone. (See Figure 10-39.) A variation on the HSV model called the hue, lightness, and saturation model (HLS) is used by Tektronix. It deforms the hexcode by stretching the white point along the value axis. This forms two hexcones placed base to base, with black at one apex and white at

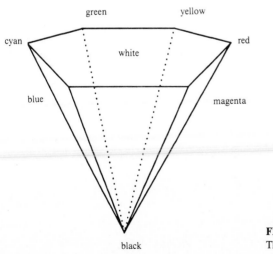

FIGURE 10-39
The HSV model hexcone of color.

the other. In this model, black has a lightness of 0 and white a lightness of 1, but fully saturated colors have a lightness value of only 0.5. The lightness is defined as the average of the maximum and minimum RGB values, which is $(V + X)/2$ in the notation of algorithm 10.13. The saturation is $(V - X)/(V + X)$ if the lightness is less than 0.5, and $(V - X)/(2 - V - X)$ for lightness greater than 0.5. (See Figure 10-40.) The HSI, HSV, and HLS color models are useful in implementing programs where the user must select colors. It is not always easy to tell which RGB values are needed to get a desired color. The HSV model corresponds to how an artist mixes colors: selecting a hue, adding white to get the proper tint, and adding black to get the desired shade. It is more intuitive. We might allow the user to specify a color using the HSV model and then convert it to RGB for display. Or the user might select a color from a displayed palette which would be converted to HSV units for later modification.

GAMMA CORRECTION

The above transformations are based on the fact that light behaves linearly, that the effect of light from two sources is simply the sum of the individual sources. While this is true for light, it probably won't be true for the voltages applied to a monitor to produce

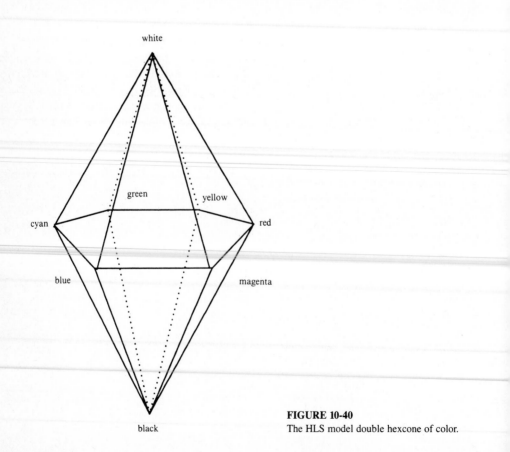

FIGURE 10-40
The HLS model double hexcone of color.

the light. Doubling the voltage at the monitor will probably not yield twice the light. Instead, there is typically a power relation.

$$I = k V^{\gamma} \tag{10.43}$$

The exponent γ is usually around 2.

Suppose we determine the value (I) for an intensity we would like to display. We still must determine the proper voltage setting for the display hardware to give this intensity. To do this, we will have to solve Equation 10.43 for (V).

$$V = \left(\frac{I}{k}\right)^{1/\gamma} \tag{10.44}$$

This is called *gamma correction*. One fast way of performing gamma correction is to construct a table of the supported intensity values and corresponding display voltages. Gamma correction then becomes a simple table lookup. For a color display, gamma correction must be applied to each of the three primary colors. Some monitors provide internal circuitry to perform the gamma correction and thus appear to be linear devices.

COLOR TABLES

Some display devices are capable of generating a large variety of colors. For example, if a device has 8 bits of control over each of the red, green, and blue channels, then each channel can have 256 intensity levels, and together 16,777,216 different colors may be produced. To fully specify all these colors we would need 24 bits per pixel in the frame buffer memory. Since we can usually get by with far fewer colors, this is not very cost-effective. An alternative is a color table. A *color table* allows us to map between a color index in the frame buffer and a color specification. Suppose our frame buffer had 8 bits per pixel. This would allow us only 256 colors; but what if we use the frame buffer entry as an index to access a color table. Suppose the color table has 256 entries, each entry containing a 24-bit color selection. Then we can show any 256 of the 16,777,216 possible colors. And by changing the values in the color table, we can change the available color selection to contain the 256 colors we most desire for the current scene. (See Figure 10-41.)

Note that changing a value in the color table can alter the appearance of large portions of the display (any part of the display which referenced that entry). Because it is the hardware which makes these changes, they usually occur very fast. Some clever techniques have been devised which take advantage of this hardware feature. For example, we might give the screen a background color from color-table entry 1 and draw a complex object using color-table entry 2. Now if table entry 2 has the same value as table entry 1, then the object will be invisible; it will be indistinguishable from the background. But if we change table entry 2 to some other color, the object will suddenly appear. Changing its color can make it visible or invisible, and this change is often far faster than we can draw or erase the object. Drawing or erasing requires changing a lot of pixel values in the frame buffer, while changing the color only requires changing a single color entry.

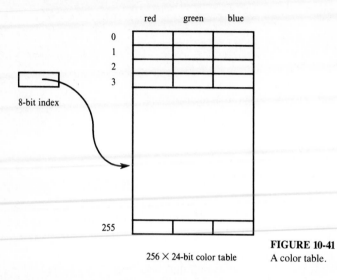

FIGURE 10-41

256 × 24-bit color table   A color table.

We can have several invisible objects (as many as there are color-table entries). By sequencing through visibility changes, animation effects can be achieved.

Color tables have been used to give false color or pseudocolor to gray-scale images. They have also been used for gamma correction, lighting and shading, and color model transformations.

EXTENDING THE SHADING MODEL TO COLOR

As we mentioned at the start of the chapter, objects have a color-dependent index of reflection which can be represented by three reflectivity values: one for red, one for green, and a third for blue. Our simple model for specular reflection is not color-dependent, but the light sources can be colored. Background light and point sources must be given three components. As a result, our shading expression of Equation 10.16 splits into three equations, one for each color component.

$$v_r = B_r R_r + \sum_j \frac{P_{rj}[R_r(L \cdot N) + D_j G_j F/(E \cdot N)]}{C + U_j}$$

$$v_g = B_g R_g + \sum_j \frac{P_{gj}[R_g(L \cdot N) + D_j G_j F/(E \cdot N)]}{C + U_j} \qquad (10.45)$$

$$v_b = B_b R_b + \sum_j \frac{P_{bj}[R_b(L \cdot N) + D_j G_j F/(E \cdot N)]}{C + U_j}$$

FURTHER READING

An introduction to the problems of realistic image generation is given in [NEW77]. First attempts at shading just used the distance from the viewpoint to determine brightness [WYL67]. An early model for shading is described in [PHO75], and an alternative computation method for it was given in [DUF79]. This model was improved in [BLI77]; it is the one used in this text. The model was further extended to include colored specular reflections in [COO82]. Extensions for light sources with intensity distributions and color are given in [WAR83]. Hardware extensions to the frame buffer have been devised to allow fast scan conversion, hidden-surface removal, clipping, smooth shading, shadows, and transparency. The method, which is based on all pixels being able to evaluate linear expression in parallel, is described in [FUC85]. The idea of imaging transparent objects by modifying the painter's algorithm was presented in [NEW72]. Improved transparency approximations are discussed in [KAY79]. Gouraud presented smooth shading by interpolation in [GOU71]. A comparison of shadow algorithms is given in [CRO77]. Shadows are also discussed in [NIS85b]. Hidden-surface techniques are used in [ATH78] to find polygons that are not in shadow. In [WIL78] shadows are determined by first computing a Z buffer using the light source as the viewpoint. Then as each point is calculated for display, it is compared against that buffer to find out if anything lies in front relative to the light source to cause a shadow. This allows curved shadows on curved objects. An extension of scan-line algorithms to include shadows is given in [BOU70]. The method of generating shadows by an extended Z buffer is described in [BRO84]. Ray tracing was first suggested in [APP68]. Modeling of light and ray tracing are discussed in [WHI80]. An introduction to ray tracing and its use with constructive solid geometry are given in [ROT82]. A system for modeling, ray tracing, and display of three-dimensional objects is described in [HAL83]; the system uses an improved illumination model including transparency. Ray tracing for shadows and reflection of diffuse radiation are described in [NIS85a]. Ray-tracing research includes methods for antialiasing and also for the elimination of sharp edges for shadows, motion blur, and translucency. See [AMA84], [COO84], [HEC84], and [LEE85]. There is also research into ray tracing of objects other than polygons. See [BLI82], [BOU85], [KAJ83a], [KAJ83b], [TOT85], and [VAN84]. And there is interest in improving the speed of ray tracing. See [AMA84], [GLA84], [HEC84], [PLU85], and [WEG84]. Ray tracing can reproduce the specular reflection of objects by objects, but does not model the interaction of diffuse radiation between objects. This is considered in [GOR84] and [COH85]. Our system allows us to shade surfaces composed of polygons of uniform color, but real objects can have textures and variations of surface color. One approach to this problem is to map texture patterns onto the surface. See [BLI76] and [CAT80]. Another is to define a three-dimensional texture pattern which can be accessed for surface points [PEA85]. Texture patterns can be used to provide perturbations to the surface normal as well as the reflectivity. This can give surfaces a rough or wrinkled appearance. See [BLI78] and [HAR84]. Reviews of techniques to obtain continuous tone images from bilevel devices are given in [ALG83] and [KNO72]. Halftoning with an ordered dither is described in [JAR76], [JUD74], [KLE70], and [LIP71]. Sometimes the halftone pattern is oriented at an angle to the scan direction; [HOL79] describes how to determine an equivalent pattern aligned with the scan direction. A more sophisticated halftone method than the one we have presented includes the error, due to threshold test of a pixel value, in calculation of the neighboring pixel's value [FLO76]. A classic introduction to the ideas of hue, value, and chroma is found in [MUN05]. Color models are presented in [JOB78], [LEH84], and [SMI78]. Some color models which we did not present strive to parameterize the color space such that equal changes in parameters are perceived as equivalent changes in color. See [MEY80] and [TAJ83]. The theory of exact color reproduction for light sources as in display monitors, transmission/absorption as in photographic transparencies, and reflection absorption as in lithography is discussed in [HOR84]. There are several reports on how to effectively use color tables. One approach is to choose colors to best cover the volume of the color space actually used in the scene. See [HEC82] and [LEH84]. A method for determining table values which compensate for nonlinearities in the hardware is presented in [CAT79]. By storing surface normals as color-table indices, the lighting of a scene can be quickly changed by altering the color table [BAS81]. Color-table techniques including animation are described in [SHO79] and [SLO79]. Some rules for the effective use of color based on the properties of vision are given in [MUR84].

[ALG83] Algie, S. H., "Resolution and Tonal Continuity in Bilevel Printed Picture Quality," *Computer Vision, Graphics, and Image Processing*, vol. 24, no. 3, pp. 329–346 (1983).

[AMA84] Amanatides, J., "Ray Tracing with Cones," *Computer Graphics*, vol. 18, no. 3, pp. 129–135 (1984).

[APP68] Appel, A., " Some Techniques for Shading Machine Renderings of Solids," *AFIPS SJCC*, vol. 32, pp. 37–45 (1968).

[ATH78] Atherton, P., Weiler, K., Greenberg, D., "Polygon Shadow Generation," *Computer Graphics*, vol. 12, no. 3, pp. 275–281 (1978).

[BAS81] Bass, D. H., "Using the Video Lookup Table for Reflectivity Calculations: Specific Techniques and Graphic Results," *Computer Graphics and Image Processing*, vol. 17, no. 3, pp. 249–261 (1981).

[BLI76] Blinn, J. F., Newell, M. E., "Texture and Reflection in Computer Generated Images," *Communications of the ACM*, vol. 19, no. 10, pp. 542–547 (1976).

[BLI77] Blinn, J. F., "Models of Light Reflection for Computer Synthesized Pictures," *Computer Graphics*, vol. 11, no. 2, pp. 193–198 (1977).

[BLI78] Blinn, J. F., "Simulation of Wrinkled Surfaces," *Computer Graphics*, vol. 12, no. 3, pp. 286–292 (1978).

[BLI82] Blinn, J. F., "Light Reflection Functions for Simulation of Clouds and Dusty Surfaces," *Computer Graphics*, vol. 16, no. 3, pp. 21–29 (1982).

[BOU70] Bouknight, J., Kelley, K., "An Algorithm for Producing Half-Tone Computer Graphics Presentations with Shadows and Movable Light Sources," *AFIPS SJCC*, vol. 36, pp. 1–10 (1970).

[BOU85] Bouville, C., "Bounding Ellipsoids for Ray-Fractal Intersection," *Computer Graphics*, vol. 19, no. 3, pp. 45–52 (1985).

[BRO84] Brotman, L. S., Badler, N. I., "Generating Soft Shadows with a Depth Buffer Algorithm," *IEEE Computer Graphics and Applications*, vol. 4, no. 10, pp. 5–12 (1984).

[CAT79] Catmull, E., "A Tutorial on Compensation Tables," *Computer Graphics*, vol. 13, no. 2, pp. 1–7 (1979).

[CAT80] Catmull, E., Smith, A. R., "3-D Transformations of Images in Scanline Order," *Computer Graphics*, vol. 14, no. 3, pp. 279–285 (1980).

[COH85] Cohen, M. F., Greenberg, D. P., "The Hemi-Cube: A Radiosity Solution for Complex Environments," *Computer Graphics*, vol. 19, no. 3, pp. 31–40 (1985).

[COO82] Cook, R. L., Torrance, K. E., "A Reflectance Model for Computer Graphics," *ACM Transactions on Graphics*, vol 1, no. 1, pp. 7–24 (1982).

[COO84] Cook, R. L., Porter, T., Carpenter, L., "Distributed Ray Tracing," *Computer Graphics*, vol. 16, no. 3, pp. 137–143 (1984).

[CRO77] Crow, F. C., "Shadow Algorithms for Computer Graphics," *Computer Graphics*, vol. 11, no. 2, pp. 242–247 (1977).

[DUF79] Duff, T., "Smoothly Shaded Renderings of Polyhedral Objects on Raster Displays," *Computer Graphics*, vol. 13, no. 2, pp. 270–275 (1979).

[FLO76] Floyd, R. W., Steinberg, L., "An Adaptive Algorithm for Spatial Grey Scale," *Proceedings of the Society for Information Display*, vol. 17, pp. 75–77 (1976).

[FUC85] Fuchs, H., et al., "Fast Spheres, Shadows, Textures, Transparencies, and Image Enhancements in Pixel-Planes," *Computer Graphics*, vol. 19, no. 3, pp. 111–120 (1985).

[GLA84] Glassner, A. S., "Space Subdivision for Fast Ray Tracing," *IEEE Computer Graphics and Applications*, vol. 4, no. 10, pp. 15–22 (1984).

[GOR84] Goral, C. M., Torrance, K. E., Greenberg, D. P., Battaile, B., "Modeling the Interaction of Light between Diffuse Surfaces," *Computer Graphics*, vol. 18, no. 3, pp. 213–222 (1984).

[GOU71] Gouraud, H., "Continuous Shading of Curved Surfaces," *IEEE Transactions on Computing*, vol. C-20, no. 6, pp. 623–629 (1971).

[HAL83] Hall, R. A., Greenberg, D. P., "A Testbed for Realistic Image Synthesis," *IEEE Computer Graphics and Applications*, vol. 3, no. 11, pp. 10–20 (1983).

[HAR84] Haruyama S., Barsky, B. A., "Using Stochastic Modeling for Texture Generations," *IEEE Computer Graphics and Applications*, vol. 4, no. 3, pp. 7–19 (1984).

[HEC82] Heckbert, P. S., "Color Image Quantization for Frame Buffer Display," *Computer Graphics*, vol. 16, no. 3, pp. 297–307 (1982).

[HEC84] Heckbert, P. S., Hanrahan, P., "Beam Tracing Polygonal Objects," *Computer Graphics*, vol. 18, no. 3, pp. 119–127 (1984).

[HOL79] Holladay, T. M., "An Optimum Algorithm for Halftone Generation for Displays and Hard Copies," *SID Digest*, vol. 10, pp. 102–103 (1979).

[HOR84] Horn, B. K. P., "Exact Reproduction of Colored Images," *Computer Vision, Graphics, and Image Processing*, vol 26, no. 2, pp. 135–167 (1984).

[JAR76] Jarvis, J. F., Judice, C. N., Ninke, W. H., "A Survey of Techniques for the Display of Continuous Tone Pictures on Bilevel Displays," *Computer Graphics and Image Processing*, vol. 5, no. 1, pp. 13–40 (1976).

[JOB78] Joblove, G. H., Greenberg, D., "Color Spaces for Computer Graphics," *Computer Graphics*, vol. 12, no. 3, pp. 20–25 (1978).

[JUD74] Judice, C. N., Jarvis, J. F., Ninke, W. H., "Using Ordered Dither to Display Continuous Tone Pictures on an AC Plasma Panel," *Proceedings of the SID*, vol. 15, no. 4, pp. 220–228 (1974).

[KAJ83a] Kajiya, J. T., "New Techniques for Ray Tracing Procedurally Defined Objects," *Computer Graphics*, vol. 17, no. 3, pp. 91–102 (1983).

[KAJ83b] Kajiya, J. T., "New Techniques for Ray Tracing Procedurally Defined Objects," *ACM Transactions on Graphics*, vol. 2, no. 3, pp. 161–181 (1983).

[KAY79] Kay, D. S., Greenberg, D., "Transparency for Computer Synthesized Images," *Computer Graphics*, vol. 13, no. 2, pp. 158–164 (1979).

[KLE70] Klensch, R. J., Meyerhofer, D., Walsh, J. J., "Electronically Generated Halftone Pictures," *RCA Review*, pp. 517–533 (Sept. 1970).

[KNO72] Knowlton, K., Harmon, L., "Computer-Produced Grey Scales," *Computer Graphics and Image Processing*, vol. 1, no. 1, pp. 1–20 (1972).

[LEE85] Lee, M. E., Redner, R. A., Uselton, S. P., "Statistically Optimized Sampling for Distributed Ray Tracing," *Computer Graphics*, vol. 19, no. 3, pp. 61–67 (1985).

[LEH84] Lehar, A. F., Stevens, R. J., "High-Speed Manipulation of the Color Chromaticity of Digital Images," *IEEE Computer Graphics and Applications*, vol. 4, no. 2, pp. 34–39 (1984).

[LIP71] Lippel, B., Kurland, M., "The Effect of Dither on Luminance Quantization of Pictures," *IEEE Transactions on Communication Technology*, vol. COM-19, no. 6, pp. 879–888 (1971).

[MEY80] Meyer, G. W., Greenberg, D. P., "Perceptual Color Spaces for Computer Graphics," *Computer Graphics*, vol. 14, no. 3, pp. 254–261 (1980).

[MUN05] Munsell, A. H., *A Color Notation*, 12th ed., Munsell Color Company, Inc., Baltimore, Md. (1971).

[MUR84] Murch, G. M., '' Physiological Principles for the Effective Use of Color,'' *IEEE Computer Graphics and Applications*, vol. 4, no. 11, pp. 49–54 (1984).

[NEW72] Newell, M. E., Newell, R. G., and Sancha, T. L., ''A Solution to the Hidden Surface Problem,'' *Proceeding of the ACM Annual Conference*, pp. 443–450 (1972).

[NEW77] Newell, M. E., Blinn, J. F., ''The Progression of Realism in Computer Generated Images,'' *ACM 77, Proceedings of the Annual Conference*, pp. 449–451 (1977).

[NIS85a] Nishita, T., Nakamae, E., ''Continuous Tone Representation of Three-Dimensional Objects Taking Account of Shadows and Interreflection,'' *Computer Graphics*, vol. 19, no. 3, pp. 23–30 (1985).

[NIS85b] Nishita, T., Okamura, I., Nakamae, E., ''Shading Models for Point and Linear Sources,'' *ACM Transactions on Graphics*, vol. 4, no. 2, pp. 124–146 (1985).

[PEA85] Peachey, D. R., ''Solid Texturing of Complex Surfaces,'' *Computer Graphics*, vol. 19, no. 3, pp. 279–286 (1985).

[PLU85] Plunkett, D. J., Bailey, M. J., ''The Vectorization of a Ray-Tracing Algorithm for Improved Execution Speed,'' *IEEE Computer Graphics and Applications*, vol. 5, no. 7, pp. 52–60 (1985).

[PHO75] Phong, Bui-Tuong, ''Illumination for Computer-Generated Pictures,'' *Communications of the ACM*, vol. 18, no. 6, pp. 311–317 (June 1975).

[ROT82] Roth, S. D., ''Ray Casting for Modeling Solids,'' *Computer Graphics and Image Processing*, vol. 18, no. 2, pp. 109–144 (1982).

[SHO79] Shoup, R. G., ''Color Table Animation,'' *Computer Graphics*, vol. 13, no. 2, pp. 8–13 (1979).

[SLO79] Sloan, K. R., Brown, C. M., ''Color Map Techniques,'' *Computer Graphics and Image Processing*, vol. 10, no. 4, pp. 297–317 (1979).

[SMI78] Smith, A. R., ''Color Gamut Transform Pairs,'' *Computer Graphics*, vol. 12, no. 3, pp. 12–19 (1978).

[TAJ83] Tajima, J., ''Uniform Color Scale Applications to Computer Graphics,'' *Computer Vision, Graphics, and Image Processing*, vol. 21, no. 3, pp. 305–325 (1983).

[TOT85] Toth, D. L., ''On Ray Tracing Parametric Surfaces,'' *Computer Graphics*, vol. 19, no. 3, pp. 171–179 (1985).

[VAN84] Van Wijk, J. J., ''Ray Tracing Objects Defined by Sweeping Planar Cubic Splines,'' *ACM Transactions on Graphics*, vol. 3, no. 3, pp. 223–237 (1984).

[WAR83] Warn, D. R., ''Lighting Controls for Synthetic Images,'' *Computer Graphics*, vol. 17, no. 3, pp. 13–21 (1983).

[WEG84] Weghorst, H., Hooper, G., Greenberg, D. P., ''Improved Computational Methods for Ray Tracing,'' *ACM Transactions on Graphics*, vol. 3, no. 1, pp. 52–69 (1984).

[WHI80] Whitted, T., ''An Improved Illumination Model for Shaded Display,'' *Communications of the ACM*, vol. 23, no. 6, pp. 343–349 (1980).

[WIL78] Williams, L., ''Casting Curved Shadows on Curved Surfaces,'' *Computer Graphics*, vol. 12, no. 3, pp. 270–274 (1978).

[WYL67] Wylie, C., Romney, G., Evans, D., Erdahl, A., ''Half-Tone Perspective Drawings by Computer,'' *AFIPS FJCC*, vol. 31, pp. 49–58 (1967).

EXERCISES

10-1 Suppose that a rectangular polygon is drawn with vertices at $(0, 0, -1)$, $(0, 1, -1)$, $(1, 1, 0)$, $(1, 0, 0)$, and is viewed with the default parallel projection. Give the shading value which would result from each of the following parameter settings.

    a) Default

    b) SET-OBJECT-SHADE(0.4, 10, 10)
        SET-LIGHT(0.5, 0.5, 1, 1, 0)

    c) SET-OBJECT-SHADE(0.4, 10, 10)
        SET-LIGHT(0.5, 0.5, 1, 1, 1)

d) SET-OBJECT-SHADE(0.4, 2, 10)
SET-LIGHT(0.5, 0.5, 1, 1, 0)

e) SET-OBJECT-SHADE(0.4, 2, 10)
SET-LIGHT(-1, 0.5, -0.5, 1, 0)

10-2 State the meaning of each of the symbols found in Equation 10.16.

10-3 Extend the shading model to include the display of objects which emit their own light as well as illuminated objects.

10-4 Could the simple Z-buffer hidden-surface algorithm be used with transparent objects? Why?

10-5 How many intensity levels can be formed from an n $\times$ n pixel cell if each individual pixel can have m intensity settings?

a) Assuming the pixel intensities are uniformly spaced

b) Assuming the pixel intensities are arbitrary (e.g., an intensity lookup table is used)

10-6 Determine the RGB to XYZ transformations matrix for the NTSC standard primaries using the definition of white given in Equation 10.29.

10-7 Develop algorithms to convert between the RGB color model and the HLS color model.

10-8 Identify the x,y value for three colors which will maximize the area of the color gamut triangle on the CIE diagram. What is the area of this triangle? Estimate the area covered by all visible colors on the diagram and determine the area of colors which cannot be produced with only three primaries. Compare the area of your maximum triangle to that for the gamut of a color monitor.

10-9 For some luminancy, describe the surface in RGB space which corresponds to the color gamut of the normalized x,y values.

PROGRAMMING PROBLEMS

10-1 Implement algorithms 10.1 through 10.11 to add automatic shading to your graphics system.

10-2 Test your shading routines by constructing a house, selecting a view which shows at least three surfaces, and generating several images, each of which differs from the others by a change of a shading parameter. Observe the effect of each parameter independently in this manner.

10-3 Write the routines

INQUIRE-SHADING(ON-OFF)
INQUIRE-LIGHT(X, Y, Z, BRIGHTNESS, BACKGROUND)
INQUIRE-OBJECT-SHADE(REFLECTIVITY, REFRACTION, GLOSS)

which return to the user the current shading parameter settings.

10-4 Extend the program of Programming Problem 9-8, which gives successive views of an object to show the object shaded.

10-5 Write a program which gives successive images of a shaded object drawn by procedure FOO within the cube $0 < X < 1, 0 < Y < 1, 0 < Z < 1$. The default viewing parameters will always be used, but in successive pictures, the light source will appear to rotate around the object.

10-6 Extend the interactive display program of Programming Problem 8-14 to include setting of the light-source parameters.

10-7 Extend the graphics system to handle transparent objects. Do this by modifying the SET-OBJECT-SHADE algorithm to include a transparency coefficient, and define a display-file style command for transparency. Finally, modify the FILLIN algorithm for polygons so that when filling a transparent polygon, each pixel value is set to the current shade plus the transparency times the old shade value of the pixel.

10-8 Extend the graphics system to show shaded images via halftoning.

*10-9 Extend the graphics system to include the Gouraud smooth shading interpolation for shades specified by the user. Polygon-entry routines should be extended to include an intensity value for each vertex. Clipping routines must supply intensity values for new vertices. The display file must be able to save these intensity values. And finally, the polygon-filling routine must interpolate over the shades.

CHAPTER
ELEVEN

CURVES
AND
FRACTALS

INTRODUCTION

Throughout this book we have dealt exclusively with straight-line segments. We saw in the first chapter that straight-line segments are fairly easy to generate. In later chapters, we learned how to represent and manipulate line segments. Straight lines have a simple mathematical form, which makes them easy to deal with in such operations as transformations or clipping. The real world, however, is not made of stick figures. Many of the things which we might like to model and display involve curves. We might like to plot a mathematical function or the path of a rocket, or we might wish to design the hood of a sports car or the wing of an airplane, or we might desire to draw a woman's face. Natural objects are neither perfectly flat nor smoothly curved but often have rough, jagged contours. In this chapter we shall introduce methods for generating curved lines. The discussion will be rather superficial, since a thorough study is beyond the scope of this book. Nevertheless, we shall develop spline interpolation algorithms for drawing curved lines and fractal curve generators for rough, natural-looking objects.

CURVE GENERATION

There are two approaches which can be taken to draw curved lines. One approach is to develop a *curve generation algorithm* such as a DDA. With this approach, a true curve is created. The second method is to approximate a curve by a number of small straight-

397

line segments. The interpolation techniques which we shall discuss later are used for this second approach. We shall begin our discussion by considering the true-curve generation method.

Suppose that we have a curve, such as the arc of a circle, that we wish to draw. If we know a differential equation for this curve, we can write a digital differential analyzer algorithm which will calculate the coordinates of points on the curve. We can then change the intensity values of the pixels which contain these points, and an image of the curve will appear on the screen.

The differential equations for simple curves such as circles and ellipses are fairly easy to solve, and generation algorithms for them can be implemented in hardware. A display device may be capable of drawing arcs as well as line segments.

Let us step through the development of a DDA algorithm for generating circular arcs. The equations for the arc coordinates can be written in terms of an angle parameter A as follows:

$$x = R \cos A + x_0$$
$$y = R \sin A + y_0 \tag{11.1}$$

where (x_0, y_0) is the center of curvature, and R is the arc radius. (See Figure 11-1.)

Differentiating tells us to change x by dx and y by dy if we change A by dA.

$$dx = - R \sin A \, dA$$
$$dy = R \cos A \, dA \tag{11.2}$$

We notice that Equation 11.1 gives

$$R \cos A = x - x_0$$
$$R \sin A = y - y_0 \tag{11.3}$$

so that

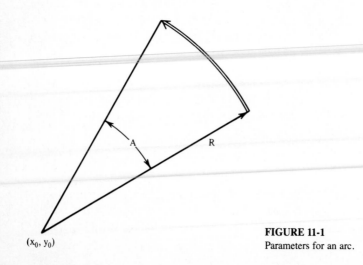

FIGURE 11-1

Parameters for an arc.

(x_0, y_0)

$$dx = -(y - y_0)dA$$
$$dy = (x - x_0)dA$$

(11.4)

Now the changes dx and dy tell us the amount to add to an old point on the arc to get a new point.

$$x_2 = x_1 + dx = x_1 - (y_1 - y_0)dA$$
$$y_2 = y_1 + dy = y_1 + (x_2 - x_0)dA$$

(11.5)

These equations form the basis for an arc generation algorithm. In this algorithm, we start with the center of curvature (x_0, y_0), the total angle of the arc to be drawn A, a point at which the arc drawing should begin (x, y), and the intensity at which to set the pixels. The step size of the parameter dA should be small enough not to leave gaps in the arc and small enough to give a good approximation to a circle. The arc-generating algorithm is as follows:

11.1 Algorithm ARCDDA(X0, Y0, A, X, Y, INTENSITY) Counterclockwise circular arc generation

Arguments   X0, Y0 the center of curvature
            A the arc angle
            X, Y the starting point for the arc drawing
Global   FRAME the frame buffer array
Local   XARC, YARC the next point to draw
            A-DRAWN the amount of angle currently covered
            DA the angle increment
Constant   ROUNDOFF some small number greater than any round-off error
BEGIN
    IF | X − X0 | + | Y − Y0 | < ROUNDOFF THEN RETURN;
    A-DRAWN ← 0;
    find a suitable angle increment
    DA ← MIN(0.01, 1 / (3.2 * (|X − X0| + |Y − Y0|)));
    set the first point of the arc
    XARC ← X;
    YARC ← Y;
    generate the arc until desired angle is covered
    WHILE A-DRAWN < A DO
        BEGIN
            find new point
            XARC ← XARC + (Y0 − YARC) * DA;
            YARC ← YARC + (XARC − X0) * DA;
            A-DRAWN ← A-DRAWN + DA;
            set the corresponding pixel
            FRAME[INT(XARC), INT(YARC)] ← INTENSITY;
        END;
    RETURN;
END;

There are, however, some problems which arise when curves are generated at this level. To specify a curve, we need more information than just its endpoints. This may mean that a different display-file structure should be used. Another problem can arise from transformations. A line segment when scaled is still a line segment, but other curves may behave differently. For example, a circle when scaled in only one direction becomes an ellipse. If we had only a circular-arc generator, we would be very limited in our ability to scale pictures. Still another problem is the fact that our clipping algorithm works only for points and straight lines. If we wished to clip arcs to some window boundary, a new clipping algorithm would have to be developed. Although these problems are not insurmountable, there is yet another limitation to the curve generation approach; not every curve which we wish to draw has a simple generation algorithm. Curves for airplane wings or sports car hoods or human faces are not simple circles or ellipses. We would have to approximate such curves by patching together pieces of circles or ellipses or spirals. But we might just as well patch together many small straight-line segments and then be able to use the display file and the transformations and the clipping algorithm which we have studied.

INTERPOLATION

How can we express a curve which has no simple mathematical definition? We can draw an approximation to such a curve if we have an array of sample points. We can then guess what the curve should look like between the sample points. If the curve is smooth and our samples are close enough together, we can make a pretty good guess as to what the missing portions should look like. Our guess will probably not be exactly right, but it will be close enough for appearances. We fill in portions of the unknown curve with pieces of known curves which pass through the nearby sample points. Since the known and unknown curves share these sample points in a local region, we assume that in this region, the two curves look pretty much alike. We fit a portion of the unknown curve with a curve that we know. Now we can fill in a gap between the sample points by finding the coordinates of points along the known approximating curve and connecting these points with line segments. (See Figure 11-2.)

The next thing which we might ask is what we should use for the known curve. What is the mathematical expression for a function which passes through the sample points in a limited region? There are many function forms which can be made to pass through sample points by adjusting parameters. Polynomial, trigonometric, exponential, and other classes of functions have been used. Furthermore, there are many options within each class. We shall use polynomial functions to approximate the curve.

Functions are often expressed in the form $y = f(x)$, but we shall prefer a parametric form.

$$x = fx(u)$$

$$y = fy(u) \tag{11.6}$$

$$z = fz(u)$$

There are a couple of reasons why the parametric form is preferable. For one thing, the difference between two and three dimensions is just the addition of a third equation for z. The parametric form treats all three directions equally, and it allows

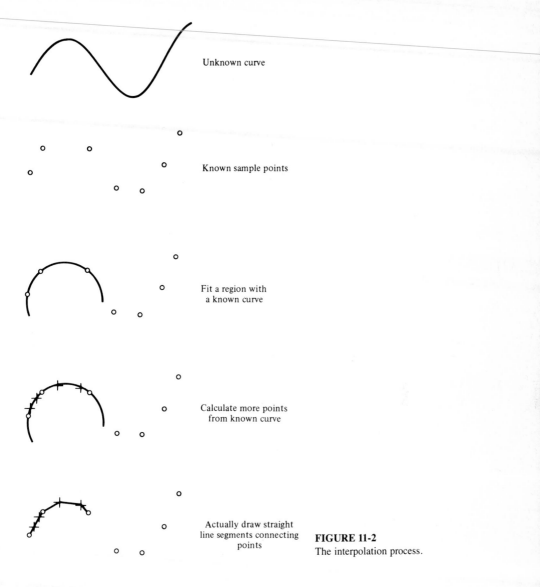

Unknown curve

Known sample points

Fit a region with
a known curve

Calculate more points
from known curve

Actually draw straight
line segments connecting
points

FIGURE 11-2
The interpolation process.

multiple values (several y or z values for a given x) so that curves can double back or even cross themselves. (See Figure 11-3.)

Now let's invent a function which can be used for interpolation. There will be a number of things wrong with this first attempt, but it will nevertheless serve to illustrate the approach.

Suppose we want a polynomial curve that will pass through n sample points.

$$(x_1, y_1, z_1), (x_2, y_2, z_2), \ldots , (x_n, y_n, z_n)$$

We shall construct the function as the sum of terms, one term for each sample point.

FIGURE 11-3
The parametric form allows representation of curves which double back or cross themselves.

$$fx(u) = \sum_{i=1}^{n} x_i B_i(u)$$

$$fy(u) = \sum_{i=1}^{n} y_i B_i(u) \qquad (11.7)$$

$$fz(u) = \sum_{i=1}^{n} z_i B_i(u)$$

The functions $B_i(u)$ are called *blending functions*. For each value of u, they determine how much the ith sample point affects the position of the curve. We can think of each sample point as trying to pull the curve in its direction. The $B_i(u)$ function tells us how hard the ith sample point is pulling. If for some value of u, $B_i(u) = 1$ and for each $j \neq i$, $B_j(u) = 0$, then the ith sample point has complete control of the curve. The curve will pass through the ith sample point. If at a different value of u, one of the other sample points has complete control, then the curve will pass through this point as well. What we want then are blending functions which for different values of u will give control of the curve to each of the sample points in turn. The particular values of the parameter u at which the curve passes through each of the sample points are not very important, just so long as the sample points get control of the curve in proper order. We shall create blending functions for which the first sample point (x_1, y_1, z_1) has complete control when $u = -1$, the second when $u = 0$, the third when $u = 1$, and so on. The reason for this selection of u values is to make the actual implementation a bit simpler. For this choice, we need for $B_1(u)$ a function which is 1 at $u = -1$, and 0 for $u = 0, 1, 2, \ldots, n - 2$. An expression which is 0 at the correct places is

$$u(u - 1)(u - 2)\ldots[u - (n - 2)]$$

At $u = -1$ it is

$$(-1)(-2)(-3)\ldots(1 - n)$$

So dividing by this constant gives us 1 at $u = -1$, and this has just the behavior we wish

$$B_1(u) = \frac{u(u - 1)(u - 2) \dots [u - (n - 2)]}{(-1)(-2)(-3) \dots (1 - n)} \tag{11.8}$$

The ith blending function can be constructed in the same way to be 1 at $u = i - 2$, and 0 at the other integers.

$$B_1(u) = \frac{(u + 1)(u)(u - 1) \dots [u - (i - 3)][u - (i - 1)] \dots [u - (i - 2)]}{(i - 1)(i - 2)(i - 3) \dots (1)(-1) \dots (i - n)} \tag{11.9}$$

Using these expressions to approximate the curve is called *Lagrange interpolation*.

Let's consider the case where there are four sample points. Then we will need four blending functions. The above definition gives

$$B_1(u) = \frac{u(u - 1)(u - 2)}{(-1)(-2)(-3)}$$

$$B_2(u) = \frac{(u + 1)(u - 1)(u - 2)}{(1)(-1)(-2)}$$

$$B_3(u) = \frac{(u + 1)u(u - 2)}{(2)(1)(-1)} \tag{11.10}$$

$$B_4(u) = \frac{(u + 1)u(u - 1)}{(3)(2)(1)}$$

Using these functions and four sample points, we can construct a curve which passes through the four sample points.

$$x = x_1 B_1(u) + x_2 B_2(u) + x_3 B_3(u) + x_4 B_4(u)$$

$$y = y_1 B_1(u) + y_2 B_2(u) + y_3 B_3(u) + y_4 B_4(u) \tag{11.11}$$

$$z = z_1 B_1(u) + z_2 B_2(u) + z_3 B_3(u) + z_4 B_4(u)$$

Now we expect this curve to lie fairly close to the actual curve in the region of these four points, particularly in the middle, between the second and third sample points. This is the portion of the curve followed as u varies between 0 and 1. We can find points on the approximation curve by plugging in values for u (between 0 and 1). The results of these calculations provide coordinates which can be used as the endpoints for small line segments which we shall draw as an approximation to the approximation curve. For example, suppose that we wish to approximate the curve between the second and third sample points by three straight-line segments. We have as sample points the values at $u = 0$ and $u = 1$. If we use our equations to calculate points at $u = 1/3$ and at $u = 2/3$, we will have four points which will serve as the endpoints of the three approximating segments. The entire curve can be approximated by repeating this process. We take four consecutive sample points (1, 2, 3, 4) and approximate the curve between the middle two (2, 3). Then we step up one sample point, picking up a new sam-

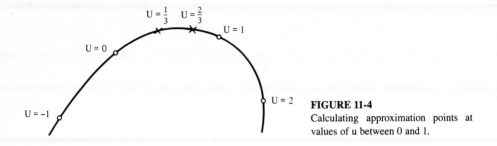

FIGURE 11-4
Calculating approximation points at values of u between 0 and 1.

ple point at one end and discarding a point at the other end (2, 3, 4, 5). We can then approximate the next portion of the curve (3, 4). We continue moving through the sample points until the curve is drawn. The initial and the final portions of the curve will require special handling. For the first four points (1, 2, 3, 4), we shall need to draw the region between points 1 and 2 with u values between -1 and 0. Likewise, the blending functions for the very last step of the curve should be evaluated with u values between 1 and 2. There is nothing particularly difficult about these special cases; we just must handle them separately.

INTERPOLATING ALGORITHMS

Before discussing the shortcomings of these blending functions and presenting an improved set, let us see how this curve-drawing program might be implemented. The first thing which we notice is that the same blending function values are needed for each section of the curve that is drawn. If each section is approximated by three straight-line segments, then each section will require the blending function values for u at 0, 1/3, 2/3, and 1. (See Figure 11-4.)

These values can be calculated once and saved in an array for use in drawing each curve section. The first algorithm which we shall present allows the user to specify how many straight-line segments should be used to complete a section of the curve. This number (NUMBER-OF-LINES) will tell us the u values at which to calculate and save the blending function values. The value of $B_i(u)$ is stored in the BLEND array at BLEND[I, U]. The blending function values needed for the first and last sections of the curve are also calculated and stored in arrays FIRST-BLEND and LAST-BLEND.

11.2 Algorithm SET-SMOOTH(NUMBER-OF-LINES) User routine to set the number of line segments per curve section

Argument	NUMBER-OF-LINES the number of line segments per curve section
Global	LINES-PER-SECTION storage for the NUMBER-OF-LINES specification
	BLEND, FIRST-BLEND, LAST-BLEND
	arrays size 4 by MAX-NUMBER-OF-LINES for blending function values
Local	U, V, W parameters for blending function evaluation
	I a variable for stepping through needed curve points

Constant   MAX-NUMBER-OF-LINES the maximum allowed number of line seg-
            ments per curve section

```
BEGIN
    IF NUMBER-OF-LINES < 1
        OR NUMBER-OF-LINES > MAX-NUMBER-OF-LINES THEN
        RETURN ERROR 'INVALID NUMBER OF LINE SEGMENTS';
    LINES-PER-SECTION ← NUMBER-OF-LINES;
    FOR I = 1 TO NUMBER-OF-LINES DO
        BEGIN
            blending function values for the middle section
            U ← I / NUMBER-OF-LINES;
            BLEND[1, I] ← U * (U − 1) * (U − 2) / (−6);
            BLEND[2, I] ← (U + 1) * (U − 1) * (U − 2) / 2;
            BLEND[3, I] ← (U + 1) * U * (U − 2) / (−2);
            BLEND[4, I] ← (U + 1) * U * (U − 1) / 6;
            V ← U − 1;
            blending function values for the first section of the curve
            FIRST-BLEND[1, I] ← V * (V − 1) * (V − 2) / (−6);
            FIRST-BLEND[2, I] ← (V + 1) * (V − 1) * (V − 2) / 2;
            FIRST-BLEND[3, I] ← (V + 1) * V * (V − 2) / (−2);
            FIRST-BLEND[4, I] ← (V + 1) * V * (V − 1) / 6;
            W ← U + 1;
            blending function values for the last section of the curve
            LAST-BLEND[1, I] ← W * (W − 1) * (W − 2) / (−6);
            LAST-BLEND[2, I] ← (W + 1) * (W − 1) * (W − 2) / 2;
            LAST-BLEND[3, I] ← (W + 1) * W * (W − 2) / (−2);
            LAST-BLEND[4, I] ← (W + 1) * W * (W − 1) / 6;
        END;
    RETURN;
END;
```

The next routine which we shall write multiplies the sample points and blending
functions to give points on the approximation curve. These points are then connected
by line segments. The sample points are assumed to be in the global arrays XSM,
YSM, and ZSM, while the array of blending function values is passed as an argument.

11.3 Algorithm MAKE-CURVE(B) A routine to fill in a section of the curve

Argument   B a 4 by LINES-PER-SECTION array of blending function values
Global   LINES-PER-SECTION the number of line segments per curve section
             XSM, YSM, ZSM four-element arrays containing the sample points
Local   I for stepping through the four sample points
             J for stepping through the line segments of the curve section
             X, Y, Z the coordinates of a point on the approximation curve

```
BEGIN
    FOR J = 1 TO LINES-PER-SECTION DO
        BEGIN
            X ← 0;
            Y ← 0;
```

```
                    Z ← 0;
                 sum the contribution from each sample point
                 FOR I = 1 TO 4 DO
                    BEGIN
                        X ← X + XSM[I] * B[I, J];
                        Y ← Y + YSM[I] * B[I, J];
                        Z ← Z + ZSM[I] * B[I, J];
                    END;
                 draw the approximation line segment
                 LINE-ABS-3(X, Y, Z);
              END;
           RETURN;
        END;
```

After a section of the curve has been drawn, we will shift the sample points so that our blending functions can be applied to the next section. This is accomplished by the following routine.

11.4 Algorithm NEXT-SECTION Routine to shift the sample points to get ready for next curve section

Global   XSM, YSM, ZSM the four-element sample point arrays
Local   I a variable for stepping through the sample points

```
BEGIN
   FOR I = 1 TO 3 DO
      BEGIN
          XSM[I] ← XSM[I + 1];
          YSM[I] ← YSM[I + 1];
          ZSM[I] ← ZSM[I + 1];
      END;
   RETURN;
END;
```

To start drawing the curve, we require the first four sample points. With these point values, we can use the FIRST-BLEND and BLEND arrays to draw the first two curve sections. The START-CURVE algorithm does this. It expects as arguments arrays containing the first four sample points. It loads these points into the XSM, YSM, and ZSM arrays, the pen is positioned at the first sample point, and the MAKE-CURVE routine is used to draw the first two sections of the curve. The sample points are then shifted to prepare for drawing the next curve section.

11.5 Algorithm START-CURVE(XA, YA, ZA) User routine to start drawing a curve

Arguments   XA, YA, ZA four-element arrays containing the first four sample points
Global   XSM, YSM, ZSM four-element arrays for holding the sample points
               FIRST-BLEND, BLEND
               4 by LINES-PER-SECTION arrays containing blending function values
Local   I for stepping through the sample points

```
BEGIN
   load the sample points
   FOR I = 1 TO 4 DO
```

```
      BEGIN
          XSM[I] ← XA[I];
          YSM[I] ← YA[I];
          ZSM[I] ← ZA[I];
      END;
  move to the start of the curve
  MOVE-ABS-3(XA[1], YA[1], ZA[1]);
  draw the first two sections
  MAKE-CURVE(FIRST-BLEND);
  MAKE-CURVE(BLEND);
  prepare for the next section
  NEXT-SECTION;
  RETURN;
END;
```

Once the curve has been started, new sections can be added one at a time. (See Figure 11-5.)

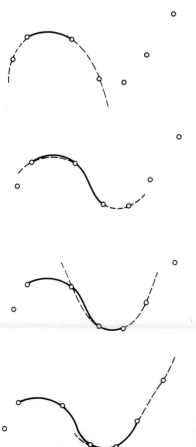

FIGURE 11-5
Drawing a curve by interpolating over consecutive four-point regions.

For each new sample point, a new section of the curve can be drawn; but since we are adding the fourth sample point while interpolating between the second and third sample points, the section of the curve being drawn always lags one sample point behind the points entered. The following is a utility routine to place a new sample point in the XSM, YSM, ZSM arrays.

11.6 Algorithm PUT-IN-SM(X, Y, Z) Routine to place a new sample point in the XSM, YSM, ZSM arrays
Arguments   X, Y, Z the new sample point
Global   XSM, YSM, ZSM four-element arrays for saving sample points
BEGIN
    XSM[4] ← X;
    YSM[4] ← Y;
    ZSM[4] ← Z;
    RETURN;
END;

The routine to extend the curve takes a new sample point as its argument and stores it in the XSM, YSM, ZSM arrays. It then uses the MAKE-CURVE routine to draw the next curve section. Finally, it shifts the sample points to make ready for the next curve section. The algorithm which does this is called CURVE-ABS-3.

11.7 Algorithm CURVE-ABS-3(X, Y, Z) User routine to extend the curve
Argument   X, Y, Z the new sample point for the curve
Global   BLEND 4 by LINES-PER-SECTION array of blending function values
BEGIN
    PUT-IN-SM(X, Y, Z);
    MAKE-CURVE(BLEND);
    NEXT-SECTION;
    RETURN;
END;

The curve may be extended as desired by repeated calls to CURVE-ABS-3, but when we are ready to end it, we must process the last section specially. This is done by the END-CURVE routine, which takes as an argument the last point on the curve. (See Figure 11-6.)

11.8 Algorithm END-CURVE(X, Y, Z) User routine to end a curve
Argument   X, Y, Z the last point on the curve.
Global   BLEND, LAST-BLEND
                  4 by LINES-PER-SECTION arrays containing blending function values
BEGIN
    PUT-IN-SM(X, Y, Z)
    MAKE-CURVE(BLEND);
    MAKE-CURVE(LAST-BLEND);
    RETURN;
END;

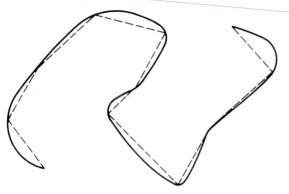

FIGURE 11-6
Interpolation smoothing.

INTERPOLATING POLYGONS

The sides of a polygon can also be rounded by means of our blending functions. In fact, a polygon is conceptually easier to deal with, since no special initial or final sections occur. We just step around the polygon, smoothing out each side by replacing it with several small line segments. We start out with a polygon that has only a few sides and end up with a polygon which has many more sides and appears smoother. (See Figure 11-7.)

The system will have some limit to the total number of sides a polygon can have. The algorithm SMOOTH-POLY-ABS-3 given below smooths a polygon. It assumes that a call has been made to the SET-SMOOTH routine to set up the proper BLEND array values and that the system is capable of handling the resulting polygons. The resulting polygon size will be the number of sides in the original polygon times the LINES-PER-SECTION factor. The algorithm steps through the sides of the original polygon and builds the new smoother polygon, which is drawn.

11.9 Algorithm SMOOTH-POLY-ABS-3(AX, AY, AZ, M) User routine to draw a smoothed polygon

Arguments   AX, AY, AZ arrays containing vertices of original polygon
             M the original number of polygon sides

Global   BLEND the array of blending function values
             LINES-PER-SECTION the number of line segments per original polygon side

Local   BX, BY, BZ arrays to hold smoothed polygon vertices
             NSIDES number of sides for the smoothed polygon
             J index variable for saving the smoothed polygon sides
             K to step through the small segments for each polygon side
             I, I1 variables for stepping through the four sample points
             L for stepping through the four blending functions

BEGIN
    IF M < 3 THEN RETURN ERROR 'POLYGON SIZE ERROR';
    NSIDES ← LINES-PER-SECTION * M;
    IF LINES-PER-SECTION = 1 THEN POLYGON-ABS-3(AX, AY, AZ, M)
    ELSE

```
          BEGIN
            J ← 1;
            FOR I1 = 1 TO M DO
              smooth all sides
              FOR K = 1 TO LINES-PER-SECTION DO
                smooth a side of the original polygon
                BEGIN
                  BX[J] ← 0;
                  BY[J] ← 0;
                  BZ[J] ← 0;
                  I ← I1;
                  FOR L = 1 TO 4 DO
                    one side of the smooth polygon
                    BEGIN
                      BX[J] ← BX[J] + AX[I] * BLEND[L, K];
                      BY[J] ← BY[J] + AY[I] * BLEND[L, K];
                      BZ[J] ← BZ[J] + AZ[I] * BLEND[L, K];
                      IF I = M THEN I ← 1 ELSE I ← I + 1;
                    END;
                  J ← J + 1;
                END;
              draw the result
              POLYGON-ABS-3(BX, BY, BZ, NSIDES);
            END;
          RETURN;
        END;
```

B SPLINES

Now that we have implemented a Lagrange interpolation program using our home-made blending functions, let's examine some of its inadequacies. One thing to notice is that the sum of the blending functions is not 1 at every value of u. The blending functions were designed to sum to 1 at integer values of u, but not at fractional values. What does this mean? Suppose that all sample points had the same x value, $x = x_0$.

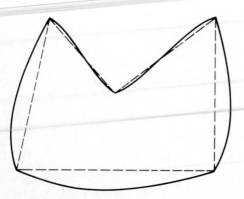

FIGURE 11-7
Smoothing of a polygon.

We would then desire the approximating curve to also have constant values for x at the points in between the sample points, but the approximating curve is

$$x = \sum_{i=1}^{n} x_i B_i(u) \tag{11.12}$$

which for $x_i = x_o$ gives

$$x = x_o \sum_{i=1}^{n} B_i(u) \tag{11.13}$$

We will get the flat behavior we desire only if the sum of the blending functions is 1 for all values of u. This shortcoming also means that curves which should lie in a plane may in fact wiggle in and out of the plane. This particular problem might be patched by dividing the blending function values calculated in SET-SMOOTH by their sum for each value of u, thereby normalizing the functions. But, alas, this is not the only problem. Each section of the curve is connected to the next section at a sample point, but the slopes of the two sections need not match at this point. This means that there can be corners at the sample points and that we may not have a completely smooth curve. Finally, in pulling the curve all the way over to pass through one of the sample points, we had to reduce the effect of all other points to zero; but as we leave the vicinity of the sample point, all points in the region have some control over the curve. Thus, we see the control of the curve by a sample point pulsing in and out as we move along in u.

A more natural behavior might be to have a sample point's control vary smoothly from zero far away from the point to a maximum near the point. We can do this if we don't try to force the curve through the sample point, but rather gently pull it into the neighborhood of the sample point. The result will be a curve which follows the general contours indicated by the sample points but may not actually pass through the points themselves. A set of blending functions which take this approach and also always sum to 1 are called *B splines*. They generate curve sections which have continuous slopes so that they fit together smoothly. (See Figure 11-8.)

The derivation of the B-spline functions is beyond the scope of this book, but we shall present and implement the *cubic B-spline* functions, which are adequate for most

FIGURE 11-8
Smoothing using B splines.

applications. The cubic B-spline blending functions interpolate over four sample points and are cubic polynomials in u, just as our homemade blending functions. The cubic B-spline functions for the middle of the curve are as follows:

$$B_1(u) = (1 - u)^3/6$$

$$B_2(u) = u^3/2 - u^2 + 2/3$$

$$B_3(u) = -u^3/2 + u^2/2 + u/2 + 1/6$$

$$B_4(u) = u^3/6$$

(11.14)

Starting or stopping the cubic B-spline blending functions requires two special curve sections. The following functions should be used for the very first section of the curve.

$$B_1'(u) = (1 - u)^3$$

$$B_2'(u) = 21u^3/12 - 9u^2/2 + 3u$$

$$B_3'(u) = -11u^3/12 + 3u^2/2$$

$$B_4'(u) = u^3/6$$

(11.15)

The last section of the curve would reverse these functions.

$$B_{1R}'(u) = B_4'(1 - u)$$

$$B_{2R}'(u) = B_3'(1 - u)$$

$$B_{3R}'(u) = B_2'(1 - u)$$

$$B_{4R}'(u) = B_1'(1 - u)$$

(11.16)

The second section of the curve also has special blending functions.

$$B_1''(u) = (1 - u)^3/4$$

$$B_2''(u) = 7u^3/12 - 5u^2/4 + u/4 + 7/12$$

$$B_3''(u) = -u^3/2 + u^2/2 + u/2 + 1/6$$

$$B_4''(u) = u^3/6$$

(11.17)

And the next-to-the-last section of the curve uses the reverse of these functions.

$$B_{1R}''(u) = B_4''(1 - u)$$

$$B_{2R}''(u) = B_3''(1 - u)$$

$$B_{3R}''(u) = B_2''(1 - u)$$

$$B_{4R}''(u) = B_1''(1 - u)$$

(11.18)

We can implement the B-spline curve-drawing method in the same way as we did our homemade blending functions. Instead of the SET-SMOOTH routine, we need an algorithm which will evaluate the five B-spline blending function groups. This is done by the SET-B-SPLINE routine. The order and form of calculation of the B-spline functions are such as to take advantage of expressions which appear more than once, to avoid repeated computation.

11.10 Algorithm SET-B-SPLINE(NUMBER-OF-LINES) User routine to set the number of line segments per curve section for B-spline interpolation

Argument	NUMBER-OF-LINES the number of line segments per curve section
Global	LINES-PER-SECTION storage for the NUMBER-OF-LINES value
	BLEND, FIRST-BLEND, SECOND-BLEND, NEXT-TO-LAST-BLEND, LAST-BLEND
	4 by MAX-NUMBER-OF-LINES arrays to store blending function values
Local	I, J to step through the needed curve points
	U for blending function evaluation
Constant	MAX-NUMBER-OF-LINES maximum line segments per curve section

```
BEGIN
    IF NUMBER-OF-LINES < 1
        OR NUMBER-OF-LINES > MAX-NUMBER-OF-LINES THEN
        RETURN ERROR 'INVALID NUMBER OF LINE SEGMENTS';
    LINES-PER-SECTION ← NUMBER-OF-LINES;
    FOR I = 1 TO NUMBER-OF-LINES DO
        BEGIN
            U ← I / NUMBER-OF-LINES;
            FIRST-BLEND[1, I] ← (1 − U) ↑ 3;
            FIRST-BLEND[4, I] ← (U ↑ 3) / 6;
            FIRST-BLEND[3, I] ← (3 / 2 − 11 * U / 12) * (U ↑ 2);
            FIRST-BLEND[2, I] ← 1 − FIRST-BLEND[1, I] − FIRST-BLEND[3, I]
                − FIRST-BLEND[4, I];
            SECOND-BLEND[1, I] ← FIRST-BLEND[1, I] / 4;
            SECOND-BLEND[4, I] ← FIRST-BLEND[4, I];
            SECOND-BLEND[3, I] ← (((1 − U) * U + 1) * U + 1 / 3) / 2;
            SECOND-BLEND[2, I] ← 1 − SECOND-BLEND[1, I]
                − SECOND-BLEND[3, I] − SECOND-BLEND[4, I];
            BLEND[1, I] ← FIRST-BLEND[1, I] / 6;
            BLEND[4, I] ← FIRST-BLEND[4, I];
            BLEND[3, I] ← SECOND-BLEND[3, I];
            BLEND[2, I] ← 1 − BLEND[1, I] − BLEND[3, I] − BLEND[4, I];
            J ← NUMBER-OF-LINES − I;
            IF J ≠ 0 THEN
                BEGIN
                    NEXT-TO-LAST-BLEND[1, J] ← SECOND-BLEND[4, I];
                    NEXT-TO-LAST-BLEND[2, J] ← SECOND-BLEND[3, I];
                    NEXT-TO-LAST-BLEND[3, J] ← SECOND-BLEND[2, I];
                    NEXT-TO-LAST-BLEND[4, J] ← SECOND-BLEND[1, I];
                    LAST-BLEND[1, J] ← FIRST-BLEND[4, I];
                    LAST-BLEND[2, J] ← FIRST-BLEND[3, I];
                    LAST-BLEND[3, J] ← FIRST-BLEND[2, I];
                    LAST-BLEND[4, J] ← FIRST-BLEND[1, I];
                END;
        END;
```

```
        NEXT-TO-LAST-BLEND[1, NUMBER-OF-LINES] ← 0;
        NEXT-TO-LAST-BLEND[2, NUMBER-OF-LINES] ← 1 / 6;
        NEXT-TO-LAST-BLEND[3, NUMBER-OF-LINES] ← 7 / 12;
        NEXT-TO-LAST-BLEND[4, NUMBER-OF-LINES] ← 1 / 4;
        LAST-BLEND[1, NUMBER-OF-LINES] ← 0;
        LAST-BLEND[2, NUMBER-OF-LINES] ← 0;
        LAST-BLEND[3, NUMBER-OF-LINES] ← 0;
        LAST-BLEND[4, NUMBER-OF-LINES] ← 1;
        RETURN;
    END;
```

To start the B-spline curve, we require the first five sample points. As with our first blending function, we start the curve by loading the sample points into the XSM, YSM, ZSM arrays and calling the MAKE-CURVE routine with the special-starting blending functions. The following algorithm starts the B-spline curve.

11.11 Algorithm START-B-SPLINE(AX, AY, AZ) User routine to start a B-spline interpolation curve

Arguments   AX, AY, AZ five-element arrays containing the first five points
Global   XSM, YSM, ZSM four-element arrays for passing sample points
            FIRST-BLEND, SECOND-BLEND
            4 by LINES-PER-SECTION arrays containing blending function values
Local   I for stepping through sample points

```
BEGIN
    FOR I = 1 TO 4 DO
        BEGIN
            XSM[I] ← AX[I];
            YSM[I] ← AY[I];
            ZSM[I] ← AZ[I];
        END;
    MOVE-ABS-3(AX[1], AY[1], AZ[1]);
    MAKE-CURVE[FIRST-BLEND];
    NEXT-SECTION;
    PUT-IN-SM(AX[5], AY[5], AZ[5]);
    MAKE-CURVE[SECOND-BLEND];
    NEXT-SECTION;
    RETURN;
END;
```

Once the curve has been started, it can be continued by calling the CURVE-ABS-3 routine. Each call of CURVE-ABS-3 adds another section to the curve.

To terminate the B-spline curve, we must draw the last two sections. This is done by the END-B-SPLINE routine. This routine takes as arguments the last two sample points for the curve. It processes these points using the NEXT-TO-LAST-BLEND and LAST-BLEND blending function values.

11.12 Algorithm END-B-SPLINE(X1, Y1, Z1, X2, Y2, Z2) User routine to terminate a B-spline curve

Arguments   X1, Y1, Z1 the next-to-the-last sample point
            X2, Y2, Z2 the last sample point

Global   NEXT-TO-LAST-BLEND, LAST-BLEND
                 4 by LINES-PER-SECTION arrays of blending function values
BEGIN
    PUT-IN-SM(X1, Y1, Z1);
    MAKE-CURVE(NEXT-TO-LAST-BLEND);
    NEXT-SECTION;
    PUT-IN-SM(X2, Y2, Z2);
    MAKE-CURVE(LAST-BLEND);
    RETURN;
END;

The special B-spline blending functions used at the beginning (and end) of the curve cause the curve to begin (end) at the first (last) sample point. So the curve will be attached to the first and last sample points. Also, the slope of the curve at the endpoints is equal to the slope of the line segment connecting the first and second (next-to-last and last) sample points.

The B-spline blending function can also be used to smooth polygons. To do so, we need only call SET-B-SPLINE instead of SET-SMOOTH before calling the SMOOTH-POLY-ABS-3 routine. (See Figure 11-9.)

B SPLINES AND CORNERS

The B-spline blending functions were designed to eliminate sharp corners in the curve, and the curve does not usually pass through sample points. However, a sharp corner and passage through a sample point can be produced in a B-spline curve, if desired. The way that this is done is to use several identical sample points. The call

CURVE-ABS-3(X0, Y0, Z0)

produces one sample point at (X0, Y0, Z0), pulling the curve in that direction. (See Figure 11-10a.)

The two calls

CURVE-ABS-3(X0, Y0, Z0)
CURVE-ABS-3(X0, Y0, Z0)

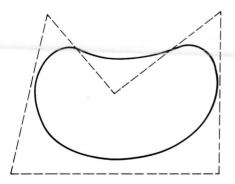

FIGURE 11-9
Smoothing a polygon using B splines.

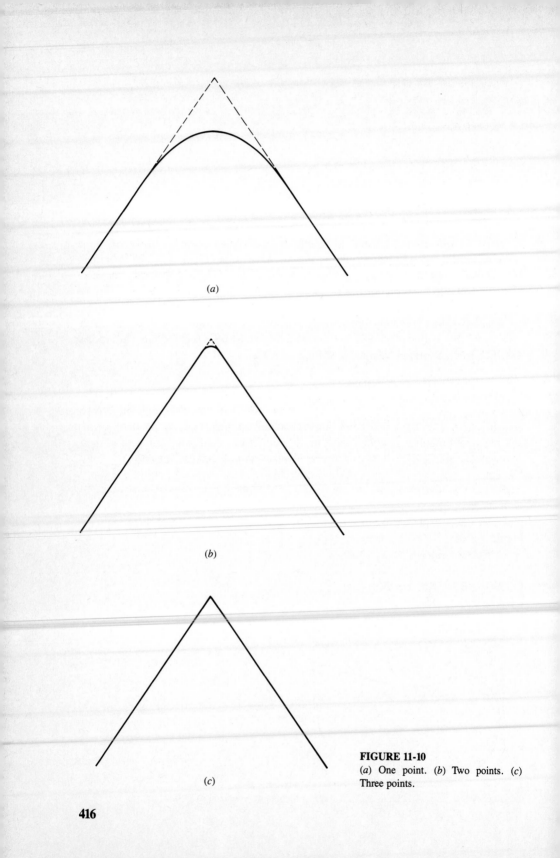

(a)

(b)

(c)

FIGURE 11-10
(a) One point. (b) Two points. (c) Three points.

produce two sample points, both pulling the curve to the same place. The curve will be pulled closer to this point, and the corner will be a little sharper. (See Figure 11-10*b*.)

If three identical sample points are used,

CURVE-ABS-3(X0, Y0, Z0)
CURVE-ABS-3(X0, Y0, Z0)
CURVE-ABS-3(X0, Y0, Z0)

the curve will be forced through this point. (See Figure 11-10*c*.)

Blending-function interpolation and approximation by small straight-line segments allow us to draw curves which may not have simple mathematical forms. The technique also lets us use the simple straight-line transformation and clipping methods which we have developed. The major drawback of this technique is the amount of display-file storage required. For each sample point, 5 or 10 small line segments may be produced, so care must be taken to assure sufficient display-file storage when curves are drawn.

CURVED SURFACE PATCHES

We have seen a way of specifying curved lines with B splines. We use a set of sample points or control points and the B-spline blending functions to determine points on the curve. This method can be generalized to describe curved surfaces such as airplane wings or car fenders. To describe a surface we shall need a grid of control points (x_{ij}, y_{ij}, z_{ij}). (See Figure 11-11.)

Stepping through i moves one direction on the grid, while changing j moves in the other direction. Such a grid can be used to define patches which will fit together to form a smooth surface, just as we previously defined curve sections which fit together to make the curve.

The coordinate values for points on the surface of a patch are given by

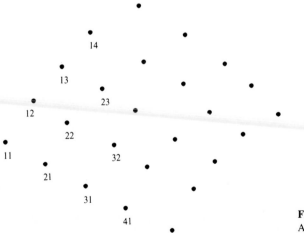

FIGURE 11-11
A grid of control points.

$$x = fx(u, v) = \sum_{i=1}^{n} \sum_{j=1}^{m} x_{ij}B_i(u)B_j(v)$$

$$y = fy(u, v) = \sum_{i=1}^{n} \sum_{j=1}^{m} y_{ij}B_i(u)B_j(v) \qquad (11.19)$$

$$z = fz(u, v) = \sum_{i=1}^{n} \sum_{j=1}^{m} z_{ij}B_i(u)B_j(v)$$

There are two parameters which specify the position on the surface patch, u and v. Just as for curves, each varies from 0 to 1. Changing u will cause movement along the patch in the same direction as changing i on the grid of control points. Changing v moves in the same direction as changing j.

As with curves, we can move from one patch to the next by simply relabeling the control points. For bicubic surface patches (cubic splines in both directions), the B functions are those presented in Equations 11.14 through 11.18. The special functions 11.15 through 11.18 are used at the boundary of the overall surface. They should be used for B_i when the patch is first or second (last or next-to-last) in the i direction on the grid, and similarly for B_j and the j direction.

To represent a curved surface on a display, we must either rely on shading techniques or show the curves which result from lines drawn on the surface. (See Figure 11-12.)

For example, for a given patch

$$x = fx(u, v), \qquad y = fy(u, v), \qquad z = fz(u, v) \qquad (11.20)$$

we can draw the curves resulting from fixing v at a constant and letting u vary from 0 to 1. We could draw the curves for several values of v. Similarly, we could draw curves for fixed values of u, letting v change from 0 to 1. Notice that for this means of display, our B-spline curve-drawing algorithms suffice. If x for the surface is given by

$$x = \sum_{i=1}^{n} \sum_{j=1}^{m} x_{ij}B_i(u)B_j(v) \qquad (11.21)$$

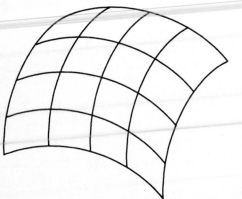

FIGURE 11-12
Displaying a curved surface patch.

and v is held constant at v_c, then $B_j(v_c)$ is a constant, so we can write

$$x = \sum_{i=1}^{n} [\sum_{j=1}^{m} x_{ij}B_i(v)]B_i(u)$$

$$(11.22)$$

$$= \sum_{i=1}^{n} \hat{x}_i B_i(u)$$

where

$$\hat{x}_1 = \sum_{j=1}^{m} x_{ij}B_j(v_c)$$

$$(11.23)$$

This is just the expression used for the B-spline curve, provided the control point at each i is replaced by the weighted sum over j of the grid points with index i. Thus for a fixed v_c, we can find the values of $B_j(v_c)$, perform the weighted sum of grid points in the j direction to determine $\hat{x}_i$ values, and use these as the control points in our curve-drawing routines. Of course, the same thing can be done for the y and z coordinates.

If we wish to employ shading to display the curved surface, one approach is to approximate the surface with a number of flat polygons. Each polygon can have a slightly different direction and shade. We have already developed the machinery for shading flat polygons, so the only thing new is the automatic decomposition of the curved surface into a patchwork of flat surfaces. This is analogous to approximating a curved path by a series of straight-line segments. One thought would be to find the rectangular polygons formed by lines of constant u and v. But there is no guarantee that four corner points of a small rectangular patch will all lie in the same plane (in fact, they probably won't). This may not bother us; if the patch is small, the points may be nearly planar and the shading software may not require planar points. An alternative is to decompose the surface into triangular pieces. Triangles are necessarily planar. Let's outline one method for converting to triangles. We have a unit square in the uv parameter space which generates the surface patch. We first imagine the diagonal (0, 0) to (1, 1) on this unit square. (See Figure 11-13.) This divides the square into two triangles. The second step is to find a rule which divides a triangle into smaller triangles. The rule is to find the midpoints of each of the three sides of the triangle and to con-

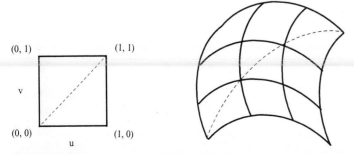

FIGURE 11-13
Form two triangles in uv parameter space.

nect them. This divides the triangle into four smaller triangles. (See Figure 11-14.) We can recursively apply this rule to break up the uv area into a mesh of small triangles. Finally, we can use the vertices of the uv triangles in our B-spline surface equations to find the corresponding xyz points. (See Figure 11-15.) These points form triangles which can be shaded and entered into the display file.

BEZIER CURVES

Now let's discuss a different curve construction called a *Bezier curve*. This is not so much a different curve as it is a different way of specifying the curve. In fact, the same shapes can be described by B splines and Bezier curves. We shall restrict our attention to the cubic Bezier curve, which is adequate for most graphics applications. The cubic Bezier curve requires four control points. These points completely specify the curve. Unlike the B-spline curve, we cannot add additional points and smoothly extend the cubic Bezier curve, but we can pick four more points and construct a second curve which can be attached to the first. And if we are careful in our choice of the points, we can make the second curve join the first curve smoothly.

A Bezier curve and its control points are shown in Figure 11-16. Note that the curve begins at the first control point and ends on the fourth. This means that if we want to connect two Bezier curves, we just make the first control point of the second curve match the last control point of the first curve. Note also that at the start of the curve, it is tangent to the line connecting the first and second control points. Likewise, at the end of the curve, it is tangent to the line connecting the third and fourth control points. That means that if we want to join two Bezier curves smoothly, we must arrange for the third and fourth control points of the first curve to be on the same line as the first and second control points of the second curve.

Equations describing the Bezier curve are as follows:

$$x = x_4u^3 + 3x_3u^2(1-u) + 3x_2u(1-u)^2 + x_1(1-u)^3$$

$$y = y_4u^3 + 3y_3u^2(1-u) + 3y_2u(1-u)^2 + y_1(1-u)^3 \qquad (11.24)$$

$$z = z_4u^3 + 3z_3u^2(1-u) + 3z_2u(1-u)^2 + z_1(1-u)^3$$

In these expressions, as u goes from 0 to 1, the curve goes from the first to the fourth control point. (This is a bit different from our previous curves, where we only covered

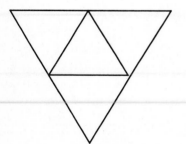

FIGURE 11-14
Subdivide triangles by connecting midpoints.

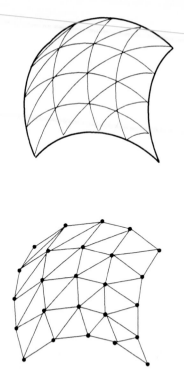

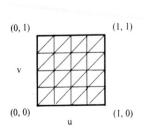

FIGURE 11-15
Approximate the surface with a grid of triangles.

the region between two control points when the parameter changed from 0 to 1.) From the expression, we could extract the blending functions for the Bezier curve and proceed as we did above; however, one of the most amazing things about Bezier curves is that they can be constructed without reference to the above defining equations. In fact, a Bezier curve can be constructed simply by taking midpoints. Consider Figure 11-17. We have drawn the lines connecting the four control points A, B, C, and D. We have determined the midpoints of these segments AB, BC, and CD. We connect these midpoints with line segments and find their midpoints ABC and BCD. Finally, we connect these two points and find the midpoint ABCD. Now the point ABCD is on the Bezier curve. It divides the curve into two sections. Furthermore, the points A, AB, ABC, and ABCD are the control points for the first section and the points ABCD, BCD, CD, and D are the control points for the second section. Thus by taking midpoints, we can find a point on the curve and also split the curve into two pieces complete with control points. We can continue to split the curve into smaller sections until we have sections so short that they can be replaced by straight lines, or even until the sections are no bigger than individual pixels.

Algorithms for adding Bezier curves to our system are given below. They assume that the first control point is at the current pen position, so only three additional points must be specified. They use the recursive subdivision approach.

FIGURE 11-16
A cubic Bezier spline.

11.13 Algorithm BEZIER-ABS-3(XB, YB, ZB, XC, YC, ZC, XD, YD, ZD, N) Adds
a Bezier curve section to the display file

Arguments XB, YB, ZB, XC, YC, ZC, XD, YD, ZD control points
               N the desired degree of subdivision

Global   DF-PEN-X, DF-PEN-Y, DF-PEN-Z the current pen position

Local   XAB, YAB, ZAB, XBC, YBC, ZBC, XCD, YCD, ZCD first-level mid-
              points
              XABC, YABC, ZABC, XBCD, YBCD, ZBCD second-level midpoints
              XABCD, YABCD, ZABCD third-level midpoint

BEGIN
  IF N = 0 THEN
    BEGIN
      LINE-ABS-3(XB, YB, ZB);
      LINE-ABS-3(XC, YC, ZC);
      LINE-ABS-3(XD, YD, ZD);
    END
  ELSE
    BEGIN
      XAB ← (DF-PEN-X + XB) / 2;
      YAB ← (DF-PEN-Y + YB) / 2;
      ZAB ← (DF-PEN-Z + ZB) / 2;
      XBC ← (XB + XC) / 2;

```
            YBC ← (YB + YC) / 2;
            ZBC ← (ZB + ZC) / 2;
            XCD ← (XC + XD) / 2;
            YCD ← (YC + YD) / 2;
            ZCD ← (ZC + ZD) / 2;
            XABC ← (XAB + XBC) / 2;
            YABC ← (YAB + YBC) / 2;
            ZABC ← (ZAB + ZBC) / 2;
            XBCD ← (XBC + XCD) / 2;
            YBCD ← (YBC + YCD) / 2;
            ZBCD ← (ZBC + ZCD) / 2;
            XABCD ← (XABC + XBCD) / 2;
            YABCD ← (YABC + YBCD) / 2;
            ZABCD ← (ZABC + ZBCD) / 2;
            BEZIER-ABS-3(XAB, YAB, ZAB, XABC, YABC, ZABC, XABCD,
                YABCD, ZABCD, N − 1);
            BEZIER-ABS-3(XBCD, YBCD, ZBCD, XCD, YCD, ZCD, XD, YD, ZD,
                N − 1);
        END;
    RETURN;
END;
```

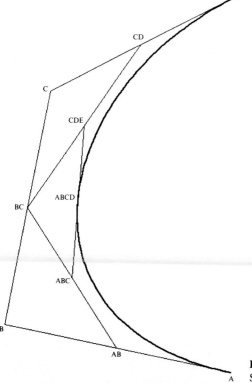

FIGURE 11-17
Subdivision of a Bezier spline.

Bezier curves satisfy the *convex hull* property. This means that the curve lies within the boundary formed by an elastic band stretched over all four of the control points. This property is useful in clipping tests.

Like B splines, the Bezier curves can be extended to surfaces. We can construct a bicubic Bezier surface from a 4×4 grid of control points. Recursive subdivision can be used to draw such patches by repeatedly quartering them until they may be replaced by polygons or pixels.

FRACTALS

Man-made or artificial objects usually have either flat surfaces, which can be described with polygons, or smooth curved surfaces, which we have just studied. But objects occurring in nature often have rough, jagged, random edges. Attempting to draw things like mountains, trees, rivers, or lightning bolts directly with lines or polygons requires a lot of specification. It is desirable to let the machine do the work of specifying the jagged lines. We would like to give the machine two endpoints and let the machine draw a jagged line between them (say for the path of a lightning bolt). Not just any jagged line will do; we want a line which closely approximates the behavior of nature, so it will look right. It is only recently that we have been able to do this because it is only recently that a branch of mathematics has been developed to describe such rough structures. They are called *fractals*, and in this section we shall give an introduction to what a fractal is and provide sample algorithms for generating them.

We begin with a discussion of dimension. Imagine that an object is composed of elastic or clay. If the object can be deformed into a line or line segment, we give it dimension $D_t = 1$. If it deforms into a plane or halfplane or a disk (as would a square), we give it dimension $D_t = 2$. And if it deforms into all space or half-space or into a ball, we give it dimension $D_t = 3$. We call D_t the *topological dimension*.

Now let's develop a second measure of an object's dimension. Imagine taking a line segment of length L and dividing it into N identical pieces, each of length $l = L/N$. The pieces each look like the original, only scaled by a factor $1/s = l \, / \, L$. To assemble the original line segment from the segments scaled by $1/s$, we must add together

$$N = s^1 \tag{11.25}$$

of them. (Pretty easy so far; we just said if you divide a line into N pieces, it takes N pieces to put it back together.) So next let's consider a square. If we scale it down by $1/s$, we will get a small square. How many small squares does it take to rebuild the original? In the case of $s = 2$, it takes 4 squares, and for $s = 3$ it takes 9. In general we have

$$N = s^2 \tag{11.26}$$

For a cube, if we scale by $1/s$, we find that the number of small cubes needed to assemble a large cube is

$$N = s^3 \tag{11.27}$$

So we see a relationship. In going from line to square to cube, the exponent goes from 1 to 2 to 3. The exponent is measuring the dimension. So we can write the following

definition for dimension. If we scale an object by s and must assemble N of them to re-
construct the full-sized object, then the dimension D of the object is given by the relation

$$N = s^D \tag{11.28}$$

We shall call D the fractal dimension. Solving for D gives

$$D = \log N / \log s \tag{11.29}$$

Now let's consider a rather strange construction call a *Peano curve* or space-filling curve. The particular Peano curve we shall focus on is called *Hilbert's curve*. This
curve can be built by the following successive approximations. Begin with a square.
The first approximation will be to divide the square into 4 quadrants and draw the
curve which connects the center points of each. (See Figure 11-18.)

The second approximation will be to further subdivide each of the quadrants and
connect the centers of each of these finer divisions before moving to the next major
quadrant. (See Figure 11-19.)

The third approximation subdivides again. It again connects the centers of the
finest level before stepping to the next level of detail. (See Figure 11-20.)

Now we can imagine continuing this process indefinitely. What will the final result look like? For one thing, the curve never crosses itself. At each subdivision, the
curve fills smaller quadrants, but never crosses into an area where it already exists.
Another interesting fact is that the curve is arbitrarily close to every point in the
square. The curve passes through the points on a grid, which becomes twice as fine
with each subdivision, and there is no limit to the subdivisions. The curve fills the
square. One more fact is that the length of the curve is infinite. With each subdivision,
the length increases by a factor of 4. Since we imagine no limit to the subdivisions,
there is also no limit to the length. So we have constructed a curve which is topologi-
cally equivalent to a line $D_t = 1$, but the curve has been so twisted and folded that it
exactly fills up a square. We can find the fractal dimension of the curve. At each sub-

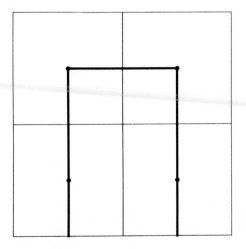

FIGURE 11-18
The first approximation to Hilbert's curve.

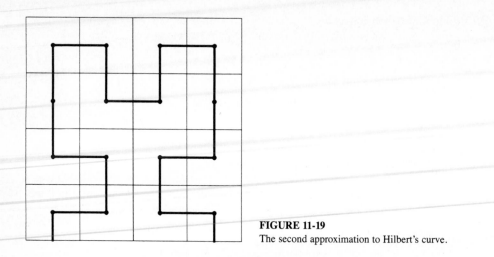

FIGURE 11-19
The second approximation to Hilbert's curve.

division the scale changes by 2, but the length changes by 4. Just as for the square, it takes 4 curves of half scale to build the full-sized object, so the dimension D given by

$$4 = 2^D \tag{11.30}$$

must be D = 2. The Hilbert curve has topological dimension 1 but fractal dimension 2. It is a line so folded that it behaves like a two-dimensional object.

Now let's look at one more strange curve called the *triadic Koch curve*. Begin with a line segment. Divide it into thirds and replace the center third by the two adjacent sides of an equilateral triangle. (See Figure 11-21.) This gives us a curve which begins and ends at the same place as the original segment but is built of 4 equal length segments, each 1/3 the original length. So the new curve has 4/3 the length of the original segment. Repeat the process for each of the 4 segments. (See Figure 11-22.) The curve has gained more wiggles, and its length is now 16/9 times the original. Now

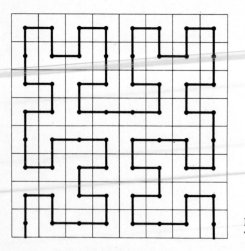

FIGURE 11-20
The third approximation to Hilbert's curve.

imagine repeating the replacements indefinitely. Since each repetition increases the length by a factor of 4/3, the length of the curve will be infinite, but it is folded in lots of tiny wiggles. Unlike the Peano curve, it does not fill an area. In fact, it does not deviate very much from its original shape. Its topological dimension is 1, but what will its fractal dimension be?

If we reduce the scale by 3, we find a curve that looks just like the original; but we must assemble 4 such curves to make the original, so we have

$$4 = 3^D \tag{11.31}$$

Solving this for the fractal dimension gives

$$D = \log_3 4 = \log 4 \,/\, \log 3 = 1.2618 \tag{11.32}$$

We get a nonintegral dimension! The curve acts like something between 1 and 2 dimensions. This is all great fun, and it has led us to the definition of a fractal. Point sets, curves, and surfaces which give a fractal dimension (a *Hausdorff Besicovitch* dimension, to be precise) that is greater than the topological dimension are called fractals. The Hilbert curve and the Koch curve are fractals because their fractal dimensions (respectively, 2 and 1.2618) are greater than their topological dimension of 1.

Nearly all the fractals which are of interest are *self-similar* under some change in scale, either strictly, as in the case of Peano and Koch curves, or statistically. As an example of a statistically self-similar fractal, consider a map of some coastline. The coastline will have a number of wiggles, bays, and peninsulas. Now if we look more carefully at the coastline, we will see a number of small variations which the mapmaker smoothed out. If we take a small section of the coast and map it more carefully (using a finer scale), we will again see wiggles, bays, and peninsulas. Furthermore, the shape and distribution of these wiggles will be the same as for the original map so that we cannot tell just by looking at the map what scale was used. The locations of the wiggles will, of course, be different, but their distribution (their likelihood) will be the same. Coastlines are one example of fractals found in nature. They typically have fractal dimension of about 1.15 to 1.25. There are many other examples. Bends and branches in rivers, bursts of noise in transmission lines, clustering of stars, craters on the moon, shapes of snowflakes, mountain landscapes, eddies and turbulence, branching of trees, lightning bolts, and many other phenomenon have been expressed as fractals.

FRACTAL LINES

We can use the computer to easily generate self-similar fractal curves. The self-similar drawing can be done by a self-referencing procedure (a recursive procedure). A curve

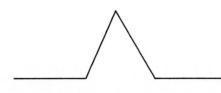

FIGURE 11-21
The replacement for a line segment for the triadic Koch curve.

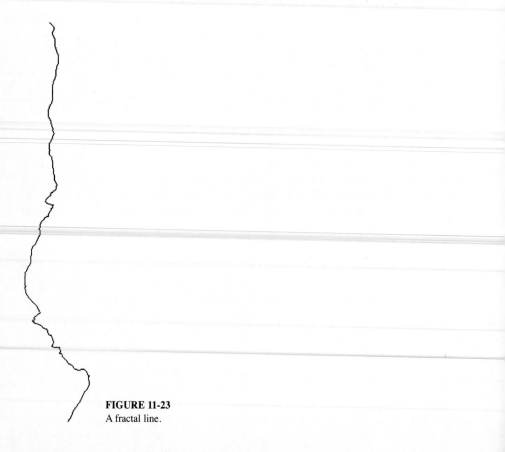

FIGURE 11-22
The second approximation to the Koch curve.

which is composed of N self-similar pieces, each scaled by 1/s, can be drawn by a routine which calls itself N times with arguments scaled by 1/s. Of course, a computer routine should terminate, which a true fractal does not. In the computer routine, each recursive call has smaller arguments, that is, smaller lengths. There will be some point where the lengths become smaller than the size of a pixel. There is not much point in continuing the recursion beyond this since the wiggles will be smaller than a pixel and cannot be displayed. So the computer procedures can terminate when lengths become less than a pixel and still provide the computer's best approximation to the fractal.

Being able to use the computer to generate fractal curves means that the user can easily generate realistic coastlines or mountain peaks or lightning bolts without concern for all the small bends and wiggles. The computer can generate the wiggles, and the user need only give the endpoints. So let's write a simple fractal line-drawing algorithm for a statistically self-similar curve. (See Figure 11-23.) Start by looking at the

FIGURE 11-23
A fractal line.

halfway point for the fractal line. If we had a perfectly straight line between (x_1, y_1, z_1) and (x_2, y_2, z_2) the halfway point would be the midpoint

$$\left(\frac{x_1 + x_2}{2}, \frac{y_1 + y_2}{2}, \frac{z_1 + z_2}{2} \right) \tag{11.33}$$

But for our fractal line, the halfway point will probably be offset a little from this, so we add an offset term to each coordinate. (See Figure 11-24.)

$$\left(\frac{x_1 + x_2}{2} + dx, \frac{y_1 + y_2}{2} + dy, \frac{z_1 + z_2}{2} + dz \right) \tag{11.34}$$

In order to get the random effect, the amount of the offset should be chosen at random. The offset is calculated as

$$dx = L * W * GAUSS \tag{11.35}$$

Identical expressions give dy and dz. The variable L is the length of the segment. The W is a weighting function governing the curve roughness (and fractal dimension). The function GAUSS returns a Gaussian variable with 0 mean. That means that (a) about half the values returned are positive and the other half are negative and (b) numbers greatly different than 0 are much less likely to appear than those near 0. The Gaussian distribution describes the way things often cluster around an average (such as the way people's height varies from average height). The pseudo-random number function (RND) available with many programming languages is usually a uniform distribution; any number between 0 and 1 is equally likely to occur. This is not what we need, but an approximate Gaussian distribution can be derived from it as shown in algorithm 11.16. The offset calculation says that the halfway point for the fractal line differs from the ideal midpoint according to the laws of chance. The scale factor tells how strongly the line tends to deviate. So far, we just have a line with a corner in it, not a full fractal line, but to further bend it we just recursively apply our method to find halfway points for each subsegment. The recursion continues until the segments become too small to matter.

We can see that this results in a fractal curve because it can be divided into two pieces (N = 2), each piece being statistically similar to the original and having a length averaging a bit greater than half the original length. The dimension will be a bit greater than 1. The greater W, the rougher the curve; and the greater the length, the smaller the value of s by which it must be scaled to give the original. We see that increasing W will increase the fractal dimension.

Algorithm 11.14 presents a procedure for drawing a fractal line segment from the current position to the specified point. It requires as arguments the endpoint, a weight

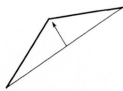

FIGURE 11-24
Offset the halfway point.

factor, and the desired recursion depth. An alternative implementation might determine the appropriate depth of recursion automatically by determining when the midpoint offset is probably less than a pixel. To be really correct, we should multiply the weight W by the length of each segment for each recursive call; but for the sake of efficiency, we shall perform the multiplication only once at the start (and with an approximation to the length) and then assume that at each level the length is close to half the previous length so that we can just divide by 2.

11.14 Algorithm FRACTAL-LINE-ABS-3 (X, Y, Z, W, N, FSEED) User routine for drawing fractal lines

Arguments   X, Y, Z the point to which to draw the line
            W describes the roughness of the curve
            N the desired depth of recursion
            FSEED seed for fractal pattern
Global   DF-PEN-X, DF-PEN-Y, DF-PEN-Z current pen position
            SEED the seed used by the random number generator
Local   L the approximate line length
BEGIN
        SEED ← FSEED;
        L ← | X − DF-PEN-X | + | Y − DF-PEN-Y| + | Z − DF-PEN-Z |;
        FRACTAL-SUBDIVIDE(DF-PEN-X, DF-PEN-Y, DF-PEN-Z, X, Y, Z, L ∗ W, N);
END;

The SEED is a number given to the random number generator. It is assumed that RND not only returns a random number calculated from SEED but also alters the value of SEED so that on the next call a different random number will be returned. The reason for giving the SEED value as an argument is that the particular shape of the fractal will depend upon the initial seed used. This means that if we wished to draw two similar fractals at different positions (for example, to represent the edges of each half of a torn piece of paper), we could do so by calling our fractal-drawing routine twice, with arguments the same except for the start and endpoints.

The routine which actually does most of the work is the following:

11.15 Algorithm FRACTAL-SUBDIVIDE(X1, Y1, Z1, X2, Y2, Z2, S, N) Draws a fractal line between points X1, Y1, Z1 and X2, Y2, Z2

Arguments   X1, Y1, Z1 the point to start the line
            X2, Y2, Z2 the point to stop the line
            S offset scale factor
            N the desired depth of recursion
Local   XMID, YMID, ZMID coordinates at which to break the line
BEGIN
    IF N = 0 THEN
        BEGIN
            recursion stops, so just draw the line segment
            LINE-ABS-3(X2, Y2, Z2)
        END
    ELSE

```
  BEGIN
     calculate the halfway point
     XMID ← (X1 + X2) / 2 + S * GAUSS;
     YMID ← (Y1 + Y2) / 2 + S * GAUSS;
     YMID ← (Y1 + Y2) / 2 + S * GAUSS;
     draw the two halves
     FRACTAL-SUBDIVIDE(X1, Y1, Z1, XMID, YMID, ZMID, S/2, N − 1);
     FRACTAL-SUBDIVIDE(XMID, YMID, ZMID, X2, Y2, Z2, S/2, N − 1);
  END;
RETURN;
END;
```

We approximate a Gaussian distribution by averaging several uniformly random numbers. Half the numbers are added and half subtracted to provide for zero mean.

11.16 Algorithm GAUSS Calculates an approximate Gaussian distribution between − 1 and 1.

```
Local      I for summing samples
BEGIN
   GAUSS ← 0;
   FOR I = 1 TO 6 DO GAUSS ← GAUSS + RND − RND;
   GAUSS ← GAUSS / 6;
   RETURN;
END;
```

As in the case of curves, we have implemented the FRACTAL-LINE-ABS-3 algorithm so that it breaks up the fractal into straight-line segments and then places them into the display file. The advantage of this is that all of the clipping and transformation machinery can be applied. The disadvantage is that a large display file is needed to hold all of the tiny line segments, and time must be spent processing each of them. For some applications it may be better to process the fractal when it is removed from the display file and not deal with all of the pieces until they are actually displayed. If this approach were to be taken, then the seed values for the fractal would have to be stored as part of the display-file entry.

FRACTAL SURFACES

A fractal line is fine for the path of a lightning bolt, but for something like a three-dimensional mountain range, we need a fractal surface. There are several ways to extend the fractal idea to surfaces. The one we shall present is based on triangles. Given three vertex points in space, we shall generate a fractal surface for the area between them. There are methods for decomposing arbitrary polygons into triangles, so the method can be used to cover more general shapes. The idea is as follows: Consider each edge of the triangle. We can imagine a fractal line along each edge and compute its halfway point by the same means as we used for fractal lines. (See Figure 11-25.)

Now by connecting these halfway points with line segments, we can subdivide the surface into four smaller triangles. (See Figure 11-26.) We can then recursively

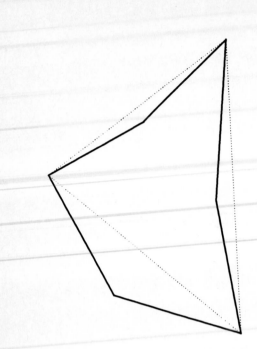

FIGURE 11-25
Find the halfway point (with offset) for each of the triangle sides.

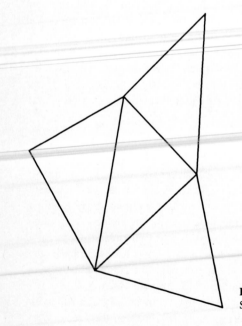

FIGURE 11-26
Subdivide the triangle into smaller triangles.

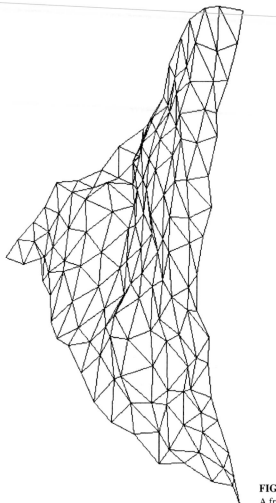

FIGURE 11-27
A fractal surface.

apply the method to each of the small triangles to subdivide the surface even further. We can continue this subdivision until the triangles are too small to matter. (See Figure 11-27.)

The algorithm presented is not very efficient in that it calculates each point twice (once for each of the triangles which border on it). Care must be taken with the seed values to ensure that the same fractal edge is generated for the two bordering triangles.

11.17 Algorithm FRACTAL-SURFACE(AX, AY, AZ, ASEED, W, N) Creates a fractal surface from a triangle
Arguments   AX, AY, AZ three-element arrays containing the triangle vertices

ASEED, a three-element array of seeds for the fractal patterns of the three triangle sides
W fractal roughness weight
N recursion depth

Local   L1, L2, L3 for the approximate lengths of the triangle sides

BEGIN

$$L1 = |AX[2] - AX[1]| + |AY[2] - AY[1]| + |AZ[2] - AZ[1]|;$$
$$L2 = |AX[3] - AX[2]| + |AY[3] - AY[2]| + |AZ[3] - AZ[2]|;$$
$$L3 = |AX[1] - AX[3]| + |AY[1] - AY[3]| + |AZ[1] - AZ[3]|;$$

FRACTAL-SURFACE-SUBDIVIDE(AX[1], AY[1], AZ[1], ASEED[1], L1 $*$ W,
                  AX[2], AY[2], AZ[2], ASEED[2], L2 $*$ W,
                  AX[3], AY[3], AZ[3], ASEED[3], L3 $*$ W, N, 1);

    RETURN;
END;

This is just a setup routine; the actual subdivision work is done in algorithm FRACTAL-SURFACE-SUBDIVIDE.

11.18 Algorithm FRACTAL-SURFACE-SUBDIVIDE(X1, Y1, Z1, S1, W1, X2, Y2, Z2, S2, W2, X3, Y3, Z3, S3, W3, N, DIR) Generates a fractal triangle

Arguments   X1, Y1, Z1, X2, Y2, Z2, X3, Y3, Z3 the three vertices of the triangle
                  S1, S2, S3 seed values for the fractal patterns of the three sides
                  W1, W2, W3 roughness weights times the lengths
                  N recursion depth
                  DIR direction indicator for drawing the triangle

Global   SEED the random number generator seed
                  DF-PEN-X, DF-PEN-Y, DF-PEN-Z the current pen position

Local   X12, Y12, Z12, X23, Y23, Z23, X31, Y31, Z31 coordinates of the division points

BEGIN
  IF N = 0 THEN
    BEGIN
      recursion stops, so draw the triangle
      DF-PEN-X ← X3;
      DF-PEN-Y ← Y3;
      DF-PEN-Z ← Z3;
      DISPLAY-FILE-ENTER(3);
      IF DIR > 0 THEN
        BEGIN
          LINE-ABS-3(X1, Y1, Z1);
          LINE-ABS-3(X2, Y2, Z2);
          LINE-ABS-3(X3, Y3, Z3);
        END
      ELSE
        BEGIN
          LINE-ABS-3(X2, Y2, Z2);
          LINE-ABS-3(X1, Y1, Z1);
          LINE-ABS-3(X3, Y3, Z3);
        END;

```
            END
      ELSE
            BEGIN
                  calculate the halfway points
                  SEED ← S1;
                  X12 ← (X1 + X2) / 2 + W1 * GAUSS;
                  Y12 ← (Y1 + Y2) / 2 + W1 * GAUSS;
                  Z12 ← (Z1 + Z2) / 2 + W1 * GAUSS;
                  SEED ← S2;
                  X23 ← (X2 + X3) / 2 + W2 * GAUSS;
                  Y23 ← (Y2 + Y3) / 2 + W2 * GAUSS;
                  Z23 ← (Z2 + Z3) / 2 + W2 * GAUSS;
                  SEED ← S3;
                  X31 ← (X3 + X1) / 2 + W3 * GAUSS;
                  Y31 ← (Y3 + Y1) / 2 + W3 * GAUSS;
                  Z31 ← (Z3 + Z1) / 2 + W3 * GAUSS;
                  draw the four subtriangles
                  FRACTAL-SURFACE-SUBDIVIDE(X1, Y1, Z1, S1 + 1, W1/2,
                                            X12, Y12, Z12, S1 + 2, W2/2,
                                            X31, Y31, Z31, S3 + 3, W3/2,
                                            N − 1, DIR);
                  FRACTAL-SURFACE-SUBDIVIDE(X2, Y2, Z2, S2 + 1, W2/2,
                                            X23, Y23, Z23, S2 + 2, W3/2,
                                            X12, Y12, Z12, S1 + 3, W1/2,
                                            N − 1, DIR);
                  FRACTAL-SURFACE-SUBDIVIDE(X3, Y3, Z3, S3 + 1, W3/2,
                                            X31, Y31, Z31, S3 + 2, W1/2,
                                            X23, Y23, Z23, S2 + 3, W2/2,
                                            N − 1, DIR);
                  FRACTAL-SURFACE-SUBDIVIDE(X12, Y12, Z12, S1 + 2, W2/2
                                            X31, Y31, Z31, S3 + 2, W1/2,
                                            X23, Y23, Z23, S2 + 2, W3/2,
                                            N − 1, − DIR);
            END;
        RETURN;
      END;
```

We have presented algorithms for drawing statistically self-similar fractal curves and surfaces, but these are by no means the only ways to construct such figures. Furthermore, there are countless fractal structures with exact self-similarity, many of which produce striking images.

AN APPLICATION

Let's consider the drawing of smooth curves once again. An area in which curve drawing is useful is the design of objects such as airplane wings or automobile fenders. Let us outline how our curve-drawing routines might be used in a program for the interactive design of a curved line such as a wing cross section. We shall provide the designer with 10 sample points. He will be able to select a sample point with the pick, and move it with the locator. The B-spline routines will be used to interpolate the sample points. As a sample point is moved, the curve will change. The designer arranges the sample points until he obtains the curve which he desires.

Our first problem will be to initialize the sample points. We shall use the character "X" to display the points. The points will be constructed at the origin, and the image transformation will be used to position them on the screen.

```
BEGIN
    FOR I = 1 TO 10 DO
        BEGIN
            CREATE-SEGMENT(I);
            MOVE-ABS-2(0, 0);
            TEXT("X");
            CLOSE-SEGMENT;
            SET-VISIBILITY(I, TRUE);
            SET-DETECTABILITY(I, TRUE);
            SET-IMAGE-TRANSLATION(I, I / 10, I / 10);
        END;
    SET-B-SPLINE(8);
    RETURN;
END;
```

Once this initialization is done, we shall have 10 points displayed along the screen diagonal. (See Figure 11-28.)

We can now enter the main part of the program, which consists of a loop allowing repeated modification and display of the curve. The part of the program for moving a sample point might look like the following:

```
BEGIN
    SAMPLE ← 0;
    WHILE SAMPLE = 0 DO AWAIT-PICK(WAIT, SAMPLE);
    BUTTON-NUM ← 0;
    WHILE BUTTON-NUM = 0 DO
        AWAIT-BUTTON-GET-LOCATOR(WAIT, BUTTON-NUM, X, Y);
    SET-IMAGE-TRANSLATION(SAMPLE, X, Y);
END;
```

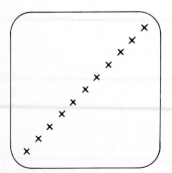

FIGURE 11-28
Ten sample points along the diagonal.

Now we need some statements which will draw the curve using the positions of the sample points. We shall need some arrays to hold the sample points, so suppose that AX, AY, and AZ are five-element arrays and that AZ contains zero values. We shall get the first five sample-point positions and place them into the arrays for use by START-B-SPLINE. The next three points will be handled by CURVE-ABS-3, while the last two points are needed for END-B-SPLINE. The curve will be drawn in display-file segment 11. (See Figure 11-29.)

```
BEGIN
    DELETE-SEGMENT(11);
    CREATE-SEGMENT(11);
    FOR I = 1 TO 5 DO INQUIRE-IMAGE-TRANSLATION(I, AX[I], AY[I]);
    START-B-SPLINE(AX, AY, AZ);
    FOR I = 6 TO 8 DO
        BEGIN
            INQUIRE-IMAGE-TRANSLATION(I, X, Y);
            CURVE-ABS-3(X, Y, 0);
        END;
    INQUIRE-IMAGE-TRANSLATION(9, X, Y);
    INQUIRE-IMAGE-TRANSLATION(10, U, V);
    END-B-SPLINE(X, Y, 0, U, V, 0);
    CLOSE-SEGMENT;
    SET-VISIBILITY(11, TRUE);
    SET-DETECTABILITY(11, FALSE);
END;
```

FURTHER READING

An introduction to ways of representing curves may be found in [FOR69]. Circle generators are described in [BRE77], [DOR79], [HOR76], [MCI83], and [SUE79]. Conic generators are given in [PIT67], [PRO83], and [SMI71]. Curve generators can be divided into those based on a parametric form $x = fx(u,v)$, $y = fy(u,v)$, and those based on an implicit form $f(x,y) = 0$. Curve generators for the implicit form are described in [COH76], [DAN70], [JOR73], [VAN84a], and [VAN85]. Conversion between the parametric and implicit forms is presented in [SED84] and [SED86]. Some texts with deeper discussions of curves are [CHA78], [DEB78], and [ROG76]. Conic curves are discussed in [COH76], [PAV83], [PIE84], and [PRA85]. Splines are surveyed in [BAR84] and [BOE82]. Bezier curves are described in [GOR74]. The sub-

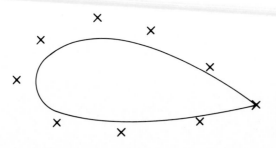

FIGURE 11-29
Positioning the sample points to produce the desired shape curve.

division of cubic Bezier and B-spline curves is presented in [LAN80*b*]. Spline techniques can be applied to all four homogeneous coordinates instead of just three, as we have done. The result is called a rational spline. Rational cubic splines can represent both cubic curves and conic sections. A description may be found in [AHU68] and [TIL83]. Representing surfaces by a number of patches is described in [FOR72]. Fitting data sample points with splines is discussed in [PLA83] and [YAM78]. The problem of finding the B-spline control points which will describe a surface passing through a grid of sample points is considered in [BAR80]. It is possible to subdivide B splines in a manner similar to that for Bezier curves [COH80]. Replacing curves with line segments is considered in [COH69], [CRA85], and [LER 69]. Several techniques have been used to image curved surfaces [FOR79]. One method is to subdivide the surface into polygons or pixels. See [CAT75], [LAN79], and [LAN80*a*]. They have also been imaged directly [SCH82]. Displaying contour lines for the surface is described in [SAT85]. Handling hidden curved surfaces is considered in [GRI84]. Ray tracing can be used to display curved objects, provided we can find the intersection of a ray with an object; methods for doing this for bicubic patches are discussed in [KAJ82] and [SWE86]. Ray tracing of objects defined by sweeping or revolving curves is discussed in [KAJ83*a*] and [KAJ83*b*] and, for curves that are cubic splines, in [VAN84*b*]. Ray tracing of parametric surfaces is discussed in [TOT85]. Mapping textures onto curved surfaces is described in [BLI76]. Programs for drawing Hilbert's curve are given in [ALE71], [GOL81], [GRI85], and [MOR82]. Fractals are defined in [MAN83] and [MAN77]. Some simple fractal curve generators are presented in [CAR86]. The statistical fractals we have presented are described in [FOU82]. Some objections to this simple approach were raised in [MAN82]. A different approach to constructing fractals based on iterated function systems is given in [BAR85] and [DEM85]. Ray-tracing techniques can be applied to fractal surfaces, provided we can find the intersection between the ray and the surface. One approach described in [BOU85] is to determine if the ray intersects a bounding ellipsoid; if so, the fractal is subdivided and the test is reapplied. Using a "cheesecake-shaped" box to bound the fractal is described in [KAJ83*a*] and [KAJ83*b*]. The idea of describing objects by statistical models has been extended to volumes of particles, which can yield impressive results (see Plates 8 and 9) for trees, grass, clouds, and flames [REE85].

[AHU68] Ahuja, D. V., "An Algorithm for Generating Spline-Like Curves," *IBM System Journal*, vol. 7, nos. 3&4, pp. 206–215 (1968).

[ALE71] Aleph Null, "Space Filling Curves, or How to Waste Time with a Plotter." *Software—Practice and Experience*, vol. 1, no. 4, pp. 403–410 (1971).

[BAR80] Barsky, B. A., Greenberg, D. P., "Determining a Set of B-Spline Control Vertices to Generate an Interpolating Surface," *Computer Graphics and Image Processing*, vol. 14, no. 3, pp. 203–226 (1980).

[BAR84] Barsky, B. A., "A Description and Evaluation of Various 3-D Models," *IEEE Computer Graphics and Applications*, vol. 4, no. 1, pp. 38–52 (1984).

[BAR85] Barnsley, M. F., Demko, S., "Iterated Functions Systems and the Global Construction of Fractals," *Proceedings of the Royal Society of London, Series A*, vol. 399, no. 1817, pp. 243–276 (1985).

[BLI76] Blinn, J. F., Newell, M. E., "Texture and Reflection in Computer Generated Images," *Communications of the ACM*, vol. 19, no. 10, pp. 542–547 (1976).

[BOE82] Boehm, W., "On Cubics: A Survey," *Computer Graphics and Image Processing*, vol. 19, no. 3, pp. 201–226 (1982).

[BOU85] Bouville, C., "Bounding Ellipsoids for Ray-Fractal Intersection," *Computer Graphics*, vol. 19, no. 3, pp. 45–52 (1985).

[BRE77] Bresenham, J., "A Linear Algorithm for Incremental Digital Display of Circular Arcs," *Communications of the ACM*, vol. 20, no. 2, pp. 100–106 (1977).

[CAR86] Carlson, P. W., "IBM Fractal Graphics," *Compute!*, vol. 8, no 3, pp. 78–80 (1986).

[CAT75] Catmull, E., "Computer Display of Curved Surfaces," *IEEE Conference on Computer Graphics, Pattern Recognition, and Data Structures*, pp. 11–17, IEEE Cat. No. 75CH0981-1c (1975).

[CHA78] Chasen, S. H., *Geometric Principles and Procedures for Computer Graphic Application*, Prentice-Hall, Englewood Cliffs, N.J. (1978).

[COH69] Cohen, D., Lee, T. M. P., "Fast Drawing of Curves for Computer Display," *AFIPS SJCC*, vol. 34, pp. 297–307 (1969).

[COH76] Cohen, E., "A Method for Plotting Curves Defined by Implicit Equations," *Computer Graphics*, vol. 10, no. 3, pp. 263–265 (1976).

[COH80] Cohen, E., Lyche, T., Risenfeld, R., "Discrete B-Splines and Subdivision Techniques in Computer-Aided Geometric Design and Computer Graphics," *Computer Graphics and Image Processing*, vol. 14, no. 2, pp. 87–111 (1980).

[CRA85] Crampin, M., Guifo, R., Read, G. A., "Linear Approximation of Curves with Bounded Curvature and a Data Reduction Algorithm," *Computer-Aided Design*, vol. 17, no. 6, pp. 257–261 (1985).

[DAN70] Danielsson, P. E., "Incremental Curve Generation," *IEEE Transactions on Computers*, vol. C-19, no. 9, pp. 783–793 (1970).

[DEB78] de Boor, C., *A Practical Guide to Splines, Applied Mathematical Sciences Series*, vol. 27, Springer-Verlag, New York (1978).

[DEM85] Demko, S., Hodges, L., Naylor, B., "Construction of Fractal Objects with Iterated Function Systems," *Computer Graphics*, vol. 19, no. 3, pp. 271–278 (1985).

[DOR79] Doros, M. "Algorithms for Generation of Discrete Circles, Rings, and Disks," *Computer Graphics and Image Processing*, vol. 10, no. 4, pp. 366–371 (1979).

[FOR69] Forrest, A. R., "Curves for Computer Graphics" in *Pertinent Concepts in Computer Graphics*, Univ. of Ill. Press (1969), pp. 31–47.

[FOR72] Forrest, A. R., "On Coons and Other Methods for the Representation of Curved Surfaces," *Computer Graphics and Image Processing*, vol. 1, no. 4, pp. 341–359 (1972).

[FOR79] Forrest, A. R., "On the Rendering of Surfaces," *Computer Graphics*, vol. 13, no. 2, pp. 253–259 (1979).

[FOU82] Fournier, A., Russell, D., "Computer Rendering of Stochastic Models," *Communications of the ACM*, vol. 25, no. 6, pp. 371–384 (1982).

[GOL81] Goldschlager, L. M., "Short Algorithms for Space-Filling Curves," *Software—Practice and Experience*, vol. 11, no. 1, pp. 99–100 (1981).

[GOR74] Gordon, W. J., Riesenfeld, R. F., "Bernstein-Bezier Methods for the Computer-Aided Design of Free-Form Curves and Surfaces," *Journal of the ACM*, vol. 21, no. 2, pp. 293–310 (1974).

[GRI84] Griffiths, J. G., "A Depth-Coherence Scanline Algorithm for Displaying Curved Surfaces," *Computer-Aided Design*, vol. 16, no. 2, pp. 91–101 (1984).

[GRI85] Griffiths, J. G., "Table-Driven Algorithms for Generating Space-Filling Curves," *Computer-Aided Design*, vol. 17, no. 1, pp. 37–41 (1985).

[HOR76] Horn, B. K. P., "Circle Generators for Display Devices," *Computer Graphics and Image Processing*, vol. 5, no. 2, pp. 280–288 (1976).

[JOR73] Jordon, B. W., Lennon, W. J, Holm, B. D., "An Improved Algorithm for the Generation of Nonparametric Curves," *IEEE Transactions on Computers*, vol. C-22, no. 12, pp. 1052–1060 (1973).

[KAJ82] Kajiya, J. T., "Ray Tracing Parametric Patches," *Computer Graphics*, vol. 16, no. 3, pp. 245–254 (1982).

[KAJ83a] Kajiya, J. T., "New Techniques for Ray Tracing Procedurally Defined Objects," *Computer Graphics*, vol. 17, no. 3, pp. 91–102 (1983).

[KAJ83b] Kajiya, J. T., "New Techniques for Ray Tracing Procedurally Defined Objects," *ACM Transactions on Graphics*, vol. 2, no. 3, pp. 161–181 (1983).

[LAN79] Lane, J., Carpenter, L., "A Generalized Scan Line Algorithm for the Computer Display of Parametrically Defined Surfaces," *Computer Graphics and Imaging Processing*, vol. 11, no. 3, pp. 290–297 (1979).

[LAN80a] Lane, J. M., Carpenter, L. C., Whitted, T., Blinn, J. F., " Scan Line Methods for Displaying Parametrically Defined Surfaces," *Communications of the ACM*, vol. 23, no. 1, pp. 23–34 (1980).

[LAN80b] Lane, J. M., Riesenfeld, R. F., "A Theoretical Development for the Computer Generation and Display of Piecewise Polynomial Surfaces," *IEEE Transactions on Pattern Analysis and Machine Intelligence*, vol. PAMI-2, no. 1, pp. 35–46 (1980).

[LER69] Le Riche, P. J., "A Curve Plotting Procedure," *Computer Journal*, vol. 12, pp. 291–292 (1969).

[MAN77] Mandelbrot, B. B., *Fractals—Form, Chance, and Dimension*, W. H. Freeman, San Francisco (1977).

[MAN82] Mandelbrot, B. B., "Comment on Computer Rendering of Fractal Stochastic Models," *Communications of the ACM*, vol. 25, no. 8, pp. 581–584 (1982).

[MAN83] Mandelbrot, B. B., *The Fractal Geometry of Nature*, W. H. Freeman, San Francisco (1982).

[MCI83] McIlroy, M. D., "Best Approximate Circles on Integer Grids," *ACM Transactions on Graphics*, vol. 2, no. 4, pp. 237–263 (1983).

[MOR82] Morrison, R., "Low Cost Computer Graphics for Micro Computers," *Software—Practice and Experience*, vol. 12, no. 8, pp. 767–776 (1982).

[PAV83] Pavlidis, T., "Curve Fitting with Conic Splines," *ACM Transactions on Graphics*, vol. 2, no. 1, pp. 1–31 (1983).

[PIE84] Piegl, L., "Defining C1 Curves Containing Conic Segments," *Computers & Graphics*, vol. 8, no. 2, pp. 177–182 (1984).

[PIT67] Pitteway, M. L. V., "Algorithm for Drawing Ellipses or Hyperbolae with a Digital Plotter," *Computer Journal*, vol. 10, no. 3, pp. 282–289 (1967).

[PLA83] Plass, M., Stone, M., "Curve-Fitting with Piecewise Parametric Cubics," *Computer Graphics*, vol. 17, no. 3, pp. 229–239 (1983).

[PRA85] Pratt, V., "Techniques for Conic Splines," *Computer Graphics*, vol. 19, no. 3, pp. 151–159 (1985).

[PRO83] Prosser, C. J., Kilgour, A. C., "An Integer Method for the Graphical Output of Conic Sections," *ACM Transactions on Graphics*, vol. 2, no. 3, pp. 182–191 (1983).

[REE85] Reeves, W. T, Blau, R., "Approximate and Probabilistic Algorithms for Shading and Rendering Structured Particle Systems," *Computer Graphics*, vol. 19, no. 3, pp. 313–322 (1985).

[ROG76] Rogers, D. F., Adams, J. A., *Mathematical Elements for Computer Graphics*, McGraw-Hill, New York (1976).

[SAT85] Satterfield, S. G., Rogers, D. F., "A Procedure for Generating Contour Lines from a B-Spline Surface," *IEEE Computer Graphics and Applications*, vol. 5, no. 4, pp. 71–75 (1985).

[SCH82] Schweitzer, D., Cobb, E. S., " Scanline Rendering of Parametric Surfaces," *Computer Graphics*, vol. 16, no. 3, pp. 265–271 (1982).

[SED84] Sederberg, T. W., Anderson, D. C., "Implicit Representation of Parametric Curves and Surfaces," *Computer Graphics and Image Processing*, vol. 28, no. 1, pp. 72–84 (1984).

[SED86] Sederberg, T. W., Goldman, R. N., "Algebraic Geometry for Computer-Aided Geometric Design," *Computer Graphics and Applications*, vol. 6, no. 6, pp. 52–59 (1986).

[SMI71] Smith, L. B., "Drawing Ellipses, Hyperbolas, or Parabolas with a Fixed Number of Points and Maximum Inscribed Area," *Computer Journal*, vol. 14, no. 1, pp. 81–86 (1971).

[SUE79] Suenaga, U. Y., Kame, T., Kobayashi, T., "A High-Speed Algorithm for the Generations of Straight Lines and Circular Arcs," *IEEE Transactions on Computers*, vol. C-28, no. 10, pp. 728–736 (1979).

[SWE86] Sweeney, M. A. J., Bartels, R. H., "Ray Tracing Free-Form B-Spline Surfaces," *Computer Graphics and Applications*, vol. 6, no. 2, pp. 41–49 (1986).

[TIL83] Tiler, W., "Rational B-Splines for Curve and Surface Representation," *IEEE Computer Graphics and Applications*, vol. 3, no. 9, pp. 61–69 (1983).

[TOT85] Toth, D. L., "On Ray Tracing Parametric Surfaces," *Computer Graphics*, vol. 19, no. 3, pp. 171–179 (1985).

[VAN84a] Van Aken, J. R., "An Efficient Ellipse-Drawing Algorithm," *IEEE Computer Graphics and Applications*, vol. 4, no. 9, pp. 24–35 (1984).

[VAN84b] Van Wijk, J. J., "Ray Tracing Objects Defined by Sweeping Planar Cubic Splines," *ACM Transactions on Graphics*, vol. 3, no. 3, pp. 223–237 (1984).

[VAN85] Van Aken, J., Novak, M., "Curve-Drawing Algorithms for Raster Displays," *ACM Transactions on Graphics*, vol. 4, no. 2, pp. 147–169 (1985).

[YAM78] Yamaguchi, F., "A New Curve Fitting Method Using a CRT Computer Display, " *Computer Graphics and Image Processing*, vol. 7, no. 3, pp. 425–437 (1978).

EXERCISES

11-1 Circular arcs may be supported by hardware drawing primitives in the display. If we are to take advantage of this feature, we need a means of allowing the user to specify an arc and also a way of describing a circular arc in our display file.

   a) How many reasonable ways of specifying an arc can you devise?

   b) Create a display-file instruction for a circular arc such that we can easily perform rotation, translation, and uniform scaling operations.

   c) Choose a representation which also preserves the proper starting and ending positions of the arc on all transformations.

11-2 Design a circle-drawing algorithm which does antialiasing.

11-3   a) Calculate the values of our homemade blending functions B_1, B_2, B_3, B_4 needed when each curve section is to be approximated by five line segments.

   b) Sketch these blending functions.

   c) If the four sample points $(1, 1, 0)$, $(2, 1, 0)$, $(2, 2, 0)$, $(1, 2, 0)$ are used, calculate and plot the interpolated curve for the center section.

11-4   a) Calculate the values of the cubic B-spline blending functions for the first, second, and middle curve sections (B_i', B_i'', B_i for $i = 1, 2, 3, 4$) when each curve section is to be approximated by three line segments.

   b) Sketch these blending functions.

   c) If the first six sample points are $(1, 1, 0)$, $(2, 1, 0)$, $(2, 2, 0)$, $(1, 2, 0)$, $(0, 2, 0)$, $(0, 3, 0)$, calculate and plot the first three sections of the interpolated curve.

11-5 Show that the four B-spline blending functions in Equation 11.14 sum to 1. What does this mean?

11-6 A fractal curve named the dragon is constructed by repeatedly replacing each line segment by two line segments forming a right angle.

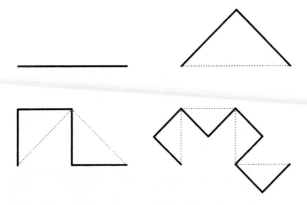

What is the fractal dimension of this curve?

PROGRAMMING PROBLEMS

11-1 a) Implement algorithm 11.1 for drawing arcs.

b) Extend your graphics system to include arc-drawing instructions as investigated in Exercise 11-1.

c) Develop and implement a clipping algorithm for circular arcs.

11-2 Suppose you wish to display the points on some function $y = f(x)$ which you can calculate. One way to do this is to calculate sample points along the function and then to connect them with line segments (as we did in Programming Problem 1-6). Write a recursive procedure which will do this, subdividing the curve with each call. If possible, let the function to be plotted be an argument to your procedure. At each recursive call you must check to see if the curve is sufficiently subdivided to be approximated by a straight line. Try the following three criteria for this test.

a) A specified number of levels has been reached.

b) The length of the approximating line segment is less than some value.

c) The angle between segments is less than some value.

Try plotting functions which vary slowly and functions with sharp corners, noting the quality of the image and the number of line segments required.

11-3 a) Implement algorithms 11.2 through 11.9 for Lagrange interpolation.

b) Also implement algorithms 11.10 through 11.12 for B splines.

11-4 Test the Lagrange and B-spline interpolation by constructing a set of sample points. Show the sample points as follows:

a) Connected by single line segments

b) Interpolated using the Lagrange interpolation scheme with eight line segments per curve section

c) Interpolated using the cubic B splines with eight line segments per curve section

11-5 Use the Lagrange interpolation routines to present a smooth curve of the widget sales data of Programming Problem 1-3.

11-6 Sketch a face and use B splines to smooth the features.

11-7 Write an interactive graphing program which draws an approximate curve for a set of data points and then allows the user to adjust the curve for the desired fit.

11-8 Show the effect of smoothing on the regular polygons with three to eight sides. Show each figure both before and after smoothing.

11-9 Write strictly two-dimensional versions of the B-spline routines.

11-10 Implement and test algorithm 11.13 for drawing Bezier curves. Also implement relative and strictly two-dimensional versions of the procedure.

11-11 Write procedures for entering and displaying bicubic Bezier surface patches.

11-12 Implement algorithms 11.14 through 11.18 for fractal lines and surfaces.

11-13 a) Write a program which generates Hilbert's curve to any desired approximation.

b) Write one for the triadic Koch curve.

11-14 Write the routines FRACTAL-LINE-ABS-2, FRACTAL-LINE-REL-2, and FRACTAL-LINE-REL-3 to extend the system to absolute and relative fractal lines in both two and three dimensions.

11-15 Generalize the fractal surface-drawing routine to arbitrary convex polygons by subdividing the polygons into triangles and then applying the FRACTAL-SURFACE-SUBDIVIDE routine.

11-16 In our graphics system, the procedures which enter a polygon into the display have available all of the polygon's vertices and know just how many sides the polygon will have. An alternative used by some graphics systems is to construct a path, a sequence of line segments, and then, at some arbitrary point, close the path to form a polygon. Polygons are built a side at a time and need not be specified all at once. This method easily generalizes to allow both straight and curved path elements, so polygons can have a mixture of straight and curved sides. Write procedures BEGIN-PATH and CLOSE-PATH which give this feature to our system. BEGIN-PATH should divert MOVE and LINE drawing display-file commands to a temporary holding area. CLOSE-PATH should transfer the collected commands to the display file as a polygon.

APPENDIX A

INFORMATION GUIDE

There is an enormous wealth of literature about computer graphics; just listing it would fill a book by itself. In this appendix we shall provide some direction on how and where to find this literature.

GUIDES

Machover, C., "Background and Source Information about Computer Graphics," *IEEE Computer Graphics and Applications*, vol. 5, no. 1, pp. 68–81 (1985).

Machover, C., "An Updated Guide to Sources of Information about Computer Graphics," *IEEE Computer Graphics and Applications*, vol. 3, no. 1, pp. 49–59 (1983).

Machover, C., "A Guide to Sources of Information about Computer Graphics," *IEEE Computer Graphics and Applications*, vol. 1, no. 1, pp. 73–85 (1981).

Schrack, G. F., "Gaining Access to the Literature of Computer Graphics," *IEEE Transactions on Education*, vol. E-26, no. 1, pp. 7–10 (1983).

BIBLIOGRAPHIES

Bibliographies cataloging each year's literature have been produced. They cover the years from 1975 to date. There are also occasional bibliographies for some subfields and related areas. The following is a list of the major ones.

Schrack, G. F., "Literature in Computer Graphics for the Year 1984: A Bibliography," *Computer Graphics*, vol. 19, no. 2, pp. 41–77 (1985).

Schrack, G. F., "Literature in Computer Graphics for the Year 1983: A Bibliography," *Computer Graphics*, vol. 18, no. 2, pp. 69–89 (1984).

Schrack, G. F., "Literature in Computer Graphics for the Year 1982: A Bibliography," *Computer Graphics*, vol. 17, no. 4, pp. 173–204 (1983).

Schrack, G. F., "Literature in Computer Graphics for the Year 1981: A Bibliography," *Computer Graphics*, vol. 17, no. 2, pp. 115–141 (1983).

Schrack, G. F., "Current Literature in Computer Graphics and Interactive Techniques: References, Eighth Series," *Computer Graphics*, vol. 16, no. 4, pp. 251–262 (1982).

Schrack, G. F., "Computer Graphics: A Keyword-Indexed Bibliography for the Year 1980," *Computer Graphics and Image Processing*, vol. 18, no. 2, pp. 145–187 (1982).

Schrack, G. F., "Current Literature in Computer Graphics and Interactive Techniques: References, Seventh Series," *Computer Graphics*, vol. 16, no. 1, pp. 101–118 (1982).

Schrack, G. F., "Current Literature in Computer Graphics and Interactive Techniques: References, Sixth Series," *Computer Graphics*, vol. 15, no. 4, pp. 458–464 (1981).

Schrack, G. F., "Computer Graphics: A Keyword-Indexed Bibliography for the Year 1979," *Computer Graphics and Image Processing*, vol. 15, no. 1, pp. 45–78 (1981).

Schrack, G. F., "Current Literature in Computer Graphics and Interactive Techniques: References, Fifth Series," *Computer Graphics*, vol. 14, no. 4, pp. 200–218 (1980).

Schrack, G. F., "Current Literature in Computer Graphics and Interactive Techniques: References, Fourth Series," *Computer Graphics*, vol. 16, nos. 1 & 2, pp. 73–83 (1980).

Schrack, G. F., "Current Literature in Computer Graphics and Interactive Techniques: References," *Computer Graphics*, vol. 13, no. 4, pp. 381–394 (1980).

Schrack, G. F., "Computer Graphics: A Keyword-Indexed Bibliography for the Years 1976, 1977, and 1978," *Computer Graphics and Image Processing*, vol. 14, no. 1, pp. 24–79 (1980).

Schrack, G. F., "Current Literature in Computer Graphics and Interactive Techniques," *Computer Graphics*, vol. 13, no. 1, pp. 148–165 (1979).

Schrack, G. F., "Current Literature in Computer Graphics and Interactive Techniques," *Computer Graphics*, vol. 12, no. 4, pp. 114–123 (1978).

Pooch, U. W., "Computer Graphics Interactive Techniques, and Image Processing 1970–1975: A Bibliography," *Computer*, vol. 9, no. 8, pp. 46–64 (1976).

Some special topic bibliographies are as follows:

Barsky, B. A., "Computer-Aided Geometric Design: A Bibliography with Keywords and Classified Index," *Computer Graphics*, vol. 16, no. 1 (1982).

Griffiths, J.G., "Bibliography of Hidden-Line and Hidden-Surface Algorithms," *Computer Aided Design*, vol. 10, no. 3 (1978).

Rosenfeld, A., "Picture Rocessing: 1972," *Computer Graphics and Image Processing*, vol. 1, no. 4, pp. 394–416 (1972).

Thalmann, N., Thalmann, D., "An Indexed Bibliography on Computer Animation," *IEEE Computer Graphics and Applications*, vol. 5, no. 7, pp. 76–86 (1985).

Thomas, J. J., Hamlin, G. "Graphical Input Interaction Technique (GIIT)," *Computer Graphics*, vol. 17, no. 1, pp. 5–30 (1983).

An overview of computer graphics and selected references may be found in

Burchi, R.S., "Interactive Graphics Today," *IBM Systems Journal*, vol 19, no. 3, pp. 299–313 (1980).

BOOK REVIEWS

Reviews of computer graphics texts may be found in the following:

Schrack, G. F., "Texts and Books in Computer Graphics," *Computer Graphics*, vol. 18, no. 4, pp. 160–165 (1984).

Schrack, G. F., "Book Reviews," *Computer Graphics*, vol. 19, no. 2, pp. 77–82 (1985).

Schrack, G. F., "A Brief Survey of Texts and Books in Computer Graphics," *Computer Graphics*, vol. 17, no. 4, pp. 90–95 (1984).

TEXTS

Some of the currently available texts are as follows:

Angell, I. O., *A Practical Introduction to Computer Graphics*, Macmillan, London and Basingstoke, England (1981).

Chasen, S. H., *Geometric Principles and Procedures for Computer Graphics Applications*, Prentice-Hall, Englewood Cliffs, N.J. (1978).

Demel, J. T., and Miller, M. J., *Introduction to Computer Graphics*, Brooks/Cole, Belmont, Calif. (1984).

Encarnacao, J., and Schlectendahl, E. G., *Computer Aided Design Fundamentals and System Architectures*, Springer-Verlag, New York (1983).

Enderle, G., Kansy, K., and Pfaff, G., *Computer Graphics Programming GKS—The Graphics Standard*, Springer-Verlag, New York (1983).

Foley, J. D., and Van Dam, A., *Fundamentals of Interactive Computer Graphics*, Addison-Wesley, Reading, Mass. (1981).

Newman, W., and Sproull, R., *Principles of Interactive Computer Graphics* (2d ed.), McGraw-Hill, New York (1979).

Pavlidis, T., *Algorithms for Graphics and Image Processing*, Computer Science Press, Rockville, Md. (1982).

Rogers, D. F., and Adams, J. A., *Mathematical Elements for Computer Graphics*, McGraw-Hill, New York (1976).

Scott, J. E., *Introduction to Interactive Computer Graphics*, Wiley Interscience, New York (1982).

Sherr, S., *Video and Digital Electronic Displays: A User's Guide*, Wiley, Somerset, N.J. (1982).

B

PIDGIN
ALGOL

The algorithms presented in this book have been written in an imaginary ALGOL-like programming language. This language was chosen for several reasons. It allows us to concentrate on the ''meat'' of the algorithm without too much concern over the details of declarations and syntax. The actual implementation of the algorithms necessitates a translation to some real programming language, so that a bit more study and thought are needed than that required for simple copying. Translation to PASCAL, PL/I, C, and FORTRAN can be carried out without much difficulty, and no single language is favored.

In this appendix we present a description of PIDGIN ALGOL to aid in understanding the algorithms which use it.

Comments. Comments may be entered at any point within the algorithm. They are distinguished by being typed in lowercase letters.

Identifiers. Names for variables and procedures consist of any number of letters, digits, and hyphens, beginning with a letter.

Variables. A variable may be either an argument, a local, or a global. Local variables exist only for the life of the routine. They do not retain their values over separate calls. They are not known outside the routine. Global variables can be accessed by any routine. They exist throughout the life of the program. Each global variable has a unique name by which it is identified. Arguments are assumed bound by a call by a reference mechanism, so that alterations in the value of the formal argument of the called routine will cause a corresponding change in the associated variable of the calling routine. No data types for variables are specified.

Arrays. Arrays of data elements may be used. Individual array elements are specified by the array name, followed by a list of indices enclosed in brackets A[I, J, K]. There is no restriction as to the number of allowed dimensions. There is also no mechanism for declaring the size of the array. An entire array may be passed between routines by using the array name (without subscripts) as the argument.

Constants. Constants may be associated with identifiers. These identifiers may be used in place of the constants to improve the comprehensibility of the routine.

Operators. The available arithmetic operators are as follows:

↑	exponentiation
*	multiplication
/	division
+	addition
−	subtraction and negation

Operators must be separated from other symbols by at least one space. The relational operators are

=	equal
≠	not equal
<	less than
>	greater than
≤	less or equal
≥	greater or equal

The result of a relational operation is a value of TRUE or FALSE. The logical operators are

NOT	negation
AND	conjunction
OR	disjunction

A few useful functions will also be assumed to be present in the language. They include

INT(X)	greatest integer part of X
MAX(X,Y)	largest of X and Y
MIN(X,Y)	smallest of X and Y
|X|	absolute value of X
SIN(X)	sine of X
COS(X)	cosine of X
ARCTAN(X)	arctangent of X
SQRT(X)	square root of X

Statements. Routines are composed of statements, where each statement causes some action to be performed. There can be several statements on one line, or a single statement may require several lines. Statements are terminated by a semicolon.

<Statement 1>; <Statement 2>; <Statement 3>; <Statement 4>;

Compound Statements. Several statements may be grouped together so as to behave as a single statement. This is done by enclosing these statements between the words BEGIN and END.

```
BEGIN
    <Statement 1>;
    <Statement 2>;
    <Statement 3>;
END;
```

Each routine consists of one compound statement.

Assignments. Variables may be assigned values by use of the assignment statement.

<Variable> ← <Expression>;

as in

X ← 3;

The assignment operator is ← .

Control Statements. Decisions are carried out by the IF statement, which has two forms

IF <Expression> THEN <Statement>;

and

IF <Expression> THEN <Statement 1> ELSE <Statement 2>;

The expression must evaluate to TRUE or FALSE. If the expression is TRUE, then for the first form the statement will be executed, and for the second form, <Statement 1> will be carried out. If the expression is FALSE, then nothing is done in the first form, and <Statement 2> is executed for the second form. In the event of nested IF statements, the ELSE clause is associated with the most recent incomplete IF. Thus in

IF <E1> THEN IF <E2> THEN <S1> ELSE <S2>;

the statement <S2> belongs with the test on <E2>.

The FOR construct allows a finite number of repetitions of a statement with varying index or counter. Its form is

FOR <Index> = <Start> TO <Finish> DO <Statement>;

With each repetition, the index is incremented by 1. The first time the <Statement> is executed, the index will have the value <Start>. Repetition continues until the value of index exceeds <Finish>. If <Finish> is less than <Start> then the index is decremented. The expressions <Start> and <Finish> are evaluated only once upon entry of the loop.

The WHILE construct has the form

WHILE <Expression> DO <Statement>;

The <Statement> is repeated until the <Expression> becomes FALSE. If the <Expression> is FALSE upon entry to this construct, the <Statement> will not be executed.

Functions and Procedures. Each routine is considered to be a separate subprogram, callable from any other subprogram. The ordering of the various subprograms is arbitrary. Each routine is headed by the routine's name, followed by a list of its formal arguments enclosed in parentheses.

Algorithm FOO(X, Y, Z)

Functions are treated the same as procedures with the exception that at some point within the function body, the function name must be assigned the value which is to be returned.

Algorithm THREE(Y)
BEGIN
    THREE ← 3 * Y;
END;

There is a RETURN; statement which may be used at any point to transfer control back to the calling routine. There is also a RETURN ERROR <String>; construct which will print an error message containing <String> before transferring control back to the calling routine.
A call of a procedure is a statement composed of only the procedure name and argument list.

FOO(2, 4, 6);

Functions are called by using them in expressions.

Z ← 2 * THREE(4) + 7;

Input/Output Statements. Input may be done by the statement

READ <Variable>;

where <Variable> is the variable identifier to be given values. Output is carried out by the statement

PRINT <Expression 1>, <Expression 2>, ... <Expression N>;

where <Expression 1>, ... <Expression N> are the expressions whose values are to be printed. Each print command utilizes a new output record (a new line). Printing of a number of array elements may be conducted by the construction

PRINT FOR <Index> = <Start> TO <Finish>, <Array>[<Index>];

GRAPHICS
ON AN
ALPHANUMERIC
TERMINAL

Throughout this book we have stated that graphics output may be obtained on an ordinary CRT terminal or line printer. In this appendix we present FORTRAN subroutines which have been used to interface our graphics system to a Decwriter. CRT terminals can be handled in a similar fashion. The routines differ from those for some line printers in that the Decwriter routines do not require any initial carriage control character. The routines display an image 90 characters wide by 50 lines high. Different characters are used to obtain different line and interior styles.

Algorithm 1.2 BRESENHAM should be included among these device-dependent interface routines. It will not be given here, but follows the form given in Chapter 1. A 90 × 50 element array IFRAME is used as the frame buffer.

Algorithm 1.3 ERASE clears the frame buffer array by setting each element to the space character.

```
SUBROUTINE ERASE
COMMON /SBLK/ IWEND,IHEND,IWSTRT,IHSTRT,IWIDTH,IHIGHT
COMMON /FBLK/ IFRAME(90,50)
DATA IBLNK /' '/
```

```
C       STEP THRU ARRAY SETTING ALL ELEMENTS TO BLANK
        DO 120 I = IWSTRT, IWEND
            DO 110 J = IHSTRT, IHEND
            IFRAME(I,J) = IBLNK
110         CONTINUE
120     CONTINUE
        RETURN
        END
```

Algorithm 1.4 DISPLAY prints out the contents of the frame buffer array in order of top to bottom. Some blank lines are also printed to position one frame per page.

```
        SUBROUTINE DISPLY
C       THIS ROUTINE DISPLAYS THE CONTENTS OF THE FRAME BUFFER
        COMMON /SBLK/ IWEND,IHEND,IWSTRT,IHSTRT,IWIDTH,IHIGHT
        COMMON /FBLK/ IFRAME(90,50)
        IHEND1 = IHEND + 1
C       DISPLAY THE ARRAY
        WRITE (6,123)
123     FORMAT(////////)
        DO 220 I = IHSTRT, IHEND
            WRITE (6,210) (IFRAME(J,IHEND1 − I), J = IWSTRT,IWEND)
210         FORMAT(90A1)
220         CONTINUE
        WRITE (6,123)
        RETURN
        END
```

Algorithm 1.5 INITIALIZE-1 sets the display size parameters, and since carriage control is not available, the user is requested to position the paper.

```
        SUBROUTINE INITL1
        COMMON /SBLK/IWEND,IHEND,IWSTRT,IHSTRT,IWIDTH,IHIGHT
        IWEND = 90
        IHEND = 50
        IWSTRT = 1
        IHSTRT = 1
        IWIDTH = IWEND − IWSTRT
        IHIGHT = IHEND − IHSTRT
        WRITE (6,10)
10      FORMAT(' POSITION AT TOP OF PAGE, PUSH RETURN')
        READ (5,20) IDUMMY
20      FORMAT(A2)
        RETURN
        END
```

Algorithm 1.6 TERMINATE can be a do-nothing dummy routine (a STOP statement might be included in this routine).

```
              SUBROUTINE TRMNAT
              RETURN
              END
```

Algorithm 2.8 DOMOVE needs only to update the variables used for the current pen position.

```
              SUBROUTINE DOMOVE(X,Y)
C             THIS ROUTINE MOVES THE CURRENT PEN POSITION
              COMMON /PDBLK/ PXAT, PYAT
              COMMON /SBLK/ IWEND,IHEND,IWSTRT,IHSTRT,IWIDTH,IHIGHT
              PXAT = AMAX1(FLOAT(IWSTRT),AMIN1(FLOAT(IWEND),X*
             1       IWIDTH + IWSTRT))
              PYAT = AMAX1(FLOAT(IHSTRT),AMIN1(FLOAT(IHEND),Y*
             1       IHIGHT + IHSTRT))
              RETURN
              END
```

Algorithm 2.9 DOLINE causes a line to be entered into the frame buffer array by a call on the BRESENHAM routine. LINCHR is the current line style character.

```
              SUBROUTINE DOLINE(X,Y)
C             THIS ENTERS A LINE INTO THE FRAME BUFFER
              COMMON /CBLK/ LINCHR
              COMMON /SBLK/ IWEND,IHEND,IWSTRT,IHSTRT,IWIDTH,IHIGHT
              COMMON /PDBLK/ PXAT, PYAT
              X1 = PXAT
              Y1 = PYAT
              PXAT = AMAX1(FLOAT(IWSTRT),AMIN1(FLOAT(IWEND),X*
             1       IWIDTH + IWSTRT))
              PYAT = AMAX1(FLOAT(IHSTRT),AMIN1(FLOAT(IHEND),Y*
             1       IHIGHT + IHSTRT))
              CALL BRSNHM(INT(X1 + 0.5),INT(Y1 + 0.5),
                          INT(PXAT + 0.5),INT(PYAT + 0.5),LINCHR)
              RETURN
              END
```

Algorithm 2.18 DOCHAR places a character into the frame buffer. The KODE routine converts from ASCII character code to a form suitable for printing.

```
              SUBROUTINE DOCHAR(IOP,X,Y)
C             THIS ROUTINE ENTERS A CHARACTER INTO THE FRAME BUFFER
              COMMON /SBLK/ IWEND,IHEND,IWSTRT,IHSTRT,IWIDTH,IHIGHT
              COMMON /FBLK/ IFRAME(90, 50)
              ICXAT = MAX0(IWSTRT,MIN0(IWEND,INT(X*IWIDTH + IWSTRT)))
              ICYAT = MAX0(IHSTRT,MIN0(IHEND,INT(Y*IHIGHT + IHSTRT)))
              ICHR = KODE(IOP)
```

```
IFRAME(ICXAT, ICYAT) = ICHR
RETURN
END
```

The initializations of algorithms 2.13, 2.19, and 2.24 can be combined into the following subroutine.

```
SUBROUTINE INITL2
COMMON /CSZBLK/ CHARHT,CHARWD,CHRSEP
COMMON /DFBLK/ IFREE
COMMON /SBLK/ IWEND,IHEND,IWSTRT,IHSTRT,IWIDTH,IHIGHT
COMMON /PINBLK/ XAT,YAT
CALL INITL1
IFREE = 1
CALL DOSTYL(0)
CHARWD = 1.0 /FLOAT(IWIDTH)
CHARHT = 1.0 / FLOAT(IHIGHT)
CHRSEP = 0.0
CALL CHARUP(0.0,1.0)
XAT = 0.0
YAT = 0.0
CALL NEWFRM
RETURN
END
```

Algorithm 3.5 DOSTYLE changes the line or interior style by changing the character used in the drawing. The default line style is an asterisk (*).

```
      SUBROUTINE DOSTYL(IOP)
      COMMON /PLYBLK/ IPLYCH
      COMMON /CBLK/ LINCHR
      IF (IOP .LT. − 15) GO TO 1228
      LCHR = 42 − IOP
      IF (LCHR .LE. 48) GO TO 1227
      LCHR = LCHR − 16
1227  LINCHR = KODE(LCHR)
      RETURN
1228  LCHR = 26 − IOP
      IF (LCHR .LE. 48) GO TO 1229
      LCHR = LCHR − 16
1229  IPLYCH = KODE(LCHR)
      RETURN
      END
```

The FILLIN routine called in algorithm 3.14 uses the BRESENHAM algorithm call to fill in a scan line.

```
      SUBROUTINE FILLIN(X1,Y1,X2,Y2)
      COMMON /PLYBLK/ IPLYCH
      IF (X1 .EQ. X2) GO TO 1301
      CALL BRSNHM(INT(X1 + 0.5),INT(Y1 + 0.5),
     1                INT(X2 + 0.5),INT(Y2 + 0.5),IPLYCH)
1301  RETURN
      END
```

INDEX